Web Standards

Mastering HTML5, CSS3 and XML

Leslie F. Sikos, Ph.D.

Apress®

Web Standards—Mastering HTML5, CSS3, and XML

ISBN-13 (pbk): 978-1-4842-0884-7

ISBN-13 (electronic): 978-1-4842-0883-0

Managing Director: Welmoed Spahr
Lead Editor: Ben Renow-Clarke
Technical Reviewer: Charles Brown
Editorial Board: Steve Anglin, Mark Beckner, Ewan Buckingham, Gary Cornell, Louise Corrigan,
    Jim DeWolf, Jonathan Gennick, Robert Hutchinson, Michelle Lowman, James Markham, Matthew Moodie,
    Jeff Olson, Jeffrey Pepper, Douglas Pundick, Ben Renow-Clarke, Dominic Shakeshaft, Gwenan Spearing,
    Matt Wade, Steve Weiss
Coordinating Editor: Christine Ricketts
Copy Editor: Linda Seifert
Compositor: SPi Global
Indexer: SPi Global
Artist: SPi Global
Cover Designer: Anna Ishchenko

Distributed to the book trade worldwide by Springer Science+Business Media New York, 233 Spring Street, 6th Floor, New York, NY 10013. Phone 1-800-SPRINGER, fax (201) 348-4505, e-mail orders-ny@springer-sbm.com, or visit www.springeronline.com. Apress Media, LLC is a California LLC and the sole member (owner) is Springer Science + Business Media Finance Inc (SSBM Finance Inc). SSBM Finance Inc is a Delaware corporation.

For information on translations, please e-mail rights@apress.com, or visit www.apress.com.

Apress and friends of ED books may be purchased in bulk for academic, corporate, or promotional use. eBook versions and licenses are also available for most titles. For more information, reference our Special Bulk Sales–eBook Licensing web page at www.apress.com/bulk-sales.

Any source code or other supplementary material referenced by the author in this text is available to readers at www.apress.com and on the companion web site of the book at www.masteringhtml5css3.com. For detailed information about how to locate your book's source code, go to www.apress.com/source-code/.

Contents at a Glance

Contents

About the Author

Leslie F. Sikos, Ph.D. is a computer scientist specializing in web standards, Responsive Web Design, Semantic Web, and Web Accessibility. Being a hand coder Web standardista and senior web designer, he is particularly interested in the Open Web Platform and Web Quality Assurance through standards-based web design and web site optimization. Living on the cutting edge of web technologies, he prides himself on creating stunning, well-structured, mobile-friendly web sites with excellent user experience.

Dr. Sikos is a member of several professional organizations, including the World Wide Web Consortium (W3C), the Internet Engineering Task Force (IETF), the Internet Society (ISOC), and the Unicode Consortium. He is also an invited editor and reviewer actively contributing to the development of open standards.

His research interests include Semantic Web technologies. He can convert unstructured web contents to structured data, especially Linked Open Data and Linking Enterprise Data, and manually add machine-readable metadata annotations to the markup. He is interested in knowledge representation with RDF, OWL, and SKOS, and the implementation of knowledge organization systems such as controlled vocabularies and ontologies.

He is also a Web Accessibility expert providing web sites with the desired level of accessibility, including WCAG 1.0 at all priority levels (1, 2, 3), WCAG 2.0 at all conformance levels (A, AA, AAA), and Section 508.

Dr. Sikos is the author of 13 books covering a wide range of topics including JavaScript, XHTML, XML, CSS, Flash, digital photography, image processing, video authoring, computer hardware, HTML5, and CSS3. Due to his pedagogical background, he can introduce technical terms and explain complex development issues in plain English.

You can read more about his publications on his fully standards-compliant web site at www.lesliesikos.com.

About the Technical Reviewer

Charles Brown is one of the most noted authors, consultants, and trainers in the industry today. His books about Dreamweaver and Fireworks have received critical acclaim and are used worldwide as teaching tools. In addition to his work in the IT industry, Charles is also a noted concert pianist, organist, and guitarist appearing in major concert centers worldwide. He began his musical studies at age 4 and went on to study with famed pianist Vladimir Horowitz. At age 14, he made his debut with Leonard Bernstein and later studied at the famed Juilliard School. Eventually he went to Paris to study with the 20th century legend, Igor Stravinsky. While working with Stravinsky, Charles developed a close friendship with one of the most powerful artistic forces of the 20th century: Pablo Picasso. What he learned about creativity from Picasso he uses today in his writings and training work. Charles is a certified Macromedia/Adobe trainer who is in heavy demand worldwide. He frequently speaks at major conferences such as MAX and NAB. You can see his blog at blog.charlesebrown.net and his web site can be found at CharlesEBrown.net.

Preface

Since its earliest stage in the 1990s, the Web has been attracting all kinds of content authors. Anybody with minimal know-how could publish web sites from anywhere, anytime. This easy access has allowed millions of web sites to appear on the "network of networks" without any kind of content review or censorship. However, the freedom to publish without limitations led to low-quality code and poor copywriting on many sites.

Online presence is increasingly important in the competitive market, but often people are unaware of the costs of web design and hosting. To keep expenses down, many try to launch and maintain a web site on their own, and are reluctant to pay for professional web design services. Such people are usually not familiar with the principles of web design, typography, color theory, or web standards, and do not have graphic design and programming skills either. Those who use a Content Management System to develop web sites often believe that there is no need for qualified professionals anymore in web design. However, while a Graphical User Interface and predefined templates are easy to use, the quality of software-generated code cannot compete with the markup and style sheets written by professional web designers. In fact, web authoring and development tools often generate codes that are not standard-compliant, longer and more complex than optimal, not well-structured, lack semantics, and are inaccessible to people with disabilities. Even if the code is standard-complaint, content authors without solid web design skills update the markup incorrectly, resulting in web sites that will violate web standards.

To ensure acceptable download speed, rendering, and functionality for poorly written web sites, browsers are extremely error tolerant and can ignore incorrect code blocks, handle missing end tags, and so on. This error tolerancy doesn't mean that web standards can be ignored! For more than a decade, the inconsistent appearance and behavior across various browsers was a real challenge, and often frustration, for web designers, a problem laypeople never understood. Even standard-compliant sites fell apart or rendered incorrectly under various browsers that did not support a particular markup element or style sheet property. Browser vendors eventually recognized the importance of standards, and gradually improved their products. In the early 2010s, modern browsers reached an acceptable (and constantly improving) level of web standards support, and creating robust web sites became almost exclusively the responsibility of web designers.

From the standardization point of view, it is not an exaggeration that most web sites—including the largest, frequently updated multi-million dollar portals—often apply obsolete technologies and bad practices, and are not optimal. Common web design practices take just a few basic principles into account, such as appearance, buzzwords, and marketing potential, while miss important factors such as document structure, properly implemented standards, user interface, user experience, and accessibility. Web designers often publish incorrect templates based on popular, emerging technologies that are not yet standardized to increase their web site traffic, and others distribute such code blocks on other sites, leading to invalid markup and style sheets. Also, there are people who keep using the same technologies, techniques, and practices for as long as possible even if better technologies and new trends appear. Unfortunately, the proper implementation of web standards is quite often a minor concern only.

The growing popularity of mobile browsing has led to a huge demand for mobile-friendly web sites. As a result, supporting smartphones, tablets, and high-resolution monitors became a standard user expectation. How can web designers create web sites that work perfectly on all these devices when they come with different screen size, resolution, aspect ratio, and scrollability? The answer to this question led to a paradigm shift in the web design industry called *Responsive Web Design* that provides an optimal viewing experience regardless of the browsing device. Responsive Web Design is based on earlier best practices such as *progressive enhancement* (which was a result of the even earlier approach, *graceful degradation*).

Practical problems are often solved by the web design community, usually in the form of a new technique or framework. The approaches and software tools that are really efficient become so popular that they are implemented globally and designers start considering them as *best practices*. However, there is no ultimate solution for web design problems. For example, how can machine-readable annotations be leveraged in modern web services? How can web site appearance and functionality be guaranteed on a variety of platforms? How can the length of the markup and styling rules be minimized while preserving site information, functionality, and behavior? How can correct character rendering be ensured on a multilingual site?

Global concerns can often be addressed by the implementation of web standards. Since the development process of technical specifications can be slow, years can pass between the initial idea, the standard release, and the practical applications. Implementing specifications that are not yet standardized is usually a bad practice, but sometimes inevitable, especially when the standard under development is shaped by the feedback from the web design community.

Users usually do not know that many web site inconsistencies, unreadable elements, and poor functionality are caused by the low-quality markup and style sheets that do not comply with web standards. Standard compliance provides backward-and forward-compatibility so web sites can be used on the widest ranges of browsers, including older, current, and future versions, and will be easy to update when new standards appear. Web standards contribute to interoperability, platform-, device- and resolution-independence so standards-based web sites are easy to use and provide excellent user experience regardless of the screen size or resolution, operating system, and browser. Correctly structured markup is a fundamental requirement for accessibility and machine-readable, semantic annotations, and also ensures that the information of your site is conveyed even if the style sheets cannot be loaded.

This book is a comprehensive collection of state-of-the-art information on both the core web standards and lesser-known standards that deserve more attention. In fact, it is written to be the most complete reference of web standardization resources ever published. The step by-step guides are based on solid theoretical design principles and standardized specifications, and are demonstrated through sample code while focusing on syntax, formal grammar, recommended annotations, and other standardization concerns. This book also introduces you to cutting-edge technologies and best practices that can be implemented in modern web sites to achieve mobile-friendliness, accessibility, machine-readability, and usability through standard compliance.

PART 1

■ ■ ■

Web Standards

In this part of the book, you learn the theory and fundamental concepts of web standards, along with the standardization bodies that develop standards and the most influential web sites that announce, promote, and distribute them. After understanding the importance of web standards, you can differentiate technical specifications under development from de facto and de jure web standards.

One of the very first steps in developing sites in languages other than English or creating multilingual sites is to select and declare the right character encoding. In these chapters you become familiar with the most powerful character encoding capable of representing all characters of the written languages of the world as well as widely used notations and historic scripts.

The history of HTML and XHTML markup languages is crucial to understanding document types, the core document structure, and the allowed elements and attributes for the selected document type. You learn the syntax, the restrictions, and benefits of XHTML, and the extension of web documents through external vocabularies as mixed-namespace documents. By enumerating the benefits of HTML5 over HTML 4.x and XHTML, you will have a solid understanding of cutting-edge markup standards. As you will see, HTML5 can be written not only in HTML, but also in XML serialization, and web designers can create so-called polyglot documents that generate the same DOM tree regardless of the parser. You learn the role of hand coding in Web Quality Assurance, and why machine-generated code cannot compete with web designers. You also learn how to add machine-readable annotations to the markup and improve the accessibility of web sites.

Without proper web server configuration, the correct appearance, operation, and behavior of web sites cannot be guaranteed. You learn about the most widely adopted application protocol, the Hypertext Transfer Protocol, and the structure of the HTTP header. The most common Internet Media Types (MIME types), the file format identifiers of the Web, are described. You see how to create permanent URIs by minimizing the information provided in them and removing file extensions on the web server.

You learn why and how to separate content from appearance using Cascading Style Sheets (CSS), and what the differences are between the major CSS versions. CSS3 offers mechanisms and properties to create conditional styles depending on the features of the browsing device, create transitions and text effects, and provide beautiful typography.

The chapters lead you through techniques to build core web site components based on standards. After reading these chapters, you will have a solid foundation of web standards and will be able to implement the right standards for your projects.

CHAPTER 1

■ ■ ■

Introduction to Web Standards

Technical standards are widely used in various fields of life—think of the standards of paper size and the standard envelopes that fit them, or AC power plugs and their corresponding sockets. *Web standards*, similar to other standards, are normative specifications of technologies and methodologies. In other words, they are well-defined sets of requirements to be satisfied. They are not only ideal from the technical point of view but also represent user needs. However, web standards are often ignored; the World Wide Web consists of billions of documents that do not consider proper restrictions or regulations, deproving user experience. This is because the Web is a "free forum" where everyone can publish pretty much anything without technical skills, content review, or censorship. Unfortunately, this approach comes at a price: you will often encounter sites that download really slow, collapse in the browser, or have poor functionality. In spite of the benefits of standard compliance, not only content authors but also web developers find it challenging to implement web standards, mainly due to the lack of widespread distribution. Even the most popular web sites can be very confusing, and in contrast to the common misconception, developers cannot use them as references to learn from. Moreover, web designers often ignore standards because of the misbelief that developing with standards means an additional workload. Due to their limited knowledge on web standards, web designers are often not familiar with the benefits of standards compliance and the best practices of standards-based web design.

In this chapter, you will learn about the significance of web standards and the reliable resources you should know in order to make the best use of web standards in your web applications. This chapter sets out the major benefits of web standards. It will also give you a solid understanding of the diversity and status of standards. After reading the chapter, you will be able to recognize finalized specifications and select the most appropriate ones for any project.

The Basic Concepts

Web standards are applicable to the World Wide Web (for short, the Web). These formal standards define and describe various aspects of the Web. According to the Web Standards Project, a major standards promoter, "Web standards are carefully designed to deliver the greatest benefits to the greatest number of web users while ensuring the long-term viability of any document published on the Web. Designing and building with these standards simplifies and lowers the cost of production, while delivering sites that are accessible to more people and more types of Internet devices. Sites developed along these lines will continue to function correctly as traditional desktop browsers evolve, and as new Internet devices come to market" [1].

Web standards are often *de facto* (in practice) standards. Since there is no law that enforces them, web standards are ignored by a large share of web developers. The Recommendations published by the World Wide Web Consortium (W3C), the largest web standardization body in the world, are not exceptions either. However, in November 2010, W3C made a big step forward when it became an ISO/IEC JTC 1 PAS Submitter because any stable core web technologies produced by W3C are also in the scope of the International Standards Organization (ISO). ISO and the International Electrotechnical Commission (IEC) can efficiently contribute to the wider, and, if possible, global, adoption of W3C standards by changing the status of de facto standards to *de jure* (in principle) [2].

Web site standardization refers to the development process of standard web sites or the correction of nonstandard sites to fulfill the requirements to become standard-compliant sites. This phrase has been recently associated with widely accepted web design technologies, principles, techniques, and best practices, and unfortunately, various tricks as well as widely adopted CSS and JavaScript hacks. Most web designers are unaware that such tricks and hacks should not be used at all.

The main goals of standardization are functionality, interoperability, and browser and resolution independence in order to maximize user experience, access to content, menu usability, mobile-friendliness, and predictable behavior.

The Role of Standardization

The goals of web design cannot be achieved without a standardized approach. How would it be possible to use printers on a daily basis without paper-size standards? How could anyone use electric devices without standardized voltage? Why do web designers assume that standards are not essential to web quality assurance?

The grammar and other rules defined by web standards should be followed in web design. Although browsers have strong built-in error-handling features capable of eliminating problems on the client side, web developers should not misuse these features.

Routine design tasks should be based on standards. Overall, designing costs of standard-compliant web design are lower because fewer design decisions are needed. A further advantage is that developers can reuse their knowledge during development.

Poor functionality and usability might have a severe impact on web site traffic and business revenue, because users switch to other web sites within a few seconds if the content is not provided in an appropriate manner or the user experience is poor.

Since various browsers interpret incorrect markup in different ways, markup errors can lead to inconsistencies, bad layout, displeasing styling, and unexpected site behavior. The best way to eliminate such problems is to fulfill all the requirements of structure, syntax, and other rules described by the appropriate Document Type Definition and W3C Recommendation (see the "W3C" section).

Web designers usually try to implement the latest popular technologies to meet client expectations and compete with other developers, but not all of these technologies are standardized. Applying up-to-date web standards can be challenging, but it is vital for providing powerful, modern features while making web sites ready for later improvements and future standard implementations. Standard compliance is an essential feature of web site development that guarantees high code quality [3] and improves overall web site usability.

The Cost of Nonstandardized Markup

All Internet users encounter web sites from time to time that break apart and show partly overlapped or incorrectly positioned elements and/or unreadable content. The cause is, in most cases, the nonstandard or browser-specific source code, and sometimes the lack of standard support of the web browser used to render the pages.

The majority of web sites are obsolete from the standardization point of view. Even the largest and most well-known companies publish nonstandard documents constantly.

The major drawbacks of nonstandardized documents are the following:

- Inadequate search engine indexing. Crawlers cannot index incorrectly coded documents efficiently, which can cause visitor loss.[1]

- Longer download time.

- Longer rendering.

---

[1]There are hundreds of other factors that affect search engine indexing.

- Incorrect rendering (one of the most significant drawbacks).
- Difficult and inefficient development cycle.
- Low level of accessibility.
- Low level of backward compatibility.
- Lost traffic, fewer visitors, and fewer sales. Because of the inconveniences and problems listed earlier, web sites that are not standard-compliant have a higher risk of losing functionality, popularity, and productivity.
- Additional bandwidth load and hosting cost. Numerous needless characters in the source code increase both file size and complexity.
- More difficult updating and maintenance.

Benefits of Standard-Compliant Markup

Valid, standard-compliant markup has several advantages. Here are the most important ones:

- Search engine crawlers can index documents more adequately, and the content is basically search engine optimized.
- Compared to those websites that violate standards, standard-compliant websites can be downloaded faster.
- Well-structured markup provides faster rendering.
- Web documents that apply standards properly are rendered accurately in modern browsers.
- More users are accommodated, and they probably stay longer because of correct appearance and layout.[2]
- Lower development costs (only in case of well-qualified developers and carefully selected software tools).
- Standard-compliant markup serves as the basis for website accessibility.
- Backward compatibility is ensured as browsers evolve.
- Optimal content lengths and file size (no unnecessary characters are listed in the source code), as well as cost-optimal storage (potential for cheaper hosting).
- Standard-compliant markup is easier to maintain and update than the markup that violates standards.
- Standard-compliant source codes become obsolete later, and upgrading is much easier when new standards are introduced.
- Compatibility with current and future browsers is guaranteed (at least from the developers' point of view).
- Inspire implementation and force web browsers to support standards progressively.

As you can see, the standard-compliant, clean code has many advantages over nonstandard code and that's why standard compliance is vital in modern web design.

---

[2]Assuming that the web site has a decent design.

Development and Announcement of Standards

Web standards are *technical specifications of web technologies* released by standardization bodies. Most web standards are published by the W3C [4]. The *W3C Recommendations* are vital in standards-based web design.[3] W3C publishes the most web specifications by far, covering markup languages, style sheets, metadata, XML technologies, semantic markup, mathematical notation, graphical formats, and other technologies. However, there are also other influential standards organizations on the web standardization scene (Table 1-1).

***Table 1-1.** Influential Organizations in Web Standardization*

Organization	Abbreviation	Web Site	Major Specifications and Standards
Dublin Core Metadata Initiative	DCMI	www.dublincore.org	Dublin Core Metadata
ECMA International (formerly ECMA)	ECMA	www.ecma-international.org	ECMAScript [5]
International Organization for Standardization	ISO[4]	www.iso.org	Web site engineering and other IT standards [6], user interface standards, PNG functional specification
Internet Assigned Numbers Authority	IANA	www.iana.org	Domain names, IP address coordination, protocol assignments [7]
Internet Engineering Task Force	IETF	www.ietf.org	Internet standard (STD) documents [8], Request for Comments (RFC) documents [9], for example, proper use of HTTP, MIME, and URI
Unicode Consortium	Unicode	www.unicode.org	Unicode Standard, Unicode Technical Reports (UTRs) [10]
Web Hypertext Application Technology Working Group	WHATWG	www.whatwg.org	HTML5, Microdata, Web Applications, Web Forms, Web Workers [11]
World Wide Web Consortium	W3C	www.w3.org	Most web recommendations, as for example, (X)HTML, CSS, DOM, XForms, SVG, RDF, GRDDL, OWL

---

[3]The term recommendation indicates the lack of legal status, which is one of the reasons why web standards are not implemented globally.

[4]Since the name of the organization would have different abbreviations in all their three official languages, English, French, and Russian, the organization adopted ISO as its abbreviated name (from the Greek word isos, meaning equal).

W3C

Founded and directed by Tim Berners-Lee (sometimes referred to as "the inventor of the Web"), the *World Wide Web Consortium* is the largest international organization for developing standards for the World Wide Web. It has several local offices throughout the world. The members of W3C are mainly universities and research groups that are keen to participate in the development of web standards. W3C works as an open forum.

Efforts are made to ease contributions to web standards. In fall 2010, W3C released the proposal "Making W3C the place for new standards" [12]. Openness could be the key to new, easier contributions from the web community, including independent web developers without W3C membership. It also contributes to the maximization of knowledge reuse [13]. Important standards such as HTML5, CSS, SVG, MathML, various APIs, RDFa, and Microdata are summarized in a suite of technical standards called the *Open Web Platform*, which is open for contributions from external organizations and the public [14]. W3C is now "an open platform for web standardization" [15].

Many problems web developers face every day have already been solved and published in earlier W3C Recommendations, often several years ago. News feeds, for example, are not as new as one might think. One of the first attempts for web syndication was described in 1995 [16], many years before news feeds first appeared on the Web and became supported by major browsers, operating systems, and office suites. Surprisingly, RSS 0.9 was published as early as 1999 [17]!

A similar trend holds for markup languages, semantic annotations, vector graphics, equations, and other specifications.

Mathematical notations are published as GIF image files all over the Internet, although the markup language for this purpose became a Recommendation in 1999 (with updates soon following).

Vector graphics are seldom used on the Web, although W3C started to develop the SVG standard in 1998, and it became a Recommendation in 2001.[5] High-resolution bitmap graphics are used instead. But why? They should be replaced by SVG whenever possible, and raster graphics should be applied for publishing photographs only. SVG is supported by Amaya, the free web editor/browser of W3C, and popular graphic suites like Adobe Illustrator and CorelDraw. From 2010, SVG has also been indexed by Google [18]. SVG 1.2 supports animation too. Editing SVG is not more complicated than editing bitmaps, so why not use them? SVG files are generally smaller in size, can be downloaded faster, and unlike bitmaps, SVG images can be resized and arbitrarily magnified without quality loss.

WHATWG

The Web Hypertext Application Technology Working Group (WHATWG) is a professional yet unofficial community founded by individuals in 2004. The WHATWG was a response to the relatively slow standards development of the W3C staff and their decision to abandon HTML in favor of XHTML. The WHATWG has an invitation-only committee, which controls the editing of specifications. Anyone can contribute to the efforts of WHATWG by joining one of its open mailing lists [19].

ERCIM

The *European Research Consortium for Informatics and Mathematics* assembles researchers to work in cooperation on various fields of ICT and applied mathematics including, but not limited to, information system applications, information storage and retrieval, information interfaces and presentation, data encryption, and database management [20]. The scientific approach is ensured by 22 organizations from different countries across Europe. ERCIM has played a major role in the formulation of standards such as SMIL and SVG [21].

---

[5]In contrast, Internet Explorer supports SVG natively from 2011 only.

IETF

The Internet Engineering Task Force (IETF) is a standardization group within the nonprofit organization Internet Society (ISOC) along with the Internet Architecture Board (IAB). IETF focuses mainly on Internet protocols. IETF standards are generally on lower levels than web site developers are interested in; however, even the well-known TCP/IP has been developed by IETF. "The mission of the IETF is make the Internet work better by producing high quality, relevant technical documents that influence the way people design, use, and manage the Internet [8]." Technical documents are listed on the Requests for Comments (RFC) web site [22].

Ecma International

Ecma International is a nonprofit standards organization that develops and promotes standards for information and communication systems [23]. One of its most important standards from a web developer's point of view is the standardized scripting language ECMAScript (which JavaScript is based on; see the section "JavaScript" for more).

Unicode Consortium

The *Unicode Consortium* coordinates the development, maintenance, and promotion of Unicode and other internationalization standards [24]. The nonprofit organization defines the behavior and relationship between Unicode characters. The consortium works in close collaboration with W3C and ISO. The most important part of the cooperation is the maintenance of ISO/IEC 10646, the International Standard synchronized with the Unicode Standard.

DCMI

The *Dublin Core Metadata Initiative* is a registered company in Singapore [25]. The open organization develops and maintains interoperable metadata standards. DCMI provides annual conferences and workshops, standards liaison, and standards promotion. The worldwide community of users and developers is supported by DCMI through collaborative work in discussion forums, communities, and task groups.

IANA

The *Internet Assigned Numbers Authority* is the organization that oversees global IP address and top-level domain allocations, root zone management in the Domain Name System (assignments of ccTLDs and gTLDs), MIME types, and other Internet Protocol–related symbols and numbers [26]. IANA is operated by the nonprofit corporation called Internet Corporation for Assigned Names and Numbers (ICANN) [27].

OASIS

The *Organization for the Advancement of Structured Information Standards* (OASIS) works on open standards for web services, interoperability, security, and ebusiness. Its slogan is "Advancing open standards for the information society" [28]. The consortium maintains influential information portals on web services as well as on XML [29, 30].

ISO

Founded in 1947, the *International Organization for Standardization* (ISO) is an international standardization body that represents various standards organizations from all over the world [31]. ISO provides both industrial and commercial standards. ISO has developed more than 19,500 international standards on a variety of subjects, many of which are also used on the Web (for example, country codes, date/time, and time duration annotations).

Standards Promotion and Distribution

Most web standards are optional only and not enforced by law (which would be the only way to achieve worldwide implementation). However, there are new trends that transform the web design industry. For example, there are accessibility standards enforced by law in some countries (see the section "Defining Web Accessibility"). Since web standards are not ubiquitous, it can be difficult for web designers to maintain up-to-date knowledge and learn new technologies. However, they can participate in a variety of events, including workshops and conferences, and use resources such as textbooks or online specifications to train themselves either as individuals or professional group members.

Groups and Associations

There are numerous groups among enthusiastic web developers that distribute and expedite standards and harmonize them with best practices. Membership fees in such groups are generally much lower than those of standardization bodies. In fact, some of them are open, and anyone can join free of charge. While appealing, many professional groups and associations focus on the latest technologies rather than standards. The following sections provide a quick overview of influential groups in web standardization.

The Web Standards Project

The Web Standards Project (WaSP) was founded in 1998 by professional web developers to spread the application of web standards published mainly by W3C. The Web Standards Project was "a grassroots coalition fighting for standards which ensure simple, affordable access to Web technologies for all" [1]. The organization focused on standard support, accessibility, and easier development.

WaSP's standardization processes were based on *task forces*. The Project's aim was to attract the attention of the most considerable companies and organizations of the world and persuade them to become as standard-compliant as possible. WaSP task forces included the following:

- Accessibility Task Force
- Adobe Task Force (formerly Dreamweaver Task Force)
- Education Task Force
- International Liaison Group
- Microsoft Task Force
- The Street Team

Among others, the Web Standards Project introduced the famous Acid tests used to compare standard support of browsers (see the section "Standard Compliance Tests"). In 2013, the Web Standards Project stopped working in its original form, and contributions can be made through other projects only.

Web Standards Group

As a web developer community, the *Web Standards Group* (WSG) focuses on web standards and best practices to achieve standard codes. WSG has thousands of members from all over the world [32].

International Webmasters Association

The *International Webmasters Association* is a W3C member that "provides and fosters professional advancement opportunities among individuals dedicated to or pursuing a Web career, and to work diligently to enhance their effectiveness, image, and professionalism as they attract and serve their clients and employers" [33].

Web Industry Professionals Association

The *Web Industry Professionals Association* (WIPA) is a technical association in Australia. WIPA assembles professional individuals working in the web industry to "exchange ideas, participate in debate, advance education and promote ethical practice" [34]. WIPA is a major organizer of web courses in Australia.

Open Digital Rights Language Initiative

The *Open Digital Rights Language* (ODRL) *Initiative* is an international organization that develops and promotes the ODRL vocabulary [35], which is an open standard for policy expressions (see the section "DC, IMS, and ODRL").

Staying Informed: Events and Courses

Beyond online resources such as official news feeds, there are several types of appearances and events that contribute to the worldwide distribution of web standards. The list includes press releases, scientific and professional conferences, talks, workshops, meetings, discussion forums, symposiums, and tutorials. The papers or presentations from these events are often available online. Web standardistas can use these documents to maintain up-to-date knowledge and keep abreast of the latest specifications.

The primary resource for major web standards events such as workshops and conferences as well as announcements of recommendations and presentations is the W3C web site at `www.w3.org` [36]. Events are classified as "Talks and appearances" and "Events." Past events are available in the News Archive [37].

The World Wide Web Consortium also offers online training courses on or related to standards such as SVG or mobile-friendly web design through a dedicated portal [38]. The courses consist of weekly modules with instructions (*lectures*), link collection, activities, and a discussion forum. The quality is guaranteed by the instructors who are either co-authors or editors of the relevant W3C standards or internationally recognized invited experts. Participants can expect to spend two to three hours per week on these courses.

The *Internationalization & Unicode Conference* (IUC) has been organized annually since 1977. It covers the latest industry standards and best practices on software and web application internationalization. Up-to-date information about this conference is available at `www.unicodeconference.org` [39].

IETF meetings are held three times a year. Information on upcoming meetings, requests, materials, proceedings, and sponsoring are published on the IETF web site [40].

The Dublin Core Metadata Initiative has held the International Conference on Dublin Core and Metadata Applications annually since 2001 [41].

WIPA provides up-to-date information on upcoming events such as Australian training courses and workshops on the WIPA web site [34].

The Association for Computing Machinery (ACM) maintains an up-to-date calendar on IT conferences and events, some of which are related to web technologies [42].

World Standards Day has been celebrated since 1970 by ISO, IEC, and ITU each year on 14 October in Geneva, Switzerland. The message of World Standards Day 2010 clearly indicated a major aim of standardization: "Standards make the world accessible for all" [43].

Not all prominent events have a long track history, though. Many promising conferences and workshops are good initiatives such as the popular conference called Future of Web Apps [44].

There are web sites that are collections of events and articles of a given topic. A good example is `www.semanticmetadata.net`, which is a comprehensive site for Semantic Web developers [45].

Resources

One of the easiest ways to keep up-to-date with web standards is to subscribe to the news feeds of standardization bodies and organizations, and regularly check their web sites. Course materials, conference proceedings, and presentation slides are also available on many of these sites. An endless variety of further resources are also available.

W3C provides a weekly newsletter [46]. Its latest news is available in both Atom [47] and RSS [48] news feeds. The vast majority of W3C documents are public and freely available.

General news on Unicode is available through the news feed of the Unicode Consortium [49].

The Dublin Core Metadata Initiative publishes news on the home page of its web site and provides a news feed [50]. The proceedings of the International Conference on Dublin Core and Metadata Applications are available at the DCMI Publications page [51].

Scientific journal papers with Digital Object Identifier (DOI) can also be found throughout the Web, although many of these documents are not in the public domain. Still, most of them provide at least a free abstract, and a reference list.

Types, Stages, and Status of Standards

The Web is a highly innovative medium where constant changes and improvements necessitate continuous standard development. This results in different document *maturity levels*. W3C Recommendations progress through five such levels, which is the *W3C process flow* [52]:

- Working Draft (WD)
- Last Call Working Draft
- Candidate Recommendation (CR)
- Proposed Recommendation (PR)
- W3C Recommendation (REC)

The last version is considered by developers as the *(de facto)* standard to be applied. W3C Recommendations are sometimes updated by separately published *erratum*. After a considerable amount of changes, new editions are published that supersede the current version. Since W3C uses permanent addresses that won't change over time, the URI of each version of their specifications is unchanged (and usually includes a datestamp), which ensures the availability of all versions of their specifications. The *document status* determines which version is the most up-to-date one and which one should be applied. The list of current W3C publications and the latest revision of technical reports can be found in the W3C technical reports folder [53].

Other standardization bodies use different status conventions. The Internet Engineering Task Force, for example, applies document status such as *Internet draft*, *informational*, and *proposed standard*. The latter one is defined as a "generally stable specification which has resolved known design choices, is believed to be well-understood, has received significant community review, and appears to enjoy enough community interest to be considered valuable. However, further experience might result in a change or even retraction of the specification before it advances [54]." The IETF RFCs are designated as *standards*, *draft standards*, *proposed standards*, *best current practices*, *informational documents*, *experimental documents*, and *historic standards* [55].

The Microformat Community uses the status *draft specification* for those documents that are "somewhat mature in the development process" and whose stability is not guaranteed [56]. Implementers of such documents are warned to keep abreast of future developments and changes.

ISO applies the following conventions:

- *Preliminary Work Item* (PWI)
- *New Work Item Proposal* (NP or NWIP, NP Amd/TR/TS/IWA)
- *Working Draft* (AWI, AWI Amd/TR/TS, WD, WD Amd/TR/TS)
- *Committee Draft* (CD, CD Amd/Cor/TR/TS, PDAmd (PDAM), PDTR, PDTS)

- *Enquiry Draft* (DIS, FCD, FPDAmd, DAmd (DAM), FPDISP, DTR, DTS)

- *Final Draft International Standard* (FDIS, FDAmd (FDAM), PRF, PRF Amd/TTA/TR/TS/Suppl, FDTR)

- *International Standard* (ISO TR, TS, IWA, Amd, Cor)

Many web standards are *open standards*, meaning that the development has been open to individual contributors; they are publicly available, and certain copyright licenses might apply.

The Variety of Rendering Engines

Web documents and files associated with style sheet files, script files, images, and XML files are processed and displayed (that is, rendered) or printed by *rendering engines* (*layout engines*). They are usually embedded in web browsers and e-mail clients.

Although the statistics of web browser market share [57, 58, 59, 60, and so on] are usually biased and inaccurate, one thing is certain: no user agent can be claimed as "the most popular" or the "most widely used" one, because usage share varies across application areas (mobile browsing, business setting, etc.). Consequently, browser independence is a fundamental need in web design that ensures interoperability and functionality.

In the early 2010s web browsers reached a really high level of web standards support, and it is now the web designers' turn to develop standard-compliant sites that leverage this standard support. To design web sites that achieve a similar (and not pixel-by-pixel identical) appearance in various browsers has always been a challenge (and often nightmare) for web designers. While the implementation of core web standards eventually became adequate in modern browsers, there are specifications under development (such as many CSS3 modules) that are already implemented partially and/or incorrectly in browsers. Due to this inconsistency and the different functioning and features, various browsers might render even standard-compliant web sites differently. For years, various tricks and hacks were used to address the problem which lost their relevance thank to best practices, but such tricks and hacks are still present in older web sites.

SVG support can serve as a good example for the limited implementation and slow adoption of web standards. The specification was published in 1999, and no one cared about it until the growing popularity of HTML5, which natively supports the format. Browsers such as Firefox, Chrome, Opera, or Safari have adopted the standard lately, although before IE, which is quite disappointing because none of them supported SVG for so many years. In the early 2000s, one (if not the only one) that did was Amaya. Until recently, many people used the Adobe SVG Viewer plug-in to display SVG images in their browsers, and most users could not open SVG files at all.

The implementation of elements and attributes does not necessarily mean proper, full support for a markup language. For example, some browser vendors claimed for years that their product supported MathML; however, MathML could not be rendered in many cases because of the lack of support for embedding mechanisms and external files. Even the appropriate MIME type was missing from most implementations.

Standards support, especially of CSS, has been incorrect and/or incomplete in most browsers for years. Moreover, the latest version of CSS, CSS3, was introduced before the previous one, CSS 2.1, could have gained complete support in browsers.

There's always been web designers who preferred one of the browsers over the others, and users who hated one or more of the major browsers, especially Internet Explorer.[6] For years, the third-party competitors of IE have been implementing the latest technologies right after their release (Figure 1-1). Since 2012, Internet Explorer keeps up with such changes through periodic updates, but previously it was lagging behind the other browsers due to rare updates and the slow release of new major versions (three years have passed between version 7 and 8, two years between version 8 and 9, compared to Firefox's rapid release at six-week intervals since version 5).

---

[6]As the built-in browser of Windows, it is more vulnerable than third-party browsers, and older versions of Windows do not support the latest versions of IE, while the latest version of third-party browsers can be installed even on really old systems. Third-party browsers have other limitations and issues. Google Chrome, for example, has well-known privacy issues.

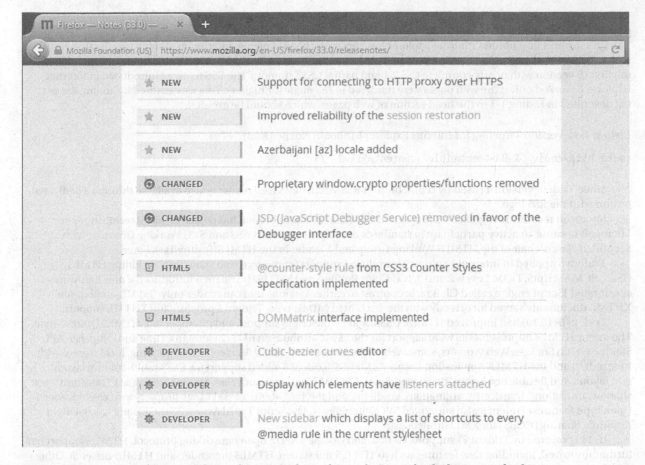

Figure 1-1. Browser updates provide new features such as advanced support for the latest standards

Trident

Used by Internet Explorer (since version 4) and IE shells, Outlook Express, Maxthon, and various media players, *Trident* is one of the most widely used rendering engines. Windows Internet Explorer (formerly Microsoft Internet Explorer) is a series of graphical web browsers developed by Microsoft. IE has been implemented in the Microsoft Windows operating systems since 1995.

Although Internet Explorer has been continuously improved in each version, even the most important standards, that is, the ones that describe the markup and style sheets, were implemented in an incomplete fashion until version 9. The limited standards support, incorrect floating positions, the expanding box problem, and especially the implementation of the individual box model of Internet Explorer 6, have caused serious problems in web design for years.

The standard-compliant mode was introduced in version 6; however, it did not solve the problem. Even some of the well-known HTML 4.01 elements (for example, abbr) were not supported prior to IE8. Several DHTML objects did not comply with standards. When web pages were rendered in IE8 mode, however, the methods and attributes updated in IE8 caused problems with web sites that expected the rendering functionality of earlier IE versions [61].

For years Trident has supported HTML 4.01, XML 1.0, XSLT 1.0, and DOM Level 1 with minor implementation gaps. CSS Level 2 and DOM Level 2 have been provided with major implementation gaps and conformance issues. The CSS support in Windows Internet Explorer has constantly been evolving. Internet Explorer 6 was the first version with full CSS Level 1 compliance. However, some selectors such as `min-height` were missing. Internet Explorer 8 is the first IE version with nearly complete CSS 2.1 and partial CSS3 support. The CSS features introduced in Internet Explorer 8 worked only if the web pages were rendered in *IE8 mode* (or higher). This was ensured by adding the `meta` tag described in Listing 1-1 to the head section of web pages, which should be avoided.

Listing 1-1. Version Targeting for Internet Explorer 8 (Should Not Be Used)

```
<meta http-equiv="X-UA-Compatible" content="IE=8" />
```

Since Trident version 4 (used by IE8), a built-in RSS/Atom news feed reader is also available through a dedicated button with the RSS logo.

Microsoft recently recognized the importance of standards support and has begun to take it seriously. First, Microsoft became an active participant in standards development in the CSS3 and SVG Working Groups at W3C. Second, it is a co-chair of the HTML5 Working Group and a leader in the HTML5 Testing Task Force.

Trident 5 applied in Internet Explorer 9 introduced support for modern web standards, including HTML5, CSS3, ECMAScript5, DOM Levels 2 and 3, ICC Color Profiles, and SVG [62]. Trident 5 introduced a new hardware-accelerated JScript engine called Chakra. In contrast to earlier versions that can render only "HTML-compatible" XHTML documents served incorrectly with the `text/html` MIME-type, Trident 5 provides full XHTML support.

Trident 6 (IE 10) had improved HTML5, CSS3, and EcmaScript5 support, and interoperable HTML5 Quirks Mode. The major HTML5 improvements were support for the `async` attribute on `HTTP/2` elements, Drag and Drop, File API, Sandbox, Web Sockets, Web Workers, some Web Performance APIs, HTML5 Video Text Captioning, local storage with IndexedDB and the HTML5 Application Cache. As for CSS, Trident 6 added support for CSS3 multi-column layout, grid layout, and flexible box layout, positioned floats, CSSOM Floating Point Value, Media Queries, 3D Transforms, text shadow, transitions, transforms, animations, gradients, and the `font-feature-settings` property to access advanced OpenType features. Trident 6 also supported SVG Filter Effects, JavaScript Typed Arrays (WebGL), and Cross-Origin Resource Sharing (CORS) for XMLHttpRequest.

IE 11 (powered by Trident 7) supports WebGL and Google's SPDY open networking protocol. HTML5 support has further improved, including new features such as HTML5 full screen, HTML5 prerender, and HTML5 prefetch. Other new features include WebGL, CSS3 border image, and HTTP/2 support, and improved JavaScript performance.

Gecko

Firefox, Camino, the Mozilla Application Suite, Netscape, Thunderbird, SeaMonkey, and other software apply the rendering engine Gecko (originally NGLayout) [63]. Netscape released the first version in 1997. In 1998, the Mozilla project was launched, and the source code was released under an open source license. Gecko is now developed by the Mozilla Foundation/Corporation. It is written in C++[7] as a cross-platform layout engine under three licenses: Mozilla Public License (MPL), GNU General Public License (GPL), and GNU Lesser General Public License (LGPL).

Gecko was originally designed with web standards support in mind and the standards implementation is improved in each version. Gecko supports HTML5, MHTML, Ruby annotations, CSS3, JavaScript, ECMAScript 3 and 5, DOM Levels 1/2/3, XML 1.0 and 1.1, SMIL, MathML, RDF, RDDL, XSLT 2.0, XSL-FO 1.0, XInclude, XForms, XFrames, XPath 2.0, GraphML and GML/XGMML, SVG 1.1, and Animated PNG (APNG) images with alpha transparency.Gecko supports `DOCTYPE` switching for backward compatibility, making it possible to render nonstandard web sites designed for older browsers correctly. Older Internet Explorer issues such as the incorrect implementation of the `document.all` property or the `marquee` element are also handled.

---

[7]The Mozilla Firefox browser has parts written in C/C++, JavaScript, CSS, XUL, and XBL.

Firefox also provides Google's Safebrowsing protocol to improve the security of data exchange.

Firefox does not support ActiveX controls by default. Although third-party plug-ins are available, they do not work safely in all versions and under all platforms.

KHTML

KHTML is the layout engine used by Konqueror. It supports HTML 4.01 and HTML 5. Both screen and paged media support is provided for CSS 2.1. Beyond the full implementation of CSS 3 selectors (from KDE 3.5.6 [64]), KHTML supports other CSS3 features, for example, multiple backgrounds, box-sizing, and text-shadow. KHTML supports DOM 1 and 2 fully and DOM 3 partially. ECMA-262 (JavaScript 1.5) can be used in KHTML, along with the graphic formats PNG, MNG, JPEG, GIF, and SVG).

WebKit

The forked (adopted) version of KHTML is the open source WebKit layout engine. The most well-known browser that uses WebKit is Apple Safari. Google Chrome used WebKit until version 27. Further browsers that use(d) WebKit are Amazon Kindle, Arora, Midori, OmniWeb, Shiira, iCab (4+), Epiphany, SRWare Iron, and Maxthon (3+). WebKit has been used on several mobile devices such as the Apple iPad, iPhone, and iPod Touch, as well as the browser on Android, Palm webOS, and Symbian S60. The desktop version of Safari is available for both Apple and Windows computers.

Being one of the first implementers of the latest standards (which have also been proved by the Acid2 and Acid3 tests), Safari has always been considered as one of the most innovative web browsers. Safari 5, for example, was amongst the first browsers that supported the newly introduced HTML5 features such as Media Support, full-screen playback for the video element, canvas, Geolocation, structuring elements, Ajax history, the draggable attribute, forms validation, the sandbox attribute, and Ruby annotation. Safari 5 handled CSS animations, CSS effects, and Web Fonts, provided JavaScript support (ECMAScript 262 version 3), and handled JSON, XML 1.0, and SVG 1.1. Advanced accessibility features have also been introduced in Safari 5 such as VoiceOver Screen Reader, ARIA Support, enhanced keyboard navigation, full-page zoom, content zoom, closed captions for HTML5 video, custom style sheets, and minimum font size. It also had a built-in news feed reader [65]. These features have further been improved in later versions.

The very first version of the other popular browser that used the WebKit rendering engine, Google Chrome, passed the Acid1 and Acid2 tests, indicating good web standards support. Chrome passes the Acid3 test from version 4.

Presto

Presto was the rendering engine used by the Opera Desktop browser from version 7 to 15, along with the Opera Devices SDK, and the Opera Mobile and Mini variants. Opera served as the basis for other browsers such as Nintendo DS and DSi, Nokia 770, and Wii Internet Channel, as well as the browser for Sony Mylo COM-1.

One of the reasons for Presto's good web standards support was Opera Software's W3C membership [66]. Opera was amongst the first browsers with HTML5 support covering the canvas, video, audio, web forms, contentEditable, the input attribute and the input type, the viewport meta element, and HTML5 APIs like Web Workers, Geolocation, Selectors, Touch Events, as well as CSS3 selectors, SVG, and SMIL [67].

Blink

The Blink rendering engine, announced in April 2013, is a fork of Webkit and used in Google Chrome 28+, Opera 15+, Webview (Android 4.4+), RockMelt, and Amazon Silk. Blink has excellent HTML5 and CSS3 support, and it deprecates vendor prefixes used in non-standard style sheets.

Amaya

Unlike other browsers that are typically used exclusively to display web documents, Amaya was a free, open source web browser and a WYSIWYG web developer environment in one. Managed by W3C, Amaya supported HTML 4.01, XHTML 1.0, XHTML Basic, XHTML 1.1, HTTP 1.1, MathML 2.0, CSS2, and SVG [68]. Distributions were available for Windows, Linux, and Mac. While still available, the latest version was released in 2012 when Amaya's development was discontinued.

Testing the Standard Support of Browsers

Web browsers can be tested from two different aspects: supported standards and user experience through performance and features. The development of browser tests depends on the approach and aim. From the web design perspective the first one is more important. The most influential browser tests are platform-independent, and can compare not only different browsers, but also the same browser running on different platforms. Incomplete or incorrect standard support is usually tested with comprehensive tests, many of which are public. Most browser tests require human evaluation to identify bugs with full certainty.

Automatic *layout tests* are difficult to execute on mobile devices because layout tests generate a screenshot and compare it to a reference image.

Two different versions of the same web page supposed to result in exactly the same rendering can be compared using *ref-tests* [69]. Mozilla also provides an automated testing framework using *MochiKit* JavaScript libraries [70]. The test applies JavaScript function calls. These browser-specific tests cannot be used for general browser comparisons.

The World Wide Web Consortium provides HTML tests [71], CSS test suites [72], mobile tests [73], a MathML test suite [74], SVG test suites [75], and internationalization tests [76]. W3C is open to browser test suggestions as well [77].

The web design community develops specialized browser tests such as the HTML5 Test [78] and the CSS3 Test [79].

Standard Compliance Tests

The most well-known browser tests for standard compliance are the *Acid tests*. The name refers to the acid tests used for gold assessment. Instead of gold purity, however, these Acid tests provide a fast and easy-to-understand indication of the standard compliance of rendering engines. In spite of that, the Acid tests have always been criticized for testing not only the core markup and style sheet compliance, but also a set of rarely used features, along with those without a finalized specification.

The first version of the Acid test, *Acid1*, was written in HTML 4.0 Strict in late 1998 to check interoperability issues between earlier web browsers. Acid1 tests several features with stress on compliance with the CSS1 specification on a page against a reference image [80]. According to the document title, Acid1 is a "display/box/float/clear test."

Acid2 is a test page published by the Web Standards Project in 2005. Again, a reference image is provided that should be compared to the rendered version. Note that the nose should change to blue when the mouse hovers over the face [81]. Beyond this hovering effect, Acid2 tests the paint order, the object element, data URIs, alpha transparency of PNG images, and several CSS features (absolute, relative, and fixed positioning, the CSS box model, CSS table formatting, CSS generated content, and CSS parsing). Safari was the first among the widely used browsers that passed Acid2 in late 2005. Others followed two to three years later. For example, Firefox passed the test from version 3.0.

Acid3 has been launched in 2008, and updated in September 2011. The 100 subtests grouped in 6 "buckets" cover various parts of the following standards: data URI scheme, HTTP 1.1 Protocol, HTTP status codes, Unicode 5.0 UTF-8 and UTF-16, the image/png and text/plain content types, the HTML 4.0 Transitional, HTML 4.01 Strict, and XHTML 1.0 Strict markup languages, DOM Level 2 (Core, HTML, Events, Style, Views, Traversal, Range), the object element, ECMAScript (including garbage collection), CSS selectors, SVG 1.1 (including fonts), and SMIL 2.1. Not only those browsers fail the test that cannot achieve the score 100/100, but also the ones that cannot render the animation smoothly or render it differently than what is presented in the reference (Figure 1-2 [82]).

To pass the test, a browser must use its default settings, the animation has to be smooth, the score has to end on 100/100, and the final page has to look exactly, pixel for pixel, like this reference rendering.

Figure 1-2. *The Acid3 test in a browser that failed to pass*

The following were the first stable, public browser releases that passed the Acid3 test:

- Apple Safari 4.0 (the very first web browser to pass Acid3 [83])
- Bolt 1.6 [84]
- Epiphany 2.28.0 [85]
- Firefox 4 (updated Acid3)
- Google Chrome 4.0.249.78 [86]
- Internet Explorer 10
- iPhone 3.1
- Iris 1.1.4
- Opera 10.6 [87]
- Opera Mobile 9.7 [88]

Comprehensive Tests

There are several other considerations in rendering engines beyond standard compliance, for example, security or CSS Selectors API [89] support.

Layout tests, Mochi tests, and RefTests can be performed by BrowserTests, a repository of browser test cases and test suites [90].

A comprehensive comparison and evaluation of overall browser functionality are provided by BrowserScope. It is a "community-driven project for profiling Web browsers" [91]. The site provides up-to-date information on recent tests performed on the latest browser versions. Browsers can be compared, and tests can be run on the browser used for rendering the site.

Standards vs. Quirks Modes, DOCTYPE Switching

Standard-compliance problems of web browsers are not recent. The situation has been constantly improved, however. After partially supporting the W3C Recommendations, browser users and web site developers faced a serious problem. Millions of web sites developed earlier for older browsers looked fine in obsolete rendering engines but had serious issues in the latest ones. In other words, compliance with W3C Recommendations became a problem.

In 1998, *Todd Fahrner* from the Web Standards Project invented the solution known as *DOCTYPE switching* [92]. Older, nonstandard documents with a missing DOCTYPE might produce different results in various rendering engines. Modern browsers check the DOCTYPE, and if the expected behavior follows W3C standards, the document is rendered in *Standards Mode* (*Strict Mode*). If the Document Type Definition is missing, browsers switch to a mode known as *Quirks Mode*[8][93] that can deal with the nonstandard, unexpected behavior of older browsers (Figure 1-3).

Figure 1-3. *W3C test file in Standards Mode [94] and Quirks Mode [95]*

---

[8]In Internet Explorer 9 and 10, the backward compatibility mode is called *Compatibility Mode*, which was renamed in Internet Explorer 11 to *Emulation*, providing a mechanism that can also be triggered manually to render version-targeted web sites with older versions of the rendering engine.

One of the most famous browser bugs was the *Internet Explorer box model bug* that made identical pixel-by-pixel rendering in various browsers impossible. It occurred as Microsoft's own box model implementation instead of the W3C CSS box model [96] in earlier versions of Microsoft Internet Explorer. (Some web developers, however, argue that the box model implemented in IE5 was more logical than that of W3C's [97]; still, it was not standard.) IE6 and newer versions eliminate the problem in Standards Mode. For the sake of compatibility, however, the bug is still present in Quirks Mode. (Internet Explorer for Mac, which was discontinued in 2006, was not affected.) According to the W3C CSS1 specification, released in 1996 (revised later several times), determining the width and height attributes of all block-level elements should affect the width and height of visible elements only while the padding, borders, and margins should be applied later. Internet Explorer 5 wrapped the content, padding, and borders within a predetermined width/height. As a result, the rendering box was different from what was expected. The box model is present in newer versions of the Cascading Style Sheets specification too, including CSS 2.1 [98] and CSS3 [99].

Standard-compliant web pages can be opened faster since browsers can use Standards Mode instead of figuring out nonstandard markup in Quirks Mode.

Internet Explorer 6 rendered all pages in Quirks Mode if anything other than a byte-order mark appeared before the DOCTYPE declaration.Modern browsers render all pages providing a DOCTYPE in Standards Mode, whether they are served with or without an XML declaration.

Problem Statement

It is a common misconception that web standardization is a well-regulated process. In reality, there is no clear set of rules to follow. Although W3C develops web technologies for markup, annotation, styles, and so on, that will sooner or later obtain an official mandate, the implementation of their "standards" (recommendations) is an expectation only. Unlike the standards announced by standardization organizations, for example, the ISO, web recommendations are adopted globally because of the lack of an official status [100]. Individual vendors and web site developers *might* follow *some* of the recommendations, might not. This approach proved to be insuffiecient in the widespread implementation of web standards. In fact, 99.9 percent of web sites are obsolete in terms of standards compliance [101], since a large share of web sites are based on invalid code.

A comprehensive validation test series was conducted in 2011 on the 350 most popular web sites in the world (selected by Alexa index[9] [102]). The test found 94 percent of those web sites failed the web standards validation tests that covered character encoding, markup, and style sheets.

While UTF-8 should be used everywhere, 12 other character encodings were also used, namely, ISO-8859-1, GB2312, Shift_JIS, GBK, Windows 1251, EUC-JP, Windows 1256, ISO-8859-15, ISO-8859-2, ISO-8859-7, ISO-8859-9, and Windows 874. As for the markup languages, nine (X)HTML versions and variants were identified which confirms web designer unawareness and lack of skills or experience. At the time of the test, 14 percent of web sites had applied HTML5 before the specification had been finalized, 23 percent used the obsolete HTML 4.01 Transitional, 45 percent the XHTML 1.0 Transitional, 8 percent the XHTML 1.0 Strict, 5 percent the HTML 4.01 Strict, and 5 percent other languages such as HTML 4.0 Transitional, HTML 4.0 Strict, and XHTML 1.1 (Figure 1-4). Although two versions, XHTML 1.0 Strict and HTML5, can be considered modern markup languages, they were applied incorrectly: the markup was full of errors on many sites. This situation was clearly indicated by the average number of markup errors, which was 6. The number of style sheet errors was even higher, with an incredible high maximum of 738 errors (!) in a single CSS file. The average number of CSS errors was 45. And these numbers represented the index files only.

---

[9]Naturally, the list of web sites changes constantly, but it does not change the conclusion.

Figure 1-4. *Many involved in web design do not know web standards at all*

In 2014, another test series indicated a much higher share of HTML5 with UTF-8 encoding (approx. 95%), while standard compliance was still an issue with not only the markup, but incorrect implementation such as that of vendor-specific CSS3 properties in the style sheets. The large number of markup errors (max. 875) and CSS errors (max. 750) is a clear indication that the implementation of web standards did not improve over the years and that many web content authors and web designers do not know what they are doing.

Many people publishing on the Web are content authors rather than web designers, and only very few web designers are experts in web standards. The majority of web content authors do not even know the underlying technologies and standards, not to mention the best practices to implement those standards. Expectations do not force people to apply web technologies and standards correctly, and the lack of consensus makes the Web chaotic. Compared to programming languages such as C, the Web is an error-tolerant environment. This featuresimplifies web publishing to the extent that everyone can create web pages without solid web design skills (through content management and templates), but without web quality assurance, often resulting in bad quality code [103].

Companies desire a professional appearance to sell their products and often focus on design and marketing exclusively. In most cases, designers know little if anything about web standardization. Without knowing the potential inherent in web standards, people won't make the effort to create standard-compliant web sites.

Incorrect or incomplete standard implementations of web browsers are responsible for further problems in web standardization. Even standardized web sites might break apart in browsers that do not support web standards fully and correctly. Optimal rendering can be expected only if standards are implemented correctly by both browser vendors and web designers.

Web publishing is often oversimplified, and only a very limited number of web designers are hand coders, which is a major key to standardized web development. Since content authors need content management via graphical interfaces and dynamic content, proper standards implementations in authoring tools and templates could contribute to web standardization significantly. For example, if a standard-compliant WordPress template is deployed, the code quality of the empty site is inherently standard-compliant, but someone without proper skills can break this standard compliance with a single character. While the markup quality of web site templates have improved in recent years, the cutting edge CSS3 implementations are usually still not standard-compliant.

Beyond a certain point, markup and style sheet errors cannot be tolerated. Web documents full of errors often contain improperly nested elements, malformed tags, and other markup errors referred to as *tag soup*. Tables should be used only for organizing data, not for layout or design. Missing tags should not be tolerated. Bad markup extends download time and rendering time since processing the errors is more complicated than rendering error-free, standard-compliant (valid) code. Efficiency can be boosted by optimizing the code. Accessibility can also be increased, along with cross-browser compatibility and forward compatibility.

Limited Standards Support in Machine-Generated Code

Server-side technologies, such as PHP, ASP, or Ruby on Rails, are popular because of their powerful assistance in creating dynamic web sites and web applications. While powerful, server-side technologies and Content Management Systems often produce markup without proper structuring and semantics that would make web sites work better [104].

Nonprofessional authors using WYSIWYG software, such as Adobe Dreamweaver, produce a large share of web sites. Until recently, many of them provided nonstandard output. Modern versions of web development authoring tools support W3C standards. The same is true for open source environments providing dynamic content such as social networking sites, blog portals, and so on.

Still, these software tools are responsible for billions of web sites published on the Web without considering standard compliance. Users often try to modify or extend the template code creating nonstandard code even if the template was originally standards-compliant (which is not always the case).

While most software tools do not reach full standard compliance, web standards implementations are constantly improved. Some content management systems support not only core standards but, like Drupal, not fundamental standards such as RDFa[10] [105].

The standard compliance of markup and styles provided by WYSIWYG authoring tools is extremely important because of the large number of authors applying them. However, even standard-compliant markup and style sheets can be easily messed up with incorrect code by those content authors who do not understand the principles and coding.

Major Concerns

Similar to documents, books, or movies, web sites that meet all criteria and user requirements cannot be created—what's suitable for one audience might not be for another, and even if you try to adhere to every relevant standard published, you will find that certain standards cannot be used in combination with others. Web designers should still strive to comply with the core web standards, which contributes to code quality . Fulfilling the fundamental requirements for standard compliance leads to best practices. Standardized web sites provide satisfactory and predictable functionality and behavior, usability, stability, and optimal performance.

Bad Practices

While best practices are widely applied in programming, web developers and unskilled content authors do not take web design best practices seriously. "It works this way—why bother with standard compliance?" This is the approach serious web developers would be best to forget. Bad markup including, but not limited to, browser-specific code fragments, heavily nested table layouts, structure mixed with layout, locally applied style attributes, attribute minimization, missing attribute values, and other anomalies significantly increase code length, complexity, download, and rendering time.

Lack of Support

Web standards support is unsatisfactory. There are no ultimate practical guidelines on web standards for the less experienced. While most web standards are freely available, most people find them too difficult to understand and implement in real-life applications.

Where standard compliance is an official requirement, such as on government portals or EU project web sites, the best solution is to hire *web standardistas* to develop suitable web sites. Web designers often focus on appearance rather than code quality while managers and directors concentrate mainly on the content. Most people cannot realize that standard compliance could be the only solution for many of their problems, such as browser-dependent web pages, incorrect rendering, or poor functionality.

---

[10]From version 7.

Unconcern

One of the major problems with web standards is that free access to them is not sufficient to convince people to use them. Standard implementations of authoring tools are limited, and the web sites produced by them seldom follow standards. While constantly evolving, the standards support of web browsers is often incomplete.

With the growing popularity of web publishing, the need to make the process easier arose. As a result, easy-to-use Content Management Systems appeared on the market, and nearly everyone became capable of publishing on the Web without advanced web design skills. To maintain web site functionality on the millions of badly coded web sites, browser vendors made their products foolproof and error-tolerant. People began to think that what was beneath the surface did not matter.

Many people still generate poor quality code web sites through easy-to-use Content Management Systems without a full understanding of web design principles and best practices. For some it is just a hobby; for others it is an income source. The importance of web standards should be highlighted by influential companies throughout the world to make these people understand the associated problems. Web design trends are forced by business and marketing to achieve popularity or fulfill business requirements. For example, because of the lack of support for Flash on the Apple iPhone, early HTML5 implementations appeared that applied unfinished specifications but at the same time expedited standards evolution and application. Everyone interested in web design, whether a professional or not, should become familiar with web standards, because they are vital in web development and worth learning (instead of copying bad practices from others).

Without several years experience, no one can understand the options. Which markup language is the most modern one? It is not possible to answer the question without knowing HTML, XHTML, XML, the Semantic Web, the maturity levels of web standards, and cutting edge web technologies.

Thanks to HTML5 and CSS3, web standards got more attention since the early 2010s; however, worldwide adoption is still far away. Manual coding is rare, so Content Management Systems have the potential to help content authors and web designers comply with web standards based on standard-compliant templates and code blocks. Some stages of web standardization, such as accessibility evaluation or error checking, cannot be fully automated (see Chapter 11). Only web standardistas can manipulate the content and the entire markup and style sheets character by character, along with all the files of a web site, but not all web designers are such experts in web standards.

Influential Sites

Developers often have the logical idea to follow the practices of the most popular and widely used web sites in the world. However, these web sites cannot serve as references in standardization simply because they often have serious problems with standard compliance.

It is shocking that the personal web sites of the top web designers in the world also suffer from markup and style sheet errors. Most of them try to avoid criticism by omitting the W3C conformance icons linking to W3C validators that would reveal their bad code with a single click.

A good starting point is to find web sites with modern features and standard-compliant code. However, this can be very difficult and misleading. Certainly, it is impossible to fulfill all user requirements, but web sites that focus on standards compliance and are labeled with the logo "Valid XHTML" or "Valid CSS" often come with a lack of design and exhibit limited use of technologies. Good examples are the web sites of web standardization bodies or web accessibility designers. Even if the source code is valid and free of errors, the code often has other issues. Expected components such as news feeds or favorites icons (favicons) are missing, semantic markup is not used, and so on. These features do not affect the validity of such web documents, which cannot be used exclusively as starting points for developing modern, standard-compliant web sites. Not only personal web sites and blogs but also precise technical documents can be presented beautifully. Remember, web standardization is not a sacrifice! Some of the largest and most popular web sites in the world apply standards successfully while proving the highest level of user experience.

But not all. Take a closer look at a code fragment from one of the largest web sites in the world (Listing 1-2).

Listing 1-2. *High-Traffic Web Sites Do Not Necessarily Apply Standard Code*

```
<body class="ego_page home hasLeftCol fbx ie8 win Locale_en_US">
<input type="hidden" id="post_form_id" name="post_form_id"
value="b053066a05f482d5739d31c033b5fd90" autocomplete="off" /><div
id="pagelet_presence"></div><div id=" HiddenContainer" style="position:absolute; top:-10000px;
width:0px; height:0px;" ></div><div id="blueBar" class=""></div><div id="globalContainer"><div
id="dialogContainer"></div><div id="c4d06220d5f2c97d20912236"><div class="ptm clearfix"
id="pageHead"><h1 id="pageLogo">
```

Such software-generated markup codes are almost impossible to understand even if you are an experienced hand-coder. There are problems with virtually every element and attribute. The `class` attribute has an empty value. Identifiers are unreasonably long and not descriptive at all, such as `c4d06220d5f2c97d20912236`. There is inline style in the source, which should be in an external style sheet.The layer positioning with -10,000 pixels is obviously a trick that could be eliminated by proper implementation of standards. Attributes should not be empty, especially if they are intended to be used for identification (a `class` without a name cannot be used to identify an element class). Even for these few lines, the error list is long.

Visual Appeal Over Functionality

Design is one of the major concerns in web site development. Adobe Flash is an ideal technology to provide a stunning appearance, catch attention, and stream videos. Full Flash sites, however, have several disadvantages. Unless the web document is a single-page, brochure-style home page that provides contact data, it is far better to develop (X)HTML content, because textual markup has several benefits over binary files. It is especially true with the exploitation of the new, interactive HTML5 elements and CSS3 properties, which are good alternatives to Flash content.

Graphic designers are not necessarily web developers. As a consequence, Flash movies are often embedded incorrectly. Although Flash files can theoretically work in any browser with an appropriate plug-in, markup codes controlling them can be browser-dependent, which should be eliminated.

There is nothing wrong with Flash, but it is better used for headers and inline animations only. The combination of XHTML and CSS can provide a similar, even more advanced, user experience, but without the need to download large files in full before showing the content of the index page. While it is not a problem for fast connections, there are millions of users around the world who have to wait for half a minute to download such contents. Even if the Flash files are streamed in certain browsers, the menus and content are unusable until downloading is completed. Web sites based on markup can be indexed and searched more effectively, are smaller in size, and have full control over the browser window by default. Text content is much more robust to render than any other format. Even if some images fail to download or there are some styling problems, the content is still there (if not absolutely positioned outside the window or written in the color identical to the background). Unlike that of Flash contents, (X)HTML text sharpness, font size, and other features can be changed upon user request directly from the browser.[11]

Some software companies recognized the advantages of markup languages over Flash and released tools to convert Flash files to HTML (for example, *FlashKeeper* [106]). Even Adobe has an FLA-HTML converter called Wallaby [107]. However, similar to other automated markup generators, extended care must be taken with them because the result is often invalid and, therefore, not optimal.

Well-Formedness

A basic requirement for XML documents and a desired one for all web documents is *well-formedness*, which is vital in standardization, because it guarantees that the list of syntax rules defined in the corresponding specifications are satisfied.

---

[11]Although there are advanced font manipulation possibilities in Flash Player from version 10, too.

To achieve well-formedness in SGML languages such as HTML, elements should be opened and closed properly. Empty elements must also be terminated. Elements should be nested properly so that overlapping does not occur. The root element of the document should contain all other elements.

Since SGML parsers are extremely error-tolerant, these rules are rarely followed completely by HTML developers, which results in markup errors. Thus, the lack of well-formedness leads directly to incorrect, nonstandard markup.

In XML languages such as XHTML, well-formedness has additional requirements. The element tags are case sensitive; that is, start and end tags must match exactly. Well-formed XML documents should contain properly encoded and legal Unicode characters only. These characters, however, can also be used directly in element names and attributes, not just in character data (document text). Characters with special meaning in XML can be used for markup instructions only, for example, <, >, or &. If they are intended to be represented as text, their entity codes should be applied (see the section "Entity references").

Characters that go against well-formedness rules can cause certain XML parsers to be unable to process XML files (XHTML documents, RDF metadata, RSS feed channels, and so on). Such special characters might also result in error messages. A single (not well-formed) character can make the whole file impossible to process. For example, the XML file of a valid RSS feed opened locally in a modern browser is presented as a tree structure. The same file retrieved from a server is represented as a news feed. If the file, however, contains just one illegal character, the browser gives an error message instead of displaying the page content (Figure 1-5).

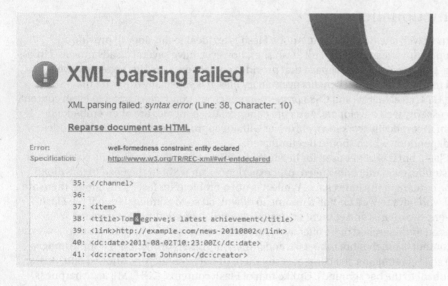

Figure 1-5. *An XML parsing error in a browser*

Interoperability

There is an endless variety of computing platforms, operating systems, and browsers available on the market. Every manufacturer and developer tries to provide additional features; thus, products are constantly competing with each other. This diversity results in different operations and functionalities. The functionality and behavior of web sites across the different systems are not guaranteed by default but can be achieved by implementing widestream standardized solutions. Naturally, users want to use various systems together that allow truly efficient communication. Data access would be restricted without standards, and platform-dependent solutions would rule the market.

Web interoperability ensures that standard-compliant web pages can be viewed in any browser under any operating system, from Windows to Mac OS and Linux, and not only on desktop computers but also on mobile devices, including tablets and smartphones.

Several technologies support interoperability and should be used in web development, including, but not limited to, UTF-8 character encoding, XML documents, structural and semantic markup with XHTML or HTML5 [108], DOM scripting, ECMAScript, CSS-based layout, separated structure, presentation and behavior, equations described in MathML, and semantic metadata.

Browser Independence

"One page, many views" has always been a nightmare for web developers. Although it is a natural user expectation for all web sites to look and behave the same way in various browsers, it is far from straightforward to fulfill.

> *Anyone who slaps a "this page is best viewed with Browser X" label on a Web page appears to be yearning for the bad old days, before the Web, when you had very little chance of reading a document written on another computer, another word processor, or another network.*

> —Tim Berners-Lee [109]

While there is a variety of web browsers on the market, the majority uses only a few browsers, namely, Internet Explorer, Mozilla Firefox, Google Chrome,Safari, and for a lesser extent, Opera. Focusing on these flagships is usually sufficient, especially when the major rendering engines behind these browsers—Trident, Gecko, WebKit, and Blink—are the ones that power the most popular mobile browsers too (Trident is used on Windows Phone smartphones, Firefox for mobile (Fennec) running on Android phones use Gecko, while iPhones and iPads use Webkit). Statistics show that only very few visitors use browsers powered by other rendering engines.

No one wants to drive potential customers away, so it is very important to avoid browser-specific coding. The best approach is to create sites that are *best viewed with any browser* which can be indicated clearly by the logo of the "Viewable with any browser" campaign [110].

To create very similar (more or less identical) appearance in all major browsers, various tricks have been applied for years to ensure functionality. However, browser-targeted code blocks do not work satisfactorily under all browsers, so more and more different hacks were added to support different browsers (and older browser versions), resulting in a mass of incorrect code. The right approach is to create standard-based web sites. Even if some standards are not fully supported in some browsers (which is actually a headache for web designers), standard-compliant codes are at least ready for the future [111], and can serve as excellent starting points for best practices and web standards evolution.

A very bad practice associated with the problem of the different rendering behavior of browsers is *code forking*. Code forking is the development of multiple versions of the same content for various browsers. Code forking should not be applied because the resulting code cannot be used in the long term.

Web standardistas agree that web sites cannot be expected to look exactly the same way in every browser, but the information published on web pages should be legible and the functionalities should be available in all major browsers [112, 113].

Eliminated Version Targeting

Since rendering engines are constantly evolving, even the various versions of the same browser support standards differently. To avoid losing users and potential customers who use older browser versions, web developers often apply various browser- and version-specific solutions in the markup or style sheets. In other words, *version targeting* means a considerable amount of additional work for developers, and the result works only in a certain version of a certain browser.

Due to the advanced standard support of current browser versions, these codes are real threats to functionality or code optimality, or both. Thus, version targeting should be eliminated, which, on the other hand, can cause problems with backward compatibility [114]. Although there are some techniques that can be used together with standard compliance to maximize version independence (for example, resetting the style sheets of the browser), creating web pages that work properly under all browsers and browser versions is unfeasible.

Browsers to be used for rendering version targeted web documents can be easily defined by a simple meta declaration in the document head (Listing 1-3).

Listing 1-3. Version Targeting Example (Should Not Be Used)

```
<meta http-equiv="X-UA-Compatible" content="IE=8;FF=3;OtherUA=4" />
```

The most up-to-date Internet Explorer version can be targeted by adding the IE=edge attribute value to the content attribute of the meta element [115] (Listing 1-4).

Listing 1-4. Version Targeting for the Latest IE Version (Should Not Be Used)

```
<meta http-equiv="X-UA-Compatible" content="IE=edge" />
```

Although targeted browsers might decide more quickly between old, backward-compatible and new, standard-compliant rendering modes when such data are provided, version targeting should be totally eliminated. Creating multiple versions of nonstandard markup for the same web page is not only costly but also unsustainable. Moreover, version targeting and browser detection scripts are not reliable and cannot target the correct browsers in many cases, because browsers often identify themselves as other browsers or other versions of the same browser.

Backward Compatibility

Standard-compliant web sites that work well under the currently used browser versions are also ready for the future but might be rendered incorrectly in older browsers because of the incorrect standards implementations of their rendering engines. Consequently, even with proper implementation, web standards do not work under all browsers. The support for old rendering engines, *backward compatibility*, should be within reasonable limits. Why bother with browsers that are no longer in use or the "very old" versions of major browsers? Netscape, for example, is "not widely used anymore" just like Internet Explorer 5 or Mozilla Firefox 3.6. The major problem with this question is how to define *browser obsoletion*. Can IE6 be labeled as "very old" and IE8 as "old"? The choice of supported browsers has a large impact on the traffic and popularity of a web site, and the lack of support for older—even obsolete—browsers can lead to loss of visitors. Satisfied users cannot be pushed to upgrade their browsers every time a new version is released, and there are users who have to use a version-targeted corporate software. Because of this, there is no ultimate decision regarding backward compatibility.

In the late 2000s and early 2010s, one of the biggest agonies regarding backward compatibility was the support for IE6. Its market share decreased slowly up to 2007 when it lost its popularity considerably, mainly because of the new versions of Windows and their new Explorer versions,[12] as well as the growing popularity of competitors such as Mozilla Firefox, Apple Safari, and Google Chrome. There was a really good reasoning against the obsolete browser. First, serious security holes have been pointed out during the years that have been partially covered by later patches. However, thanks to growing needs, new functions have been introduced in other browsers and in the newer versions of Internet Explorer. All modern browsers support XML technologies, RSS feeds, and tabbed browsing, for example. IE8, IE9, and especially IE10 were big steps toward standard compliance and modern functions. Even Microsoft recommended IE6 users to upgrade [116, 117]. Software giants like Google stopped supporting older browsers, which is another reason for the upgrade [118]. In 2014, the support for Windows XP has ended, and with the more and more affordable and powerful modern computers and mobile devices, there is no reason not to use a modern browser with satisfactory HTML5 and CSS3 support. It is also a great relief for web designers that don't have to deal with obsolete browsers anymore.

The major drawback of backward compatibility is that it hinders the widespread use of new technologies at some point. Still, backward compatibility should be maximized whenever possible. Because of the incomplete or unsatisfactory standard support of older browsers, providing backward compatibility often results in browser-targeted hacks and code fragments, as well as nonstandard and even deprecated markup that should be eliminated.

A useful tool to achieve or maximize backward compatibility is the JavaScript library "Modernizr," which detects browser support for the latest web standards, including HTML5 and CSS3 modules [119]. This software determines whether a currently used browser has implemented a given feature, so web designers can apply new technologies in the browsers that support them and create a fallback mechanism for those browsers that do not.

Forward Compatibility

While a new browser release can be a problem for developers of nonstandard and especially browser-specific web sites, those web designers who write standard-compliant code do not have to worry, because standard compliance ensures *forward compatibility*. Standardized web documents can be easily upgraded to newer standards.

Functionality

Beyond content, functionality is one of the most important web site features, without which all other efforts would be useless, including a fancy design. While functionality can be ensured by developing with web standards, this often seems like some kind of sacrifice. For example, the latest standards are not necessarily supported by some rendering engines, so web designers have to make a decision: either write standard-compliant code and not support some browsers or provide nonstandard, browser-independent code. The better the standards support in web browsers, the less frequent this dilemma.

Device Independence

Internet access is no longer restricted to desktop computers. Mobile devices such as tablets, smartphones, and some e-book readers also have Internet-browsing capabilities. However, some devices—especially the handheld ones— have limited screen size and scrollability. Mobile-readiness is more important than ever, which also contributes to web accessibility and usability.

---

[12]Internet Explorer 6 was shipped with Windows XP. Versions 7 and 8 can be used on XP, too, while IE9 requires Windows Vista or Windows 7. IE10 runs under Windows 7 and above.

There is a wide choice of computer monitors and displays, all of which come with a different size, aspect ratio, resolution, pixel density, contrast ratio, and color fidelity. To support the wide variety of screens, web sites should be *resolution-independent*. Functionality should be satisfactory and similar on a variety of devices regardless of different hardware controls and features. *Device independence* provides support for different access mechanisms and different modes of use (for example, visual and auditory use). The aim of device independence is to "match Web content to the needs, capabilities, and limitations of the delivery environment" [120]. The popularity of mobile browsing makes device independence a major concern in modern web design.

Markup languages are good examples for device independence standards. CSS also provides web design techniques to achieve device independence through device-specific style sheets for mobile phones, projectors, and printers,[13] as well as conditional styles depending on viewport size and device features. Java applets can be executed on a variety of devices under different platforms, because Java is a cross-platform programming language. Image file formats such as JPEG, TIFF, or GIF are also device-independent files. In document publishing and sharing, PDF is a classic example for device independence.

Separating Content from Presentation

In the early days of the Web, the major concern in web publishing was the web presence itself. At that time, web documents were limited mainly to the combination of lightly formatted text content and images. When the possibilities widened, the Web soon became a full multimedia platform, and inline styles flooded the markup of web documents. To update the color or the font size of an element throughout a site, the style attributes had to be updated one by one on each page.

To solve this problem, the W3C introduced a new Golden Rule in web design: formatting should be separated from structure, which centralizes styling, making it possible to change the styles of an entire web site from a single location. A further benefit is that the markup becomes shorter, less redundant and complex, clearer, and easier to interpret and render.

Usability

Usability can be defined as "setting clear and concise goals for a web site, determining a correct and exhaustive set of user requirements, ensuring that the web site meets user's expectations, setting usability goals, and providing useful content" [121]. It is a measure of how easily a system can be used. Usability can be achieved by optimizing user experience via browser independence, accessibility, expected behavior, logical site structure, and reliable layout. Confusing content and disturbing effects should be avoided. Usability should not be confused with accessibility, which means access to all, regardless of user disabilities or device limitations.

Web sites should provide useful content that is relevant and appropriate to the audience. There are numerous requirements for the appearance of texts, links, lists, controls, graphics, and multimedia objects. Beyond content, the navigation and site structure should be organized in a way that meets user expectations. This can be achieved by assessing the site with test users. User experience and user interface design should precede web design and coding.

Reliable Layout

Reliable positioning of web site elements has always been a major concern in web site development. Because of the enormous number of factors to consider, some elements should be positioned absolutely while others relatively. There are elements that are meant to be fixed, even if the content exceeds the browser window and the content is scrolled (see the section "Reliable Positioning"). Layout is in strong correlation with device, resolution, and browser independence. On mobile-ready web sites, the objects should rescale according to the viewport size and be proportional to each other, while the text should reflow dynamically on smaller screens.

---

[13]The same web site rendered without the background image on mobile phones is a good example.

CSS provides both absolute and relative measurement units for defining element dimensions, lengths, and distances. The appropriate units should be chosen according to the overall design and layout of a web site (see the section "Sizes and Proportions"). Unreliable or browser-dependent positioning and improperly combined units can result in unreadable content or limited functionality. The overlapping order of layers might also be a problem if it makes the content unreadable.

Code Optimality

Web standards provide a way to develop reliable, fully functional, interoperable, device-independent, future-ready web sites. However, they cannot guarantee *optimal code length* by default. Even if each character in the source code has its meaning, that is, none of them is unnecessary, code length might still be far from optimal. Incorrect structuring in the markup and especially the ignored inheritance in CSS (see the section "Ignored Inheritance") can increase complexity and length, resulting in larger file size, slower download and longer rendering time (see the section "Nonoptimal Code Length").

Summary

In this chapter, you learned about the importance of web standards, the benefits of standards-based web design, and the resources where open standards can be accessed and standardization stages followed. Proper standards implementation is independent from site popularity and the latest web design trends. Software tools with incorrect or incomplete standards implementations and unskilled content authors produce the most nonstandard markup and style sheets. The only way to maximize interoperability and secure your web sites for the future is to implement web standards correctly.

In the next chapter, I will discuss language and character settings on servers and in markup to ensure proper character representation and provide advanced hints for software agents that search and process web documents. The internationalization settings of web documents typically precede coding and can be considered as one of the first steps in standards-based web design.

References

1. Featherstone D, Gustafson A, et al (2013) http://www.webstandards.org. The Web Standards Project. Accessed 24 October 2014

2. Dardailler D (2010) W3C PAS FAQ. World Wide Web Consortium. http://www.w3.org/2010/04/pasfaq. Accessed 24 November 2014

3. Hazaël-Massieux D (2003) Buy standards compliant Web sites. World Wide Web Consortium. http://www.w3.org/QA/2002/07/WebAgency-Requirements. Accessed 24 October 2014

4. W3C (2014) Standards. World Wide Web Consortium. http://www.w3.org/standards/. Accessed 24 October 2014

5. ECMA International (2014) Formal publications. http://www.ecma-international.org/publications/. Accessed 24 October 2014

6. ISO (2014) World Wide Web standards at the ISO website. http://www.iso.org/iso/search.htm?qt=world+wide+web&published=on&active_tab=standards. International Organization for Standardization. Accessed 24 October 2014

7. IANA (2014) Website of IANA. http://www.iana.org. Internet Assigned Numbers Authority. Accessed 24 October 2014

8. IETF (2014) IETF website. `http://www.ietf.org`. The Internet Engineering Task Force. Accessed 24 October 2014

9. IETF (2014) RFC pages. `http://www.ietf.org/rfc.html`. The Internet Engineering Task Force. Accessed 24 October 2014

10. Unicode Consortium (2010) Technical Reports. `http://www.unicode.org/reports/`. Unicode, Inc. Accessed 24 October 2014

11. WHATWG (2011) Web Hypertext Application Technology Working Group. `http://www.whatwg.org`. Accessed 24 October 2014

12. Jacobs I (2010) Making W3C the place for new standards. `http://www.w3.org/2010/07/community`. Accessed 24 October 2014

13. Dardailler D (2010) Open Standards Policies. In: W3C: An Open Platform for Web Standardisation. Future Internet Conference - Standardization Workshop. World Wide Web Consortium. `http://www.w3.org/2010/12/dd-w3c.html#(3)`. Accessed 24 October 2014

14. Dardailler D (2010) W3C Exec Summary. In: W3C: An Open Platform for Web Standardisation. World Wide Web Consortium. `http://www.w3.org/2010/06/dd-diplo.html#(7)`. Accessed 24 October 2014

15. Dardailler D (2010) W3C: An Open Platform for Web Standardisation. World Wide Web Consortium. `http://www.w3.org/2010/12/dd-w3c.html`. Accessed 24 October 2014

16. Guha RV, Bray T (1997) Meta Content Framework using XML. World Wide Web Consortium. `http://www.w3.org/TR/NOTE-MCF-XML/`. Accessed 24 October 2014

17. Netscape Communications (1999) My Netscape Network: Quick Start. Netscape. `http://web.archive.org/web/20001208063100/http://my.netscape.com/publish/help/quickstart.html`. (archived version accessed 24 October 2014, original version is no longer available)

18. Stanescu B, Sarapata J (2010) Google now indexes SVG. Google Inc. `http://googlewebmastercentral.blogspot.com/2010/08/google-now-indexes-svg.html`. Accessed 24 October 2014

19. WHATWG (2014) WHATWG Mailing List. Web Hypertext Application Technology Working Group. `http://www.whatwg.org/mailing-list`. Accessed 24 October 2014

20. ERCIM (2014) ERCIM website. `http://www.ercim.org`. The European Research Consortium for Informatics and Mathematics. Accessed 24 October 2014

21. Jeffery K (2009) Twenty Years of ERCIM: History and Outlook. European Research Consortium for Informatics and Mathematics. `http://ercim-news.ercim.eu/en77/joint-ercim-actions/twenty-years-of-ercim-history-and-outlook`. Accessed 24 October 2014

22. IETF (2014) RFC-Editor Webpage. `http://www.rfc-editor.org`. The Internet Engineering Task Force. Accessed 24 October 2014

23. ECMA International (2014) ECMA Website. `http://www.ecma-international.org`. Accessed 24 October 2014

24. Unicode (2014) The Unicode Consortium. Unicode Inc. `http://www.unicode.org`. Accessed 24 October 2014

25. DCMI (2014) The Dublin Core Metadata Initiative. Dublin Core Metadata Initiative Limited. `http://dublincore.org`. Accessed 24 October 2014

26. IANA (2014) Internet Assigned Numbers Authority. `http://www.iana.org`. Accessed 24 October 2014

27. ICANN (2014) Internet Corporation for Assigned Names and Numbers. `http://www.icann.org`. Accessed 24 October 2014

28. OASIS (2014) OASIS: Advancing open standards for the global information society. `http://www.oasis-open.org`. OASIS. Accessed 24 October 2014

29. OASIS (2014) The Cover Pages. `http://xml.coverpages.org`. OASIS. Accessed 24 October 2014

30. OASIS (2014) XML.org. `http://www.xml.org`. Accessed 24 October 2014

31. ISO (2014) International Organization for Standardization. `http://www.iso.org`. Accessed 24 October 2014

32. WSG (2014) WSG website. `http://webstandardsgroup.org`. Web Standards Group. Accessed 24 October 2014

33. IWA (2014) The International Webmasters Association website. International Webmasters Association. `http://www.iwanet.org`. Accessed 24 October 2014

34. WIPA (2014) The Web Industry Professionals Association website. Web Industry Professionals Association Incorporated. `http://www.wipa.org.au`. Accessed 24 October 2014

35. ODRL Initiative (2014) ODRL website. Open Digital Rights Language Initiative. `http://odrl.net`. Accessed 24 October 2014

36. W3C (2014) World Wide Web Consortium. `http://www.w3.org`. Accessed 24 October 2014

37. W3C (2014) News Archive. World Wide Web Consortium. `http://www.w3.org/News/`. Accessed 24 October 2014

38. W3C (2014) W3DevCampus. World Wide Web Consortium. `http://www.w3devcampus.com`. Accessed 24 October 2014

39. OMG (2014) Internationalization & Unicode Conference. Object Management Group. `http://www.unicodeconference.org`. Accessed 24 October 2014

40. IETF (2014) IETF Meetings. The Internet Engineering Task Force. `http://www.ietf.org/meeting/`. Accessed 24 October 2014

41. DCMI (2014) International Conference on Dublin Core and Metadata Initiatives. Dublin Core Metadata Initiative. `http://dcevents.dublincore.org/`. Accessed 24 October 2014

42. ACM (2014) Calendar. Association for Computing Machinery. `http://www.acm.org/calendar-of-events`. Accessed 24 October 2014

43. Régis J, Morrison A, Touré H (2010) Standards make the world accessible for all – 41st World Standards Day. International Organization for Standardization. `http://www.iso.org/iso/wsd_message_2010.pdf`. Accessed 24 October 2014

44. Carsonified (2014) The Future of Web Apps Conference. Carsonified. `http://futureofwebapps.com`. Accessed 24 October 2014

45. Lux M (2014) SemanticMetadata.net. Mathias Lux. http://www.semanticmetadata.net. Accessed 24 October 2014

46. W3C (2014) Weekly newsletter. World Wide Web Consortium. http://www.w3.org/News/Public/. Accessed 24 October 2014

47. W3C (2014) W3C News (Atom new feed). World Wide Web Consortium. http://www.w3.org/News/atom.xml. Accessed 24 October 2014

48. W3C (2014) W3C News (RSS new feed). World Wide Web Consortium. http://www.w3.org/News/news.rss. Accessed 24 October 2014

49. Unicode (2014) The Unicode Blog (news feed). Unicode Consortium. http://unicode-inc.blogspot.com/feeds/posts/default?alt=rss. Accessed 24 October 2014

50. DCMI (2014) News feed of the Dublin Core Metadata Initiative. Dublin Core Metadata Initiative. http://dublincore.org/news.rss. Accessed 24 October 2014

51. DCMI (2014) DCMI Publications. Dublin Core Metadata Initiative. http://dcpapers.dublincore.org/. Accessed 24 October 2014

52. Dardailler D (2010) W3C Process Flow. In: W3C: An Open Platform for Web Standardisation. Future Internet Conference - Standardization Workshop. World Wide Web Consortium. http://www.w3.org/2010/12/dd-w3c.html#(7). Accessed 24 October 2014

53. W3C (2014) All Standards and Drafts. World Wide Web Consortium. http://www.w3.org/TR/. Accessed 24 October 2014

54. Bradner S (1996) The Internet Standards Process – Revision 3. The Internet Engineering Task Force. http://tools.ietf.org/html/rfc2026. Accessed 24 October 2014

55. IETF (2008) RFC overview. The Internet Engineering Task Force. http://www.rfc-editor.org/overview.html. Accessed 3 May 2011

56. TMC (2013) Drafts. In: The microformats wiki. The Microformats Community. http://microformats.org/wiki/Main_Page. Accessed 24 October 2014

57. Net Apps (2013) Browser Market Share. Net Applications. http://www.netmarketshare.com/browser-market-share.aspx?qprid=0. Accessed 21 October 2014

58. STAT OWL (2014) Web Browser Market Share. STAT OWL. http://statowl.com/web_browser_market_share.php. Accessed 21 October 2014

59. StatCounter (2014) StatCounter Global Stats. StatCounter. http://gs.statcounter.com/. Accessed 21 October 2014

60. W3Counter (2014) Global Web Stats. Awio Web Services LLC. http://www.w3counter.com/globalstats.php. Accessed 21 October 2014

61. Microsoft Developer Network (2010) Standards Compliance Updates in Internet Explorer 8. Microsoft Corporation. http://msdn.microsoft.com/library/dd433047(VS.85).aspx. Accessed 24 October 2014

62. Microsoft (2010) http://www.beautyoftheweb.com/#/highlights/html5. Microsoft Corporation. Accessed 31 December 2010

63. Scholz F et al (2014) Gecko. Mozilla Developer Network.
    https://developer.mozilla.org/en/Gecko. Accessed 24 October 2014

64. KDE Webmasters (2014) KDE 3.5.6 Changelog. KDE e.V.
    http://www.kde.org/announcements/changelogs/changelog3_5_5to3_5_6.php.
    Accessed 24 October 2014

65. Apple (2014) Safari features. Apple Inc. http://www.apple.com/safari/.
    Accessed 24 October 2014

66. W3C (2014) Current members. World Wide Web Consortium.
    http://www.w3.org/Consortium/Member/List. Accessed 24 October 2014

67. Opera Software (2012) Web specifications support in Opera products. Opera Software ASA.
    http://www.opera.com/docs/specs/productspecs/. Accessed 24 October 2014

68. Quint V (ed) (2012) Amaya. W3C's editor/browser. World Wide Web Consortium.
    http://www.w3.org/Amaya/. Accessed 24 October 2014

69. Baron LD (2006) Layout Engine Visual Tests (reftest). Mozilla Corporation.
    http://mxr.mozilla.org/mozilla-central/source/layout/tools/reftest/README.txt.
    Accessed 24 October 2014

70. Shepherd E (ed) (2014) Mochitest. Mozilla Developer Network.
    https://developer.mozilla.org/en/Mochitest. Accessed 24 October 2014

71. W3C (2014) Testing area. World Wide Web Consortium. http://w3c-test.org/html/.
    Accessed 2 October 2014

72. Bos B (ed) (2010) Official W3C Test Suites. World Wide Web Consortium.
    http://www.w3.org/Style/CSS/Test/. Accessed 24 October 2014

73. Andersen W, Hazael-Massieux D (eds) (2010) Mobile Tests. World Wide Web Consortium.
    http://www.w3.org/2005/MWI/Tests/. Accessed 10 February 2011

74. Flon PD (ed) (2010) MathML Test Suite. World Wide Web Consortium.
    http://www.w3.org/Math/testsuite/. Accessed 24 October 2014

75. W3C (2010) SVG test suites. World Wide Web Consortium.
    http://www.w3.org/Graphics/SVG/WG/wiki/Test_Suite_Overview. Accessed 24 October 2014

76. Ishida R (ed) (2010) Internationalization tests. World Wide Web Consortium.
    http://www.w3.org/International/tests/. Accessed 24 October 2014

77. Le Hégaret P (2010) How do we test a Web browser? World Wide Web Consortium.
    http://www.w3.org/QA/2010/09/how_do_we_test_a_web_browser_o.html.
    Accessed 24 October 2014

78. Leenheer N (2013) HTML5 Test. How well does your browser support HTML5?
    http://html5test.com/. Accessed 22 October 2014

79. Verou L (2014) The CSS3 Test. http://css3test.com. Accessed 22 October 2014

80. Fahrner T (1998) The Acid1 test. World Wide Web Consortium, the National Insititute of
    Standards and Technology, Case Western Reserve University.
    http://www.w3.org/Style/CSS/Test/CSS1/current/test5526c.htm. Accessed 24
    October 2014

81. Hickson I (2005) The Acid2 test. Web Standards Project. http://acid2.acidtests.org.
    Accessed 24 October 2014

82. Hickson I (2008) The Acid 3 test. Web Standards Project. http://acid3.acidtests.org. Accessed 24 October 2014

83. Apple (2010) Safari – Learn about the features available in Safari. Apple Inc. http://www.apple.com/safari/features.html. Accessed 23 September 2010

84. Scott (2009) Bolt Browser gets Updated to Version 1.6 – Brings New Features! Smartphone Blogs Network. http://blackberrysync.com/2009/12/bolt-browser-gets-updated-to-version-1-6-brings-new-features/. Accessed 24 October 2014

85. Ryan P (2009) Linux garden gets a new GNOME with version 2.28. Ars Technica. http://arstechnica.com/open-source/news/2009/09/linux-garden-gets-a-new-gnome-with-version-228.ars. Accessed 24 October 2014

86. Laforge A (2010) Google Chrome Releases: Stable Channel Update. Google Inc. http://googlechromereleases.blogspot.com/2010/01/stable-channel-update_25.html. Accessed 24 October 2014

87. Opera Software (2009) Turbocharge your Web experience with Opera 10. Opera Software ASA. http://www.opera.com/press/releases/2009/09/01/. Accessed 23 September 2010

88. Engebø HL (2009) Opera Mobile 9.7 with Opera Turbo. Opera Software ASA. http://my.opera.com/operamobile/blog/2009/03/26/opera-mobile-9-7-beta-for-windows-mobile. Accessed 23 September 2010

89. Van Kesteren A, Hunt L (eds) (2013) Selectors API Level 1. W3C Recommendation. World Wide Web Consortium. http://www.w3.org/TR/selectors-api/. Accessed 24 October 2014

90. Pasche S (2010) BrowserTests. Cross-browser automated tests. Google Inc. http://code.google.com/p/browsertests/wiki/StartPage. Accessed 24 October 2014

91. Simon L et al (2014) Browserscope. http://www.browserscope.org. Accessed 24 October 2014

92. Fahrner T (2002) Geocrawler.com - mozilla-layout - NG layout and 5.0 Navigator. An e-mail of Todd Fahrner archived by archive.com. Open Source Development Network. http://web.archive.org/web/20030212115103/http://www.geocrawler.com/archives/list-name.mbox/123/1998/7/0/1037920/. Accessed 24 October 2014

93. Ishida R (2010) Serving HTML & XHTML. 'Standards' vs 'Quirks' modes. World Wide Web Consortium. http://www.w3.org/International/articles/serving-xhtml/. Accessed 24 October 2014

94. Ishida R (2010) XHTML test document for Standards Mode. In: Serving HTML & XHTML. 'Standards' vs 'Quirks' modes. World Wide Web Consortium. http://www.w3.org/International/articles/serving-xhtml/standards.html. Accessed 24 October 2014

95. Ishida R (2010) XHTML test document for Quirks Mode. In: Serving HTML & XHTML. 'Standards' vs 'Quirks' modes. World Wide Web Consortium. http://www.w3.org/International/articles/serving-xhtml/quirks.html. Accessed 24 October 2014

96. Lie HW, Bos B (2008) Formatting model. In: Cascading Style Sheets, level 1. W3C Recommendation. http://www.w3.org/TR/REC-CSS1/#formatting-model. World Wide Web Consortium. Accessed 24 October 2014

97. Bowman D (2005) Douglas Bowman declares his love to CSS ... Vorsprung durch Webstandards. http://www.vorsprungdurchwebstandards.de/interviews/fallinginlovewithcss/douglas-bowman/. Accessed 24 October 2014

98. Bos B, Çelik T, Hickson I, Lie HW (2009) CSS 2.1 Box model. In: Cascading Style Sheets Level 2 Revision 1 (CSS 2.1) Specification, W3C Candidate Recommendation. World Wide Web Consortium. http://www.w3.org/TR/CSS2/box.html. Accessed 24 October 2014

99. Bos B (2007) CSS basic box model. World Wide Web Consortium. http://www.w3.org/TR/css3-box/. Accessed 24 October 2014

100. Gertner M (2008) Is Web Standardization Obsolete? Just Browsing. http://browsing.justdiscourse.com/2008/01/22/is-web-standardization-obsolete/. Accessed 9 September 2010

101. Zeldman J, Marcotte E (2009) 99.9% of websites are obsolete. In: Designing with Web standards, 3rd edn. New Riders, Berkeley

102. Alexa (2011) Alexa Top 500 Global Sites. Alexa Internet, Inc. http://www.alexa.com/topsites. Accessed 14 March 2011

103. Anderson E, DeBolt V, Featherstone D, Gunther L, Jacobs DR, Jensen-Inman L, Mills C, Schmitt C, Sims G, Walter A (2010) InterACT With Web Standards – A Holistic Approach to Web Design. New Riders, Berkeley

104. Zeldman J, Marcotte E (2009) Core forking can be hazardous to your site's long-term health. In: Designing with Web standards, 3rd edn. New Riders

105. Herman I, Corlosquet S, Clark L (2010) Combine the Web of Data and the Web of Documents (RDFa and Drupal 7). Proceedings of the International Semantic Web Conference 2010, 8 November 2010, Shanghai. http://www.w3.org/2010/Talks/RDFa-Drupal-Tutorial/. Accessed 24 October 2014

106. Sparkle Media (2010) Publishing Flash Animations to HTML format. Sparkle Media Systems. http://www.flashkeeper.com/publishhtml.htm. Accessed 12 January 2011

107. Adobe Labs (2011) Convert Adobe Flash FLA files into HTML and reach more devices. Adobe Systems Incorporated. http://labs.adobe.com/technologies/wallaby/. Accessed 22 June 2011

108. Çelik T (2010) HTML5 Now: A Step-by-Step Video Tutorial for Getting Started Today. New Riders Publishing, Berkeley

109. Berners-Lee T (1996) Technology Review, July 1996. http://en.wikiquote.org/wiki/Tim_Berners-Lee. Accessed 24 October 2014

110. Burstein CD (2011) Viewable with Any Browser: Campaign. Cari D. Burstein. http://www.anybrowser.org/campaign/. Accessed 24 October 2014

111. Kyrnin J (2006) Browser Specific Web Designs – Why Should You Care. The New York Times Company. http://webdesign.about.com/od/browsers/a/aa111797.htm. Accessed 24 October 2014

112. Allsopp J (2009) It doesn't have to look the same in every browser. In: Developing with Web standards. New Riders, Berkeley

113. Zeldman J (2010) Gentle persuasion. In: Designing with Web standards. New Riders, Berkeley

114. Gustafson A (2008) Beyond DOCTYPE: Web Standards, Forward Compatibility, and IE8. A List Apart Magazine. http://www.alistapart.com/articles/beyonddoctype. Accessed 24 October 2014

115. Microsoft Developer Network (2010) Standards by Default: What Does It Mean? Microsoft Corporation. http://msdn.microsoft.com/en-us/library/cc817575.aspx. Accessed 24 October 2014

116. Shankland S (2009) Microsoft actively urges IE 6 users to upgrade. CNET News. http://news.cnet.com/8301-30685_3-10406468-264.html. Accessed 24 October 2014

117. Microsoft (2014) The Internet Explorer 6 Countdown. Microsoft Corporation. http://ie6countdown.com. Accessed 24 October 2014

118. Protalinski E (2010) Google to send Internet Explorer 6 users packing come March. Ars Technica. http://arstechnica.com/microsoft/news/2010/01/google-to-send-internet-explorer-6-users-packing-come-march.ars. Accessed 24 October 2014

119. Ateş F, Irish P, Sexton A (2014) Modernizr: the feature detection library for HTML5/CSS3. Faruk Ateş, Paul Irish, and Alex Sexton. http://www.modernizr.com. Accessed 24 October 2014

120. Gimson R, Finkelstein SR, Maes S, Suryanarayana L (eds) (2003) Device Independence Principles. World Wide Web Consortium. http://www.w3.org/TR/di-princ/. Accessed 24 October 2014

121. Leavitt MO, Shneiderman B, Bailey RW, Barnum C, Bosley J, Chaparro B, Dumas J, Ivory MY, John B, Miller-Jacobs H, Koyani SJ, Lewis JR, Page S, Ramey J, Redish J, Scholtz J, Wigginton S, Wolfson CA, Wood LE, Zimmerman D (eds) (2006) Research-based Web Design & Usability Guidelines. Department of Health & Human Services (HHS), U.S. Government. http://guidelines.usability.gov/. Accessed 24 October 2014

CHAPTER 2

■ ■ ■

Internationalization

Web documents are published in all languages of the world, using a variety of character repertoires and features such as text direction. Several technologies support multilingual websites. To display characters correctly on websites, a character encoding that supports the required characters should be used to encode the markup files. The character encoding should be properly declared in the document header, and the documents served with proper server settings. Capable of representing any characters and ideographs of all natural languages, both ancient and modern, Unicode can be considered as the ultimate character encoding. To use Unicode, you need to understand the byte-order marks which provide information about the ordering of individually addressable subcomponents of this multibyte character encoding. Special characters and symbols can be written in various ways from entity sets and escape codes to hexadecimal notation.

In this chapter, you will learn how to ensure correct character rendering on web sites, and use the same markup structures for different language versions of multilingual sites. While the many characters are supported by more than one character encoding system, Unicode should always be used unless you have a very good reason not to do so. Most characters can be typed in directly into the markup, but there are some exceptions too. You will also learn the proper application of character entities and whitespace characters to add special characters to web sites, such as invisible, unprintable control characters.

The Importance of Character Encoding

Until the mid-1990s, computers mainly supported the characters of the English alphabet only (partly because of the American dominance on the computer market), and the need for international characters has been satisfied through hardware code pages, such as CP852 or CP1252, supported by the then-used operating systems (for example, DOS, Windows 3.1, and Windows 95). The proper display of Central-European characters, for example, depended on the hardware configuration, the operating system, and the settings of the operating system. A few years later, with the introduction of the Web, such limitations were no longer acceptable. In 1997, HTML 4.0 added advanced support for international characters.

The American Standard Code for Information Interchange (ASCII) has been the most widely supported character encoding scheme, which stores 128 characters on 7 bits. Additional characters have been provided by 8-bit character sets, such as the ISO/IEC 8859 series of ASCII-based standard character encodings (informally referred to as Latin-1). They were first published in 1987 and supported most Western European languages and partly supported some other languages.

Most modern character encoding systems are based on ASCII; however, they support many more characters.

If anything other than the most basic Latin characters is needed, many characters on your web site will be incorrect unless an appropriate *character encoding* is specified. These standards define not only the identification of each character and the associated numeric value (*codepoint*[1]), but also the way this value is represented in the bits of the file to be encoded.

---

[1]Codepoints are code positions that can be any of the numerical values that form the codespace of a character encoding.

If the character encoding is declared properly, browsers can use the appropriate encoding to render web documents correctly, including all special characters. Browsers usually have an automatic character encoding recognition feature as well, which is activated if the character encoding declaration is missing. Based on the setting and features of the file, the browser might identify the character encoding being used. Users can also select an encoding scheme manually in most browsers which is not needed if all server and document settings are correct.

As an example, let us assume that we want to publish Christmas greetings in several languages on a web page, as in Table 2-1.

Table 2-1. *Christmas Greetings in Different Languages*

Language	Greetings
Albanian	Gëzuar Krishtlindjet e Vitin e Ri
Arabic	أجمل التهاني بمناسبة الميلاد و حلول السنة الجديدة
	(Ajmel altehani bemonasebt almīlad wa helol alseneh aljedīdah)
Bulgarian	Честита Коледа! (Čestita Koleda!)
Dutch	Prettige kerstdagen en een Gelukkig Nieuwjaar!
English	Merry Christmas and a Happy New Year!
Finnish	Hyvää joulua ja onnellista uutta vuotta
French	Joyeux Noël et bonne année
German	Frohes Fest und guten Rutsch [ins neue Jahr]
Hindi	नये साल की हारदकि शुभकामनायें (Naye sāl kī hārdik śubhkāmnaye ṅ)
Hungarian	Kellemes karácsonyi ünnepeket és boldog új évet!
Italian	Buon Natale e felice anno nuovo
Persian	کرابم ناهج یمامت رب یدالیم ون لاس
	(Sale noe miladi bar tamami marodme jahan mobarak!)
Russian	С Рождеством Христовым и С наступающим Новым Годом
Urdu	Sale No Mobarak

Not all character encoding systems can represent such a character variety. Without choosing the right character encoding system, undesirable characters such as squares (□) or question marks (�) would appear instead of the correct form of special characters.[2] Inappropriate character encoding (or incorrect encoding declaration) can cause additional problems too; for example, users might not be able to search in the text. In web documents that contain characters beyond the English alphabet and not encoded correctly, there might be legible characters (sharing the same codepoint in the advanced and the basic character encoding), and meaningless characters throughout the document. Due to wrong encoding, databases might become inaccessible too.

Not only incorrect or missing encoding information can spoil text readability, but also missing fonts or fonts that do not support all characters of the language(s) of the site.

---

[2]Special characters in English, but basic characters in another language.

The set of supported characters depends on the character encoding, which is usually one of the following:

- *UTF*: UTF-8/UTF-16/UTF-32 (Unicode, worldwide)

- *ISO standards*: ISO-8859-1 (Western Europe), ISO-8859-2 (Central Europe), ISO-8859-3 (Southern Europe), ISO-8859-4 (Northern Europe), ISO-8859-5 (Cyrillic), ISO-8859-6-i (Arabic), ISO-8859-7 (Greek), ISO-8859-8 (Hebrew, visual), ISO-8859-8-i (Hebrew, logical), ISO-8859-9 (Turkish), ISO-8859-10 (Latin 6), ISO-8859-11 (Latin/Thai), ISO-8859-13 (Latin 7, Baltic Rim), ISO-8859-14 (Latin 8, Celtic), ISO-8859-15 (Latin 9), ISO-8859-16 (Latin 10), ISO-2022-jp (Japanese, e-mails), ISO-ir-111 (Cyrillic KOI-8)

- *US-ASCII (basic English)*

- *Windows*: Windows-1250 (Central Europe), Windows-1251 (Cyrillic), Windows-1252 (Western Europe), Windows-1253 (Greek), Windows-1254 (Turkish), Windows-1255 (Hebrew), Windows-1256 (Arabic), Windows-1257 (Baltic Rim)

- *Encodings for eastern languages*: EUC-JP (Japanese, Unix), Shift_JIS (Japanese, Win/Mac), EUC-kr (Korean), gb2312 (Chinese, simplified), gb18030 (Chinese, simplified), big5 (Chinese, traditional), Big5-HKSCS (Chinese, Hong Kong), tis-620 (Thai)

- *Other*: koi8-r (Russian), koi8-u (Ukrainian), Macintosh (MacRoman), and so on.

In spite of this wide variety, only the variants of a single character encoding—Unicode—should be used unless there is a very good reason not to do so.

Unicode

Unicode is a standard for universal character encoding, which is capable of representing all characters of the written languages of the world [1]. Beyond the characters of natural languages and widely used notations, all historic scripts of the world are also covered. Unicode provides codes for approximately 137,000 characters covering 122 scripts (even historic ones such as Egyptian hieroglyphs), including alphabets, ideograph sets, and symbols. Moreover, the Unicode codespace supports more than a million codepoints. The Unicode Character Code Charts provide quick access to any characters and their codepoints [2]. These classifications also give an insight into the wonderful richness of languages and fields supported by Unicode:

- Scripts

    - *European scripts*: Armenian (including ligatures), Coptic (including Coptic in Greek block), Cypriot syllabary, Cyrillic, Georgian, Glagolitic, Gothic, Greek, Latin (extended, including ligatures and fullwidth Latin letters), Linear B (with syllabary and ideograms), Ogham, Old Italic, Phaistos Disc, Runic, and Shavian

    - *Phonetic symbols*: IPA extensions, phonetic extensions, modifier tone letters, spacing modifier letters, superscripts and subscripts

    - *Combining diacritics*: Combining diacritical marks and combining half marks

    - *African scripts*: Bamum, Egyptian hieroglyphs, Ethiopic, N'Ko, Osmanya, Tifinagh, and Vai

    - *Middle Eastern scripts*: Arabic, Imperial Aramaic, Avestan, Carian, Cuneiform (including numbers and punctuation, Old Persian, and Ugaritic), Hebrew, Lycian, Lydian, Mandaic, Old South Arabian, inscriptional Pahlavi, inscriptional Parthian, Phoenician, Samaritan, and Syriac

- *Central Asian scripts*: Mongolian, Old Turkic, Phags-Pa, and Tibetan

- *South Asian scripts*: Bengali, Brahmi, Devanagari, Gujarati, Gurmukhi, Kaithi, Kannada, Kharoshthi, Lepcha, Limbu, Malayalam, Meetei Mayek, Ol Chiki, Oriya, Saurashtra, Sinhala, Syloti Nagri, Tamil, Telugu, Thaana, and Vedic extensions

- *Southeast Asian scripts*: Batak, Balinese, Buginese, Cham, Javanese, Kayah Li, Khmer (with symbols), Lao, Myanmar (extended), New Tai Lue, Rejang, Sundanese, Tai Le, Tai Tham, Tai Viet, and Thai

- *Philippine scripts*: Buhid, Hanunoo, Tagalog, and Tagbanwa

- *East Asian scripts*: Bopomofo (extended), CJK unified ideographs (Han, extended), CJK compatibility ideographs (with supplement), CJK / KangXi radicals, Hangul Jamo (extended) and syllables, Hiragana, Katakana (with phonetic extensions, Kana supplement, and half-width Katakana), Kanbun, Lisu, and Yi (with syllables and radicals)

- *American scripts*: Cherokee, Deseret, and Unified Canadian Aboriginal Syllabics

- *Other scripts*: Alphabetic presentation forms, half-width and full-width forms, and ASCII characters

- Symbols and punctuation

- *Punctuation*: General punctuation (ASCII punctuation, Latin-1 punctuation, small form variants), supplemental punctuation (CJK symbols and punctuation, CJK compatibility forms, full-width ASCII punctuation, and vertical forms)

- *Alphanumeric symbols*: Letterlike symbols (including Roman symbols), mathematical alphanumeric symbols, enclosed alphanumerics, enclosed CJK letters and months, CJK compatibility symbols (including additional squared symbols)

- *Numbers and digits*: Aegean numbers, Ancient Greek numbers, ASCII digits (including fullwidth ASCII digits), common Indic number forms, counting Rod numerals, Cuneiform numbers and punctuation, number forms, Rumi numeral symbols, superscripts, and subscripts

- *Mathematical symbols*: Arrows, mathematical alphanumeric symbols, mathematical operators, and geometric shapes

- *Other symbols*: Alchemical symbols, ancient symbols, Braille patterns, and currency symbols, dingbats, emoticons, game symbols, miscellaneous symbols, musical symbols (including Ancient Greek musical notation and Byzantine musical symbols), transport and map symbols, and Yijing symbols

- *Special characters*: Layout controls, invisible operators, tags, and variation selectors

The standard supports three encoding forms (UTF-8, UTF-16, UTF-32) that use a common repertoire of characters. They support the same data transmission but in 8, 16, or 32 bits per code unit format, respectively (byte, word, or double word). They can even be transformed into one another. All three encoding forms need a maximum of 4 bytes (32 bits) of data for each character. Depending on the encoding form chosen (UTF-8, UTF-16, or UTF-32), each character is represented as a sequence of either one to four 8-bit bytes, one or two 16-bit code units, or a single 32-bit code unit. Since UTF-8 and UTF-16 are variable-width encodings, UTF-8 results in smaller file size for English texts. However, UTF-8 requires 3 bytes for an Asian character for which UTF-16 requires only 2 bytes. UTF-32 codepoint calculations can be performed quickly, but all codepoints require 4 bytes (fixed-width encoding).

For web publishing, UTF-8 is recommended, which provides interoperability and backward compatibility with US-ASCII[3] and has further advantageous characteristics [3]. UTF-8 supports *internationalized resource identifiers* (IRIs, multilingual web addresses) [4, 5]. UTF-8 uses at least one byte for encoding while UTF-16 uses two, so a UTF-8 encoded file tends to be smaller than a UTF-16 encoded file. UTF-8 is byte oriented, while UTF-16 and UTF-32 are not; in other words, the byte order should be declared for UTF-16 and UTF-32 files by the byte-order mark (see the section "The Byte-Order Mark (BOM)"). UTF-8 is better in recovering from errors than the other Unicode flavors.

There are further variants of UTF-16 and UTF-32, depending on the *endianness*, which is the order of individually addressable subcomponents within the character set. If the most significant byte is the first byte (lowest address) and the least significant byte is the last byte (highest address), the file is called *big-endian* (UTF-16BE, UTF-32BE). If these bytes are reversed, the file is referred to as *little-endian* (UTF-16LE, UTF-32LE). Table 2-2 summarizes the differences between UTF-8 and the variants of UTF-16 and UTF-32.

Table 2-2. Comparison of Unicode Encoding Schemes

Encoding	UTF-8	UTF-16	UTF-16BE	UTF-16LE	UTF-32	UTF-32BE	UTF-32LE
Smallest code point	0000	0000	0000	0000	0000	0000	0000
Largest code point	10FFFF	10FFFF	10FFFF	10FFFF	10FFFF	10FFFF	10FFFF
Code unit size	8 bits	16 bits	16 bits	16 bits	32 bits	32 bits	32 bits
Byte order	Not provided	*BOM*	Big-endian	Little-endian	*BOM*	Big-endian	Little-endian
Fewest bytes per character	1	2	2	2	4	4	4
Most bytes per character	4	4	4	4	4	4	4

According to the HTML5 specification, "authors are encouraged to use UTF-8. Conformance checkers may advise authors against using legacy encodings [6]. Authoring tools should default to using UTF-8 for newly created documents [7]."

Characters That Should Be Avoided In the Markup

Some Unicode characters should not be applied in HTML markup and XML documents (see Table 2-3) because of one or more of the following reasons:

- They are deprecated in the Unicode standard.
- They cannot be supported without additional data.
- They are difficult to handle because they are stateful.[4]
- They can be handled more efficiently with markup.
- They should be avoided because of the potential conflict they could cause with equivalent markup.

---

[3]All US-ASCII characters use exactly the same bytes in UTF-8 as in US-ASCII; i.e., a UTF-8 file that contains only ASCII characters is identical to an ASCII file.

[4]A character represented by a particular value in the text depends on values provided earlier in the text stream, e.g., escape sequences or bidirectional embedding controls.

Table 2-3. *Unicode Characters Not Suitable for Markup [8]*

Codepoint(s)	Description	Comment
U+0340..U+0341	Clones of grave and accent	Deprecated in Unicode.
U+17A3, U+17D3	Obsolete characters for Khmer	Deprecated in Unicode.
U+2028..U+2029	Line and paragraph separator	`<xhtml:br />`, `<xhtml:p></xhtml:p>`, or equivalent should be used instead.
U+202A..U+202E	BIDI (bidirectional) embedding controls (LRE, RLE, LRO, RLO, PDF)	Strongly discouraged in HTML 4.01.
U+206A..U+206B	Activate/Inhibit Symmetric swapping	Deprecated in Unicode.
U+206C..U+206D	Activate/Inhibit Arabic form shaping	Deprecated in Unicode.
U+206E..U+206F	Activate/Inhibit National digit shapes	Deprecated in Unicode.
U+FFF9..U+FFFB	Interlinear annotation characters	Ruby markup should be used instead.
U+FEFF	As ZWNBSP	U+2060 word joiner should be used instead.
	As Byte Order Mark	Use only at the start of a file, not as part of markup.
U+FFFC	Object replacement character	Markup should be used instead, e.g., `<object>`, `<img>`.
U+1D173..U+1D17A	Scoping for Musical Notation	An appropriate markup language should be used instead.
U+E0000..U+E007F	Language Tag code points	`xhtml:lang` or `xml:lang` should be used instead.

Formatting Characters Suitable Also for Markup

There are special formatting characters in Unicode that can also be used in markup languages (see Table 2-4). They affect text and can be applied for markup simultaneously. These formatting characters are interpreted by rendering engines.

Table 2-4. *The Most Important Formatting Characters That Can Also Be Used for Markup [9]*

Codepoint(s)	Name or Function	Comment
U+00A0	Nonbreakable space	Line break control.
U+00AD	Soft hyphen	Line break control.
U+200B	Zero-width space	Line break control.
U+200C..U+200D	Zero-width join controls (ZWJ and ZWNJ)	Required for Persian and many Indic scripts.
U+200E..U+200F	Implicit directional marks (LRM and RLM)	LRM and RLM are allowed.
U+2011	Nonbreaking hyphen	Line break control.
U+2044	Fraction slash	Alternatively, MathML markup can be used.
U+2060	Word joiner	This should be used for word joiner instead of U+FEFF (ZWNBSP).
U+2061..U+2064	Invisible mathematical operators	Mathematical use.
U+2FF0..U+2FFB	Ideographic character description	Graphic characters (not controls).
U+303E	Ideographic variation indicator	Graphic character (not a control).
FE00..FE0F	Variation selectors	Modify graphic characters.
E0100..E01DF	Variation selectors	Modify graphic characters.

Special Characters

Certain Unicode characters deserve extended attention because they should be used with caution.

The Byte-Order Mark (BOM)

Unicode files can contain special bytes at the very beginning known as the *byte-order mark* (BOM). This codepoint is the U+FEFF (Zero-width non-breaking space, ZWNBSP). As mentioned earlier, the byte order of UTF-16 and UTF-32 encoded files should be declared, and the BOM provides this information.

In UTF-16, the 2 or 4 bytes of characters can be ordered in two ways (little-endian or big-endian—defining the direction the bytes should be read in). To choose from the two, documents encoded in UTF-16 should always start with the BOM. In UTF-8, the BOM is optional since there are no alternate byte sequences, but if it is still provided, it is called the *UTF-8 signature*. According to the I18N Activity Group at W3C, the byte-order mark should be omitted in UTF-8 [10], mainly because it could cause display problems in some browsers. Typically it produces an extra line or unwanted characters at the top of the page [11]. An advanced text editor or Richard Ishida's *UTF-8 BOM tester* [12] can be used to check the presence of UTF-8 signatures.

Whitespace Characters

Some Unicode characters are (invisible) *whitespace* characters that have different line-breaking properties, different ligating properties, and different widths. These characters are used to separate different parts of the document with line breaks, tabulators, and spaces. They represent horizontal or vertical spaces on web pages and contribute to the appearance and layout of content blocks or the entire page. Whitespace characters are typically not visible but reserve some space when rendered. The list of whitespace characters varies from context to context. For example, the form feed control character is considered as whitespace in HTML but not in XML. Each markup language defines those few whitespace characters that can be applied as part of the markup syntax. The XML specification defines whitespace as a combination of one or more of the following characters: space (U+0020), carriage return (U+000D), line feed (U+000A), or tab (U+0009). HTML 4.01 also supports the form feed character (U+000C) which cannot be used in XHTML.

Not all whitespace characters can be typed in from the keyboard, although the most common ones, such as a blank space (the basic word divider in Western languages) or a single tabulator, can be typed using the spacebar and the Tab key, respectively. Advanced text editors usually provide inserting options for whitespaces (see the later section "Development Tools").

A very bad practice from the 1990s is to provide whitespaces for typography or layout by embedding blank images, such as 1×1 pixel `spacer.gif` files, instead of whitespace characters, margins, or paddings. The biggest disadvantage of this technique is the lack of structure or semantic meaning in the markup. Such images also have a negative effect on searchability and accessibility (text browsers and screen readers would read aloud "spacer.gif" repeatedly). Another huge problem with spaceholder images is that even the slightest changes in the markup can completely destroy the site layout.

NFC Normalization Is Recommended

In Unicode the same text can be provided with different character sequences. The accentuated a (in other words, á), for example, can be represented either as the *pre-composed* U+00E1 (Latin small letter a with acute) or as the *decomposed* sequence of U+0061 (Latin small letter a) and U+0301 (Combining acute accent).

The Unicode standard supports four *normalization forms*: *NFC*, *NFD*, *NFKC*, and *NFKD* where *C* stands for composed (precomposed), *D* for decomposed, and *K* represents compatibility.

The normalization form is especially important when accents or other diacritics are used in (X)HTML identifiers or CSS selectors and class names. If such a word is used in precomposed form in the HTML (for example, `<div id="hangsúlyos">`), but in decomposed form in the CSS (for example, `#hangsúlyos { color: red; }`), then the selector won't match the class name. This problem can be avoided by completely eliminating accented characters in markup attributes and CSS properties, and use standard English characters only, which is the best practice.

W3C recommends NFC normalization—which is supported by advanced text editors by default—on the Web to improve interoperability [13].

Unicode Should Be Preferred

Web pages should use one character encoding at a time. Different parts of the same document should not be encoded with different encoding schemes.

UTF-8 character encoding can simplify multilingual sites. Unicode allows more languages to be used on a single page than any other encoding system, which makes it ideal for content, forms, scripts, and databases. Due to its powerful features, Unicode should be used wherever possible [14]. Thanks to the increasing popularity of HTML5 templates and best practices, web designers tend to use UTF-8 for all their projects. The global distribution of UTF-8 eliminates incorrect automatic encoding detection in browsers rendering documents with special characters.

Using Unicode does not guarantee that texts will be displayed correctly in browsers. Several scripting languages such as Arabic require additional techniques to ensure the appropriate character sequence of glyphs.

Declaring Character Encoding for the Markup

Character encoding of web documents can be determined in many ways:

- Using the HTTP header
- Using in-document declarations
  - Using the *pragma directive* (HTML 4, XHTML, (X)HTML5)
  - Using the meta charset attribute (HTML5)
  - Using the XML declaration[5] (XHTML)

The last three options are used in the markup, but not the first one, which is applied by the web server. Not all in-document declarations can be used in all markup languages, but the pragma directive can be used in most. Since browsers retrieve the character encoding declaration to use the right encoding scheme and display the content correctly, these declarations must correspond to the actual character encoding of the file.

If the different encoding declarations are inconsistent or contradictory, the following precedence rules determine the encoding to apply:

1. HTTP Content-Type header
2. Byte-order mark[6]
3. XML declaration
4. The meta element
5. The link charset attribute

Encoding Declaration in the HTTP Header

The highest precedence declaration sets the character encoding in the HTTP header. Listing 2-1 shows an example.

Listing 2-1. Setting the Character Encoding in the HTTP Header

```
HTTP/1.1 200 OK
Date: Tue, 02 Aug 2011 14:18:05 GMT
Server: Apache/2.2.3 (Oracle)
...
Content-Type: text/html; charset=UTF-8
Content-Language: en
```

These declarations should be consistent with the in-document declarations.

Documents using UTF-16 should be declared as UTF-16 rather than UTF-16BE or UTF-16LE and provide a byte-order mark in the file.

HTTP headers are used for other purposes too. For more information on the HTTP header, see Chapter 4.

---

[5]The character encoding declaration, if provided exclusively using the XML declaration, is ignored by some rendering engines.
[6]The BOM was added to the hierarchy in the HTML5 specification, but this is not implemented in all browsers yet.

In-Document Declarations

In HTML 4, the *pragma directive* should be used at the top of the head element in the form shown in Listing 2-2.

Listing 2-2. Declaring the Character Encoding with the Pragma Directive

```
<meta http-equiv="Content-type" content="text/html;charset=UTF-8">
```

The previous declaration can be used in HTML5 as well, but HTML5 introduced another option, namely the meta charset attribute (see Listing 2-3). Either of them can be used, but only one at a time. The whole declaration must fit within the first 512 bytes of the page.

Listing 2-3. HTML5 meta charset

```
<meta charset="UTF-8">
```

The encoding declaration of XHTML documents depends on which MIME type they are served with. If they are served as text/html, the *pragma directive* in Listing 2-2 can be used at the top of the head element.

XHTML documents served as XML can use the encoding information of the XML declaration (see Listing 2-4) in the first line of the document (see Chapter 3).

Listing 2-4. Setting the Character Encoding in XML Documents

```
<?xml version="1.0" encoding="utf-8"?>
```

The XML declaration is required for all XML documents that use character encoding other than UTF-8 or UTF-16 or when the encoding is missing from the HTTP header (see later in Chapter 3).

Declaring Character Encoding for CSS

Character encoding declarations can usually be omitted in style sheets. The encoding of external CSS files needs to be declared if and only if there are non-ASCII characters in the file. The best practice is to use characters from the English alphabet only, or write non-Latin characters in descriptive selector names or other CSS content without accents.

HTTP Header Declarations

CSS encoding can also be declared in the HTTP Content-Type header. For example, if the character encoding is UTF-8, the HTTP declaration looks like Listing 2-5.

Listing 2-5. Declaring the Character Encoding for CSS (Rarely Used)

```
Content-Type: text/css; charset=UTF-8
```

Using an in-document declaration on top of the HTTP declaration can guarantee that the encoding of the external CSS file can be determined even if the file is moved or used locally (see the next section).

The character encoding declared in the HTTP header should coincide with the one declared in the CSS file, and the first one has higher precedence.

In-Document Declarations

Character encoding can be set by the @charset *at-rule* with the syntax shown in Listing 2-6.

Listing 2-6. Syntax of the @charset At-Rule

```
@charset "<charset-name>";
```

Only one @charset rule can be used per CSS file. It should be declared at the very beginning of the file. No characters should precede the declaration (only BOM if the CSS file is Unicode encoded[7]).

The charset-name can be one of the character sets defined by IANA [15]. Some encodings have multiple names in the IANA registry (the one marked as preferred should be used). Listing 2-7 shows a typical example for character encoding declaration of external CSS files.

Listing 2-7. Setting the Character Encoding of CSS with an At-Rule

```
@charset "UTF-8";
```

These rules can be used only in external style sheets. In-document style sheet declarations cannot use @charset rules.

The HTML 4.01 specification defined a charset attribute to the link element for identifying the character encoding of the target document. In HTML5, however, this attribute is obsolete and should not be used.

Escape Codes, Special Characters, and Symbols

In HTML and XHTML documents, each character can be typed in directly or represented by a character sequence (also known as a *character reference*). Two types of character sequences exist: *numeric character references* and *character entity references*.

Assume a document fragment contains an a character with an accent (á). This character can be declared by either the á or á numeric character references or by the á entity reference in (X)HTML documents (see the following sections for details). However, the best practice is to type in the á character directly in the markup. The same is true for the copyright sign (© instead of ©), the registered trademark sign (® instead of ®), and so on.

Characters should always be preferred to escape codes unless they are special characters with syntactic meaning in (X)HTML or XML, or characters that are invisible or ambiguous. In such cases, using entities is mandatory [16]. In other words, markup characters used in textual content or attribute values must be *escaped*. For example, when we demonstrate (X)HTML source code blocks on a web page and want to avoid processing, the < and > characters should be provided by their entity names (< and >) in the source code rather than typing them in directly. Analogously, if an & character is needed as text within an RSS feed or an RDF file, the & entity should be used instead (see the "Entity References" section for more information).

Numeric References

Numeric character references identify characters by *Universal Character Set* or *Unicode codepoints* in the form &#nnnn; where *nnnn* is the codepoint in decimal form. Both HTML and XHTML support *hexadecimal references* as well. In HTML, they can be applied in either the &#Xhhhh; or &#xhhhh; form. Since XML is case sensitive, in XHTML they must be in lowercase (&#xhhhh;) [17]. The nnnn or hhhh can be any number of digits and may include leading zeros.

---

[7]External CSS files are usually encoded in US-ASCII.

Wherever possible, type in the characters directly instead of their corresponding numeric references. Usually there is no reason to insert a single apostrophe in the markup as ’ rather than the ' character itself. If a character, such as a Japanese ideograph, cannot be typed in with the keyboard, the corresponding character can be inserted using advanced software tools or copy-pasted from other applications, codecharts, or web sites via the clipboard. Note that even advanced text editors display many of these directly inserted characters incorrectly during development; however, browsers will display them correctly if the character encoding of the containing file has been set properly and the file served correctly.

Entity References

Character entity references refer to characters by the name of the appropriate entity that has the desired character as its replacement text in the form &*name*;.

HTML supports 252 character entities [18]. In XHTML, there are 253 entities (including the 5 predefined entities of XML 1.0) [19]; however, their application is affected by the way XHTML documents are processed. Keep in mind that XHTML documents, if served correctly, are processed by XML parsers instead of SGML parsers that interpret HTML documents. Those characters that have a meaning in XML, such as the less-than sign (<), cause parsing errors if they are provided directly rather than using entities. There are only four character entities whose processing is guaranteed in all XML environments: &, >, <, and " (&, >, <, and " respectively). Fortunately, this short list contains those very important character entities that can be used for syntactic notation (ampersand, greater than, less than). W3C recommends the use of ampersand characters in href attributes of XHTML documents [20]. Particular attention should be paid to URIs that include parameters. Single ampersand characters in these URIs should be replaced by the & entity [21].

Although the ' entity (apostrophe, U+0027) is among the five predefined entities of XML, it should not be used in XHTML [22].

Character references should be eliminated since virtually all characters can be represented directly in Unicode including, but not limited to, all letters and ideograms of natural languages, accentuated letters, special characters, mathematical signs, and symbols [23]. Direct character use is easier to interpret, maintain, and modify than numeric or entity references (see Listing 2-8). Texts filled with character references are more difficult to extend and almost impossible to search. Many characters cannot be represented by references, which often resulted in incorrect characters on web pages in the 1990s. For example, the small o with tilde, õ, has been displayed instead of o with the double acute accent (also known as the Hungarumlaut), ő, which is a different character.

Listing 2-8. Three Versions of the Same Central-European Text with Characters, Numeric, and Entity References

```
Áttekintés</h1>
<p>
A HTML5 a HTML teljes megújulása, új funkciókkal felvértezve.
</p>


&#193;ttekint&#233;s</h1>
<p>
A HTML5 a HTML teljes meg&#250;jul&#225;sa, &#250;j funkci&#243;kkal felv&#233;rtezve.
</p>


&Aacute;ttekint&eacute;s</h1>
<p>
A HTML5 a HTML teljes meg&uacute;jul&aacute;sa, &uacute;j funkci&oacute;kkal felv&eacute;rtezve.
</p>
```

Checking I18N

Those settings and markup segments that support internationalization can be checked by the *W3C Internationalization Checker* [24]. It can determine whether the HTML/XHTML documents contain non-NFC class names and identifiers, the language settings of pages, and so on. The validator is described in detail in the "Validating I18N" section in Chapter 14.

Summary

In this chapter, you learned the importance of internationalization settings that enable properly displayed special characters on web sites. You know by now that there is a wide choice of character encoding systems, many of which have been used for decades but became obsolete in recent years. There is an ultimate variable-width character encoding, called UTF-8, which is a flavor of Unicode, omits the BOM, and is backward compatible with the once most widely used encoding scheme, ASCII.

The next chapter will describe the markup, where most standardization efforts take place. The markup not only provides the document structure and content but also serves as the basis for accessibility support and semantic annotations. As you will see, there is a wide choice of markup languages, not just HTML5, the latest and most popular one. You will learn the HTML and XHTML elements and attributes that can be safely applied in a variety of documents while maintaining standard compliance. The chapter will also demonstrate the benefits of strict markup.

References

1. The Unicode Consortium (2014) The Unicode Standard: A Technical Introduction. Unicode, Inc. http://www.unicode.org/standard/principles.html. Accessed 14 October 2014

2. Unicode (2014) Unicode 7.0 Character Code Charts. Unicode Consortium. http://www.unicode.org/charts/. Accessed 14 October 2014

3. Yergeau F (2003) UTF-8, a transformation format of ISO 10646 [RFC3629]. The Internet Society. http://www.ietf.org/rfc/rfc3629.txt. Accessed 14 October 2014

4. Duerst M, Suignard M (2005) Internationalized Resource Identifiers (IRIs). The Internet Society. http://www.ietf.org/rfc/rfc3987. Accessed 14 October 2014

5. Ishida R (2010) An Introduction to Multilingual Web Addresses. World Wide Web Consortium. http://www.w3.org/International/articles/idn-and-iri/. Accessed 14 October 2014

6. Hickson I (ed) (2010) HTML5 (Edition for Web Authors) revision 1.4439. A vocabulary and associated APIs for HTML and XHTML. Editor's Draft. World Wide Web Consortium. http://dev.w3.org/html5/spec-author-view/semantics.html. Accessed 29 September 2010

7. Hickson I (ed) (2014) HTML5 (including next generation additions still in development). Draft Standard. Apple Computer, Inc., Mozilla Foundation, and Opera Software ASA. http://www.whatwg.org/specs/web-apps/current-work/multipage/semantics.html. Accessed 14 October 2014

8. Dürst M, Freytag A (2013) Characters not suitable for use with markup. In: Unicode in XML and other Markup Languages. Unicode Technical Report #20. W3C Working Group Note. World Wide Web Consortium. `http://www.w3.org/TR/unicode-xml/#Suitable`. Accessed 14 October 2014

9. Dürst M, Freytag A (2013) Format Characters Suitable for Use with Markup. In: Unicode in XML and other Markup Languages. Unicode Technical Report #20. W3C Working Group Note. World Wide Web Consortium. `http://www.w3.org/TR/unicode-xml/#Format`. Accessed 14 October 2014

10. Ishida R (2013) What do I need to know about the BOM? In: The byte-order mark (BOM) in HTML. World Wide Web Consortium. `http://www.w3.org/International/questions/qa-byte-order-mark#bomhow`. Accessed 14 October 2014

11. Cawkwell D, Ishida R (2013) Display problems caused by the UTF-8 BOM. World Wide Web Consortium. `http://www.w3.org/International/questions/qa-utf8-bom`. Accessed 14 October 2014

12. Ishida R (2007). UTF-8 BOM tester. Richard Ishida. `http://rishida.net/utils/bomtester/`. Accessed 30 September 2010

13. Ishida R (2010) Normalization in HTML and CSS. World Wide Web Consortium. `http://www.w3.org/International/questions/qa-html-css-normalization`. Accessed 14 October 2014

14. Ishida R (2014) Use UTF-8, if you can. In: Choosing & applying a character encoding. World Wide Web Consortium. `http://www.w3.org/International/questions/qa-choosing-encodings#useunicode`. Accessed 14 October 2014

15. Simonsen K et al (2013) Character sets. The Internet Assigned Numbers Authority. `http://www.iana.org/assignments/character-sets`. Accessed 30 September 2010

16. Ishida R (2010) When to use escapes. In: Using character escapes in markup and CSS. World Wide Web Consortium. `http://www.w3.org/International/questions/qa-escapes#use`. Accessed 14 October 2014

17. Pemberton S et al (2002) Entity references as hex values. In: XHTML 1.0 – The Extensible HyperText Markup Language (2nd edn). A Reformulation of HTML 4 in XML 1.0. W3C Recommendation. World Wide Web Consortium. `http://www.w3.org/TR/xhtml1/#h-4.12`. Accessed 14 October 2014

18. Le Hors A, Jacobs I (ed.) (1999) Character entity references in HTML 4. In: HTML 4.01 Specification. W3C Recommendation. World Wide Web Consortium. `http://www.w3.org/TR/html4/sgml/entities.html`. Accessed 14 October 2014

19. Pemberton S et al (2002) Entity Sets. In: XHTML 1.0 – The Extensible HyperText Markup Language (2nd edn). A Reformulation of HTML 4 in XML 1.0. W3C Recommendation. World Wide Web Consortium. `http://www.w3.org/TR/xhtml1/#h-A2`. Accessed 14 October 2014

20. Pemberton S et al (2002) Using Ampersands in Attribute Values (and Elsewhere). In: XHTML 1.0 – The Extensible HyperText Markup Language (2nd edn). A Reformulation of HTML 4 in XML 1.0. W3C Recommendation. World Wide Web Consortium. `http://www.w3.org/TR/2002/REC-xhtml1-20020801/#C_16`. Accessed 14 October 2014

21. Ishida R (2010) By the way. In: Using character escapes in markup and CSS. World Wide Web Consortium. `http://www.w3.org/International/questions/qa-escapes#bytheway`. Accessed 14 October 2014

22. Pemberton S et al (2002) The Named Character Reference '. In: XHTML 1.0 – The Extensible HyperText Markup Language (2nd edn). A Reformulation of HTML 4 in XML 1.0. W3C Recommendation. World Wide Web Consortium. `http://www.w3.org/TR/2002/REC-xhtml1-20020801/#C_16`. Accessed 14 October 2014

23. Ishida R (2010) When not to use escapes. In: Using character escapes in markup and CSS. World Wide Web Consortium. `http://www.w3.org/International/questions/qa-escapes#not`. Accessed 14 October 2014

24. W3C I18N Activity Group (2013) W3C Internationalization Checker. World Wide Web Consortium. `http://qa-dev.w3.org/i18n-checker/`. Accessed 14 October 2014

CHAPTER 3

■ ■ ■

Markup Languages: More Than HTML5

Since markup is the essence of web documents, it provides the largest place for standardization efforts. The popularity of HTML has not decreased since the birth of the Web. Becoming familiar with the versions and variants of that language and understanding the differences between HTML and XHTML are crucial for understanding the techniques for changing the document type. The general structure of all web documents follows the same logic. The latest core version and by far the most popular markup language of the World Wide Web, HTML5, introduced new structuring elements as well as multimedia element annotations that can be used to create rather sophisticated document structures. By examining well-structured document examples, you will be able to build correct document structures on your own. To achieve well-structuredness, the block-line and inline-level elements should be differentiated, which is also important in understanding how to embed elements into each other (element nesting). You should also know how to use Formal Public Identifiers and Document Type Definitions for creating standard-compliant documents. The strict rules of XML declarations are vital for XHTML authoring. HTML5 can be used to create HTML or XHTML documents (HTML5 or XHTML5, respectively), and documents that can be interpreted either as HTML or XHTML (polyglot markup).

In this chapter, you will learn about the most important markup standards in web design, covering the most advanced markup languages along with mixed-namespace document types. I provide sample HTML and XHTML documents for the sake of easier understanding. You will understand how to distinguish deprecated elements and attributes to avoid from the ones that can be used in almost all versions and variants of markup languages. Beyond HTML, you will learn about the XML-powered mixed-namespace documents that display text-based vector graphics and mathematical annotations. After reading the chapter, you will be able to apply semantically meaningful markup elements and attributes, eliminate obsolete markup, and create web documents with correct element nesting and DOM structure.

■ **Note** The detailed description of markup basics is beyond the scope of this book. Several resources are available for both beginner and intermediate developers such as "Getting started with HTML," a very short overview written by the author/editor of HTML specifications, Dave Raggett [1], or "HTML: The Markup Language Reference" by Michael Smith [2]. There are also many books on HTML5 [e.g., 3, 4, 5, 6] and XHTML[1] but the first HTML5 textbooks were published before the standardization of HTML5, and often contain incorrect, obsolete, or incomplete descriptions. If you need a short summary about a particular markup element, the W3C Cheatsheet can be very helpful too [7].

---

[1]XHTML hand coders can write HTML markup with ease.

SGML Languages

Standard Generalized Markup Language (SGML) is a markup language family. It has been used since the mid-1980s. One of the major features of SGML is flexibility.

The most important SGML language for web designers is HTML, which has been the core language of the World Wide Web from the very beginning.

■ **Caution**   Despite the similarities in the markup syntax of earlier HTML versions and HTML5, the latest version is no longer based on SGML; however, it is backward-compatible with conventional HTML parsing.

HTML

The idea behind *Hypertext Markup Language (HTML)* was born at the European Laboratory for High-Energy Physics (CERN) in Geneva, Switzerland, as early as 1989 [8]. One year later, the World Wide Web project was also started there. In the beginning, HTML was used to share information between scientists. The major elements of the language were formed at that time, including headings, paragraphs, and hyperlinks, but the semantics of the first documents were limited [9]. New elements and multimedia capabilities were added later that caused interoperability problems for documents used across different platforms.

The relatively simple syntax and vocabulary of the language made rapid and wide distribution possible, but it is also the reason for invalid markup found in more than 90 percent of HTML documents.

XML Languages

Extensible Markup Language (XML) is a universal format for structured documents and data on the World Wide Web. Since XML has been extended from SGML, it can be considered as a restricted, machine-readable form of SGML that removes those features of SGML that might result in loose source code.

In contrast to most computer languages, XML has no fixed, predefined set of tags. With XML, individual markup formats can be defined. Some of the most well-known and frequently used XML formats and/or XML serializations on the Web are XML, XHTML, SVG, MathML, RDF, and Atom.

Many markup languages were originally designed for textual content, later followed by other types of information such as music and video, playlists, vector graphics, and news feeds. The big advantage of XML is that it is strict, well-defined, and extendible. With XML you can combine multiple markup languages into single profiles, such as XHTML + MathML + SVG or XHTML + SMIL. The additional vocabularies (elements, attributes, and further components) of other XML applications can be used through the namespace mechanism declared by the `xmlns` attribute. This is one of the major advantages of XHTML over HTML[2].

XHTML

Extensible Hypertext Markup Language (XHTML) is an XML language family that can be used as an alternative to HTML. XHTML is an application of XML and thus more restrictive than HTML. In contrast to HTML, XHTML documents must be written without errors; otherwise, rendering engines give error messages instead of rendering the content. XHTML documents require an XML parser rather than an SGML parser.

---

[2]HTML5 provides additional features through its Application Programming Interfaces (APIs). Before the introduction of HTML5, the XHTML modules and external vocabularies provided the only way to extend the core markup features, which was available in XHTML documents only.

Documents served with an XML MIME type, such as `application/xhtml+xml`, are treated as XML documents by browsers; in other words, they are parsed by an XML processor. Consequently, XML and HTML are processed differently. In fact, even minor syntactic errors will prevent an XML document from being rendered correctly. In contrast, the errors of such documents would be ignored in the HTML syntax. A parsing error of XML documents can easily result in the "Yellow Screen of Death."

Version Overview

Understanding the major differences and capabilities of the different markup language versions and variants and analyzing sample documents with minimum content known as *skeleton documents* is very useful. These documents can serve as the basis for hand coding from scratch. While indentation is used to provide clear, easy-to-understand code, tabulators can be omitted to obtain optimal code length. Since all provided documents are valid character by character on an as-is basis, they can be used to create standards-compliant documents from scratch, and should be extended with valid markup only to maintain validity. All these documents can be downloaded from the book's web page at www.apress.com, as well as from the companion web site of the book at www.masteringhtml5css3.com.

HTML Versions and Variants

This section will highlight the milestones of HTML history. The described HTML versions have made a significant impact on the evolution of the Web, and were used to form newer standards. Some of these old HTML versions were used for more than 10 years.

The formal specification of HTML was created in 1992, and this specification has evolved constantly, introducing new SGML Document Type Definitions. HTML soon became the *lingua franca* of web publishing. HTML documents can be created manually in plain-text editors as well as in WYSIWYG environments.[3] HTML is not case-sensitive.

HTML 2.0 was created by the HTML Working Group of the Internet Engineering Task Force in 1995 as the RFC 1866 specification [10]. HTML 2.0 was the first standardized form of the core HTML elements. HTML 2.0 was used for platform-independent hypertext documents [11]. The HTML 2.0 document type is obsolete and considered as historic.

HTML 3.2 is the first HTML Recommendation from W3C. HTML 3.2 introduced new elements for tables, applets, superscripts, subscripts, and text flows around images [12]. HTML 3.2 was backward-compatible with version 2.0. The code in Listing 3-1 is a fragment of an HTML 3.2 document which demonstrates bad practices.

Listing 3-1. Bad Practices in an Old HTML Document (Just Demonstration, Should Not Be Used)

```
<!DOCTYPE HTML PUBLIC "-//W3C//DTD HTML 3.2//EN">
<title>An HTML 3.2 example</title>
<body bgcolor="#FFF6F0"
 text="#000000" link="#C00000">
<h1 align=center>Example header</h1>
  <p><A HREF=http://www.example.com/><img align=left border=0 alt="Example:"
width=102 height=52
src=http://www.example.com/images/author.jpg></A> <i>The Author</i>
</body>
```

This is very poor quality code, because some of the attributes are not quoted (for example, `width=102` instead of `width="102"`), strictly presentational attributes (`bgcolor`, `align`) are used that should be written in CSS instead, the paragraph is not closed (the `</p>` tag is missing), and so forth.

---

[3]Web Quality Assurance relies on hand coding.

■ **Tip**   Although HTML allows both capitalized and lowercase letters in element and attribute names, it is better to use lowercase letters, which are allowed in every markup (including XHTML, which is case-sensitive).

HTML 4 was an ISO-conforming version (ISO 8879) and the *de facto* standard, the "publishing language of the World Wide Web," for years [13]. The specification was released in 1997 and revised in 1998. Listing 3-2 shows a fragment of a typical HTML 4.0 document.

Listing 3-2. A Typical HTML 4 Document (Obsolete)

```
<!DOCTYPE HTML PUBLIC "-//W3C//DTD HTML 4.0 Transitional//EN">
<html>
<head>
<title>An HTML 4.0 example</title>
</head>
<body>
 ...
</body>
</html>
```

Note the similarity between the structure of this document and the previous one. The core HTML structure is still the same.

HTML 4 was superseded by *HTML 4.01*, the most well-known HTML version before HTML5, and the primary markup language of the Web for more than a decade. The HTML 4.01 W3C Recommendation was released in late 1999. The language had three variants: the Strict, the Transitional, and the Frameset [14]. At that time, the best choice was the Strict flavor, which contained those elements only that had been selected for inclusion in future versions. The Transitional variant was created to make it easier for web designers to stop using deprecated tags and gave time to learn writing strict markup without these obsolete tags (hence the name). In the late 1990s, web sites often had a layout where the menu on the top or left was written in one file and the main content in another (frames), while the index file was used to control and open these files simultaneously. Such frameset documents are obsolete and should not be used anymore due to the associated issues. If you accessed a web site with a broken frameset, for example, missing contents took up the whole window. If a visitor arrived through a direct link to a framed page, the text was out of context. Search engines could not index frameset documents effectively. There were linking and bookmarking issues, and further problems such as the Back button did not work in browsers. Frames also reduced the amount of usable space on a web page and caused problems with printing.

XHTML Versions and Variants

XHTML is a document type family that is the reformulation of HTML in XML rather than SGML. Typical XHTML *file extensions* are .html, .htm, .xhtml, .xht, and .xml. XHTML documents usually apply the application/xhtml+xml *Internet media type*; however, there are occasional exceptions (see next chapter).

Beyond the core versions of XHTML (Table 3-1), several compounds, extensions, and special profiles are known (Table 3-2), and further ones can also be defined. The additional mechanisms allow XHTML subsets or supersets. XHTML 1.1 + MathML 2.0 + SVG 1.1 and XHTML+RDFa documents are typical examples for supersets of XHTML. Because of the additional (external) element sets, these mixed-namespace documents have a wider variety of markup elements than plain XHTML documents.

Table 3-1. *Core XHTML Versions*

Version	Descriptive Name	Site	Status	Date
XHTML 1.0	A reformulation of HTML 4 in XML 1.0	www.w3.org/TR/xhtml1/	R	1/26/2000 r. 8/1/2002
XHTML 1.1	Module-based XHTML	www.w3.org/TR/xhtml11/	R	5/31/2001 r. 10/7/2010
XHTML 2.0 (XHTML2)	–	www.w3.org/TR/xhtml2/	WD[4]	7/26/2006
XHTML5	A vocabulary and associated APIs for XHTML	www.w3.org/TR/html5/	PR	1/22/2008
XHTML 5.1	A vocabulary and associated APIs for HTML and XHTML	www.w3.org/TR/html51/	WD	12/17/2012

R: W3C Recommendation   PR: Proposed Recommendation   WD: W3C Working Draft   r: revised

Table 3-2. *Special and Mixed-Namespace XHTML Document Types*

Version	Descriptive Name	Status	Date
XHTML 1.1 + MathML 2.0 + SVG 1.1	An XHTML + MathML + SVG Profile [15]	WD	8/9/2002
XHTML-MP 1.2	XHTML Mobile Profile	R[5]	7/29/2008
XHTML-Print	XHTML for Printing	R	9/20/2006
XHTML-Print 2nd ed.		R	11/23/2010
XHTML+RDFa 1.0	RDFa in XHTML [16]	R	10/14/2008
XHTML+RDFa 1.1	Support for RDFa via XHTML Modularization [17]	R	6/7/2012
XHTML+RDFa 1.1 2nd ed.	Support for RDFa via XHTML Modularization [18]	R	8/22/2013

R: W3C Recommendation   WD: W3C Working Draft

XHTML 1.1 + MathML 2.0 + SVG 1.1 documents can be written in any of the compound languages, all of which have their own document format (XHTML document, MathML document, or SVG document). The selected language is the *host language* (see the "XHTML + MathML + SVG" section later in the chapter).

XHTML 1.0

According to the subtitle of its specification released in 2000 (and revised in 2002), XHTML 1.0 is "a reformulation of HTML 4 in XML 1.0" [19]. Similar to the three flavors of HTML 4.01, XHTML 1.0 also defines the Strict, Transitional, and Frameset variants, all of which are the XML serialization of their corresponding predecessors. XHTML 1.0 Strict includes those elements and attributes only that have not been deprecated in HTML 4.01. Every "missing" element and attribute can be substituted by CSS styles. Similar to HTML 4.01 Transitional, XHTML 1.0 Transitional also provides the presentational elements such as center or font that are not allowed in the Strict variant. Listings 3-3 and 3-4 show an example.

---

[4]The XHTML2 specification is no longer actively developed, and was last updated in 2010.
[5]The specification was standardized by Open Mobile Alliance not W3C.

Listing 3-3. An Element Deprecated a Long Time Ago Is Still Used in XHTML 1.0 Transitional Documents

```
<center>
  <p>
  A paragraph aligned to center.
  </p>
</center>
```

Listing 3-4. The Code of Listing 3-3 Written in XHTML 1.0 Strict and Styled by CSS

```
.center {
  text-align: center;
}

<p class="center">
A paragraph aligned to center.
<p>
```

XHTML 1.0 also has a Frameset variant, although, as we saw earlier, framesets should not be used anymore. Listing 3-5 presents an XHTML 1.0 Strict skeleton document.

Listing 3-5. An XHTML 1.0 Strict Skeleton Document

```
<?xml version="1.0" encoding="UTF-8"?>
<!DOCTYPE html ↵
 PUBLIC "-//W3C//DTD XHTML 1.0 Strict//EN" ↵
 "http://www.w3.org/TR/xhtml1/DTD/xhtml1-strict.dtd">
<html xmlns="http://www.w3.org/1999/xhtml" xml:lang="en" lang="en">
  <head>
    <title>Minimal XHTML 1.0 Document</title>
    <meta http-equiv="Content-Type" content="application/xhtml+xml; charset=utf-8" />
  </head>
  <body>
    <p>
    This is a minimal XHTML 1.0 document.
    </p>
  </body>
</html
```

■ **Tip** The XHTML 1.0 Strict skeleton document is the best starting point for any kind of XHTML documents, because this document type contains fundamental markup elements only that have been derived from HTML and are still current in most markup languages. This markup can also be extended using external vocabularies (which changes the document type to a mixed-namespace document type). If you update XHTML 1.0 Strict documents to HTML5, minimal changes are needed (such as removing the DTD and using new elements).

XHTML 1.1

Over the years markup language developers realized that there are presentational components in markup languages that can be handled more efficiently with style sheets. Moreover, web documents developed for mobile devices can use limited resources more effectively if a subset of selected elements is applied in a document rather than the whole set of elements. This is the basic idea behind *XHTML modularization*, and these element subsets are called *element modules*.

XHTML 1.1, the "module-based XHTML," contains exclusively those elements that are defined by the "Modularization of XHTML" [20]. Elements deprecated in HTML 4 and XHTML 1.0 cannot be used in XHTML 1.1. The modules of XHTML 1.1 are the following [21]:

- Structure Module: `body`, `head`, `html`, `title`
- Text Module: `abbr`, `acronym`, `address`, `blockquote`, `br`, `cite`, `code`, `dfn`, `div`, `em`, `h1`, `h2`, `h3`, `h4`, `h5`, `h6`, `kbd`, `p`, `pre`, `q`, `samp`, `span`, `strong`, `var`
- Hypertext Module: `a`
- List Module: `dl`, `dt`, `dd`, `ol`, `ul`, `li`
- Object Module: `object`, `param`
- Presentation Module: `b`, `big`, `hr`, `i`, `small`, `sub`, `sup`, `tt`
- Edit Module: `del`, `ins`
- Bi-Directional Text Module: `bdo`
- Forms Module: `button`, `fieldset`, `form`, `input`, `label`, `legend`, `select`, `optgroup`, `option`, `textarea`
- Table Module: `caption`, `col`, `colgroup`, `table`, `tbody`, `td`, `tfoot`, `th`, `thead`, `tr`
- Image Module: `img`
- Client-Side Image Map Module: `area`, `map`
- Server-Side Image Map Module: `ismap` attribute on `img`
- Intrinsic Events Module: event attributes
- Metainformation Module: `meta`
- Scripting Module: `noscript`, `script`
- Stylesheet Module: `style` element
- Style Attribute Module (deprecated): `style` attribute
- Link Module: `link`
- Base Module: `base`

The description of the previous modules, their elements and attributes, and their minimal content are defined by the "Modularization of XHTML" [20].

Listing 3-6 shows an XHTML 1.1 skeleton document.

Listing 3-6. An XHTML 1.1 Skeleton Document

```
<?xml version="1.0" encoding="utf-8"?>
<!DOCTYPE html PUBLIC "-//W3C//DTD XHTML 1.1//EN" ↵
 "http://www.w3.org/TR/xhtml11/DTD/xhtml11.dtd">
<html xmlns="http://www.w3.org/1999/xhtml" xml:lang="en">
  <head>
    <title>XHTML 1.1 sample document title</title>
    <meta http-equiv="Content-Type" content="application/xhtml+xml; charset=utf-8" />
  </head>
  <body>
    <p>
    XHTML 1.1 sample document body
    </p>
  </body>
</html>
```

XHTML 1.1 can also be used in mixed-namespace documents to support mathematical markup and vector graphics (see "XTHML+MathML+SVG").

XHTML 2.0

XHTML 2.0 (also denoted as XHTML2) could have been the next-generation markup language and the successor of XHTML 1.0 and 1.1. However, it remained on the Working Draft level and never became a Recommendation.

Although XHTML 2.0 reused elements from earlier versions of markup languages, it had backward compatibility issues. However, web designers familiar with XHTML 1.0 and 1.1 could easily develop XHTML 2.0 documents.

The "Modularization of XHTML" refers to XHTML 2.0 as not just another markup language but as an *XHTML host language* [20]. In XHTML 2.0, there were several updated modules compared to the "Modularization of XHTML."

After the W3C shifted its focus from XHTML 2.0 to HTML5, many features originally introduced in the XHTML 2.0 working draft were assigned to independent working groups to continue their development (RDFa, XForms, XML Events, etc.).

HTML5

HTML5 was initially proposed by individuals from Apple, the Mozilla Foundation, and Opera Software, known as the *Web Hypertext Application Technology Working Group* (*WHATWG*) [22]. Later, the W3C validated the WHATWG proposal and announced to work on a new HTML specification [23]. WHATWG found XHTML 2.0 too document-centric and inappropriate for blogs, forums, web stores, and multimedia sites. Their major goal was to create a platform for dynamic web applications [24].

While its name might be misleading, *HTML5* is not just another HTML language. It is the complete reformulation of former markup languages with new capabilities. HTML5 is designed to be backward-compatible with older browsers, and uses a syntax that is compatible with both HTML and XHTML documents. In HTML5, you can use the well-known `text/html` media type, or a new media type called `text/html-sandboxed`, which makes it possible to interpret a file without giving the content access to the rest of the web site. Because of a new approach that separates authoring and rendering conformance requirements, deprecated tags are not needed anymore.

All modern browsers released in or after 2012 have good HTML5 support. The HTML5 support of older browsers can be tested with services such as the "HTML5 test" for backward compatibility [25]. For those who want to contribute to the development of HTML5, several tests are available on the W3C testing web page, where current tests can be reviewed and new tests submitted [26].

HTML5 introduced new structural and multimedia elements for the markup, and Application Programming Interfaces (APIs) to extend the capabilities of the core specification, and provide the option to develop web applications. The web applications written in HTML5 are accessible and device-independent, and need declarative programming (much less coding) compared to traditional procedural programming [27], while code reuse is easy. To use HTML5 in its full glory, it is usually used together with other technologies such as CSS3, XML, and JavaScript libraries.

Listing 3-7 shows an HTML5 skeleton document.

Listing 3-7. An HTML5 Skeleton Document

```
<!DOCTYPE html>
<html>
  <head>
    <title>Sample HTML5 document</title>
    <meta charset="UTF-8" />
  </head>
  <body>
    <header>
      <h1>Document sample</h1>
    </header>
    <section>
      <article>
        <h2>Article1</h2>
          The first article of the document.
      </article>
      <article>
        <h2>Article2</h2>
          The second article of the document.
      </article>
    </section>
    <footer>
      Copyright © 2015 John Smith. All rights reserved.
    </footer>
  </body>
</html>
```

HTML5 Modules

HTML5 is modular, providing the option to use extension specifications that define new elements, new attributes, new attribute values, and new APIs. There are three types of HTML5 modules:

1. Technologies that were originally parts of the HTML5 specification, but later moved to separate specifications: HTML5 Microdata, HTML5 Canvas, Web Messaging, Web Workers, Web Storage, WebSocket, Server-Sent Events, WebRTC, WebVTT

2. Specifications developed as HTML5 extensions: HTML+RDFa, Polyglot Markup, HTML Editing APIs, Media Capture and Streams, Media Source Extensions

3. Initially standalone specifications that have been adopted by the HTML5 specification: SVG, MathML, WAI-ARIA

The elements and attributes of external vocabularies such as Scalable Vector Graphics (SVG) or MathML can be embedded directly into the HTML5 markup. For example, an SVG image can be embedded between the `<svg>` and `</svg>` tags such as in Listing 3-8.

Listing 3-8. Directly Embedded SVG in HTML5

```
<svg xmlns="http://www.w3.org/2000/svg">
<rect stroke="black" fill="blue" x="50px" y="50px" width="300px" height="150px"
stroke-width="2">
</svg>
```

MathML equations can be embedded similarly. These elements can also be nested for more complex content [28].

■ **Caution**   The different HTML5 modules are in various stages of development, and are being standardized separately (Microdata, Canvas, etc.), including the HTML5 core, which has minor revisions in separate specifications (HTML 5.1, HTML 5.2).

XHTML5

HTML5 can be written either in HTML syntax (HTML5) or in XML syntax (XHTML5). XHTML5 is the XML serialization of HTML5. In other words, HTML5 and XHTML5 share the same vocabulary (set of elements and attributes) defined by the HTML5 specification, but their syntax and parsing rules are different.

HTML5 documents can also be written in a way that they are HTML5 and XHTML5 documents at the same time, called *polyglot markup* (overlap language of HTML and XML). A polyglot web document is a valid HTML document and a well-formed XML document, and produces an identical DOM tree when processed as HTML and when parsed as XML[6] [29]. HTML5 and XHTML5 documents are cross-compatible, but XHTML5 has a stricter syntax. XML processing instructions can only be used in XHTML5.

Listing 3-9 shows an XHTML5 skeleton document.

Listing 3-9. An XHTML5 Skeleton Document

```
<?xml version="1.0" encoding="utf-8"?>
<!DOCTYPE html>
<html xmlns="http://www.w3.org/1999/xhtml">
  <head>
    <title>An XHTML5 example</title>
    <meta charset="UTF-8" />
  </head>
  <body>
    <header>
      <h1>Document sample</h1>
    </header>
```

---

[6]Except for those `xml`, `xmlns`, and `xlink` attributes for which HTML and XML parsers generate different DOMs, e.g., `xml:lang`, `xml:space`, `xml:base`, `xmlns=""`, `xmlns:xlink=""`, and `xlink:href`.

```
<section>
  <article>
    <h2>Article1</h2>
      The first article of the document.
  </article>
  <article>
    <h2>Article2</h2>
      The second article of the document.
  </article>
</section>
<footer>
  Copyright © 2015 John Smith. All rights reserved.
</footer>
</body>
</html>
```

(X)HTML 5.1, (X)HTML 5.2, and Beyond

On December 17, 2012, the W3C published the Candidate Recommendation of HTML5 [30], and introduced the first minor revision of HTML5 under the name HTML 5.1 (and its XML serialization as XHTML 5.1) [31].

This new version added new features for web applications and new elements based on developers' feedback. From this version onward, the W3C will separate controversial or unstable parts of the specification into extension specifications if needed (such as HTML 5.2 on the roadmap). This makes it possible to finalize the core specification in a relatively short timeframe without affecting quality (the approach of the original editorial team of HTML5 was proved inefficient and the standardization of HTML5 was progressing too slowly).

Markup Syntaxes

While similar, there are some significant differences between the HTML and the XHTML syntax as described in the following sections.

The HTML Syntax

The individual markup components are called *elements*. In HTML, keywords provided in angle brackets called *tags* delimit document fragments to which they are applied. Elements should have a starting tag and an ending tag in the form shown in Listing 3-10.

Listing 3-10. Pseudocode of Starting and Closing Tags

```
<element_name> element_content </element_name>
```

The *start tag* contains the name of the element, surrounded by angle brackets (in the form <element>). Element features such as appearance, behavior, or functioning are determined by the optional *attributes* specified on the start tag (Figure 3-1). They are separated by spaces.

Figure 3-1. *HTML element structure*

To distinguish the *end tag* from the start tag, the end tag has a slash after the opening angle bracket (in the form `</element>`). For example, a simple HTML paragraph looks like Listing 3-11.

Listing 3-11. A Simple Paragraph in HTML

```
<p>A simple paragraph.</p>
```

The elements can provide the structure and meaning to web documents through the indication of coherent sections such as headings, paragraphs, lists, tables, image embeddings, forms, and so on.

The default style sheet of the browser used to render the document determines the default appearance. However, the default appearance can be arbitrarily overridden by external style sheets as will be discussed later when we look at Cascading Style Sheets (CSS).

Two special tags in HTML are different from all the others. Comments can be added by the `<!-- ... -->` tag. The document type can be defined by the `<!DOCTYPE>` tag (see the "Document Type Declaration" section later in the chapter).

The XHTML Syntax and Restrictions

The element and attribute sets of the HTML and XHTML languages largely overlap, and most HTML elements can be used in the corresponding XHTML 1.0 flavor (HTML 4.01 Transitional elements in XHTML 1.0 Transitional, and HTML 4.01 Strict elements in XHTML 1.0 Strict). However, some elements introduced in the XHTML specifications can be applied in XHTML exclusively (compare the elements of the various markup language versions in Table 3-7). The major difference between earlier HTML and XHTML versions is that XHTML is stricter than HTML and it is extensible while HTML is not.[7] The difference between the HTML and XHTML vocabularies completely disappeared with the introduction of the latest markup versions, HTML5 and XHTML5, since HTML5 has exactly the same elements and attributes as XHTML5.

The difference between HTML and XHTML can be demonstrated by the fundamental requirements of XHTML. In fact, these strict rules point out best practices for superior markup that can also be extended with semantic annotations, and boosted to the desired level of web accessibility. By applying these rules, you can write web documents that are backward- and forward-compatible at the same time.

---

[7]Up to version 4.01. From HTML5, external vocabularies, such as SVG and MathML, can be used in HTML, too, as you will see later.

Well-formedness

According to *well-formedness*, a basic concept in XHTML, all elements must be closed and element nesting should be done in the proper order (Listing 3-12). Overlapping elements are incorrect in XHTML (Listing 3-13).

Listing 3-12. Properly Nested Elements

```
<p>Part of this <strong>bold text should be <em>italic as well</em></strong>.</p>
```

Listing 3-13. Overlapping Elements (Incorrect)

```
<p>Part of this <strong>bold text should be <em>italic as well</strong></em>.</p>
```

Names Are in Lowercase

Since XML is case-sensitive, all XHTML element and attribute names must be in lowercase.

Required End Tags

In HTML, the end tag of several elements can be omitted, which is not allowed in XHTML (Listings 3-14 and 3-15).

Listing 3-14. Properly Closed Elements

```
<p>This is the first paragraph.</p>
<p>This is the second one.</p>
```

Listing 3-15. Unterminated Elements Are Incorrect in XHTML

```
<p>This is the first paragraph. <p>This is the second one.
```

All elements that are declared in the DTD as *empty elements* (meta, link, br, hr, img, input) can be closed either by an end tag (similar to nonempty elements) or by the shorthand notation; in other words, a space and a slash character are inserted prior to the end of the declaration, as shown in Listing 3-16.

Listing 3-16. Pseudocode of Element Closing with Shorthand Notation (Self-closing)

```
<element_name attrib1="value1" ... attribn="valuen" />
```

which provides shorter code. Although the space before the slash is optional, it is preferred because the result is easier to read (Listing 3-17). Tags without a closing tag are also known as *self-closing tags*.

Listing 3-17. Terminated Empty Element

```
<br />
```

In XHTML, all unterminated elements are incorrect, including unterminated empty elements (Listing 3-18).

Listing 3-18. Unterminated Empty Elements Are Incorrect in XHTML

```
<br> unterminated elements are incorrect in XHTML <hr>
```

The script element applies either to the full form (with the end tag) or to the shorthand notation, depending on the number of parameters and the behavior of the element.

Quoted Attribute Values

All attributes must include values in XHTML. All attribute values must be quoted (Listing 3-19). Unquoted attribute values are not allowed in XHTML (Listing 3-20).

Listing 3-19. Defining XHTML Attributes Correctly

```
<input type="checkbox" name="checkbox" id="checkbox" value="True" checked="checked" />
```

Listing 3-20. Unquoted and Minimized Attributes (Incorrect in XHTML)

```
<input type=checkbox name=checkbox id=checkbox value=True checked />
```

No Attribute Minimization

Attribute-value pairs must be written in full (Listing 3-21). Attribute minimization is not supported by XHTML (Listing 3-22). Attribute names such as compact and checked cannot be used in elements without specifying their values (Table 3-3).

Listing 3-21. Attributes Should Be Written in Full

```
<option value="eng" selected="selected">English</option>
```

Listing 3-22. Minimized Attribute (Incorrect in XHTML)

```
<option value="eng" selected>English</option>
```

Table 3-3. Attributes That Can Be Minimized in HTML, but Not in XHTML

Minimized Attribute (HTML)	Full Form (HTML/XHTML)
compact	compact="compact"
checked	checked="checked"
declare	declare="declare"
readonly	readonly="readonly"
disabled	disabled="disabled"
selected	selected="selected"
defer	defer="defer"
ismap	ismap="ismap"
nohref	nohref="nohref"
noshade	noshade="noshade"
nowrap	nowrap="nowrap"
multiple	multiple="multiple"
noresize	noresize="noresize"

Whitespace Handling

Leading and trailing whitespace characters are stripped in XHTML. In contrast to HTML, whitespace characters in XHTML attribute values are normalized to single spaces. According to the XML specification, a single interword space (#x20) is appended to whitespace character sequences (#x20, #xD, #xA, #x9) [32].

Using Script and Style Elements

While the content type of the script and style HTML elements is *character data* (CDATA), it is *processed character data* (#PCDATA) in XHTML. The script and style elements are defined with #PCDATA content; in other words, < is handled as the beginning of markup code, while < is recognized as an entity (Listing 3-23).

Listing 3-23. Unescaped Script Content to Display x<y in XHTML through Javascript

```
<script type="text/javascript">
  <![CDATA[
unescaped script content x&lt;y
  ]]>
</script>
```

XML processors recognize these CDATA sections, and display the content rather than processing it as XML. If there is no script content to unescape, the <![CDATA[and]]> lines would be omitted, which is identical to the usual script embedding in HTML. The CDATA sections are represented as nodes in the Document Object Model.

The unescaped script or style contents are not needed in external script files and styles sheet files.

Identifiers

Instead of the name attribute defined in HTML 4, the id attribute should be used in XHTML for identifiers. XHTML documents must use the id attribute when defining fragment identifiers on the a, applet, form, frame, iframe, img, and map elements. This ensures the well-structuredness required by XML.

Element Prohibitions

In XHTML, elements cannot be nested arbitrarily. Those who are not familiar with XHTML often commit nesting errors. The nesting rules should not be confused with overlapping, which is strictly forbidden in XHTML. The nesting rules of XHTML 1.0 are similar to those of HTML 4.01, but there are some differences. The table element can contain a direct tr child element in XHTML, which is not allowed in HTML. In such cases, a tbody element is implied in HTML but not in XHTML. This behavior is important when tbody is used as a CSS selector. Table 3-4 summarizes those parent-child element relationships that are not allowed in XHTML.

Table 3-4. *XHTML Elements with Prohibitions*

Element	Prohibition(s)
a	Cannot contain other a elements
pre	Cannot contain img, object, big, small, sub, or sup elements
button	Cannot contain input, select, textarea, label, button, form, fieldset, iframe, or isindex elements
label	Cannot contain other label elements
form	Cannot contain other form elements

Since the additional nesting restrictions are defined by XHTML specifications, some nesting violations are not recognized by validators in XHTML documents, while such errors can be clearly identified in HTML.

Unlike in HTML, texts cannot be provided directly in the XHTML body without wrapping them in container elements (such as p). Omitting containers in XHTML results in the "character data is not allowed here" error message in the W3C Markup Validator (see Chapter 14).

Invalid Characters

Web documents containing non-Latin characters or special characters such as the copyright sign (©) or the registered trademark sign (®), and older HTML documents, especially the ones from the late 1990s and early 2000s, often contain character entities. While eliminating most character entities is recommended in HTML, it is mandatory in XHTML. The best practice is to type in the characters directly in the UTF-8 encoded XHTML markup.

Dashes Are Allowed for Comments Only

In XHTML, double dashes are allowed only at the beginning and end of comments (Listing 3-24).

Listing 3-24. A Comment in XHTML

```
<!-- Comment -->
```

Avoid Using Deprecated Elements

While a large set of HTML elements can be used in certain XHTML versions and variants as well, the blackface, blockquote, embed, layer, noembed, and shadow deprecated elements are not allowed in XHTML 1.0 Strict, only in XHTML 1.0 Transitional and XHTML 1.0 Frameset. These elements should be replaced by style sheets except embed and noembed whose contents can be provided with object. (Table 3-5).

Table 3-5. *Elements Not Allowed in XHTML 1.0 Strict Must Be Avoided*

Element	Deprecated in Favor of
applet	object
basefont	Style sheets
center	Style sheets
dir	ul
font	Style sheets
isindex	input element, CGI forms
menu	ul, nl
s	Style sheets
u	Style sheets

In XHTML 1.0 Strict, XHTML 1.1, and XHTML5, the ul element should be used instead of the menu element. XHTML2 introduced the nl element for menus, which is not supported in any other markup language.

The most arguable elements are i and b that are not deprecated and can be used in every XHTML version to create italic and bold texts, respectively. However, they are purely presentational elements without structural meaning. Although most user agents render the appropriate structural elements (em and strong) similarly if not identically to the i and b basic character formatting elements, em and strong are preferred.

As a general rule, use the XHTML 1.0 Strict elements and attributes only, and if you author XHTML5, extend the markup with the new XHTML5 elements and attributes where needed.

Avoid Deprecated Attributes

Several HTML attributes are deprecated in XHTML in favor of other attributes or style sheets (see Table 3-6).

Table 3-6. *Attributes Deprecated in XHTML*

Attribute	Deprecated in Favor of
alink	Style sheets
align	Style sheets
background	Style sheets
border	Style sheets
color	Style sheets
compact	Style sheets
face	Style sheets
height	Style sheets
language	type attribute
link	Style sheets
name	id attribute
noshade	Style sheets
nowrap	Style sheets
size	Style sheets
start	Style sheets
text	Style sheets
type	Style sheets
value	Style sheets
version	DTDs
vlink	Style sheets
width[8]	Style sheets

---

[8]It is deprecated on certain elements only (e.g., cannot be used on td, but allowed on img).

Data Types

The data types that can be used in element contents and attribute values are defined by DTDs and specifications of the markup language being used. While many elements and attributes allow most Unicode characters (such as the p, div, and section elements), there are elements and attributes that have specific restrictions. For example, a link in the href attribute of an a element must contain a valid URL or file path (Listing 3-25). The width attribute of an img element should be a value expressed by a number, with or without the unit of a certain type (Listing 3-26). Always make sure that you use valid attribute values only.

Listing 3-25. Correct and Incorrect URLs in the href Attribute Value

```
<a href="http://www.example.com/about/"> <!-- correct -->
<a href="contact.htm"> <!-- correct -->
<a href="a;b.html"> <!-- incorrect (contains an illegal character) -->
```

Listing 3-26. Correct and Incorrect Width Attribute Values

```
<img src="/images/logo.png" width="128" height="128" alt="logo" /> <!-- correct -->
<img src="/images/logo.png" width="100px" height="100px" alt="logo" /> <!-- correct -->
<img src="/images/logo.png" width="78pt" height="64pt" alt="logo" /> <!-- incorrect
(not allowed unit) -->
```

Markup elements and attributes can contain a variety of data types, such as case information, SGML basic data types, text strings, URIs, colors, lengths, content types, language codes, character encodings, single characters, dates and times, link types, media descriptors, script data, and style sheet data [33].

The syntax of the core markup element content values and attribute values are derived from SGML tokens such as the following:

- *PCDATA*: Parsed Character Data. Mixed content; in other words, an element can contain any number of character data and/or child elements in arbitrary order.

- *CDATA*: Character data. A sequence of characters from the document character set and may include character entities. CDATA attribute values should not contain leading or trailing whitespace characters. User agents replace character entities with characters, replace carriage returns and tabs with a single space, and ignore line feeds when interpreting CDATA attribute values. For script and style elements, CDATA sections are treated as raw text and passed forward as is. The end tag open delimiter </ is considered as the terminator of the element content.

- *NAME, ID*: Identifier tokens that must begin with a letter (A–Z, a–z) and may be followed by any number of letters, digits (0–9), hyphens (-), underscores (_), colons (:), and periods (.)

- *NUMBER*: Tokens containing a minimum of one digit (0–9).

The SGML tokens were introduced in the ISO 8879 standard [34], and they determine the allowed values of the data types to be used in markup attributes such as URLs, text, numbers, and so on. The supported characters in the markup depend on the data type as some characters are reserved or considered unsafe for a particular data type.

The PCDATA and CDATA data types are used mainly in XML applications and serialization, including XHTML, RSS, Atom, and so on (Chapter 7). SGML and XML Document Type Definition files also use PCDATA and CDATA for markup declarations.

■ **Caution**   In HTML, `<![CDATA[...]]>` is a *bogus comment*; that is, the sequence of characters is considered as regular character data. In XHTML, `<![CDATA[...]]>` is a *character data* section; in other words, a sequence of characters to be displayed rather than processed as XML. Without unescape, these sections would result in a well-formedness error in XML.

HTML5 supports the following data types:

- *Text*: If Unicode encoded, a sequence of Unicode characters that does not contain U+0000 characters, control characters other than space characters, or any permanently undefined Unicode characters.

- *String*: An arbitrary mixture of text and character references.

- *Token*: A string without space characters.

- *Browsing-context name*: A string that does not start with an underline (_) character and is at least one character long.

- *Browsing-context name or keyword*: A string that is either a browsing-context name or one of the following literal strings: _blank, _self, _parent, or _top.

- *ID*: A string without space characters that is at least one character long.

- *Name*: A string without space characters that is at least one character long.

- *Hash-name reference*: A string that starts with a # character.

- *Number*: Integer, positive integer, non-negative integer, floating-point number, positive floating-point number, or non-negative floating-point number.

- *Date and time*: A date-time as defined in RFC 3339, with the additional constraints that the literal letters *T* and *Z* must always be uppercase and that the date + full year is described as four or more digits representing a number greater than 0.

- *URL*: A valid IRI reference as defined in RFC 3987.

- *MIME type*: A string identifying a valid MIME media type defined by RFC 2046.

- *Character encoding name*: A character encoding a name or alias from the IANA registry.

- *Meta-charset string*: A string with the following parts (in that order): the literal string text/html;, one or more optional space characters, the literal string charset=, and a character encoding name (HTML5) or the string UTF-8 (XHTML5).

- *Refresh value*: Either a non-negative integer or a string containing a non-negative integer, a ; character, one or more space characters, the string url=, and finally a URL (in this order).

- *Default-style name*: A string.

- *Media-query list*: A media query list as defined in the W3C specification "Media Queries" [35].

- *Language tag*: A language tag as defined in BCP 47 [36].

- *List of key labels*: An ordered set of unique space-separated tokens, each of which is exactly one Unicode codepoint in length.

- *Dropzone value*: An unordered set of unique space-separated tokens, each of which is one of the values copy, move, or link, or any string with a minimum of three characters, beginning with the literal string s: (Plain Unicode string) or f: (File items). The default value is copy.

- *Functionbody*: Any JavaScript code that is a FunctionBody production according to ECMA 262.

- *Coordinates*: Rectangle coordinates (four integers), circle coordinates (two integers and a non-negative integer number), or polygon coordinates (minimum six integers).

- *Sandbox allow keywords list*: An unordered set of unique space-separated tokens that can be the literal string allow-forms, allow-scripts, allow-top-navigation, or allow-same-origin.

- *Pattern*: A regular expression that is a JavaScript pattern production according to ECMA 262.

- *E-mail address*: Any string that matches the ABNF production 1*(atext / ".") "@" ldh-str 1*("." ldh-str), where atext is as defined in RFC 5322, and ldh-str is as defined in RFC 1034.

- *Color*: A string exactly seven characters long, starting with a # character, followed by six characters in the range 0–9, a–f, and A–F.

Markup Elements

The various versions and variants of HTML support a different set of elements; in other words, they have different vocabularies, although there are many common elements and attributes that can be used in many or all markup languages (see Table 3-7, historic versions not included).

Table 3-7. *Overview of Markup Elements*

Element	HTML 4.01			XHTML					(X)HTML	Meaning
	T	F	S	1.0 T	1.0 F	1.0 S	1.1	2.0	5	
a	+	+	+	+	+	+	+	+	+	Hyperlink anchor
abbr	+	+	+	+	+	+	+	+	+	Abbreviation
access	–	–	–	–	–	+	+	–	–	Accessibility mapping
acronym	+	+	+	+	+	+	+	–	–	Acronym
action	–	–	–	–	–	–	–	+	–	Action
address	+	+	+	+	+	+	+	+	+	Author information
applet	+	–	–	+	+	–	–	–	–	Java applet
area	+	+	+	+	+	+	+	–	+	Client-side image map
article	–	–	–	–	–	–	–	–	+	Logically separate section
aside	–	–	–	–	–	–	–	–	+	Additional content section
audio	–	–	–	–	–	–	–	–	+	Audio stream
b	+	+	+	+	+	+	+	–	+	Bold text style
base	+	+	+	+	+	+	+	–	+	Document base URI
basefont	+	–	–	+	+	–	–	–	–	Base font size

(continued)

Table 3-7. (*continued*)

Element	HTML 4.01				XHTML					(X)HTML	Meaning
	T	F	S	1.0 T	1.0 F	1.0 S	1.1	2.0	5		
bdi	–	–	–	–	–	–	–	–	+	Text directionality isolation
bdo	+	+	+	+	+	+	+	–	+	Writing direction
big	+	+	+	+	+	+	+	–	–	Large text style
blockquote	+	+	+	+	+	+	+	+	+	Long quotation
body	+	+	+	+	+	+	+	+	+	Document body
br	+	+	+	+	+	+	+	+	+	Line break ("break row")
button	+	+	+	+	+	+	+	–	+	Push button
canvas	–	–	–	–	–	–	–	–	+	Bitmap canvas
caption	+	+	+	+	+	+	+	+	+	(Table/figure) caption
center	+	–	–	+	+	–	–	–	–	Content alignment to center
cite	+	+	+	+	+	+	+	+	+	Citation
code	+	+	+	+	+	+	+	+	+	Code fragment
col	+	+	+	+	+	+	+	+	+	Table column
colgroup	+	+	+	+	+	+	+	+	+	Table column group
data	–	–	–	–	–	–	–	–	+	Machine-readable equivalent
datalist	–	–	–	–	–	–	–	–	+	Data list
dd	+	+	+	+	+	+	+	+	+	Definition description
del	+	+	+	+	+	+	+	–	+	Deleted text
delete	–	–	–	–	–	–	–	+	–	Delete
dfn	+	+	+	+	+	+	+	+	+	Definition
di	–	–	–	–	–	–	–	+	–	Definition item
dir	+	–	–	+	+	–	–	–	–	Directory list
dispatch	–	–	–	–	–	–	–	+	–	Dispatch
div	+	+	+	+	+	+	+	+	+	Generic (block) container ("division")
dl	+	+	+	+	+	+	+	+	+	Definition list
dt	+	+	+	+	+	+	+	+	+	Definition term
em	+	+	+	+	+	+	+	+	+	Emphasized text style
embed	–	–	–	+	–	–	–	–	+	Embedded content
ev:listener	–	–	–	–	–	–	–	+	–	Event listener
fieldset	+	+	+	+	+	+	+	–	+	Form control group
figcaption	–	–	–	–	–	–	–	–	+	Legend

(*continued*)

Table 3-7. (*continued*)

Element	HTML 4.01			XHTML					(X)HTML	Meaning
	T	F	S	1.0 T	1.0 F	1.0 S	1.1	2.0	5	
figure	−	−	−	−	−	−	−	−	+	Paragraph with embedded content and caption
font	+	−	−	+	+	−	−	−	−	Font properties (local)
footer	−	−	−	−	−	−	−	−	+	(Document or section) footer
form	+	+	+	+	+	+	+	−	+	Interactive form
frame	−	+	−	−	+	−	−	−	−	Subwindow (frame)
frameset	−	+	−	−	+	−	−	−	−	Window subdivision
group	−	−	−	−	−	−	−	+	−	Element group
h	−	−	−	−	−	−	−	+	−	Heading
h1	+	+	+	+	+	+	+	+	+	Level 1 heading
h2	+	+	+	+	+	+	+	+	+	Level 2 heading
h3	+	+	+	+	+	+	+	+	+	Level 3 heading
h4	+	+	+	+	+	+	+	+	+	Level 4 heading
h5	+	+	+	+	+	+	+	+	+	Level 5 heading
h6	+	+	+	+	+	+	+	+	+	Level 6 heading
handler	−	−	−	−	−	−	−	+	−	Handler definition
head	+	+	+	+	+	+	+	+	+	Document head
header	−	−	−	−	−	−	−	−	+	Section header
hr	+	+	+	+	+	+	+	−	+	Horizontal rule
html	+	+	+	+	+	+	+	+	+	Document root
i	+	+	+	+	+	+	+	−	+	Italic text style
iframe	+	−	−	+	+	−	−	−	+	Inline frame
img	+	+	+	+	+	+	+	+	+	Embedded image
input	+	+	+	+	+	+	+	+	+	Form input
ins	+	+	+	+	+	+	+	−	+	Inserted text
insert	−	−	−	−	−	−	−	+	−	Insert
isindex	+	−	−	+	+	−	−	−	−	Keyword index that can be searched by entering keywords
kbd	+	+	+	+	+	+	+	+	+	Text to be entered by the user ("keyboard")
keygen	−	−	−	−	−	−	−	−	+	Key generator
l	−	−	−	−	−	−	−	+	−	Line of text

(*continued*)

Table 3-7. (*continued*)

Element	HTML 4.01 T	F	S	1.0 T	XHTML 1.0 F	1.0 S	1.1	2.0	(X)HTML 5	Meaning
label	+	+	+	+	+	+	+	+	+	Form field label
legend	+	+	+	+	+	+	+	−	+	Fieldset legend
li	+	+	+	+	+	+	+	+	+	List item
link	+	+	+	+	+	+	+	+	+	Media-independent link
load	−	−	−	−	−	−	−	+	−	Load
main	−	−	−	−	−	−	−	−	+	Main document content
map	+	+	+	+	+	+	+	−	+	Client-side image map
mark	−	−	−	−	−	−	−	−	+	Marked text
menu	+	+	−	+	+	−	−	−	−	Menu list
message	−	−	−	−	−	−	−	+	−	Message
meta	+	+	+	+	+	+	+	+	+	Generic metadata
meter	−	−	−	−	−	−	−	−	+	Scalar measurement
model	−	−	−	−	−	−	−	+	−	Model
nav	−	−	−	−	−	−	−	−	+	Navigation links section
nl	−	−	−	−	−	−	−	+	−	Navigation list
noframes	−	+	−	+	+	−	−	−	−	Alternate content for frames
noscript	+	+	+	+	+	+	+	−	+	Alternate content for scripts
object	+	+	+	+	+	+	+	+	+	Generic embedded object (Flash, applet, inline frame)
ol	+	+	+	+	+	+	+	+	+	Ordered list
optgroup	+	+	+	+	+	+	+	−	+	Option group
option	+	+	+	+	+	+	+	−	+	Select box item
output	−	−	−	−	−	−	−	+	+	Output
p	+	+	+	+	+	+	+	+	+	Paragraph
param	+	+	+	+	+	+	+	+	+	Named property value ("parameter")
pre	+	+	+	+	+	+	+	+	+	Preformatted text
progress	−	−	−	−	−	−	−	−	+	Task progress
q	+	+	+	+	+	+	+	+	+	Short (inline) quotation
range	−	−	−	−	−	−	−	+	−	Range definition
rb	−	−	−	−	−	−	+	+	+	Ruby base
rbc	−	−	−	−	−	−	+	+	−	Ruby base container

(*continued*)

Table 3-7. (*continued*)

Element	HTML 4.01			XHTML			(X)HTML			Meaning
	T	F	S	1.0 T	1.0 F	1.0 S	1.1	2.0	5	
rebuild	–	–	–	–	–	–	–	+	–	Rebuild
recalculate	–	–	–	–	–	–	–	+	–	Recalculate
refresh	–	–	–	–	–	–	–	+	–	Refresh
repeat	–	–	–	–	–	–	–	+	–	Repeat
reset	–	–	–	–	–	–	–	+	–	Reset
revalidate	–	–	–	–	–	–	–	+	–	Revalidate
rp	–	–	–	–	–	–	+	+	+	Ruby parentheses
rt	–	–	–	–	–	–	+	+	+	Ruby text
rtc	–	–	–	–	–	–	+	+	+	Ruby text container
ruby	–	–	–	–	–	–	+	+	+	Ruby markup
s	+	–	–	+	+	–	–	–	+	Strike-through text style
samp	+	+	+	+	+	+	+	+	+	Sample output
script	+	+	+	+	+	+	+	–	+	Script statements
secret	–	–	–	–	–	–	–	+	–	Secret input
section	–	–	–	–	–	–	–	+	+	Document section
select	+	+	+	+	+	+	+	+	+	Option selector
select1	–	–	–	–	–	–	–	+	–	Single select
send	–	–	–	–	–	–	–	+	–	Send
separator	–	–	–	–	–	–	–	+	–	Separator
setfocus	–	–	–	–	–	–	–	+	–	Set focus
setindex	–	–	–	–	–	–	–	+	–	Set index
setvalue	–	–	–	–	–	–	–	+	–	Set value
small	+	+	+	+	+	+	+	–	+	Small text style Side comment (HTML5)
source	–	–	–	–	–	–	–	–	+	Media resource
span	+	+	+	+	+	+	+	+	+	Generic (inline) container
standby	–	–	–	–	–	–	–	+	–	Message (while loading)
strike	+	–	–	+	+	–	–	–	–	Strike-through text
strong	+	+	+	+	+	+	+	+	+	Strong emphasis, importance
style	+	+	+	+	+	+	+	+	+	Style information
sub	+	+	+	+	+	+	+	+	+	Subscript
submit	–	–	–	–	–	–	–	+	–	Submit

(*continued*)

Table 3-7. (*continued*)

Element	HTML 4.01			XHTML					(X)HTML	Meaning
	T	F	S	1.0 T	1.0 F	1.0 S	1.1	2.0	5	
summary	–	–	–	–	–	–	–	+	–	Table summary
sup	+	+	+	+	+	+	+	+	+	Superscript
switch	–	–	–	–	–	–	–	+	–	Selection
table	+	+	+	+	+	+	+	+	+	Table
tbody	+	+	+	+	+	+	+	+	+	Table body
td	+	+	+	+	+	+	+	+	+	Table data cell
template	–	–	–	–	–	–	–	–	+	Template
textarea	+	+	+	+	+	+	+	+	+	Multiline text field
tfoot	+	+	+	+	+	+	+	+	+	Table footer
th	+	+	+	+	+	+	+	+	+	Table header cell
thead	+	+	+	+	+	+	+	+	+	Table header
time	–	–	–	–	–	–	–	–	+	Date and/or time
title	+	+	+	+	+	+	+	+	+	Document title
tr	+	+	+	+	+	+	+	+	+	Table row
track	–	–	–	–	–	–	–	–	+	Timed track
trigger	–	–	–	–	–	–	–	+	–	Trigger
tt	+	+	+	+	+	+	+	–	–	Teletype (monospace) text style
u	+	–	–	+	+	–	–	–	+	Underlined text style
ul	+	+	+	+	+	+	+	+	+	Unordered list
upload	–	–	–	–	–	–	–	+	–	File upload
var	+	+	+	+	+	+	+	+	+	Variable
video	–	–	–	–	–	–	–	–	+	Video
wbr	–	–	–	–	–	–	–	–	+	Conditional line break

The core markup elements were introduced in the early versions of HTML, and later versions gradually updated the set of elements. Some elements became *obsolete* over time, others were *deprecated*,[9] removed, or replaced. New specifications often introduce new elements. There are 70 elements listed in the HTML 3.2 specification [37], 91 in HTML 4.01 [38], and 108 in HTML5 [39].

There is a large similarity between the elements of the Transitional, Frameset, and Strict flavors of HTML as well as their XHTML counterparts. XHTML 1.0 Frameset is the XML equivalent of HTML 4.01 Frameset, the document type that provides the definition of frameset documents, which was a common web feature of the late 1990s. XHTML 1.0 Transitional is the XML equivalent of HTML 4.01 Transitional, the document type that includes the presentational

---

[9]Prior to HTML5

elements, such as center and font that are excluded from the Strict variant. XHTML 1.0 Strict is the XML equivalent of HTML 4.01 Strict, which includes strictly those elements that have not been deprecated.

The XHTML versions and variants provide a different set of elements. There are 89 elements in XHTML 1.0 Transitional, 92 in XHTML 1.0 Frameset, 78 in XHTML 1.0 Strict, 83 in XHTML 1.1, 99 in XHTML 2.0, and 108 in XHTML5 (the same as in HTML5) [40]. The applet, basefont, center, dir, font, isindex, menu, s, strike, and u elements have been deprecated in XHTML 1.0. Consequently, they can be used in XHTML 1.0 Transitional or XHTML 1.0 Frameset but not in XHTML 1.0 Strict or above. Many web designers did not understand this important fact and applied the Transitional variant of HTML4 or XHTML 1.0 for more than a decade. A Transitional variant, even in standard-compliant files, allows obsolete elements deprecated in the specification with the intention to indicate that these elements will be removed from future markup versions and thus should not be used. In other words, millions of web sites have used a markup until recently that allowed elements already obsoleted in HTML 4.01!

XHTML 1.0 Strict and XHTML 1.1 have a very similar set of elements. The most important differences are that XHTML 1.1 introduced the *Ruby elements* and removed the access element. Prior to XHTML 1.1, the lang attribute was used (instead of xml:lang which is preferred today). The name attribute for anchors and client-side maps was used until XHTML 1.0, which should be replaced by the id attribute from XHTML 1.1. The essence of XHTML 1.1 is that elements are collected to *modules*, making it possible to apply subsets of the full element set in environments with limited resources (for example, mobile devices), known as *XHTML modularization* (as mentioned earlier in the chapter).

XHTML 2.0 has several elements that are not found in any other markup language, namely, action, delete, di, dispatch, ev:listener, group, h, handler, insert, l, load, message, model, nl, output, range, rebuild, recalculate, refresh, repeat, reset, revalidate, secret, section, select1, send, bseparator, setfocus, setindex, setvalue, standby, submit, summary, switch, trigger, and upload. These elements were introduced in XHTML 2.0 but discontinued in (X)HTML5. XHTML 2.0 supports some XHTML 1.1 elements too, some of which are also included in (X)HTML5, such as ruby, while others have been excluded, such as rtc. The core elements were derived from earlier versions.

The latest version of XHTML, XHTML5, has the same set of elements as HTML5, as mentioned earlier. The most significant extension of markup elements and attributes in the past decade has been realized in (X)HTML5, especially because of the newly introduced structuring and multimedia elements not supported by any earlier versions.

Block vs. Inline Elements

To provide full control over different document sections, HTML elements are on different levels. Similar to the character, paragraph, and document formatting levels used in word processors, HTML provides tags with different scopes. Certain elements, known as *inline elements*, can be applied both on individual characters and on strings, such as font features, italic or bold texts, subscripts, and superscripts.[10] They are usually placed in paragraphs (p) or divisions (div) that contain text and/or inline elements. These containers are the block elements that form the basic structure of web documents. These elements can also be the containers of other block elements. Block-level elements have their own block margins, width, and height properties that can be set independently from other parts of the document (see Chapter 5). Block-level elements are usually rendered on a new line. In contrast, inline elements are treated as parts of the text flow and cannot have margins, cannot have width or height properties, and do break across lines.

In Listing 3-27, the paragraph below the heading begins in a new line, because both h1 and p are block-level elements. The emphasized text in the paragraph (between <em> and </em>) is rendered continuously and does not begin in a new line, because em is an inline element. While the div might have margins (set from CSS), the em cannot.

---

[10]Obsolete HTML elements used exclusively for character formatting should be substituted by CSS. (These styling elements have been removed from the Strict variants, and later from all other versions.)

Listing 3-27. Block vs. Inline Elements

```
<div>
  <h1>Attention</h1>
  <p>View our <em>special offers</em> now!</p>
</div>
```

Most HTML elements that can be used within the document body are classified as either block-level elements or inline elements. There are some elements that can be used in both contexts (such as buttons, objects, and scripts).

Block-Level Elements

The following elements are handled as block-level elements in HTML5: article, aside, blockcode, blockquote, body, button, canvas, caption, col, colgroup, dd, div, dl, dt, embed, fieldset, figcaption, figure, footer, form, h1, h2, h3, h4, h5, h6, header, hr, li, map, object, ol, output, p, pre, progress, section, table, tbody, textarea, td, tfoot, th, thead, tr, ul, and video.

Inline Elements

Generally, inline elements can contain text or other inline elements only. They are usually rendered within the current line. The inline elements of HTML5 are a, abbr, address, area, b, cite, code, del, details, dfn, datalist, em, font, i, iframe, img, input, ins, kbd, label, legend, link, mark, meter, nav, optgroup, option, q, samp, small, select, source, span, strong, sub, summary, sup, textarea, tt, u, time, and var.

Elements That Can Be Either Block or Inline Elements

Elements such as button, del, iframe, ins, map, object, and script can be used as either block-level elements or inline elements. If used as inline elements (e.g., within another inline element or a paragraph), these elements should not contain any block-level elements.

Attributes

The HTML5 element attributes are summarized in Table 3-8 [41].

Table 3-8. *HTML5 Attributes*

Attribute	Element(s)	Description	Value
abbr	th	Alternative label for header cell (reference in different context)	Text
accept	input	Hint for expected file type in file upload controls	Set of comma-separated tokens
accept-charset	form	Character encodings (form submission)	Ordered set of unique space-separated tokens (ASCII case-insensitive)
accesskey	HTML elements	Keyboard shortcut to activate or focus element	Ordered set of unique space-separated tokens (case-sensitive; one Unicode codepoint)
action	form	URL (form submission)	URL
alt	area, img, input	Alternate text for images or input fields	Text
async	script	Execute script asynchronously	Boolean attribute
autocomplete	form	Prevent autocompletion for form control(s)	on | off
autocomplete	input, select, textarea	Hint for form autofill	Autofill field name and related tokens
autofocus	button, input, keygen, select, textarea	Gives focus to form control automatically when the page is loaded	Boolean attribute
autoplay	audio, video	Media playback starts automatically	Boolean attribute
border	table	Indication that the table element is used for tabular data, not layout	Empty string or 1
challenge	keygen	String to package with the generated and signed public key	Text
charset	meta	Character encoding declaration	Preferred MIME name of an encoding
charset	script	Character encoding of external script file	Preferred MIME name of an encoding
checked	input	Determines whether the control is checked	Boolean attribute
cite	blockquote, del, ins, q	Link to quotation source or additional information	URL
class	HTML elements	Element class	Set of space-separated tokens

(continued)

Table 3-8. (*continued*)

Attribute	Element(s)	Description	Value
cols	textarea	Maximum number of characters per line	Non-negative integer greater than zero
colspan	td, th	Number of columns that the cell is to span	Non-negative integer greater than zero
content	meta	Meta content	Text
contenteditable	HTML elements	Determines whether the element is editable	true | false
controls	audio, video	Playback controls	Boolean attribute
coords	area	Shape coordinates (image map)	List of integers
crossorigin	audio, img, link, script, video	Determines how the element handles crossorigin requests	anonymous | use-credentials
data	object	Resource URL	URL
datetime	del, ins	Date and (optionally) time of modification	Date string with optional time
datetime	time	Time value	Date or time string
default	track	Enable the track if there is no more suitable track	Boolean attribute
defer	script	Defers script execution	Boolean attribute
dir	HTML elements	Text directionality	ltr | rtl | auto[11]
dirname	input, textarea	Form field name to send directionality (form submission)	Text
disabled	button, fieldset, input, keygen, optgroup, option, select, textarea	Determines whether the form control is disabled	Boolean attribute
download	a, area	Indicates resource to be downloaded rather than navigating to it, and declares the filename	Text
enctype	form	Encoding type (form submission)	application/x-www-form-urlencoded | multipart/form-data | text/plain
for	label	Associates the label with a form control	ID
for	output	Specifies controls from which the output was calculated	Unordered set of unique space-separated tokens (case-sensitive)

(*continued*)

---

[11]The auto attribute value cannot be used on the bdo element.

Table 3-8. (*continued*)

Attribute	Element(s)	Description	Value
form	button, fieldset, input, keygen, label, object, output, select, textarea	Associates the control with a form element	ID
formaction	button, input	URL to use for form submission	URL
formenctype	button, input	Encoding type to use for form submission	application/x-www-form-urlencoded | multipart/form-data | text/plain
formmethod	button, input	HTTP method to use for form submission	GET | POST
formnovalidate	button, input	Bypass form control validation for form submission	Boolean attribute
formtarget	button, input	Browsing context for form submission	Browsing context name or keyword
headers	td, th	Header cells for the cell	Unordered set of unique space-separated tokens (case-sensitive)
height	canvas, embed, iframe, img, input, object, video	Vertical dimension	Non-negative integer
hidden	HTML elements	Hides element	Boolean attribute
high	meter	Low limit of high range	Floating-point number
href	a, area, link	Hyperlink URL	URL[12]
href	base	Document base URL	URL
hreflang	a, area, link	Language of the linked resource	BCP 47 language tag
http-equiv	meta	Pragma directive	Text
icon	command	Command icon	URL
id	HTML elements	Element identifier	Text
ismap	img	Determines whether the image is a server-side image map	Boolean attribute
keytype	keygen	The type of cryptographic key to generate	Text
kind	track	The type of text track	subtitles | captions | descriptions | chapters | metadata
label	optgroup, option, track	Label	Text

(*continued*)

---

[12]The href attribute value cannot be empty on link elements.

Table 3-8. (*continued*)

Attribute	Element(s)	Description	Value
lang	HTML elements	Element language	BCP 47 language tag or empty string
list	input	List of autocomplete options	ID
loop	audio, video	Determines whether to loop the media	Boolean attribute
low	meter	High limit of low range	Floating point number
manifest	html	Application cache manifest	URL
max	input	Maximum value	*Varies*
max	meter, progress	Upper bound of range	Floating-point number
maxlength	input, textarea	Maximum length of value	Non-negative integer
media	link, source, style	Applicable media	Media query
mediagroup	audio, video	Groups media elements that have an implicit MediaController	Text
method	form	HTTP method to use for form submission	GET	POST
min	input	Minimum value	*Varies*
min	meter	Lower bound of range	Floating-point number
minlength	input, textarea	Minimum length	Non-negative integer
multiple	input, select	Whether to allow multiple values	Boolean attribute
muted	audio, video	Whether to mute the media resource by default	Boolean attribute
name	button, fieldset, input, keygen, output, select, textarea	Name of form control (form submission or form.elements API)	Text
name	form	Form name (document.forms API)	Text
name	iframe, object	Name of nested browsing context	Browsing context name or keyword
name	map	Image map name to reference from the usemap attribute	Text
name	meta	Metadata name	Text
name	param	Parameter name	Text
novalidate	form	Bypasses form control validation for form submission	Boolean attribute
optimum	meter	Optimum value in gauge	Floating-point number

(*continued*)

Table 3-8. (*continued*)

Attribute	Element(s)	Description	Value
pattern	input	Pattern to be matched by the value of the form control	Regular expression matching the JavaScript pattern production
placeholder	input, textarea	Visible label placed within the form control	Text
poster	video	Poster frame displayed prior to video playback	URL
preload	audio, video	Buffering hint for media	none | metadata | auto
readonly	input, textarea	Determines whether the value is editable	Boolean attribute
rel	a, area, link	Relationship between the document containing the hyperlink and the destination resource	Set of space-separated tokens
required	input, select, textarea	Determines whether the control is required for form submission	Boolean attribute
reversed	ol	List with reversed numbering	Boolean attribute
rows	textarea	Number of lines to show	Non-negative integer greater than zero
rowspan	td, th	Number of rows that the cell is to span	Non-negative integer
sandbox	iframe	Security rules for nested content	Unordered set of unique space-separated tokens consisting of allow-same-origin, allow-forms, and allow-scripts (ASCII case-insensitive)
spellcheck	HTML elements	Specifies the need for spelling and grammar check	true | false
scope	th	Specifies header cell scope	row | col | rowgroup | colgroup
selected	option	Option selected by default	Boolean attribute
shape	area	Shape type in an image map	circle | default | poly | rect
size	input, select	Control size	Non-negative integer greater than zero
sizes	link	Icon size for rel="icon"	Unordered set of unique space-separated tokens (ASCII case-insensitive)

(*continued*)

Table 3-8. (*continued*)

Attribute	Element(s)	Description	Value
span	col, colgroup	Number of columns spanned by the element	Non-negative integer greater than zero
src	audio, embed, iframe, img, input, script, source, track, video	Resource URL	URL
srcdoc	iframe	A document source of the inline frame	An iframe srcdoc resource
srclang	track	Text track language	BCP 47 language tag
start	ol	Ordinal value of the first item	Integer
step	input	Granularity to be matched by the form control value	Floating-point number greater than zero, or any
style	HTML elements	Styles (formatting and presentation)	CSS declarations
tabindex	HTML elements	Focus order	Integer
target	a, area	Hyperlink target	Browsing context name or keyword
target	base	Default browsing context (hyperlink navigation, form submission)	Browsing context name or keyword
target	form	Browsing context for form submission	Browsing context name or keyword
title	HTML elements	Additional visible information	Text
title	abbr, dfn	Reveals abbreviation or definition	Text
title	input	Input field hint	Text
title	link	Link title	Text
title	link, style	Alternate style sheet set name	Text
translate	HTML elements	Determines whether the element is to be translated when the page is localized	yes | no
type	a, area, link	Hint for resource type	MIME type
type	button	Button type	submit | reset | button
type	input	Form control type	input type keyword
type	ol	List marker type	1 | a | A | i | I
type	embed, object, script, source, style	Resource type	MIME type

(*continued*)

Table 3-8. (*continued*)

Attribute	Element(s)	Description	Value
typemustmatch	object	Determines whether the type attribute and the Content-Type value need to match the resource	Boolean attribute
usemap	img, object	Image map to use	Hash-name reference
value	button, option	Value to be used for form submission	Text
value	data	Machine-readable metadata	Text
value	input	Form control value	*Varies*
value	li	Ordinal value of the list item	Integer
value	meter, progress	Current value of the element	Floating point number
value	param	Parameter value	Text
width	canvas, embed, iframe, img, input, object, video	Horizontal dimension	Non-negative integer
wrap	textarea	Wrap type of the form control (form submission)	soft | hard

The global attributes and event handlers are described in the following sections by category.

Global Attributes

Table 3-9 summarizes those attributes that can be applied to all HTML5 elements.

Table 3-9. *Global HTML5 Attributes*

Attribute	Value
accesskey	List of unique space-separated key labels
class	Set of space-separated tokens (class name)
contenteditable	true | false | "" | empty
dir	ltr | rtl
hidden	hidden | "" | empty
id	Identifier
lang	Language code
spellcheck	true | false | "" | empty
style	String (style definition)
tabindex	Integer
title	Normal character data (text)
translate	yes | no

The accesskey, class, dir, id, lang, style, tabindex, and title attributes can also be used in HTML 4.

Event Handlers

The interactivity of web sites is achieved by checking whether an element received focus, a key is pressed, the user touched the touchscreen, and so forth. When such an event occurs, the script declared as the attribute value of the *event handler* attribute is executed. The name of event handlers starts with on and is followed by the name of the corresponding event (onclick, onkeypress, etc.).

When an HTML or XHTML document is loaded into a web browser, it becomes a Document object. An open browser window can be represented by the Window object. Some event handlers can be applied not only to markup elements, but also to the Document or Window objects.

Event handlers can be used as *content attributes* (markup element attributes and some event handlers on the Window object, Listing 3-28), *Interface Definition Language (IDL) attributes* [42] (scripting attributes, common to all event handlers, Listing 3-29), or both.

Listing 3-28. Content Attributes in the Markup

```
<div id="stunning" class="decoration"><p>...</p></div>
```

Listing 3-29. IDL Attributes in Scripting (Sets the Same Value as the class Attribute in Listing 3-28)

```
document.getElementById('stunning').className='decoration'
```

The following example demonstrates a simple onclick event handler (Listing 3-30).

Listing 3-30. A Button That Displays the Current Time When the User Clicks on It

```
<p>Click the button to display the date.</p>
<p><button onclick="displayDate()">What's the time?</button></p>
<script>
  function displayDate() {
  document.getElementById("demo").innerHTML = Date();
  }
</script>
<p id="demo"></p>
```

Global Event Handlers

The event handlers that are supported by all HTML5 elements (as both event handler content attributes and event handler IDL attributes) as well as by all Document and Window objects (as event handler IDL attributes) are the keyboard event handlers, the mouse event handlers, the media event handlers, the form event handlers, and the document event handlers.

Keyboard Event Handlers

HTML supports three keyboard events: the user pressed down a key, the user is holding down a key, and the user released a key (see Table 3-10).

***Table 3-10.** Keyboard Event Handlers*

Attribute	Runs the Script When...
onkeydown	A key is pressed
onkeypress	A key is pressed and released
onkeyup	A key is released

Mouse Event Handlers

On Graphical User Interfaces (GUIs), user actions are often triggered by the mouse. The mouse event attributes described in Table 3-11 apply to all HTML5 elements.

***Table 3-11.** Mouse Event Handlers*

Attribute	Runs the Script...
onclick	On a single click
ondblclick	On a double-click
onmousedown	When the mouse button is pressed
onmouseenter	When the mouse pointer reaches an area
onmouseleave	When the mouse pointer leaves an area
onmousemove	When the mouse pointer moves
onmouseout	When the mouse pointer moves out of an element
onmouseover	When the mouse pointer moves over an element
onmouseup	When the mouse button is released
onmousewheel	When the mouse wheel is being rotated
onscroll	When the scrollbar of an element is being scrolled

Media Event Handlers

Media event handlers can be used to control audio and video playback (see Table 3-12).

Table 3-12. *Media Event Attributes*

Attribute	Runs the Script...
onabort	When element loading is aborted
oncanplay	When the media data can be started to play with potential buffering
oncanplaythrough	When the media data can be played to the end without buffering
oncuechange	When the text of the track cue is changed
ondurationchange	When the length of the media object is changed
onemptied	When the media resource becomes empty
onended	When the media object has reached the end
onerror	When file loading is unsuccessful
onloadeddata	When the media data is loaded
onloadedmetadata	When media metadata such as duration is loaded
onloadstart	When the browser starts to load the media data
onpause	When the media data is paused
onplay	When the media data is going to start playing
onplaying	When the media data has started playing
onprogress	When the browser is fetching the media data
onratechange	When the playing rate of the media data has changed
onseeked	When the seeking attribute is no longer true and seeking has ended
onseeking	When the seeking attribute is true and seeking has begun
onstalled	When the media data cannot be fetched
onsuspend	When fetching media data has been started but stopped before the entire media file was fetched
ontimeupdate	When the media object changes its playing position
onvolumechange	When the media object changes the volume or when volume is set to mute
onwaiting	When the media content has stopped playing but is expected to resume

Form Event Handlers

Form event handlers can be used to make forms interactive (see Table 3-13).

Table 3-13. *Form Event Handlers*

Attribute	Runs the Script...
onblur	When an element lost focus
oncancel	When cancelling a file upload
onchange	On element change
onfocus	When an element received focus
oninput	On user input
oninvalid	On invalid user input
onreset	When the user clicks on the Reset button of a form
onselect	After some text has been selected in an element
onshow	When a menu element is shown as a context menu
onsubmit	On form submit
ontoggle	When the user opens or closes the details element

Window Event Handlers

The window event handlers supported by all `Window` objects are summarized in Table 3-14.

Table 3-14. *Window Event Handlers*

Attribute	Runs the Script ...
onafterprint	After the document is printed
onbeforeprint	Before the document is printed
onbeforeonload	Before the document is loaded
onhashchange	When the anchor of a URL is changed
onmessage	When the message is activated
onoffline	When the document goes offline
ononline	When the document comes online
onpagehide	When the window is hidden
onpageshow	When the window becomes visible
onpopstate	When the window history changes

(continued)

Table 3-14. (*continued*)

Attribute	Runs the Script ...
onresize[13]	When the browser window is resized
onstorage	When loading
onunload	When the user leaves the web page

The onreadystatechange Event Handler

The only event handler supported exclusively by the Document objects is onreadystatechange, which is triggered every time the readyState changes which holds the status of the server response to our request.

Clipboard Event Handlers

The clipboard event handlers supported by HTML5 [43] are summarized in Table 3-15.

Table 3-15. *Clipboard Event Handlers in HTML5*

Attribute	Runs the Script...
oncopy	When the user copies the content of an element
oncut	When the user cuts the content of an element
onpaste	When the user pastes some content in an element
onbeforecopy	When initiating a copy operation
onbeforecut	When initiating a cut operation
onbeforepaste	When initiating a paste operation

Touch Event Handlers

In HTML5 web applications, you can handle touch events from a mobile device or computer touchscreen by using touch event handlers on the HTML5 canvas to capture the user's movements and allow them to draw on the canvas. Table 3-16 summarizes the touch event handlers supported by HTML5 [44].

Table 3-16. *Touch Event Handlers*

Attribute	Runs the Script When...
ontouchcancel	A touch point has been disrupted
ontouchend	The user removes a touch point from the touch surface, or the touch point physically left the touch surface
ontouchmove	The user moves a touch point along the touch surface
ontouchstart	The user places a touch point on the touch surface

---

[13]Unlike all the other window event handlers, onresize is a global event handler which is supported by all HTML5 elements as well as all Document and Window objects.

HTML Document Structure

HTML documents apply a platform- and language-independent interface known as the *Document Object Model* (*DOM*) that makes it possible to refer to and manipulate markup elements as objects [45]. This model provides dynamic content access and updates as well as document styling for scripts [46]. The DOM can be considered a mechanism that makes web pages behave like applications [47]. The DOM can be visualized as a tree structure for the hierarchy of markup elements within a document (Listing 3-31, Figure 3-2).

Listing 3-31. A Well-Structured HTML Document

```
<!DOCTYPE html>
<html>
  <head>
    <title>A DOM example</title>
    <link rel="stylesheet"
     type="text/css"
     href="main.css">
  </head>
  <body>
    <p>Paragraph content</p>
  </body>
</html>
```

Figure 3-2. The DOM tree of Listing 3-31

Improperly closed elements and the missing closing tags destroy the DOM structure, which often has serious consequences such as disrupted layout or incorrect styling. Thanks to the built-in error-handling feature of web browsers, many markup errors are corrected on-the-fly, but the intended structure can be presumed only so the correct web site layout and styling is not guaranteed. Developers should not rely on this error-handling feature!

An HTML document usually consists of a Document Type Declaration (DTD), a Formal Public Identifier (FPI), and a link associating the document with the appropriate DTD at the very beginning of the file (except HTML5 documents that usually omit the DTD). All HTML documents must have an html root element[14] that contains the document head and the document body [48].

---

[14]Even if the element was marked optional in the HTML 4.01 specification.

The document head provides processing information and metadata relating to the whole document. The style sheets are usually linked here too.

The document body holds the content of the document. This can contain simple text, formatted text, images, videos, applets, or dynamic content, for example. The most common generic containers are the div elements (Figure 3-3), while the generic inline container is the span element. Blocks of texts that can be considered paragraphs should be written as the content of the p element.

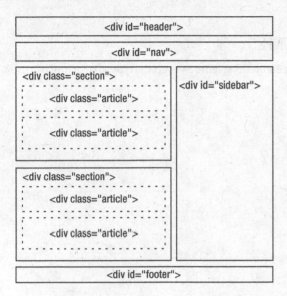

Figure 3-3. *Typical document structure within the body up to HTML 4.01*

In older versions of HTML, the typical web document structure looked like Listing 3-32.

Listing 3-32. The Document Structure Up to HTML 4.01

```
<!DOCTYPE HTML PUBLIC
"-//W3C//DTD HTML 4.01//EN"
"http://www.w3.org/TR/html4/strict.dtd">
<html>
  <head>
    <title>Sample HTML document structure</title>
  </head>
  <body>
    <div class="section">
      <div class="article">
        <h2>Abstract</h2>
        <p>... first paragraph of main content ...</p>
      </div>
      <div class="article">
        <h2>Overview</h2>
        <p>... second paragraph of main content ...</p>
      </div>
    </div>
```

```
<div id="footer">
  <p>
  Copyright © 2011 John Smith. All rights reserved.
  </p>
</div>
</body>
</html>
```

New Semantic Structuring Elements In HTML5

In HTML5 there are additional, meaningful (semantic) structuring elements (Figure 3-4), so the typical structure of HTML5 documents is more sophisticated and logical (Listing 3-33).

Listing 3-33. Typical HTML5 Document Structure

```
<!DOCTYPE html>
<html>
  <head>
    <title>Sample HTML5 document structure</title>
  </head>
  <body>
    <header>
      <h1>Document structure sample</h1>
    </header>
    <section>
      <article>
        <h2>Abstract</h2>
        <p>This sample document demonstrates the structure of HTML5 documents.</p>
      </article>
      <article>
        <h2>Overview</h2>
        <p>
        HTML5 adds more semantics to the document stucture. Instead of using general purpose
        divisions, it provides meaningful elements.
        </p>
      </article>
    </section>
    <footer>
      <p>
      Copyright © 2015 John Smith. All rights reserved.
      </p>
    </footer>
  </body>
</html>
```

Figure 3-4. *Document structure in HTML5*

The new structuring elements of HTML5 can be summarized as follows:

- `article`: Articles, blog posts, forum posts, and so on

- `aside`: Sidebars, such as cross-references to an article

- `section`: Group of elements (typically with a `header` and a `footer`)

- `header`: The header of a section (usually with a title and maybe a short overview)

- `footer`: Footer information of the entire page or a part of it (consequently, there might be more footer tags in a page)

- `nav`: Navigation elements

While useful, not all these structuring elements can be used on all web pages as they are not always suitable for the content.

Document Type Declaration

The various markup language versions have different features that should be handled differently. As discussed earlier, elements of one document type are not always allowed in others so the appropriate rendering strongly relies on the identification of the document type being used.

The document type must be declared in the top of the document that associates it with a formally defined specification. The document type declaration can be defined by a *Formal Public Identifier* (*FPI*) and the URI of the so-called *Document Type Definition* (*DTD*). These URIs are used for identification, and they are not hyperlinks. This is a machine-readable way to express "this document is HTML" or "this document is XHTML." Most DTD driver files are provided by the World Wide Web Consortium.

An FPI is a human-readable, descriptive name that identifies the HTML version, while the DTD defines the location of the `.dtd` file (machine-readable grammar) on the W3C server (this file specifies the rules the document type should follow).

You can see the general syntax of the HTML document type declaration in Listing 3-34. Note that HTML5 has a simplified DOCTYPE, as you will see.

Listing 3-34. General Syntax of Document Type Declaration

```
<!DOCTYPE root-element PUBLIC "FPI" ↵
  SYSTEM "URI"
>
```

The root element is html since it is the element opened first and closed last in HTML files (see "Core Structure Elements").

The various versions of HTML use similar syntax (except HTML5):

- HTML 2.0 (historical, not used anymore)

  ```
  <!DOCTYPE html PUBLIC "-//IETF//DTD HTML 2.0//EN">
  ```

- HTML 3.2 (historical, not used anymore)

  ```
  <!DOCTYPE html PUBLIC "-//W3C//DTD HTML 3.2 Final//EN">
  ```

- HTML 4.0 Transitional (should not be used)

  ```
  <!DOCTYPE HTML PUBLIC "-//W3C//DTD HTML 4.0 Transitional//EN" ↵
    "http://www.w3.org/TR/REC-html40/loose.dtd">
  ```

- HTML 4.0 Frameset (obsolete, should not be used)

  ```
  <!DOCTYPE HTML PUBLIC "-//W3C//DTD HTML 4.0 Frameset//EN" ↵
    "-//W3C//DTD HTML 4.0 Frameset//EN">
  ```

- HTML 4.0 Strict

  ```
  <!DOCTYPE HTML PUBLIC "-//W3C//DTD HTML 4.0//EN" ↵
    "http://www.w3.org/TR/REC-html40/strict.dtd">
  ```

- HTML 4.01 Transitional (should not be used)

  ```
  <!DOCTYPE HTML PUBLIC "-//W3C//DTD HTML 4.01 Transitional//EN" ↵
    "http://www.w3.org/TR/html4/loose.dtd">
  ```

- HTML 4.01 Frameset (obsolete, should not be used)

  ```
  <!DOCTYPE HTML PUBLIC "-//W3C//DTD HTML 4.01 Frameset//EN" ↵
    "http://www.w3.org/TR/html4/frameset.dtd">
  ```

- HTML 4.01 Strict

  ```
  <!DOCTYPE HTML PUBLIC "-//W3C//DTD HTML 4.01//EN" ↵
    "http://www.w3.org/TR/html4/strict.dtd">
  ```

- HTML 4.01+RDFa

  ```
  <!DOCTYPE HTML PUBLIC "-//W3C//DTD HTML 4.01+RDFa 1.1//EN" ↵
    "http://www.w3.org/MarkUp/DTD/html401-rdfa11-1.dtd">
  ```

- HTML5 (DOCTYPE without DTD). Unlike the former, SGML-based HTML versions, HTML5 requires neither an FPI nor a reference to a DTD. The document type can be defined by the DOCTYPE declaration `<!DOCTYPE html>`. Since the `text/html` serialization of HTML5 is not SGML-based, HTML5 applies the document type for mode selection only.

  ```
  <!DOCTYPE HTML>
  ```

Core Structure Elements

HTML documents must contain one element that is the parent of all other elements, that is, the `html` element. This element is called the *root element*. It has been standardized in the HTML 2.0 specification, along with the other two fundamental structure elements, `head` and `body`.

The `html` *root element* contains all other elements within the document; in other words, the `<html>` starting tag and the `</html>` closing tag delimit the document.

The HTML Head

The head section of HTML documents is the container of processing information and metadata. The document head should be provided between the `<head>` and `</head>` tags and precede the document body.

Common elements in the HTML head (with one example for each) include the following:

- `title` element (required)

  ```
  <title>Document title</title>
  ```

- `meta` elements[15] (optional, one or more)

  ```
  <meta name="keywords" content="web standardization, valid XHTML5, valid ↵
  XHTML+RDFa, tableless CSS layout, W3C validation, WCAG, semantic web, ↵
  accessibility">
  ```

- `link` elements (optional, one or more)

  ```
  <link rel="stylesheet" type="text/css" media="all" href="alt2.css" ↵
  title="Alternate style 2">
  ```

- `script` elements (optional, one or more)

  ```
  <script type="text/javascript" src="js/loading.js"></script>
  ```

The document body is the main content of a web document. It might contain both block and inline elements including, but not limited to, plain and formatted text, lists, headers, paragraphs, divisions, images, objects, forms, and tables. However, there are prohibitions that determine which elements can be included in other elements.

Element Nesting

To maintain a logical document structure, certain HTML elements cannot contain all types of data or elements. For example, elements of a table such as table body and data cells should be within a table; the `ins` element cannot contain block-level content when it is used as an inline element, and so on. Some elements cannot contain other enclosed elements of the same kind (e.g., `form`, `label`). The content delimited by some elements can be a certain type of data only (e.g., `script`, `style`).

---

[15]See Chapter 7 for details.

Some nesting rules require the knowledge of content categories. In HTML5, the following kinds of content are differentiated [49]:

- *Metadata content*: Content that determines the presentation or behavior of the page content, sets up the relationship of the document with other documents, or provides additional information.

  base, command, link, meta, noscript, script, style, title

- *Flow content*: Most elements that are used in the document and application body are referred to as flow content.

  a, abbr, address, area (as a descendant of a map element), article, aside, audio, b, bdi, bdo, blockquote, br, button, canvas, cite, code, datalist, del, details, dfn, div, dl, em, embed, fieldset, figure, footer, form, h1, h2, h3, h4, h5, h6, header, hr, i, iframe, img, input, ins, kbd, keygen, label, map, mark, math, meter, nav, noscript, object, ol, output, p, pre, progress, q, ruby, s, samp, script, section, select, small, span, strong, style (only with the scoped attribute), sub, sup, svg, table, textarea, time, u, ul, var, video, wbr, and textual content

- *Sectioning content*: Content that defines the scope of headings and footers.

  article, aside, nav, section

- *Heading content*: Content that defines the header of a section.

  h1, h2, h3, h4, h5, h6

- *Phrasing content*: The document text and elements in paragraphs.

  a (only with phrasing content), abbr, area (as a descendant of a map element), audio, b, bdi, bdo, br, button, canvas, cite, codedatalist, del (only with phrasing content), dfn, em, embed, i, iframe, img, input, ins (only with phrasing content), kbd, keygen, label, map (only with phrasing content), mark, math, meter, noscript, object, output, progress, q, ruby, s, samp, script, select, small, span, strong, sub, sup, svg, textarea, time, u, var, video, wbr, and textual content

- *Embedded content*: Imported content from external resources or content from another vocabulary directly embedded into the document.

  audio, canvas, embed, iframe, img, math, object, svg, video

- *Interactive content*: Content dedicated to user interaction.

  a, audio (only with the controls attribute), button, details, embed, iframe, img (only with the usemap attribute), input (only if the type attribute is not set to hidden), keygen, label, object (only with the usemap attribute), select, textarea, video (only with the controls attribute)

The most common elements can be nested as follows:

- html
  - head
    - title (required)
    - script, style
      - CDATA
    - base, meta, link (empty)
    - object
      - param (empty)
      - flow

- body
  - ins, del
    - flow
      - block
      - inline
  - script
    - CDATA
  - block
    - address
      - inline
    - article
      - header
      - sectioning (article, aside, section)
    - aside
      - header
      - sectioning (article, aside, section)
    - audio, video
    - blockquote
      - block
      - script
        - CDATA
    - div
      - flow
    - dl
      - dt
        - inline
      - dd
        - flow
    - fieldset
      - #PCDATA
      - inline
      - flow
      - legend
        - inline

- form
  - block except an enclosed form
  - script
    - CDATA
- footer
  - flow
- h1, h2, h3, h4, h5, h6, p
  - inline
    - #PCDATA
    - a
      - inline except an enclosed a element
    - button
      - flow except a, button, fieldset, form, input, label, select, textarea
    - abbr, b, bdo, cite, code, dfn, em, i, kbd, q, samp, small, span, strong, sub, sup, var
      - inline
    - img, br (empty)
    - input (empty)
    - label
      - label except enclosed label
    - map
      - area (empty)
      - block
    - object
      - param (empty)
      - flow
    - script
      - CDATA
    - select
      - optgroup
        - option
      - option
    - textarea

- header
  - h1, h2, h3, h4, h5, h6
  - form
  - img
  - flow
- hr (empty)
- nav
  - header
  - sectioning (article, aside, section)
- noscript
  - flow
- pre
  - inline except img, object, small, sub, sup
- section
  - header
    - h1, h2, h3, h4, h5, h6
    - form
    - img
    - flow
  - footer
  - sectioning (article, aside, section)
- table
  - caption
    - inline
  - colgroup
    - col (empty)
  - col (empty)
  - thead, tbody
    - tr
      - th, td
        - flow
- ul, ol
  - li
    - flow

After understanding the difference between block-level and inline elements, nesting elements is rather straightforward. Empty elements, such as img or hr, cannot contain other elements. Some elements have restrictions for not only the elements but also the data types they can contain (for example, the contents of script elements should be CDATA). Violating the nesting order of element might destroy the DOM structure of the document, which makes rendering unreliable, risking the usability of the web page.

XHTML Document Structure

The XHTML document structure is similar to that of HTML in the sense that there is a head and a body section; however, additional restrictions apply. Since XHTML documents are XML documents too, they begin with an XML declaration not used in HTML. Moreover, there are several document types and profiles to choose from, depending on the main purpose of the web document being developed.

XML Declaration

The very first line in XHTML documents is usually the optional XML prolog (its application is recommended by W3C). The most commonly used XML declaration looks like Listing 3-35.

Listing 3-35. The Most Commonly Used XML Declaration

```
<?xml version="1.0" encoding="utf-8"?>
```

No content is allowed to precede the declaration (except an optional byte-order mark).

Although the character encoding is optional only, it is highly recommended.

Some older browsers cannot handle the XML declaration. The web page might become invisible, or the content is rendered incorrectly (for example, in IE6). IE7 ignores the XML prolog and correctly renders the content in Strict Mode (discussed in Chapter1).

Document Type Declaration

Similar to HTML, XHTML documents use a specific *Document Type Declaration*[16] to identify the document type being used.

Generally, transforming an XHTML document into another XHTML document type is straightforward, especially if XHTML 1.0 Strict elements are applied exclusively. However, care must be taken when performing such an action because of the differences between the specifications. XHTML 1.0 Transitional is much more permissive, and changing the Document Type Declaration of these documents will probably result in numerous errors that should be justified in order to obtain a valid XHTML 1.0 Strict, XHTML 1.1, or XHTML5 document.

Until recently, the former Quality Assurance Interest Group at W3C maintained a "Recommended list of Doctype declarations" [50]. Although it could be considered a "list of valid DTDs," it is not complete; thus, some of the newer as well as the most up-to-date document types are not listed (e.g., Mobile Profile, XHTML 2.0, or XHTML+RDFa), partly because the group closed in 2007. This does not affect the application or validation of such documents. Some non-W3C validators use the previous list and give warnings if a document type missing from that list is used. Such warnings are often false positives, because some of the less used, earlier DTDs as well as the latest document types are not on the list.

---

[16]Prior to XHTML5

The document type declaration of the various XHTML versions and variants are summarized here:

- General documents

    - XHTML Basic 1.0

        ```
        <!DOCTYPE html PUBLIC "-//W3C//DTD XHTML Basic 1.0//EN" ↵
           "http://www.w3.org/TR/xhtml-basic/xhtml-basic10.dtd">
        ```

    - XHTML Basic 1.1

        ```
        <!DOCTYPE html PUBLIC ↵
           "-//W3C//DTD XHTML Basic 1.1//EN" ↵
           "http://www.w3.org/TR/xhtml-basic/xhtml-basic11.dtd">
        ```

    - XHTML 1.0 Transitional (should not be used)

        ```
        <!DOCTYPE html PUBLIC "-//W3C//DTD XHTML 1.0 Transitional//EN" ↵
           "http://www.w3.org/TR/xhtml1/DTD/xhtml1-transitional.dtd">
        ```

    - XHTML 1.0 Frameset (obsolete, should not be used)

        ```
        <!DOCTYPE html PUBLIC "-//W3C//DTD XHTML 1.0 Frameset//EN" ↵
           "http://www.w3.org/TR/xhtml1/DTD/xhtml1-frameset.dtd">
        ```

    - XHTML 1.0 Strict

        ```
        <!DOCTYPE html PUBLIC "-//W3C//DTD XHTML 1.0 Strict//EN" ↵
           "http://www.w3.org/TR/xhtml1/DTD/xhtml1-strict.dtd">
        ```

    - XHTML Basic 1.1

        ```
        <!DOCTYPE html PUBLIC "-//W3C//DTD XHTML Basic 1.1//EN" ↵
           "http://www.w3.org/TR/xhtml-basic/xhtml-basic11.dtd">
        ```

    - XHTML 1.1

        ```
        <!DOCTYPE html PUBLIC "-//W3C//DTD XHTML 1.1//EN" ↵
           "http://www.w3.org/TR/xhtml11/DTD/xhtml11.dtd">
        ```

    - XHTML 2.0 (XHTML2) (suspended [51])

        ```
        <!DOCTYPE html PUBLIC "-//W3C//DTD XHTML 2.0//EN" ↵
           "http://www.w3.org/MarkUp/DTD/xhtml2.dtd">
        ```

    - XHTML5 (DOCTYPE without DTD)

        ```
        <!DOCTYPE html>
        ```

    - XHTML+RDFa

        ```
        <!DOCTYPE html PUBLIC "-//W3C//DTD XHTML+RDFa 1.0//EN" ↵
           "http://www.w3.org/MarkUp/DTD/xhtml-rdfa-1.dtd">
        ```

- Mobile profiles

  - XHTML Mobile Profile 1.0

    ```
    <!DOCTYPE html PUBLIC "-//WAPFORUM//DTD XHTML Mobile 1.0//EN" ↵
        "http://www.wapforum.org/DTD/xhtml-mobile10.dtd">
    ```

  - XHTML Mobile Profile 1.1

    ```
    <!DOCTYPE html PUBLIC "-//WAPFORUM//DTD XHTML Mobile 1.1//EN" ↵
        "http://www.openmobilealliance.org/tech/DTD/xhtml-mobile11.dtd">
    ```

  - XHTML Mobile Profile 1.2

    ```
    <!DOCTYPE html PUBLIC "-//WAPFORUM//DTD XHTML Mobile 1.2//EN" ↵
        "http://www.openmobilealliance.org/tech/DTD/xhtml-mobile12.dtd">
    ```

- Mathematical markup

  - MathML 1.01

    ```
    <!DOCTYPE math SYSTEM ↵
    "http://www.w3.org/Math/DTD/mathml1/mathml.dtd">
    ```

  - MathML 2.0

    ```
    <!DOCTYPE math PUBLIC "-//W3C//DTD MathML 2.0//EN" ↵
        "http://www.w3.org/TR/MathML2/dtd/mathml2.dtd">
    ```

  - MathML 3.0

    ```
    <!DOCTYPE math PUBLIC "-//W3C//DTD MathML 3.0//EN" ↵
        "http://www.w3.org/Math/DTD/mathml3/mathml3.dtd">
    ```

- Graphical markup

  - SVG 1.0

    ```
    <!DOCTYPE svg PUBLIC "-//W3C//DTD SVG 1.0//EN" ↵
        "http://www.w3.org/TR/2001/REC-SVG-20010904/DTD/svg10.dtd">
    ```

  - SVG 1.1 Tiny

    ```
    <!DOCTYPE svg PUBLIC "-//W3C//DTD SVG 1.1 Tiny//EN" ↵
        "http://www.w3.org/Graphics/SVG/1.1/DTD/svg11-tiny.dtd">
    ```

  - SVG 1.1 Basic

    ```
    <!DOCTYPE svg PUBLIC "-//W3C//DTD SVG 1.1 Basic//EN" ↵
        "http://www.w3.org/Graphics/SVG/1.1/DTD/svg11-basic.dtd">
    ```

  - SVG 1.1 Full

    ```
    <!DOCTYPE svg PUBLIC "-//W3C//DTD SVG 1.1//EN" ↵
        "http://www.w3.org/Graphics/SVG/1.1/DTD/svg11.dtd">
    ```

- Compound documents

  - XHTML + MathML + SVG (using XHTML as the host)

    ```
    <!DOCTYPE html PUBLIC ↵
      "-//W3C//DTD XHTML 1.1 plus MathML 2.0 plus SVG 1.1//EN" ↵
      "http://www.w3.org/2002/04/xhtml-math-svg/xhtml-math-svg.dtd">
    ```

  - XHTML + MathML + SVG (using SVG as the host)

    ```
    <!DOCTYPE svg:svg PUBLIC ↵
      "-//W3C//DTD XHTML 1.1 plus MathML 2.0 plus SVG 1.1//EN" ↵
      "http://www.w3.org/2002/04/xhtml-math-svg/xhtml-math-svg.dtd">
    ```

The Root Element in XHTML

All XML documents must contain a root element with the syntax shown in Listing 3-36.

Listing 3-36. Pseudocode of the Root Element

```
<root>
  <child>
    <subchild>.....</subchild>
  </child>
</root>
```

The root element of XHTML documents must be `html`. Furthermore, the root element must contain an `xmlns` attribute to associate it with the XHTML namespace. The namespace URI is `http://www.w3.org/1999/xhtml` for XHTML 1.0 and XHTML5 documents, and it is `http://www.w3.org/2002/06/xhtml2/` for XHTML2 documents. Consequently, the most common XHTML namespace declaration looks like Listing 3-37.

Listing 3-37. The Most Common XHTML Namespace Declaration

```
<html xmlns="http://www.w3.org/1999/xhtml">
```

The natural language of XML documents is often identified by the `xml:lang` attribute of the `html` element[17] (Listing 3-38).

Listing 3-38. Common Use of the `xml:lang` Attribute

```
<html xmlns="http://www.w3.org/1999/xhtml" xml:lang="en">
```

Namespace Declaration

Beyond the default XHTML namespace `http://www.w3.org/1999/xhtml`, additional ones can also be used in XHTML documents. For example, XHTML+RDFa documents often use additional namespaces for semantic markup (for more details, see Chapter 7). In the example shown in Listing 3-39, the namespace of the FOAF Vocabulary Specification follows the default namespace declaration.

---

[17]Although it is used frequently, this is just one of the many options to identify the XML document language (see Chapter 4).

Listing 3-39. Additional Namespace Declaration

```
<html version="XHTML+RDFa 1.0" ↵
 xmlns="http://www.w3.org/1999/xhtml" xmlns:foaf="http://xmlns.com/foaf/0.1/" ↵
 xml:lang="en">
```

In mixed-namespace documents, such as XHTML + MathML + SVG, multiple namespace declarations occur throughout the document body (unlike the previous ones that are declared in the document head). Listing 3-40 shows an example.

Listing 3-40. Namespace Declarations in the body of a Compound Document

```
<!-- ... XHTML content ... -->
  <math xmlns="http://www.w3.org/1998/Math/MathML">
    <!-- ... MathML notation ... -->
  </math>
  <!-- ... XHTML content ... -->
  <svg:svg version="1.1" ↵
   xmlns:svg="http://www.w3.org/2000/svg" xmlns:xlink="http://www.w3.org/1999/xlink">
    <!-- ... SVG graphic ... -->
  </svg>
<!-- ... XHTML content ... -->
```

The XHTML Head

The title of XHTML documents can be written exactly the same way as in HTML, that is, between the start and end tags (Listing 3-41).

Listing 3-41. XHTML Document Title

```
<title>Title of the sample XHTML document</title>
```

The meta, link, and script elements can be provided in the document head of XHTML like in HTML documents. However, in XHTML these elements (along with all other elements) should be closed. These empty elements apply the XHTML shorthand notation (self-closing) (Listing 3-42).

Listing 3-42. A Self-Closing Link Element in XHTML

```
<link rel="stylesheet" type="text/css" media="all" href="alt2.css" ↵
 title="Alternative style 2" />
```

In the following example, the title attribute is used to indicate search engines that show where to locate the German and Hungarian versions of the original English document (Listing 3-43). The xml:lang attribute declares the language of the target documents.

Listing 3-43. Links to Other Language Versions of the Same Document

```
<head>
  <title>The document in English</title>
  <link title="Das Dokument auf Deutsch" ↵
   rel="alternate" ↵
   href="http://example.com/german/"
   xml:lang="de" />
```

```
<link lang="hu" title="A dokumentum magyarul" ↵
  rel="alternate" ↵
  xml:lang="hu" ↵
  href="http://example.com/hungarian/" />
</head>
```

The character encoding of the page specified as the link target can be declared by the charset attribute. The media attribute specifies the medium the link applies to. Table 3-17 summarizes the possible values.

Table 3-17. Values of the media Attribute on the link Element

Value	Description
screen	Computer screens (default)
tty	TeleTypes (fixed character width)
tv	Televisions and similar devices (low resolution, limited scrollability)
projection	Projectors
handheld	Mobile devices, smartphones (small screens, limited bandwidth)
print	Print preview/printed pages
braille	Braille devices
aural	Speech synthesizers
all	Suitable for all devices

Listing 3-44 shows an example for three different style sheets written for three different media types (all, handheld, print).

Listing 3-44. CSS Files for Different Media Types

```
<link rel="stylesheet" type="text/css" media="all" href="main.css" ↵
 title="Default style" />

<link rel="stylesheet" type="text/css" media="handheld" href="mobile.css" ↵
 title="Styles for mobile devices" />

<link rel="stylesheet" type="text/css" media="print" href="print.css" ↵
 title="Styles for printing" />
```

The rel attribute (which stands for relationship) is a space-separated list of one or more values specifying the relationship between the current page and the target resource (Listing 3-45). Possible values are alternate, appendix, bookmark, chapter, contents, copyright, glossary, help, index, next, prev, section, stylesheet, and subsection.

Listing 3-45. Application Example for the rel Attribute

```
<link rel="alternate" type="application/rss+xml" title="New feed of example page" ↵
 href="http://www.example.com/rss.xml" />
<link rel="glossary" title="Glossary" href="glossary/" />
<link rel="copyright" title="Copyright" href="copy/" />
```

```
<link rel="bookmark" title="About" href="about/" />
<link rel="bookmark" title="Services" href="services/" />
<link rel="bookmark" title="Portfolio" href="portfolio/" />
<link rel="bookmark" title="Contact" href="contact/" />
```

The author of the document can be declared similarly (Listing 3-46).

Listing 3-46. A Link to the Author

```
<link rel="author"> href="http://www.example.com/" />
```

The favorites icon (favicon[18]), a 16×16 pixel square icon by default, can be determined by the shortcut icon or icon link (Listing 3-47). The first one is supported in all browsers; however, it is not declared in HTML specifications.

Listing 3-47. A Link to the Web Site Icon

```
<link rel="shortcut icon" href="favicon.ico" type="image/x-icon" />
```

Although the default image format is ICO, modern browsers support other formats too such as PNG, animated PNG, JPEG, GIF, animated GIF, and SVG. They can be used in the form shown in Listing 3-48.

Listing 3-48. Link Examples for rel="icon"

```
<link rel="icon" type="image/vnd.microsoft.icon"> href="http://www.example.com/image.ico" />

<link rel="icon" type="image/png"> href="http://www.example.com/image.pgn" />

<link rel="icon" type="image/gif"> href="http://www.example.com/image.gif" />
```

■ **Tip** Since the attribute value icon was not standardized until HTML5 and browser support varies, it is a common practice to declare the same icon file with both the shortcut icon and icon attribute values.

The files can also be 32×32, 48×48, or 64×64 pixels in size with 8-, 24-, or 32-bit color depth. However, because of the different browser support, the preferred format for favicons is the *de facto* file name and type (favicon.ico) provided in the root directory of the web site. Note that the larger the resolution and color depth, the longer the download time. File size should be kept within reasonable limits (see Chapter 9 for more on this).

The rel attribute is often used in other contexts as well. The microformats rel="license", rel="nofollow", and rel="tag", for example, provide various metadata on (X)HTML elements, most commonly on the a element. Generally they are parts of the document body but are used for specific purposes; thus, they are described later in Chapter 7.

In the XHTML document head, further attribute values can also be used from namespaces other than the default XHTML namespace. Listing 3-49 shows an example for that.

Listing 3-49. Linking to an Additional Namespace

```
<link rel="foaf:primaryTopic" type="application/rdf+xml" title="FOAF" ↵
href="http://www.example.com/metadata/foaf.rdf" />
```

---

[18]Also known as bookmark icon, URL icon, shortcut icon, or web site icon

In this case, the FOAF namespace is also required to make the `foaf:primaryTopic` meaningful. The declaration of the additional namespace should be provided on the `html` element, as discussed in the previous section (Listing 3-39).

The XHTML Body

The XHTML document body is similar to the HTML body from the document structuring point of view. However, XHTML is case-sensitive. Consequently, the JavaScript event handler `onload` cannot be written with the same camel case notation `onLoad` used in HTML. It should be in lowercase (Listing 3-50).

Listing 3-50. Case-Sensitive Event Handler in XHTML

```
<body onload="function();">
```

Moving from HTML to XHTML

For over a decade, a common task in web site standardization was to convert HTML documents into XHTML. However, with the release of a brand new line of HTML, more and more web developers intend to use HTML5, mainly due to its vocabulary and APIs. This does not mean, however, that HTML syntax must be preferred, because HTML5 documents can be written in XML serialization too (XHTML5). There are several reasons to use stricter markup. Although some changes to be made on HTML documents while upgrading to XHTML are straightforward, there are significant differences between the two formats in features and behavior that need to be considered. Since XHTML is the reformulation of HTML 4 as an application of XML, it can be used as an XML-conforming language with all of its attendant benefits:

- *Strict markup*: Unlike HTML, XHTML complies with strict conventions. As a result, there are no missing end tags, overlapping elements, or unnecessary attributes, just pure code. XHTML is well-formed and easy to write, interpret, and read. Content and styles are separated.

- *Easy introduction of new markup*: New elements and attributes can be added quite easily through XHTML modules.

- *XML conformance*: As such, they are readily viewed, edited, and validated with standard XML tools.

- *DOM choice*: Applets and scripts, and other applications can apply either the HTML Document Object Model or the XML Document Object Model.

- *Interoperability*: As web markup languages evolve, documents that conform to XHTML conventions will be more likely to interoperate within different user agents of the future.

Additionally, backward- as well as forward-compatibility can be ensured with appropriate markup.

Specific Markup Languages

Beyond the general-purpose HTML and XHTML markup languages, there are more specific languages such as the ones that represent vector graphics (SVG), mathematical annotations (MathML), multimedia presentations (SMIL), or textual information synchronized with other media (TTML [53]). Such languages are used either in a specific external file or their reserved words are written directly in general-purpose markup. The following sections provide an overview of SVG and MathML.

SVG

In contrast to raster graphic formats such as GIF, PNG, or JPEG that have been handled by browsers for years, native support of vector graphics did not appear until the introduction of HTML5. Although the *Vector Markup Language* (*VML*) and the *Precision Graphics Markup Language* (*PGML*) appeared in 1998, they were soon followed by *Scalable Vector Graphics* (*SVG*) in 1999; however, implementers had to wait for a decade.

SVG is an XML-based markup for describing two-dimensional static and dynamic (animated or interactive) vector graphics [54]. The first version, SVG 1.0, became a W3C Recommendation in 2001, followed by SVG 1.1 in 2003. Beyond the full version, SVG also has a Tiny specification and a Basic specification optimized for mobile devices [55]. They are described as profiles of SVG 1.1. SVG Tiny 1.2 became a W3C Recommendation in 2008. The full version of SVG 1.2 has been stalled in the Working Draft stage and dropped in favor of SVG 2.0, which is a completely new version with advanced support for HTML5, CSS3, and Web Fonts (Chapter 9). Because of the native SVG support in (X)HTML5 along with the increasing browser support, the SVG format has gradually gained popularity.[19] Internet Explorer 9+, Firefox 3.5+, Safari 3.1+, and Opera 9.5+ have native SVG rendering and embedding support and do not require a plugin for SVG images.

■ **Caution**   The browser support for SVG in modern browsers, which do not require a plug-in for displaying SVG, is different for each embedding method (inline, via `img`, via `object`) and feature (SVG effects, SVG in SMIL animation, SVG filters, SVG in CSS background, and SVG fonts).

Most browsers that support SVG do not render SVG files unless they are served as `image/svg+xml`. The most common rendering error with embedded SVG files is that they are served with an incorrect MIME type.

SVG is suitable for logos, graphs, geographical information systems, and so on. The major benefits of the SVG format can be summarized as follows:

- *Accessibility*: Images are often magnified by mobile users as well as for the visually impaired. SVG images are scalable without distortions or quality loss. Moreover, in SVG, text is rendered as text. Textual equivalents of objects can also be developed.

- *Optimal file size*: Although it depends on image content complexity, SVG files are generally smaller in size than their bitmap equivalents.

- *Scriptability*: All features of SVG images can be manipulated through JavaScript and the DOM.

- *Animation*: SVG elements and element groups can also be animated without scripting. This can be achieved by using Synchronized Multimedia Integration Language (SMIL) together with SVG.

■ **Note**   SMIL is an XML markup language that defines markup for media synchronization, layout, animations, visual transitions, and media embedding. It supports presentations with text, images, audio, video, and links to other SMIL presentations. SMIL is a W3C Recommendation [56].

---

[19]Although it can be used in XHTML 1.x/2.0 too.

Syntax

The root element of both embedded and inline SVG images is svg. Listing 3-51 shows an example.

Listing 3-51. The svg Root Element

```
<svg xmlns="http://www.w3.org/2000/svg">
  <rect x="10" y="10" rx="0" ry="0" width="80" height="80" fill="#898989" />
</svg>
```

The namespace prefix can also be specified on the xmlns attribute. Doing so, the corresponding namespace is not the default namespace. Consequently, an explicit namespace prefix must be assigned to all elements such as in Listing 3-52.

Listing 3-52. Explicit Namespace Prefix

```
<svg:svg xmlns:svg="http://www.w3.org/2000/svg">
  <svg:rect x="10" y="10" rx="0" ry="0" width="80" height="80" fill="#898989" />
</svg:svg>
```

Both examples draw a rectangle using the rect element with a top-left positioning (x, y), dimensions (width, height), and optional horizontal and vertical corner radii (rx, ry). If length units are omitted, they are assumed to be in pixels. The default fill color for such objects is black, which can be overridden by the fill attribute.

Other geometrical shapes can be drawn in SVG similarly. Circles, for example, can be declared by a horizontal and vertical center and a radius (Listing 3-53).

Listing 3-53. A Circle in SVG

```
<circle cx="100" cy="100" r="90" stroke="#666" fill="#fff" />
```

For ellipses, a horizontal and a vertical center, as well as a horizontal and a vertical radius, are required (Listing 3-54).

Listing 3-54. An Ellipsis in SVG

```
<ellipse cx="100" cy="100" rx="120" ry="80" fill="blue" />
```

The svg element can contain any of the following elements, in any order [57]: animation elements (animate, animateColor, animateMotion, animateTransform, set), descriptive elements (desc, metadata, title), shape elements (circle, ellipse, line, path, polygon, polyline, rect), structural elements (defs, g, svg, symbol, use), gradient elements (linearGradient, radialGradient), a, altGlyphDef, clipPath, color-profile, cursor, filter, font, font-face, foreignObject, image, marker, mask, pattern, script, style, switch, text, and view.

Embedding

SVG images can be embedded in the markup by using the img or object element or by writing the SVG code directly into the markup (*inline SVG*).

The first approach applies the markup element img, which is used for other images such as JPEG or PNG (Listing 3-55).

Listing 3-55. Embedding SVG with the img Element

```
<img src="images/cover.svg" width="400" height="300" alt="Book cover" />
```

However, this embedding type has become supported in browsers with native SVG support only recently. In browsers and browser versions that do not support SVG embedding via the img element, the object element can be used (it cannot be ensured that users have an SVG plug-in installed). Listing 3-56 shows an example.

Listing 3-56. Embedding SVG Using object

```
<object type="image/svg+xml" data="images/cover.svg" width="400" height="300">
  <img src="images/cover.png" alt="Book cover" />
</object>
```

The disadvantage of the technique is that an image is provided as a general object rather than an image, which is not optimal from the semantic point of view: the meaning of an element representing an image is logically provided by the img element with more specific information about the content. The major advantage is that it displays the alternate (in this case PNG) version of the image in browsers that cannot display SVG. Moreover, object elements are included in the DOM, which allows the SVG image to be scripted.

The third option for providing SVG content is to write it directly into the XHTML or HTML5 markup. The major risk associated with the direct SVG embedding in XHTML is that XHTML documents containing inline SVG files should be valid, served as application/xml or application/xml+xhtml, and have an XHTML DOCTYPE. Otherwise, the SVG images are not displayed in the browser. Moreover, if XHTML documents are served correctly for browsers with a real XML parsing, Internet Explorer does not render the document at all (not only the SVG images).[20] This problem does not exist in HTML5, where direct SVG embedding is a native feature.

Because of these issues, providing external SVG files is generally a better solution especially if the same file (such as a logo) is used throughout the site.

There are nonstandardized approaches called *SVG Support Libraries* such as the JavaScript API "Raphaël" [58]. It supports SVG and VML in a manner that all graphical objects are also DOM objects, with the potential to attach JavaScript event handlers. Raphaël provides a cross-browser solution; however, it requires JavaScript to be enabled and applies a programmer interface via JavaScript rather than SVG markup. The advantage of Raphaël is that it provides VML for IE8 or earlier and provides SVG for all browsers with SVG support.

MathML

The *Mathematical Markup Language (MathML)* is an XML application for describing mathematical annotations on the Web. It provides content and structure, making it possible to index and process equations.

The first version of the Mathematical Markup Language, MathML 1.0, has become a W3C Recommendation in 1998 [59] and slightly modified in 1999 as MathML 1.01 [60]. After three years of development, MathML2 has obtained the Recommendation status in 2001, which has been further improved as the second edition until 2003 [61]. After recognizing the limitations of the second version, several new features have been introduced in MathML3, such as advanced line breaking and indentation, elementary math notation, alignment of Content MathML with OpenMath, support for bi-directional languages, new attributes for the math tag, semantic annotations, interaction with the host environment, linking, and new elements such as mglyph and mpadded [62].

MathML is supported by a variety of applications including web pages, e-books, screen readers, Braille displays, equation editors, ink input devices, and e-learning and computational software tools. However, the rendering engine implementation for MathML varies, and no browser provides full MathML support.

Internet Explorer has no native MathML support, and the MathPlayer plug-in has been used for versions up to IE8. Unfortunately, MathPlayer does not work under IE9. Native rendering support for MathML is available in Gecko-based browsers such as Firefox and Camino from the first versions and in Safari from version 5.1. Opera supports MathML since version 9.5. Google added MathML support to Chrome 24 which was removed from later versions.

---

[20]This problem can be eliminated by specifying the MIME type text/html for Internet Explorer and application/xml for other browsers on the server.

Syntax

MathML has presentational, content, and mixing markup elements. There are two types of flavor for MathML markup. The first one focuses on the display of equations, known as *Presentation MathML*. The second, *Content MathML*, stresses the semantic meaning of the mathematical annotation.

Similar to XHTML, there are two types of elements in MathML: the ones with the start and end tags and the empty elements that are self-closing. However, the ratio of empty elements is much higher in MathML than in XHTML. Elements can have optional attributes that consist of a name and a value (the latter one is quoted in double or single quotes). The majority of MathML attribute values must be in a predetermined format such as a positive integer or the keyword true.

In MathML there are *container elements* such as mrow (a group of subexpressions) and *token elements* such as mi (identifier; i.e., a name of a constant, a variable, or a function). The element mo represents an operator (e.g., +), a fence (e.g., {), or a separator (e.g., ,). Numeric literals are specified by mn. The proper use of mi, mo, and mn is vital to provide adequate information for rendering engines to apply the correct typographic rules. Containers can contain other elements only while token elements delimit plain-text characters, special entity references, or symbols (the smallest units with meaning). Listing 3-57 shows an example.

Listing 3-57. A Simple Example for Container and Token Elements in MathML

```
<mrow>
  <mi>a</mi>
  <mo>+</mo>
  <mi>b</mi>
</mrow>
```

Entity references begin with an ampersand (&) and end with a semicolon (;). Beyond keywords such as α, a numeric format referring to the Unicode codepoint of the symbol is also allowed. More than 1,800 symbols are supported.

The MathML namespace is http://www.w3.org/1998/Math/MathML. It can be declared in two ways: using the xmlns attribute or an attribute with an xmlns prefix. In the first case, the default namespace applies to the element on which it is provided, as well as all child elements (Listing 3-58).

Listing 3-58. A Presentation MathML Document Fragment Applying the MathML Namespace

```
<math mode="display" xmlns="http://www.w3.org/1998/Math/MathML">
  <mrow>
  <mi>x</mi>
  <mo>=</mo>
  <mfrac>
    <mrow>
      <mrow>
        <mo>-</mo>
        <mi>b</mi>
      </mrow>
      <mo>&#xB1;<!--PLUS-MINUS SIGN--></mo>
      <msqrt>
        <mrow>
          <msup>
            <mi>b</mi>
            <mn>2</mn>
          </msup>
```

```
          <mo>-</mo>
          <mrow>
            <mn>4</mn>
            <mo>&#x2062;<!--INVISIBLE TIMES--></mo>
            <mi>a</mi>
            <mo>&#x2062;<!--INVISIBLE TIMES--></mo>
            <mi>c</mi>
          </mrow>
        </mrow>
      </msqrt>
    </mrow>
    <mrow>
      <mn>2</mn>
      <mo>&#x2062;<!--INVISIBLE TIMES--></mo>
      <mi>a</mi>
    </mrow>
    </mfrac>
  </mrow>
</math>
```

This is identical to the Content notation in Listing 3-59.

Listing 3-59. The Content MathML Equivalent of Listing 3-58

```
<math>
  <apply>
    <eq/>
    <ci>x</ci>
      <apply>
        <divide/>
      <apply>
        <plus/>
        <apply>
          <minus/>
          <ci>b</ci>
        </apply>
        <apply>
          <root/>
          <apply>
            <minus/>
            <apply>
              <power/>
              <ci>b</ci>
              <cn>2</cn>
            </apply>
            <apply>
              <times/>
              <cn>4</cn>
              <ci>a</ci>
              <ci>c</ci>
            </apply>
          </apply>
        </apply>
```

```
          </apply>
        </apply>
        <apply>
          <times/>
          <cn>2</cn>
          <ci>a</ci>
        </apply>
      </apply>
    </apply>
  </apply>
</math>
```

Both should be rendered as the following well-known quadratic formula in browsers that support MathML:

$$x = \frac{-b \pm \sqrt{b^2 - 4ac}}{2a}$$

In the second case, the prefix associates other elements and attributes with a particular namespace. For example, the namespace and the prefix are declared on the body element, as shown in Listing 3-60.

Listing 3-60. Namespace and Prefix Declaration on the body

```
<body xmlns:m="http://www.w3.org/1998/Math/MathML">
```

which adds meaning to mathematical notations such as the ones in Listing 3-61.

Listing 3-61. An Example for Using the MathML Prefix

```
<m:math>
  <m:mrow>
    <m:mi>x</m:mi>
    <m:mo>+</m:mo>
    <m:mn>y</m:mn>
  </m:mrow>
</m:math>
```

Embedding

Since MathML is an XML language, it can be directly embedded into XML files, including XHTML (see the next section). Because of the lack of support for namespaces, MathML embedding was not supported by HTML versions up to 4.01. HTML5 is the first version of HTML that supports MathML.

Combinations, Profiles, and Mixed-Namespace Documents

Several newly developed web site features are very useful but not required for basic documents. These technologies are defined by various specifications that can be used as the extensions of certain versions of (X)HTML. One of them combines markup and additional semantics, while another supports mathematical markup and vector graphics within (X)HTML documents. Some of these compound documents have their own DTDs they can be validated against and namespaces[21] that provide containers for the context of identifiers, including uniquely named elements and attributes.

---

[21]By utilizing namespaces, XHTML documents can provide extensibility by including fragments from other XML-based languages such as SVG and MathML. This option was the privilege of XHTML languages, and was not supported by HTML before HTML5.

(X)HTML+RDFa

The need for publishing semantically meaningful structured data, such as metadata in RDFa, is not recent. RDFa in XHTML became a World Wide Web Consortium (W3C) Recommendation on 14 October, 2008 [63]. XHTML+RDFa (Extensible Hypertext Markup Language + Resource Description Framework in attributes) is an extended version of the XHTML markup language for supporting RDF through a collection of attributes and processing rules in the form of well-formed XML documents. This combination is one of the most advanced markup codes. XHTML+RDFa provides the option to develop Semantic Web content by embedding rich semantic markup. Version 1.1 of the language is a superset of XHTML 1.1, integrating the attributes according to RDFa Core 1.1. In other words, it is RDFa support through XHTML Modularization. The RDFa Core 1.1 specification describes how attributes can be used to express structured data in any markup language, with an emphasis on HTML (instead of XHTML), SVG, the Open Document Format, and other web-enabled document formats [64]. If the host language is XHTML, it is called XHTML+RDFa 1.1 [65].

The RDFa markup in XHTML+RDFa reuses the markup code, thus eliminating the need for unnecessary duplications. XHTML+RDFa can provide machine-readable metadata within the markup code, which makes additional user functionalities available. Most important of all, actions can be performed automatically that enable up-to-date publishing, structured searches, and sharing [66].

XHTML+RDFa has never been widely distributed, mainly because of the lack of support in authoring tools and content management systems [67] and because web designers are not familiar with RDFa. Although the specification HTML+RDFa 1.1 is primarily an extension of HTML5, it describes rules and guidelines for applying RDFa, not only in HTML5 but also in HTML 4.01 and XHTML5 [68].

Listing 3-62 presents an XHTML+RDFa skeleton document.

Listing 3-62. An XHTML+RDFa Skeleton Document with an Additional Namespace

```
<?xml version="1.0" encoding="UTF-8"?>
<!DOCTYPE html PUBLIC "-//W3C//DTD XHTML+RDFa 1.0//EN" ↵
 "http://www.w3.org/MarkUp/DTD/xhtml-rdfa-1.dtd">
<html  version="XHTML+RDFa 1.0" ↵
 xmlns="http://www.w3.org/1999/xhtml" ↵
 xmlns:foaf="http://xmlns.com/foaf/0.1/" xml:lang="en">
  <head>
    <title>An XHTML+RDF example</title>
    <meta http-equiv="Content-Type" content="application/xhtml+xml; charset=utf-8" />
  </head>
  <body>
    <p>This is a paragraph with semantic content. It was written by ↵
     <span about="#smith" typeof="foaf:person" property="foaf:name">John Smith</span>.
    </p>
  </body>
</html>
```

The RDFa notation is described in Chapter 7.

XHTML-Print

XHTML-Print is defined in the W3C Recommendation "Modularization of XHTML" [19]. This profile can be used in printing environments without installing printer-specific drivers. XHTML-Print can also be useful for mobile devices and low-cost printers that often come with a lack of large (full-page) buffers and that generally print from top-to-bottom and left-to-right with portrait orientation.

The XHTML-Print document structure is based on the XHTML 1.0 specification. However, application and usage restrictions apply for images, styles, and forms.

XHTML + MathML + SVG

One of the easiest ways to demonstrate the power of XML is to create mixed-namespace documents. General and mathematical markup as well as vector graphics can be described within the same document by the XHTML + MathML + SVG profile. This profile combines XHTML 1.1, MathML 2.0, and SVG 1.1.

The *host language* of XHTML + MathML + SVG documents can be either XHTML or SVG.

XHTML as the Host Language

Listing 3-63 shows a typical XHTML + MathML + SVG document.

Listing 3-63. An XHTML + MathML + SVG Skeleton Document in XHTML

```
<?xml version="1.0" encoding="UTF-8"?>
<!DOCTYPE html PUBLIC ↵
 "-//W3C//DTD XHTML 1.1 plus MathML 2.0 plus SVG 1.1//EN" ↵
 "http://www.w3.org/2002/04/xhtml-math-svg/xhtml-math-svg.dtd">
<html xmlns="http://www.w3.org/1999/xhtml" xml:lang="en" dir="ltr">
  <head>
    <title>Sample XHTML 1.1 plus MathML 2.0 plus SVG 1.1 document</title>
    <meta http-equiv="Content-Type" content="application/xhtml+xml; charset=utf-8" />
    <link rel="stylesheet" type="text/css" href="style/style.css"/>
  </head>
  <body>
    <h2 id="math">MathML sample</h2>
    <p>Math expression
      <math xmlns="http://www.w3.org/1998/Math/MathML">
        <mrow>
          <mi>y</mi>
          <mo>=</mo>
          <mfrac>
            <mn>1</mn>
            <msqrt>
              <mrow>
                <msup>
                  <mi>x</mi>
                  <mn>2</mn>
                </msup>
                <mo>+</mo>
                <mn>1</mn>
              </mrow>
            </msqrt>
          </mfrac>
        </mrow>
      </math>
    inside an XHTML paragraph.</p>
    <h2 id="svg">SVG sample</h2>
```

```
    <p>
      <svg:svg xmlns:svg="http://www.w3.org/2000/svg" width="5em" height="4em"
       viewBox="0 0 500 400" version="1.1">
       <svg:title>A star</svg:title>
       <svg:polygon style="fill:red; stroke:blue; stroke-width:10"
        points="210,46 227,96 281,97 238,129
        254,181 210,150 166,181 182,129
        139,97 193,97" />
      </svg:svg>
    </p>
  </body>
</html>
```

Developers have the freedom to change the parameter entities of the DTD if required. Since MathML and SVG require additional support, the validity of the previous code does not guarantee that the document will be rendered correctly by all web browsers.

SVG as the Host Language

A mixed document can be created by inserting XHTML and MathML into SVG with foreignObject (Listing 3-64).

Listing 3-64. An XHTML+MahtML+SVG Skeleton Document in SVG

```
<?xml version="1.0"?>
<!DOCTYPE svg PUBLIC
 "-//W3C//DTD XHTML 1.1 plus MathML 2.0 plus SVG 1.1//EN"
 "http://www.w3.org/2002/04/xhtml-math-svg/xhtml-math-svg.dtd"[
  <!ENTITY % SVG.prefixed "IGNORE" >
  <!ENTITY % XHTML.prefixed "INCLUDE" >
  <!ENTITY % XHTML.prefix "xhtml" >
  <!ENTITY % MATHML.prefixed "INCLUDE" >
  <!ENTITY % MATHML.prefix "math" >
]>
<svg version="1.1" xml:lang="en"
 xmlns="http://www.w3.org/2000/svg"
 xmlns:xlink="http://www.w3.org/1999/xlink">
  <desc>SVG as the host language</desc>
  <!-- ... SVG content ... -->
  <switch>
    <foreignObject width="800px" height="600px">
      <xhtml:p xmlns:xhtml="http://www.w3.org/1999/xhtml">
      <!-- ... XHTML content ... -->
        <math:math xmlns:math="http://www.w3.org/1998/Math/MathML">
        <!-- ... MathML content ... -->
        </math:math>
      <!-- ... XHTML content ... -->
      </xhtml:p>
    </foreignObject>
  </switch>
  <!--... SVG content ... -->
</svg>
```

Choosing a Markup Language

Since web designers tend to implement the latest markup language even when it is not standardized, rendering web pages written in the most up-to-date markup always involves some risks.

The Transitional variants of HTML 4.01 and XHTML 1.0 have been developed to ease the work of web developers by providing features whose replacements have already been planned (tagged as deprecated elements). Their purpose was to give developers time to change obsolete markup, not to maintain them. The Traditional variants intended to provide a way to make the transition to modern web standards. Frameset documents are contradictory with the philosophy of XHTML. Consequently, the Frameset variant of XHTML 1.0 had a purpose similar to that of the Transitional variant. Both variants have been designed with backward compatibility in mind. In other words, XHTML 1.0 Strict should have been used exclusively after its introduction wherever possible. Although many content authors have done so, error-free markup has always been very rare. But what is the point of applying a strictly regulated markup in implementations full of errors? To be fair, web designers are not the only ones to blame because they often have to deal with incorrect markup in the form of third-party and CMS-generated dynamic content based on templates that are not standard-compliant.

The potential for modularization in XHTML 1.1 has not been exploited either. XHTML 2.0 has been criticized by web developers, and the W3C was pushed to suspend the development of the specification.

Because of the new, advanced features introduced in (X)HTML5, it became the recommended markup language. However, there is no reason to change a valid XHTML 1.0 Strict markup of conventional web documents to HTML5 unless some new features introduced in HTML5 would be really beneficial for the content.

The Benefits of XHTML 1.*x* over HTML 4.*x*

In spite of the advantages of strict XML codes, it took several years for developers to realize the power of XHTML and to implement XHTML instead of HTML. Both HTML and XHTML have their advantages and disadvantages (see Table 3-18).

Table 3-18. *HTML vs. XHTML*

Benefits of HTML	Benefits of XHTML
• Backward compatibility	• Strict XML syntax, well-formed markup
• Well-known syntax	• Easier maintenance
• Error-tolerance	• Direct integration with other XML vocabularies, e.g., SVG, MathML
• "Loose" syntax that might be convenient for some developers (permissive nesting, omission of certain tags and attributes)	• XML processing
	• Forced elimination of presentational markup

It is easy to see that some HTML features that claimed to be advantageous are not necessarily real benefits because precise, strict markup should always be considered better than loose markup.

The Benefits of HTML5 over HTML 4.*x* and XHTML

The latest version of HTML overcame several limitations and inconsistencies of earlier HTML versions and XHTML. The new parsing rules of HTML5 are not based on SGML, which makes parsing more flexible and improves compatibility. The new elements provide more sophisticated document structuring (article, aside, figure, footer, section, etc.), new types of form controls, and advanced multimedia embedding (audio, video). The obsolete markup elements were dropped, including acronym, applet, basefont, big, center, dir, font, frame, frameset, isindex, noframes, strike, and tt. New attributes have been introduced, such as the id, tabindex, and hidden global attributes, and the custom data attribute `data-*`. The `charset` attribute on the `meta` element and the `async` attribute on the `script` element have been improved. Inline SVG and MathML can be embedded in `text/html` documents. HTML5 provides advanced features for web applications through its APIs, introducing a new area in web site development.

Most web designers and the W3C recommend HTML5 for most web sites and web applications.

HAML: Markup Preprocessing

Haml (**H**TML **a**bstraction **m**arkup **l**anguage) is a lightweight markup language used to describe XHTML web documents without traditional inline coding. Haml is created to overcome the limitations of traditional template engines, accelerating and simplifying template creation while making markup as neat as possible [69]. The functions of Haml can be used to replace inline page templating systems, such as ASP, RHTML, and PHP. The main principle of Haml is beautiful, *DRY* (Don't Repeat Yourself), well-indented markup with a clear HTML structure.

Alternatives to Web Markup

Although the lion's share of web documents are published in (X)HTML files, forms, brochures, flyers, posters, animations, source codes, presentations, and office documents are often provided in other formats such as in the ones indexed by Google [70]:

- Adobe Flash (`.swf`)
- Adobe Portable Document Format (`.pdf`)
- Adobe PostScript (`.ps`)
- Autodesk Design Web Format (`.dwf`)
- Basic source code (`.bas`)
- C/C++ source code (`.c`, `.cc`, `.cpp`, `.cxx`, `.h`, `.hpp`)
- Google Earth (`.kml`, `.kmz`)
- GPS eXchange Format (`.gpx`)
- Hancom Hanword (`.hwp`)
- Java source code (`.java`)
- Microsoft Excel (`.xls`, `.xlsx`)
- Microsoft PowerPoint (`.ppt`, `.pptx`)
- Microsoft Word (`.doc`, `.docx`)
- OpenOffice presentations (`.odp`)
- OpenOffice spreadsheet (`.ods`)
- OpenOffice text (`.odt`)
- Perl source code (`.pl`)
- Python source code (`.py`)
- Rich Text Format (`.rtf`, `.wri`)
- Text (`.ans`, `.asc`, `.cas`, `.txt`, `.text`)

Always use the appropriate file type for web publishing. Markup documents are preferred for general contents and should be used whenever possible. With the introduction of HTML5, the share of documents published as markup has become larger than ever before. HTML5—especially empowered by CSS3 style sheets and jQuery scripts—has all the features to create animations instead of Flash, presentations instead of PowerPoint presentations, and so forth. Still, editable documents should not be converted into markup. Downloading a Word document and modifying it to fit your needs can be very convenient. Printable documents that need to be signed only are frequently provided in PDF. Special file types are confusing and cannot be processed by user agents.[22] It is the web author's responsibility to provide documents in the right file format.

Summary

In this chapter, you learned about the versions and variants of markup languages, which is beneficial for many reasons. First, it is required to know the history of markup languages to become capable of choosing the most suitable markup for your projects. Second, the relationship between these markup languages is vital when moving from one document type to another. Third, becoming familiar with the vocabulary of HTML and XHTML languages can be useful not only for comparison but also to ensure that you use only those elements and attributes that are allowed in the chosen document type. While most modern web sites are written in HTML5, there are millions of sites written in older markup languages. More and more owners of obsolete web sites order an HTML5 upgrade or a complete site redesign based on HTML5, CSS3, and jQuery, while most new projects are based on these technologies.

Error-free markup code is among the most important features of standard-compliant web sites, but its full potential can be used only if it is served with proper settings. The next chapter will discuss the basics of server configuration, the most common content types, and the URIs used to query and link web sites.

References

1. Raggett D (2005) Getting started with HTML, revised version. World Wide Web Consortium. http://www.w3.org/MarkUp/Guide/. Accessed 18 October 2014

2. Smith M (2010) HTML: The Markup Language Reference. World Wide Web Consortium. http://dev.w3.org/html5/markup/. Accessed 21 January 2011

3. Pilgrim M (2010) HTML5: Up and Running. O'Reilly Media, Sebastopol

4. Meloni JC, Morrison M (2009) Teach Yourself HTML and CSS in 24 Hours (8th edn). Sams, Indianapolis

5. Lemay L, Colburn R (2010) Teach Yourself Web Publishing with HTML and CSS in One Hour a Day: Includes New HTML5 Coverage (6th edn). Sams, Indianapolis

6. Powell TA (2010) HTML & CSS: The Complete Reference (5th edn). McGraw-Hill Osborne

7. W3C (2010) W3C Cheat Sheet. World Wide Web Consortium. http://www.w3.org/2009/cheatsheet/. Accessed 18 October 2014

8. Quittner J (1999) Tim Berners Lee - Time 100 People of the Century. Time Magazine. http://205.188.238.181/time/time100/scientist/profile/bernerslee.html. Accessed 11 September 2010

---

[22]Unknown file types that browsers cannot recognize by extension might still be processed or rendered (such as unknown formats provided in XML serialization are probably be represented as an XML tree).

9. Lie HW, Saarela J (1998) Multi-purpose publishing using HTML, XML, and CSS. Association for Computing Machinery, Inc. http://www.w3.org/People/Janne/porject/paper.html. Accessed 18 October 2014

10. Berners-Lee T (2013) Hypertext Markup Language – 2.0, RFC 1866. Network Working Group, Internet Engineering Task Force. http://datatracker.ietf.org/doc/rfc1866/. Accessed 18 October 2014

11. Connolly D (1999) HTML 2.0 Materials. World Wide Web Consortium. http://www.w3.org/MarkUp/html-spec/. Accessed 18 October 2014

12. Raggett D (1997) HTML 3.2 Reference Specification, W3C Recommendation. World Wide Web Consortium. http://www.w3.org/TR/REC-html32. Accessed 18 October 2014

13. Raggett D, Le Hors A, Jacobs I (1998) HTML 4.0 Specification, W3C Recommendation. World Wide Web Consortium. http://www.w3.org/TR/1998/REC-html40-19980424/. Accessed 18 October 2014

14. Raggett D, Le Hors A, Jacobs I (1999) HTML 4.01 Specification, W3C Recommendation. World Wide Web Consortium. http://www.w3.org/TR/html401/. Accessed 18 October 2014

15. Masayasu I (ed) (2002) An XHTML + MathML + SVG Profile. World Wide Web Consortium. http://www.w3.org/TR/XHTMLplusMathMLplusSVG/xhtml-math-svg.html. Accessed 18 October 2014

16. Adida B, Birbeck M, McCarron S, Pemberton S (2008) RDFa in XHTML: Syntax and Processing. A collection of attributes and processing rules for extending XHTML to support RDF. W3C Recommendation. World Wide Web Consortium. http://www.w3.org/TR/2008/REC-rdfa-syntax-20081014/. Accessed 18 October 2014

17. McCarron S (2010) XHTML+RDFa 1.1. Support for RDFa via XHTML Modularization. W3C Recommendation. World Wide Web Consortium. http://www.w3.org/TR/2012/REC-xhtml-rdfa-20120607/. Accessed 18 October 2014

18. McCarron S (2010) XHTML+RDFa 1.1 – Second Edition. Support for RDFa via XHTML Modularization. W3C Recommendation. World Wide Web Consortium. http://www.w3.org/TR/xhtml-rdfa/. Accessed 18 October 2014

19. Pemberton S et al (2002) XHTML 1.0 The Extensible HyperText Markup Language (2nd edn). A Reformulation of HTML 4 in XML 1.0. W3C Recommendation. World Wide Web Consortium. http://www.w3.org/TR/xhtml1/. Accessed 18 October 2014

20. Altheim M, Boumphrey F, Dooley S, McCarron S, Schnitzenbaumer S, Wugofski T (2001) Modularization of XHTML. W3C Recommendation. World Wide Web Consortium. http://www.w3.org/TR/2001/REC-xhtml-modularization-20010410/. Accessed 18 October 2014

21. Altheim M, McCarron S (eds) (2001) The XHTML 1.1 Document Type. W3C Recommendation. World Wide Web Consortium. http://www.w3.org/TR/xhtml11/doctype.html. Accessed 18 October 2014

22. Hickson I (2010) Welcome to the WHATWG community. Maintaining and evolving HTML since 2004. Web Hypertext Application Technology Working Group. http://www.whatwg.org. Accessed 18 October 2014

23. Hickson I (2007) W3C restarts HTML effort. In: The WHATWG Blog, 7 March 2007. Web Hypertext Application Technology Working Group. http://blog.whatwg.org/w3c-restarts-html-effort. Accessed 18 October 2014

24. Hickson I (2008) Relationship to XHTML2. In: HTML 5. A vocabulary and associated APIs for HTML and XHTML, W3C Working Draft. World Wide Web Consortium. http://www.w3.org/TR/2008/WD-html5-20080122/#relationship0. Accessed 18 October 2010

25. Leenheer N (2013) The HTML5 test – How well does your browser support HTML5? Niels Leenheer. http://www.html5test.com/. Accessed 18 October 2014

26. W3C (2011) Testing – HTML Wiki. World Wide Web Consortium. http://www.w3.org/html/wiki/Testing. Accessed 18 October 2014

27. Pemberton S (2010) XML and Applications. World Wide Web Consortium. http://www.w3.org/2010/Talks/11-11-steven-applications/. Accessed 18 October 2014

28. Van Kesteren A (2010) HTML5 differences from HTML4. World Wide Web Consortium. http://www.w3.org/TR/2010/WD-html5-diff-20100624/. Accessed 18 October 2014

29. Graff E, Silli LH (2014) Polyglot Markup: A robust profile of the HTML5 vocabulary. World Wide Web Consortium. http://www.w3.org/TR/html-polyglot/. Accessed 18 October 2014

30. Berjon, R, Leithead, T, Navara, ED, O'Connor, E, Pfeiffer, S (eds) (2012) HTML5. A vocabulary and associated APIs for HTML and XHTML. W3C Candidate Recommendation. World Wide Web Consortium. http://www.w3.org/TR/2012/CR-html5-20121217/. Accessed 18 October 2014

31. Berjon, R, Leithead, T, Navara, ED, O'Connor, E, Pfeiffer, S (eds) (2012) HTML 5.1. A vocabulary and associated APIs for HTML and XHTML. World Wide Web Consortium. http://www.w3.org/TR/2012/WD-html51-20121217/. Accessed 18 October 2014

32. Bray T, Paoli J, Sperberg-McQueen CM, Maler E, Yergeau F (2013) Extensible Markup Language (XML) 1.0, Section 3.3.3 Attribute-Value Normalization. World Wide Web Consortium. http://www.w3.org/TR/REC-xml/#AVNormalize. Accessed 18 October 2014

33. Raggett D, Le Hors A, Jacobs I (eds) (1999) Basic HTML data types. In: HTML 4.01 Specification. World Wide Web Consortium. http://www.w3.org/TR/html4/types.html. Accessed 18 October 2014

34. ISO (1996) "Information Processing — Text and Office Systems — Standard Generalized Markup Language (SGML)". ISO 8879:1986/Cor 1:1996. International Organization for Standardization. http://www.iso.org/iso/iso_catalogue/catalogue_tc/catalogue_detail.htm?csnumber=28557. Accessed 18 October 2014

35. Lie H W, Çelik T, Glazman D, van Kesteren A (eds) (2012) Media Queries. W3C Recommendation. World Wide Web Consortium. http://www.w3.org/TR/css3-mediaqueries/. Accessed 18 October 2014

36. Phillips A, Davis M (eds) (2009) Tags for Identifying Languages. Internet Engineering Task Force. http://tools.ietf.org/html/bcp47. Accessed 18 October 2014

37. Raggett D (1997) HTML 3.2 Reference Specification. W3C Recommendation. World Wide Web Consortium. http://www.w3.org/TR/REC-html32. Accessed 18 October 2014

38. Raggett D, Le Hors A, Jacobs I (eds) (1999) Index of Elements. In: HTML 4.01 Specification. W3C Recommendation. World Wide Web Consortium. http://www.w3.org/TR/html401/index/elements.html. Accessed 18 October 2014

39. Hickson I, Berjon R, Faulkner S, Leithead T, Navara ED, O'Connor E, Pfeiffer S (eds) (2014) Index of elements. In: HTML5. A vocabulary and associated APIs for HTML and XHTML. World Wide Web Consortium. http://www.w3.org/TR/html5/index.html#elements-1. Accessed 18 October 2014

40. Hickson I, Berjon R, Faulkner S, Leithead T, Navara ED, O'Connor E, Pfeiffer S (eds) (2014) HTML vs XHTML. In: HTML5. A vocabulary and associated APIs for HTML and XHTML. World Wide Web Consortium. http://www.w3.org/TR/html5/introduction.html#html-vs-xhtml. Accessed 18 October 2014

41. Hickson I, Berjon R, Faulkner S, Leithead T, Navara ED, O'Connor E, Pfeiffer S (eds) (2014) HTML5 attributes. In: HTML5. A vocabulary and associated APIs for HTML and XHTML. World Wide Web Consortium. http://www.w3.org/TR/html5/index.html#attributes-1. Accessed 18 October 2014

42. McCormack C (2012) Web IDL. World Wide Web Consortium. http://www.w3.org/TR/WebIDL/. Accessed 28 October 2014

43. Steen HRM (ed) (2014) Clipboard API and events. World Wide Web Consortium. http://www.w3.org/TR/clipboard-apis/. Accessed 28 October 2014

44. Schepers D, Moon S, Brubeck M, Barstow A (eds) (2013) Touch Events. W3C Recommendation. World Wide Web Consortium. http://www.w3.org/TR/touch-events/. Accessed 28 October 2014

45. Le Hégaret P (2009) Document Object Model (DOM). World Wide Web Consortium. http://www.w3.org/DOM/. Accessed 18 October 2014

46. Le Hors A, Le Hégaret P, Wood L, Nicol G, Robie J, Champion M, Byrne S (eds) (2004) Document Object Model (DOM) Level 3 Core Specification 1.0. W3C Recommendation. World Wide Web Consortium. http://www.w3.org/TR/2004/REC-DOM-Level-3-Core-20040407/. Accessed 18 October 2014

47. Zeldman J, Marcotte E (2010) A Standard Way to Make Web Pages Behave Like Applications. In: Designing with Web standards, 3rd Ed., New Riders, Berkeley

48. Raggett D, Le Hors A, Jacobs I (1999) The global structure of an HTML document. In: HTML 4.01 Specification. W3C Recommendation. World Wide Web Consortium. http://www.w3.org/TR/REC-html40/struct/global.html. Accessed 18 October 2014

49. Hickson I (ed) (2011) Kinds of content. In: HTML5 - A vocabulary and associated APIs for HTML and XHTML. World Wide Web Consortium. http://www.w3.org/TR/html5/content-models.html#kinds-of-content. Accessed 14 August 2011

50. Dubost K, Curran P (2011) Recommended Doctype Declarations to use in your Web document. Quality Assurance Interest Group, World Wide Web Consortium. http://www.w3.org/QA/2002/04/valid-dtd-list.html. Accessed 18 October 2014

51. Axelsson J, Birbeck M, Dubinko M, Epperson B, Ishikawa M, McCarron S, Navarro A, Pemberton S (2006) The XHTML 2.0 Document Type. In: XHTML 2.0, W3C Working Draft. World Wide Web Consortium. http://www.w3.org/TR/xhtml2/xhtml2-doctype.html#s_doctype. Accessed 23 September 2010

52. Adams G (ed), Dolan M, Freed G, Hayes S, Hodge E, Kirby D, Michel T, Singer D (2013) Timed Text Markup Language (TTML) 1.0. W3C Recommendation. World Wide Web Consortium. http://www.w3.org/TR/ttaf1-dfxp/. Accessed 18 October 2014

53. W3C SVG Working Group (2014) What is SVG? Graphics Markup for the Web. World Wide Web Consortium. http://www.w3.org/Graphics/SVG/. Accessed 18 October 2014

54. Andersson O, Berjon R, Dahlström E, Emmons A, Ferraiolo J, Grasso A, Hardy V, Hayman S, Jackson D, Lilley C, McCormack C, Neumann A, Northway C, Quint A, Ramani N, Schepers D, Shellshear A (eds) et al (2008) Scalable Vector Graphics (SVG) Tiny 1.2 Specification. W3C Recommendation. World Wide Web Consortium. http://www.w3.org/TR/SVGTiny12/. Accessed 18 October 2014

55. Bulterman D, Jansen J, Cesar P, Mullender S, Hyche E, DeMeglio M, Quint J, Kawamura H, Weck D, Pañeda XG, Melendi D, Cruz-Lara S, Hanclik M, Zucker DF, Michel T (eds) (2008) Synchronized Multimedia Integration Language (SMIL 3.0). W3C Recommendation. World Wide Web Consortium. http://www.w3.org/TR/SMIL/. Accessed 18 October 2014

56. Dahlström E, Dengler P, Grasso A, Lilley C, McCormack C, Schepers D, Watt J, Ferraiolo J, Fujisawa J, Jackson D (eds) (2011) The svg element. In: Scalable Vector Graphics (SVG) 1.1 (Second Edition). W3C Recommendation. World Wide Web Consortium. http://www.w3.org/TR/SVG11/struct.html#SVGElement. Accessed 18 October 2014

57. Baranovskiy D (2012) Raphaël — JavaScript Library. Dmitry Baranovskiy. http://raphaeljs.com/. Accessed 18 October 2014

58. Ion P, Miner R (eds), Buswell S, Devitt S, Diaz A, Poppelier N, Smith B, Soiffer N, Sutor R, Watt S et al (1998) Mathematical Markup Language (MathML) 1.0 Specification. W3C Recommendation. World Wide Web Consortium. http://www.w3.org/TR/1998/REC-MathML-19980407/. Accessed 18 October 2014

59. Buswell S, Devitt S, Diaz A, Ion P, Miner R, Poppelier N, Smith B, Soiffer N, Sutor R, Watt S et al (1999) Mathematical Markup Language (MathML) 1.01 Specification. W3C Recommendation. World Wide Web Consortium. http://www.w3.org/TR/REC-MathML/. Accessed 18 October 2014

60. Ausbrooks R, Buswell S, Carlisle D, Dalmas S, Devitt S, Diaz A, Froumentin M, Hunter R, Kohlhase M, Poppelier N, Smith B, Soiffer N, Sutor R, Watt S et al (2003) Mathematical Markup Language (MathML) Version 2.0 (Second Edition). W3C Recommendation. World Wide Web Consortium. http://www.w3.org/TR/MathML2/. Accessed 18 October 2014

61. Carlisle D, Ion P, Miner R (eds), Ausbrooks R, Buswell S, Carlisle D, Chavchanidze G, Dalmas S, Devitt S, Diaz A, Dooley S, Hunter R, Kohlhase M, Lazrek A, Libbrecht P, Miller B, Rowley C, Sargent M, Smith B, Soiffer N, Sutor R, Watt S et al (2010) Mathematical Markup Language (MathML) Version 3.0 2nd Edn. W3C Recommendation. World Wide Web Consortium. http://www.w3.org/TR/MathML3/. Accessed 18 October 2014

62. Adida B, Birbeck M, McCarron S, Pemberton S (eds) (2008) RDFa in XHTML: Syntax and Processing. A collection of attributes and processing rules for extending XHTML to support RDF. W3C Recommendation. World Wide Web Consortium. http://www.w3.org/TR/2008/REC-rdfa-syntax-20081014/. Accessed 18 October 2014

63. Adida B, Birbeck M, McCarron S, Herman I (eds) (2010) RDFa Core 1.1. Syntax and processing rules for embedding RDF through attributes. World Wide Web Consortium. http://www.w3.org/TR/2010/WD-rdfa-core-20101026/. Accessed 18 October 2014

64. McCarron S (ed) (2010) XHTML+RDFa 1.1 – Support for RDFa via XHTML Modularization. World Wide Web Consortium. http://www.w3.org/TR/2010/WD-xhtml-rdfa-20100422/. Accessed 18 October 2014

65. Pollock JT (2009) Semantic Web for Dummies. Wisley Publishing, Hoboken

66. Watson M (2009) Scripting Intelligence: Web 3.0 Information, Gathering and Processing. Apress, Berkeley

67. Sporny M, McCarron S (eds), Adida B, Birbeck M, Pemberton S (authors) (2010) HTML+RDFa 1.1. Support for RDFa in HTML4 and HTML5. World Wide Web Consortium. http://www.w3.org/TR/2010/WD-rdfa-in-html-20101019/. Accessed 18 October 2014

68. Catlin H, Weizenbaum N, Clarke N, Walsh N (2014) Haml. http://haml.info/. Accessed 21 October 2014

69. Google Inc. (2014) What file types can Google index? Google Webmaster Central. http://www.google.com/support/webmasters/bin/answer.py?hl=en&answer=35287. Accessed 18 October 2014

CHAPTER 4

■■■

Serving and Configuration

The correct appearance and web documents handling cannot be guaranteed simply by applying strict, error-free markup. Web server configuration has a significant impact on web site appearance, operation, and behavior. Documents should be served with the proper media type and character encoding. Content negotiation can be used to serve various document versions to browsers supporting the corresponding media types. XHTML documents can be served as either HTML or XML, but there is a huge difference in processing. XML files are processed by XML parsers that are far more error-sensitive than SGML parsers. XHTML served as XML involves the risk that the document cannot be rendered at all. On the other hand, backward-compatible serving cannot use the benefits of strict XML markup. There are several aspects of sending HTML and XHTML from the server to the rendering engine, all of which should be considered to achieve proper settings.

In this chapter, you will learn how to configure your web site, browser, and server in order to serve web documents correctly. Becoming familiar with the most important MIME types is crucial for properly serving web documents and the files used by them, for example, style sheets, images, audio and video files, ZIP archives, and office documents. Beyond Internet media types, you will also learn domain configuration; the difference between URIs, URLs, and URNs; the application of base directories; and practices to eliminate file extensions.

The HTTP Header

The foundation of data communication on the World Wide Web is the Hypertext Transfer Protocol (HTTP). It is a networking protocol that functions as a request-response protocol in a client-server computing model. In this model, a typical client is a web browser, while an application that runs on the host of a web site is a server. During each query, the client submits an HTTP request message to the server. In return, the server sends a response message to the client that contains additional data, such as completion status information about the request, which is sent along with web documents from the server to the user agent. These header fields form the *HTTP header*. The header fields determine the parameters of the HTTP communication. HTTP requests are used to indicate which content types and character sets are acceptable (Accept, Accept-Charset), the date and time the message was sent (Date), the domain name (Host), a string representing a user agent (User-Agent), and so on.

As you can see in Listing 4-1, HTTP responses provide the name of the server (Server), an alternate location for the returned data (Content-Location), and the date and time after which the response expires (Expires). The Vary field confirms whether the cached response can be used rather than repeat the request. The Platform for Privacy Preferences Project (P3P) policy can be set by the P3P field. An identifier of a specific version of the resource is provided by ETag. These are the most common HTTP header fields, but there are many more, all of which are described by RFC 4229 [1].

Listing 4-1. HTTP Header Example

```
HTTP/1.1 200 OK
Date: Fri, 10 Sep 2010 10:05:08 GMT
Server: Apache/2.2.16 (Unix) PHP/5.3.3
Content-Location: index.html
Vary: negotiate,accept-language,accept-charset
TCN: choice
P3P: policyref=http://example.com/p3p.xml
Cache-Control: max-age=21600
Expires: Fri, 10 Sep 2010 16:05:08 GMT
Last-Modified: Fri, 21 Aug 2009 22:18:49 GMT
ETag: "3668bab8;37e77d1c"
Accept-Ranges: bytes
Content-Length: 11537
Connection: close
Content-Type: text/html; charset=UTF-8
Content-Language: en
```

Internet Media Types (MIME)

Internet media types (also known as *MIME types* or *content-types*) determine the way browsers handle web documents. They are the file format identifiers of the Web. Thus, it is crucial to set the right media type for web site components and web pages.

The Multipurpose Internet Mail Extensions (MIME) specification was introduced in 1992 by the Internet Engineering Task Force (see Chapter 1 for more information on the IETF). Most specifications are available as an IETF/ISOC Request for Comments (RFCs). Although the original MIME concept was designed to format non-ASCII messages,[1] it is used in web browsers to make it possible to render or process files other than (X)HTML. The Internet media types are standardized by IANA registration (again, see Chapter 1 for more information on the IANA) [2]. Nonstandard MIME types and subtypes can be recognized by their prefix, since they all begin with x-. Vendor-specific subtypes begin with vnd., while personal subtypes begin with prs.

Media types consist of a minimum of two parts: a type, a subtype, and optional parameters.

XML data can be assigned to two MIME media types: application/xml and text/xml. They are defined by RFC 3023 [3]. Further, MIME types can be identified by the suffix +xml. The most important media type from a web standardista's point of view is the XML media type registered for XHTML, namely, application/xhtml+xml, which is defined in RFC 3236 [4]. Although XHTML documents could be served with the application/xhtml+xml, application/xml, or text/xml media type, W3C recommends serving XHTML as XML with its dedicated MIME type application/xhtml+xml [5]. However, using this media type cannot guarantee proper XML handling without a correct XML header (see Chapter 3 for more on XML headers). Furthermore, Internet Explorer 6 and earlier IE versions do not render the contents of documents served as application/xhtml+xml; instead, users are prompted to download the file.

■ **Caution**   If the media type for an XHTML web page is set to text/html, it will be parsed as HTML. If the media type is set to application/xhtml+xml, browsers will parse the document as XML. This is a huge difference! XHTML files served with the proper MIME cannot contain a single error; otherwise, the document will not be rendered, and the XML parser will give an error, as already mentioned earlier in Chapters 1 and 3.

---

[1]The advanced version, S/MIME, supports message encryption too.

Another registered XML media type is `application/atom+xml`, which is used for the Atom Syndication Format (see Chapter 8) defined by RFC 4287 [6]. Other frequently used XML media types of this kind are `application/rss+xml` (RSS; see Chapter 8), `application/mathml+xml` (MathML; see Chapter 3), `image/svg+xml` (SVG; see Chapter 3), and `application/xslt+xml` (XSLT; see Chapter 5). The full list of MIME types is published on the IANA web site [2].

The `Content-Type` field of the HTTP header describes the data format as a MIME media type (Listing 4-2). Additionally, this entry can also provide the character encoding of the document (as discussed earlier in Chapter 2).

Listing 4-2. A Content-Type Example

```
Content-Type: application/xhtml+xml; charset=UTF-8
```

The MIME type of web pages can also be set on the document level with the `meta` element such as in Listing 4-3.

Listing 4-3. MIME Type Declaration with the `meta` Element

```
<meta http-equiv="Content-Type" content="application/xhtml+xml; charset=utf-8" />
```

Generally, the MIME type `text/html` is used for HTML documents, and the `application/xhtml+xml` is used for XHTML documents. However, XHTML documents can be served with both (as we'll see later in the chapter).

The wide variety of Internet media types is not fixed. Custom MIME types can also be registered at IANA [7].

Common Media Types

The most common media types are listed in the next sections. Note that this is not a full list by any means.

Application-Specific Media Types

Table 4-1 summarizes the most common application-specific MIME types.[2]

Table 4-1. *Common Application-Specific Media Types*

Media Type	Specification	Description
application/atom+xml	RFC 4287 [6], RFC 5023 [8]	Atom news feed
application/ecmascript	RFC 4329 [9]	ECMAScript
application/javascript	RFC 4329 [9]	JavaScript
application/json	RFC 4627 [10]	JavaScript Object Notation
application/mathml-content+xml	MathML 3.0, Appendix B [11]	Content MathML
application/mathml-presentation+xml	MathML 3.0, Appendix B [11]	Presentation MathML
application/mathml+xml	MathML 3.0, Appendix B [11]	MathML
application/octet-stream	RFC 2046 [12]	Nonspecified binary data
application/ogg	RFC 5334 [13]	Ogg multimedia container

(*continued*)

---

[2]Cannot be used in IE8 or earlier

Table 4-1. (*continued*)

Media Type	Specification	Description
application/pdf	RFC 3778 [14]	PDF document
application/postscript	RFC 2045 [15] RFC 2046 [12]	PostScript
application/rdf+xml	RFC 3870 [16]	RDF document
application/rtf	IANA registration [17]	RTF document
application/sgml	RFC 1874 [18]	SGML document
application/smil+xml	RFC 4536 [19]	SMIL document
application/soap+xml	RFC 3902 [20]	Simple Object Access Protocol
application/sparql-query	In: SPARQL Query Language for RDF [21]	SPARQL
application/sparql-results+xml	In: SPARQL Query Results XML Format [22]	SPARQL Query Results
application/xhtml+xml	RFC 3236 [4]	XHTML document
application/xml	RFC 3023 [3]	XML document
application/xml-dtd	RFC 3023 [3]	DTD file
application/xslt+xml	In: XSLT 2.0 [23]	XSL Transformations
application/zip	IANA registration [24]	ZIP archive file

Vendor-Specific Media Types

Table 4-2 summarizes the most common vendor-specific MIME types.

Table 4-2. *Common Vendor-Specific Media Types*

Media type	Specification	Description
application/vnd.google-earth.kml+xml	IANA registration [25]	Google Earth file in XML
application/vnd.google-earth.kmz	IANA registration [26]	Google Earth file
application/msword	IANA registration [27]	Microsoft Word file
application/vnd.ms-excel	IANA registration [28]	Microsoft Excel file
application/vnd.ms-powerpoint	IANA registration [29]	Microsoft PowerPoint file
application/vnd.oasis.opendocument.graphics	IANA registration [30]	OpenDocument Graphics
application/vnd.oasis.opendocument.presentation	IANA registration [31]	OpenDocument Presentation
application/vnd.oasis.opendocument.spreadsheet	IANA registration [32]	OpenDocument Spreadsheet
application/vnd.oasis.opendocument.text	IANA registration [33]	OpenDocument Text

It is highly probable that nonstandardized MIME types associated with widely used file formats will become registered in the near future. The application/x-dvi represents device-independent documents, which is not a standard. The MIME type of LaTeX files, application/x-latex, is not standardized yet either, similar to the widely adopted media type, application/x-shockwave-flash used for Adobe Flash. The application/x-rar-compressed MIME type of RAR archives are also still not standardized.

Audio Media Types

Table 4-3 summarizes the most common audio MIME types.

Table 4-3. *Common Audio Media Types*

Media Type	Specification	Description
audio/mpeg	RFC 3003 [34]	MPEG audio, for example, MP3
audio/ogg	RFC 5334 [13]	Ogg Vorbis, Flac, and other audio
audio/vorbis	RFC 5215 [35]	Vorbis Encoded Audio
audio/x-ms-wma	MS KB 288102 [36]	Windows Media Audio
audio/vnd.wave	RFC 2361 [37]	WAV audio

Image Media Types

Table 4-4 summarizes the most common image MIME types.

Table 4-4. *Common Image Media Types*

Media Type	Specification	Description
image/gif	RFC 2045 [15], RFC 2046 [12]	GIF image
image/jpeg	RFC 2045 [15], RFC 2046 [12]	JPEG image
image/png	RFC 2083 [38]; IANA registered [39]	PNG image
image/svg+xml	In: SVG Tiny 1.2 Appendix M [40]	SVG vector image
image/tiff	RFC 3302 [41]	TIFF image
image/vnd.microsoft.icon	IANA registered [42]	ICO image (icon)

Multipart Object Media Types

Table 4-5 summarizes the most common multipart object media types.

Table 4-5. *Common Multipart Object Media Types*

Media Type	Specification	Description
multipart/mixed	RFC 2045 [15], RFC 2046 [12]	MIME e-mail
multipart/alternative	RFC 2045 [15], RFC 2046 [12]	MIME e-mail
multipart/related	RFC 2387 [43]	MIME e-mail; used by MHTML (HTML mail)
multipart/form-data	RFC 2388 [44]	MIME web form
multipart/signed	RFC 1847 [45]	Digital signature
multipart/encrypted	RFC 1847 [45]	Encrypted message

Text Media Types

Table 4-6 summarizes the most common text media types.

Table 4-6. *Common Text Media Types*

Media Type	Specification	Description
text/css	RFC 2318 [46]	Cascading Style Sheets (CSS)
text/csv	RFC 4180 [47]	Comma-separated values
text/html	RFC 2854 [48]	HTML
text/javascript	RFC 4329 [9]	JavaScript; obsoleted in favor of application/javascript
text/plain	RFC 2046 [12] RFC 3676 [49]	Textual data
text/xml	RFC 3023 [3]	Extensible Markup Language

Video Media Types

Table 4-7 summarizes the most common video media types.

Table 4-7. *Common MIME Types for Video*

Media Type	Specification	Description
video/mpeg	RFC 2045 [15], RFC 2046 [12]	MPEG-1 video
video/mp4	RFC 4337 [50]	MP4 video
video/ogg	RFC 5334 [13]	Ogg Theora or other video
video/quicktime	IANA registered [51]	QuickTime video
video/x-ms-wmv	MS KB 288102 [36]	Windows Media Video

Serving XHTML

There are two approaches for serving XHTML, both of which have their advantages and disadvantages. They are described in the following sections.

Serving XHTML as HTML

In the early days of the Web, HTML was the exclusive markup language. After several years, new innovations appeared that could not have been covered by HTML. XML rules have been added to HTML, creating XHTML, a new line of markup languages. These best practices are the rules applied when converting HTML documents to XHTML, as discussed earlier in Chapter 3.

However, the vocabulary of HTML 4.01 has been more or less preserved; thus, it is similar to that of XHTML 1.0. Consequently, XHTML documents can be served as HTML to rendering engines. This approach provides backward compatibility. Media types can be used to request browsers to handle XHTML as HTML instead of XML. If the media type of an XHTML document is defined as text/html, the rendering engine will parse the web page as if it were HTML. If the media type is given as application/xhtml+xml, browsers will process the document as XML.

Several server and server-side scripting platforms (PHP, ASP, and so on) apply the text/html media type for web content by default. The "dirty secret" of XHTML is that several browsers with an XML parser treat documents served as text/html with XHTML syntax and DOCTYPE as HTML.[3] But backward compatibility comes at a price: the impressive features of XML cannot be used at all in XHTML served this way. And what is the point of applying strict rules if documents cannot use their full potential? Where backward compatibility is not a major concern, the solution is to serve XHTML as XML.

Serving XHTML as XML

While code quality strongly depends on markup structure and correctness, the reliability of rendering is also determined by the browser. The browsers' behavior of refusing to render invalid XHTML markup might seem frustrating; however, the browsers have a really good reason to do so. Browsers process those HTML documents that contain markup errors by guessing the intentions of the content author or web designer, often resulting in undesirable layout and poor styling.

There are scenarios where errors cannot be tolerated. In scientific publishing, for example, the representation of mathematical equations should be reliable. If such documents are published on the Web with MathML embedded in XHTML, errors cannot be tolerated because the consequences can cost millions or be fatal. This is the main reason for the extreme error sensitivity of XML parsers.

Being an XML language family, XHTML is meant to be served as XML to leverage all the benefits of XML. However, it also involves a serious risk. Web documents served as application/xhtml+xml request browsers to process them according to the rules of XML. Since invalid XHTML markup is not rendered at all in web browsers, extended care should be taken when serving XHTML as XML. One simple character at the wrong location in the source code results in an XML parsing error message instead of the web page content (as already hinted in Chapter 1). This is one of the reasons why HTML has always been preferred by most content authors and web designers. However, you should not be afraid of writing pure XHTML code. If you learn how to use the practices described in the previous chapter, you will be able to create not only error-free XHTML documents but also any kind of structured markup.

Although modern browsers support the application/xhtml+xml MIME type, some older browsers do not. One of the options to preserve backward compatibility with older browsers and support advanced XML applications for modern ones is the technique called *content negotiation*. It can be done through .htaccess[4] settings or using server-side scripting languages.

---

[3]Real XML parsers such as that of Firefox or Safari consider the MIME type of documents (as sent by the server) rather than file syntax and DOCTYPE only.
[4]A common configuration file on web servers such as Apache. Note that the file begins with a period and has no extension.

The HTTP specification defines the mechanism for serving different versions of the same resource [1]. Document types, document languages, and image types are some examples [52]. The preferred and acceptable document format(s)—in our case, the preference between HTML and XHTML files—can be defined in the HTTP header, as shown in Listing 4-4.

Listing 4-4. Content Negotiation in the HTTP Header

```
Accept: text/html, application/xhtml+xml, application/xml; q=0.9, */*; q=0.8
```

Using the previous example, the browser can specify that HTML and XHTML are preferred to XML. The "relative quality parameter" (q) and its value (qvalue) are considered as follows. All items without a specified preference value get the default value 1 (in this case text/html and application/xhtml+xml). The specified value for application/xml is 0.9, and all the other formats 0.8. The precedence values ordered in descending order reveal the actual precedence, in other words, 1 for text/html and application/xhtml+xml, 0.9 for application/xml, and 0.8 for any other content types.

On Apache servers, the directive shown in Listing 4-5 should be added to your .htaccess (or httpd.conf) file to set the HTTP headers required for the correct MIME type.

Listing 4-5. Preference Between text/html and application/xhtml+xml

```
Options +Multiviews
AddType application/xhtml+xml;qs=0.8
AddType text/html;qs=0.9
```

The "quality of source" parameter (qs), set to 0.8 in our example, determines whether the AddType directive applies the specified MIME type. Since the qs value for application/xhtml+xml is smaller than that of text/html, application/xhtml+xml will be used by compliant browsers only; otherwise, the preferred version will be the MIME type text/html.

Content negotiation can also be implemented in server-side scripting languages such as PHP (Listing 4-6), ASP (Listing 4-7), and C# (Listing 4-8).

Listing 4-6. Content Negotiation in PHP

```php
$accept = $_SERVER["HTTP_ACCEPT"];
$ua = $_SERVER["HTTP_USER_AGENT"];
if (isset($accept) && isset($ua)) {
  if (stristr($accept, "application/xhtml+xml") || stristr($ua, "W3C_Validator")) {
    header("Content-Type: application/xhtml+xml");
  }
}
```

Listing 4-7. Content Negotiation in ASP

```asp
Dim strAccept, strUA
strAccept = Request.ServerVariables("HTTP_ACCEPT").Item
strUA = Request.ServerVariables("HTTP_USER_AGENT").Item
If InStr(1, strAccept, "application/xhtml+xml") > 0 Or InStr(1, strUA, "W3C_Validator") > 0
  Then Response.ContentType = "application/xhtml+xml"
End If
```

Listing 4-8. Content Negotiation in C# in ASP .NET

```
string accept = Request.ServerVariables["HTTP_ACCEPT"];
string ua = Request.ServerVariables["HTTP_USER_AGENT"];
if (accept != null && ua != null) {
  if (accept.IndexOf("application/xhtml+xml") >=0 || ua.IndexOf("W3C_Validator") >= 0) {
    Response.ContentType = "application/xhtml+xml";
  }
}
```

The previous codes perform content negotiation with their own syntax. In PHP, for example, the server variables contained in the $_SERVER array are used to evaluate the HTTP Accept header of the user agent and set the appropriate MIME type via the header function (Listing 4-6).

URIs, URLs, and URNs

A *Uniform Resource Identifier* (*URI*) is a character string that identifies a name or a resource on the Internet (RFC 2396 [53]). URIs can be classified as *Uniform Resource Locators* (*URLs*; RFC 1738 [54]), *Uniform Resource Names* (*URNs*), or both. A URN defines the identity of a resource, while the URL provides a method for finding it (including protocol and path). URIs are often used incorrectly as the synonym for URL, although URI is a wider term (RFC 3305 [55]). Both the URN and the URL are subsets of URI, but they are generally disjoint sets.

The best-known examples for URLs are the web site addresses on the World Wide Web. Listing 4-9 shows the general URL syntax.

Listing 4-9. URL Syntax

```
protocol://domain:port/path?query_string#fragment_identifier
```

The *protocol* (*scheme name*) is followed by a colon. The other parts of URLs depend on the scheme being used. Usually there is a domain name or an IP address, an optional port number, and an optional path to the resource or script. Programs such as PHP or CGI scripts might have a query string. The end of the URL can be an optional fragment identifier.

Since many of these sections are optional, one or more of them are omitted. Listing 4-10 shows an example, where http is the protocol, www.masteringhtml5css3.com is the domain, and the path leads to the shop directory.

Listing 4-10. A Typical URL

```
http://www.masteringhtml5css3.com/shop/
```

URI references are widely used in markup languages, for example, as the attribute value of the href attribute on the a element in HTML or as the system identifier after the SYSTEM keyword in an XML DTD.

Persistent URIs

Everyone knows the frustrating feeling when a web site address typed into the address bar of the browser is not available, or when clicking on a hyperlink generates a File not found error.

There are many reasons why URIs can be temporarily or permanently unavailable. The simplest reason is that the requested files have been moved to another folder or they have removed from the server. Another reason is that technologies applied on the server have been changed. For example, a company used CGI scripts but recently changed to Perl, and the URIs of the files located in the cgi-bin directory have become obsolete.

There are only a few cases when it is acceptable to discontinue a web address, such as if the company or organization has been closed. Unless there is a really good reason to do so, we addresses should not be changed.

Poorly designed URIs are responsible for a large share of dead links on the Web. While challenging, URIs can be designed in a way that there will be no need to change them for the years to come.

Designing URIs

URIs can be designed to be persistent by minimizing the information provided in them [56]. The author of an updated document can be different from that of the original one, and thus the author should not be included. The subject should also be eliminated since it changes very fast. For example, a web technology blog should apply the directory name markup instead of the names of exact technologies that are currently the most up-to-date one (HTML5). Directory names that indicate the status of documents such as draft or latest should not be used in URIs simply because document status changes over time. A persistent URI is required for the latest version of each document.

Some parts of a web site might be restricted to members only. The access should also be eliminated from URIs because documents might be moved from the private section to the public one, or vice versa.

The most frequently provided needless information in URIs is the file extension. Technologies and tools that are currently considered as the most advanced will probably change in the near future, or the developer might change the applied technologies. Changed URIs can affect not only the findability of web pages or web page components but also your maintenance tasks. Carefully selected directory names are logical and seldom should be changed in the references in the markup.

■ **Tip** Use the name script or scripts for the directory where you store the script files of a web site instead of php or javascript, because if you adopt further scripting languages later, the URIs in the files of the site will reflect a specific language rather than a common name. Similarly, the directory name style or styles is more practical than css or xsl, and the name news or feed is more fortunate than rss or atom. The name images is better than jpg, and a doc or docs directory can hold a variety of documents from PDF to Word documents, not just a certain type.

Directory names that indicate software mechanisms such as cgi-bin should also be eliminated from URIs. They might change. Topic names, company sections, access levels, or security levels are also inappropriate for URIs. Classifications can also change. The creation date is constant so it can be included in web addresses, however, dates are not the best strings for SEO. Keep in mind that multiple web servers can be hidden behind an apparent server with proxying and redirection.

Beyond providing descriptive names for users and machines, URIs should be simple, stable, and manageable. Properly designed URIs are fundamental parts of the Semantic Web [57].

Domain Names

Web resources can be located by unique IP addresses. However, they are hard to remember. Consequently, *domain names* are used instead in most cases. Figure 4-1 shows the relationship between a domain name and a URL; www.example.com is a subdomain of the node example.com, which is the subdomain of the com domain (stands for commercial). The domain name syntax rules are defined by RFC 1035 [58], RFC 1123 [59], and RFC 2181 [60].

Figure 4-1. *The domain within the URL*

The tree of subdomains can contain a maximum of 127 levels. Each label may contain up to 63 characters. According to RFC 2181, the full length of a domain name is 253 characters.

Conventional domain names cannot contain Latin alphabet-based characters with diacritics, non-Latin characters, or scripts. With the introduction of Internationalized Domain Names (IDN), it is possible to represent names and words in several languages in native alphabets and scripts.

Domain names should be thought over before they are registered. They should be easy to remember and easy to spell [61]. There are also SEO considerations. While the name of a person generally remains the same over the years, a product or technology name can change. For example, the owner of a DVD store has probably changed from DVD sales to Blu-ray sales with the beginning of the HD era. However, the domain name containing the word *DVD* still represents the old technology. If the word *movie* or *films* would have been used, the domain name would not have become obsolete. Finding an appropriate domain name, which is still free and contains popular keywords, can be a real challenge, though.

No WWW

Although the www subdomain is very common on the Web, some webmasters consider it outdated or inappropriate [62]. Similar to mail servers that do not use the request@mail.example.com format, web servers can allow access to web pages though the main domain.

On Apache servers, the www. can be removed from the URIs within the domain by adding the code in Listing 4-11 to the .htaccess file. Its name stands for hypertext access. This file provides directory-level access control that can be used for authorization, authentication, redirection, blocking, customized error response, and cache control.

Listing 4-11. Removing www. from URIs with .htaccess Configuration

```
RewriteEngine On
RewriteCond %{HTTP_HOST} ^www\.example\.com$ [NC]
RewriteRule ^(.*)$ http://example.com/$1 [R=301,L]
```

This code makes it unnecessary to remove the www. from every hyperlink of the web site one by one. However, a large share of webmasters disagrees with removing the www. from URIs [63]. According to their reasoning, www. is a reminder that the World Wide Web (WWW) is just one of the many services on the Internet.

■ **Tip** The previous code is usually not needed since an unlimited number of subdomains are generally included in the domain registration price. It is a common practice that domain owners point both the main domain and the `www` subdomain to the same directory of the web server. In other words, `www.domain.com` is the preferred URI, and users retrieving `domain.com` are redirected to `www.domain.com`. Doing so, users can access the same content with and without `www`.

Base href

The previous sections discussed absolute URLs. Since many web page components are located in the subdirectories of the root directory associated with the domain, relative URLs can also be used. They are shorter, however, and not always convenient. For example, if the hierarchy is too deep and the style sheets are located in a `styles` directory three directories above a web page, the path becomes rather long (Listing 4-12).

Listing 4-12. A Long Path in a Complex Web Site

```
<link rel="stylesheet" type="text/css" href="../../../styles/main.css" />
```

While the parent directory references and the delimiters (`../../../`) can be shortened by referring to the root directory (`/`) instead, this can be omitted by declaring all locations according to the root directory (Listing 4-13).[5]

Listing 4-13. Setting a Base Directory for a Web Site

```
<base href="http://example.com/" />
```

The specified URL is used as the base for all relative URLs in the document. By adding the `base` element to the document head, the original example can be simplified (Listing 4-14).

Listing 4-14. A Short Path According to the Base Directory

```
<link rel="stylesheet" type="text/css" href="styles/main.css" />
```

Eliminating File Extensions

One of the key techniques for creating permanent URIs is to remove file extensions. On a file-based web server such as Apache, this can be done by *content negotiation* [64]. We used content negotiation earlier in the chapter to set the precedence between MIME types; now we will use it for creating a precedence order for file types. As a result, file extensions can be kept on the files but can safely be removed from links [65].

Using a type map file, Apache servers can check the directory for all files with the given name and any extension and select the appropriate one (the one with the highest precedence). A type map file takes precedence over the extension of the file (even if the special search for implicit file name pattern match, *Multiviews*, is enabled). The precedence of a higher-quality image file variant can be set by the `qs` parameter. In Listing 4-15, the file `logo.svg` will be used for all URIs that refer to the file without extension. If there is no SVG version of that file in the directory, the PNG version will be used.

---

[5]Starting the file path with a `/` is relative while defining a base directory is absolute referencing.

Listing 4-15. Precedence Order of File Types Set by the qs Parameter

```
URI: logo

URI: logo.svg
Content-type: image/svg+xml; qs=0.8

URI: logo.png
Content-type: image/jpeg; qs=0.5
```

The qs value varies from 0.000 to 1.000. Variants with a qs value of 0.000 will never be chosen. Entries of the different variants are separated by blank lines that cannot be used within entries.

Explicitly setting paths to specific file variants is not feasible for larger sites with hundreds or thousands of files. The second option for content negotiation on Apache servers is to use the MultiViews search feature, where the server performs an implicit file name pattern match within directories and chooses from the results. MultiViews is a fine option for eliminating file extensions that contributes to easy maintenance (in case new file versions will be used) and optimal markup (because of shorter links). MultiViews can be enabled in the server configuration or .htaccess file (Listing 4-16).

Listing 4-16. MultiViews Enabled

```
<Directory /home/www/example/htdocs>
Options + MultiViews
</Directory>
```

Now when the server receives a request for /images/logo and /images/logo does not exist, the server searches inside the images directory looking for all files named logo.*, assigning MIME types based on the extension of each file. The server then chooses the best match based on the preferences and delivers that resource. For example, let's assume that the images directory contains the following file variants: logo.svg, logo.png, and logo.gif. When there is a query for /images/logo, the precedence order will be considered in the answer to the query (Listing 4-17).

Listing 4-17. The Precedence Order of Image File Formats

```
Accept: image/svg+xml; q=.8, image/png; q=.5, image/gif;q=0.2, */*;q=0.1
```

When MultiViews is enabled, the server will search the referenced directory and deliver the image with the highest quality (thanks to the highest precedence), in other words, logo.svg. This is achieved in a way that URIs in HTML/XHTML files do not need to contain the file extension, which makes maintenance easier and reduces file size. URIs can now omit the technology behind the resource. Since example.com/images/logo.svg becomes example.com/images/logo, the logo embedding used throughout the site becomes <img src="logo" alt="Company logo"> instead of <img src="logo.svg" alt="Company logo">.

While a URI ending in .html or .php will probably remain the same in the near future, even widely used file types might soon become obsolete or less frequently used within a few years. Flash animations (.swf) are often replaced by HTML5 markup (.html), a PNG image (.png) by its SVG equivalent (.svg), and so on. As a consequence, all currently created internal links of the site as well as the external links on other sites will be invalid.

The World Wide Web Consortium has mastered eliminating extensions in links. Even images of the site are provided without extension in links (the files have extensions), so the links pointing to the file in thousands of web documents should not be modified if the image will be changed, as, for example, from logo.png to logo.svg.

References with extensions remain usable; however, they do not allow the server to select the best of currently available and future formats. With a *type map* declaration or with enabled *MultiViews search* [66], on the other hand, raster images used for ages can be updated to their new, SVG versions in no time. The file name without the extension is *content-type generic*, while file names with extensions are *content-type specific*.

There is a special file supported by all web servers, called index.html. When users do not specify a file in the address bar, browsers open this file by default (with content negotiation, the extension can be not only .html but also .php, .jsp, .aspx, and so on). This is the reason why web sites can be opened without typing the file name and extension to the end of the domain name such as www.example.com/index.html. This server behavior can also be used for creating permanent access to web pages within a site. Instead of adding the about.html, services.html, portfolio.html, and contact.html files to the root directory of the domain, they can be provided as index.html files within their own subdirectories. As a result, the pages of the site can be accessed as www.example.com/about/, www.example.com/services/, and so on, without file extensions. Naturally, original file names can also be kept if the default file of each directory is set on the server. However, in that case, server settings should also be migrated if the hosting provider of the web site is changed.

Namespace URIs

Namespace URIs are used to uniquely identify an XML application and separate it from other XML languages. The prefixes associated with a namespace URI are handy when you want to associate an element or an attribute with a particular XML namespace. Although a namespace URI does not necessarily point to a particular document, many do, such as the http://www.w3.org/1999/xhtml namespace used by XHTML 1.x/5 (discussed earlier in Chapter 3). The previous namespace URI will let the XML parser know that the elements and attributes used in the document are from the XHTML vocabulary.

■ **Note** Some namespace URIs point to the web page of the corresponding specification or standard, but many do not and are strings only.

Even if they are generally designed stable, namespaces might evolve over time [67]. To eliminate the problem, namespaces are often registered as *Persistent Uniform Resource Locators* at purl.org [68]. If the resource they point to changes, the URI can be modified in the profile settings on purl.org, which will provide the up-to-date URI with the persistent address.

The XML namespaces are standardized according to the corresponding W3C Recommendation [69].

Summary

In this chapter, you learned about the general structure of an HTTP header, which provides information about web documents sent by the server. You know the most common MIME types and their declaration by now, which can be used to ensure that browsers will properly handle your web site components. You also know how to use content negotiation on the server to eliminate file extensions, which makes future maintenance easier. Furthermore, you learned how to serve XHTML properly, which makes all the difference, because XHTML documents served as application/xhtml+xml will be parsed by an XML parser rather than a much less error-sensitive HTML parser. You know how to design URIs in order to maximize their persistence.

By now you are ready to create standard-compliant markup and use the proper settings for serving the files of your web sites. In the next chapter, you will learn techniques for separating web site content from its presentation by using Cascading Style Sheets (CSS).

References

1. Nottingham M, Mogul J (2005) HTTP Header Field Registrations. RFC 4229. The Internet Society. http://tools.ietf.org/html/rfc4229. Accessed 19 October 2014

2. IANA (2014) MIME Types. The Internet Assigned Numbers Authority. http://www.iana.org/assignments/media-types/. Accessed 19 October 2014

3. Murata M, Laurent S, Kohn D (2001) XML Media Types. The Internet Society. http://tools.ietf.org/html/rfc3023. Accessed 19 October 2014

4. Baker M, Stark P (2002) The 'application/xhtml+xml' Media Type. The Internet Society. http://tools.ietf.org/html/rfc3236. Accessed 19 October 2014

5. Masayasu I (2002) XHTML Media Types. World Wide Web Consortium. http://www.w3.org/TR/2002/NOTE-xhtml-media-types-20020801/. Accessed 19 October 2014

6. Nottingham M, Sayre R (eds) (2005) The Atom Syndication Format. The Internet Society. http://tools.ietf.org/html/rfc4287. Accessed 19 October 2014

7. IANA (2002) Application for Media Type. The Internet Assigned Numbers Authority. http://www.iana.org/cgi-bin/mediatypes.pl. Accessed 19 October 2014

8. Gregorio J, de Hora B (eds) (2007) The Atom Publishing Protocol. Proposed standard. The Internet Society. http://tools.ietf.org/html/rfc5023. Accessed 19 November 2014

9. Hoehrmann B (2006) Scripting Media Types. The Internet Society. http://tools.ietf.org/html/rfc4329. Accessed 19 October 2014

10. Crockford D (2006) The application/json Media Type for JavaScript Object Notation (JSON). RFC 4627. The Internet Society. http://tools.ietf.org/html/rfc4627. Accessed 19 October 2014

11. Carlisle D, Ion P, Miner R (eds) et al (2014) Selection of Media Types for MathML Instances. In: Mathematical Markup Language (MathML) Version 3.0 2nd edn. W3C Recommendation. World Wide Web Consortium. http://www.w3.org/TR/MathML3/appendixb.html. Accessed 19 October 2014

12. Freed N, Borenstein N (1996) Octet-Stream Subtype. In: Multipurpose Internet Mail Extensions (MIME) Part Two: Media Types. RFC 2046. The Internet Society. http://tools.ietf.org/html/rfc2046. Accessed 19 October 2014

13. Goncalves I, Pfeiffer S, Montgomery C (2008) Ogg Media Types. RFC 5334. The Internet Society. http://tools.ietf.org/html/rfc5334. Accessed 19 October 2014

14. Taft E, Pravetz J, Zilles S, Masinter L (2004) The application/pdf Media Type. RFC 3778. The Internet Society. http://tools.ietf.org/html/rfc3778. Accessed 19 October 2014

15. Freed N, Borenstein N (1996) Multipurpose Internet Mail Extensions (MIME) Part One: Format of Internet Message Bodies. RFC 2045. Internet Engineering Task Force. http://tools.ietf.org/html/rfc2045. Accessed 19 October 2014

16. Swartz A (2004) The application/rdf+xml Media Type Registration. RFC 3870. The Internet Society. http://www.ietf.org/rfc/rfc3870.txt. Accessed 19 October 2014

17. IANA (2007) Registration of the MIME type application/rtf. Internet Assigned Numbers Authority. http://www.iana.org/assignments/media-types/application/rtf. Accessed 19 October 2014

18. Levinson E (1995) SGML Media Types. Internet Assigned Numbers Authority. http://www.rfc-editor.org/rfc/rfc1874.txt. Accessed 19 October 2014

19. Hoschka P (2006) The application/smil and application/smil+xml Media Types. RFC 4536. The Internet Society. http://www.ietf.org/rfc/rfc4536.txt. Accessed 19 October 2014

20. Baker M, Nottingham M (2004) The "application/soap+xml" media type. RFC 3902. The Internet Society. http://tools.ietf.org/html/rfc3902. Accessed 19 October 2014

21. Prud'hommeaux E, Seaborne A (2007) Internet Media Type, File Extension and Macintosh File Type. In: SPARQL Query Language for RDF. World Wide Web Consortium. http://www.w3.org/TR/2007/CR-rdf-sparql-query-20070614/#mediaType. Accessed 19 October 2014

22. Beckett D, Broekstra J (eds) (2007) Internet Media Type, File Extension and Macintosh File Type. In: SPARQL Query Results XML Format. World Wide Web Consortium. http://www.w3.org/TR/2007/CR-rdf-sparql-XMLres-20070925/#mime. Accessed 19 October 2014

23. Kay M (ed) (2007) The XSLT Media Type. In: XSL Transformations (XSLT) Version 2.0. W3C Recommendation. World Wide Web Consortium. http://www.w3.org/TR/2007/REC-xslt20-20070123/#media-type-registration. Accessed 19 October 2014

24. Paul Lindner (ed) (1993) Registration of the new MIME Content-Type/Subtype application/zip. Internet Assigned Numbers Authority. http://www.iana.org/assignments/media-types/application/zip. Accessed 19 October 2014

25. Ashbridge M (2006) Registration of the MIME type application/vnd.google-earth.kml+xml. Internet Assigned Numbers Authority. http://www.iana.org/assignments/media-types/application/vnd.google-earth.kml+xml. Accessed 19 October 2014

26. Ashbridge M (2006) Registration of the MIME type application/vnd.google-earth.kmz. Internet Assigned Numbers Authority. http://www.iana.org/assignments/media-types/application/vnd.google-earth.kmz. Accessed 19 October 2014

27. Lindner P (1993) Registration of the Media Type application/msword. Internet Assigned Numbers Authority. http://www.iana.org/assignments/media-types/application/msword. Accessed 19 October 2014

28. Gill SS (1996) Registration of the MIME type application/vnd.ms-excel. Internet Assigned Numbers Authority. http://www.iana.org/assignments/media-types/application/vnd.ms-excel. Accessed 19 October 2014

29. Gill SS (1996) Registration of the MIME type application/vnd.ms-powerpoint. Internet Assigned Numbers Authority. http://www.iana.org/assignments/media-types/application/vnd.ms-powerpoint. Accessed 19 October 2014

30. Schubert S (2009) The application/vnd.oasis.opendocument.graphics MIME type. Internet Assigned Numbers Authority. http://www.iana.org/assignments/media-types/application/vnd.oasis.opendocument.graphics. Accessed 19 October 2014

31. Schubert S (2009) The application/vnd.oasis.opendocument.presentation MIME type. Internet Assigned Numbers Authority. http://www.iana.org/assignments/media-types/application/vnd.oasis.opendocument.presentation. Accessed 19 October 2014

32. Schubert S (2009) The application/vnd.oasis.opendocument.spreadsheet MIME type. Internet Assigned Numbers Authority. http://www.iana.org/assignments/media-types/application/vnd.oasis.opendocument.spreadsheet. Accessed 19 October 2014

33. Schubert S (2009) The application/vnd.oasis.opendocument.text MIME type. Internet Assigned Numbers Authority. http://www.iana.org/assignments/media-types/application/vnd.oasis.opendocument.text. Accessed 19 October 2014

34. Nilsson M (2000) The audio/mpeg Media Type. RFC 3003. The Internet Society. http://tools.ietf.org/html/rfc3003. Accessed 19 October 2014

35. Barbato L (2008) RTP Payload Format for Vorbis Encoded Audio. RFC 5215. The Internet Society. http://tools.ietf.org/html/rfc5215. Accessed 19 October 2014

36. Microsoft Support (2003) MIME Type Settings for Windows Media Services. KB 288102. Microsoft Corporation. http://support.microsoft.com/kb/288102. Accessed 19 October 2014

37. Fleischman E (1998) WAVE and AVI Codec Registries. RFC 2361. The Internet Society. http://tools.ietf.org/html/rfc2361. Accessed 19 October 2014

38. Boutell T et al (1997) PNG (Portable Network Graphics) Specification Version 1.0. RFC 2083. Internet Engineering Task Force. http://tools.ietf.org/html/rfc2083. Accessed 14 November 2014

39. Randers-Pehrson G (1996) Registration of the Media Type image/png. Internet Assigned Numbers Authority. http://www.iana.org/assignments/media-types/image/png. Accessed 19 October 2014

40. Andersson O et al (2008) Media Type Registration for image/svg+xml. In: Scalable Vector Graphics (SVG) Tiny 1.2 Specification. W3C Recommendation. http://www.w3.org/TR/SVGTiny12/mimereg.html. Accessed 19 October 2014

41. Parsons G, Rafferty J (2002) Tag Image File Format (TIFF) – image/tiff MIME Sub-type Registration. RFC 3302. The Internet Society. http://tools.ietf.org/html/rfc3302. Accessed 19 October 2014

42. Butcher S (ed) (2003) Vendor Tree - vnd.microsoft.icon. Internet Assigned Numbers Authority. http://www.iana.org/assignments/media-types/image/vnd.microsoft.icon. Accessed 19 October 2014

43. Levinson E (1998) The MIME Multipart/Related Content-type. RFC 2387. The Internet Society. http://tools.ietf.org/html/rfc2387. Accessed 19 October 2014

44. Masinter L (1998) Returning Values from Forms: multipart/form-data. RFC 2388. The Internet Society. http://tools.ietf.org/html/rfc2388. Accessed 19 October 2014

45. Galvin J, Murphy S, Crocker S, Freed N (1995) Security Multiparts for MIME: Multipart/Signed and Multipart/Encrypted. RFC 1847. The Internet Engineering Task Force. http://tools.ietf.org/html/rfc1847. Accessed 19 October 2014

46. Lie H, Bos B, Lilley C (1998) The text/css Media Type. RFC 2318. The Internet Society. http://tools.ietf.org/html/rfc2318. Accessed 19 October 2014

47. Shafranovich Y (2005) Common Format and MIME Type for Comma-Separated Values (CSV) Files. RFC 4180. The Internet Society. http://tools.ietf.org/html/rfc4180. Accessed 19 October 2014

48. Connolly D, Masinter L (2000) The 'text/html' Media Type. RFC 2854. The Internet Society. http://tools.ietf.org/html/rfc2854. Accessed 19 October 2014

49. Gellens R (2004) The Text/Plain Format and DelSp Parameters. The Internet Society. http://tools.ietf.org/html/rfc3676. Accessed 19 October 2014

50. Lim Y, Singer D (2006) MIME Type Registration for MPEG-4. RFC 4337. `http://tools.ietf.org/html/rfc4337`. Accessed 19 October 2014

51. Lindner P (ed) (1993). Registration of the MIME content-type/subtype video/quicktime. Internet Assigned Numbers Authority. `http://www.iana.org/assignments/media-types/video/quicktime`. Accessed 19 October 2014

52. Fielding R, Irvine UC, Gettys J, Mogul J, Frystyk H, Masinter L, Leach P, Berners-Lee T (1999) Hypertext Transfer Protocol – HTTP/1.1. World Wide Web Consortium and The Internet Society. `http://www.w3.org/Protocols/rfc2616/rfc2616-sec14.html`. Accessed 19 October 2014

53. Berners-Lee T, Fielding R, Masinter L (1998) Uniform Resource Identifiers (URI): Generic Syntax. RFC 2396. The Internet Society. `http://tools.ietf.org/html/rfc2396`. Accessed 19 October 2014

54. Berners-Lee T, Masinter L, McCahill M (eds) (1994) Uniform Resource Locators (URL). RFC 1738. The Internet Engineering Task Force. `http://tools.ietf.org/html/rfc1738`. Accessed 19 October 2014

55. Mealling M, Denenberg R (eds) (2002) Report from the Joint W3C/IETF URI Planning Interest Group: Uniform Resource Identifiers (URIs), URLs, and Uniform Resource Names (URNs): Clarifications and Recommendations. RFC 3305. The Internet Society. `http://tools.ietf.org/html/rfc3305`. Accessed 14 November 2014

56. Berners-Lee T (1998) Cool URIs don't change. World Wide Web Consortium. `http://www.w3.org/Provider/Style/URI`. Accessed 19 October 2014

57. Sauermann L, Cyganiak R (eds), Ayers D, Völkel M (2008) Cool URIs for the Semantic Web. World Wide Web Consortium. `http://www.w3.org/TR/cooluris/`. Accessed 19 October 2014

58. Mockapetris P (1987) Domain names – Implementation and specification. RFC 1035. The Internet Engineering Task Force. `http://tools.ietf.org/html/rfc1035`. Accessed 19 October 2014

59. Braden R (ed) (1989) Requirements for Internet Hosts – Application and Support. RFC 1123. The Internet Engineering Task Force. `http://tools.ietf.org/html/rfc1123`. Accessed 19 October 2014

60. Elz R, Bush R (1997) Clarifications to the DNS Specification. RFC 2181. The Internet Engineering Task Force. `http://tools.ietf.org/html/rfc2181`. Accessed 19 October 2014

61. Nielsen J (1999) URL as UI. Jakob Nielsen. `http://www.nngroup.com/articles/url-as-ui/`. Accessed 19 October 2014

62. No WWW (2012) www. is deprecated. `http://no-www.org/`. Accessed 19 October 2014

63. Hampton M (2011) www. is not deprecated. Michael Hampton. `http://www.yes-www.org`. Accessed 19 October 2014

64. Fielding R, Irvine UC, Gettys J, Mogul J, Frystyk H, Masinter L, Leach P, Berners-Lee T (1999) Content Negotiation. In: Hypertext Transfer Protocol – HTTP/1.1. The Internet Society. `http://www.w3.org/Protocols/rfc2616/rfc2616-sec12.html`. Accessed 19 October 2014

65. TASF (2013) Content Negotiation. Apache HTTP Server Version 2.0. The Apache Software Foundation. http://httpd.apache.org/docs/2.0/content-negotiation.html. Accessed 19 October 2014

66. TASF (2013) Apache Module mod_negotiation. The Apache Software Foundation. http://httpd.apache.org/docs/2.0/mod/mod_negotiation.html#typemaps. Accessed 19 October 2014

67. Berners-Lee T (ed) (2006) Namespace Changes over Time. In: URIs for W3C namespaces. World Wide Web Consortium. http://www.w3.org/2005/07/13-nsuri. Accessed 19 October 2014

68. OCLC, Zepheira (2014) Persistent Uniform Resource Locators (PURL). OCLC Online Computer Library Center Inc., Zepheira LLC. http://purl.org. Accessed 19 October 2014

69. Bray T, Hollander D, Layman A, Tobin R, Thompson HS (eds) (2009) Namespaces in XML 1.0 (Third Edition). W3C Recommendation. World Wide Web Consortium. http://www.w3.org/TR/xml-names/. Accessed 19 October 2014

CHAPTER 5

■ ■ ■

Style Sheets

A golden rule in web site standardization is to separate content from appearance. External style sheets should be preferred to inline styles except when only a small portion of a web page is styled. The syntax and naming convention of external style sheets and the style attribute values are slightly different. To achieve the highest code quality, the style sheets must be valid (error-free), and optimized in terms of scope, inheritance, and declaration order.

In this chapter, you will learn frequently used standards for styling web sites, including general CSS grammar rules and selector syntaxes that are vital for every web site. After examining the differences between properties of different CSS versions, you will gain a solid understanding of standardization issues and the challenges of providing backward-compatibility. You will also become familiar with fundamental principles in CSS ruleset optimization. Furthermore, you will analyze the methods used by rendering engines for determining the styles to apply.

Cascading Style Sheets

Cascading Style Sheets (*CSS*) is a style sheets language (style language) introduced by W3C. *Cascading* refers to the process of determining the priority of styling rules. CSS is used to define the presentational semantics of structured documents. It provides control over visual as well as aural[1] characteristics of HTML and XHTML documents and their elements. Some typical features are, for example, fonts, colors, backgrounds, margins, borders, and layers. CSS provides a powerful feature to support more than just visual media and target special browsers running on different types of devices: media types. CSS supports not only the most commonly used visual media type but also other media types that can be grouped as follows:

- *Aural*: Properties for aural browsers. Examples: `pitch`, `pitch-range`, `play-during`, `richness`, `voice-family`.

- *Interactive*: Properties for devices that allow user interaction. Examples: `nav-down`, `nav-index`, `nav-left`, `nav-right`, `nav-up`.

- *Paged and noncontinuous*: Properties for the content of documents split into one or more discrete pages, such as the pages of documents to print. Examples: `image-orientation`, `page`, `page-break-before`, `page-break-inside`, `page-policy`, `size`.

- *Speech*: Properties for styling speech. Examples: `cue`, `cue-after`, `cue-before`, `mark`, `mark-after`, `mark-before`, `pause`, `speak-header`, `speak-numeral`, `speak-punctuation`, `speech-rate`, `stress`.

---

[1]Although most styles associated with web documents are visual, CSS supports aural properties as well, including volume, speaking, pause, cue, spatial properties, and voice characteristics. They are used for aural presentation, such as when a document is converted to plain text and fed to a screen reader. Beyond improved accessibility, aural style sheets also have a potential in online education, entertainment, in-car use, and so on.

147

As you will see later in the chapter, most CSS properties are visual properties or can be applied to all media, but there are many properties designed for a specific media type.

One of the major concepts of CSS is to separate HTML/XHTML content from appearance, in other words, to distinguish style from structure. Another aim is centralization, which means providing full control over the styles of multiple documents from a single location.

Although CSS is used primarily for styling (X)HTML web documents, it can also be applied to all kinds of XML documents, for example XUL or SVG [1]. In SVG, many CSS properties are reused for styling, such as font properties, text properties, and other visual properties. SVG also uses CSS features such as the CSS syntax, selectors, external style sheets, cascading, inheritance, and at-rules, each of which will be described later in detail. Since SVG is an XML application, internal CSS style sheets can be provided as CDATA sections (Listing 5-1).

Listing 5-1. Embedded CSS in SVG

```
<?xml version="1.0" standalone="no"?>
<!DOCTYPE svg PUBLIC "-//W3C//DTD SVG August 1999//EN"
 "http://www.w3.org/Graphics/SVG/SVG-19990812.dtd">
<svg>
  <defs>
    <style>
      <![CDATA[ main { font-size: 14px; font-family: Georgia, serif; } ]]>
    </style>
  </defs>
  <text class="main">Here is my title</text>
</svg>
```

CSS can even be used for mathematical notations with or without MathML, the markup language discussed in Chapter 3, which is especially designed for publishing equations and mathematical symbols on the Web [2, 3].

Levels, Profiles, and Modules

The various versions of CSS are often referred as *CSS levels*. Each CSS level is based on the previous level and adds new properties and features. The three most significant versions are CSS1, CSS 2.1, and CSS3.

Subsets of at least one level of CSS created for a particular device are called *CSS profiles*, such as the CSS Print Profile [4], the CSS TV Profile [5], and the CSS Mobile Profile [6].

The specifications that form CSS3 are called *CSS modules*.

■ **Caution**   Profiles are not equal to media types, which were introduced in CSS2.

The three major CSS versions are described in the following sections.

CSS1

CSS Level 1, the first Cascading Style Sheet specification, was published in 1996. It is a W3C Recommendation, but its development has been closed by W3C [7]. CSS1 introduced styles for font properties, element color, alignment, tables, margin, border, padding, and positioning. CSS1 properties can be applied to uniquely identified elements or element groups.

CSS2 and CSS 2.1

CSS Level 2 was developed as a superset of CSS1 and has been extended with several new features. The most important ones are layer order (z-index), three types of element positioning (absolute, relative, and fixed), the aural media type, and bidirectional text.

CSS Level 2 Revision 1, often abbreviated as CSS 2.1 [8], has been the ultimate styling solution on the Web for many years. CSS 2.1 became a W3C Recommendation in 2011.

CSS3

The development of CSS Level 3 (CSS3) started in 2005. In contrast to further CSS specifications, CSS3 is modularized [9]. The CSS3 modules are described in separate specifications such as Selectors, Media Queries, Text, Backgrounds and Borders, Colors, 2D Transformations, 3D Transformations, Transitions, Animations, and Multi-Columns. The modules are in different stages of development and browser implementation. Until recently, only a few modules had been standardized, such as the Color module [10], the Namespaces module [11], the Selectors module [12], and the Media Queries module [13].

A variety of new functions and features have been introduced in CSS3 such as border-radius, box-shadow, background-origin; color declaration in HSL, HSLA, and RGBA; text-shadow; text-overflow; word-wrap; box-sizing; attribute selectors; transitions; multiple backgrounds; multicolumn layout; Web Fonts; and speech.

Grammar and Conventions

Parsing errors caused by nonexisting properties, incorrect values, malformed declarations, and so on, can be eliminated by following the proper *CSS syntax*. The grammar ensures syntactically correct CSS, which makes it possible for browsers to handle parsing rules, selector, property, value, and unit notations correctly. Although the fundamental rules are similar, each CSS version has its own syntax [14]. Being a superset of CSS 2.1, CSS3 introduced additional semantic constraints.

Identifiers and Classes

The ID and class identifiers should always start with a letter. These identifiers correspond to the id and class markup attributes. Since an element with an id attribute is unique within a web page, ID identifiers can be used to style a unique element of a page. If the same styles are applied to multiple elements, class identifiers should be used. Identifier names are case sensitive. Using the letters a-z and the numbers 0-9 is highly recommended, although underscores and hyphens are also allowed. Names should be meaningful and semantic. Unique names should be applied.

Units

CSS3 supports both absolute measurement values (Table 5-1) and relative length units, including font-relative and viewport-relative units.

Table 5-1. *Absolute CSS Units*

Unit	Description
in	Inch.
cm	Centimeter.
mm	Millimeter.
pt	1 point is equal to 1/72 inch.
pc	1 pica is equal to 12 points.
px	1 pixel is a dot on the screen.

Font-relative lengths can be expressed in em, ex, and in CSS3 also in ch or rem (Table 5-2).

Table 5-2. *Font-Relative CSS Units*

Unit	Description
em	1 em is equal to the current font size, which can be used to automatically adapt the font size proportions to the font size chosen by the user in the browser. The em unit defines the proportion of the width and height of a given letter with respect to the point size of a given font. This unit originates in typography.
ex	1 ex is the x-height of a font (approximately half the font size).
ch	The used advance measure of the 0 glyph (ZERO, U+0030) of the font used to render the text.
rem	The computed value of font-size on the root element.

In CSS3, lengths can also be expressed relative to the viewport size (Table 5-3), which is very useful in mobile-friendly website design.

Table 5-3. *Viewport-Relative CSS3 Units*

Unit	Description
vw	1% of the width of the initial containing block.
vh	1% of the height of the initial containing block.
vmin	The smallest vw and vh.
vmax	The largest vw or vh.

■ **Note**   In spite of this variety, only three of these units are used most of the time: %, em, and px.

Color Declarations

There are several notations in CSS for declaring colors. A brief overview is provided in the following sections, which is important because color declaration examples will be used intensively in the demonstrational rulesets throughout the chapter.

Hexadecimal Notation

Hexadecimal notation is by far the most commonly used notation for declaring colors in CSS. In the RGB color space used on the Web, any color can be represented by additive color mixing, using the different intensity variants of three colors: Red, Green, and Blue (RGB). Two hundred and fifty-six shades of the three base colors are sufficient to mix any color, because any two adjacent shades of red, green, or blue with an intensity difference of 1/256 cannot be distinguished by the human eye. Since there are 256 shades for each channel, the values vary from 0 to 255 (00 to ff in hexadecimal notation) per channel; 0 is the darkest shade of the channel, and 255 is the lightest.

The hexadecimal numeral system applies the positional (also known as *place-value*) notation. In contrast to the 10 digits of the decimal numeral system, in the hexadecimal system there are 16 symbols from 0 to 9 and a to f (the letters represent the values from 10 to 15). The latest symbol corresponds to the value multiplied by the 0th power[2] of 16, the symbol preceding the last symbol represents the value multiplied by the 1st power of 16, and so forth.

Consequently, the symbols 0–9 in hexadecimal notation correspond to the identical numbers in decimal notation, while a in hex is equal to 10 in the decimal system, b to 11, c to 12, d to 13, e to 14, and f to 15. Further numbers can be computed by the place-value (starting from 0). For example, the hexadecimal value e8 corresponds to the decimal value 232, because $14 \cdot 16^1 + 8 \cdot 16^0 = 14 \cdot 16 + 8 \cdot 1 = 224 + 8 = 232$. Conversion from decimal to hexadecimal can be performed similarly, but with the reverse computation. For example, 86 in decimal notation is 56 in hexadecimal notation, because $86/16 = 5.375$, so the first digit is 5. $5 \cdot 16 = 80$, and the remainder is 6, which is the second digit, because $5 \cdot 16^1 + 6 \cdot 16^0 = 5 \cdot 16 + 6 \cdot 1 = 80 + 6 = 86$.

In CSS, hexadecimal color declarations begin with a number sign (#), followed by six hexadecimal (hex) values, two for each channel (this can be abbreviated to three digits if the groups of digits are identical). They are used to mix colors arbitrarily. For example, pure red can be set by #ff0000. In other words, the intensity of the red channel is maximal (ff), while the intensity of green and blue are minimal (00). Similarly, pure green is #00ff00, while pure blue is #0000ff. If the values of each channel are set to 00, the result is black (#000000). If all values are maximal, you get white (#ffffff). If the values for each channel are identical, the result is a shade of gray (Listing 5-2).

Listing 5-2. A Gray Font Color Declared for All Paragraphs

```
p {
  color: #898989;
}
```

■ **Tip** If the two digits of each channel are identical, they can be abbreviated by omitting the second digit. For example, #f00 represents red, #0f0 represents green, #00f represents blue, #000 represents black, #fff represents white, and so on.

---

[2] Any nonzero number raised to the power 0 is 1.

The RGB and RGB(a) Notations

The saturation of each color channel in the RGB model can also be declared by either decimal numbers or percentages (Listing 5-3).

Listing 5-3. Simple RGB Notation

```
p {
  color: rgb(0, 255, 0) /* equivalent to rgb(0, 100%, 0), #00ff00 and #0f0 */
}
```

The previous notation is supported by CSS 2.1 but has been extended in CSS3 with the transparency (alpha channel) of the color. This notation is known as RGB(a). For example, the pure green with 75 percent transparency (which corresponds to 25 percent opacity) can be declared as shown in Listing 5-4. Note that the alpha is always a percentage (a value from 0 to 1) rather than running from 0–255 as the colors do.

Listing 5-4. An RGB(a) Notation in CSS3

```
p {
  color: rgb(0, 255, 0, 0.25);
}
```

The HSL(a) Notation

In CSS, colors can also be denoted by the HSL(a) notation, where the colors are represented by their hue, saturation, and lightness. The first value can be a number from 0 to 360, while the second and third values can be declared as a percentage. The alpha channel works the same way as in RGB(a) (Listing 5-5).

Listing 5-5. A Transparent Color in HSL(a) Notation

```
#warning {
  background-color: hsl(240, 78%, 50%, 0.25);
}
```

■ **Tip** If you want to use a color seen on a photograph or on a web site, you can obtain the code in many ways. First, you can check the style sheet of the page or site for the color code. If this is not convenient, there are other techniques to get the color code. If there are no advanced image-processing applications installed on your computer, you should simply create a screenshot using the Print Screen button and copy and paste it to a basic image manipulation application, such as Microsoft Paint. Select the Color Picker tool, and click the color of your choice. Choose the Edit Colors option from the Color menu, and click Define custom colors.[3] You get the hue, lightness, and saturation of the color, along with the red, green, and blue components. Since they are provided in decimal, they need to be converted into hexadecimal with an application such as the Windows Calculator (in Scientific Mode). If you have a more advanced image manipulator than Paint, such as Adobe Photoshop, you can use the Color Picker tool on the pasted image to get the color code in different color spaces and notations, including decimal and hexadecimal.

---

[3]The version of Paint in Windows 7 has a ribbon interface instead of the conventional menu found in earlier versions.

Web-Safe Colors

In the early days of color computer screens, only 256 different colors were supported. In that era, a list of 216 colors was referred to as *web-safe colors*. This cross-browser color palette was used to ensure that all computers, including the ones using a 256-color palette, would display the colors correctly. Web-safe colors consist of 00, 33, 66, cc, and ff values for each channel (for example, 00ff00, 663300, 993300, cc6600, and ff9966).

■ **Note**   Web-safe colors are not interesting from the presentational point of view anymore, since all modern screens, monitors, and projectors are capable of representing any colors from the RGB color space.

Color Names

CSS supports the names of 16 basic colors. These keywords are easier to read than their corresponding hexadecimal values[4] (Table 5-4). Using hexadecimal notation, however, is strictly recommended (see Chapter 13).

Table 5-4. *CSS Color Names Handled by All Browsers*

Color	Hexadecimal Equivalent
aqua (= cyan)	#00ffff (can be abbreviated as #0ff)
black	#000000 (can be abbreviated as #000)
blue	#0000ff (can be abbreviated as #00f)
magenta (= fuchsia)	#ff00ff (can be abbreviated as #f0f)
gray	#808080
green	#008000
lime	#00ff00 (can be abbreviated as #0f0)
maroon	#800000
navy	#000080
olive	#808000
purple	#800080
red	#ff0000 (can be abbreviated as #f00)
silver	#c0c0c0
teal	#008080
white	#ffffff (can be abbreviated as #fff)
yellow	#ffff00 (can be abbreviated as #ff0)

---

[4]After learning color mixing with hexadecimal notation, using these values becomes a routine task.

Selector Syntaxes

A *CSS selector* identifies those markup elements to which the CSS style(s) will be applied. Specific element groups are styled by various types of selectors. The general structure of a *CSS rule* (or *CSS ruleset* for multiple declarations), as shown in Figure 5-1, can be written with the pseudocode shown in Listing 5-6.

Figure 5-1. *CSS rule structure*

Listing 5-6. Pseudocode of CSS Rulesets

```
selector [, selector2, ..., selectorn] [:pseudo-class] {
  property: value;
  [property2: value2;
  ...
  propertym: valuem;]
}
```

Multiple declarations of the same selector can be organized into groups separated by semicolons (;).

■ **Tip** Although it is legal to omit the semicolon after the last declaration in a ruleset, it is strongly recommended to always provide it. It makes maintenance and modifications easier and becomes handy when a declaration is moved to another location in the CSS.

For example, the rules in Listing 5-7 can be written as shown in Listing 5-8.

Listing 5-7. It Is Not Optimal to Declare Rules of the Same Element Separately

```
h1 { font-weight: bold }
h1 { font-size: 1.6em }
h1 { font-family: Verdana, sans-serif }
```

Listing 5-8. Rules of the Same Element Should Be Grouped

```
h1 {
  font-weight: bold;
  font-size: 1.6em;
  font-family: Verdana, sans-serif;
}
```

Although they are equivalent, the second version should be preferred for many reasons. First, it is shorter and thus contributes to code length optimality. Second, further declarations of other selectors might accidentally be inserted between the single lines, making the CSS file much harder to maintain. Finally, the second arrangement is easier to read, which makes development easier.

Element Selectors

If all paragraphs of a web site are intended to be written in Garamond with 1.2em font size, the ruleset looks like Listing 5-9.

Listing 5-9. A Ruleset for All Paragraphs

```
p {
  font-size: 1.2em;
  font-family: Garamond, serif;
}
```

This applies to all paragraphs in the markup such as the ones in Listing 5-10.

Listing 5-10. Paragraphs to Be Styled by the Ruleset of Listing 5-9

```
<p>
 A paragraph.
</p>
<p>
 Another paragraph.
</p>
```

Naturally, a subset of paragraphs might have a different ruleset that partially or fully overrides the general rules (see the "Cascading" section later in the chapter).

In the previous example, the selector selects a markup element. Such selectors are called *element selectors* and apply the corresponding element names themselves. The curly braces contain the properties of the element to style, along with the values to which they should be changed. The curly braces and the content between them is the *declaration block*. The property-value pairs are separated from each other by semicolons. The properties are separated from their values by colons. Each line is called a *declaration* or *statement*.

The selectors are separated by *combinators*, that is, whitespace, **>** or **+**. Further whitespace characters might be present between the combinators and the simple selectors around them [15].

Selectors can also be grouped if the same CSS rules apply to them. The comma (**,**) should be used as the combinator. Grouping common rules contributes to CSS code optimality. For example, Listing 5-11 changes the color and font size of both div elements with the id attribute articles and relatedlinks, respectively.

Listing 5-11. Common Rules Can Be Grouped to Avoid Duplication

```
#articles, #relatedlinks {
  color: white;
  font-size: 1.8em;
}
```

Class Selectors

Class selectors, which begin with a period (.), select all elements with a class attribute identical to the value specified in them. Since the class attribute can be applied multiple times in a web page, class selectors can style any element within the document with the same class identifier. For example, the rule in Listing 5-12 is referred in the markup, as shown in Listing 5-13 and Listing 5-14.

Listing 5-12. Class Selector Example

```
.abstract {
  font-size: 1.1em;
}
```

Listing 5-13. The Class Selector in Listing 5-12 Can Be Applied to Headings

```
<h3 class="abstract">Abstract</h3>
```

Listing 5-14. The Same Class Selector Can Also Be Applied to Paragraphs

```
<p class="abstract">
The abstract of the first Chapter
</p>
```

If the ruleset should be applied for certain types of elements with the specified class name, a more specific rule can be written by providing the element name before the period. For example, if the previous rule should be valid exclusively for paragraphs, it should be extended by declaring the desired element type (Listing 5-15).

Listing 5-15. A Rule for All Paragraphs with the Class Name abstract

```
p.abstract {
  font-size: 1.1em;
}
```

ID Selectors

Certain markup elements are intended to be unique throughout a web document; that is, they can occur only once per web page. They are identified by the identifier attribute id. Those selectors that select the unique element on the web page with the id attribute equal to the value specified in them are called *ID selectors* and begin with a hash mark (#). Listing 5-16 shows an example.

Listing 5-16. An ID Selector Example

```
#main {
  margin-left: 120px;
}
```

Listing 5-17 shows a markup example where the previous rule is applied.

Listing 5-17. Example Content for Which the ID Selector #main Can Be Applied

```
<div id="main">
The main content has a left margin of 120 pixels.
</div>
```

Universal Selectors

A *universal selector* matches the name of any element type on a web page (any elements regardless of the type). The universal selector is referred to with an asterisk (*). Listing 5-18 shows an example.

Listing 5-18. A Universal Selector Example

```
*.caution {
  color: #ff2318;
}
```

The asterisk can be omitted if the universal selector is not the only component of a simple selector (Listing 5-19).

Listing 5-19. A Rule from Which the Asterisk Can Be Safely Omitted

```
.caution {
  color: #ff2318;
}
```

Considering the markup shown in Listing 5-20, the selector `div * em` will match most em elements and apply to the content of the em element in h1 (favorite), p (impressive), the first li element (hybrid electric), and the second li (fuel efficient). In the last two cases, the * matches the ul or the li.

Listing 5-20. A Demonstration Markup for the Universal Selector

```
<body>
  <div>
    <h1>My <em>favorite</em> car</h1>
    <p>The Lexus CT 200h is <em>impressive</em> due to the following reasons:</p>
    <ul>
      <li>It is a <em>hybrid electric</em> car.</li>
      <li>It is a <em>fuel efficient</em> car.</li>
    </ul>
    That's why it is a nice <em>entry-level luxury</em> hatchback.
  </div>
</body>
```

Since the em element with the content entry-level luxury is an immediate child of the div element, there is nothing for the * to match between div and em.

■ **Caution** The implementation of universal selectors is imperfect in Internet Explorer 7 and earlier.

Attribute Selectors

Attribute selectors select every element with the attribute specified within square brackets. An attribute type or an attribute with a specific value can be styled with them. For example, all img elements with the title attribute within the document can have a yellow border by applying the rule shown in Listing 5-21.

Listing 5-21. An Attribute Selector Example with an Attribute

```
img[title] {
  border-color: #ff0;
}
```

Attribute selectors can be used not only for attributes but also for attribute-attribute value pairs. For example, a 10-pixel border can be added to all `logo.png` images within the web page with the CSS rule shown in Listing 5-22.

Listing 5-22. An Attribute Selector with an Attribute and an Attribute Value

```
img[src="logo.png"] {
  border: 10px;
}
```

This applies to multiple instances of the markup in Listing 5-23 throughout the web page.

Listing 5-23. A Markup Code Where Listing 5-22 Is Applied

```
<img src="logo.png" alt="logo" />
```

Child Selectors

Child selectors select the right-hand element in the selector if and only if it is a direct child of the left-hand element. The greater-than sign (>) is used between the child and the ancestor. Listing 5-24 shows an example.

Listing 5-24. Child Selector Example

```
td > a {
  font-weight: bold;
}
```

This is applied to all hyperlinks within table data cells, such as in Listing 5-25, but does not affect hyperlinks in general such as in Listing 5-26.

Listing 5-25. A Hyperlink Example for the Child Selector in Listing 5-24

```
<td><a href="http://www.privatecloud.services">Private Cloud Services</a></td>
```

Listing 5-26. The Child Selector Example Is Not Applied to Anchors That Are Not Children of a Data Cell

```
<a href="http://www.domainregistrationwebhosting.com.au">Domain registration</a>
```

■ **Caution** Child selectors are not supported in Internet Explorer 6 and earlier.

Descendant Selectors

Styles of elements that are lower on the DOM tree can be provided by *descendant selectors* that use the element names separated by spaces. In contrast to child selectors, descendant selectors do not require the child element to be a direct child of the ancestor. Listing 5-27 shows an example.

Listing 5-27. Descendant Selector Example

```
td a {
  font-weight: bold;
}
```

This is applied to all hyperlinks within table data cells, for example to Listing 5-25 (similar to the child selector shown previously) or Listing 5-28. This rule does not affect hyperlinks in general, however.

Listing 5-28. An Anchor Example Where Listing 5-27 Is Applied

```
<td><p>The textbook <a href="http://www.masteringhtml5css3.com">Web Standards</a> is a comprehensive
guide to current and future standards for the World Wide Web.</p></td>
```

Note the difference between the child selector and the descendant selector.

Adjacent Sibling Selectors

Adjacent sibling selectors select the element on the right-hand side of the selector if and only if it has an instance of the element on the left-hand side next to it. The **+** sign is applied as the combinator. Sibling elements are on the same level within the DOM hierarchy. Listing 5-29 shows an example.

Listing 5-29. Adjacent Sibling Selector Example

```
h2 + p {
  color: #0f0;
}
```

This selector applies to Listing 5-30, but neither to Listing 5-31 nor Listing 5-32.

Listing 5-30. Elements That Apply the Green Color from Listing 5-29

```
Heading</h2>
<p>A paragraph</p>
```

Listing 5-31. A Paragraph That Does Not Apply the Rule Shown in Listing 5-29

```
<p>A paragraph</p>
```

Listing 5-32. Because of the Missing Level 2 Heading Preceding the Paragraph, the Style Is Not Applied Here Either

```
Heading</h1>
<p>A paragraph</p>
```

■ **Caution**   Adjacent sibling selectors are not supported in IE6 or earlier.

Pseudoclasses

Pseudoclasses, which use colons to separate an element from its state, are more sophisticated selectors. They are frequently used to determine the style of hyperlinks, depending on their states. For example, Listing 5-33 applies to all a elements but only when the mouse hovers over the link.

Listing 5-33. Link Color to Be Applied in Case an Anchor Is Being Hovered Over

```
a:hover {
  color: #000080;
}
```

Another example is Listing 5-34, which changes the color of all hyperlinks that have already been visited[5] to green.

Listing 5-34. Link Color Set to Visited Hyperlinks

```
a:visited {
  color: #0f0;
}
```

Pseudoelements

Pseudoelements can be used to add style to specific element parts instead of whole elements. They can also be applied for inserting content before or after certain elements. The combinator is a colon (:). For example, the CSS rule in Listing 5-35 changes the font size of the first letter of all paragraphs within the web page to 2 em.

Listing 5-35. A Rule for the First Letter of Paragraphs

```
p:first-letter {
  font-size: 2em;
}
```

Property Value Types

CSS property values can be the following:

- Keywords (for example, auto)

- Basic data types (for example, %)

- Combination of keyword and custom data (for example, url ('http://www.masteringhtml5css3.com/img/webstandardsbook.jpg')

Shorthand Notation

Certain CSS properties can be grouped into a single property declaration. The most common shorthand notations are described in the following sections.

---

[5]According to the current browser history.

Shorthand Notation for Font Properties

Font properties can be written either in the full form shown in Listing 5-36 or with the shorthand notation of Listing 5-37.

Listing 5-36. If Several Font Properties Should Be Set for the Same Element, the Ruleset Becomes Too Long

```
p {
  font-weight: bold;
  font-size: 1em;
  line-height: 1.2em;
  font-family: Garamond;
  font-style: normal;
}
```

Listing 5-37. Shorthand Notation for Font Properties

```
p { font: bold 1em/1.2em Garamond }
```

■ **Note** In the second case, the font-style property is not set and thus takes the value defined as the *default value* for that property in the CSS specification, which is normal.

Shorthand Notation for Background Properties

Separate background properties (Listing 5-38) have the shorthand property background (Listing 5-39).

Listing 5-38. Separate Background Properties That Can Be Shortened

```
body {
  background-color: #232323;
  background-image: url('images/bg.jpg');
  background-repeat: no-repeat;
  background-position: 100% 0%;
  background-attachment: fixed;
}
```

Listing 5-39. Background Properties Combined into a Single Background Property

```
body {
  background: #232323 url('images/bg.jpg') no-repeat 100% 0% fixed;
}
```

Shorthand Notation for List Properties

List styles, such as the ones in Listing 5-40, can also be shortened by the enumeration of the individual property values for the list-style shorthand property (Listing 5-41).

Listing 5-40. List Styles That Can Be Shortened

```
ul.tick {
  list-style-image: url('tick.png');
  list-style-type: none;
  list-style-position: inside;
}
```

Listing 5-41. A One-Line Rule for Three List Styling Property Values

```
ul.tick {
  list-style: url('tick.png') none inside;
}
```

Shorthand Notation for Padding, Border, and Margin Properties

There are five properties for setting the top, right, bottom, and left padding (padding-top, padding-right, padding-bottom, padding-left, respectively) or all of them together with the shorthand property padding. Similar conventions exist for borders (border-top, border-right, border-bottom, border-left, border) and margins (margin-top, margin-right, margin-bottom, margin-left, margin). There are various options for shortening the enumeration of property values in a certain order:

- Four values set the padding of each side: the top, the right, the bottom, and finally the left padding (clockwise, starting from top) (Listing 5-42).

    Listing 5-42. Padding Shorthand Property with Four Values

    ```
    #decor {
      padding: 10px 5px 20px 30px;
    }
    ```

■ **Tip**   This order is worth memorizing, because it can be used not only for padding but also for borders, margins, and CSS3 properties such as border-radius.

- Three values set the top, right, and left (equally), and the bottom padding (Listing 5-43).

    Listing 5-43. Padding Shorthand Property with Three Values

    ```
    #decor {
      padding: 10px 20px 15px;
    }
    ```

- Two values set an equal padding for the top and bottom sides, and then an equal padding for the right and left sides (Listing 5-44).

    Listing 5-44. Padding Shorthand Property with Two Values

    ```
    #decor {
      padding: 30px 20px;
    }
    ```

- One value sets an equal padding for all sides (Listing 5-45).

Listing 5-45. Padding Shorthand Property with One Value

```
#decor {
    padding: 10px;
}
```

Similar shorthand notations can be used for setting border and margin property values with the `border` and `margin` shorthand properties. Further padding, border, and margin properties can also be written in shorthand notation. Listing 5-46 shows an example.

Listing 5-46. Border Properties That Can Be Shortened

```
.book {
    border-width: 1px;
    border-style: solid;
    border-top-color: #000;
    border-right-color: #000;
    border-bottom-color: #000;
    border-left-color: #000;
}
```

Since the border color of each side is the same in this example, the properties in the third, fourth, fifth, and sixth lines can be written as `border-color` (Listing 5-47).

Listing 5-47. The `border-color` Shorthand Property Sets the Border Color of Each Side of the Element

```
.book {
    border-width: 1px;
    border-style: solid;
    border-color: #000;
}
```

Even if the border colors are different, they can be declared by the `border-color` shorthand property by simply enumerating the desired colors in the top, right, bottom, left order (clockwise, starting from top).

All the previous properties can be shortened further to a single line, as shown in Listing 5-48.

Listing 5-48. The Shortest Border Declaration for Multiple Properties

```
.book {
    border: 1px solid #000;
}
```

Implementation

There are three ways to implement CSS. The chosen method determines the scope of styling.

- *Inline style*: Styling with the most limited scope. An inline style is embedded in an (X)HTML tag to which it exclusively applies. This CSS fragment is defined by the `style` attribute that can be provided on most markup elements. The attribute value has the same syntax as the contents of a CSS declaration block except that the delimiting braces are omitted [16]. Listing 5-49 shows an example.

Listing 5-49. Inline Style Declaration Example

```
<img src="logo.png" style="margin: 10px;" alt="logo" />
```

- *Embedded (internal) style*: A code block usually located in the document head. Embedded styles are used for styling rules unique to that web page (the element to style does not occur in other pages on the site). Listing 5-50 shows an example.

Listing 5-50. An Example for Embedded Styles

```
<head>
  ...
  <style type="text/css">
    #disclaimer {
      text-align: center;
      margin-top: 30px;
      margin-bottom: 60px;
    }
  </style>
  ...
<head>
```

- *External style sheet*: An external style sheet is a separate file with the `.css` extension that contains style rules for multiple web documents, such as an entire web site. This is a plain-text file usually encoded in US-ASCII. CSS files cannot contain the `style` element, just the CSS style rules themselves. Each page refers to that file with the `link` element in the (X)HTML head section. Listing 5-51 shows an example.

Listing 5-51. Link to an External Style Sheet File in XHTML

```
<link rel="stylesheet" type="text/css" href="main.css" />
```

In XML documents (XML, XUL, SVG, and so on), external style sheets can be provided by the *XML processing instruction* `xml-stylesheet` in the first document section [17] (Listing 5-52).

Listing 5-52. Link to an External Style Sheet File in XML

```
<?xml-stylesheet type="text/css" href="default.css" title="Default style" ?>
```

Embedded styles override the corresponding styles declared in an external CSS file, which makes it possible to use the main styling rules of the web site while declaring some specific ones for a single web page. Inline styles are even more specific and locally override the styles of the external style sheet as well as the embedded styles (if any).

Style sheets can also import CSS rules from other style sheet files with the `@import` rule. It should be provided after the `@charset` rules (if any) but before all other rules. If the additional CSS files are in the same directory structure, the path is adequate (Listing 5-53).

Listing 5-53. Reusing an External Style Sheet

```
@import "styles/alter.css";
```

The rulesets of the file containing this rule will override the corresponding rules of the imported styles (if any). For example, if different pages of a site have the same styles except background-color, which is modified as part of the design, then all the styles can be imported and the background-color property is overwritten (alter.css in Listing 5-54). Similarly, a style sheet designed for mobile devices can reuse the main styles but remove the background image[6] and set the maximum width of the document body to the largest screen width available on smartphones today (mobile.css in Listing 5-54). All other styles are imported, including the color and the font-family.

Listing 5-54. Reusing and Extending Styles of the Main CSS File of a Site

main.css	alter.css	mobile.css
body {	@import ("main.css");	@import ("main.css");
background: url('http://example.com/	body {	body {
images/bg.jpg') no-repeat 100% 0% fixed;	background-color:#00254c;	background-image: none;
background-color:#004c25;	}	max-width: 640px;
color: #fff;		}
font-family: Garamond, serif;		
}		
...		

A more robust declaration provides not the path but the URL of the file. Listing 5-55 shows an example.

Listing 5-55. Importing a Style Sheet File by Providing a Full URL

```
@import url("http://www.example.com/alter.css");
```

One of the applications of importing style sheets is to provide alternate styles for web sites that can serve several purposes. For example, accessibility can be improved by providing different style sheets for different media. The media-specific CSS files of a site can be controlled in the markup by the media attribute on the link element, as discussed earlier in Chapter 3. The rulesets of such CSS files have an intersection defined by the main CSS file of the site. The files of media-specific rules rely on each other and often import rules from each other (Listing 5-56). Multiple CSS files can also be used for site design.

Listing 5-56. Importing Media-Specific Styles

```
@import url("print.css") print;
@import url("mobile.css") handheld and (max-width: 480px);
```

Display and Visibility

The element levels of HTML and XHTML documents have already been discussed. In CSS, (X)HTML elements can generally be displayed in the following ways:

- *Block*: Uses the full width available, along with a new line before and after (Listing 5-57)

---

[6]In the example, the background-image property is set using the shorthand property background in the main.css file.

Listing 5-57. Rule for Elements to Be Displayed As Block

```
display: block;
```

- *Inline*: Uses only as much width as needed without breaking the row (Listing 5-58)

Listing 5-58. Rule for Elements to Be Displayed Inline

```
display: inline;
```

- *Not di.yed*: Removes the element completely from the document so it does not take up any space, even though its corresponding markup is still in the source code (Listing 5-59)

Listing 5-59. Rule for Elements to Hide Without Spaceholder

```
display: none;
```

- *Hidden*: Hides the element but still takes up space in the layout (Listing 5-60)

Listing 5-60. Rule for Elements to Hide with Spaceholder

```
visibility: hidden;
```

Cascading

The *C* in CSS stands for *Cascading*. It is a mechanism that determines one declaration among a set of styling rules that should be applied for a certain element-property pair. Browsers consider three features in the following order to choose that declaration [18]:

1. *Weight*: The declaration with the highest weight is chosen. In CSS3, the weight of a declaration is based on the *origin of the declaration* and its *level of importance*. The origin can be of three kinds: *author*, *user*, and *user agent*. CSS declarations have two levels of importance: *normal* and *important* (the first one is the default level; the second one is optional and should be marked). An important declaration looks like Listing 5-61.

Listing 5-61. A Rule with the Highest Level of Importance

```
#menu {
  margin-top: 12px !important;
}
```

■ **Tip** The proper exploitation of the cascading mechanism eliminates the need for !important rules.

The weight of style sheets derived from the different origins, in descending order, is as follows:

a. User style sheets (important)

b. Author style sheets (important)

c. Author style sheets (normal)

d. User style sheets (normal)

e. Default style sheets of rendering engines

As a result, declarations written by developers generally have more weight than that of user style sheets, which have more weight than the default styles of the browser. This is the reason why links are generally rendered in the font color defined by the web designer rather than the default anchor color (Listing 5-62).

Listing 5-62. A Rule in a CSS File That Has More Weight Than the Corresponding Rule in the Default Style Sheet of Browsers

```
a {
    font-color: #12ee12;
}
```

2. *Specificity*: The declaration with the highest specificity is chosen. The specificity of selectors can be calculated as follows [19]:

- The number of ID attributes in the selector is counted.

- The number of other attributes and pseudoclasses in the selector is counted.

- The number of element names in the selector is counted.

- The concatenation of these numbers is the specificity.

- Negative selectors are counted similar to their simple selectors' argument.

- Pseudoelements are ignored.

In Listing 5-63, the specificity of the first declaration is the lowest, and the specificity of the last one is the largest. The font color of all paragraphs is the same (black), except those paragraphs that are included in a division, which have a different font color (green). The div elements with the tip value declared for the class attribute have an even more specific rule, which makes their font color distinctive (red, which is different from the color of any other paragraphs).

Listing 5-63. Declarations with Increasing Specificity

```
p {
    color: #000;
}
div p {
    color: #0f0;
}
.tip p {
    color: #00f;
}
```

3. *Declaration order*: If two declarations have the same weight, origin, and specificity, the last declaration is chosen (imported style sheets should also be considered). Imported style rules are processed prior to the rules of the style sheet. The rules of further imported style sheets are taken into account in the order of the @import rules.

Inheritance

In web markup languages and style sheets, certain codes are automatically reused. In CSS, property values of parent elements can be set to their children. The specified value of an element-property combination is copied from the corresponding computed value of the parent element. This procedure is called *inheritance*. It eliminates the need for defining properties that are straightforward. If, for example, the background color of a web document is defined, all container elements, divisions, and paragraphs within the document will inherit that property. Certainly, any of them can be arbitrarily overridden.

Certain CSS property values are defined as *inherited*. Unless a value is specified for these element-property combinations, the value is determined by inheritance.

The inherit value can be used for all properties to be determined by inheritance. For example, color is an inheritable property. However, the color of anchor elements is commonly set to blue by the user agent style sheet. By using the value inherit, the declaration of the user agent style sheet can be overridden: all child anchor elements inherit the value of the foreground color from the parent element (Listing 5-64).

Listing 5-64. Inherited Property Value

```
#warning {
  color: #000;
}
#warning a:link {
  color: inherit;
}
```

■ **Note**   The more specific a property, the fewer elements it can be applied to. As you will see in the overview of CSS properties, a large share of CSS properties are not inherited at all.

Scopes and Structure

In contrast to the underlined blue hyperlinks used in the first years of the Web, modern web sites often apply different colors and decorations to accommodate the overall design. When using a dotted underline for hyperlinks, however, it is rather frustrating that linking images share the same style. To solve the problem, image borders should be removed and more specific styles set. Listing 5-65 shows an example.

Listing 5-65. Specific Rules to Eliminate the Underline for Links Declared by General Rules

```
img {
  border: 0;
}

a.nounder {
  border-bottom: none;
}
```

The *scope* of rules has a large impact on their application. The rules that apply to more (most) elements within the same category should be identified in an early stage of web site development. For example, if the vast majority of paragraphs have the same indent, that value should be applied as a general CSS rule to all p elements (for example, p { text-indent: 3em; }), and another rule should be written to the class of paragraphs that are different (for example, p.morein { text-indent: 5em; }).

In the optimal case, both the scope and the inheritance are considered for those properties that can be used as the basis for the entire web site, such as the default font size (Listing 5-66).

Listing 5-66. The Default Font Size of the Entire Web Site Can Be Inherited from the Document Body

```
body {
  font-size: 0.8em;
}
```

For those elements that require a different font size, such as headings, the property can be set specifically (Listing 5-67), and all the other elements inherit the default font size set for the document body. Consequently, there is no need to declare the font size for, say, all p and div elements, if the desired font size for them is the default one, because the property is inherited from the body element.

Listing 5-67. Specific Declarations That Override the Default Font Size Set in the Previous Listing

```
h1 {
  font-size: 1.4em;
}
h2 {
  font-size: 1.2em;
}
h3 {
  font-size: 1em;
}
```

The Box Model

The actual markup content of block elements is wrapped around by optional *paddings*, *borders*, and *margins*, called the *CSS box model* (Figure 5-2) [20]. These rectangular boxes are generated for certain markup elements in the document tree.

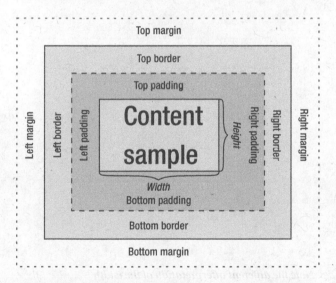

Figure 5-2. *The CSS box model*

Text and images appear in the content. The padding clears the area around the content. The padding is affected by the background color of the box similar to the border area around the padding. The margin is the outermost area around the border. It has no background color and is transparent. The size of each area can be determined by CSS properties. Since they are optional, they can also be collapsed to 0 (that is, totally eliminated).

The margins of two vertically adjacent block elements normally collapse into one another; that is, a margin is rendered according to the size of the larger bottom margin of the first box and that of the top margin of the other below it.

The IE Box Model Bug

From the first version of CSS, the width and height of all block-level elements specified explicitly determine only the width or height of the visible element, and the padding, borders, and margins are applied afterward. In earlier versions of Internet Explorer, the CSS specifications were implemented incorrectly, which is often referred to as the *Internet Explorer box model bug*. Internet Explorer 5 included the content, padding, and borders within a specified width or height, resulting in a narrower or shorter rendering of the box [21] (Figure 5-3).

Figure 5-3. *Comparison of the W3C and the IE5 box model. Note the different interpretation of the width*

Internet Explorer 6 and newer IE versions[7] apply the correct implementation in their standards-compliant mode, but for compatibility reasons, the bug still exists when a page is rendered in Quirks Mode.

Overview of CSS Properties

Table 5-5 summarizes the rich selection of CSS properties. There are 53 properties in CSS1, 122 in CSS2, 115 in CSS 2.1, and more than 300 (and counting) in CSS3.[8]

---

[7]The bug was not present in Internet Explorer for Mac (discontinued in 2006).
[8]The value none applies to all media.

Table 5-5. *Overview of CSS Properties*

Property	CSS1	CSS2	CSS2.1	CSS3	Applicability	Inherited	Media
align-content	–	–	–	+	Block containers, flex containers, and grid containers	–	V
align-items	–	–	–	+	Block-level elements	–	V
align-self	–	–	–	+	Block-level elements	–	V
alignment-adjust	–	–	–	+	Inline elements	–	V
alignment-baseline	–	–	–	+	Inline elements	–	V
all	–	–	–	+	Depends on the property to which all is used for as a shorthand property	d	d
anchor-point	–	–	–	+	All elements	–	V
animation	–	–	–	+	Block and inline elements	–	V
animation-delay	–	–	–	+	Block and inline elements	–	V
animation-direction	–	–	–	+	Block and inline elements	–	V
animation-duration	–	–	–	+	Block and inline elements	–	V
animation-fill-mode	–	–	–	+	All elements, ::before and ::after pseudo-elements	–	V
animation-iteration-count	–	–	–	+	Block and inline elements	–	V
animation-name	–	–	–	+	Block and inline elements	–	V
animation-play-state	–	–	–	+	Block and inline elements	–	V
animation-timing-function	–	–	–	+	Block and inline elements	–	V
azimuth	–	+	+	–	All elements	+	A
backface-visibility	–	–	–	+	Block and inline elements	–	V
background	+	+	+	+	All elements	–	V
background-attachment	+	+	+	+	All elements	–	V
background-clip	–	–	–	+	All elements	–	V
background-color	+	+	+	+	All elements	–	V
background-image	+	+	+	+	All elements	–	V
background-origin	–	–	–	+	All elements	–	V
background-position	+	+	+	+	All elements	–	V
background-repeat	+	+	+	+	All elements	–	V
background-size	–	–	–	+	All elements	–	V
baseline-shift	–	–	–	+	Inline elements	–	V

(continued)

Table 5-5. *(continued)*

Property	CSS1	CSS2	CSS2.1	CSS3	Applicability	Inherited	Media
binding	–	–	–	+	All elements (but not pseudoelements)	–	All
bleed	–	–	–	+	Page media elements	–	P
bookmark-label	–	–	–	+	All elements	–	All
bookmark-level	–	–	–	+	All elements	–	All
bookmark-target	–	–	–	+	All elements	–	All
border	+	+	+	+	All elements	–	V
border-bottom	+	+	+	+	All elements	–	V
border-bottom-color	–	+	+	+	All elements	–	V
border-bottom-left-radius	–	–	–	+	All elements	–	V
border-bottom-right-radius	–	–	–	+	All elements	–	V
border-bottom-style	–	+	+	+	All elements	–	V
border-bottom-width	+	+	+	+	All elements	–	V
border-collapse	–	+	+	?	Table and inline-table elements	–	V
border-color	+	+	+	+	All elements	–	V
border-image	–	–	–	+	Depends on individual properties	–	V
border-image-outset	–	–	–	+	All elements except internal table elements when border-collapse is set to collapse	–	V
border-image-repeat	–	–	–	+	All elements except table elements when border-collapse is set to collapse	–	V
border-image-slice	–	–	–	+	All elements except internal table elements when border-collapse is set to collapse	–	V
border-image-source	–	–	–	+	All elements except internal table elements when border-collapse is set to collapse	–	V
border-image-width	–	–	–	+	All elements, except internal table elements when border-collapse is set to collapse	–	V

(continued)

Table 5-5. (*continued*)

Property	CSS1	CSS2	CSS2.1	CSS3	Applicability	Inherited	Media
border-left	+	+	+	+	All elements	–	V
border-left-color	–	+	+	+	All elements	–	V
border-left-style	–	+	+	+	All elements	–	V
border-left-width	+	+	+	+	All elements	–	V
border-radius	–	–	–	+	All elements except table elements when border-collapse is set to collapse	–	V
border-right	+	+	+	+	All elements	–	V
border-right-color	–	+	+	+	All elements	–	V
border-right-style	–	+	+	+	All elements	–	V
border-right-width	+	+	+	+	All elements	–	V
border-spacing	–	+	+	?	Table and inline-table elements (also frameset elements in certain document types)	+	V
border-style	+	+	+	+	All elements	–	V
border-top	+	+	+	+	All elements	–	V
border-top-color	–	+	+	+	All elements	–	V
border-top-left-radius	–	–	–	+	All elements	–	V
border-top-right-radius	–	–	–	+	All elements*	–	V
border-top-style	–	+	+	+	All elements	–	V
border-top-width	+	+	+	+	All elements	–	V
border-width	+	+	+	+	All elements	–	V
bottom	–	+	+	+	Positioned elements	–	V
box-decoration-break	–	–	–	+	All elements	–	V
box-shadow	–	–	–	+	All elements	–	V
box-sizing	–	–	–	+	All elements that accept width or height	–	V
box-snap	–	–	–	+	Block-level boxes and internal table elements except table cells	+	V
box-suppress	–	–	–	+	All elements	–	All
break-after	–	–	–	+	Block-level elements	–	V
break-before	–	–	–	+	Block-level elements	–	V
break-inside	–	–	–	+	Block-level elements	–	V

(*continued*)

Table 5-5. (*continued*)

Property	CSS1	CSS2	CSS2.1	CSS3	Applicability	Inherited	Media
caption-side	–	+	+	?	Table-caption elements	+	V
chains	–	–	–	+	Template elements	–	V
clear	+	+	+	+	Block-level elements	–	V
clip	–	+	+	?	Absolutely positioned elements	–	V
clip-path	–	–	–	+	All elements. In SVG, it applies to container elements excluding the defs element and all graphics elements	–	V
clip-rule	–	–	–	+	SVG graphics elements	+	V
color	+	+	+	+	All elements	+	V
color-interpolation-filters	–	–	–	+	All filter primitives	+	V
column-count	–	–	–	+	Nonreplaced block-level elements (except table elements), table cells, and inline-block elements	–	V
column-fill	–	–	–	+	Multicolumn elements	–	N
column-gap	–	–	–	+	Multicolumn elements	–	V
column-rule	–	–	–	+	Multicolumn elements	–	V
column-rule-color	–	–	–	+	Multicolumn elements	–	V
column-rule-style	–	–	–	+	Multicolumn elements	–	V
column-rule-width	–	–	–	+	Multicolumn elements	–	V
columns	–	–	–	+	Nonreplaced block-level elements (except table elements), table cells, and inline-block elements	–	V
contain	–	–	–	+	All elements	–	All
content	–	+	+	+	All elements, ::before, ::after, ::alternate, ::marker, ::line-marker, margin areas, and @footnote areas	–	All
counter-increment	–	+	+	+	All elements, ::before, ::after, ::alternate, ::marker, ::line-marker, margin areas, @footnote areas, and @page context	–	All

(*continued*)

Table 5-5. (*continued*)

Property	CSS1	CSS2	CSS2.1	CSS3	Applicability	Inherited	Media
counter-reset	–	+	+	+	All elements, ::before, ::after, ::alternate, ::marker, ::line-marker, margin areas, @footnote areas, and @page context	–	All
counter-set	–	–	–	+	All elements	–	All
crop	–	–	–	+	Replaced elements	–	V
cue	–	+	+	+	All elements	–	S
cue-after	–	+	+	+	All elements	–	S
cue-before	–	+	+	+	All elements	–	S
cursor	–	+	+	+	All elements	+	V, I
direction	–	+	+	+	All elements*	+	V
display	+	+	+	+	All elements	–	V[8]
display-inside	–	–	–	+	All elements	–	All
display-list	–	–	–	+	All elements	–	All
display-outside	–	–	–	+	All elements	–	All
dominant-baseline	–	–	–	+	Inline-level elements*	–	V
elevation	–	+	+	–	All elements	+	A
empty-cells	–	+	+	?	Table-cell elements	+	V
filter	–	–	–	+	All elements. In SVG, it applies to container elements without the defs element and all graphics elements	–	V
flex	–	–	–	+	Flex items	d	V
flex-basis	–	–	–	+	Flex items	–	V
flex-direction	–	–	–	+	Flex containers	–	V
flex-flow	–	–	–	+	Flex containers	d	V
flex-grow	–	–	–	+	Flex items	–	V
flex-shrink	–	–	–	+	Flex elements	–	V
flex-wrap	–	–	–	+	Flex containers	–	V
float	+	+	+	+	All elements*	–	V
float-offset	–	–	–	+	Floated elements	–	V, P

(*continued*)

Table 5-5. (*continued*)

Property	CSS1	CSS2	CSS2.1	CSS3	Applicability	Inherited	Media
flood-color	–	–	–	+	feFlood, feDropShadow	–	V
flood-opacity	–	–	–	+	feFlood, feDropShadow	–	V
flow-from	–	–	–	+	Non-replaced block containers	–	V
flow-into	–	–	–	+	All elements except pseudo-elements	–	V
font	+	+	+	+	All elements	+	V
font-family	+	+	+	+	All elements	+	V
font-feature-settings	–	–	–	+	All elements	+	V
font-kerning	–	–	–	+	All elements	+	V
font-language-override	–	–	–	+	All elements	+	V
font-size	+	+	+	+	All elements	+	V
font-size-adjust	–	+	–	+	All elements	+	V
font-stretch	–	–	–	+	All elements	+	V
font-style	+	+	+	+	All elements	+	V
font-synthesis	–	–	–	+	All elements	+	V
font-variant	+	+	+	+	All elements	+	V
font-variant-alternates	–	–	–	+	All elements	+	V
font-variant-caps	–	–	–	+	All elements	+	V
font-variant-east-asian	–	–	–	+	All elements	+	V
font-variant-ligatures	–	–	–	+	All elements	+	V
font-variant-numeric	–	–	–	+	All elements	+	V
font-variant-position	–	–	–	+	All elements	+	V
font-weight	+	+	+	+	All elements	+	V
grid	–	–	–	+	Grid containers	d	V
grid-area	–	–	–	+	Grid items	d	V
grid-auto-columns	–	–	–	+	Grid containers	–	V
grid-auto-flow	–	–	–	+	Grid containers	–	V
grid-auto-rows	–	–	–	+	Grid containers	–	V
grid-column	–	–	–	+	Grid items	d	V
grid-column-end	–	–	–	+	Grid items	–	V
grid-column-start	–	–	–	+	Grid items	–	V
grid-row	–	–	–	+	Grid elements	d	V

(*continued*)

Table 5-5. (*continued*)

Property	CSS1	CSS2	CSS2.1	CSS3	Applicability	Inherited	Media
grid-row-end	–	–	–	+	Grid items	–	V
grid-row-start	–	–	–	+	Grid items	–	V
grid-template	–	–	–	+	Grid containers	d	V
grid-template-areas	–	–	–	+	Grid containers	–	V
grid-template-columns	–	–	–	+	Grid containers	–	V
grid-template-rows	–	–	–	+	Grid containers	–	V
hanging-punctuation	–	–	–	+	Block and inline-block elements, table cells	+	V
height	+	+	+	+	All elements except nonreplaced inline elements, table columns, and column groups	–	V
hyphens	–	–	–	+	All elements	+	V
icon	–	–	–	+	All elements	–	All
image-orientation	–	–	–	+	Images	?	P
image-resolution	–	–	–	+	Replaced elements and background images	+	V
ime-mode	–	–	–	+	Text fields	–	I
initial-letter	–	–	–	+	::first-letter pseudo elements and inline level first child of a block container	–	V
inline-box-align	–	–	–	+	Inline block-level elements	–	V
justify-content	–	–	–	+	Flex containers	–	V
justify-items	–	–	–	+	Block containers, flex containers, and grid containers	–	V
justify-self	–	–	–	+	Block-level boxes, absolutely-positioned boxes, and grid items	–	V
left	–	+	+	+	Positioned elements	–	V
letter-spacing	+	+	+	+	All elements	+	V
lighting-color	–	–	–	+	feDiffuseLighting, feSpecularLighting	–	V
line-box-contain	–	–	–	+	Block-level elements	+	V
line-break	–	–	–	+	All elements	+	V

(*continued*)

Table 5-5. (*continued*)

Property	CSS1	CSS2	CSS2.1	CSS3	Applicability	Inherited	Media
line-grid	–	–	–	+	Block containers	–	V
line-height	+	+	+	+	All elements	+	V
line-snap	–	–	–	+	All elements	+	V
line-stacking	–	–	–	+	Block-level elements	+	V
line-stacking-ruby	–	–	–	+	Block-level elements	+	V
line-stacking-shift	–	–	–	+	Block-level elements	+	V
line-stacking-strategy	–	–	–	+	Block-level elements	+	V
list-style	+	+	+	+	All elements with display: list-item	N	V
list-style-image	+	+	+	+	All elements with display: list-item	+	V
list-style-position	+	+	+	+	All elements with display: list-item	+	V
list-style-type	+	+	+	+	All elements with display: list-item	+	V
margin	+	+	+	+	All boxes except certain table boxes and certain inline-level boxes	–	V
margin-bottom	+	+	+	+	All boxes except certain table boxes and certain inline-level boxes	–	V
margin-left	+	+	+	+	All boxes except certain table boxes and certain inline-level boxes	–	V
margin-right	+	+	+	+	All boxes except certain table boxes and certain inline-level boxes	–	V
margin-top	+	+	+	+	All boxes except certain table boxes and certain inline-level boxes	–	V
marker-offset	–	+	–	–	Elements with display: marker	–	V
marker-side	–	–	–	+	List items	+	V
marks	–	+	–	+	Page context	–	V, P

(*continued*)

Table 5-5. (*continued*)

Property	CSS1	CSS2	CSS2.1	CSS3	Applicability	Inherited	Media
mask	–	–	–	+	All elements. In SVG, it applies to container elements, excluding the defs element and all graphics elements	–	V
mask-border	–	–	–	+			
mask-border-mode	–	–	–	+	All elements. In SVG, it applies to container elements, excluding the defs element and all graphics elements	–	V
mask-border-outset	–	–	–	+	All elements. In SVG, it applies to container elements, excluding the defs element and all graphics elements	–	V
mask-border-repeat	–	–	–	+	All elements. In SVG, it applies to container elements, excluding the defs element and all graphics elements	–	V
mask-border-slice	–	–	–	+	All elements. In SVG, it applies to container elements, excluding the defs element and all graphics elements	–	V
mask-border-source	–	–	–	+	All elements. In SVG, it applies to container elements, excluding the defs element and all graphics elements	–	V
mask-border-width	–	–	–	+	All elements. In SVG, it applies to container elements, excluding the defs element and all graphics elements	–	V
mask-clip	–	–	–	+	All elements. In SVG, it applies to container elements, excluding the defs element and all graphics elements	–	V

(*continued*)

Table 5-5. (*continued*)

Property	CSS1	CSS2	CSS2.1	CSS3	Applicability	Inherited	Media
mask-composite	–	–	–	+	All elements. In SVG, it applies to container elements, except the defs element and all graphics elements	–	V
mask-image	–	–	–	+	All elements. In SVG, it applies to container elements, excluding the defs element and all graphics elements	–	V
mask-origin	–	–	–	+	All elements. In SVG, it applies to container elements, excluding the defs element and all graphics elements	–	V
mask-position	–	–	–	+	All elements. In SVG, it applies to container elements, excluding the defs element and all graphics elements	–	V
mask-repeat	–	–	–	+	All elements. In SVG, it applies to container elements, excluding the defs element and all graphics elements	–	V
mask-size	–	–	–	+	All elements. In SVG, it applies to container elements, excluding the defs element and all graphics elements	–	V
mask-type	–	–	–	+	All mask elements	–	V
max-height	–	+	+	+	All elements except nonreplaced inline elements, table rows, and row groups	–	V
max-lines	–	–	–	+	Fragment boxes	–	V
max-width	–	+	+	+	All elements except nonreplaced inline elements, table rows, and row groups	–	V

(*continued*)

Table 5-5. (*continued*)

Property	CSS1	CSS2	CSS2.1	CSS3	Applicability	Inherited	Media
min-height	–	+	+	+	All elements except nonreplaced inline elements, table rows, and row groups	–	V
min-width	–	+	+	+	All elements except nonreplaced inline elements, table rows, and row groups	–	V
move-to	–	–	–	+	All elements, ::before, ::after, ::alternate	–	All
nav-down	–	–	–	+	All enabled elements	–	I
nav-index	–	–	–	+	All enabled elements	–	I
nav-left	–	–	–	+	All enabled elements	–	I
nav-right	–	–	–	+	All enabled elements	–	I
nav-up	–	–	–	+	All enabled elements	–	I
object-fit	–	–	–	+	Replaced elements	–	V
object-position	–	–	–	+	Replaced elements	–	V
opacity	–	–	–	+	All elements	–	V
order	–	–	–	+	Flex items and absolutely-positioned children of flex containers	–	V
orphans	–	+	+	+	Block-level elements	+	V
outline	–	+	+	+	All elements	–	V
outline-color	–	+	+	+	All elements	–	V
outline-offset	–	–	–	+	All elements	–	V
outline-style	–	+	+	+	All elements	–	V
outline-width	–	+	+	+	All elements	–	V
overflow	–	+	+	+	Nonreplaced block-level elements and nonreplaced inline-block elements	–	V
overflow-wrap	–	–	–	+	All elements	+	V
overflow-x	–	–	–	+	Nonreplaced block-level elements and nonreplaced inline-block elements	–	V
overflow-y	–	–	–	+	Nonreplaced block-level elements and nonreplaced inline-block elements	–	V

(*continued*)

Table 5-5. (*continued*)

Property	CSS1	CSS2	CSS2.1	CSS3	Applicability	Inherited	Media
padding	+	+	+	+	All elements	−	V
padding-bottom	+	+	+	+	All elements	−	V
padding-left	+	+	+	+	All elements	−	V
padding-right	+	+	+	+	All elements	−	V
padding-top	+	+	+	+	All elements	−	V
page	−	+	−	+	Block-level elements	+	P
page-break-after	−	+	+	+	Block-level elements	−	V, P
page-break-before	−	+	+	+	Block-level elements	−	V, P
page-break-inside	−	+	+	+	Block-level elements	+	P
page-policy	−	−	−	+	@counter and @string blocks	?	P
pause	−	+	+	+	All elements	−	S
pause-after	−	+	+	+	All elements	−	S
pause-before	−	+	+	+	All elements	−	S
perspective	−	−	−	+	Block-level and inline-level elements	−	V
perspective-origin	−	−	−	+	Block-level and inline-level elements	−	V
pitch	−	+	+	−	All elements	+	A
pitch-range	−	+	+	−	All elements	+	A
play-during	−	+	+	−	All elements	−	A
position	−	+	+	+	All elements	−	V
presentation-level	−	−	−	+	All elements	+	All
quotes	−	+	+	+	All elements, ::before, ::after, ::alternate, ::marker, ::line-marker, margin areas, and @ footnote areas	−	V
region-fragment	−	−	−	+	CSS regions	−	V
resize	−	−	−	+	Elements with overflow other than visible	−	V
rest	−	−	−	+	All elements	−	S
rest-after	−	−	−	+	All elements	−	S
rest-before	−	−	−	+	All elements	−	S

(*continued*)

Table 5-5. (*continued*)

Property	CSS1	CSS2	CSS2.1	CSS3	Applicability	Inherited	Media
richness	–	+	+	–	All elements	+	A
right	–	+	+	+	Positioned elements	–	V
rotation	–	–	–	+	Block-level elements, inline-table elements, and inline-block elements	–	V
rotation-point	–	–	–	+	Block-level elements	–	V
ruby-align	–	–	–	+	All elements and generated content	–	V
ruby-merge	–	–	–	+	Ruby annotation containers	+	V
ruby-position	–	–	–	+	The parent of elements with display: ruby-text	+	V
shape-image-threshold	–	–	–	+	Floats	–	V
shape-outside	–	–	–	+	Floats	–	V
shape-margin	–	–	–	+	Floats	–	V
size	–	+	–	+	Page context	?	P
speak	–	+	+	+	All elements	+	S
speak-as	–	–	–	+	All elements	+	S
speak-header	–	+	+	–	Elements that have table header information	+	A
speak-numeral	–	+	+	–	All elements	+	A
speak-punctuation	–	+	+	–	All elements	+	A
speech-rate	–	+	+	–	All elements	+	A
stress	–	+	+	–	All elements	+	A
string-set	–	–	–	+	All elements	–	All
table-layout	–	+	+	?	Table and inline-table elements	–	V
tab-side	–	–	–	+	Elements with display: stack	+	V
text-align	+	+	+	+	Block containers	+	V
text-align-last	–	–	–	+	Block containers	+	V
text-combine-upright	–	–	–	+	Non-replaced inline elements	+	V
text-decoration	+	+	+	+	All elements	–	V
text-decoration-color	–	–	–	+	All elements	–	V

(*continued*)

Table 5-5. (*continued*)

Property	CSS1	CSS2	CSS2.1	CSS3	Applicability	Inherited	Media
text-decoration-line	–	–	–	+	All elements	–*	V
text-decoration-skip	–	–	–	+	All elements	+	V
text-decoration-style	–	–	–	+	All elements	–	V
text-emphasis	–	–	–	+	All elements	+	V
text-emphasis-color	–	–	–	+	All elements	+	V
text-emphasis-position	–	–	–	+	All elements	+	V
text-emphasis-style	–	–	–	+	All elements	+	V
text-height	–	–	–	+	Inline elements and parents of element with display: ruby-text	+	V
text-indent	+	+	+	+	Block containers	+	V
text-justify	–	–	–	+	Block containers, inline elements	+	V
text-orientation	–	–	–	+	All elements except table rows and columns	+	V
text-overflow	–	–	–	+	Block containers	–	V
text-shadow	–	+	–	+	All elements	+	V
text-space-collapse	–	–	–	+	All elements	+	V
text-transform	+	+	+	+	All elements	+	V
text-underline-position	–	–	–	+	All elements	+	V
text-wrap	–	–	–	+	All elements	+	V
top	–	+	+	+	Positioned elements	–	V
transform	–	–	–	+	Block and inline elements	–	V
transform-origin	–	–	–	+	Block and inline elements	–	V
transform-style	–	–	–	+	Block and inline elements	–	V
transition	–	–	–	+	All elements, :before and :after pseudoelements	–	I
transition-delay	–	–	–	+	All elements, :before and :after pseudoelements	–	I
transition-duration	–	–	–	+	All elements, :before and :after pseudoelements	–	I
transition-property	–	–	–	+	All elements, :before and :after pseudoelements	–	V
transition-timing-function	–	–	–	+	All elements, :before and :after pseudoelements	–	I

(*continued*)

Table 5-5. (*continued*)

Property	CSS1	CSS2	CSS2.1	CSS3	Applicability	Inherited	Media
unicode-bidi	–	+	+	+	All elements*	–	V
vertical-align	+	+	+	+	Inline-level elements	–	V
visibility	–	+	+	+	All elements	+	V
voice-balance	–	–	–	+	All elements	+	S
voice-duration	–	–	–	+	All elements	–	S
voice-family	–	+	–	+	All elements	+	S
voice-pitch	–	–	–	+	All elements	+	S
voice- range	–	–	–	+	All elements	+	S
voice-rate	–	–	–	+	All elements	+	S
voice-stress	–	–	–	+	All elements	+	S
voice-volume	–	–	–	+	All elements	+	S
volume	–	+	+	–	All elements	+	A
white-space	+	+	+	+	All elements	+	V
widows	–	+	+	+	Block-level elements	+	V
width	+	+	+	+	All elements except nonreplaced inline elements, table rows, and row groups	–	V
word-break	–	–	–	+	All elements	+	V
word-spacing	+	+	+	+	All elements	+	V
word-wrap	–	–	–	+	All elements	+	V
wrap-flow	–	–	–	+	Block-level elements	–	V
wrap-through	–	–	–	+	Block-level elements	–	V
writing-mode	–	–	–	+	All elements except table rows and table columns	+	V
z-index	–	+	+	+	Positioned elements	–	V

Legend

*   Special rules might apply
n   Not defined for shorthand properties
d   Depends on the individual property
?   Not finalized yet
V   Visual media
I   Interactive media
A   Aural media
P   Paged media
N   Noncontinuous media (continuous media only if column length is constrained)
S   Speech media

The browser support of CSS properties varies and is gradually improving. However, even the CSS 2.1 properties gained a more or less complete and correct implementation only recently. Consequently, old browsers do not support all properties and have incorrect implementation for many properties. This was the major reason for the huge difference in rendering the same site under different browsers for years. With the proper, if not full, implementation of CSS properties in modern browsers, this difference has been decreased to a minimum.

Most Common CSS3 Features and Properties

With CSS3, you can create rounded borders, add shadow to boxes, use an image as a border, and other advanced styling without creating images in an image processing program such as Photoshop.

border-radius

With CSS3, you can add rounded borders to elements individually using the border-top-left-radius, border-top-right-radius, border-bottom-right-radius, and border-bottom-left-radius properties (Listing 5-68), or together with their shorthand property, border-radius (Listing 5-69).

Listing 5-68. Border Radii Set Individually for the Four Corners

```
div {
  border: 2px solid;
  border-top-left-radius: 2em;
  border-top-right-radius: 1.8em;
  border-bottom-right-radius: 2.2em;
  border-bottom-left-radius: 1.6em;
}
```

The property value (the radius) can be declared in pixels, ems, or %, which defines the shape of the corners.

Listing 5-69. Identical Border Radius for All Corners

```
div {
  border: 2px solid;
  border-radius: 25px;
}
```

The radii values are declared in the order top-left, top-right, bottom-right, and bottom-left. If bottom-left is omitted, it is the same as top-right. If bottom-right is omitted, it is the same as top-left. If top-right is omitted, it is the same as top-left. If all four radii values are the same, the border-radius shorthand property should be used with that value.

box-shadows

In CSS3, the box-shadow property is used to add shadow to divisions (Listing 5-70).

Listing 5-70. Shadow on the div Elements

```
div {
    box-shadow: 10px 10px 5px #848484;
}
```

text-shadow

In CSS3, the text-shadow property adds shadow to texts (Listing 5-71).

Listing 5-71. Simple Text Shadow Effect

```
h2 {
  text-shadow: 2px 3px 5px #00f;
}
```

The first property value defines the x-offset, the second value is the y-offset, the third value is the z-offset (blur), and the last value is the color of the shadow. If you want to add multiple shadows, a comma should be used as the separator (Listing 5-72).

Listing 5-72. Outline Effect Using Multiple Text Shadows

```
h2 {
  text-shadow: 0 1px 0 #000, 0 -1px 0 #000, 1px 0 0 #000, -1px 0 0 #000;
  color: #fff;
}
```

Background Size

In CSS3, background images are resizable, making it possible to implement the background image to take up all available space (Listing 5-73) or be proportional to the screen, regardless of the width of the browser window.

Listing 5-73. Stretched Background

```
body {
  background: url('/img/bg.jpg') no-repeat;
  background-size: 100% 100%;
}
```

Multiple Backgrounds

In CSS3, multiple backgrounds can be declared (Listing 5-74). The separate background images are separated by a comma.

Listing 5-74. Two Background Images for One Element

```
#container {
  background: url('/img/bg.jpg') 0 0 no-repeat, url('/img/bg2.jpg') 100% 0 no-repeat;
}
```

In this example, the first image is placed to the top-left position (0 0), while the second to the top-right position (100% 0). Multiple backgrounds can be especially useful when applying a texture or gradient as the main background, and a photo as the other.

Transitions

With CSS3, we can add effects to elements that will gradually change from one style to another without JavaScript or Flash animations. transition-delay determines when the transition effect should start. transition-duration specifies the length of the transition effect in seconds or milliseconds. transition-property identifies the CSS property the transition effect is applied for. transition-timing-function specifies the speed curve of the transition effect. transition is the shorthand property of the four transition properties.

One of the typical transition effects is associated with the event when a user is moving the mouse over an element (Listing 5-75).

Listing 5-75. Specifying a :hover Effect for div Elements

```
div:hover {
  width: 400px;
}
```

If there is no duration specified, the transition will have no effect, because the default value is 0. To specify the duration, the CSS property to which the transition will be applied must be defined, followed by the transition length such as transition: width 2s;.

Transition effects can be added to more than one CSS property by separating the properties with a comma (Listing 5-76).

Listing 5-76. Transition Effects for Width, Height, and Transformation

```
div {
  transition: width 2s, height 2s, transform 2s;
}
```

■ **Tip**   It is recommended to apply CSS3 rules with caution, because most modules of CSS3 are not standardized yet, and browser support varies. Web designers should ensure the graceful degradation of user experience on older browsers that do not support CSS3. While the rounded corners declared by using the CSS3 property border-radius are not rendered by older browsers, the general layout and styling provide a similar appearance in old browsers as with modern browsers with CSS3 support. Similarly, if Web Fonts—that are not supported by older browsers—are used on a site, a common font and at least a generic font family should be declared as a fallback mechanism (see Chapter 9 for details).

Initial Property Values

All CSS properties have their *initial values* that are applied when the property values are set neither by cascading nor by inheritance. The initial value of each property is defined by the CSS specifications. An initial value is one of the allowed values of the corresponding CSS property. For example, a color declaration (in any of the allowed formats, typically in hexadecimal notation), transparent, and inherit are all legal values of the background-color property, from which transparent is the initial value that can be easily overridden by declaring the desired value in your CSS file (Listing 5-77).

Listing 5-77. The Declared Value Overrides the Initial Value Defined by the CSS Specification

```
body {
  background-color: #198c00;
}
```

This is the reason why the background of all paragraphs, divisions, and other elements is transparent. Another example is the bullet type of lists, which is often used without override. If the value of the property `list-style-type` is not set by the developer, the initial value is used for rendering, which is `disc`. However, it can be overridden by any other allowed values of that property, including `circle`, `square`, `decimal`, `decimal-leading-zero`, `lower-roman`, `upper-roman`, `lower-greek`, `lower-latin`, `upper-latin`, `armenian`, `georgian`, `lower-alpha`, `upper-alpha`, `none`, and `inherit`. The last value, `inherit`, can be applied not only to `list-style-type` but also to any other CSS property in order to explicitly apply the initial value of the corresponding property.

Since the root element has no parent element, its value is set to the initial property value by default.

Default Styles of Rendering Engines

Since the default style sheet of rendering engines contains different property values for certain properties, the property values that are not declared by the web site developer might look different under various browsers. Because of the different line heights, margins, font sizes, and other properties, the overall appearance of a web site is typically not uniform. Although some of the default property values differ slightly only, developers cannot rely on the default styles of rendering engines.

■ **Tip** The inconsistencies between the CSS implementations of browsers can be minimized by overriding the CSS property values of the default style sheet of rendering engines. This technique is called *CSS reset*. One of the most well-known CSS reset files was written and maintained by Eric A. Meyer (Listing 5-78) and can be used on your web site for free [22].

Listing 5-78. A CSS Reset

```
/* http://meyerweb.com/eric/tools/css/reset/
   v2.0 | 20110126
   License: none (public domain)
*/
html, body, div, span, applet, object, iframe, h1, h2, h3, h4, h5, h6, p, blockquote, pre, a,
abbr, acronym, address, big, cite, code, del, dfn, em, img, ins, kbd, q, s, samp, small, strike,
strong, sub, sup, tt, var, b, u, i, center, dl, dt, dd, ol, ul, li, fieldset, form, label, legend,
table, caption, tbody, tfoot, thead, tr, th, td, article, aside, canvas, details, embed, figure,
figcaption, footer, header, hgroup, menu, nav, output, ruby, section, summary, time, mark, audio,
video {
  margin: 0;
  padding: 0;
  border: 0;
  font-size: 100%;
  font: inherit;
  vertical-align: baseline;
}
/* HTML5 display-role reset for older browsers */
article, aside, details, figcaption, figure, footer, header, hgroup, menu, nav, section {
  display: block;
}
```

```
body {
  line-height: 1;
}
ol, ul {
  list-style: none;
}
blockquote, q {
  quotes: none;
}
blockquote:before, blockquote:after, q:before, q:after {
  content: '';
  content: none;
}
table {
  border-collapse: collapse;
  border-spacing: 0;
}
```

XSL

Although it is not widely used and only a limited number of web developers are familiar with it, since 1999 a technology other than CSS can also be used for styling XML-serialized web documents [23]. *Extensible Stylesheet Language* (*XSL*) is a language family that can be used for styling, manipulation, and transformation of XML files. There are three XSL languages; however, only one of them is a style sheet language:

- *XSL Transformations* (XSLT): An XML style sheet language that can be used for transforming XML documents into other XML documents or other formats such as HTML or plain text. The original document remains unchanged, and a new document is created based on the existing one.

- *XSL Formatting Objects* (XSL-FO): An XML markup language applied for specifying the visual formatting of XML documents. Several software support XSL-FO that can provide various output formats, including plain text, PDF, PS, SVG, PCL, and MIF.

- *XML Path Language* (XPath): A non-XML query language that can also be used by XSLT.

XSLT Style Sheets

XSLT style sheets consist of one or more style sheet modules that are part of XML documents or form entire XML documents by themselves. The typical file extensions of XSLT are .xsl and .xslt. XSLT style sheets use the media type application/xslt+xml.

Namespaces

The XSLT namespace is http://www.w3.org/1999/XSL/Transform. However, further (reserved) namespaces are also recognized by XSLT processors [24], including the following:

- The standard function namespace, http://www.w3.org/2005/xpath-functions

- The XML namespace, http://www.w3.org/XML/1998/namespace

- The schema namespace, http://www.w3.org/2001/XMLSchema

- The schema instance namespace, http://www.w3.org/2001/XMLSchema-instance

Structure

The structure of XSLT style sheets looks like Listing 5-79.

Listing 5-79. XSLT Style Sheet Structure

```
<xsl:stylesheet version="1.0" xmlns:xsl="http://www.w3.org/1999/XSL/Transform">
  <xsl:import href="..."/>
  <xsl:include href="..."/>
  <xsl:strip-space elements="..."/>
  <xsl:preserve-space elements="..."/>
  <xsl:output method="..."/>
  <xsl:key name="..." match="..." use="..."/>
  <xsl:decimal-format name="..."/>
  <xsl:namespace-alias stylesheet-prefix="..." result-prefix="..."/>
  <xsl:attribute-set name="...">
    ...
  </xsl:attribute-set>
  <xsl:variable name="...">...</xsl:variable>
  <xsl:param name="...">...</xsl:param>
  <xsl:template match="...">
    ...
  </xsl:template>
  <xsl:template name="...">
    ...
  </xsl:template>
</xsl:stylesheet>
```

Note that the previous example shows all allowed element types; however, style sheets might contain zero or more of these elements.

Elements

XSLT style sheets are represented by the xsl:stylesheet or xsl:transform element in XML documents. An xsl:stylesheet element must have a version attribute. The xsl:stylesheet element may contain the following types of elements: xsl:import, xsl:include, xsl:strip-space, xsl:preserve-space, xsl:output, xsl:key, xsl:decimal-format, xsl:attribute-set, xsl:param, xsl:variable, xsl:namespace-alias, and xsl:template. Table 5-6 provides an overview of XSLT 1.0 elements.

Table 5-6. *Overview of XSLT Elements*

Element	Description
apply-imports	Applies a template rule from an imported style sheet
apply-templates	Applies a template rule to the current element or to the child nodes of the current element
attribute	Adds an attribute
attribute-set	Defines a named attribute set
call-template	Calls a named template
choose	Multiple conditional test (used with when and otherwise)
comment	Creates a comment node
copy	Creates a copy of the current node
copy-of	Creates a copy of the current node (with child nodes and attributes)
decimal-format	Defines the format to be used for converting numbers into strings with the format-number function
element	Creates an element node in the output document
fallback	Declares an alternate code for XSLT elements
for-each	Provides a loop within a node set
if	Provides a template to be applied in case of a specified condition
import	Imports an external style sheet (with lower precedence)
include	Includes an external style sheet (with same precedence)
key	Declares a key to be used with the key function
message	Writes a message (typically error message)
namespace-alias	Replaces a namespace in the style sheet to another one in the output
number	Determines the position of the current node
otherwise	Specifies a default action for the choose element
output	Defines the format of the output document
param	Adds a (local or global) parameter
preserve-space	Defines elements with preserved whitespace
processing-instruction	Writes a processing instruction to the output
sort	Sorts the output
strip-space	Defines the elements from which whitespace should be removed
stylesheet	Defines the root element of a style sheet
template	Applies a template when a specified node is matched
text	Writes text to the output
transform	Defines the root element of a style sheet
value-of	Extracts the value from the selected node
variable	Declares a (local or global) variable
when	Specifies an action for the choose element
with-param	Defines the parameter value to be passed into a template

The application of XSLT elements is straightforward and follows general XML authoring principles. Listing 5-80 shows an example.

Listing 5-80. XSLT Elements and Attributes Correspond to XML Guidelines

```
<xsl:param name="page-header-margin">20px</xsl:param>
```

Standard Attributes

Several standard attributes are associated with XSLT elements, including `version`, `exclude-result-prefixes`, `extension-element-prefixes`, `xpath-default-namespace`, `default-collation`, and `use-when`. To distinguish them from attributes defined by authors, they should be written with the namespace notation as `xsl:version`, `xsl:exclude-result-prefixes`, `xsl:extension-element-prefixes`, `xsl:xpath-default-namespace`, `xsl:default-collation`, and `xsl:use-when`.

Combining CSS and XSL

XSL can also be used as a bridge between complex XML-based documents and the CSS formatting model. Since CSS has no XML syntax, CSS properties become XML attributes in the XSL syntax. The main CSS object is `chunk`. Additional objects might also be required. Usually they are other `chunk` objects with functionality such as `anchor`, or further objects such as `switch`. For example, the CSS ruleset in Listing 5-81 can be written in XSL syntax, as shown in Listing 5-82.

Listing 5-81. CSS Ruleset Example to Be Converted into XSL

```
{
  font-size: 1.2em;
  text-indent: 1em;
}
```

Listing 5-82. The XSL Equivalent of Listing 5-81

```
<css:chunk
  font-size="1.2em"
  text-indent="1em">
```

CSS Preprocessing

Although CSS is a powerful language, it has limitations compared to traditional programming languages and especially object-oriented programming languages. For example, CSS does not support *mixins* such as classes that contain a combination of methods from other classes. Another desirable CSS feature would be selector inheritance, which is not supported by CSS. CSS has a set of selectors and pseudo-selectors that group rules that apply to them. *CSS preprocessors* extend CSS by providing additional mechanisms available in traditional programming languages, particularly object-oriented languages, but that are not available in CSS. Such extensions are very useful in the development of large, complex websites and web applications,[9] providing concise style sheets that are faster to write, and easier to maintain or update. One of the principles in CSS preprocessing is *DRY* (Don't Repeat Yourself (as opposed to *WET*, Write Everything Twice). The most popular CSS preprocessors are Sass, LESS, and Stylus.

---

[9]Since CSS is abstracted, there is an additional step to updates and changes, which is not always worthwhile in small web projects.

Sass

Sass (**S**yntactically **a**wesome **s**tylesheets) is a scripting language that is interpreted into Cascading Style Sheets. Sass has two syntaxes: the original syntax ("the indented syntax", typically with the file extension `.sass`), and the newer syntax, known as SCSS (with the extension `.scss`). The original syntax is similar to the syntax of Haml, applying indentation to separate code blocks and newline characters to separate rules. SCSS uses block formatting similar to that of CSS, braces to denote code blocks, and semicolons to separate lines within a block [25].

LESS

LESS is another CSS preprocessor to make CSS more maintainable, themable, and extendable [26]. LESS is influenced by Sass and the SCSS syntax. LESS is a nested metalanguage, meaning that any valid CSS code is also valid LESS code (sharing the same semantics). LESS provides programming mechanisms such as variables, nesting (selectors inside other selectors), mixins, operators (addition, subtraction, division, and multiplication of property values and colors to create complex relationships between properties), and functions (manipulation of values through JavaScript). A distinctive feature of LESS compared to other CSS preprocessors is that LESS allows real-time compilation via `less.js` within the browser. LESS can be used on the client-side or the server-side, or compiled into CSS. The file extension of LESS files is `.less`.

Stylus

The third most popular CSS preprocessor is Stylus, a dynamic style sheet language influenced by Sass and LESS [27]. Stylus runs on the Node platform [28]. In Stylus, colons, semicolons, commas, and braces are optional. Stylus supports variables, interpolation, mixins, arithmetics, type coercion, dynamic importing, conditionals, iteration, selector nesting, parent referencing, variable function calls, lexical scoping, functions, optional compression, character escaping, and robust error reporting. The typical file extension for Stylus files is `.styl`.

Summary

In this chapter, you learned how to separate presentation from content, which is imperative in web site standardization. You know the syntax of Cascading Style Sheets, the language used by virtually every web site. You have mastered the use of CSS selectors and can apply them in your daily work to control the appearance of exactly those elements or sets of elements that need to be styled. By now you know how to use the cascading feature of CSS with confidence, which makes it possible to create CSS files that are optimal in length and easy to maintain. You also know how to ensure backward-compatibility by applying a fallback mechanism and properties supported even by older browsers. You learned that XML files can be styled not only by CSS but also by using XSL.

In the next chapter, you will learn about the standardization issues of server-side scripting and web applications.

References

1. Dahlström E, Dengler P, Grasso A, Lilley C, McCormack C, Schepers D, Watt J, Ferraiolo J, Jun F, Jackson D (eds) (2011) Styling with CSS. In: SVG 1.1 (2nd Edn). World Wide Web Consortium. http://www.w3.org/TR/SVG/styling.html#StylingWithCSS. Accessed 20 October 2014

2. Chavchanidze G (2004) Formatting Mathematical Articles with Cascading Style Sheets. Andrea Razmadze Mathematical Institute. http://www.princexml.com/samples/math.pdf. Accessed 20 October 2014

3. Bos B, Carlisle D, Chavchanidze G, Ion PDF, Miller BR (2011) A MathML for CSS Profile. W3C Recommendation. World Wide Web Consortium. http://www.w3.org/TR/mathml-for-css/. Accessed 20 October 2014

4. Grant M (ed) (2013) CSS Print Profile. World Wide Web Consortium.
    http://www.w3.org/TR/css-print/. Accessed 20 October 2014

5. Hayes S, Adams G, Çelik T, Lie HW (2014) CSS TV Profile 1.0. World Wide Web
    Consortium. http://www.w3.org/TR/css-tv. Accessed 20 October 2014

6. Bos B (ed) (2014) CSS Mobile Profile 2.0. World Wide Web Consortium.
    http://www.w3.org/TR/css-mobile/. Accessed 20 October 2014

7. Lie HW, Bos B (2008) Cascading Style Sheets, level 1. W3C Recommendation (revised
    version). World Wide Web Consortium. http://www.w3.org/TR/CSS1/. Accessed
    20 October 2014

8. Bos B, Çelik T, Hickson I, Lie HW (eds) (2011) Cascading Style Sheets Level 2 Revision 1
    (CSS 2.1) W3C Recommendation. World Wide Web Consortium.
    http://www.w3.org/TR/CSS21/. Accessed 20 October 2014

9. Meyer EA, Bos B (eds) (2001) Module Descriptions and Related Information. In:
    Introduction to CSS3. W3C Working Draft. World Wide Web Consortium.
    http://www.w3.org/TR/css3-roadmap/#module. Accessed 09 October 2010

10. Çelik T, Lilley C, Baron LD, Pemberton S, Pettit B (eds) (2011) CSS Color Module Level 3.
    W3C Recommendation. World Wide Web Consortium.
    http://www.w3.org/TR/css3-color/. Accessed 20 October 2014

11. Etemad EJ (ed) (2014) CSS Namespaces Module Level 3. W3C Recommendation. World
    Wide Web Consortium. http://www.w3.org/TR/css3-namespace/.
    Accessed 20 October 2014

12. Çelik T, Etemad EJ, Glazman D, Hickson I, Linss P, Williams J (eds) (2011) Selectors Level 3.
    W3C Recommendation. http://www.w3.org/TR/selectors/. Accessed 20 October 2014

13. Rivoal F (ed) (2012) Media Queries. W3C Recommendation.
    http://www.w3.org/TR/css3-mediaqueries/. Accessed 20 October 2014

14. Bos B, Çelik T, Hickson I, Lie HW (eds) (2011) Grammar of CSS 2.1. In: Cascading Style
    Sheets Level 2 Revision 1 (CSS 2.1) Specification. W3C Recommendation. World Wide Web
    Consortium. http://www.w3.org/TR/CSS21/grammar.html. Accessed 20 October 2014

15. Bos B, Çelik T, Hickson I, Lie HW (eds) (2011) Selector syntax. In: Cascading Style Sheets
    Level 2 Revision 1 (CSS 2.1) Specification. W3C Recommendation. World Wide Web
    Consortium. http://www.w3.org/TR/CSS21/selector.html#selector-syntax.
    Accessed 20 October 2014

16. Çelik T, Etemad EJ (eds) (2010) Syntax and Parsing. In: CSS Style Attributes. World Wide
    Web Consortium. http://www.w3.org/TR/2010/CR-css-style-attr-20101012/#syntax.
    Accessed 20 October 2014

17. Clark J, Pieters S, Thompson HS (eds) (2010) Associating Style Sheets with XML
    documents 1.0 (Second Edition). W3C Recommendation. World Wide Web Consortium.
    http://www.w3.org/TR/xml-stylesheet/. Accessed 20 October 2014

18. Lie HW (ed) (2005) Cascading. In: CSS3 module: Cascading and inheritance.
    W3C Working Draft. World Wide Web Consortium.
    http://www.w3.org/TR/2005/WD-css3-cascade-20051215/#cascading.
    Accessed 20 October 2014

19. Glazman D, Çelik T, Hickson I, Linss P, Williams J (eds) (2001) Calculating a selector's specificity. In: Selectors. World Wide Web Consortium. http://www.w3.org/TR/2001/CR-css3-selectors-20011113/#specificity. Accessed 20 October 2014

20. Bos B, Çelik T, Hickson I, Lie HW (2011) Box model. In: Cascading Style Sheets Level 2 Revision 1 (CSS 2.1) Specification. W3C Recommendation. World Wide Web Consortium. http://www.w3.org/TR/CSS21/box.html. Accessed 20 October 2014

21. Silver L (2006) Fix the Box Instead of Thinking Outside It. In: CSS Enhancements in Internet Explorer 6. Microsoft Corporation. http://msdn.microsoft.com/en-us/library/bb250395.aspx#cssenhancements_topic3. Accessed 20 October 2014

22. Meyer EA, Meyer KS (2014) CSS Tools: Reset CSS. Eric A. Meyer, Kathryn S. Meyer. http://meyerweb.com/eric/tools/css/reset/. Accessed 20 October 2014

23. Clark J (ed) (1999) XSL Transformations (XSLT) Version 1.0 W3C Recommendation. World Wide Web Consortium. http://www.w3.org/TR/xslt. Accessed 20 October 2014

24. Kay M (ed) (2007) XSL Transformations (XSLT) Version 2.0. W3C Recommendation. World Wide Web Consortium. http://www.w3.org/TR/xslt20/. Accessed 20 October 2014

25. Catlin H, Weizenbaum N, Eppstein C (2014) Sass: Syntactically Awesome Style Sheets. http://sass-lang.com/. Accessed 20 October 2014

26. Sellier A, Schlinkert J, Page L, Bointon M, Jurčovčová M, Dean M, Mikhailov M (2014) Getting started | Less.js. http://lesscss.org/. Accessed 20 October 2014

27. LearnBoost (2014) Stylus—expressive, robust, feature-rich CSS preprocessor. http://learnboost.github.io/stylus/. Accessed 20 October 2014

28. Joyent (2014) Node.js. http://nodejs.org/. Accessed 20 October 2014

CHAPTER 6

■ ■ ■

Scripting and Applications

Modern web sites are meant to be dynamic. Very few web sites are based purely on document structure and style sheets. Web site sections often behave differently or react to user input. While small programs can run in the browser, complex functions are usually executed on the web server. Most dynamic sites are powered by databases that are handled by server-side scripts. Since server-side languages frequently use variables and reuse large code blocks, the validity of the generated code relies on the code quality of the development framework, the Content Management System, or the templates, often resulting in incorrect markup and styles. Even so, web designers can modify the code so that the server-side system will generate valid, error-free markup and style sheets. This can be challenging if the framework or CMS core uses invalid syntax and multiplies incorrect code blocks throughout the site.

In this chapter, you will learn why the standardization of dynamic content is more challenging than that of static pages. Becoming familiar with the basic syntax of the most widely used client-side and server-side scripting languages is crucial, because small programs written in these languages are often embedded into the markup. The inline scripts might have an impact on the standards compliance of a whole web page. You will also learn how to provide alternate content for scripts. Although the standard compliance of the markup generated on the server side using web programming languages, frameworks, and development platforms to provide web applications is constantly improving, the generated code is often incorrect. Many of these development technologies are not standardized but are implemented worldwide and considered *de facto* standards. Many technologies rely on a number of other technologies and standards. This chapter provides a quick overview of some of the most common scripting and application development technologies that often determine the standard compliance of dynamic web sites.

Client-Server Architectures

The distributed application structure that divides tasks and/or workloads between resource or service providers, called *servers*, and service requesters, called *clients*, is known as the *client-server model*. Clients and servers communicate over the Web to exchange data and perform tasks.

The *client-server* architecture represents relationships between cooperating programs in a web application. For example, a contact form can be evaluated on the client side and processed on the server side.

The general syntax and grammar conventions of the most popular client-side and server-side scripting and programming languages, technologies, and frameworks are discussed in the following sections. Note that a detailed description of scripts and applications is beyond the scope of the book.

Scripting and Standards Implementation

A *script* is program code that does not require preprocessing (such as compiling) before execution [1]. Small dynamic components of web documents such as the current date or interactive content and behavior can be added by *scripting languages*. Modifications can be performed on the web page content without reloading the new version of the page. Content can be added to or sent from a web page with *Asynchronous JavaScript and XML* (*Ajax*) without reloading the entire updated page.

Static web pages have constant content that is either valid or not, but can be relatively easily validated and, if necessary, updated to make the markup and styles standard-compliant. Server-side scripting, on the other hand, provides *content generated on the fly*. The source code of the program that generates the markup on the server-side is quite complex to check for markup errors. Server-side scripts often rely on hard-coded codeblocks that cannot be easily modified. Validating and standardizing large web sites with hundreds of thousands of web pages relying on incorrect code can be practically infeasible.

The major problem with web sites relying on data stored in databases and processed by server-side scripts is the higher complexity and the lack of full control. Templates used by Content Management Systems are not always standards-compliant which is distributed on all sites that apply the same templates. Moreover, a single problem of either the script or the database can result in an error message instead of the web page content (Figure 6-1).

Figure 6-1. *Content replaced by error message*

There is a huge difference between small programs running on web pages and programs created for generating web pages. Server-side scripting languages are powerful and provide features that cannot be achieved by static content. There is nothing wrong with small contact forms, for example. However, server-side scripts should be used only where really needed. A huge advantage of server-side scripts is that they can provide the same headers, footers, and so on, as templates for identical markup fragments (header, sidebar, main area, footer, etc.) throughout the web site that can be easily maintained from a single location (in contrast to static web pages). However, the application of server-side scripting should be minimized on web sites that do not rely on databases and dynamically generated content, such as small-scale, brochure-style web sites. Undoubtedly, a large share of invalid markup code on the Web is generated by server-side scripting languages. In many cases, additional practices are required to obtain valid markup, such as to handle the ampersand characters used as an argument separator in URLs of PHP sessions [2]

Client-Side Development

Client-side development refers to those web programs that run on the client side, generally a web browser, instead of being executed on the server side (on a web server). Client-side programs can be used to provide different and changing content on a web page, depending on user input and other variables. For example, "dynamic" greetings can be added to a web page according to the current time of day.

Ajax

Ajax is an acronym for *Asynchronous JavaScript and XML*. It is not a programming language but a group of web technologies that can be used together, such as HTML, CSS, DOM, JavaScript, XML, and XSLT. Ajax can be used on the client side to create interactive web applications. Web site applications empowered with Ajax can send data to and retrieve data from servers asynchronously (which is the reason for the name). Ajax is suitable for avoiding full-page reloads when exchanging data asynchronously. This approach ensures that the display and behavior of the current page won't be affected. Despite the name, Ajax does not require XML; the JavaScript Object Notation (JSON), a lightweight text-based open standard [3], is often used instead. The requests are not necessarily asynchronous either. Ajax usually retrieves data using the XMLHttpRequest object [4]. The DOM is used along with JavaScript to dynamically display information and allow the user to interact with the information presented. The data interchanged using Ajax can be manipulated using XSLT.

■ **Note**   Modern browsers have a built-in XMLHttpRequest object. Before IE7, Internet Explorer provided an object called ActiveXObject.

To demonstrate Ajax, the code in Listing 6-1 creates a link that will replace the content of a div element with the content of a text file. The Document Object Model is used to manipulate the object. The XMLHTTPRequest object is used to make the HTTP request load the file ajaxdemo.txt and display its content.

Listing 6-1. Ajax Demonstration

```
<script type="text/javascript">
  var http = false;
  if (navigator.appName == "Microsoft Internet Explorer") {
    http = new ActiveXObject("Microsoft.XMLHTTP");
    } else {
    http = new XMLHttpRequest();
  }

  function replace() {
    http.open("GET", "ajaxdemo.txt", true);
    http.onreadystatechange=function() {
      if (http.readyState == 4) {
        document.getElementById('repdiv').innerHTML = http.responseText;
      }
    }
    http.send(null);
  }
</script>
```

In the document body, we need a function call and a div with the text to replace (Listing 6-2).

Listing 6-2. The Function Call and the div with the Original Text

```
<p>
  <a href="javascript:replace()">Click here to replace text</a>
</p>

<div id="repdiv">
  Original text in the markup
</div>
```

The http.open() argument is the asynchronous argument that sends the request in the background.

Flex

Adobe Flex is a software development kit (SDK) for cross-platform, rich Internet applications based on the Adobe Flash technology [5]. The user interface layout and behavior are described by a declarative XML-based language, MXML, while the client logic is created by using the ActionScript 3.0 programming language.

■ **Note**   ActionScript is an object-oriented language and a dialect of ECMAScript. Consequently, ActionScript is a superset of the syntax and semantics of JavaScript. Most frequently, ActionScript is implemented in SWF files.

As an example, let's create a simple RSS news feed reader! First, we need to write a common XML declaration, followed by an MXML declaration (Listing 6-3).

Listing 6-3. The XML and MXML Declaration

```
<?xml version="1.0" ?>
<mx:Application xmlns:mx="http://www.macromedia.com/2003/mxml">

</mx:Application>
```

Within the mx:Application, our HTTPService should be defined, and the custom controls (DataGrid, TextArea, and Button) are prepared for the panel (Listing 6-4).

Listing 6-4. The HTTPService and the Panel for the Custom Controls

```
<mx:Application xmlns:mx="http://www.macromedia.com/2003/mxml">
  <mx:HTTPService id="httpRSS" url="http://www.example.com/rss/" resultFormat="object" />
  <mx:Panel id="reader" title="Simple RSS Reader" width="600">
  </mx:Panel>
</mx:Application
```

Now it is time to define the DataGrid. The horizontal dimension of the panel should be set by the width parameter. Each item tag of the RSS file is bound to a DataGrid row by the dataProvider attribute. Next we create an event handler to display the contents of the description tags inside the RSS items selected by the user. The entries.selectedIndex variable is used to determine which item was clicked. The description of the corresponding item is retrieved by httpRSS.result.rss.channel.item[entries.selectedIndex].description. The value of the RSS description is assigned to the htmlText property of the TextArea (Listing 6-5).

Listing 6-5. Creating the DataGrid for the RSS Reader

```
<mx:DataGrid id="entries" width="{reader.width-15}"↵
 dataProvider="{httpRSS.result.rss.channel.item}"↵
  cellPress=↵
 "{body.htmlText=httpRSS.result.rss.channel.item[entries.selectedIndex].description}">
  <mx:columns>
    <mx:Array>
      <mx:DataGridColumn columnName="title" headerText="Title" />
      <mx:DataGridColumn columnName="pubDate" headerText="Date" />
    </mx:Array>
  </mx:columns>
</mx:DataGrid>
```

Finally, a TextArea needs to be created using the mx:TextArea tag, and a button needs to be created with a click event handler to call the send() method on the HTTPService object (Listing 6-6).

Listing 6-6. The TextArea and the Button

```
<mx:TextArea id="body" editable="false" width="{reader.width-15}" height="400" />
<mx:Button label="Load
RSS channel items" click="{httpRSS.send()}" />
```

HTML5 APIs

HTML5 provides much more than just new structuring elements. HTML5 supports many features that were available originally through plug-ins or sophisticated code only [6]. Beyond markup elements and attributes, HTML5 specifies Application Programming Interfaces (APIs) as well [7]. A native drawing API, native sockets, and so on, eliminate the problems associated with plug-ins.

The HTML5 APIs have separate specifications under W3C standardization. Some of the most frequently used HTML5 APIs are discussed in the following sections.

The HTML5 Canvas API

The canvas markup element was introduced with HTML5, and the second level of the HTML Canvas 2D Context [8] was published on December 17, 2012. The HTML5 canvas allows dynamic, scriptable rendering of 2D shapes and bitmap images on a drawing surface.

■ **Note**   The HTML5 canvas has no built-in scene graph, which is a general data structure to arrange the logical (and often spatial) representation of a graphical scene. The scene graph is commonly used by vector-based graphical systems, including SVG. In SVG, all drawn shapes are stored as an object in the scene graph or the DOM and then rendered as bitmap graphics. Consequently, if the SVG object attributes are changed, the browser can automatically rerender the scene, which is not possible on the canvas. From this point of view, SVG graphics are more advanced than shapes on the HTML5 canvas.

In Listing 6-7, you can see how to draw a simple triangle on the HTML5 canvas. First, a custom-size canvas is declared with alternate textual content for older browsers that do not support the HTML5 canvas. Second, a `script` element specifies two variables to shorten the code, a two-dimensional canvas, an emerald fill color, the coordinates of the three corners of a triangle, and the triangle with the fill color.

Listing 6-7. Drawing on the HTML5 Canvas

```
<canvas id="samplecanvas" width="200" height="200">
  A triangle (requires HTML5 Canvas support)
</canvas>
<script>
  var mycanvas = document.getElementById("samplecanvas"),
  context2d = mycanvas.getContext("2d");
  context2d.fillStyle = "#2ad3a8";
  context2d.beginPath();
  context2d.moveTo(100, 0);
  context2d.lineTo(0, 55);
  context2d.lineTo(165, 100);
  context2d.fill();
</script>
```

The HTML5 canvas is supported by IE9+, Firefox 3.0+, Chrome 1.0+, Safari 3.0+, and Opera 9.5+.

The HTML5 File and DnD APIs

The HTML5 File API provides easy-to-use file control in web browsers. The File API is being standardized by the World Wide Web Consortium [9]. The Drag & Drop (DnD) API specification defines an event-based mechanism that adds additional markup for declaring elements to be draggable on web pages. The DnD API is being developed by the Web Hypertext Application Technology Working Group [10].

The code in Listing 6-8 creates an interface to choose files either through browsing the directories on your computer or by using drag and drop. The name, size, and MIME type of the selected files will be retrieved using the HTML5 File API.

Listing 6-8. File API Demonstration

```
<h1>Choose file(s)</h1>
<p>
  <input id="upload" type="file" multiple="multiple">
</p>
<div id="drop">
  You can also drag and drop your files here
</div>
<h1>Retrieved file information</h1>
<ul id="fileList">
  <li class="no-items">&lt;no files uploaded yet&gt;</li>
</ul>
<script>
  (function () {
    var filesUpload = document.getElementById("upload"),
    dropArea = document.getElementById("drop"),
    fileList = document.getElementById("fileList");
    function fileTransfer (files) {
```

```
      var li,
      file,
      fileInfo;
      fileList.innerHTML = "";
      for (var i = 0, fl = files.length; i < fl; i++) {
        li = document.createElement("li");
        file = files[i];
        fileInfo = file.name; // Name
        fileInfo += " (" + file.type + "), "; // Type
        fileInfo += file.size + " bytes"; // Size
        li.innerHTML = fileInfo;
        fileList.appendChild(li);
      };
    };
      filesUpload.onchange = function () {
        fileTransfer(this.files);
      };
      dropArea.ondragenter = function () {
        return false;
      };
      dropArea.ondragover = function () {
        return false;
      };
      dropArea.ondrop = function (evt) {
        fileTransfer(evt.dataTransfer.files);
        return false;
      };
  })();
</script>
```

The division representing the drop area in the previous example (`<div id="drop">`) should be styled either with a border or with a background color to make it visible (Listing 6-9).

Listing 6-9. CSS Ruleset for the Previous Example

```
#drop {
  border: 2px dashed #f00;
  padding: 10px;
}
```

Next, create a very simple drag-and-drop example with five words that can be dragged from one division to another and back. First, declare the `div` items and make them draggable with the `draggable` attribute. Then, put them into a container `div` and create the second `div` (the target) (Listing 6-10).

Listing 6-10. The Markup for the DnD Example

```
<section>
  <header>
    <h3>Drag the word "DnD" to the other box and back</h3>
  </header>
  <div id="leftDiv" ondragover="dragOver(event)" ondrop="dragDrop(event)">
   <div id="word1" class="dragbox" draggable="true" ondragstart="return
   dragDefine(event)" ondragend="dragEnd(event)">My</div>
   <div id="word2" class="dragbox" draggable="true" ondragstart="return
   dragDefine(event)" ondragend="dragEnd(event)">dog</div>
   <div id="word3" class="dragbox" draggable="true" ondragstart="return
   dragDefine(event)" ondragend="dragEnd(event)">is</div>
   <div id="word4" class="dragbox" draggable="true" ondragstart="return
   dragDefine(event)" ondragend="dragEnd(event)">called</div>
   <div id="word5" class="dragbox" draggable="true" ondragstart="return
   dragDefine(event)" ondragend="dragEnd(event)">Bobby</div>
</div>
  <div id="rightDiv" ondragover="return dragOver(event)" ondrop="dragDropped(event)"></div>
</section>
```

In the document head, declare a `script` element, and create the functions to be called (Listing 6-11) when the following happens:

- The item starts to be dragged

- The item being dragged is over another item

- The drag is complete

- The item being dragged is dropped

Listing 6-11. The Functions for Handling Drag and Drop

```
<script>
  function dragStarted(evt) {
    evt.dataTransfer.effectAllowed = 'move';
    evt.dataTransfer.setData("text/plain", evt.target.getAttribute('id'));
    evt.dataTransfer.setDragImage(evt.target, 0, 0);
  return true;
}

function dragOver(evt) {
  evt.preventDefault();
}

function dragEnded(evt) {
  return true;
}
```

```
function dragDropped(evt) {
  var idDrag = evt.dataTransfer.getData("Text");
  evt.target.appendChild(document.getElementById(idDrag));
  evt.preventDefault();
}
</script>
```

Finally, declare styles, including the layout and colors for the boxes, in the document head or an external file (Listing 6-12).

Listing 6-12. The Styles for the Boxes

```
body {
  width: 800px;
  margin: 100px auto;
}

#leftDiv, #rightDiv {
  float: left;
  width: 200px;
  height: 100px;
  margin: 50px;
  background-color: #bbdeee;
  border: 1px solid #000;
}

.word {
  width: 60px;
  height: 20px;
  margin: 5px;
  text-align: center;
  font-weight: bold;
  background-color: #ff6;
  display: inline-block;
  cursor: move;
}
```

The File API is supported by Firefox 3.6+, IE10+, Safari 6+, Chrome 6.0+, and Opera 11.5+. The Drag & Drop API is supported by Firefox 3.5+, Chrome 21+, Opera 12+, and IE9+.

The HTML5 Forms API

HTML5 introduced new attributes for the input element (autocomplete, autofocus, form, formaction, formenctype, formmethod, formnovalidate, formtarget, height, list, max, min, multiple, pattern, placeholder, required, step, and width) and new attribute values for the type attribute of the input element (including email, url, number, range), search, color, and date pickers (date, month, week, time, datetime, and datetime-local), as well as form validation [11].

As an example, create an (X)HTML5 form for a registration page of a web site (Listing 6-13).

Listing 6-13. A Registration Form

```
<form action="newaccount.php" method="post">
  <fieldset title="Create account">
    <p>
      <label for="mailadd">E-mail address:</label>
      <input id="mailadd" type="email" required="required" name="mail"
       placeholder="email@example.com" />
    </p>
    <p>
      <label for="passwd1">Password:</label>
      <input id="passwd1" type="password" required="required" name="pwd" />
    </p>
    <p>
      <label for="passwd2">Confirm password:</label>
      <input id="passwd2" type="password" required="required" name="pwd2" />
    </p>
    <p>
      <label for="website">Website:</label>
      <input type="url" name="website" placeholder="http://www.example.com" />
    </p>
    <p>
      <label for="number">Number:</label>
      <input type="number" name="number" min="0" max="10" placeholder="0-10" />
    </p>
    <p>
      <label for="range">Range:</label>
      <input type="range" name="range" min="0" max="10" step="2" />
    </p>
    <p>
      <input type="submit" value="Create account" />
    </p>
  </fieldset>
</form>
```

The HTML5 Geolocation API

The Geolocation API provides an interface to retrieve information on the geographical location for a client-side device. In other words, it can be used in web browsers to find the current position of the user. The location of the user is not shared until the user confirms the request. The Geolocation API became a W3C Recommendation in 2013 [12].

Listing 6-14 shows an example for the application of the Geolocation API. In the example, the setOnLoadCallback function is used to create a map. The if-then construct is used to check whether the Geolocation API is supported, get the current position, and, in case it is successfully retrieved, mark it on the map. If necessary, we inform the user to accept the Geolocation request, or the location cannot be determined. The location is hard-coded to Garden Island in Port Adelaide, Australia, which is used until the user enables geolocation. In the else branch, a nice location is set for users that use a browser without geolocation support.

Listing 6-14. Retrieving the Location of the User

```
<div id="map">
</div>
<script src="http://www.google.com/jsapi?key=ABQIAAAAlJFc1lrstqhgTl3ZYo38bBQcfCcww1WgMTx↵
EFsdaTsnOXOVOUhTplLhHcmgnaYOu87hQyd-n-kiOqQ">
</script>
<script>
  (function () {
    google.load("maps", "2");
    google.setOnLoadCallback(function () {
      var map = new google.maps.Map2(document.getElementById("map")),
      markerText = "<h2>You are here</h2><p>This is your current position</p>",
      markOutLocation = function (lat, long) {
        var latLong = new google.maps.LatLng(lat, long),
        marker = new google.maps.Marker(latLong);
        map.setCenter(latLong, 15);
        map.addOverlay(marker);
        marker.openInfoWindow(markerText);
        google.maps.Event.addListener(marker, "click", function () {
          marker.openInfoWindow(markerText);
        });
      };
      map.setUIToDefault();
      if (navigator.geolocation) {
        navigator.geolocation.getCurrentPosition(function (position) {
          markOutLocation(position.coords.latitude, position.coords.longitude);
        },
        function () {
          markerText = "<p>You should accept the Geolocation request, otherwise your↵
            position cannot be determined.</p>";
          markOutLocation(59.3325215, 18.0643818);  // Garden Island, Port Adelaide, Australia
        });
      }
      else {
        markerText = "<p>Geolocation is not supported. Welcome to my favourite location.</p>";
        markOutLocation(-34.928621, 138.599959);  // Rundle Mall, Adelaide, Australia
      }
    });
  })();
</script>
```

■ **Tip** The position is approximate only. In the previous example, we get a marker that does not necessarily mark the exact location of the user. More sophisticated interfaces, such the "Location-Aware Browsing" test page of Firefox [13], provide a semitransparent circle above the map rather than a marker pointing to an exact position.

The HTML5 Geolocation API is supported by IE9+, Firefox 3.5+, Chrome 5.0+, Opera 10.6+, and Safari 5+.

The HTML5 Web Storage API

Web Storage is an API for persistent data storage of key-value pair data (similar to cookies) in browsers (`sessionStorage`) and window-local storage saved between sessions (`localStorage`). The Web Storage API became a W3C Recommendation in 2013 [14].

Table 6-1 summarizes the methods of `localStorage` and `sessionStorage`.

Table 6-1. *Web Storage Methods*

Method with Parameters	Description
setItem(string name, string value)	Adds or updates a value in the store
getItem(string name)	Retrieves a named value from the stored name-value pairs
removeItem(string name)	Removes a named value from the stored name-value pairs
length	Number of values stored
key(long index)	Name of the key at the index
clear()	Clears the store

As an example, create two input fields for the local storage of name-value pairs, as well as a push button to let the user set the items entered (Listing 6-15). Display the name-value pairs in a table. Create a text field where the user can add the item to remove from the stored pairs after clicking the associated button. Add a push button that can be used to clear the stored items. Provide another text field where the item name can be typed to retrieve its value. Since the table is created by the `displayItems` function, that function should be loaded by the `onload` attribute on the body element as `<body onload="displayItems()">`.

Listing 6-15. A `localStorage` Example

```
<form name="lsform">
  <fieldset title="WebStorage">
    <legend>Local storage of name-value pairs</legend>
    <p>
      <label>Value:</label>
      <input name="data">
    </p>
    <p>
      <label>Name:</label>
      <input name="name">
    </p>
    <p>
      <input type="button" value="Set item" onclick="setTheItem()">
    </p>
    <table id="pairs"></table>
    <p>
    Enter name to remove item:
      <input name="remove">
      <input type="button" value="Remove item" onclick="removeTheItem()">
      <input type="button" value="Clear items" onclick="clearItems()">
    </p>
```

```
    <p>
      Enter name to retrieve value:
      <input name="retrieve">
      <input type="button" value="Get value" onclick="getTheItem()">
    </p>
    <script type="text/javascript">
      function setTheItem() {
        var name = document.forms.lsform.name.value;
        var data = document.forms.lsform.data.value;
        localStorage.setItem(name, data);
        displayItems();
      }
      function getTheItem() {
        var name = document.forms.lsform.retrieve.value;
        window.alert('The value associated with the name ' + name + ' is ' +↵
         localStorage.getItem(name));
        displayItems();
      }
      function removeTheItem() {
        var name = document.forms.lsform.remove.value;
        document.forms.lsform.data.value = localStorage.removeItem(name);
        displayItems();
      }
      function clearItems() {
        localStorage.clear();
        displayItems();
      }
      function displayItems() {
        var key = "";
        var pairs = "<tr><th>Name</th><th>Value</th></tr>\n";
        var i = 0;
        for (i = 0; i <= localStorage.length-1; i++) {
          key = localStorage.key(i);
          pairs += "<tr><td>" + key + "</td>\n<td>" + localStorage.getItem(key) +↵
           "</td></tr>\n";
        }
        if (pairs == "<tr><th>Name</th><th>Value</th></tr>\n") {
          pairs += "<tr><td><em>&lt;not set&gt;</em></td>\n<td><em>&lt;not↵
          set&gt;</em></td></tr>\n";
        }
        document.getElementById('pairs').innerHTML = pairs;
      }
    </script>
  </fieldset>
</form>
```

The Web Storage API is supported by IE 8+, Firefox 3.5+, Google Chrome 4+ (sessionStorage from 5+), Safari 4+, and Opera 10.50+.

The HTML5 Web Workers API

Web Workers is an API that can be used to execute scripts in the background independent from any user interface scripts. Consequently, the user interface is not affected, and all browser tasks are performed without any delay.

The "worker" in Web Workers refers to a script stored in an external file, which is loaded and executed in the background (Listing 6-16).

Listing 6-16. Creating a "Worker"

```
new Worker("worker.js");
```

While complex JavaScript codes might hang your browser (such as giving an "unresponsive script" warning), the Web Workers API makes it possible to avoid user interruption, while the browser performs tasks such as event handling, DOM manipulations, queries, and processes.

■ **Note**   Since JavaScript was originally designed to run in a single-threaded environment—that is, multiple scripts cannot be run simultaneously—Web Workers can be considered as an API that brings threading to JavaScript.

In our example, we create a "worker" that counts up from 0 to 10,000 in the background. First, two push buttons are needed in the document body to start and stop counting (two input elements with unique identifiers), and a paragraph is needed with an identifier (`<p id="result">`) where the result will be displayed (Listing 6-17).

Listing 6-17. Markup of a Web Worker Example

```html
<h1>Start/Stop the Worker</h1>
<p>
  <input id="start" type="button" value="Start">
  <input id="stop" type="button" value="Stop">
</p>
<h1>The results</h1>
<p id="result">Click Start to start the Worker</p>
<script>
  (function () {
    function createWorker () {
      worker = new Worker("webworker.js");
    }
    document.getElementById("start").onclick = function () {
      createWorker();
      worker.postMessage(0);  // initial value
      worker.onmessage = function (evt) {
        document.getElementById("result").innerHTML = evt.data;
      };
      worker.onerror = function (evt) {
        document.getElementById("result").innerHTML = "Error";
      };
    };
```

```
    document.getElementById("stop").onclick = function () {
      if (worker) {
        worker.terminate();
      }
    };
  })();
</script>
```

We also need a function for the Start button, an error event handler, and a function for the Stop button. The function that actually performs the counting takes place in an external `.js` file (Listing 6-18).

Listing 6-18. The webworker.js File

```
onmessage = function (evt) {
  for (var i = evt.data, t = 10000; i < t; i++) {
    postMessage(i);
  };
};
```

The Web Workers API is supported by IE10+, Firefox 3.5+, Chrome 5.0+, Safari 4.0+, and Opera 10.6+.

The HTML5 WebSocket API

The WebSocket API can be used for bidirectional, full-duplex communication over a Transmission Control Protocol (TCP) socket.

The WebSocket API is being standardized by the World Wide Web Consortium [15].

After building a WebSocket connection with the web server, data can be retrieved from the server using the `onmessage` event handler and can be sent from the client to the server by the `send()` method.

A new `WebSocket` object can be created as shown in Listing 6-19.

Listing 6-19. A New WebSocket Object

```
var Socket = new WebSocket(http://example.com/ws/);
```

Optionally, the protocol can also be specified after the URI.

The WebSocket object has two read-only attributes: `Socket.readyState` and `Socket.bufferedAmount`. The first one represents the connection state (0 is no connection yet, 1 is connection has been built, 2 is closing handshake, 3 is connection closed or cannot be established). The second attribute gives the number of bytes queued using the `send()` method.

The WebSocket API supports four events: `open` (socket connection established), `message` (client receives data from server), `error` (error in communication), and `close` (the connection is closed). They can be handled by the `Socket.onopen`, `Socket.onmessage`, `Socket.onerror`, and `Socket.onclose` event handlers, respectively.

The two methods of WebSocket are `Socket.send()` (the `send()` method transmits data through the connection), and `Socket.close()` (the `close()` method is used to terminate the existing connection).

As an example, we create a bidirectional TCP socket between the client and the server in the document head (Listing 6-20).

Listing 6-20. Creating a WebSocket

```
<script type="text/javascript">
  function myWS() {
    if ("WebSocket" in window) {
      alert("WebSocket is supported by your Browser!");
      var ws = new WebSocket("ws://localhost:9998/echo");
      ws.onopen = function() {
        ws.send("Message to send");
        alert("Message sent...");
      };
      ws.onmessage = function (evt) {
        var received_msg = evt.data;
        alert("Message received...");
      };
      ws.onclose = function() {
        alert("Connection closed...");
      };
    }
    else {
      alert("WebSocket is not supported by your browser!");
    }
  }
</script>
```

In the document body, the myWS() function should be called to start the WebSocket (Listing 6-21).

Listing 6-21. An Anchor to Start the WebSocket

```
<p>
  <a href="javascript:myWS()">Start WebSocket</a>
</p>
```

The client program is now ready, but we also need a server with WebSocket support to test it. For example, pywebsocket, which can be used as a WebSocket stand-alone server and a WebSocket extension for Apache HTTP servers, is suitable for testing [16].

After the HTTP handshake, the TCP socket is ready for use, and the connection is live; both the server and the client can send data.

On the client side, the WebSocket API is supported by Firefox 4+, Google Chrome 4+, Safari 5+, and Opera 11+.

Offline Web Applications

The offline web application feature in HTML5 allows online applications to work without interruption even when the Internet connection is not available. For example, users can compose a message in their webmail client when they cannot find a Wi-Fi hotspot.

Since the browser has no access to web site files when it is offline, the first step is to specify the required resources (a simple list of fundamental files) for caching in a file called offline.manifest (Listing 6-22).

Listing 6-22. An `offline.manifest` File

```
CACHE MANIFEST
index.html
styles.css
main.js
```

This file should be provided as the attribute value of the `manifest` attribute on the `html` element (Listing 6-23). The file should be served with the MIME type `text/cache-manifest`.

Listing 6-23. Using the Manifest File

```
<html manifest="offline.manifest">
```

Users will be requested to allow caching on their computer.

The online/offline state of the browser can be determined by JavaScript using `navigator.onLine`.

When the browser is offline, the data can be easily stored locally using the Web Storage API discussed earlier, that is, the `sessionStorage` to retrieve data during a session or the `localStorage` to retain values for longer periods.

Offline web applications are supported by Firefox 3.5+, Chrome 1.0+, Safari 4.0+, and Opera 10.6+.

Java Applets

Java is an object-oriented, structured, imperative, cross-platform programming language. Java was originally developed by Sun Microsystems, which is now owned by Oracle Corporation. Java can be used in a variety of contexts on the client side as well as the server side, including applets, servlets, Swing applications, and JavaServer Pages (JSP).

Java applets are small applications for performing a specific task and are provided on web sites in a format called Java bytecode, which can be executed by the Java Virtual Machine (JVM). Although Java applets can be substituted by alternate technologies such as Flash, Curl, or Microsoft Silverlight, they are still present on the Web.

A Java applet should be provided by two `object` elements and self-closing parameters. The inner object is used by Trident and the outer object by Gecko and other rendering engines. Listing 6-24 shows an example.

Listing 6-24. Java Applet Embedding with `object`

```
<object classid="java:bookflip.class"
 type="application/x-java-applet"
 archive="bookflip.jar"
 height="120" width="120">
  <param name="res" value="1" />
  <param name="image1" value="01.jpg" />
  <param name="link1" value="NO" />
  <param name="flip1" value="0" />
  <param name="image2" value="02.jpg" />
  <param name="link2" value="NO" />
  <param name="flip2" value="0" />
  <param name="speed" value="4" />
  <object classid="clsid:8AD9C840-044E-11D1-B3E9-00805F499D93" height="120" width="120" >
    <param name="code" value="bookflip" />
    <param name="archive" value="bookflip.jar" />
    <param name="res" value="1" />
```

213

```
      <param name="image1" value="01.jpg" />
      <param name="link1" value="NO" />
      <param name="flip1" value="0" />
      <param name="image2" value="02.jpg" />
      <param name="link2" value="NO" />
      <param name="flip2" value="0" />
      <param name="speed" value="4" />
   </object>
</object>
```

Objects must be rendered only once per page. As you will see, a similar approach exists for Flash objects too (Chapter 9).

ECMAScript, JavaScript, and jQuery

A widely used scripting language is ECMAScript, which is standardized by Ecma International (ECMA-262 [17], ECMA-290 [18], ECMA-327 [19], ECMA-357 [20]) and the International Organization for Standardization (ISO/IEC 16262 [21]). The Internet media type of ECMAScript is application/ecmascript, and the file extension is .es.

The three best-known dialects of ECMAScript are JavaScript, JScript, and ActionScript. The first one, JavaScript, is the primary client-side scripting language on the Web. It is used by millions of web sites to add interaction and functionality.

jQuery is a comprehensive, cross-platform JavaScript library for simplifying client-side scripting and interactions. jQuery provides the code blocks for rapid prototyping and developing a unique user interface with minimum coding and effort. Instead of writing JavaScript code from scratch for an advanced image gallery such as nanoGALLERY [22], an image slider such as Unslider [23], manipulated content such as Avgrund Modal [24], or animations such as jQuery UI Effects Core [25], you can reuse the free, open source code licensed under the MIT License. jQuery can be downloaded from the jQuery web site as an uncompressed or a compressed file [26]. For production environments, the compressed .js file is recommended. This file can be loaded in the document head with the script element as any other JavaScript file (Chapter 3). Beyond the core functions of jQuery, the web design community offers thousands of plug-ins developed and maintained independently.

■ **Caution**   JavaScript should not be confused with Java. Although both languages have a C-like syntax, JavaScript is a scripting language, while Java is general programming language. JavaScript has dynamic typing, while Java has static typing. JavaScript is a weakly typed language, while Java is strongly typed. JavaScript is loaded from human-readable source code, while Java is retrieved from a compiled bytecode. In contrast to JavaScript objects, which are prototype-based, Java objects are class-based.

JScript is the Microsoft implementation of ECMAScript [27]. The major implementations of JScript are Windows Script, and JScript .NET. The typical file extensions of JScript are .js, .jse, .wsf, .wsc, and, if embedded, .htm, .html, and .asp.

ActionScript is an object-oriented language originally developed by Macromedia, which is now owned by Adobe Systems. It is implemented in Adobe Flash and, as mentioned earlier, Adobe Flex. The typical file extension of external ActionScript files is .as. ActionScript reuses the MIME type of ECMAScript.

Embedding and Loading JavaScript

JavaScript codes applied to a whole web page are usually declared in the (X)HTML head. JavaScript can also be used locally in the body section of web documents. Those JavaScript codes that are used throughout the entire web site are written in external files.

Generally, there are three ways to use JavaScript on web sites. They are discussed in the following sections.

Loading JavaScript from an External File

This technique is used when the same script applies to multiple documents. The file extension of external JavaScript files is `.js`. The character encoding of these files is usually US-ASCII. JavaScript files encoded in other encoding schemes might have interoperability problems. While UTF-8 is the perfect choice for (X)HTML web documents and can be applied as the default character encoding in the text editor of any developer, care must be taken to encode JavaScript files (similar to CSS files) in US-ASCII whenever possible.

External JavaScript files should contain JavaScript code exclusively (Listing 6-25). The script tags must also be avoided (Listing 6-26)!

Listing 6-25. JavaScript Code in the Markup

```
<script type="text/javascript">
  document.write("Nice coding");
</script>
```

Listing 6-26. The Same Code in an External `.js` File

```
document.write("Nice coding");
```

External JavaScript files can be loaded with the `src` attribute on the `script` element.[1] Listing 6-27 shows an example.

Listing 6-27. Loading JavaScript from an External File

```
<script type="text/javascript" src="scripts/click.js"></script>
```

This embedding is commonly used for the scripts loaded in the document head and any scripts that are too long to write directly into the markup. Alternate style selectors, font resizers, and hidden layer controller scripts are some examples for this approach.

Inline JavaScript

JavaScript can also be written directly in the markup as the content of the `script` element. Assume we have the JavaScript function shown in Listing 6-28 and variables in Listing 6-29 either in the document head or in an external `.js` file.

Listing 6-28. A Short JavaScript Function

```
function fourdigits(number) {
  return (number < 1000) ? number + 1900 : number;
}
```

---

[1]In the early days of the Web, the `language="javascript"` attribute-value pair was used on the `script` element, which was later deprecated in favor of `type="text/javascript"`.

Listing 6-29. Variables

```
var now = new Date();
var year = fourdigits(now.getYear());
```

This code provides the current year, which can be used for a "dynamic" copyright content as Listing 6-30.

Listing 6-30. Inline JavaScript Example

Copyright © **<script type="text/javascript">document.write(year);</script>** John Smith

This is an inline JavaScript code. In this case, it will represent the current year between the copyright sign and the name, as shown in Listing 6-31.

Listing 6-31. The Result of Listings 6-28, 6-29, and 6-30

```
Copyright © 2011 John Smith
```

Note that if the JavaScript code cannot run for whatever reasons, the other parts of the document are still rendered (Listing 6-32).

Listing 6-32. The Result of the Same Code with JavaScript Disabled or Without JavaScript Support

```
Copyright © John Smith
```

Event Handlers

JavaScript is often used to provide control over document elements or the browser window according to user interaction such as clicking an element with the mouse.

Assume three images on a web page intended to modify the font size of the main layer when the user clicks them. Listing 6-33 shows a possible solution.

Listing 6-33. Functions to Manipulate the Font Size

```
function normal() {
  var esize = document.getElementById('main').style;
  esize.fontSize = "1.1em";
}

function larger() {
  var esize = document.getElementById('main').style;
  esize.fontSize  = "1.4em";
}

function huge() {
  var esize = document.getElementById('main').style;
  esize.fontSize = "1.8em";
}
```

These three functions can be written either within the script tags in the document or in the external file font.js. In the latter case, they can be loaded with the src attribute of the script element as discussed earlier in Listing 6-27 (the file path and name can be arbitrarily modified).

Now the appropriate event handler function can be loaded with the onclick attribute (Listing 6-34).

Listing 6-34. Event Handlers That Load the Appropriate Function Upon User Click

```
<a href="#" onclick="javascript:normal();">
  <img src="images/normal.png" alt="Normal font" title="Normal" />
</a>
<a href="#" onclick="javascript:larger();">
  <img src="images/larger.png" alt="Larger font" title="Larger" />
</a>
<a href="#" onclick="javascript:huge();">
  <img src="images/huge.png" alt="Huge font" title="Huge" />
</a>
```

Which function will run depends on which image link the user clicks.

Determining JavaScript Support

JavaScript support can be easily determined by a script with an alternate content such as in Listing 6-35.

Listing 6-35. JavaScript with Alternate Content

```
<script type="text/javascript">
  document.write("If this text is displayed, your browser supports scripting, and↵
  JavaScript is enabled!")
</script>
<noscript>JavaScript is NOT enabled!</noscript>
```

Browsers that do not support JavaScript will show the content of the noscript element.

The Most Common jQuery Functions

jQuery offers a variety of selectors to manipulate markup elements. The most common selectors are summarized in Listing 6-36.

Listing 6-36. Common jQuery Selectors

```
// Select element by identifier
$("#ElementID").something();

// Select element by CSS class
$(".ClassName").something();

// Select elements that have an identifier with a string
$("[id*='value']").something();

// Select elements that have an identifier that begins with a string
$("[id^='value']").something();

// Select elements that have an identifier ending with a string
$("[id$='value']").something();

// Select elements of a particular type
$("div").something();
```

Toggle Show and Hide

You can use the toggle function to toggle hide/show of an element in jQuery. An element can be hidden or shown using the hide and show functions, respectively (Listing 6-37).

Listing 6-37. Toggle, Show, and Hide Functions in jQuery

```
// Toggle hide/show of an element
$("#DivID").toggle(1000);

// Perform an action after the animation is completed
$("#DivID").toggle(1000, function () {
  alert("Toggle Complete");
});

// Hide an element
$("#DivID").hide(1000);

// Perform an action after the animation is completed
$("#DivID").hide(1000, function () {
  alert("Hide Complete");
});

// Show an element
$("#DivID").show(1000);

// Perform an action after the animation is completed
$("#DivID").show(1000, function () {
  alert("Show Complete");
});
```

Slide Functions

In jQuery, the basic slide functions are slideToggle, slideUp, and slideDown (Listing 6-38).

Listing 6-38. Toggle, Show, and Hide Functions in jQuery

```
// Toggle slide up and down
$("#DivID").slideToggle(1000);

// Perform an action after the animation is completed
$("#DivID").slideToggle(1000, function () {
  alert("Slide Toggle Complete");
});

// Slide up
$("#DivID").slideUp(1000);

// Perform an action after the animation is completed
$("#DivID").slideUp(1000, function () {
  alert("Slide Up Complete");
});
```

```
// Slide down
$("#DivID").slideDown(1000);

// Perform an action after the animation is completed
$("#DivID").slideDown(1000, function () {
  alert("Slide Down Complete");
});
```

Fade Functions

jQuery has the fadeIn, fadeOut, and fadeTo functions to fade an element in or out, or fade it to a specified style (Listing 6-39).

Listing 6-39. Fade an Element in, out, and to

```
// Fade in
$("#DivID").fadeIn(1000);

// Perform an action after the animation is completed
$("#DivID").fadeIn(1000, function () {
  alert("Fade In Complete");
});

// Fade out
$("#DivID").fadeOut(1000);

// Perform an action after the animation is completed
$("#DivID").fadeOut(1000, function () {
  alert("Fade Out Complete");
});

// Fade to (fades to specified opacity)
$("#DivID").fadeTo(1000, 0.25);

// Perform an action after the animation is completed
$("#DivID").fadeTo(1000, 0.25, function () {
  alert("Fade To Complete");
});
```

Animation Functions

Markup elements can be animated by changing the value of their CSS properties with animate (Listing 6-40).

Listing 6-40. Animation with jQuery

```
$("#DivID").animate({ opacity: 0.75 }, 1000);

// Perform an action after the animation is completed
$("#DivID").animate({ opacity: 0.75 }, 1000, function () {
  alert("Opacity Animation Complete");
});
```

219

Set and Retrieve Input Values

jQuery can set and retrieve the property value of input elements such as textboxes (Listing 6-41).

Listing 6-41. Get and Set Textbox Values

```
// Get the value of a textbox
var TextboxValue = $("#TextboxID").val();

// Set the value of a textbox
$("#TextboxID").val("New Textbox Value");
```

Set and Retrieve Element Markup Content

The markup content of elements can be manipulated with the html function (Listing 6-42).

Listing 6-42. Get and Set Markup Content

```
// Get the markup content of an element
var DivHTML = $("#DivID").html();

// Set markup content
$("#DivID").html("<p>The updated markup content.</p>");
```

Set and Retrieve Element Text

The textual content of elements can be manipulated with the text function (Listing 6-43).

Listing 6-43. Get and Set Textual Content

```
// Retrieve the textual content of an element
var DivText = $("#DivID").text();

// Set the textual content of element
$("#DivID").text("The new textual content.");
```

Set and Retrieve Element Dimensions

The dimensions of markup elements can be retrieved and changed using the height and width jQuery functions (Listing 6-44).

Listing 6-44. Get and Set Element dimensions

```
// Get element height
var ElementHeight = $("#DivID").height();

// Set element height
$("#DivID").height(300);

// Get element width
var ElementWidth = $("#DivID").width();

// Set element width
$("#DivID").width(400);
```

Handling CSS Classes

CSS Classes can be created and removed using the addClass and removeClass jQuery functions (Listing 6-45).

Listing 6-45. Add and Remove CSS Classes

```
// Create a CSS class
$("#DivID").addClass("newclassname");

// Remove a CSS class
$("#DivID").removeClass("classname");

// Create a new class and remove the old one
$("#DivID").removeClass("classname").addClass("newclassname");

// Create and remove multiple classes
$("#DivID").removeClass("classname classname2").addClass("newclassname newclassname2");
```

Change CSS Properties

The CSS properties of markup elements can be manipulated by the css jQuery function (Listing 6-46).

Listing 6-46. Change the CSS Property for an Element

```
$("#DivID").css("border", "solid 1px #00f");
```

Silverlight

Silverlight is a freeware application framework created by Microsoft Corporation for developing rich Internet applications [28]. The runtime environment for Silverlight is available as a web browser plug-in. Silverlight provides many features similar to those of Adobe Flash, such as animations, drawing objects, reflection effects, glyphs, and so on.

Silverlight uses the Extensible Application Markup Language (XAML) instead of Scalable Vector Graphics (SVG). XAML is a declarative, XML-based user interface markup language developed by Microsoft and used extensively in .NET.

Similar to Flash, a common embedding option for Silverlight is using the object tag (Listing 6-47).

Listing 6-47. Silverlight Embedding with Alternate Content (Determining Support)

```
<object id="SilverlightPlugin1" width="300" height="300"
 data="data:application/x-silverlight-2,"
 type="application/x-silverlight-2" >
  <param name="source" value="SilverlightApplication1.xap" />
  <a href="http://go.microsoft.com/fwlink/?LinkID=149156&v=4.0.60310.0">
    <img src="http://go.microsoft.com/fwlink/?LinkId=161376" alt="Get Silverlight" />
  </a>
</object>
```

Silverlight can be written not only in your text editor but also in the Microsoft Visual Studio software development platform, which makes it easier to create graphical interfaces displayed simultaneously with the source code.

Server-Side Development

Although static content is adequate for many web site components, advanced web site features, such as web applications, content management, online banking, form submission, database management, and so on, require server-side programming.

■ **Note** The main difference between client-side and server-side programming is that client-side scripts are downloaded, interpreted, and executed by the browser, while server-side scripts and applications run on the server.

■ **Tip** In contrast to client-side technologies, where the support is embedded in most browsers (such as for JavaScript) or can be set easily by installing a free plug-in (such as for SilverLight), the support for server-side technologies should be provided by the hosting service provider. While widely adopted technologies such as PHP and MySQL are supported by most hosting services, it is strongly recommended that you ask the provider about the support for special technologies before selecting and paying for a service, because hosting companies usually refuse to install any software components not included in, or supported by, one of their packages (for example, FFMPEG, ionCube PHP Loader, Apache Ant, Ivy, JTA, JAXP). Some technologies rely on others, and there might be a prerequisite to install certain software components.

There is a wide variety of server-side scripting and programming languages used to create server-side applications. Some of the most widely adopted ones are described in the following sections.

ColdFusion

ColdFusion is an application server offered by Adobe [29] to process the ColdFusion Markup Language (CFML). CFML is a scripting language that uses tags with a structure similar to that of HTML (which is the reason for the name) [30]; it has a functionality similar to that of PHP. CFML has several implementations beyond Adobe ColdFusion, such as the .NET Framework, the Java Virtual Machine, and the Google App Engine. Because of its scalability, ColdFusion is ideal not only for desktop environments but also for the increasingly popular mobile web applications.

The most significant technologies that compete with ColdFusion are BlueDragon [31], Coral Web Builder [32], IgniteFusion [33], Railo [34], and SmithProject [35].

Java

The Java programming language was already mentioned earlier in the chapter regarding Java applets. However, Java is also used on the server side.

JavaServer Pages (JSP) is a Java technology for dynamically generated web pages. The syntax of JSP combines scriptlet elements and markup (typically HTML or XML) [36]. The content of scriptlet elements is Java code that might be mixed with the markup.

The Java Platform, Enterprise Edition (Java EE) is a popular platform for server-side programming in Java. The platform and the associated APIs are defined in separate specifications [37, 38].

WebObjects is a Java web application server and web application framework for Mac OS X developed by Apple. WebObjects is described by Apple specifications [39, 40, 41].

The .NET Framework

Microsoft .NET is a popular software framework with a wide-ranging library [42]. The .NET Framework supports several programming languages (C#, J#, VB .NET, and so on). Any of these languages can use code written in other languages, which provides a high level of interoperability. A fundamental part of the framework architecture is the application virtual machine called *Common Language Runtime (CLR)*, which is Microsoft's implementation of the *Common Language Infrastructure (CLI)*. CLI is an ECMA standard (ECMA 335 [43]).

Some applications of the .NET Framework, such as ADO.NET, ASP.NET, and Windows Forms, are not parts of the previously mentioned standards.

ASP.NET

Active Server Pages, often referred to as ASP or ASP Classic, was a web application framework developed by Microsoft for creating interactive and dynamic web pages. It has been superseded by ASP.NET, which provides powerful features for web applications and services [44]. The typical file extensions are `.asp` for ASP and `.aspx` for ASP.NET files.

As you can see in Listing 6-48, an ASP script can be embedded in the document body of a web page by delimiting the script with <% and %>.

Listing 6-48. ASP Script in the Markup

```
<!DOCTYPE html>
<html>
  <head>
    <title>Simple ASP embedding example</title>
    <meta charset="UTF-8">
  </head>
  <body>
    <%
    response.write("Hello, World!")
    %>
  </body>
</html>
```

Before introducing HTML5 support in Visual Studio and ASP.NET in 2011, ASP.NET generated error-free XHTML markup in most cases. Since ASP.NET does not modify static text and nonserver markup elements, however, the final markup was not necessarily standards-compliant per XHTML 1.0 Strict. According to Microsoft, some markup controls providing optional functionality, especially those with a target attribute for specifying their client-side behavior (AdRotator, BulletedList, HyperLink, HyperLinkColumn, ImageMap, MenuItem, TreeNode), might result in markup code that is not standard compliant [45].

223

C#

A popular programming language often used in .NET is C# (pronounced *See Sharp*), which has been standardized by ECMA [46] and ISO [47, 48]. C# is a multiparadigm programming language, which is declarative, generic, functional, and imperative, and it has strong typing. C# applies object-oriented (class-based) as well as component-oriented disciplines.

Perl

Perl is a high-level, interpreted, general-purpose, dynamic programming language. The specification of the language is available at Perl.org [49]. In the late 1990s, Perl became popular as a CGI scripting language because of its parsing abilities. The core syntax of Perl is summarized in the "Perl style guide" [50]. A very impressive text-processing feature of Perl is that it can handle text files of arbitrary length if enough memory is available.

PHP

PHP: Hypertext Preprocessor is one of the most popular open source server-side scripting languages. It is a cross-platform, general-purpose language originally designed for generating dynamic web pages. Some programmers have tried to introduce "standardized" best practices for PHP over the years [e.g., 51, 52, 53, 54], none of which gained an official status yet. The major specification of PHP is being maintained by the PHP Group [55], which is considered as the *de facto* standard of the language, because there is no formal specification.

PHP is the widely used, free, and efficient alternative to competitors such as ASP.NET.

Embedding and Loading PHP

While some PHP code is embedded in (X)HTML documents and mixed with markup elements, complex PHP applications are provided in external files.

PHP in the Markup

PHP code is usually delimited by `<?php` and `?>` or `<script language="php">` and `</script>`. The less portable short tags `<?` and `<?=` and ASP-style tags such as `<%` and `<%=` should not be used. PHP parsers parse code only within the delimiters. In XML documents (including XHTML), the first embedding method provides well-formed XML processing instructions. Since they are not part of the character data in the document, there is the potential that the combination of markup and PHP code provides valid markup on the server before PHP parsing.

The simplest example for embedding PHP in the markup is a "Hello World" script such as `hello.php` (Listing 6-49).

Listing 6-49. "Hello World" in PHP

```
<!DOCTYPE html>
<html xmlns="http://www.w3.org/1999/xhtml" xml:lang="en" lang="en">
  <head>
    <title>Hello World in PHP</title>
    <meta charset="UTF-8" />
  </head>
  <body>
    <?php echo '<p>Hello World</p>'; ?>
  </body>
</html>
```

Depending on the proper server configuration, the PHP code should be parsed, and the output in Listing 6-50 will be sent to the browser.

Listing 6-50. The Output with Parsed PHP

```
<!DOCTYPE html>
<html xmlns="http://www.w3.org/1999/xhtml" xml:lang="en" lang="en">
  <head>
    <title>Hello World in PHP</title>
    <meta charset="UTF-8" />
  </head>
  <body>
    <p>Hello World!</p>
  </body>
</html>
```

The resulting markup validates as XHTML5. To make the markup easier to understand, the structural elements and additional contents were omitted.

PHP in External Files

The typical file extensions of external PHP files are .php, .phtml, .php5, and .phps. External PHP files usually contain the PHP code between the opening and closing delimiters. In other words, they start with <?php and end with ?>. However, many PHP files, such as the ones used for settings, do not necessarily have a closing delimiter.

The include command can be used to insert the content of a specified external PHP file into the markup (Listing 6-51).

Listing 6-51. Embedding a PHP File

```
<?php include("copyright.php"); ?>
```

An external PHP file might contain PHP code, markup, or a combination of the two.

■ **Tip** It is a common practice to collect the markup fragment of common—frequently repeated—web page contents, such as menus and legal information, and embed them from an external PHP file. This approach eliminates the redundancy of common scripting requirements of a site.

Python

Python is a general-purpose high-level programming language [56]. Python, similar to other dynamic languages, is often used as a scripting language as well. Multiple programming paradigms are supported by Python. Although Python is mainly object-oriented, it also involves functional programming styles. The capabilities of the language can be extended by third-party tools; for example, Python code can be provided as stand-alone executables. Python interpreters are available for a variety of operating systems, which makes Python a cross-platform language.

Ruby

Ruby is a general-purpose, dynamic, and reflective object-oriented programming language. One of the most common Ruby implementations is the open source web application framework called *Ruby on Rails*. The major documentation of Ruby includes the Ruby Core Reference [57], the Ruby Standard Library Reference [58], the Ruby C API Reference [59], and the document on Rails Searchable APIs [60].

SSJS

Although JavaScript is used primarily on the client side, it has server-side implementations as well. Server-side JavaScript (SSJS) was first implemented in 1996 in the Netscape Enterprise Server 2.0 and Netscape LiveWire. The common specifications for SSJS development are provided by the CommonJS community [61]. The Server-Side JavaScript Google Group makes efforts to create cross-platform SSJS standard APIs [62].

Combinations of Client-Side and Server-Side Technologies

Not all programming environments are purely client-side or server-side technologies. For example, the *Google Web Toolkit* has tools for programming JavaScript front-end applications in Java. Ajax applications and rich Internet applications can be developed in Python using the development tool and framework *Pyjamas*. An open source platform for developing rich Internet applications with client-side functionality and server-side processing is *Tersus*.

Database Technologies

A large share of server-side applications and services rely on data stored in databases. One of the most commonly used databases on the Web is the cross-platform relational database management system *MySQL* [63]. It is considered as a *de facto* standard and also used by the highest-traffic web sites in the world. Although it is very popular, languages such Ruby and Python often apply database servers other than MySQL. Some other frequently used database technologies on the Web are Apache Derby [64], IBM DB2 [65], Firebird [66], Microsoft SQL Server [67], Oracle [68], PostgreSQL [69], SQLite [70], and Sybase [71].

Alternate Content and Fallback Mechanism for Scripts

In web site standardization, it is vital to provide alternate content for scripts and also design web documents for user agents that do not support scripting. You can provide the alternate content by using the noscript element. A script is not executed, and user agents render the content of noscript elements only if the browser configuration eliminates scripting or in rare cases when the scripting language used in the script element is not supported. Browsers without client-side scripting support must render the contents of noscript elements.

For example, if dynamically created data is provided by the script element, a direct link to the resource can be used if scripting is not supported (Listing 6-52).

Listing 6-52. Useful Alternate Content

```
<noscript>
  <p><a href="http://example.com/news/">Latest News</a></p>
</noscript>
```

There is a practice of commenting out script written in the markup to eliminate rendering element content by browsers that cannot handle the script element. Advanced rendering engines recognize that scripts in comments should be executed. This could eliminate the need for comments if external script files are used.

As you learned earlier in the chapter, a properly embedded script does not break page layout or content flow when JavaScript is not supported. Still, this approach usually cannot provide the same functionality or behavior as the script would (the provided information should be similar). The importance of alternate content or fallback mechanism for JavaScript code can be best demonstrated by "dynamic" menus that should not rely on JavaScript alone, since the functionality of the site will be lost if JavaScript is disabled or the script cannot be loaded.

Let's assume that you have a special Help screen, contained by a layer that is not shown by default (Listing 6-53) and displayed only when the user clicks the menu "Help".

Listing 6-53. A Help div Which Is Not Rendered by Default

```
#help {
  display: none;
}
```

Since the help is displayed using JavaScript (Listing 6-54), it will be not available if JavaScript is disabled or not supported.

Listing 6-54. The Function That Displays the Hidden div

```
function display_help() {
  document.getElementById("help").style.display = 'block';
}
```

A good fallback mechanism is to provide a conventional hyperlink—which looks the same as the link calling the JavaScript code that displays the special Help layer above the page—as an alternate content (Listing 6-55). If the layer cannot be displayed because of the lack of JavaScript support, the link opens another web document with the same content the Help div would provide. Although the visual appearance of the "Help screen" and the Help document is different, the content is the same. One of them is always available.

Listing 6-55. An Advanced Menu Item with Fallback Mechanism

```
<li>
  <script type="text/javascript">
    <a href="javascript:display_help();" title="Guide and access keys" accesskey="h"↵
      tabindex="22">Help</a>
  </script>
  <noscript>
    <a href="http://example.com/help/" title="Guide and access keys" accesskey="h"↵
      tabindex="22">Help</a>
  </noscript>
</li>
```

Summary

In this chapter, you learned about client-side and server-side scripting and programming languages used to create scripts, applets, and web applications. Using these technologies on a daily basis is inevitable, and you know by now that they are vital in web applications and web services. However, many of them are vendor-specific and have not been standardized yet. You also know that a large share of incorrect markup is generated by server-side applications, even though more and more provide standard-compliant web documents.

In the next chapter, you will learn about emerging Semantic Web technologies and machine-readable metadata annotations.

References

1. Dominique Hazaël-Massieux D (2013) What is scripting? In: Scripting and Ajax. World Wide Web Consortium. http://www.w3.org/standards/webdesign/script. Accessed 21 October 2014

2. Dorward D (2011) Ampersands, PHP Sessions and Valid HTML. World Wide Web Consortium. http://www.w3.org/QA/2005/04/php-session. Accessed 21 October 2014

3. Crockford D (2006) The application/json Media Type for JavaScript Object Notation (JSON). The Internet Society. http://tools.ietf.org/html/rfc4627. Accessed 21 October 2014

4. van Kesteren A, Aubourg J, Song J, Steen HRM (eds) (2014) XMLHttpRequest Level 1. World Wide Web Consortium. http://www.w3.org/TR/XMLHttpRequest/. Accessed 21 October 2014

5. Adobe (2014) Adobe Flex – One codebase, multiple devices. Adobe Systems Inc. http://www.adobe.com/products/flex/. Accessed 21 October 2014

6. Lubbers P, Albers B, Salim F (2010) Pro HTML5 programming – Powerful APIs for Richer Internet Application Development. Apress Media LLC, New York

7. Pieters S (2014) APIs. In: HTML5 differences from HTML4. World Web Web Consortium. https://rawgit.com/whatwg/html-differences/master/Overview.html#apis. Accessed 21 October 2014

8. Cabanier R, Mann J, Munro J, Wiltzius T, Hickson I (eds) (2014) HTML Canvas 2D Context, Level 2. World Wide Web Consortium. http://www.w3.org/TR/2dcontext2/. Accessed 1 November 2014

9. Ranganathan A, Sicking J (2013) File API. World Wide Web Consortium. http://www.w3.org/TR/FileAPI/. Accessed 21 October 2014

10. Hickson I (ed) (2014) Drag and drop. In: HTML. Web Hypertext Application Technology Working Group. https://html.spec.whatwg.org/multipage/interaction.html#dnd. Accessed 21 October 2014

11. Hickson I (ed) (2014) Forms. In: HTML. Web Hypertext Application Technology Working Group. http://www.whatwg.org/specs/web-apps/current-work/multipage/forms.html. Accessed 21 October 2014

12. Popescu A (ed) (2010) Geolocation API Specification. W3C Recommendation. World Wide Web Consortium. http://www.w3.org/TR/geolocation-API/. Accessed 21 October 2014

13. Mozilla (2014) Location-Aware Browsing. http://www.mozilla.com/en/firefox/geolocation/. Mozilla Corporation. Accessed 21 October 2014

14. Hickson I (ed) (2013) Web Storage. W3C Recommendation. World Wide Web Consortium. http://www.w3.org/TR/webstorage/. Accessed 21 October 2014

15. Hickson I (ed) (2012) The WebSocket API. World Wide Web Consortium. http://www.w3.org/TR/websockets/. Accessed 21 October 2014

16. Google (2013) pywebsocket - WebSocket server and extension for Apache HTTP Server for testing. Google Inc. http://code.google.com/p/pywebsocket/. Accessed 21 October 2014

17. ECMA (2011) The ECMA 262 standard, 5.1 Edition. Ecma International. http://www.ecma-international.org/publications/files/ECMA-ST/ECMA-262.pdf. Accessed 21 October 2014

18. ECMA (1999) ECMAScript Components Specification. The ECMA-290 standard. ECMA International. http://www.ecma-international.org/publications/files/ECMA-ST/ECMA-290.PDF. Accessed 21 October 2014

19. ECMA (2001) ECMAScript 3rd Edition Compact Profile. The ECMA-327 standard. ECMA International. http://www.ecma-international.org/publications/files/ECMA-ST/Ecma-327.pdf. Accessed 21 October 2014

20. ECMA (2005) ECMAScript for XML (E4X) Specification, 2nd edition. The ECMA-357 standard. ECMA International. http://www.ecma-international.org/publications/files/ECMA-ST/Ecma-357.pdf. Accessed 21 October 2014

21. ISO (2002) ISO/IEC 16262:2002. International Organization for Standardization. http://www.iso.org/iso/catalogue_detail.htm?csnumber=33835. Accessed 21 October 2014

22. Brisbois C (2014) nanoGALLERY. http://nanogallery.brisbois.fr/. Accessed 30 October 2014

23. Unslider.com (2014) Unslider—the super-tiny jQuery slider. http://unslider.com/. Accessed 30 October 2014

24. Voronianski D (2014) Avgrund Modal. http://labs.voronianski.com/jquery.avgrund.js/. Accessed 30 October 2014

25. The jQuery Foundation (2014) jQuery UI Effects Core. http://plugins.jquery.com/ui.effect/. Accessed 30 October 2014

26. The jQuery Foundation (2014) Downloading jQuery. http://jquery.com/download/. Accessed 30 October 2014

27. Microsoft (2014) JScript (ECMAScript3) – Windows Scripting 5.8. Microsoft Corporation. http://msdn.microsoft.com/en-us/library/hbxc2t98%28v=VS.85%29.aspx. Accessed 21 October 2014

28. Microsoft (2014) Silverlight. Microsoft Corporation. http://www.silverlight.net. Accessed 21 October 2014

29. Adobe (2014) Adobe ColdFusion 11 family. Adobe Systems Inc. http://www.adobe.com/products/coldfusion-family.html. Accessed 21 October 2014

30. Brooks-Bilson R (2009) Core CFML Tags. CFML Advisory Committee. http://www.opencfml.org/display/cfmladvisory/Core+CFML+Tags. Accessed 23 August 2011

31. New Atlanta (2009) Upgrading from ColdFusion. In: BlueDragon 7.1 User Guide. New Atlanta Communications LLC. http://www.newatlanta.com/products/bluedragon/self_help/docs/7_1/BlueDragon_71_User_Guide.pdf. Accessed 21 October 2014

32. rave7 (2014) rave7. http://www.pcaonline.com/index.cfm?DocID=10082&fkb=y. Accessed 21 October 2014

33. FindMySoft (ed) (2011) IgniteFusion CFML engine. http://www.findmysoft.com/scripts/IgniteFusion-CFML-engine-download.html. Accessed 24 August 2011

34. Railo (2014) Railo - Open Source CFML - Training, Consulting and Support. http://www.getrailo.com. Accessed 21 October 2014

35. Placona M (2011) Yet another free ColdFusion engine. Marcos Placona Blog. http://www.placona.co.uk/52/coldfusion/yet-another-free-coldfusion-engine/. Accessed 24 August 2011

36. Sun (2001) JAVASERVER PAGES (JSP) SYNTAX version 1.2. Sun Microsystems, Inc. http://java.sun.com/products/jsp/syntax/1.2/card12.pdf. Accessed 23 August 2011

37. Oracle (2014) Your First Cup: An Introduction to the Java EE Platform Release 7 for Java Platform, Enterprise Edition. Oracle Corporation. http://docs.oracle.com/javaee/7/firstcup/doc/firstcup.pdf. Accessed 21 October 2014

38. Oracle (2013) Java EE 7 Specification APIs. Oracle Corporation. http://docs.oracle.com/javaee/7/api/. Accessed 21 October 2014

39. Apple (2007) WebObjects Overview. Apple Inc. http://developer.apple.com/legacy/mac/library/documentation/WebObjects/WebObjects_Overview/WebObjects_Overview.pdf. Accessed 21 October 2014

40. Apple (2007) WebObjects Web Applications Programming Guide. Apple Inc. http://developer.apple.com/legacy/mac/library/documentation/WebObjects/Web_Applications/Web_Applications.pdf. Accessed 21 October 2014

41. Apple (2007) WebObjects Enterprise Objects Programming Guide. Apple Inc. http://developer.apple.com/legacy/mac/library/documentation/WebObjects/Enterprise_Objects/EnterpriseObjects.pdf. Accessed 21 October 2014

42. Microsoft (2014) Microsoft .NET Framework. Microsoft Corporation. http://www.microsoft.com/net. Accessed 21 October 2014

43. ECMA (2012) Common Language Infrastructure (CLI), 6th edition. ECMA-335 Standard. ECMA International. http://www.ecma-international.org/publications/files/ECMA-ST/ECMA-335.pdf. Accessed 21 October 2014

44. Microsoft (2014) The Official Microsoft ASP.NET Site. Microsoft Corporation. http://www.asp.net. Accessed 21 October 2014

45. Microsoft (2010) XHTML Standards in Visual Studio and ASP.NET. Microsoft Corporation. http://msdn.microsoft.com/en-us/library/exc57y7e.aspx. Accessed 21 October 2014

46. ECMA (2006) C# Language Specification, 4th edition. ECMA-334 Standard. ECMA International. http://www.ecma-international.org/publications/files/ECMA-ST/Ecma-334.pdf. Accessed 21 October 2014

47. ISO (2012) Information technology – Programming languages – C#. ISO/IEC 23270:2006. International Organization for Standardization. `http://www.iso.org/iso/iso_ catalogue/catalogue_ics/catalogue_detail_ics.htm?csnumber=42926`. Accessed 21 October 2014

48. ISO (2012) Information technology – Common Language Infrastructure (CLI) Partitions I to VI. ISO/IEC 23271:2006. International Organization for Standardization. `http://www.iso.org/iso/iso_catalogue/catalogue_ics/catalogue_detail_ics. htm?csnumber=42927`. Accessed 21 October 2014

49. Allen J (ed) (2014) Perl 5 version 14.1 documentation – Full version. Official documentation for the Perl programming language. Perl5 Porters. `http://perldoc.perl.org/perldoc.tar.gz`. Accessed 21 October 2014

50. Allen J (ed) (2014) Perl version 5.20.1 documentation – Perl style guide. `http://perldoc.perl.org/perlstyle.pdf`. Accessed 21 October 2014

51. Hoff T, Kristiansen F (2003) PHP Coding Standard. Todd Hoff, Fredrik Kristiansen. `http://www.dagbladet.no/development/phpcodingstandard/`. Accessed 24 August 2011

52. Google (2011) PHP Standards Working Group. Google Inc. `http://groups.google.com/group/php-standards`. Accessed 24 August 2011

53. Icontem (2014) PHP standards discussion group opens to the world - PHP Classes. Icontem. `http://www.phpclasses.org/blog/post/96-PHP-standards-discussion-group-opens-to-the-world.html`. Accessed 21 October 2014

54. Donat J (ed) (2014) PHP Standards. `http://phpstandards.net`. Accessed 15 November 2014

55. Olson P (ed), Achour M, Betz F, Dovgal A, Lopes N, Magnusson H, Richter G, Seguy D, Vrana J, et al (2014) PHP Manual. PHP Documentation Group. `http://www.php.net/manual/en/`. Accessed 21 October 2014

56. PSF (2014) Welcome to Python.org. Python Software Foundation. `http://www.python.org`. Accessed 21 October 2014

57. Britt J, Neurogami (2014) Index of Files, Classes & Methods in Ruby. James Britt, Neurogami. `http://www.ruby-doc.org/core/`. Accessed 21 October 2014

58. Britt J, Neurogami (2014) Ruby Standard Library Reference. James Britt, Neurogami. `http://www.ruby-doc.org/stdlib/`. Accessed 21 October 2014

59. Britt J, Neurogami (2006) Ruby C API Reference. James Britt, Neurogami. `http://www.ruby-doc.org/doxygen/current/`. Accessed 24 August 2011

60. Kolesnikov V (2009) Rails Searchable API Doc. Vladimir Kolesnikov. `http://railsapi.com`. Accessed 24 August 2011

61. Dangoor K *et al* (2009) CommonJS: JavaScript Standard Library. The CommonJS community. `http://www.commonjs.org`. Accessed 24 August 2011

62. Google (2014) The CommonJS Google Group. Google Inc. `http://groups.google.com/group/commonjs`. Accessed 21 October 2014

63. Oracle (2014) MySQL: The world's most popular open source database. Oracle Corporation. `http://www.mysql.com`. Accessed 21 October 2014

64. ASF (2014) Apache Derby. Apache Software Foundation. `http://db.apache.org/derby/`. Accessed 15 November 2014

65. IBM (2014) DB2 database software. International Business Machines. `http://www-01.ibm.com/software/data/db2/`. Accessed 21 October 2014

66. Firebird Project (2014) Firebird: True universal open source database. Firebird Foundation Incorporated. `http://www.firebirdsql.org`. Accessed 21 October 2014

67. Microsoft (2014) SQL Server. Microsoft Corporation. `http://www.microsoft.com/sqlserver/en/us/default.aspx`. Accessed 21 October 2014

68. Oracle (2014) Oracle Database. Oracle Corporation. `http://www.oracle.com/database/`. Accessed 21 October 2014

69. PostgreSQL GDG (2014) PostgreSQL: The world's most advanced open source database. PostgreSQL Global Development Group. `http://www.postgresql.org`. Accessed 21 October 2014

70. Hipp DR (2014) SQLite. `http://sqlite.org`. Accessed 21 October 2014

71. Sybase (2014) Database Management. Sybase Inc. `http://www.sybase.com/products/databasemanagement`. Accessed 21 October 2014

■■■

Metadata and the Semantic Web

The basic structure of web documents provides the desired appearance and functionality. By default, however, the content is human-readable only. You can use additional technologies to provide meaning to web documents, making them machine-readable and human-readable at the same time. There is a wide choice of metadata available, along with microformats and various annotations that can significantly extend the processability of web documents and the efficiency of web searches. Structured data should be added to web sites and conventional search engines changed from brute-force approaches to semantic parsing.

In this chapter, you will learn machine-readable metadata annotations and semantically meaningful attributes. You will also become familiar with the Resource Description Framework, the fundamental standard behind Semantic Web technologies. After reading the chapter, you will be able to create new vocabularies, schemes, and ontologies, and use existing technologies such as

- *General metadata in the markup*: Conventional meta tags

- *Microformats*: Metadata provided as attribute values of markup elements

- *Microdata*: A metadata annotation for general metadata embedding in HTML5

- *RDF*: A standardized framework for Semantic Web data models

- *OWL*: A knowledge representation language for describing and sharing web ontologies that formally represent knowledge as a set of concepts within a domain and the relationships between those concepts

- *FOAF and DOAC*: Machine-readable ontologies for people and their professional capabilities

- *XMP, Rich Snippets, SearchMonkey RDFa*: Metadata formats for images and video clips

The Semantic Web

Until recently, software agents could not handle many kinds of information that could have been associated with files. Although file structure and extensions provided some information about files, much information could not be expressed. For example, a file with a .jpg extension has always represented a JPEG image but provided no information about the shutter speed, exposure program, f-stop, aperture, ISO speed rating, or focal length until the introduction of metadata formats such as Exif and XMP (see Chapter 9). However, sharing metadata stored in binary files is still not the most efficient way to share metadata, especially if it is much more generic. In the digital era, electronic files are being sold (e-books, MP3 files, and so on) that might be retrieved or played on many types of devices. A variety of metadata technologies can be used to express arbitrary information and represent any kind of knowledge associated with electronic documents in a machine-readable format. Machine-readable data (automated data) is data stored in a machine-readable format, making it possible for automated software agents to access and process it without human intervention.

To browsers, web documents consisted of human-readable data only. In fact, information was confused with the containers that contained them. In contrast to the conventional Web (the "Web of documents"), the Semantic Web is the "Web of data" [1]. The Semantic Web provides machine-processable data, making it possible for software agents to "understand" the meaning of information (in other words, semantics) presented by web documents. This feature can be used for a variety of services [2], such as museums [3], community sites [4], podcasting [5], Big Data processing, and search engines.

■ **Caution**   The word *semantic* is used on the Web in other contexts as well. For example, in HTML5 there are semantic (in other words, meaningful) structuring elements, but this expression refers to the "meaning" of elements. In this context, the word *semantic* contrasts the "meaning" of elements, such as that of `section` (a thematic grouping), with the generic elements of older HTML versions, such as the "meaningless" `div`. The semantics of markup elements should not be confused with the semantics (in other words, machine-processability) of metadata annotations and web ontologies used on the Semantic Web. The latter can provide far more sophisticated data than the meaning of a markup element.

Conventional web documents can be extended with additional data that add meaning to them rather than structure alone. *Semantic Web* is a new approach that is going to change the world of the Web. Surprisingly, Tim Berners-Lee described the reason for the existence of the Semantic Web as early as 2001 [6]. On the Semantic Web, data can be retrieved from seemingly unrelated fields automatically in order to combine them, find relations, and make discoveries [7]. The machine-processability can also be used in huge and complex datasets that are considered *Big Data*.

The Semantic Web should be considered an extension of the conventional Web [8]. *Web 2.0* is an umbrella term used for a collection of technologies that form the second generation of the Web, such as Extensible Markup Language (XML), Asynchronous JavaScript and XML (Ajax), Really Simple Syndication (RSS), and Session Initiation Protocol (SIP). They are the underlying technologies and standards behind instant messaging, Voice over IP, wikis, blogs, forums, and web syndication.

The next generation of web services is denoted as *Web 3.0*, which is an umbrella term usually referring to customization and semantic contents and more sophisticated web applications toward artificial intelligence, including computer-generated contents [9].

The Semantic Web is a major aspect of Web 2.0 [10] and Web 3.0 [11]. Web 3.0 can be considered a superset of the Semantic Web that features social connections and personalization.

Several technologies contribute to the sharing of such information instead of web pages alone, and the number of Semantic Web applications is constantly increasing.

All data controlled by conventional web applications are kept by the applications themselves, making a significant share of data and their relationships virtually unavailable for automated processing. Semantic Web applications, on the other hand, can access this data through the general web architecture and transfer structured data between applications and web sites [12]. Semantic web technologies can be widely applied in a variety of areas, such as data integration, resource discovery and classification, cataloging, intelligent software agents, content rating, and intellectual property right descriptions [13]. A much wider range of tasks can be performed on semantic web pages than on conventional ones; for example, relationships between data and even sentences can be automatically processed (see the next sections). Additionally, the efficiency is much higher. For example, a very promising approach provides direct mapping of relational data to RDF, making it possible to share data of relational databases on the Semantic Web [14]. Since relational databases are extremely popular in computing, databases that are publicly unavailable can now be shared on the Semantic Web. Commercial RDF database software packages are already available on the market (5Store, AllegroGraph, BigData, Oracle, OWLIM, Talis Platform, Virtuoso, and so on) [15]. Semantic tools can also be used in a variety of other areas, including business process modeling or diagnostic applications [16].

Along with these benefits, there are several open issues that need further investigation and, in some cases, the development of new approaches. The largest challenge of Semantic Web applications is to resolve semantic data quality problems and identify useful and meaningful information [17]. There are more and more promising approaches; however, they have a common feature: all rely on standard annotations, taxonomies, vocabularies, and ontologies. We analyze these essential technologies and their features throughout the chapter from a standardization point of view.

Structured Data

Data should be structured to support advanced processability and searchability by data type. Structured data is data organized in a structure to become identifiable. Such data has been used for decades in computing, such as in the form of Access and SQL databases, where queries can be performed to retrieve information (for example, a ZIP code). In contrast to relational databases, most data on the Web is stored in (X)HTML documents that contain *unstructured data*.

Conventional web documents contain large amounts of unstructured data that can be rendered in web browsers. This approach works satisfactorily for publishing purposes; however, a large amount of data stored in, or associated with, web documents cannot be processed this way. According to Berners-Lee, the data used to describe social connections between people is a good example for that kind of data [18]: "The Web is more a social creation than a technical one. I designed it for a social effect—to help people work together—and not as a technical toy. The ultimate goal of the Web is to support and improve our weblike existence in the world. We clump into families, associations, and companies. We develop trust across the miles and distrust around the corner. What we believe, endorse, agree with, and depend on is representable and, increasingly, represented on the Web. We all have to ensure that the society we build with the Web is of the sort we intend."

On the Semantic Web, there is a variety of *structured data*, usually expressed in, or based on, the Resource Description Framework (RDF), which will be described later in detail. Similar to conventional conceptual modeling approaches, such as class diagrams and entity relationships, the RDF data model is based on statements that describe and feature resources, especially web resources, in the form of subject-predicate-object expressions. The subject corresponds to the resource. The predicate expresses a relationship between the subject and the object. Such expressions are called *triples*.

For example, the statement "The grass is green" can be expressed in an RDF triple as follows:

- Subject: "The grass"

- Predicate: "is"

- Object: "green"

RDF is an abstract model that has several serialization formats. Consequently, the syntax of the triple varies from format to format (see later in the section "Resource Description Framework").

■ **Caution** RDF is a data representation model, not a language like XML.

The authors of the "conventional" Web usually publish unstructured data, because they do not know about the power of structured data, find RDF too complex, or do not know how to create and publish RDF in any of its serialization formats. The following are solutions to the problem that add structured data to conventional (X)HTML markup, which can be extracted by appropriate software and converted to RDF:

- Microformats, which reuse markup attributes

- Microdata, which extends HTML5 markup with structured metadata

- RDFa, which expresses RDF in markup attributes that are not part of (X)HTML vocabularies

Linked Open Data

Linked Data (also known as *Linking Data*) can be applied to improve the exploitation of the "Web of data." The expression refers to the publishing of structured data in a way that typed links are created between data from different sources [19] to provide a higher level of usability. By using Linked Data, it is possible to find other, related datasets. Structured data should meet four requirements to be called Linked Data [20]:

- URIs should be assigned to all entities of the dataset.

- HTTP URIs are required to ensure that all entities can be referenced and cited by users and user agents.

- Entities should be described using standard formats such as RDF/XML.

- Links should be created to other, related entity URIs.

All data that fulfill these requirements and are released for the public are called *Linked Open Data* (LOD). The variety of datasets published as Linked Data is represented by the LOD cloud diagram (Figure 7-1) [21].

Figure 7-1. *The LOD cloud diagram (courtesy of Max Schmachtenberg, Christian Bizer, Anja Jentzsch, and Richard Cyganiak)*

The image collects the datasets published according to the Linked Data principles and represents links between them. The size of the bubbles corresponds to the number of triples stored in each dataset. Contributors include the Linking Open Data community project, individuals, and organizations.

Machine-Readable Metadata

Metadata is structured data describing information about features and content of web sites. The meta *tags* written in (X) HTML head sections, which do not require additional technologies, can be used to describe general data about web pages (as mentioned earlier in Chapter 3 and will be described in detail in the next section). Semantic, machine-readable labels can be provided as attribute values of (X)HTML or XML elements by microdata, microformats, or RDFa.

There are several metadata technologies; many apply different annotations. For example, the description of a person can be expressed in RDFa, microdata, the vCard microformat, and further vocabularies such as FOAF or DOAC.

Special metadata such as licensing can be provided with different notations. Licensing information of images and of the web pages containing them can be different. Providing license metadata can be beneficial to every web site, especially the ones that have different copyright than the user content, such as image-sharing portals like Flickr [22]. Image licenses can be provided in basic markup, microdata, rel="license" microformat, and RDFa.

Several metadata technologies have multiple syntaxes. The syntax of microformats, for example, depends on the host markup languages. In the case of RDF, some syntaxes have the same capabilities but different complexity.

Semantic Annotations
The meta Tags

In the 1990s, meta elements had a large effect on web search results. Since then, their significance has been decreasing, partly because of the unethical tricks that have been used to manipulate search engine rankings. A good example is *keyword stuffing*, which was used to load a web page with popular keywords that were not necessarily relevant to the page content, either in the meta tags or in the content. In the latter case, the keywords were often hidden, but the web page that contained them was indexed by search engines. Such tricks made it possible for developers to achieve higher ranking on search results but significantly increased the number of irrelevant links on search result lists. Although they are less important nowadays, meta tags still should be used to provide information on web page contents for search engines.

The meta tags in HTML/XHTML can define a variety of metadata, for example, content type, author, publication date, keywords, page content description, character encoding, and so on. These tags were introduced in HTML 2.0 and are still current.

The following attributes can be used on the meta element: content, http-equiv, name, and scheme. The first one is the only required attribute. In HTML5, the scheme attribute is not supported on the meta element, and there is another attribute called charset. The meta element attributes can specify the following:

- *Alternatives to HTTP headers* that are sent by web servers prior to the web page content. Listing 7-1 shows an example.

  Listing 7-1. Document Expiry Date Provided by the meta Tag

  ```
  <meta http-equiv="expires" content="Fri, 15 October 2010 14:15:00 GMT" />
  ```

- *Names and associated content attributes* describing aspects of (X)HTML pages. Listing 7-2 shows an example.

  Listing 7-2. Keyword Declaration with the meta Tag

  ```
  <meta name="keywords" content="standardization, accessibility" />
  ```

- Meta schemes specify a semantic framework defining the meaning of the key and its value (prior to HTML5). They can also prevent potential ambiguity. Listing 7-3 shows an example.

Listing 7-3. A Meta Scheme

```
<meta name="foo" content="bar" scheme="DC" />
```

In this case, the meta scheme is Dublin Core (DC).

The `language`, `keywords`, `description`, and `robots` attributes contribute to more precise web searches by defining document language, the most relevant keywords, and a short description. The value of the last attribute, `robots`, provides control over search engine behavior for a limited extent [23]. Web pages can be prevented from being indexed (`noindex`), crawled (`nofollow`), cached (`noarchive`), described (`nosnippet`), or described according to the *Open Directory Project* (`noodp`) [24]. The combination of the `noindex, nofollow` values can be substituted by the value none [25]. This setting can be used, for example, for confidential documents whose content and links should not be indexed by search engines.[1] Web page descriptions retrieved from ODP used by Google, Yahoo!, and Bing can be disallowed specifically. The `meta` name to be applied is `Googlebot` for Google, `Slurp` for Yahoo!, and `msnbot` for Bing (Listing 7-4).

Listing 7-4. `meta` Tags for Different Crawlers

```
<meta name="Googlebot" content="noodp" />
<meta name="Slurp" content="noodp" />
<meta name="msnbot" content="noodp" />
```

If you want to prevent the descriptions and titles retrieved from the Yahoo! Directory from being displayed in search results, you can use the `noydir` value [26] (Listing 7-5).

Listing 7-5. Using the `noydir` Attribute Value

```
<meta name="robots" content="noydir" />
```

In spite of the variety of attribute values, using `meta` tags for preventing search engine indexing or crawling is not the best solution. The `robots.txt` file should be used instead for this purpose.

The typical general metadata provided in the head section of web documents looks like Listing 7-6.

Listing 7-6. A Complete Example for `meta` Tags in XHTML5

```
<meta charset="UTF-8" />
<meta name="robots" content="index, follow" />
<meta name="content-language" content="en" />
<meta name="author" content="John Smith" />
<meta name="keywords" content="My Darling, pet shop, pet accessories, dog, collar,↩
 harness, dog lead, dog kennel, dog bowl, dog coats" />
<meta name="description" content="The website of the pet shop My Darling." />
```

Since the attribute value of the `name` attribute on the `meta` element is `robots`, the value of the `content` attribute (`index, follow`) is applied to all search engines rather than a specific one.

---

[1]There are other techniques to achieve similar results. For example, web documents contained by a directory that is disallowed in `robots.txt` will usually be excluded from search results.

Microformats

A special approach to metadata is a set of simple open data formats called *microformats* (μF). They are highly correlated with the Semantic Web by applying and reusing features of existing technologies (for example, the (X) HTML rel attribute) and by introducing new ones with the simplest approaches possible—based on *Plain Old Semantic HTML* (*POSH*) (for example, hCard). They can be applied not only in (X)HTML markup but also in XML, RSS, Atom, and so on.

Microformats can express site structure, link weight, content type, and human relationships with the class, rel, and rev attribute values [27]. They are very easy to write, and the number of software supporting them is increasing (for example, the Operator [28] and Tails Export [29] add-ons for Firefox, the Michromeformats Google Chrome extension [30], the microformats transformer Optimus [31], or the Microformats Bookmarklet for Safari, Firefox, and IE [32]).

However, there are still some open issues. For example, applying various microformats as multiple values on the a element should be avoided (for example, rel="nofollow" and rel="friend"). The rev attribute used by the Vote Links microformat cannot be used in HTML5.

Profile URIs provided by the profile attribute cannot be used on the head element in HTML5, where the profile attribute values can be declared for the rel attribute on anchors (a) or link elements (link). As an example, a profile URI is presented for the hCalendar microformat with all the three options. The hCalendar microformat is based on the iCalendar standard (RFC 2445 [33]). All contents that use hCalendar notation should refer to the hCalendar XMDP profile, in other words, http://microformats.org/profile/hcalendar, as shown in Listing 7-7 or Listing 7-8 for the document head or in Listing 7-9 as part of the document body. These methods can also be combined.

Listing 7-7. Providing the hCalendar Head Profile in the Document Head (Cannot Be Used in HTML5)

```
<head profile="http://microformats.org/profile/hcalendar">
```

Listing 7-8. Linking to the hCalendar Profile in the Document Head

```
<link rel="profile" href="http://microformats.org/profile/hcalendar">
```

Listing 7-9. Using the hCalendar Profile in the Document Body

```
<a rel="profile" href="http://microformats.org/profile/hcalendar">hCalendar</a>
```

New structural elements introduced by HTML5, such as article, nav, and section, are not recognized by certain microformat parsers.

In the next sections, we will give you an overview of some of the most popular microformats, namely, hCalendar, hCard, rel="license", rel="nofollow", rel="tag", Vote Links, and XFN.

hCalendar

You can use the hCalendar microformat to create calendar entries for sport events, anniversaries, reminders, meetings, workshops, conferences, and other events. The root class name for hCalendar is vcalendar. The root class name for events is vevent, which is required for all event listings.

The properties are represented by the elements of hCalendar. The required properties are dtstart, which should be provided in the ISO date format,[2] and summary.

---

[2]Beyond microformats such as hAtom, hCalendar, hCard, and hReview, several web technologies apply the ISO 8601 date format for date-time representation, such as XML, XML schema datatypes, RDF, and Atom.

Listing 7-10 shows an hCalendar example.

Listing 7-10. A Three-Day Conference Represented in hCalendar

```
<div class="vevent">
  <h1 class="summary">Semantic Web Conference '15</h1>
  <div class="description">Semantic Web Conference 2015 was announced yesterday.</div>
  <div>Posted on: <abbr class="dtstamp" title="20150825T080000Z">Aug 25, 2015</abbr></div>
  <div class="uid">uid1@host.com</div>
  <div>Organized by: <a class="organizer" href="mailto:js@expl.com">js@expl.com</a></div>
  <div>Dates: <abbr class="dtstart" title="20151012T093000Z">October 12 2015, 9.30am⮐
   UTC</abbr> – <abbr class="dtend" title="20151014T200000Z">October 14 2015, 8.00pm⮐
   UTC</abbr></div>
  <div>Status: <span class="status">Confirmed</span></div>
  <div>Filed under:</div>
  <ul>
    <li class="category">Conference</li>
  </ul>
</div>
```

Optional properties include, but are not limited to, `location`, `url`, `dtend` (in ISO date format), `duration` (in ISO date duration format), `rdate`, `rrule`, `category`, `description`, `uid`, `geo`, `attendee`, `contact`, `organizer`, `attach`, and `status`. The geo property has the subproperties `latitude` and `longitude`, while `attendee` has the subproperties `partstat` and `role`. According to the specification, the property list is not final and is being extended [34].

Those who have to publish new events regularly might find the hCalendar generator *hCalendar-o-matic* useful [35].

hCard

The hCard microformat standard can be used to represent contact data of people, companies, and organizations by semantic markup [36]. hCard metadata should be provided on the contact pages of web sites. In summer 2010, hCard crossed the 2 billion mark according to Yahoo! Search Monkey, making it the most popular metadata format for people and organizations on the Web.

hCard is based on the vCard standard (RFC 2426 [37]). In fact, existing vCards can be easily converted to hCard.[3]

■ **Tip**   The vCard standard is widely used for storing electronic business cards. For example, Microsoft Outlook uses this format for the business cards available under Contacts.

The hCard class names should be in lowercase.

■ **Caution**   The root class name for an hCard is `vcard`. An element with a class name `vcard` is itself called an hCard.

---

[3]The vCard notation BEGIN:VCARD is `class="vcard"` in hCard, N: is `class="n"`, FN: is `class="fn"`, and so on.

The two required attributes in hCard are fn and n. However, the second one is optional if any *implied "N" optimization rules* are in effect.[4] The property n might have the subproperties family-name, given-name, additional-name, honorific-prefix, and honorific-suffix.

All other properties are optional, including adr, agent, bday, category, class, email, geo, key, label, logo, mailer, nickname, note, org, photo, rev, role, sort-string, sound, tel2, title, tz, uid, and url. Allowed subproperties are post-office-box, extended-address, street-address, locality, region, postal-code, country-name, type, and value for adr; type and value for email; latitude and longitude for geo; organization-name and organization-unit for org; and type and value for tel2.

A typical hCard code looks like Listing 7-11.

Listing 7-11. A Typical hCard

```
<div id="hcard-John-Smith" class="vcard">
  <img src="http://www.example.com/jsmith.jpg" alt="Photo of John Smith" class="photo" />
  <a class="url fn" href="http://www.example.com">John Smith</a>
  <div class="org">Smith and Sons</div>
  <a class="email" href="mailto:smith@example.com">smith@example.com</a>
  <div class="adr">
    <div class="street-address">123 Nice Street</div>
    <span class="locality">Vancouver</span>,
    <span class="region">BC</span>,
    <span class="postal-code">V5K</span>
    <span class="country-name">Canada</span>
  </div>
  <div class="tel">+12345678</div>
</div>
```

The following hCard elements are singular and can be provided just once: fn, n, bday, tz, geo, sort-string, uid, class, and rev. All other properties are allowed to have multiple instances.

Generally, the visible property values of markup elements represent the value of the hCard property. However, there are some exceptions.

For hyperlinks that are represented by the a element for one or multiple hCard properties, the href attribute provides the property value for all properties with a URL value (for example, photo). In case the img element is used, the src attribute holds the property value for all properties with a URL value. For object elements, the data attribute provides the property value. The content of the element is the property value for all other properties.

If the title attribute is provided for abbr elements with hCard notation, its value is considered as the hCard property instead of the element contents used otherwise.

Although it is easy to create it manually, hCard metadata can be generated by the hCard creator *hCard-o-matic* on the web site of the authors of the specification [38]. You simply fill in a form about the name, organization, country, e-mail, and other contact data, and the software generates the hCard.

To provide additional information, microformats can also be nested. For example, a sport event review might contain not only the review but also personal information (hCard) at the same time (Listing 7-12).

---

[4]If n is omitted but fn is present, the value of n will be equal to the value of fn.

Listing 7-12. A Combination of hReview and hCard

```
<div class="hreview">
  <span class="item"><strong class="item"><span class="fn">The winner takes it all</span>
Review</strong></span>
  <span class="reviewer vcard">
  By <span class="fn">John Smith</span>, <span class="title">Editor</span>↵
  at <span class="org">Consumer Reviews</span>
  </span>
  Rating: <span class="rating">4.5</span> out of 5.
  <span class="description">A fascinating performance.</span>
</div>
```

The review is described by the hReview microformat (`class="hreview"`). The name of the reviewer is revealed by `span class="reviewer"`. The hCard microformat is nested inside the hReview microformat in order to provide additional information about him (a space-separated list of attribute values in `<span class="reviewer vcard">`). The hCard properties describe the name (`fn`), job title (`title`), and organization (`org`) of the reviewer.

rel="license"

There are millions of web resources with some or all rights reserved. Many licenses associated with documents and objects are sophisticated, and users cannot be expected to know them.

The `rel="license"` microformat can be added to hyperlinks that point to the description of the license. This is especially useful for images but can be used for any resources.

Basic image embeddings apply only the `src` and `alt` attributes on the `img` element, such as in Listing 7-13.

Listing 7-13. A Basic Image Embedding

```
<img src="hotel.jpg" alt="The Palace Hotel" />
```

To declare the image license, the `rel` and `href` attributes should also be used. In the case of the *Creative Commons Attribution ShareAlike license*, for example, it should be in the form shown in Listing 7-14.

Listing 7-14. Declaring an Image License

```
<img src="hotel.jpg" alt="The Palace Hotel" rel="license"↵
 ref="http://creativecommons.org/licenses/by-sa/3.0/" />
```

The value of the `href` attribute provides the associated URI of the resource where the license is described. Some of the most commonly used *license deeds* are [39] as follows:

- Creative Commons Attribution (cc by)

  http://creativecommons.org/licenses/by/3.0/

- Creative Commons Attribution Share Alike (cc by-sa)

  http://creativecommons.org/licenses/by-sa/3.0

- Creative Commons Attribution No Derivatives (cc by-nd)

  http://creativecommons.org/licenses/by-nd/3.0

- Creative Commons Attribution Non-Commercial (cc by-nc)

  http://creativecommons.org/licenses/by-nc/3.0

- Creative Commons Attribution Non-Commercial Share Alike (cc by-nc-sa)

  `http://creativecommons.org/licenses/by-nc-sa/3.0`

- Creative Commons Attribution Non-Commercial No Derivatives (cc by-nc-nd)

  `http://creativecommons.org/licenses/by-nc-nd/3.0`

You should select a license that matches what you let others do with your work (distribute commercially or noncommercially, remix, tweak, share with proper crediting, alter, and so on).

The profile of this microformat is `http://microformats.org/profile/rel-license` [40], which can be specified on the head (X)HTML tag as shown in Listing 7-15.

Listing 7-15. The Head Profile of "rel=license"

```
<head profile="http://microformats.org/profile/rel-license">
```

rel="nofollow"

One value of the `rel` attribute deserves extended attention, because it is often used in *search engine optimization* (SEO). When `rel="nofollow"` is added to a hyperlink, the link destination should not be considered for additional ranking by search engines. This attribute value can be applied if document owners need hyperlinks without affecting the ranking of their web pages or links to external web sites. For example, if a hyperlink is vital on the web page but its destination page has a very low PageRank, the hyperlink should be provided with `rel="nofollow"` to avoid search engine penalty.

■ **Note** PageRank (PR) is a link analysis algorithm used to assign a numerical weighting to each web document in order to express its relative importance on a 0–10 scale.

For example, if `lowprsite.com` has a low PR but you have to link to it because of the content presented there, you can use the `rel="nofollow"` microformat as shown in Listing 7-16.

Listing 7-16. A Link That Will Be Not Considered by Search Engines While Indexing a Page

```
<a href="http://www.lowprsite.com" rel="nofollow">Low PR site</a>
```

Listing 7-17 shows the profile URI of this microformat.

Listing 7-17. The Profile URI of `rel="nofollow"`

```
<link rel="profile" href="http://microformats.org/profile/rel-nofollow">
```

Although it is widely used, there are several open issues about this microformat [41]. The `rel="nofollow"` microformat indicates a behavior rather than a relationship, so the definition is illogical. The name of the microformat does not reflect the real meaning. It is not a noun. It does not affect spamming. Finally, many legitimate nonspam links might be ignored or given reduced weight, which is an unfortunate side effect that should be eliminated [42].

rel="tag"

The rel="tag" is still a draft specification since 2005 [43]. Unlike other microformats and general meta keywords, this microformat can be used for visible links. It can be applied on hyperlink elements to indicate that the destination of the link is a general author-designated tag (keyword) for the current page.

Within this microformat, spaces can be provided either as + or as %20. Unicode characters are encoded according to the generic syntax rules of URIs described by the Internet Society (RFC 3986 [44]).

Vote Links

Vote Links is an elemental microformat with three possible values on the rev attribute of the a element: vote-for, vote-against, and vote-abstain. The values are mutually exclusive. Optionally, visible rollovers can be provided by the title attribute. Listing 7-18 shows an example.

Listing 7-18. A Vote Links Example

```
<a rev="vote-for" href="http://example.com/thumbsup/"↩
 title="HTML should be the primary markup language">HTML5</a>
<a rev="vote-against" href="http://example.com/thumbsdown/"↩
 title="XHTML should be the primary markup language">XHTML5</a>
```

Initially, the draft specification applied Vote Links on the rel attribute, which is now deprecated [45]. Listing 7-19 shows the URI profile reference.

Listing 7-19. The URI Profile for Vote Links

```
<link rel="profile" href="http://microformats.org/profile/vote-links">
```

XFN

The very first HTML microformat, XHTML Friends Network (XFN), was introduced in December 2003 [46]. XFN was designed by Global Multimedia Protocols Group to express human relationships with simple hyperlinks [47]. XFN is especially useful for brochure-style home pages and blog entries.

The name of the person should be provided as the text of the hyperlink (between <a> and </a>). The personal web site is the target of the hyperlink, in other words, the value of the href attribute. All relationship data can be provided by the rel attribute on a elements. Multiple values are allowed and should be separated by spaces. The friendship type can be contact, acquaintance, or friend. If the person is known personally, it can be expressed by the met attribute value of the rel attribute. For example, a friend of Leslie Sikos whom he knows personally can publish that relationship on his web site by XFN, as shown in Listing 7-20.

Listing 7-20. Link to the Web Site of a Friend

```
I am an old friend of <a href="http://lesliesikos.com" rel="friend met">Leslie Sikos</a>.
```

The distance between the residence of the person and that of his friend can be expressed by the co-resident and neighbor values. Relatives can set to child, parent, sibling, spouse, or kin. The professional relationships co-worker and colleague are also supported. Feelings can also be expressed (muse, crush, date, sweetheart) [48].

CSS styles can also be added to XFN metadata. For example, friends can be provided in bold and colleagues in italic with the CSS rules shown in Listing 7-21.

Listing 7-21. Styling XFN

```
a[rel~="friend"] {
  font-weight: bold;
}

a[rel~="colleague "] {
  font-style: italic;
}
```

Although it is easy to create XFN from scratch, XFN creators such as XFN Creator [49] or Exefen [50] might speed up development.

XMDP

XHTML MetaData Profiles (XMDP) metadata is an XHTML-based format for defining metadata profiles that are both machine- and human-readable. XMDP consists of a property definition list, an optional description, and then, if applicable, one or more definition list items. The profile definition list is identified by the class (Listing 7-22).

Listing 7-22. XMDP Profile Definition

```
<dl class="profile">
```

The definition term is identified by the id (Listing 7-23).

Listing 7-23. Definition Term and Data for XMDP

```
<dt id="property1">property1</dt>
<dd>propertydesc</dd>
```

The informatively used meta properties author and keywords, for example, can be defined by XMDP as shown in Listing 7-24 [51].

Listing 7-24. A Complete XMDP Example

```
<dl class="profile">
  <dt id="author">author</dt>
  <dd>A person who wrote (at least part of) the document.</dd>
  <dt id="keywords">keywords</dt>
  <dd>A comma and/or space separated list of the keywords or keyphrases of the document.</dd>
</dl>
```

Listing 7-25 shows the structure of an XMDP profile URI.

Listing 7-25. An XMDP Profile URI

```
<link rel="profile" href="http://gmpg.org/xmdp/samplehtmlprofile.html">
```

Drafts and Future Microformats

The number of newly developed microformats is increasing. You can apply them to provide specific metadata on a wide variety of resources.

Address information can be described by adr [52]. Geographic coordinates (latitude-longitude pairs) can be provided according to the *World Geodetic System* (WGS) with the geo microformat [53]. hAtom can be used for web syndication [54]. Information about audio recordings can be embedded by using the hAudio microformat [55]. The hListing microformat can be applied for open, distributed listings [56]. Image, video, and audio media components can be described by hMedia [57]. hNews is a microformat to provide news content on web sites [58]. Product descriptions can be expressed in hProduct [59]. Cooking and baking recipes can be described on the Web with hRecipe [60]. Resumes and CVs can be published with hResume [61]. Document reviews can be written in hReview [62]. The rel-directory microdata can indicate that a link destination is a directory listing that refers to the current page [63]. File attachments provided for downloading can be indicated by the rel-enclosure microformat [64]. rel-home provides a hyperlink to the home page of the web site [65]. The rel-payment microformat is an online payment mechanism [66]. The reworking of the robots meta tag is the robots-exclusion microformat [67]. The xFolk microformat (stands for xFolksomony) was designed for publishing collections of bookmarks [68].

The Microformats Community welcomes metadata enthusiasts to create new microformats [69].

HTML5 Microdata

The concept of *microdata* was introduced in HTML5 for labeling content to describe a specific type of information [70]. HTML5 microdata can be used for semantical descriptions of people, organizations, events, products, reviews, and links.

■ **Note**   Many descriptions provided in HTML5 microdata can also be expressed in microformats (discussed earlier), as well as in RDFa (as you will see later). However, each format has its strengths and weaknesses, as will be described later in detail.

People

A variety of metadata can be used to describe a person on the Web. One of the options to express properties such as name, job title, or address is microdata. A person can be described with microdata as shown in Listing 7-26.

Listing 7-26. Describing a Person with Microdata

```
<div itemscope itemtype="http://data-vocabulary.org/Person">
  <span itemprop="name">Leslie Sikos</span> is the↵
  <span itemprop="title">manager</span> of
<span itemprop="affiliation">Sikos Web Consulting</span>.
</div>
```

Events

Events, such as workshops, conferences, sport events, and so on, can be described by the following microdata properties:

- description: A description of the event
- duration: The duration date of the event in ISO duration format
- endDate (dtend): The ending date and time of the event in ISO date format
- eventType (category): The category of the event, for example, Concert, Festival, Lecture
- geo: Geographical coordinates of the location with two elements: latitude and longitude
- location: Location or venue of the event
- photo: Hyperlink to a photo or image related to the event
- startDate (dtstart): The starting date and time of the event in ISO date format (required)
- summary: The name of the event (required)
- url: Hyperlink of the web page describing the details of the event

For example, a sport event can be described as shown in Listing 7-27.

Listing 7-27. Describing a Sport Event with Microdata

```
<div>
  <a href="http://www.example.com/ncws.htm">National flyball competition</a>
  <img src="flyball.jpg" alt="Flyball" />
  The national flyball competition is approaching.
  When: Nov 13, 9:00AM—12:00AM
  Where: Dog Park, 123 Arena Eve, Melbourne, VIC
  Category: Sport
</div>
```

Image Licensing with Microdata

One of the options to provide image licensing information is HTML5 microdata. Listing 7-28 shows an example.

Listing 7-28. Describing the Image License with Microdata

```
<figure itemscope itemtype="http://example.org/pics" itemref="licenses">
  <img itemprop="name" src="images/amdb9.jpg" alt="My Aston Martin DB9.">
  <figcaption itemprop="title">The DB9.</figcaption>
</figure>
<footer>
  <p id="licenses">All images are licensed under the <a itemprop="license"↵
  href="http://creativecommons.org/licenses/by-sa/3.0/">Creative Commons↵
  Attribution Share Alike license</a>.
  </p>
</footer>
```

It is strongly recommended you publish photographs on the Web with licensing metadata. This can eliminate copyright issues and licensing problems as well as contribute to advanced web searches.

Knowledge Organization Systems: Schemas, Vocabularies, and Ontologies

Taxonomies or *controlled vocabularies* are structured collections of terms that can be used as metadata element values. They are parts of conceptual data *schemas* (conceptual data models) that map concepts and their relationships. The *namespaces* reveal the meaning of tags and attributes and form *vocabularies*. Formalized conceptual structures can be defined as *ontologies*, in other words, knowledge representations of sets of concepts in a domain and the relationships between them. Web ontologies make it possible to describe complex statements in any topic in a machine-readable format.

Namespaces provide a mechanism to extend the vocabulary of markup languages. To use external vocabularies and ontologies of various metadata technologies, the XML namespace facility is applied in order to associate all properties with the appropriate schema that defines them. Specific metadata can be provided this way such as friends of the author, the nearest airport to the author, GPS coordinates of the office, and so on. User-defined namespaces (schemas) can be created for additional classes and instances of resources.

Shorthand notations are used throughout the Semantic Web to reduce document length. A popular mechanism is called the *qualified name* (*Qname*), which is applied in XML, XML Schema, RDF, RDF Schema, OWL, Dublin Core, and so on. The following are the most common Qnames:

- `dc`

  Refers to the namespace URI http://purl.org/dc/elements/1.1/

- `owl`

  Refers to the namespace URI http://www.w3.org/2002/07/owl#

- `rdf`

  Refers to the namespace URI http://www.w3.org/1999/02/22-rdf-syntax-ns#

- `rdfs`

  Refers to the namespace URI http://www.w3.org/2000/01/rdf-schema#

- `xsd`

  Refers to the namespace URI http://www.w3.org/2001/XMLSchema#

The selection of Semantic Web applications is increasing. For example, OntosMiner runs ontology-driven multilingual information extraction and provides the output in various formats, including RDF(S), XML, OWL, and N3 [71]. Clinical archetypes can be represented and managed as web ontologies in OWL. OWL can also be applied for e-government representations. Web ontologies can be applied for considering viewpoints of learning resources such as online programming courses [72]. Financial headline news can also be represented by ontologies [73]. The following is a short list of some of the more established knowledge organization systems:

- *Functional Requirements for Bibliographic Records*, often abbreviated as *FRBR*, can be used to express bibliographic records with properties such as `creator`, `part`, `embodiment`, `successor`, and `subject`. FRBR has four classes: `Work`, `Expression`, `Manifestation`, and `Item` [74].

- Licenses of creative works can be denoted by *Creative Commons*. The Creative Commons Rights Expression Language is ideal to describe copyright in RDF. It has properties such as `permits`, `requires`, `prohibits`, `jurisdiction`, `legalcode`, and `deprecatedOn`, as well as the classes `Work`, `License`, `Jurisdiction`, `Permission`, `Requirement`, and `Prohibition` [75].

- The *Open Digital Rights Language* is an open standard for policy expressions and is being developed and promoted by the ODRL Initiative [76]. The digital management of rights performed using ODRL has also caught attention, and ODRL is also described as a W3C Note [77].

- Data related to video files, films, and video production can be described using *VidOnt*, the Video Ontology [78].

- Geographic positions can be precisely annotated in *Geo*. It has the lat, long, and alt properties and the SpatialThing and Point classes [79].

- Biographical information can be expressed by the *Bio* vocabulary [80].

- In education, the IMS/IEEE *Learning Object Metadata* (*LOM*) can do a service [81].

- Math-Net can be applied to standardize the presentation of information on mathematical departments and research institutes [82].

- People and their social networks can be precisely described in RDF/XML or OWL by Friend of a Friend (FOAF) properties such as name, homepage, knows, weblog, and interest (see the section "FOAF") [83]. FOAF should be used on all social networking sites.

- Professional capabilities and achievements can be described by Description of a Career (DOAC) (see the section "DOAC") [84]. DOAC is compatible with the European Curriculum (Europass) that can be generated from a FOAF+DOAC file.

- Software projects, in particular open source ones, can be expressed in Description of a Project (DOAP) [85].

These schemas, vocabularies, and ontologies are just demonstrations for the endless variety. The list is not complete by any means. VocabularyMarket [86], vocab.org [87], and other libraries collect further specific and sophisticated vocabularies, schemas, and ontologies such as the Beer Ontology [88], the Music Vocabulary [89], or the Music Ontology [90]. You can also find many vocabularies with a Google search.

Web ontologies have their limitations and open issues, however. For example, the verification of OWL ontologies with rule extensions is rather complex. However, they can be verified at the symbolic level by using a declarative approach (a new language called Datalog) [91]. The semantic differences between various ontologies should be resolved. The effort to achieve that goal is known as *ontology alignment*. Storing and retrieving data from large RDFs can be performed by advanced techniques only [92].

FOAF

FOAF is a machine-readable ontology to describe people and their contact data, interests, and relationships with other people. In 2007, Berners-Lee defined a new Semantic Web concept known as the "Giant Global Graph". He stated that FOAF is an important part of the GGG: "I express my network in a FOAF file, and that is a start of the revolution" [93].

Unlike conventional online social networks developed in PHP or JSP, FOAF networks can be built without a centralized database. Additionally, FOAF content can be processed automatically. No one has to search for friends in FOAF networks because the system itself describes the connections.[5] According to the original FOAF project started in 2000, these systems are open networks [94].

There are more and more FOAF search engines, for example, QDOS FOAFNet [95], netEstate Friend Of A Friend (FOAF) Search Engine [96], the Semantic Web Search [97], or Quatuo [98]. The latter one, for example, can also be used for creating FOAF files. However, there are dedicated FOAF generators as well. The most well-known is FOAF-O-MATIC developed by Leigh Dodds. FOAF files can be generated by filling in a form (Figure 7-2) [99].

---

[5]However, anybody can provide their own FOAF file and search for others'.

Figure 7-2. FOAF-a-matic in action

Some of the popular content management systems, such as Drupal, also support FOAF [100]. Prior to these tools, the lack of a graphical user interface could have been the major reason why this powerful technology has not come into general use until recently.

The FOAF vocabulary provides a variety of classes and properties to express personal data and relationships [83]:

- Basic information

  - Classes: Agent, Person

  - Properties: name, nick, title, homepage, mbox, mbox_sha1sum, img, depiction (depicts), surname, family_name, givenname, firstName

- Personal information

  - Properties: weblog, knows, interest, currentProject, pastProject, plan, based_near, workplaceHomepage, workInfoHomepage, schoolHomepage, topic_interest, publications, geekcode, myersBriggs, dnaChecksum

- Online accounts

  - Classes: OnlineAccount, OnlineChatAccount, OnlineEcommerceAccount, OnlineGamingAccount

  - Properties: holdsAccount, accountServiceHomepage, accountName, icqChatID, msnChatID, aimChatID, jabberID, yahooChatID

- Projects and memberships

  - Classes: Project, Organization, Group

  - Properties: member, membershipClass, fundedBy, theme

- Documents and images

  - Classes: Document, Image, PersonalProfileDocument

  - Properties: topic (page), primaryTopic, tipjar, sha1, made (maker), thumbnail, logo

A complete FOAF description looks like Listing 7-29.

Listing 7-29. Describing Personal Metadata with FOAF

```
<foaf:Person>
  <foaf:name>Thomas Davis</foaf:name>
  <foaf:gender>Male</foaf:gender>
  <foaf:title>Mr</foaf:title>
  <foaf:givenname>Thomas</foaf:givenname>
  <foaf:family_name>Davis</foaf:family_name>
  <foaf:homepage rdf:resource="http://www.example.com"/>
  <foaf:weblog rdf:resource="http://www.example.com/blog/"/>
</foaf:Person>
```

As you will see, such descriptions can be embedded in XML and RDF files. In contrast to the profiles of conventional community portals, such as the ones driven by PHP and MySQL, the entire content of such files can be automatically processed. Anyone who publishes a FOAF or DOAC file on their web site can provide a machine-readable personal introduction, resources, and links to colleagues and friends.

DOAC

FOAF properties can be considered as the semantic equivalents of personal characteristics and relationships described on Facebook, and DOAC properties are the semantic counterparts of LinkedIn features. The DOAC vocabulary not only provides classes and properties to describe professional capabilities but also reapplies FOAF properties from the foaf:Person domain, including doac:summary, doac:experience, doac:education, doac:skill, doac:reference, and doac:publication [84].

Employment history and career experience can be described by the doac:title, doac:date-starts, doac:date-ends, doac:position, doac:activity, and doac:location properties of the doac:Experience class.

Education and training information can be provided by the doac:title, foaf:organization, doac:date-starts, doac:date-ends, doac:subject, and doac:level properties of the doac:Education class.

The doac:Skill class has the subclasses doac:Skill, doac:LanguageSkill, doac:SocialSkill, doac:OrganizationalSkill, doac:ComputerSkill, and doac:DrivingSkill.

A FOAF+DOAC file looks like Listing 7-30.

Listing 7-30. A Complete FOAF+DOAC Example

```
<foaf:Person>
  <foaf:name>John Smith</foaf:name>
  <foaf:mbox rdf:resource="mailto:john@jsmith.com" />
  <foaf:homepage rdf:resource="http://www.jsmith.com" />
  <doac:experience>
    <doac:VolunterExperience>
      <doac:title>CEO</doac:title>
      <doac:organization>ABC Company</doac:organization>
      <doac:start-date>2010-04-06</doac:start-date>
      <doac:end-date>2011-09-18</doac:end-date>
    </doac:VolunterExperience>
  </doac:experience>
  <doac:education>
    <doac:Degree>
      <doac:title>Information Management</doac:title>
      <doac:organization>Nanyang Technological University</doac:organization>
      <doac:start-date>2000-09-01</doac:start-date>
      <doac:end-date>2005-06-15</doac:end-date>
    </doac:Degree>
  </doac:education>
  <doac:skill>
    <doac:LanguageSkill>
      <doac:language>en</doac:language>
      <doac:reads rdf:resource="http://ramonantonio.net/doac/0.1/#nativelevel" />
      <doac:writes rdf:resource="http://ramonantonio.net/doac/0.1/#nativelevel" />
      <doac:speaks rdf:resource="http://ramonantonio.net/doac/0.1/#nativelevel" />
    </doac:LanguageSkill>
  </doac:skill>
</foaf:Person>
```

Such metadata is especially beneficial when someone is looking for a job or wants to describe the cornerstones of their career in a machine-processable format. Consequently, DOAC files could be used to enable software agents to make automatic job offers according to their qualification and experience.

Dublin Core

Dublin Core is a fundamental group of metadata elements developed and distributed by the Dublin Core Metadata Initiative (DCMI) and standardized by the International Organization for Standardization (ISO 15836 [101]), the Internet Engineering Task Force (IETF) (RFC 5013 [102]), and the American National Standards Institute (ANSI/NISO Z39.85-2007 [103]). Dublin Core metadata is often used in (X)HTML document head sections (similar to general meta tags), in attributes of XHTML+RDFa documents, and in other files such as feed channels. It can be expressed using meta and link (X)HTML elements, RDFa, RDF/XML representation, and plain XML [104]. The Dublin Core syntax is provided in the reference model defined by the *Dublin Core Abstract Model* specification [105].

The *Dublin Core Metadata Element Set* defines the 15 fundamental elements of Dublin Core, including contributor, coverage, creator, date, description, format, identifier, language, publisher, relation, rights, source, subject, title, and type [106]. If these elements are used exclusively, we are talking about *Simple Dublin Core*. The extended set of elements is a higher level of Dublin Core called *Qualified Dublin Core*, which provides more specific elements. In addition to the general rules of Simple Dublin Core, further rules apply for Qualified Dublin Core. Qualified Dublin Core properties can be not only the 15 Dublin Core elements but also other elements recommended by the Dublin Core Metadata Initiative or DCMI element refinements. Optionally, Qualified Dublin Core values might have associated encoding schemes, each of which is identified by a name. Element refinements are handled similarly to properties (element refinement name associated with a Dublin Core namespace).

Dublin Core Namespaces

Dublin Core namespaces can be declared by the rel attribute on the (X)HTML link element or with the xmlns attribute in XML. The (X)HTML declaration consists of a prefix and a namespace URI (see Listing 7-31).

Listing 7-31. A Dublin Core Namespace Declaration

```
<link rel="schema.DC" href="http://purl.org/dc/elements/1.1/" />
```

The namespace URIs of all DCMI properties, classes, and encoding schemes are defined by the following DCMI namespace URIs [107]:

- http://purl.org/dc/dcmitype/

  Classes in the DCMI Type Vocabulary

- http://purl.org/dc/dcam/

  Terms used in the DCMI Abstract Model

- http://purl.org/dc/elements/1.1/

  The Dublin Core Metadata Element Set, Version 1.1 (the 15 original elements)

- http://purl.org/dc/terms/

  All other DCMI properties, classes, and encoding schemes

The DCMI Abstract Model also applies some semantic concepts of the Resource Description Framework and RDF Schema (RDFS), including resource, property/element, class, syntax encoding scheme, some relationships (has domain, has range, sub-property of, sub-class of), and the concept of plain and typed value strings [108].

Simple Dublin Core

Dublin Core records consist of one or more properties and their associated property values (Listing 7-32).

Listing 7-32. A DC Property (Creator) and a Value Associated with It (John Smith)

```
<meta name="DC.Creator" content="John Smith" />
```

Each property should be an element from the *Dublin Core Metadata Element Set*. All properties are optional and may be repeated [109]. The DC property values are considered as literal strings and might have an associated language (for example, en-US). Dublin Core records and the resources they are applied to are not linked; however, such a linkage can optionally be provided by the identifier element with the resource URI as the property value (Listing 7-33).

Listing 7-33. Dublin Core Metadata with `identifier`

```
<dc:title>
  Tutorials
</dc:title>
<dc:description>
  HTML5 and CSS3 tutorials.
</dc:description>
<dc:publisher>
  Dr. Leslie F. Sikos
</dc:publisher>
<dc:identifier>
  http://www.lesliesikos.com/tutorials/
</dc:identifier>
```

The Dublin Core Metadata Initiative recommends three general rules for Dublin Core implementation:

1. Dublin Core properties should be provided as XML elements. Property values should be the contents of those elements. Listing 7-34 shows an example.

    Listing 7-34. Dublin Core Properties as XML Elements

    ```
    <dc:title>Dublin Core in XML element format</dc:title>
    ```

2. All Dublin Core property names should be lowercase. Listing 7-35 shows an example.

    Listing 7-35. Dublin Core Property Names in Lowercase

    ```
    <dc:title>Dublin Core example</dc:title>
    ```

3. Multiple property values should be declared by repeating the XML element for that property (see Listing 7-36).

    Listing 7-36. Repeated XML Elements for Multiple Dublin Core Property Values

    ```
    <dc:creator>John Smith</dc:creator>
    <dc:creator>Robert Johnson</dc:creator>
    ```

Qualified Dublin Core

Qualified Dublin Core makes more specific and advanced (meaningful) annotations possible than Simple Dublin Core. Using Qualified Dublin Core metadata is similar to adding Simple Dublin Core, except that Qualified Dublin Core properties can be not only from the set of the original 15 DC elements but also from additional elements or element refinements defined by the DCMI Metadata Terms recommendation [110]. Furthermore, all Qualified Dublin Core property values might have an associated encoding scheme with a unique name listed as the `Term` name in the DCMI Metadata Terms recommendation.

Beyond the general implementation guidelines, the following rules apply for Qualified Dublin Core:

1. Similar to DC properties, the element refinement names should be XML *qualified names* (*QName*) that link to the associated DCMI namespace name (Listing 7-37).

Listing 7-37. XML QName with Dublin Core

```
<dcterms:available>2011-04</dcterms:available>
```

In this example, the date or period when the resource became or will become available is expressed with Qualified Dublin Core.

Element refinements might have further embedded element refinements.

2. Encoding schemes should be declared by the xsi:type attribute on the XML element for the property. The name of the encoding scheme is provided as the attribute value in the form of a QName. Listing 7-38 shows an example.

Listing 7-38. Encoding Scheme Declaration

```
<dc:identifier xsi:type="dcterms:URI">
   http://www.example.com/
</dc:identifier>
```

3. The names of both the element refinements and the encoding schemes should be those that are specified in the DCMI Metadata Terms recommendation. The first letter of the element and element refinement names should always be in lowercase. The first letter of encoding scheme names should be in uppercase. Scheme names are often provided in all uppercase. Listing 7-39 shows an example.

Listing 7-39. Element Refinement and Encoding Scheme

```
<dcterms:isPartOf xsi:type="dcterms:URI">
   http://www.example.com/
</dcterms:isPartOf>
```

4. The language of the property value can optionally be provided by using the xml:lang attribute (Listing 7-40).

Listing 7-40. Setting the Natural Language for Dublin Core

```
<dc:subject xml:lang="en">
   website standardization
</dc:subject>
<dc:subject xml:lang="hu">
   weblap-szabványosítás
</dc:subject>
```

Dublin Core Expressed by (X)HTML Meta and Link Elements

A URI reference can be either a URI or a relative reference expressed in the RFC 3986 format [111]. URI references should be represented in full (Listing 7-41).

Listing 7-41. A Full URI Reference for the subject Metadata

```
<link rel="DCTERMS.subject" href="http://example.org/docs" />
```

Relative references are allowed only if they can be resolved by the base URI (href attribute on the base element or from the document URI). Listing 7-42 shows an example.

Listing 7-42. A Relative URI Reference for Dublin Core

```
<base href="http://example.org/docs/" />
<link rel="schema.DCTERMS" href="http://purl.org/dc/terms/" />
<link rel="DCTERMS.isReferencedBy" href="doc1" />
```

A *prefixed name* is an abbreviation for a URI used in the DC-HTML format [112]. A DC-HTML prefixed name consists of a *prefix* followed by a *period* (.) and a *local name*. For example, a DC-HTML prefixed name is expressed as attribute value in the form shown in Listing 7-43.

Listing 7-43. A DC-HTML Prefixed Name

```
<link rel="schema.DC" href="http://purl.org/dc/elements/1.1/" />
<meta name="DC.title" content="Smartphone descriptions" />
```

A Dublin Core statement is represented by either an (X)HTML meta or a link element, depending on the content of the statement (literal or nonliteral value surrogate). For example, the document title can be provided by the meta element as presented in Listing 7-44, while the subject is represented by the link element as in Listing 7-45.

Listing 7-44. Document Title Declared Using Dublin Core

```
<meta name="DC.title" content="Smartphone descriptions" />
```

Listing 7-45. Document Subject Declared Using Dublin Core

```
<link rel="DCTERMS.subject" href="http://example.org/topic" title="Topic" />
```

Dublin Core metadata on the document language, author, and so on, can be declared in the XHTML document head, as shown in Listing 7-46.

Listing 7-46. Document Language and Creator Described with Dublin Core

```
<meta name="DC.language" content="en" />
<meta property="dc:creator" content="John Smith" />
```

Dublin Core Expressed in XML

Creating XML applications with Simple Dublin Core metadata according to XML schemas instead of XML DTDs is recommended. XML namespaces should be applied to identify Dublin Core elements, element refinements, or encoding schemes. Properties should be encoded as XML elements and values. The names of these XML elements should be XML qualified names (QNames). Property names should be all lowercase. The XML element should be repeated when providing multiple property values.

The `xsi:type` attribute of the XML element should be applied for implementing encoding schemes. Element refinements and encoding schemes use the names specified by the DCMI Metadata Terms. The `xml:lang` attribute should be applied to provide the language of Qualified Dublin Core values in XML [113]. Listing 7-47 shows a complex example.

Listing 7-47. Dublin Core in XML

```
<?xml version="1.0"?>
<metadata
 xmlns="http://example.org/myapp/"
 xmlns:xsi="http://www.w3.org/2001/XMLSchema-instance"
 xsi:schemaLocation="http://example.com/xmlapp/ http://example.com/schemata/schema.xsd"
 xmlns:dc="http://purl.org/dc/elements/1.1/">
  <dc:title>
    DC in XML sample document
  </dc:title>
  <dc:description>
    The description of the XML application.
  </dc:description>
  <dc:publisher>
    John Smith
  </dc:publisher>
  <dc:identifier>
    http://www.example.com
  </dc:identifier>
</metadata>
```

Dublin Core Description Sets (DC-DS-XML) can also be expressed in XML [114]. These sets consist of one or more descriptions containing zero or one described resource URI, and one or more statements. The statements contain one property URI and one value surrogate. Depending on the type of the value surrogate, it can be one value string (in case of literal value surrogates) or zero or one value URIs, zero or one vocabulary encoding scheme URI, and zero or more value strings (in case of nonliteral value surrogates). A value string can be a plain value string or a typed value string. The first one can optionally be associated with a value string language, while the latter one has a syntax encoding scheme URI. Nonliteral values can also be described by other descriptions.

A *description set element* has an expanded name with the pair of the XML namespace name http://purl.org/dc/xmlns/2008/09/01/dc-ds-xml/ and the local name descriptionSet (Listing 7-48).

Listing 7-48. A Description Set Element

```
<?xml version="1.0" encoding="UTF-8" ?>
<dcds:descriptionSet
 xmlns:dcds="http://purl.org/dc/xmlns/2008/09/01/dc-ds-xml/">
  <dcds:description>
    <dcds:statement
     dcds:propertyURI="http://purl.org/dc/terms/title">
      <dcds:literalValueString>
        Smith and Sons Inc Home Page
      </dcds:literalValueString>
    </dcds:statement>
  </dcds:description>
</dcds:descriptionSet>
```

Description elements are XML elements that are child elements of description set elements with the name `dcds:description`.

A statement element is a single Dublin Core statement represented by a child XML element of a description element. Statement elements have the name `dcds:statement`.

Value string elements are child elements of statement elements. Literal value surrogates, the value surrogates for literal values containing one value string representing a literal, can be encoded by the value string element `dcds:literalValueString`, which can be provided just once per statement element.

Nonliteral value surrogates optionally contain a value URI represented as the value of the XML attribute `dcds:valueURI` of the statement element (Listing 7-49).

Listing 7-49. Optional Value URI in a Nonliteral Value Surrogate

```
<dcds:statement⏎
 dcds:propertyURI="http://purl.org/dc/terms/publisher"⏎
 dcds:valueURI="http://example.com">
  <dcds:valueString>Smith and Sons Inc</dcds:valueString>
</dcds:statement>
```

For nonliteral value surrogates, the *vocabulary encoding scheme URI* can optionally be provided by the `dcds:vesURI` attribute.

The *value string language* of plain value strings can be provided by the `xml:lang` attribute of the value string element. Language identifiers of IETF RFC 4646 or later [115] should be applied. Listing 7-50 shows an example.

Listing 7-50. Value String Language Declaration

```
<?xml version="1.0" encoding="UTF-8" ?>
  <dcds:descriptionSet⏎
   xmlns:dcds="http://purl.org/dc/xmlns/2008/09/01/dc-ds-xml/">
    <dcds:description⏎
     dcds:resourceURI="http://example.com">
    <dcds:statement⏎
      dcds:propertyURI="http://purl.org/dc/terms/title">
      <dcds:literalValueString xml:lang="en-US">
        Example document
      </dcds:literalValueString>
    </dcds:statement>
  </dcds:description>
</dcds:descriptionSet>
```

For typed value strings, the syntax encoding scheme URI attribute `dcds:sesURI` should be used.

Dublin Core Expressed in RDF

Simple Dublin Core can be expressed also in RDF, including RDF/XML serialization [116]. Listing 7-51 shows an example that includes an XML declaration, a reference to the XML DTD, an RDF declaration, and the resource descriptions.

Listing 7-51. Dublin Core in RDF/XML

```
<?xml version="1.0"?>
<!DOCTYPE rdf:RDF PUBLIC "-//DUBLIN CORE//DCMES DTD 2002/07/31//EN"↩
 "http://dublincore.org/documents/2002/07/31/dcmes-xml/dcmes-xml-dtd.dtd">
<rdf:RDF xmlns:rdf="http://www.w3.org/1999/02/22-rdf-syntax-ns#"↩
 xmlns:dc="http://purl.org/dc/elements/1.1/">
  <rdf:Description>
    <dc:title>Internet for everyone</dc:title>
    <dc:creator>Leslie Sikos</dc:creator>
    <dc:format>Book</dc:format>
    <dc:identifier>ISBN 963 9425 08 7</dc:identifier>
  </rdf:Description>
</rdf:RDF>
```

XML character-encoding rules apply. Optionally, the language of any element in these documents can be provided by the xml:lang attribute.

Expressing Qualified Dublin Core in RDF is described by another DCMI specification [117]. In contrast, properties such as dc:creator and dc:date are considered in this document as entities rather than names. Listing 7-52 shows an example.

Listing 7-52. Qualified Dublin Core in RDF

```
<http://www.example.com> dc:creator <http://www.example.org/pj>
```

The original specifications defining the RDF implementations of DC have been superseded by the 2008 specification [118] and notes [119]. For example, the RDF schemas for DCMI properties and classes have been removed from the specification.

Knowledge Representation Standards

Resource Description Framework (RDF)

Although it was originally designed as a metadata data model, *Resource Description Framework* (*RDF*) has become a general web resource description and modeling language. It can be used for conceptual description or modeling of information stored in web resources. RDF can be used to create a machine-readable description about any kind of resource, because RDF files can be extended with an arbitrary number of external vocabularies. In contrast to many W3C standards, RDF has no single specification but is defined by a set of documents [120].

The RDF data model can be used for describing any kind of resources that can be identified by a URI. As mentioned earlier, an RDF document is a sequence of statements called *RDF triples* (resource–property–value or subject–predicate–object). The predicate (property) that denotes a relationship between the subject and the object can be binary only. Any expression in RDF is a collection of triples. A set of triples is called an *RDF graph*, which is a directed, labeled graph that represents information on the Web. The nodes of the RDF graph are the resources and values [121].

As shown earlier, a person can be described using the FOAF vocabulary. Such descriptions can be written either in XML or in RDF. Listing 7-53 shows how to write FOAF in RDF.

Listing 7-53. Describing a Person in RDF

```
<rdf:RDF↵
 xmlns:rdf="http://www.w3.org/1999/02/22-rdf-syntax-ns#"↵
 xmlns:foaf="http://xmlns.com/foaf/0.1/"↵
 xmlns="http://www.example.com/johnsmith/contact.rdf#">
  <foaf:Person rdf:about="http://www.example.com/johnsmith/contact.rdf#johnsmith">
    <foaf:mbox rdf:resource="mailto:john.smith@example.com" />
    <foaf:homepage rdf:resource="http://www.example.com/johnsmith/" />
    <foaf:family_name>Smith</foaf:family_name>
    <foaf:givenname>John</foaf:givenname>
  </foaf:Person>
</rdf:RDF>
```

Figure 7-3 represents this file as an RDF graph.

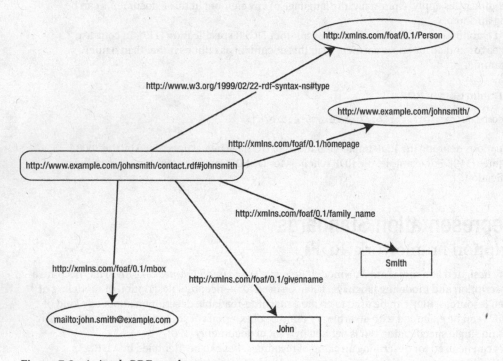

Figure 7-3. *A simple RDF graph*

As you will see, RDF can be expressed in a variety of formats. For example, Listing 7-54 is another notation of Listing 7-53. This notation, N3, will also be described later in detail.

Listing 7-54. The N3 Equivalent of the Previous Example

```
@prefix :      <http://www.example.org/~joe/contact.rdf#> .
@prefix foaf: <http://xmlns.com/foaf/0.1/> .
@prefix rdf:  <http://www.w3.org/1999/02/22-rdf-syntax-ns#> .

:joesmith a foaf:Person ;
  foaf:givenname "Joe" ;
  foaf:family_name "Smith" ;
  foaf:homepage <http://www.example.org/~joe/> ;
  foaf:mbox <mailto:joe.smith@example.org>.
```

The RDF namespace is http://www.w3.org/1999/02/22-rdf-syntax-ns#, which is conventionally associated with the namespace prefix rdf:.

The Unicode strings in URI references of RDF graphs cannot contain control characters (#x00–#x1F, #x7F–#x9F). These URIs should be absolute URIs with optional fragment identifiers.

RDF literals are used to identify values such as numbers and dates. RDF literals are Unicode strings containing one or two named components. They should be written in *UTF-8 normalized in Normalization Form C* (Canonical Decomposition followed by Canonical Composition [122]). RDF literals can be either plain or typed. Plain literals are strings combined with an optional language tag (normalized to lowercase). They correspond to plain text in a natural language. Typed literals are strings combined with a datatype URI for applying the lexical-to-value mapping to the literal string.

The Formal Grammar of the Resource Description Framework was introduced in 1999 [123]. RDF has the following vocabulary:

- rdf:Alt, rdf:Bag, rdf:Seq

  Containers of alternatives, unordered containers, and ordered containers (rdfs:Container is a superclass of the three)

- rdf:List

  The class of RDF lists

- rdf:nil

  An empty list (an instance of rdf:List)

- rdf:Property

  The class of properties

- rdf:Statement, rdf:subject, rdf:predicate, rdf:object

  Reification

- rdf:type

  A predicate that identifies the class that the resource is an instance of

- rdf:XMLLiteral

  The class of typed literals

This vocabulary is also used as the basis for the extensible knowledge representation language, *RDF Schema* (see the section "RDF Schema").

There is a *query language* called *SPARQL* (pronounced "Sparkle") that can be used to retrieve and manipulate information stored in RDF or in any format that can be retrieved as RDF [124]. The output can be a results set or an RDF graph. It is also possible to update RDF graphs through a protocol known as the *SPARQL 1.1 Uniform HTTP Protocol* [125].

The Resource Description Framework technology is important from the standardization point of view for many reasons. First, the basic data model of RDF is a standard graph. Second, the naming system applies standard URLs. The data retrieval and composition mechanisms used by RDF are also standard technologies.

RDF can be provided in a variety of syntaxes/serialization formats, for example, RDF XML serialization (RDF/XML), RDFa, Turtle, Notation3, JSON-LD, N-Triples [126], TRiG [127], and TRiX [128]. The most common ones are described in the next sections.

RDF in XML Serialization Syntax

The recommended and most frequently used syntax for RDF applications is the XML serialization format, RDF/XML [129]. Although there are other notations of RDF that are easier to read and write (see the next sections), RDF/XML provides widely accepted XML documents. However, the fundamental problem with RDF/XML is the contradiction of representing a graph with a tree structure.

The Internet media type for RDF/XML is `application/rdf+xml`. The recommended file extension is `.rdf`.

The XML serialization of RDF provides well-formed XML documents (Chapter 1).

A person's Wikipedia page, for example, can be described in a machine-readable form in RDF/XML, as shown in Listing 7-55.

Listing 7-55. A Wikipedia Page Described in RDF/XML

```
<rdf:RDF
 xmlns:rdf="http://www.w3.org/1999/02/22-rdf-syntax-ns#"
 xmlns:dc="http://purl.org/dc/elements/1.1/">
  <rdf:Description rdf:about="http://en.wikipedia.org/wiki/Rowan_Atkinson">
    <dc:title>Rowan Atkinson</dc:title>
    <dc:publisher>Wikipedia</dc:publisher>
  </rdf:Description>
</rdf:RDF>
```

RDF in N3 Syntax

Notation 3, often abbreviated as *N3*, is a shorthand non-XML serialization of RDF. It is a superset of RDF and is more compact than the XML serialization of RDF. The grammar of N3 is defined by W3C in many formats [130], for example, in *Extended Backus-Naur Form* (*EBNF*)[6] [131].

The MIME type and character encoding of N3 should be declared as `text/n3; charset=utf-8`. The typical file extension is `.n3`. Tokenizing and whitespace handling are not specified in the grammar.

Base URIs to be used for the parsing of relative URIs can be set with the `@base` directive in the form `@base <http://example.com/overview/>`.

A prefix can be associated to a namespace URI by the `@prefix` directive.

Several rules for string escaping are derived from Python, namely, `stringliteral`, `stringprefix`, `shortstring`, `shortstringitem`, `longstring`, `longstringitem`, `shortstringchar`, and `longstringchar`. Additionally, the `\U` extension, also used in another RDF serialization (N-Triples), can be applied. Legal escape sequences are `\newline`, `\\` (backslash, `\`), `\'` (single quote, `'`), `\"` (double quote, `"`), `\n` (ASCII Linefeed, LF), `\r` (ASCII Carriage Return, CR), `\t` (ASCII Horizontal Tab, TAB), `\uhhhh` (Unicode character in BMP), and `\U00hhhhhh` (Unicode character in plane 1–16 notation). The escapes `\a`, `\b`, `\f`, and `\v` cannot be used because the corresponding characters are not allowed in RDF.

---

[6]EBNF is a family of metasyntax notations that can be used to express context-free grammars.

Shorthand notation can be used for the following common predicates:

- a (stands for <http://www.w3.org/1999/02/22-rdf-syntax-ns#type>)

- = (stand for <http://www.w3.org/2002/07/owl#sameAs>)

- => (stands for <http://www.w3.org/2000/10/swap/log#implies>)

- <= (stands for <http://www.w3.org/2000/10/swap/log#implies>)

New classes and new properties can be defined in new vocabularies [132]. A class can be defined as Listing 7-56 because the rdf:type property is abbreviated as a in N3.

Listing 7-56. An RDF Class in N3

```
:Sport a rdfs:Class.
```

An object of the class can be defined as shown in Listing 7-57.

Listing 7-57. Declare an Object of a Class in N3

```
:Kayak a :Sport.
```

Objects can be in multiple classes. Relationships between classes can be written as shown in Listing 7-58.

Listing 7-58. Class Relationships in N3

```
:Watersport a rdfs:Class; rdfs:subClassOf :Sport.
```

A property can be defined as shown in Listing 7-59.

Listing 7-59. Property Declaration in N3

```
:paddle a rdf:Property.
```

Relationships between classes are not necessarily hierarchical relationships. You can see an example in Listing 7-60.

Listing 7-60. Nonhierarchical Relationships in N3

```
:paddle rdfs:domain :Sport;
        rdfs:range :Watersport.
```

The person's Wikipedia page described in the previous section can be written in N3 as shown in Listing 7-61.

Listing 7-61. A Wikipedia Page Description in N3

```
@prefix dc: <http://purl.org/dc/elements/1.1/>.

<http://en.wikipedia.org/wiki/Rowan_Atkinson>
  dc:title "Rowan Atkinson";
  dc:publisher "Wikipedia".
```

Notation3 has several subsets, including Turtle, N-Triples, N3 RDF, and N3 Rules. The most popular of them is discussed in the next section.

RDF in Turtle Syntax

A subset of N3 is the *Terse RDF Triple Language*, often referred to as *Turtle*. Turtle provides a syntax to describe RDF graphs in a compact textual form, which is easy to develop. It is a subset of Notation 3 (N3) and a superset of N-Triples. Turtle is popular among Semantic Web developers and considered as an easy-to-read alternative to RDF/XML. Turtle is being standardized by the World Wide Web Consortium [133]. The typical file extension of Turtle files is .ttl. The character encoding of Turtle files should be UTF-8. The MIME type of Turtle is text/turtle. Turtle is supported by many software frameworks that can be used for querying and analyzing RDF data, such as Jena [134], Redland [135], and Sesame [136].

Turtle files consist of a sequence of directives, statements representing triples, and blank lines. Triples can be written in Turtle as a sequence of subject – predicate – object terms, separated by whitespace, and terminated by a period (.). URIs should be written in angle brackets (<>). Literals are delimited by double quotes (""). Listing 7-62 shows an example.

Listing 7-62. A Basic Example for the Turtle Syntax

```
<http://example.com/shop> <http://example.com/contact> "Text content".
```

URI length can be reduced by the @PREFIX (Listing 7-63).

Listing 7-63. A URI Prefix Declaration

```
@PREFIX ex: <http://example.com/>.
```

In that case, the first example can be written as in Listing 7-64.

Listing 7-64. Using a Prefix

```
ex:shop ex:contact "Text content".
```

where ex:shop declares the concatenation of http://example.com/ with shop, revealing the original URI http://example.com/shop.

RDFa

The power of RDF, which was demonstrated earlier, can be exploited through external files written in rather complex syntax. However, there is a nice exception: RDFa. RDFa (RDF in attributes) adds attribute-level extensions to any markup language (from this point of view, the host language, as discussed earlier in Chapter 3) in order to describe structured data. In other words, RDFa notations can be declared in attributes, rather than elements (which is the approach used by other RDF serialization formats). Although many attributes are defined by RDFa, some markup attributes (such as href and rel) are reused. Wherever possible, the textual content is also reused. RDFa can serve as a bridge between the "human and data Webs," since RDFa makes it possible to write RDF triples in the (X)HTML markup [137]. Structured information can be extracted and utilized from web documents via an RDFa application programming interface (RDFa API) [138]. The mechanism of the RDF data model mapping allows RDF triples to be embedded within web documents as well as the extraction of RDF model triples by compliant software.

RDFa provides the option to embed rich metadata within certain attributes of web documents [139]. The set of attributes to be used for this purpose is as follows:

- about, src

  The Unified Resource Identifier (URI) or compact URI (CURIE) [140] of the resource that describes the metadata

- `rel, rev`

  Relationship with another resource

- `href, resource`

  The partner resource

- `property`

  A property for the content of an element

- `content`

  Element content override when using the `property` attribute (optional)

- `datatype`

  The datatype of text specified for use with the `property` attribute (optional)

- `typeof`

  The RDF type(s) of the subject (optional)

RDFa makes it possible to arbitrarily mix multiple independently developed vocabularies. It can be parsed without analyzing the specific vocabularies being applied. This is one of the most advanced technologies to provide different types of machine-readable structured data in the markup.

Since the "a" in RDFa stands for attributes whose styles are provided most commonly in Cascading Style Sheets, it is straightforward to use CSS selectors to style the code [141]. For example, if the name of the creator and the book title of the previous example appear throughout the site, all instances can be styled using universal selectors (Listing 7-65).

Listing 7-65. Styling RDFa

```
* [property="dc:creator"] {
  color: #2a56d3;
  font-style:italic;

}
* [property="dc:title"] {
  font-size: 2em;
  font-family: Georgia, serif;
}
```

The latest news on RDFa can be tracked on the web site of the RDFa Working Group of W3C [142].

As an example, let's describe a person with RDFa notation using the FOAF vocabulary! First we need to declare the FOAF namespace (either in the document head or on the body element). The about attribute of RDFa can be used to express the subject, while the RDFa attribute `property` sets the predicate (Listing 7-66).

Listing 7-66. An RDFa Annotation Using FOAF

```
<body xmlns:foaf="http://xlmns.com/foaf/0.1/">
  <p about="#smith" property="foaf:name">John Smith</p>
</body>
```

The content of the p element is both a human- and machine-readable text that will be rendered on the web page.

Now extend the previous example with another person and express a relationship between the two persons (Listing 7-67)! The class of the entity can be declared by the `typeof` attribute. In this case, we use the `Person` class from the FOAF vocabulary to "let the browser know" that John Smith is a person. The second person is declared exactly the same way. Finally, we use the term `knows` from the FOAF vocabulary and pass it as the value of the `rel` attribute to express that John Smith knows Peter Johnson (declared by the `resource` attribute).

Listing 7-67. Two People and the Relationship Between Them Expressed Using FOAF in RDFa

```
<body xmlns:foaf="http://xmlns.com/foaf/0.1">
  <p>
    <span about="#john" typeof="foaf:Person" property="foaf:name">John Smith</span> is
    interested in smartphones. <span about="#jane" typeof="foaf:Person"
    property="foaf:name">Peter Johnson</span> is an Android developer. <span
    about="#john" rel="foaf:knows" resource="#peter">John and Peter knows each other.
    </span>
  </p>
</body>
```

Compare this machine-readable statement with MySQL database records displayed using PHP, and you have a glimpse of the power of the Semantic Web!

Other vocabularies can be similarly used with RDFa. For example, Dublin Core metadata can be embedded to the markup using RDFa, as shown in Listing 7-68.

Listing 7-68. An RDFa Annotation Using DC

```
<p xmlns:dc="http://purl.org/dc/elements/1.1/"
about="#standardweb" property="dc:title">
Web standardista <span about="#sikos" property="dc:creator">Dr. Sikos</span> describes
web standardization, accessibility, and web semantics in the second edition of
<cite about="#webstandards" property="dc:title">Web Standards</cite>. The first blog
post has been published on <span about="#webstandards" property="dc:date"
content="2014-10-11">11 October 2014</span>.
</p>
```

Microformats vs. Microdata vs. RDFa

You should have noticed that there are similar concepts defined by certain microformats and HTML5 microdata to describe people, events, or licenses. RDFa, on the other hand, is not limited to such concepts and can be used to annotate any kind of resource.

As discussed earlier, microformats reuse HTML attributes (for example, `class`, `title`) and have separate vocabularies that are difficult to combine, because microformats do not use the namespace mechanism. Last but not least, microformats do not define an RDF representation.[7]

HTML5 microdata, as also presented earlier, provides new attributes for HTML5 markup. HTML5 microdata is easy to write and works well in documents that use a single external vocabulary. Combining different vocabularies is rather complex in HTML5 microdata. Some vocabulary mappings, such as that of Dublin Core elements, are supported by the technology by default. A missing feature is the concept of data types and namespaces. Fortunately, however, HTML5 microdata defines a generic mapping to RDF, so it can be used to express triples.

---

[7]It is possible to transform microformats to RDF using technologies such as XSLT and GRDDL, but such transformations depend on the vocabularies being used.

In contrast to microformats and microdata, RDFa is a complete serialization of RDF and hence provides the most advanced annotation of them all. RDFa defines new markup attributes and uses URIs and namespaces by default. Consequently, combining vocabularies is very easy (similar to RDF). RDFa is completely flexible regarding literals and URI resources.

RDF Schema

According to the W3C Metadata Activity, *RDF Schema* (*RDFS*) is "a declarative representation language influenced by ideas from knowledge representation" [143]. RDF Schema extends RDF with structure (classes, properties of properties, and so on). It can be used to formalize metadata exchange between human-readable and machine-processable vocabularies. Beyond the basic RDF vocabulary discussed earlier, RDFS has several additional constructs [144]:

- Classes
  - rdf:Property
  - rdf:XMLLiteral
  - rdfs:Class
  - rdfs:Datatype
  - rdfs:Literal
  - rdfs:Resource
- Properties
  - rdf:type
  - rdfs:comment
  - rdfs:domain
  - rdfs:isDefinedBy
  - rdfs:label
  - rdfs:range
  - rdfs:seeAlso
  - rdfs:subClassOf
  - rdfs:subPropertyOf

These classes and properties provide an even more advanced level of knowledge representation than RDF does and can be used for basic description of web ontologies. This is the reason why a more expressive language, the Web Ontology Language (OWL), reuses many RDFS components (see next section).

For example, the resource "macaw" can be declared as a subclass of the class "birds," as shown in Listing 7-69.

Listing 7-69. A Simple RDFS Example

```
<?xml version="1.0"?>
<rdf:RDF↵
 xmlns:rdf="http://www.w3.org/1999/02/22-rdf-syntax-ns#"↵
 xmlns:rdfs="http://www.w3.org/2000/01/rdf-schema#"↵
 xml:base="http://www.example.com/birds#">
  <rdf:Description rdf:ID="bird">
    <rdf:type rdf:resource="http://www.w3.org/2000/01/rdf-schema#Class"/>
  </rdf:Description>
  <rdf:Description rdf:ID="macaw">
    <rdf:type rdf:resource="http://www.w3.org/2000/01/rdf-schema#Class"/>
    <rdfs:subClassOf rdf:resource="#bird"/>
  </rdf:Description>
</rdf:RDF>
```

This notation can also be shortened by using `rdfs:Class` instead of `rdf:Description` and omitting `rdf:type` (Listing 7-70).

Listing 7-70. An Optimized Version of the Previous Example

```
<?xml version="1.0"?>
<rdf:RDF↵
 xmlns:rdf="http://www.w3.org/1999/02/22-rdf-syntax-ns#"↵
 xmlns:rdfs="http://www.w3.org/2000/01/rdf-schema#"↵
 xml:base="http://www.example.com/birds#">
  <rdfs:Class rdf:ID="bird" />
    <rdfs:Class rdf:ID="macaw">
    <rdfs:subClassOf rdf:resource="#bird"/>
  </rdfs:Class>
</rdf:RDF>
```

Web Ontology Language (OWL)

Web Ontology Language is a knowledge representation language with the primary purpose of creating *web ontologies*. Web ontologies can be used for a variety of purposes, such as searching, query formation, indexing, and agent or service metadata management, or to improve application and database interoperability. Web ontologies are especially useful for knowledge-intensive applications, where text extraction, decision support, or resource planning are common tasks, as well as in knowledge repositories used for knowledge acquisition.

The abbreviation of the Web Ontology Language, OWL, is not straightforward on purpose [145]. OWL ontologies are RDF graphs, in other words, sets of RDF triples. Similar to RDF graphs, OWL ontology graphs can be expressed in various syntactic notations. There are three variants of OWL: *OWL Lite*, *OWL DL*, and *OWL Full* [146]. OWL is a higher-level language than RDF; in fact, it is a vocabulary extension of RDF. Consequently, RDF graphs are OWL Full ontologies.

The default OWL namespace is `http://www.w3.org/2002/07/owl#`, which defines the OWL vocabulary. There is no MIME type defined specifically for OWL. Using the `application/rdf+xml` or the `application/xml` MIME type for OWL documents is recommended. The recommended file extension is either `.rdf` or `.owl`.

The development of the first version of OWL was started in 2002, and the second version, OWL2, in 2008. OWL became a W3C Recommendation in 2004 [147], and OWL2 was standardized in 2009 [148, 149].

Syntaxes

At the high level, the OWL abstract syntax [150] and the OWL2 functional syntax [151] can be used. OWL also supports several exchange syntaxes, including RDF syntaxes [152] (RDF/XML [153], RDF/Turtle [154]), the OWL2 XML syntax [155], and the Manchester syntax [156]. RDF/XML is the normative syntax [157].

For example, a class declaration for a smartphone ontology can be written in various syntaxes, as shown in Listings 7-71 to 7-75.

Listing 7-71. OWL2 Functional Syntax Example

```
Ontology(<http://example.com/smartphone.owl>
  Declaration( Class( :Smartphone ) )
)
```

Listing 7-72. OWL2 XML Syntax Example

```
<Ontology ontologyIRI="http://example.com/smartphone.owl">
  <Prefix name="owl" IRI="http://www.w3.org/2002/07/owl#"/>
  <Declaration>
    <Class IRI="Smartphone"/>
  </Declaration>
</Ontology>
```

Listing 7-73. RDF/XML Syntax Example

```
<rdf:RDF>
  <owl:Ontology rdf:about=""/>
  <owl:Class rdf:about="#Smartphone"/>
</rdf:RDF>
```

Listing 7-74. RDF/Turtle Example

```
<http://example.com/smartphone.owl> rdf:type owl:Ontology.
:Smartphone rdf:type owl:Class.
```

Listing 7-75. Manchester Syntax Example

```
Ontology: <http://example.com/smartphone.owl>
Class: Smartphone
```

Properties

In OWL, the following types of properties exist:

- *Object properties* that link individuals to other individuals
- *Datatype properties* that link individuals to data values (subclasses of object properties)
- *Annotation property* (owl:AnnotationProperty)
- *Ontology property* (owl:OntologyProperty)

Property features are defined by the property axioms. The basic form expresses the existence only. For example, in a smartphone ontology, the property hasTouchscreen can be declared to express a major feature of mobile phones (see Listing 7-76).

Listing 7-76. A Property Declaration in OWL

```
<owl:ObjectProperty rdf:ID="hasTouchscreen"/>
```

OWL property axioms can also define additional characteristics. OWL supports RDF Schema constructs such as rdfs:subPropertyOf, rdfs:domain, and rdfs:range. Relations to other properties can be expressed by owl:equivalentProperty and owl:inverseOf (Listing 7-77).

Listing 7-77. Two Equivalent Smartphone Properties (Accelerometer and G-sensor)

```
<owl:ObjectProperty rdf:ID="hasAccelerometer">
  <owl:equivalentProperty>
    <owl:ObjectProperty rdf:ID="hasGsensor"/>
  </owl:equivalentProperty>
</owl:ObjectProperty>
```

Global cardinality constraints are defined by owl:FunctionalProperty and owl:InverseFunctionalProperty. Logical property features are defined by owl:SymmetricProperty and owl:TransitiveProperty [158] (Listing 7-78).

Listing 7-78. A Symmetric Property in OWL

```
<owl:SymmetricProperty rdf:ID="hasLiveConnection">
  <rdfs:domain rdf:resource="#Smartphone"/>
  <rdfs:range rdf:resource="#Smartphone"/>
</owl:SymmetricProperty>
```

OWL provides precise declarations for expressing relationships, even if they are evident. For example, the *property hierarchy* of two smartphone features can be expressed in functional syntax, as presented in Listing 7-79.

Listing 7-79. Property Hierarchy in OWL

```
SubObjectPropertyOf( :hasGeotagging :hasCamera )
```

Classes

Similar to RDF, OWL provides classes to group resources. There are six different *class descriptions* in OWL:

- Class identifier (URI reference). A named instance of owl:Class, a subclass of rdfs:Class.[8] Listing 7-80 shows an example.

   Listing 7-80. A Class Identifier in OWL

   ```
   <owl:Class rdf:ID="Handheld"/>
   ```

---

[8]In OWL Lite and OWL DL. In OWL Full they are equivalent.

- Set of individuals (instances of a class) defined by the owl:oneOf property. For example, the class of smartphones can be declared in the RDF/XML syntax with the RDF construct rdf:parseType="Collection", as shown in Listing 7-81.

Listing 7-81. Class Instances in OWL

```
<owl:Class>
  <owl:oneOf rdf:parseType="Collection">
    <owl:Thing rdf:about="#Touch"/>
    <owl:Thing rdf:about="#Type"/>
    <owl:Thing rdf:about="#TouchType"/>
    <owl:Thing rdf:about="#Business"/>
  </owl:oneOf>
</owl:Class>
```

- Property restriction: a value constraint or a cardinality constraint (for example, Listing 7-82).

Listing 7-82. Property Restrictions in OWL

```
<owl:Restriction>
  <owl:onProperty rdf:resource="hasGPS" />
  <owl:allValuesFrom rdf:resource="#Smartphone" />
</owl:Restriction>
```

- Intersection of two or more class descriptions. For example, the intersection of two Brochures enumerations can be described by the statement owl:intersectionOf, as presented in Listing 7-83.

Listing 7-83. Intersection in OWL

```
<owl:Class>
  <owl:intersectionOf rdf:parseType="Brochures">
    <owl:Class>
      <owl:oneOf rdf:parseType="Brochures">
        <owl:Thing rdf:about="#Manual" />
        <owl:Thing rdf:about="#Guide" />
        <owl:Thing rdf:about="#Prospectus" />
      </owl:oneOf>
    </owl:Class>
    <owl:Class>
      <owl:oneOf rdf:parseType="Brochures">
        <owl:Thing rdf:about="#Specs" />
        <owl:Thing rdf:about="#Overview" />
        <owl:Thing rdf:about="#Guide" />
      </owl:oneOf>
    </owl:Class>
  </owl:intersectionOf>
</owl:Class>
```

where the intersection is a class with the only common individual, Guide.

- Union of two or more class descriptions. For example, the union of the previous example contains the individuals Manual, Guide, Prospectus, Specs, and Overview (if they are all different).

- Complement of a class description. The class extension contains exactly those individuals that do not belong to the class extension of the class description that forms the object of the statement. The complement can be described by the owl:complementOf property.

Class descriptions can be combined into *class axioms*. Class hierarchy can be expressed by *subclass axioms* (Listing 7-84).

Listing 7-84. Class Hierarchy in OWL

```
SubClassOf( :Slide :Smartphone )
```

The equivalence of two classes express that the individuals contained by them are identical. Listing 7-85 shows an example.

Listing 7-85. Equivalent Classes in OWL

```
EquivalentClasses( :Virtualkeyboard :Softquerty )
```

Although individuals can be members of several classes in general, in many cases memberships are exclusive. For example, a smartphone belongs to either the bar or the slide form factor. This *class disjointness* can be expressed as shown in Listing 7-86.

Listing 7-86. Class Disjointness in OWL

```
DisjointClasses( :Bar :Slide )
```

Simple Knowledge Organization System (SKOS)

Simple Knowledge Organization System (SKOS) is a W3C recommendation for representing taxonomies, thesauri, classification schemes, subject-heading systems, and structured controlled vocabularies. Being one of the most frequently implemented Semantic Web standards in industrial applications, SKOS is built upon RDF and RDFS to enable easy publication of controlled vocabularies as linked data. RDF provides interoperability, consistency, and integrity, and allows knowledge organization systems to be used in distributed, decentralized metadata applications where metadata are retrieved from multiple resources.

The SKOS standard defines the SKOS data model as an OWL Full ontology [159]. The elements of the SKOS data model are OWL classes and properties with individual URIs that form the SKOS vocabulary.

Combining Metadata

Schemas are often combined on the Semantic Web in order to apply all those specific vocabularies that are designed to express metadata on the topic of the web pages being described. The longest lists of namespaces occur in web documents that provide a significant amount of additional metadata, most commonly, in (X)HTML+RDFa. Listing 7-87 shows an example.

Listing 7-87. A Long List of Namespaces in an XHTML+RDFa Document

```
<html version="XHTML+RDFa 1.0" xmlns="http://www.w3.org/1999/xhtml"
 xmlns:air="http://www.daml.org/2001/10/html/airport-ont#"
 xmlns:bio="http://vocab.org/bio/0.1/"
 xmlns:bibo="http://purl.org/ontology/bibo/"
 xmlns:cc="http://creativecommons.org/ns#"
 xmlns:contact="http://www.w3.org/2000/10/swap/pim/contact#"
 xmlns:dbp="http://dbpedia.org/property/"
 xmlns:dbr="http://dbpedia.org/resource/"
 xmlns:dc="http://purl.org/dc/elements/1.1/"
 xmlns:dcterms="http://purl.org/dc/terms/"
 xmlns:fb="http://www.facebook.com/2008/fbml"
 xmlns:foaf="http://xmlns.com/foaf/0.1/"
 xmlns:geo="http://www.w3.org/2003/01/geo/wgs84_pos#"
 xmlns:ical="http://www.w3.org/2002/12/cal/icaltzd#"
 xmlns:og="http://opengraphprotocol.org/schema/"
 xmlns:openid="http://xmlns.openid.net/auth#"
 xmlns:owl="http://www.w3.org/2002/07/owl#"
 xmlns:rdf="http://www.w3.org/1999/02/22-rdf-syntax-ns#"
 xmlns:rdfa="http://www.w3.org/ns/rdfa#"
 xmlns:rdfs="http://www.w3.org/2000/01/rdf-schema#"
 xmlns:rel="http://vocab.org/relationship/"
 xmlns:rss="http://web.resource.org/rss/1.0/"
 xmlns:sioc="http://rdfs.org/sioc/ns#"
 xmlns:smap="http://purl.org/net/ns/sitemap#"
 xmlns:vcard="http://www.w3.org/2006/vcard/ns#"
 xmlns:wot="http://xmlns.com/wot/0.1/"
 xmlns:xhv="http://www.w3.org/1999/xhtml/vocab#"
 xmlns:xsd="http://www.w3.org/2001/XMLSchema#">
```

These *vocabulary prefixes* allow the use of terms defined by the listed external vocabularies in the current document. It is highly recommended to list only those namespaces that are actually used in the document, which contributes to code optimality and easier maintenance. Although unnecessary namespaces do not cause any error messages in the browser, they make the markup more complex.

Because of the different features of vocabularies, the combined application is not always straightforward. For example, many terms are included in various vocabularies, and choosing one of them is often driven by personal preference only. In fact, you should take the specification of the candidate properties into account in order to choose the most suitable one for your scenario.

Combining Vocabularies in RDF

The easiest way to mix properties from any vocabulary is to create an RDF file. For example, a completely machine-readable personal profile uses FOAF terms to describe the title, name, gender, IM accounts, home page, phone number, and relationships of a person. The nearest airport to the office of the person can be expressed with a term from the Contact vocabulary, the date when the file has been created can be declared by Dublin Core, and so on (Listing 7-88).

Listing 7-88. Several Vocabularies Used for a Personal Profile Written in RDF

```
<?xml version="1.0" encoding="UTF-8"?>
<rdf:RDF↵
 xmlns:contact="http://www.w3.org/2000/10/swap/pim/contact#"↵
 xmlns:dc="http://purl.org/dc/terms/"↵
 xmlns:foaf="http://xmlns.com/foaf/0.1/"↵
 xmlns:google="http://rdf.data-vocabulary.org/#"↵
 xmlns:owl="http://www.w3.org/2002/07/owl#"↵
 xmlns:rdf="http://www.w3.org/1999/02/22-rdf-syntax-ns#"↵
 xmlns:rdfs="http://www.w3.org/2000/01/rdf-schema#"↵
 xmlns:wot="http://xmlns.com/wot/0.1/"↵
 xmlns:xhv="http://www.w3.org/1999/xhtml/vocab#"
>
  <rdf:Description rdf:about="http://www.example.com/metadata/foaf.rdf">
    <foaf:title>Dr</foaf:title>
    <foaf:givenname>John</foaf:givenname>
    <foaf:surname>Smith</foaf:surname>
    <foaf:gender>male</foaf:gender>
    <foaf:depiction rdf:resource="http://www.example.com/images/jsmith.jpg"/>
    <foaf:based_near rdf:resource="http://dbpedia.org/resource/New_York "/>
    <contact:nearestAirport rdf:resource="http://www.panynj.gov/airports/jfk.html"/>
    <foaf:phone rdf:resource="tel:+1123456789"/>
    <foaf:homepage rdf:resource="http://www.example.com"/>
    <google:url rdf:resource="http://www.example.com"/>
    <foaf:holdsAccount rdf:resource="http://www.linkedin.com/in/jsmith"/>
    <foaf:holdsAccount rdf:resource="http://www.facebook.com/jsmith"/>
    <foaf:holdsAccount rdf:resource="http://www.twitter.com/jsmith"/>
    <foaf:interest rdf:resource="http://dbpedia.org/resource/Photography"/>
    <foaf:interest rdf:resource="http://dbpedia.org/resource/Semantic_Web"/>
    <foaf:interest rdf:resource="http://dbpedia.org/resource/Classical_music"/>
    <rdfs:seeAlso rdf:resource="http://www.example.com/metadata/foaf.rdf"/>
    <rdfs:seeAlso rdf:resource="http://www.example.com/metadata/doac.rdf"/>
    <rdf:type rdf:resource="http://xmlns.com/foaf/0.1/Person"/>
    <rdf:type rdf:resource="http://rdf.data-vocabulary.org/#Person"/>
    <rdf:type rdf:resource="http://purl.org/dc/terms/Agent"/>
    <owl:sameAs rdf:resource="http://www.example.com/about/"/>
    <foaf:publications rdf:resource="http://www.example.com/metadata/doac.rdf"/>
    <foaf:knows rdf:resource="http://www.1stfriendswebsite.net/foaf.rdf"/>
    <foaf:knows rdf:resource="http://www.2ndfriendssite.com/foaf/"/>
    <dc:date rdf:datatype="http://www.w3.org/2001/XMLSchema#date">2010-08-22</dc:date>
    <dc:creator>John Smith</dc:creator>
    <rdf:type rdf:resource="http://xmlns.com/foaf/0.1/PersonalProfileDocument"/>
    <xhv:stylesheet rdf:resource="http://www.example.com/styles.css"/>
    <wot:assurance rdf:resource="http://www.example.com/signature.asc"/>
    <foaf:primaryTopic rdf:resource="http://www.example.com/about/"/>
    <dc:title>Dr. John Smith associate professor</dc:title>
  </rdf:Description>
</rdf:RDF>
```

Microdata and Microformats

As mentioned earlier, overlapping features can be described by both microdata and microformats, as well as arbitrary features using RDFa. Microformats can also be used simultaneously with (X)HTML5 microdata. For example, hCard can be written together with microdata, as shown in Listing 7-89.

Listing 7-89. Combining hCard with Microdata

```
<dl class="vcard" itemscope itemtype="http://data-vocabulary.org/Person">
  <dt class="fn" itemprop="name"><a href="http://example.com"
  itemprop="url">John Smith</a></dt>
  <dd class="title" itemprop="title">Photographer</dd>
  <dd class="adr" itemprop="address" itemscope
  itemtype="http://data-vocabulary.org/Address"><span class="locality"
  itemprop="locality">Memphis</span>, <abbr title="Tennessee" class="region"
  itemprop="region">TN</abbr>
  <span class="postal-code" itemprop="postal-code">38145</span></dd>
</dl>
```

Dublin Core and vCard in RDF

The flexibility of the Resource Description Framework makes it simple to use more than one kind of metadata from external namespaces at the same time. Consequently, rich semantics can be added to documents from a variety of vocabularies simultaneously (Listing 7-90).

Listing 7-90. Dublin Core and vCard in RDF

```
<?xml:namespace ns="http://www.w3.org/RDF/RDF/" prefix="RDF" ?>
<?xml:namespace ns="http://purl.oclc.org/DC/" prefix="DC" ?>
<?xml:namespace ns="http://person.org/BusinessCard/" prefix="CARD" ?>
<RDF:RDF>
  <RDF:Description RDF:HREF="http://uri-of-Document-1">
    <DC:Creator RDF:HREF="#Creator_001"/>
  </RDF:Description>
  <RDF:Description ID="Creator_001">
    <CARD:Name>John Smith<CARD:Name>
    <CARD:Email>jsmith@example.net<CARD:Email>
    <CARD:Affiliation>ABC Ltd.<CARD:Affiliation>
  </RDF:Description>
</RDF:RDF>
```

Dublin Core, vCard, and Math-Net

The introduction of a person on a brochure-style home page can be described in many ways. One of them is the combination of Dublin Core and vCard. Indexing and processing such data can be enhanced by providing them in RDF. Listing 7-91 shows an example.

Listing 7-91. Combining DC and vCard with Math-Net

```
<?xml version="1.0"?>
<rdf:RDF xmlns:rdf="http://www.w3.org/1999/02/22-rdf-syntax-ns#"↵
 xmlns:dc="http://purl.org/dc/elements/1.1/"↵
 xmlns:rdfs="http://www.w3.org/2000/01/rdf-schema#"↵
 xmlns:vCard="http://www.w3.org/2001/vcard-rdf/3.0#">
  <rdf:Description>
    <dc:creator>
      <rdf:Description rdf:about="http://jsmith.com/about.htm">
        <rdfs:label>John Smith</rdfs:label>
        <vCard:FN>John Smith</vCard:FN>
        <vCard:N rdf:parseType="Resource">
          <vCard:Family>Smith</vCard:Family>
          <vCard:Given>John</vCard:Given>
          <vCard:Prefix>Dr</vCard:Prefix>
        </vCard:N>
        <vCard:BDAY>1976-05-12</vCard:BDAY>
      </rdf:Description>
    </dc:creator>
  </rdf:Description>
</rdf:RDF>
```

It is important to keep in mind that Dublin Core element name conventions and XML element nestings do not consequently apply to all the other metadata schemas.

Some vocabulary from the Math-Net schemes can be used to extend descriptions of persons expressed by other vocabularies, including Dublin Core and vCard [160].

DC, IMS, and ODRL

When using the XML or RDF/XML syntax, Dublin Core can be used in combination with external metadata vocabularies such as IEEE Learning Object Metadata (IMS) [161] or Open Digital Rights Language (ODRL) metadata [162]. For example, the storage, preservation, and retrieval of digital learning materials at universities can be properly provided by the combination of Dublin Core, LOM, and local labels describing learning materials when using the Greenstone digital library software [163].

For example, an online educational system can be described accurately by three different types of metadata (Listing 7-92).

Listing 7-92. A Combination of DC, IMS, and ODRL

```
<record↵
 xmlns="http://www.example.org/virtualtutor/"↵
 xmlns:xsi="http://www.w3.org/2001/XMLSchema-instance"↵
 xsi:schemaLocation="http://www.example.org/virtualtutor/↵
 http://www.example.org/virtualtutor/schema.xsd"↵
 xmlns:dc="http://purl.org/dc/elements/1.1/"↵
 xmlns:dcterms="http://purl.org/dc/terms/"↵
 xmlns:oex="http://odrl.net/1.0/ODRL-EX"↵
 xmlns:odd="http://odrl.net/1.0/ODRL-DD"↵
```

```
xmlns:ims="http://www.imsglobal.org/xsd/imsmd_v1p2">
  <dc:title>
    Virtual Tutor
  </dc:title>
  <dc:identifier xsi:type="dcterms:URI">
    http://www.example.org/virtualtutor/
  </dc:identifier>
  <dc:description>
    Online educational system.
  </dc:description>
  <ims:typicallearningtime>
    <ims:datetime>
      2011-08-02T08:00
    </ims:datetime>
  </ims:typicallearningtime>
  <dc:rights>
    All rights reserved.
  </dc:rights>
  <oex:rights>
    <oex:asset>
      <oex:context>
        <odd:uid idscheme="URI">
          http://www.example.org/virtualtutor/
        </odd:uid>
      </oex:context>
    </oex:asset>
  </oex:rights>
</record>
```

Special Applications

There are metadata approaches that are specialized for images or a given media content type such as YouTube video. Some of them are provided in the markup, while others are embedded into binary files such as images.

Image Metadata and XMP

Digital photographs and custom images form integral parts of web sites. Various types of metadata can be provided with them, including descriptive, technical, and administrative metadata.

An advanced approach is to provide image metadata by markup. The alt attribute is vital for validity. Properly provided attribute values can improve accessibility too (see Chapter 10). The longdesc attribute, however, which could be used to provide a link to a long description for images and other nontext contents, has poor software support and is obsoleted in (X)HTML5.

Beyond the image descriptions provided in markup and the descriptions or image licensing written in RDFa discussed earlier, advanced and professional image manipulation software such as Adobe Photoshop can be used to add or modify metadata contained in the image files themselves (Figure 7-4). To a limited extent, file explorers of modern operating systems can also perform this task.

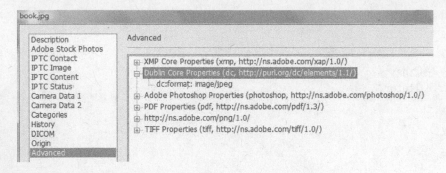

Figure 7-4. *Manipulating image file metadata in Photoshop*

Depending on the image format, a wide variety of metadata can be applied, including, but not limited to, title, author, copyright holder, keywords, orientation, point of view, color space, photographer's contact data, camera data, origin, advanced metadata, and more.

■ **Note**   Several types of metadata about the exposition are embedded in JPEG files taken by digital cameras that can be retrieved in image viewer and processing applications.

Behind the scenes, Adobe Photoshop applies the Extensible Metadata Platform (XMP) standard created by Adobe Systems. The serialization of XMP can be embedded into several popular file formats, including GIF, JPEG, JPEG 2000, PNG, and TIFF images, as well as PDF files[9] [164]. GIF supports XMP embedding as an *application extension* with the identifier XMP Data and authentication code XMP. In JPEG files, the XMP metadata is embedded at *application segment 1* (0xFFE1) with segment header http://ns.adobe.com/xap/1.0/\x00. In JPEG 2000 images, the XMP metadata can be located at the uuid atom identified by the UID 0xBE7ACFCB97A942E89C71999491E3AFAC. In PNG files, XMP is embedded inside an iTXt text block with the keyword XML:com.adobe.xmp. XMP is located at *Tag 700* in TIFF images. The Portable Document Format supports XMP embedding in a metadata stream within a PDF object.

The major problem with images from this aspect is that they are binary files (Figure 7-5) that need different approaches to be indexed or searched than text files do. For example, in *Google Image Search* there are additional aspects, including the techniques applied for eliminating very small (for example, 1×1 pixel) images, scams, and so forth. Textual metadata used on top of the metadata stored in the image files themselves always provides an advanced level of processing and sharing options.

---

[9]External .xmp sidecar files can be provided for all other file formats that do not support embedded XMP metadata.

```
<x:xmpmeta xmlns:x="adobe:ns:meta/" x:xmptk="Adobe XMP Core 4.1-c036 46.276720, Fri Oct 15 2010 09:16:05      ">
  <rdf:RDF xmlns:rdf="http://www.w3.org/1999/02/22-rdf-syntax-ns#">
    <rdf:Description rdf:about="" xmlns:xap="http://ns.adobe.com/xap/1.0/" xmlns:dc="http://purl.org/dc/elements/1.1/"
xmlns:photoshop="http://ns.adobe.com/photoshop/1.0/" xmlns:Iptc4xmpCore="http://iptc.org/std/Iptc4xmpCore/1.0/xmlns/"
xmlns:xapMM="http://ns.adobe.com/xap/1.0/mm/" xmlns:tiff="http://ns.adobe.com/tiff/1.0/" xmlns:exif="http://ns.adobe.com/exif/1.0/"
xap:CreateDate="2010-10-15T08:51:07+02:00" xap:ModifyDate="2010-10-15T09:12:35+02:00"
xap:MetadataDate="2010-10-15T09:12:35+02:00" xap:CreatorTool="Adobe Photoshop CS3 Windows" dc:format="image/jpeg"
photoshop:ColorMode="3" photoshop:History="" xapMM:InstanceID="uuid:CA5BF9872BD8DF11AB8EF78C7944688B" tiff:Orientation="1"
tiff:XResolution="720000/10000" tiff:YResolution="720000/10000" tiff:ResolutionUnit="2"
tiff:NativeDigest="256,257,258,259,262,274,277,284,530,531,282,283,296,301,318,319,529,532,306,270,271,272,305,315,33432;6966157B8
458EA730AB07D7DBE4" exif:PixelXDimension="213" exif:PixelYDimension="174" exif:ColorSpace="-1"
exif:NativeDigest="36864,40960,40961,37121,37122,40962,40963,37510,40964,36867,36868,33434,33437,34850,34852,34855,34856,37377,
8,37379,37380,37381,37382,37383,37384,37385,37386,37396,41483,41484,41486,41487,41488,41492,41493,41495,41728,41729,41730,419
986,41987,41988,41989,41990,41991,41992,41993,41994,41995,41996,42016,0,2,4,5,6,7,8,9,10,11,12,13,14,15,16,17,18,20,22,23,24,25,26,
,30;CD88C06C74D97B1DDDDC1F0AA87E0AAB">
      <Iptc4xmpCore:CreatorContactInfo Iptc4xmpCore:CiUrlWork="http://www.example.com"/>
    </rdf:Description>
    <rdf:Description xmlns:dc="http://purl.org/dc/elements/1.1/"><dc:creator><rdf:Seq
xmlns:rdf="http://www.w3.org/1999/02/22-rdf-syntax-ns#"><rdf:li>John Smith</rdf:li></rdf:Seq>
    </dc:creator></rdf:Description><rdf:Description xmlns:tiff="http://ns.adobe.com/tiff/1.0/"><tiff:artist>John
Smith</tiff:artist></rdf:Description></rdf:RDF>
</x:xmpmeta>
<?xpacket end='w'?>
```

Figure 7-5. *Textual RDF metadata in a binary JPEG image file*

Metadata for YouTube Videos

YouTube, the popular video sharing web site provides a convenient option to embed videos stored on YouTube servers to custom web pages. RDFa notation can be used to improve the effectiveness of web searches on such videos.

The details on how to create standard-compliant markup from the YouTube embedding code by eliminating the embed tag and moving the required attributes to the `object` tag will be described later in Chapter 13.

There are two video metadata formats to be written in the markup that are recognized by Google: Facebook Share and Yahoo! SearchMonkey RDFa [165]. They can be used alternately or simultaneously. They should be written directly into the markup in a way that they can be read without JavaScript or Flash.

Facebook Share and RDFa Rich Snippets

The image and video resource URLs are required for Facebook Share (`image_src` and `video_src`). The `medium` property supports the values `audio`, `image`, `video`, `news`, `blog`, and `mult`. Video size can be provided using the `video_width` and `video_height` properties. The MIME type of videos can be identified by `video_type` (with the value `application/x-shockwave-flash`). A brief description of up to 200 characters can be written by using the `description` property. The title of the video, which can be a maximum of 60 characters long, can be added by the `title` property. These properties are also recognized by Google.

A complete Facebook Share example looks like Listing 7-93.

Listing 7-93. *A Facebook Share Example*

```
<meta name="title" content="Smith plays BWV543" />
<meta name="description" content="Organist John Smith plays Praeludium and Fuge in A minor
 by J. S. Bach" />
<link rel="image_src" href="http://example.com/543thumb.jpg" />
<link rel="video_src" href="http://example.com/bach/543vid.swf" />
<meta name="video_width" content="640" />
<meta name="video_height" content="385" />
<meta name="video_type" content="application/x-shockwave-flash" />
```

279

Yahoo! SearchMonkey RDFa

Yahoo! SearchMonkey metadata can be provided on the `object` tag as demonstrated in Listing 7-94.

Listing 7-94. A Yahoo! SearchMonkey Example

```
<object type="application/x-shockwave-flash" width="480" height="385"↵
 data="http://www.youtube.com/v/a38-oj8VEXI&amp;hl=en_US&amp;fs=1&amp;" rel="media:video"↵
 resource="http://www.youtube.com/v/a38-oj8VEXI&amp;hl=en_US&amp;fs=1&amp;"↵
 xmlns:media="http://search.yahoo.com/searchmonkey/media/"↵
 xmlns:dc="http://purl.org/dc/terms/">
  <a rel="media:thumbnail" href="http://example.com/preview.jpg" />
</object>
```

The SearchMonkey media namespace `xmlns:media` is required, and the only acceptable value is `"http://search.yahoo.com/searchmonkey/media/"`. The GIF, JPEG, or PNG image with a resolution of 105×93 pixels that previews the video before the user clicks the Play button should be defined by the URI as the `href` attribute value of `media:thumbnail`. The video to be played when the user clicks the Play button should be defined by the resource of `media:video`.

All other tags are optional, including the Dublin Core namespace (`xmlns:dc`) and Dublin Core metadata (`dc:contributor`, `dc:creator`, `dc:date`, `dc:description`, `dc:identifier`, `dc:license`, `dc:subject`), the media metadata (`media:duration`, `media:height`, `media:player`, `media:region`, `media:title`, `media:type`, `media:views`, `media:width`), as well as `review:rating` [166].

Metadata in SEO

Although there is no strict correlation between higher page ranking or better search list positions and standardized web sites, several technologies contribute to better, higher-quality web documents. Semantic content adds meaning to web documents, making information indexing, searching, and processing easier. Metadata annotations considerably extend the potential of web searches.

The potential in web documents enriched with RDFa is increasing since major search engines have begun to index and process these annotations. Google, for example, started to apply the hCard, hProduct, and hReview microformats as well as RDFa in 2009 on search result pages as what it calls *Rich Snippets* [167]. Yahoo! has indexed RDFa and microformats since 2008 [168]. Web site content enriched with RDFa or microformats can enhance web searches by providing useful structured data [169].

Google indexes microdata, microformats, and RDFa contact properties derived from the hCard microformat, including `name`, `nickname`, `photo`, `title`, `role`, `url`, `affiliation`, `friend`, `contact`, `acquaintance`, and `address`. The `fn`, `org`, and `adr` microformats properties that stand for name, affiliation, and address, respectively, are also displayed on search engine result pages.[10] Additionally, Google recognizes the `friend`, `contact`, and `acquaintance` XFN microformats [170]. Relationships and connections expressed in XFN and FOAF are also processed by Google [171].

As discussed earlier, the `nofollow` attribute value of the `rel` attribute on anchor elements can be used to ensure that the web page will gain no PageRank from the destination link. Such links are followed by Google, but PageRank is not added. Bing does not follow the link, and the page is not indexed. Yahoo! follows the link and indexes the page. Listing 7-95 shows an example.

---

[10]Google displays human-readable content only. Machine-readable metadata is not displayed. For example, the date declared as the content of the `span` element `<span class="value-title" title="2011-12-06T20:00-08:00" /> 06 December, 8 PM</span>` is the human-readable content, which is specified independently from the machine-readable attribute value of the `title` attribute in the ISO date format (`2011-12-06T20:00-08:00`).

Listing 7-95. Applying the `nofollow` Attribute on a Link

```
<a href="http://www.lowprsite.com" rel="nofollow">External site</a>
```

Yahoo! SearchMonkey supports the following metadata [172]:

- Microformats, including hCard, hCalendar, hReview, hAtom, hResume, adr, geo, tag, and XFN
- RDFa
- eRDF (embedded RDF)

Microformat searches in Yahoo! can be performed easily with queries in the form shown in Listing 7-96.

Listing 7-96. Microformat Search Syntax used by Yahoo!

```
searchmonkeyid:com.yahoo.page.uf.metadata_name
```

where `metadata_name` is the name of the metadata in lowercase. RDFa and eRDF searches are similar. The only difference is that the string `uf` should be changed to `rdf`. For example, the hCard microformat can be searched with the query `searchmonkeyid:com.yahoo.page.uf.hcard`, RDF in attributes with `searchmonkeyid:com.yahoo.page.rdf.rdfa`, and so on.

Metadata annotations such as RDFa can effectively contribute to better search results. The more semantic content is provided on the Web, the more reasonable and relevant search results can be expected from search engines.[11] Properly set metadata can help search engines better process and provide personal introductions, contact data, and full descriptions of persons and human relationships in search results. The indexing of brochure-style business cards and personal information described in (X)HTML markup, XML, RDF, FOAF, and DOAC is straightforward. However, semantic contents embedded in conventional markup can be processed only if they are supported by the mechanisms used by web crawlers. Fortunately, search engines can process more and more metadata types.

In spite of the huge potential of metadata implementations in search engine optimization, there are several limitations in real-life applications. For example, image metadata cannot be fully exploited since a large share of social media and photo-sharing web sites either remove all embedded metadata during upload or apply a new, on-the-fly generated file without them (even in another file format). Images uploaded to the Internet by anonymous Wikipedia editors, on the other hand, can be found by their embedded metadata indexed by Google (if available). It is arguable whether this feature is advantageous.

Similar to any other data, it is important to decide wisely what to publish on the Web. It is no problem at all to publish the ISBN number of a book or a link to the DBpedia description of a web site item; however, several types of metadata are risky to publish since they can be abused. Especially e-mail addresses, phone numbers, and instant messenger screen names should be provided with extreme precaution.

Metadata embedding goes hand in hand with accessibility. Accessibility guidelines can ensure that alternate content is provided for objects and that the document structure is well organized (Chapter 10).

Some SEO practices do not contribute to user experience (UX) such as frequently repeated keywords that can decrease human readability [173].

---

[11]Markup is only one thing considered by search engines. For example, well-written, unique, and frequently updated site content is becoming more and more important for gaining better positions on search results.

Summary

In this chapter, you learned the fundamental concepts of the Semantic Web. You know by now how to create machine-readable metadata annotations and external metadata files manually. You are familiar with the most common schemas, vocabularies, and ontologies; the major serializations of the Resource Description Framework; and the basics of creating ontologies with OWL. You know how to combine annotations derived from different vocabularies, describe licenses and images in machine-readable formats, and use this metadata to boost the searchability of the files of your web site.

The next chapter will show you how to create standard-compliant news feed channels from scratch and maximize their interoperability.

References

1. Herman I (ed) (2009) How would you define the main goals of the Semantic Web? In: W3C Semantic Web FAQ. World Wide Web Consortium. http://www.w3.org/2001/sw/SW-FAQ#swgoals. Accessed 1 November 2014

2. Sbodio LM, Martin D, Moulin C. Discovering Semantic Web services using SPARQL and intelligent agents. Web Semantics: Science, Services and Agents on the World Wide Web 2010, 8(4):310–328

3. Hyvönen E, Mäkelä E, Salminen M, Valo A, Viljanen K, Saarela S, Junnila M, Kettula S. MuseumFinland — Finnish museums on the semantic web. Web Semantics: Science, Services and Agents on the World Wide Web 2005, 3(2–3):224–241

4. Bojārs U, Breslin JG, Finn A, Decker S. Using the Semantic Web for linking and reusing data across Web 2.0 communities. Web Semantics: Science, Services and Agents on the World Wide Web 2008, 6(1):21–28

5. Celma Ò, Raimond Y. ZemPod: A semantic web approach to podcasting. Web Semantics: Science, Services and Agents on the World Wide Web 2008, 6(2):162–169

6. Berners-Lee T (2001) Business Model for the Semantic Web. World Wide Web Consortium. http://www.w3.org/DesignIssues/Business. Accessed 1 November 2014

7. Murphy T (2010) Lin Clark On Why Drupal Matters. Socialmedia. http://socialmedia.net/2010/09/07/lin-clark-on-why-drupal-matters. Accessed 9 September 2010

8. Hausenblas M, Adida B, Herman I (2008) RDFa – Bridging the Web of Documents and the Web of Data. Joanneum Research, Creative Commons, World Wide Web Consortium. http://www.w3.org/2008/Talks/1026-ISCW-RDFa/. Accessed 1 November 2014

9. Kobie N (ed) (2011) Q&A: Conrad Wolfram on communicating with apps in Web 3.0. Dennis Publishing Ltd. http://www.itpro.co.uk/621535/q-a-conrad-wolfram-on-communicating-with-apps-in-web-3-0. Accessed 25 August 2011

10. Ankolekar A, Krötzsch M, Tran T, Vrandečić, D. The two cultures: Mashing up Web 2.0 and the Semantic Web. Web Semantics: Science, Services and Agents on the World Wide Web 2008, 6(1):70–75

11. Shannon V (2006) A "more revolutionary" Web. International Herald Tribune. The New York Times Company. http://www.nytimes.com/2006/05/23/technology/23iht-web.html?scp=1&sq=A+%27more+revolutionary%27+Web&st=nyt. Accessed 1 November 2014

12. Adida B, Birbeck M, McCarron S, Herman I (eds) (2013) Abstract. In: RDFa Core 1.1. Syntax and processing rules for embedding RDF through attributes. W3C Recommendation. World Wide Web Consortium. http://www.w3.org/TR/rdfa-core/. Accessed 1 November 2014

13. Herman I (2009) W3C Semantic Web Frequently Asked Questions. World Wide Web Consortium. http://www.w3.org/RDF/FAQ. Accessed 1 November 2014

14. Arenas M, Bertails A, Prud'hommeaux E, Sequeda J (eds) (2012) A Direct Mapping of Relational Data to RDF. W3C Recommendation. World Wide Web Consortium. http://www.w3.org/TR/rdb-direct-mapping/. Accessed 1 November 2014

15. Clark K (2010) The RDF Database Market. Clark & Parsia, LLC. http://weblog.clarkparsia.com/2010/09/23/the-rdf-database-market/. Accessed 1 November 2014

16. Oinonen K (2005) On the road to business application of Semantic Web technology. Semantic Web in Business – How to proceed. In: Industrial Applications of Semantic Web: Proceedings of the 1st IFIP WG12.5 Working Conference on Industrial Applications of Semantic Web. International Federation for Information Processing. Springer Science+Business Media Inc., New York

17. Nagy M, Vargas-Vera M (2010) Towards an Automatic Semantic Data Integration: Multi-agent Framework Approach. In: Semantic Web. In-Teh, Vukovar

18. Dertouzos LM, Berners-Lee T, Fischetti M (1999) Weaving the Web: The Original Design and Ultimate Destiny of the World Wide Web by Its Inventor. Harper San Francisco, San Francisco

19. Bizer C, Heath T, Berners-Lee T. Linked data — The story so far. Semantic Web and Information Systems 2009, 5(3):1–22

20. Berners-Lee T (2009) Linked Data. World Wide Web Consortium. http://www.w3.org/DesignIssues/LinkedData.html. Accessed 1 November 2014

21. Cyganiak R, Jentzsch A (2014) Linking Open Data cloud diagram. http://lod-cloud.net. Accessed 1 November 2014

22. Yahoo (2014) Flickr - Photo sharing. Yahoo! Inc. http://www.flickr.com. Accessed 1 November 2014

23. Google Webmaster Central Team (2007) Using the robots meta tag. Google Inc. http://googlewebmastercentral.blogspot.com/2007/03/using-robots-meta-tag.html. Accessed 1 November 2014

24. AOL (2014) ODP - Open Directory Project. AOL Inc. http://www.dmoz.org. Accessed 1 November 2014

25. TWRP (2007) About the Robots <META> tag. The Web Robots Pages. http://www.robotstxt.org/meta.html. Accessed 1 November 2014

26. Sullivan D (2007) Yahoo Provides NOYDIR Opt-Out Of Yahoo Directory Titles & Descriptions. Search Engine Land. Third Door Media. http://searchengineland.com/yahoo-provides-noydir-opt-out-of-yahoo-directory-titles-descriptions-10631. Accessed 1 November 2014

27. Smarty A (2010) How to Use Various REL Attributes - Learning Microformats. Search Engine Journal. http://www.searchenginejournal.com/how-to-use-various-rel-attributes-learning-microformats/16144/. Accessed 1 November 2014

28.   Kaply M (2010) Operator Add-on for Firefox. Michael Kaply.
      https://addons.mozilla.org/en-US/firefox/addon/4106/. Accessed 1 November 2014

29.   De Bruin R (2010) Tails Export Add-on for Firefox. Robert de Bruin.
      https://addons.mozilla.org/en-US/firefox/addon/2240/. Accessed 1 November 2014

30.   Ryckbost B (2014) Michromeformats Google Chrome extension. Brian Ryckbost.
      https://chrome.google.com/extensions/detail/oalbifknmclbnmjlljdemhjjlkmppjjl.
      Accessed 1 November 2014

31.   Baranovskiy D (2014) Optimus – Microformats Transformer. Dmitry Baranovskiy.
      http://microformatique.com/optimus/. Accessed 1 November 2014

32.   Left Logic (2010) Microformats Bookmarklet. Left Logic Ltd. http://leftlogic.com/
      projects/microformats_bookmarklet. Accessed 17 November 2010

33.   Dawson F, Stenerson D (1998) Internet Calendaring and Scheduling Core Object
      Specification (iCalendar). The Internet Society. http://www.ietf.org/rfc/rfc2445.txt.
      Accessed 1 November 2014

34.   Çelik T, Suda B (2013) hCalendar 1.0. The Microformats Community.
      http://microformats.org/wiki/hcalendar. Accessed 1 November 2014

35.   King R, Çelik T (2012) hCalendar Creator. The Microformats Community.
      http://microformats.org/code/hcalendar/creator. Accessed 1 November 2014

36.   Çelik T, Suda B (2013) hCard 1.0. The Microformats Community.
      http://microformats.org/wiki/hcard. Accessed 1 November 2014

37.   Dawson F, Howes T (1998) vCard MIME Directory Profile. The Internet Society.
      http://www.ietf.org/rfc/rfc2426.txt. Accessed 1 November 2014

38.   Çelik T (2005) hCard Creator. The Microformats Community. http://microformats.org/
      code/hcard/creator. Accessed 1 November 2014

39.   Casserly C, Domicone A, Green L, Heung A, Kinkade N, Linksvayer M, Park J, Peters
      D, Rees J, Roberts A, Rose T, Ruttenberg A, Schultz AJ, Stcucr E, Vollmcr T, Webber C,
      Wilbanks J, Yergler N, Yip J et al (eds) (2014) Licenses. Creative Commons.
      http://creativecommons.org/about/licenses/. Accessed 1 November 2014

40.   Çclik T (2013) rel="license". http://microformats.org/wiki/rel-license.
      The Microformats Community. Accessed 1 November 2014

41.   Olbertz D (2010) No to rel="nofollow". Fight Spam not Blogs. Dirk Olbertz.
      http://nonofollow.net. Accessed 13 November 2010

42.   Çelik T, Marks K (eds), Cutts M, Shellen J (2013) rel="nofollow". The Microformats
      Community. http://microformats.org/wiki/rel-nofollow. Accessed 1 November 2014

43.   Çelik T, Marks K (eds), Powazek D (2014) rel="tag". The Microformats Community.
      http://microformats.org/wiki/rel-tag. Accessed 1 November 2014

44.   Berners-Lee T, Fielding R, Masinter L (2005) Uniform Resource Identifier (URI): Generic
      Syntax. The Internet Society. http://www.ietf.org/rfc/rfc3986.txt. Accessed 1
      November 2014

45.   Çelik T, Marks K (2010) Vote Links. The Microformats Community.
      http://microformats.org/wiki/vote-links. Accessed 1 November 2014

46. Paul A (2003) Social networking beginning to take shape on the Web. The Seattle Times. http://community.seattletimes.nwsource.com/archive/?date=20031229&slug=paul29. Accessed 1 November 2014

47. GMPG (2014) XFN – XHTML Friends network. Global Multimedia Protocols Group. http://gmpg.org/xfn/. Accessed 1 November 2014

48. Lewis EP (2008) Getting Semantic With Microformats, Part 2: XFN. Emily P. Lewis. http://ablognotlimited.com/index.php/articles/getting-semantic-with-microformats-part-2-xfn/. Accessed 1 November 2014

49. Mullenweg M, Çelik T (2004) XFN 1.1 Creator. Global Multimedia Protocols Group. http://gmpg.org/xfn/creator. Accessed 1 November 2014

50. Mullenweg M (2014) Exefen. Matthew Mullenweg. http://ma.tt/tools/exefen.php/. Accessed 1 November 2014

51. Çelik T (2003) XMDP: Introduction and Format Description. Global Multimedia Protocols Group. http://gmpg.org/xmdp/description. Accessed 1 November 2014

52. Çelik T (2013) The adr microformat Draft Specification. The Microformats Community. http://microformats.org/wiki/adr. Accessed 1 November 2014

53. Çelik T (2013) The geo microformat Draft Specification. The Microformats Community. http://microformats.org/wiki/geo. Accessed 1 November 2014

54. Janes D, Carlyle B, Tantek Çelik T (2013) The hAtom microformat. The Microformats Community. http://microformats.org/wiki/hatom. Accessed 1 November 2014

55. Sporny M, McEvoy M et al (2013) The hAudio microformat. The Microformats Community. http://microformats.org/wiki/haudio. Accessed 1 November 2014

56. Çelik T, Khare R, Rădulescu A (eds), Arkin A, Donato C, King R (2014) The hListing microformat. The Microformats Community. http://microformats.org/wiki/hlisting. Accessed 1 November 2014

57. McEvoy M, Çelik T, Marks K, Hodder M, Beghie R, Kinberg J, Messina C, Rein L, Newell C, Sporny M, Johnson M (2014) The hMedia microformat. The Microformats Community. http://microformats.org/wiki/hmedia. Accessed 1 November 2014

58. Malek J, Myles S, Moore M, Ng M, Martin TB (2013) The hNews microformat. The Microformats Community. http://microformats.org/wiki/hnews. Accessed 1 November 2014

59. Lee P, Myers J, Cook C, Gustafson A (2013) The hProduct microformat. The Microformats Community. http://microformats.org/wiki/hproduct. Accessed 1 November 2014

60. Lörtsch T (ed), Berriman F, Ward B, Inkster T (2013) The hRecipe microformat. The Microformats Community. http://microformats.org/wiki/hrecipe. Accessed 1 November 2014

61. Çelik T, Jones G (eds), King R, Levine J, Marks K (2013) The hResume microformat Draft Specification. The Microformats Community. http://microformats.org/wiki/hresume. Accessed 1 November 2014

62. Çelik T (ed) (2014) The hReview microformat. The Microformats Community. http://microformats.org/wiki/hreview. Accessed 1 November 2014

63. King R, Cook B, Çelik T, Marks K (2013) The rel-directory microformat. The Microformats Community. http://microformats.org/wiki/rel-directory. Accessed 1 November 2014

64. Marks K (2013) The rel="enclosure" microformat. The Microformats Community. http://microformats.org/wiki/rel-enclosure. Accessed 1 November 2014

65. Ayers D (2014) The rel="home" microformat. The Microformats Community. http://microformats.org/wiki/rel-home. Accessed 1 November 2014

66. Pedersen AH, Kinberg J, Dedman J, van Dijk P (2014) The rel-payment microformat. The Microformats Community. http://microformats.org/wiki/rel-payment. Accessed 1 November 2014

67. Janes P (2013) The Robot Exclusion Profile. The Microformats Community. http://microformats.org/wiki/robots-exclusion. Accessed 1 November 2014

68. Gibson B (2013) The xFolk microformat. The Microformats Community. http://microformats.org/wiki/xfolk. Accessed 1 November 2014

69. Çelik T (ed) (2013) So you wanna develop a new microformat? The Microformats Community. http://microformats.org/wiki/process. Accessed 1 November 2014

70. Hickson I (2013) HTML Microdata. World Wide Web Consortium. http://www.w3.org/TR/microdata/. Accessed 1 October 2014

71. Ontos (2014) OntosMiner. Ontos AG. http://www.ontos.com/products/ontosminer/. Accessed 1 November 2014

72. Wu G (ed) (2010) Semantic Web. In-Tech, Vukovar

73. Mellouli S, Bouslama F, Akande A (2010) An ontology for representing financial headline news. doi:10.1016/j.websem.2010.02.001

74. Davis I, Newman R, D'Arcus B (2005) Expression of Core FRBR Concepts in RDF. Richard Newman, Ian Davis. http://vocab.org/frbr/core.html. Accessed 1 November 2014

75. Creative Commons (2011) Describing Copyright in RDF. Creative Commons Rights Expression Language. Creative Commons. http://creativecommons.org/ns. Accessed 1 November 2014

76. ODRL (2014) ODRL Community Group. http://www.w3.org/community/odrl/. Accessed 1 November 2014

77. Iannella R (2002) Open Digital Rights Language (ODRL) Version 1.1. World Wide Web Consortium. http://www.w3.org/TR/odrl. Accessed 1 November 2014

78. Sikos LF (2014) VidOnt – the video ontology. Leslie F. Sikos. http://vidont.org/. Accessed 2 November 2014

79. Berners-Lee T (ed) (2009) WGS84 Geo Positioning: an RDF vocabulary. World Wide Web Consortium. http://www.w3.org/2003/01/geo/wgs84_pos.rdf. Accessed 1 November 2014

80. Davis I, Galbraith D (2011) BIO: A vocabulary for biographical information. Ian Davis, David Galbraith. http://vocab.org/bio/0.1/. Accessed 1 November 2014

81. IMS (2006) IMS Meta-data Best Practice Guide for IEEE 1484.12.1-2002 Standard for Learning Object Metadata. Version 1.3 Final Specification. IMS Global Learning Consortium. http://www.imsglobal.org/metadata/mdv1p3/imsmd_bestv1p3.html. Accessed 1 November 2014

82. Universität Osnabrück (2002) Math-Net RDF Collection. Universität Osnabrück. http://www.iwi-iuk.org/material/RDF/1.1/. Accessed 1 November 2014

83. Brickley D, Miller L et al (2014) FOAF Vocabulary Specification. Dan Brickley and Libby Miller. http://xmlns.com/foaf/spec/. Accessed 1 November 2014

84. Parada RA (2008) DOAC Vocabulary Specification. Ramon Antonio Parada. http://ramonantonio.net/doac/0.1/. Accessed 21 February 2011

85. Dumbill E (2011) DOAP. Edd Dumbill. http://trac.usefulinc.com/doap. Accessed 22 February 2011

86. W3C (2013) VocabularyMarket. http://www.w3.org/wiki/VocabularyMarket. Accessed 1 November 2014

87. Davis I (2006) vocab.org - A URI space for vocabularies. Ian Davis. http://vocab.org. Accessed 21 February 2011

88. Aumueller D (2006) Beer Ontology. David Aumueller. http://www.purl.org/net/ontology/beer.owl. Accessed 1 November 2014

89. Kanzaki M (2007) Music Vocabulary. http://www.kanzaki.com/ns/music.rdf. Accessed 1 November 2014

90. Pickering R (2014) The Music Ontology. http://musicontology.com. Accessed 2 November 2014

91. Baumeister J, Seipel D (2010) Anomalies in ontologies with rules. Web Semant 2010, 8(1):55–68. doi:10.1016/j.websem.2009.12.003

92. Khan L (2009) Semantic Web and Cloud Computing. In: Research of Dr. Latifur Khan. The University of Dallas. http://www.utdallas.edu/~lkhan/research.html. Accessed 13 November 2010

93. Berners-Lee T (2007) Giant Global Graph. Massachusetts Institute of Technology. http://dig.csail.mit.edu/breadcrumbs/node/215. Accessed 1 November 2014

94. Brickley D (2014) The FOAF Project. http://www.foaf-project.org. Accessed 1 November 2014

95. QDOS (2010) FOAFNet. QDOS. http://foaf.qdos.com/. Accessed 23 September 2010

96. NetEstate (2014) Friend Of A Friend (FOAF) Search Engine. NetEstate. http://www.foaf-search.net. Accessed 1 November 2014

97. Intellidimension (2010) Semantic Web Search. Intellidimension. http://www.semanticwebsearch.com/query/. Accessed 23 September 2010

98. Quatuo (2010) Search FOAF profiles / Create, manage, store and publish your Friend of a Friend (FOAF) profile – A Semantic Web project. Quatuo. http://www.quatuo.com. Accessed 23 September 2010

99. Dodds L (2014) FOAF-a-matic. http://www.ldodds.com/foaf/foaf-a-matic.en.html. Leigh Dodds. Accessed 1 November 2014

100. Walker J (2013) The Drupal FOAF module. http://drupal.org/project/foaf. Dries Buytaert. Accessed 1 November 2014

101. ISO (2014) Information and documentation — The Dublin Core metadata element set. ISO 15836:2009. International Organization for Standardization. `http://www.iso.org/iso/iso_catalogue/catalogue_ics/catalogue_detail_ics.htm?csnumber=52142`. Accessed 1 November 2014

102. Kunze J, Baker T (2007) The Dublin Core Metadata Element Set. The IETF Trust. `http://www.ietf.org/rfc/rfc5013.txt`. Accessed 1 November 2014

103. ANSI, NISO (2007) The Dublin Core Metadata Element Set. ANSI/NISO Z39.85. National Information Standards Organization. `http://www.niso.org/kst/reports/standards/kfile_download?id%3Austring%3Aiso-8859-1=Z39-85-2007.pdf&pt=RkGKiXzW643Y eUaYUqZ1BFwDhIG4-24RJbcZBWg8uE4vWdpZsJDs4RjLzOt9o_d5_ymGsj_IKVa86hjP37r_ hFEijh12LhLqJw52B-5udAaMy22WJJl0y5GhhtjwcI3V`. Accessed 1 November 2014

104. Hillmann D (2005) Syntax Issues. In: Using Dublin Core. Dublin Core Metadata Initiative. `http://dublincore.org/documents/usageguide/#whichsyntax`. Accessed 1 November 2014

105. Powell A, Nilsson M, Naeve A, Johnston P, Baker T (2007) DCMI Abstract Model. DCMI Recommendation. Dublin Core Metadata Initiative. `http://dublincore.org/documents/abstract-model/`. Accessed 1 November 2014

106. DCMI (2012) Dublin Core Metadata Element Set, Version 1.1. DCMI Recommendation. Dublin Core Metadata Initiative. `http://dublincore.org/documents/dces/`. Accessed 1 November 2014

107. Powell A, Wagner H (eds), Weibel S, Baker T, Matola T, Miller E, Johnston P (2007) Namespace Policy for the Dublin Core Metadata Initiative (DCMI). Dublin Core Metadata Initiative. `http://dublincore.org/documents/dcmi-namespace/`. Accessed 1 November 2014

108. Powell A, Nilsson M, Naeve A, Johnston P, Baker T (2007) DCMI Abstract Model semantics. In: DCMI Abstract Model. Dublin Core Metadata Initiative. `http://dublincore.org/documents/2007/02/05/abstract-model/#sect-5`. Accessed 1 November 2014

109. Hillmann D (2005) Using Dublin Core – The Elements, Dublin Core Metadata Initiative. Dublin Core Metadata Initiative. `http://dublincore.org/documents/usageguide/elements.shtml`. Accessed 1 November 2014

110. DCMI Usage Board (2012) DCMI Metadata Terms. DCMI Recommendation. Dublin Core Metadata Initiative. `http://dublincore.org/documents/dcmi-terms/`. Accessed 1 November 2014

111. Berners-Lee T, Fielding R, Masinter L (2005) RFC 3986: Uniform Resource Identifier (URI): Generic Syntax. Internet Engineering Task Force. `http://www.ietf.org/rfc/rfc3986.txt`. Accessed 1 November 2014

112. Johnston P, Powell A (2008) Expressing Dublin Core metadata using HTML/XHTML meta and link elements. Dublin Core Metadata Initiative. `http://dublincore.org/documents/dc-html/`. Accessed 1 November 2014

113. Powell A, Johnston P (2003) Guidelines for implementing Dublin Core in XML. Dublin Core Metadata Initiative. `http://dublincore.org/documents/dc-xml-guidelines/`. Accessed 1 November 2014

114. Johnston P, Powell A (2008) Expressing Dublin Core Description Sets using XML (DC-DS-XML). Dublin Core Metadata Initiative. `http://dublincore.org/documents/dc-ds-xml/`. Accessed 1 November 2014

115. Phillips A, Davis M (2006) Tags for Identifying Languages. The Internet Society. http://www.ietf.org/rfc/rfc4646.txt. Accessed 1 November 2014

116. Beckett D, Miller E, Brickley D (2002) Expressing Simple Dublin Core in RDF/XML. Dublin Core Metadata Initiative. http://dublincore.org/documents/dcmes-xml/. Accessed 1 November 2014

117. Kokkelink S, Schwänzl R (2002) Expressing Qualified Dublin Core in RDF / XML. Dublin Core Metadata Initiative. http://dublincore.org/documents/dcq-rdf-xml/. Accessed 1 November 2014

118. Nilsson M, Powell A, Johnston P, Naeve A (2008) Expressing Dublin Core metadata using the Resource Description Framework (RDF). Dublin Core Metadata Initiative. http://dublincore.org/documents/dc-rdf/. Accessed 1 November 2014

119. Nilsson M, Baker T (2008) Notes on DCMI specifications for Dublin Core metadata in RDF. Dublin Core Metadata Initiative. http://dublincore.org/documents/dc-rdf-notes/. Accessed 1 November 2014

120. Beckett D, McBride B (eds) (2004) Introduction. In: RDF/XML Syntax Specification. W3C Recommendation. World Wide Web Consortium. http://www.w3.org/TR/rdf-syntax-grammar/#section-Introduction. Accessed 1 November 2014

121. Klyne G, Carroll JJ, McBride B (eds) (2014) RDF 1.1 Concepts and Abstract Syntax. W3C Recommendation. World Wide Web Consortium. http://www.w3.org/TR/rdf11-concepts/. Accessed 1 November 2014

122. Davis M, Whistler K (eds) (2014) Unicode Standard Annex #15. Unicode Normalization Forms. The Unicode Consortium. http://www.unicode.org/reports/tr15/#Norm_Forms. Accessed 1 November 2014

123. Ora Lassila O, Swick RR (eds) (1999) Formal Grammar for RDF. In: Resource Description Framework (RDF) Model and Syntax Specification. World Wide Web Consortium. http://www.w3.org/TR/1999/REC-rdf-syntax-19990222/#grammar. Accessed 1 November 2014

124. The W3C SPARQL Working Group (eds) (2013) SPARQL 1.1 Overview. W3C Recommendation. World Wide Web Consortium. http://www.w3.org/TR/sparql11-overview/. Accessed 1 November 2014

125. Ogbuji C (ed) (2013) SPARQL 1.1 Graph Store HTTP Protocol. W3C Recommendation. World Wide Web Consortium. http://www.w3.org/TR/sparql11-http-rdf-update/. Accessed 1 November 2014

126. Carothers G, Seaborne A (2014) RDF 1.1 N-Triples. A line-based syntax for an RDF graph. W3C Recommendation. World Wide Web Consortium. http://www.w3.org/TR/n-triples/. Accessed 1 November 2014

127. Chris Bizer C, Cyganiak R (2014) RDF 1.1 TriG. RDF Dataset Language . W3C Recommendation. World Wide Web Consortium. http://www.w3.org/TR/trig/. Accessed 1 November 2014

128. Carroll JJ, Stickler P (2004) RDF Triples in XML. HP Laboratories. http://www.hpl.hp.com/techreports/2003/HPL-2003-268.pdf. Accessed 1 November 2014

129. Gandon F, Schreiber G (eds) (2014) RDF 1.1 XML Syntax. World Wide Web Consortium. http://www.w3.org/TR/rdf-syntax-grammar/. Accessed 1 November 2014

130. Berners-Lee T, Connolly D (2011) Notation3 (N3): A readable RDF syntax. W3C Team Submission. World Wide Web Consortium. `http://www.w3.org/TeamSubmission/n3/`. Accessed 1 November 2014

131. Berners-Lee T, Connolly D (2008) Grammar of N3 in EBNF as used in XML 1.1 format. World Wide Web Consortium. `http://www.w3.org/2000/10/swap/grammar/n3-ietf.txt`. Accessed 1 November 2014

132. Berners-Lee T (2005) Primer: Getting into RDF & Semantic Web using N3. World Wide Web Consortium. `http://www.w3.org/2000/10/swap/Primer`. Accessed 1 November 2014

133. Prud'hommeaux E, Carothers G (ed), Beckett D, Berners-Lee T (2011) Terse RDF Triple Language. World Wide Web Consortium. `http://www.w3.org/TR/2011/WD-turtle-20110809/`. Accessed 11 November 2014

134. The Apache Software Foundation (2014) Apache Jena – A free and open source Java framework for building Semantic Web and Linked Data applications. `http://openjena.org`. Accessed 11 November 2014

135. Beckett D (2014) Redland RDF Libraries. Dave Beckett. `http://librdf.org`. Accessed 11 November 2014

136. Broekstra J, Ansell P, Visser D, Leigh J, Kampman A, Schwarte A (2014) Sesame. `http://rdf4j.org/`. Accessed 11 November 2014

137. Zeldman J, Marcotte E (2009) Designing with Web standards, 3rd edn. New Riders, Berkeley

138. Sporny M, Adrian B (eds), Rixham N, Birbeck M, Herman I (2012) RDFa API. An API for extracting structured data from Web documents. World Wide Web Consortium. `http://www.w3.org/TR/rdfa-api/`. Accessed 1 November 2014

139. Adida B, Birbeck M, McCarron S, Herman I (eds) (2010) RDFa Core 1.1 2nd Ed. Syntax and processing rules for embedding RDF through attributes. W3C Recommendation. World Wide Web Consortium. `http://www.w3.org/TR/rdfa-core/`. Accessed 1 November 2014

140. Birbeck M, McCarron S (2009) CURIE Syntax 1.0. A syntax for expressing Compact URIs, W3C Candidate Recommendation. World Wide Web Consortium. `http://www.w3.org/TR/curie/`. Accessed 1 November 2014

141. Lewis JR, Moscovitz M (2009) AdvancED CSS. Friends of ED, Berkeley

142. Adida B, Herman I (eds) (2012) W3C RDFa Working Group. World Wide Web Consortium. `http://www.w3.org/2010/02/rdfa/`. Accessed 1 November 2014

143. Swick R (ed) (2002) Metadata Activity Statement. World Wide Web Consortium. `http://www.w3.org/Metadata/Activity.html`. Accessed 1 November 2014

144. Brickley D, Guha RV, McBride B (eds) (2014) RDF Schema 1.1. W3C Recommendation. World Wide Web Consortium. `http://www.w3.org/TR/rdf-schema/`. Accessed 1 November 2014

145. Herman I (2010) "Why OWL and not WOL?" Tutorial on Semantic Web Technologies. World Wide Web Consortium. `http://www.w3.org/People/Ivan/CorePresentations/RDFTutorial/Slides.html#%28114%29`. Accessed 1 November 2014

146. Smith MK, Welty C, McGuinness DL (eds) (2004) The Species of OWL. In: OWL Web Ontology Language Guide. W3C Recommendation. `http://www.w3.org/TR/2004/REC-owl-guide-20040210/#OwlVarieties`. Accessed 1 November 2014

147. Dean M, Schreiber G (eds), Bechhofer S, van Harmelen F, Hendler J, Horrocks I, McGuinness DL, Patel-Schneider PF, Stein LA (2004) OWL Web Ontology Language Reference. W3C Recommendation. World Wide Web Consortium. http://www.w3.org/TR/owl-ref/. Accessed 1 November 2014

148. Hitzler P, Krötzsch M, Parsia B, Patel-Schneider PF, Rudolph S (eds) (2012) OWL 2 Web Ontology Language – Primer 2nd Ed. W3C Recommendation. World Wide Web Consortium. http://www.w3.org/TR/owl-primer/. Accessed 1 November 2014

149. Motik B, Grau BC, Horrocks I, Wu Z, Fokoue A, Lutz C (eds), Calvanese D, Carroll J, De Giacomo G, Hendler J, Herman I, Parsia B, Patel-Schneider PF, Ruttenberg A, Sattler U, Schneider M (2012) OWL 2 Web Ontology Language - Profiles. W3C Recommendation. World Wide Web Consortium. http://www.w3.org/TR/owl2-profiles/. Accessed 1 November 2014

150. Patel-Schneider PF, Horrocks I (eds) (2004) Abstract Syntax. In: OWL Web Ontology Language. Semantics and Abstract Syntax. World Wide Web Consortium. http://www.w3.org/TR/2004/REC-owl-semantics-20040210/syntax.html. Accessed 1 November 2014

151. Motik B, Patel-Schneider PF, Parsia B (eds), Bock C, Fokoue A, Haase P, Hoekstra R, Horrocks I, Ruttenberg A, Sattler U, Smith M (2012) OWL 2 Web Ontology Language. Structural Specification and Functional-Style Syntax 2nd Ed. W3C Recommendation. World Wide Web Consortium. http://www.w3.org/TR/owl-syntax/. Accessed 1 November 2014

152. Patel-Schneider PF, Motik B (eds), Grau BC, Horrocks I, Parsia B, Ruttenberg A, Schneider M (2009) OWL 2 Web Ontology Language. Mapping to RDF Graphs. W3C Recommendation. World Wide Web Consortium. http://www.w3.org/TR/2009/REC-owl2-mapping-to-rdf-20091027/. Accessed 1 November 2014

153. Gandon F, Schreiber G (eds) (2014) RDF 1.1 XML Syntax. W3C Recommendation. World Wide Web Consortium. http://www.w3.org/TR/rdf-syntax-grammar/. Accessed 1 November 2014

154. Beckett D, Berners-Lee T (2011) Turtle - Terse RDF Triple Language. World Wide Web Consortium. http://www.w3.org/TeamSubmission/turtle/. Accessed 1 November 2014

155. Motik B, Parsia B, Patel-Schneider PF (eds), Bechhofer S, Grau BC, Fokoue A, Hoekstra R (2012) OWL 2 Web Ontology Language. XML Serialization 2nd Ed. W3C Recommendation. World Wide Web Consortium. http://www.w3.org/TR/owl-xml-serialization/. Accessed 1 November 2014

156. Horridge M, Patel-Schneider PF (2009) OWL 2 Web Ontology Language. Manchester Syntax. W3C Working Group Note. World Wide Web Consortium. http://www.w3.org/TR/owl-xml-serialization/www.w3.org/TR/2009/NOTE-owl2-manchester-syntax-20091027/. Accessed 1 November 2014

157. W3C OWL Working Group (eds) (2009) Syntaxes. In: OWL 2 Web Ontology Language. Document Overview. W3C Recommendation. World Wide Web Consortium. http://www.w3.org/TR/owl2-overview/#Syntaxes. Accessed 1 November 2014

158. Dean M, Schreiber G (eds), Bechhofer S, van Harmelen F, Hendler J, Horrocks I, McGuinness DL, Patel-Schneider PF, Stein LA (2004) Properties. In: OWL Web Ontology Language Reference. W3C Recommendation. World Wide Web Consortium. http://www.w3.org/TR/owl-ref/#Property. Accessed 1 November 2014

159.   Miles A, Bechhofer S (2009) SKOS Simple Knowledge Organization System
        Reference. W3C Recommendation. World Wide Web Recommendation.
        `http://www.w3.org/TR/skos-reference/`. Accessed 2 November 2014

160.   Kokkelink S, Schwänzl R (2002) DC in collaboration with other vocabularies and
        DumbDown. In: Expressing Qualified Dublin Core in RDF / XML. Dublin Core Metadata
        Initiative. `http://dublincore.org/documents/dcq-rdf-xml/#sec3`. Accessed 1
        November 2014

161.   Barker P, Campbell LM, Roberts A, Smythe C (eds) (2006) IMS Meta-data Best Practice
        Guide for IEEE 1484.12.1-2002 Standard for Learning Object Metadata. Final Specification.
        IMS Global Learning Consortium. `http://www.imsglobal.org/metadata/mdv1p3/imsmd_`
        `bestv1p3.html`. Accessed 1 November 2014

162.   Iannella R (ed) (2002) ODRL 1.1 Expression Language Schema. Open Digital Rights
        Language Initiative. `http://odrl.net/1.1/ODRL-EX-11-DOC/index.html`. Accessed 23
        October 2010

163.   Rivera-Aguilera AB, Vega-López M, Pozo-Marrero A (2010) Metadata Application Profile:
        Integrating Different Metadata Schemes for Cataloguing the Digital Learning Materials
        Collections. In: Proceedings of the International Conference on Dublin Core and Metadata
        Applications. Dublin Core Metadata Initiative, Pittsburgh

164.   Adobe Systems Inc. (2010) Embedding XMP metadata in application files. In: XMP
        specification, Part 3 – Storage in files. `http://www.adobe.com/content/dam/Adobe/en/`
        `devnet/xmp/pdfs/XMPSpecificationPart3.pdf`. Accessed 1 November 2014

165.   Sikos LF (2011) Advanced (X)HTML5 metadata and semantics for Web 3.0 videos.
        DESIDOC Journal of Library and Information Technology 2011, 31(4):247–252

166.   Yahoo! Inc. (2009) SearchMonkey – Video. Yahoo! Developer Network. Inc.
        `http://developer.search.yahoo.com/help/objects/video`. Accessed 15 October 2010

167.   Goel K, Guha RV, Hansson O (2009) Introducing Rich Snippets. Google Inc.
        `http://googlewebmastercentral.blogspot.com/2009/05/introducing-rich-`
        `snippets.html`. Accessed 1 November 2014

168.   Birbeck M (2009) Introduction to RDFa. A List Apart Magazine.
        `http://www.alistapart.com/articles/introduction-to-rdfa`. Accessed
        1 November 2014

169.   Goel K, Gupta P, Hansson O (2009) Help us make the web better: An update on Rich
        Snippets. Google Inc. `http://googlewebmastercentral.blogspot.com/2009/10/help-`
        `us-make-web-better-update-on-rich.html`. Accessed 1 November 2014

170.   Google Webmaster Central (2010) People. About contact information. Google Inc.
        `http://www.google.com/support/webmasters/bin/answer.py?answer=146646`. Accessed
        1 November 2014

171.   Google (2010) Social Graph API. Google Code Labs. `http://code.google.com/intl/hu/`
        `apis/socialgraph/`. Accessed 11 November 2010

172.   Yahoo! Developer Network (2008) Monkey Finds Microformats and RDF. Yahoo!
        Inc. `http://developer.yahoo.com/blogs/ydn/posts/2008/12/monkey_finds_`
        `microformats_and_rdf/`. Accessed 13 November 2010

173.   Anderson E, DeBolt V, Featherstone D, Gunther L, Jacobs DR, Jensen-Inman L, Mills C,
        Schmitt C, Sims G, Walter A (2010) Web writing that works (or doesn't). In: InterACT With
        Web Standards – A Holistic Approach to Web Design. New Riders, Berkeley

CHAPTER 8

Web Syndication

The amount of up-to-date information shared on the Internet is constantly growing. Web syndication provides news feed channels in order to publish a summary of recently updated web site contents, latest news, or forum posts. These web feeds make it possible for users to stay informed without browsing web sites. Moreover, the same feed can also be shared among multiple web sites. Although the two popular web syndication formats, RSS and Atom, have relatively easy vocabularies, news feed channels are desired to conform to strict standards, first of all XML.

In this chapter, you will learn how to create standard-compliant news feed channels manually and update them frequently while maintaining standard compliance. You will be familiarized with the pros and cons of the two major rivals, RSS and Atom. Moreover, you will learn about the data formats used for news feed elements, along with the default and legal property values. You will also become familiar with the required channel and item elements, as well as the ones that should be provided to maximize interoperability.

News Feeds

Web syndication makes web site components available to multiple sites without logging in or downloading irrelevant components of other sites. The phrase often refers to *web news feeds* (*news channels*) that provide an up-to-date summary of recently added contents and the latest changes of web sites. Most commonly news feeds are used for the latest news, news headlines, blog entries, and forum posts.

The first technologies for web syndication appeared in 1997, including the *Channel Definition Format* [1], *Meta Content Framework* [2], and *scriptingNews* [3]. The first version of *Really Simple Syndication* (*RSS*), which later became the most widely used news feed format, was published by Netscape in 1999 [4]. The first part of the specification of *Atom*, the other popular news feed, was introduced in 2005.

Since feed readers and aggregators run on a variety of software platforms and devices including, but not limited to, web browsers, Windows news feed reader gadgets, Microsoft Outlook, and news feed readers on smartphones, interoperability is vital.

Really Simple Syndication

Really Simple Syndication (RSS) is the most widely used web syndication format. Since RSS is an XML application, it can be extended through XML namespaces. Beyond its conventional use of representing news and press releases, RSS also has special applications such as providing up-to-date exchange rates for banks [5].

The typical file extensions for RSS are `.rss` and `.xml`. The Internet media type associated with RSS is `application/rss+xml`, which is not standardized yet [6].

RSS describes lightweight syndication channels with the properties `title`, `link`, `description`, `channel`, and `item`.

RSS has the following versions: RSS 0.90, RSS 0.91, RSS 0.92, and RSS 2.0. In 2000, the name *RDF Site Summary* was in use, which referred to the extensibility with RDF-based modularization [7]. Version 0.91 was called *Rich Site Summary*, which dropped the RDF structure and imported elements from the scriptingNews syndication format developed by Dave Winer for his news site "Scripting News." The current acronym is *Really Simple Syndication*. The latest version of the RSS Specification has a permanent URI at the RSS Advisory Board web site [8]. The most widely used and most advanced version, RSS 2.0.11 [9], is discussed in the next sections.

Creating an RSS File

To create an RSS file, you first need an XML declaration and an rss element. The rss element is the root element of RSS files and is the container of a channel element, which provides information about the file and contains item elements (news feed entries). Listing 8-1 shows the general structure of an RSS file. The version attribute on the rss element is required, and its value must be 2.0 for RSS 2.0.11 (without indicating the subversion).

Listing 8-1. General Structure of an RSS File with Maximized Interoperability

```
<?xml version="1.0" encoding="utf-8" ?>
<rss version="2.0" ↵
 xmlns:content="http://purl.org/rss/1.0/modules/content/" ↵
 xmlns:dc="http://purl.org/dc/elements/1.1/" ↵
 xmlns:sy="http://purl.org/rss/1.0/modules/syndication/" ↵
 xmlns:atom="http://www.w3.org/2005/Atom">
  <channel>
    <title>An RSS news feed example</title>
    <link>http://www.example.com</link>
    <pubDate>Mon, 08 Aug 2011 08:03:00 +0200</pubDate>
    <image>
      <url>http://www.example.com/images/logo.png</url>
      <title>An RSS news feed example</title>
      <link>http://www.example.com</link>
    </image>
    <dc:creator>John Smith</dc:creator>
    <description>The news feed of rock star John Smith. Concerts, CDs, and more.</description>
    <language>en</language>
    <sy:updatePeriod>daily</sy:updatePeriod>
    <sy:updateFrequency>1</sy:updateFrequency>
    <atom:link href="http://www.example.com/rss.xml" rel="self" type="application/rss+xml" />
    <item>
      <title>News item 2</title>
      <link>http://www.news2link.com</link>
      <pubDate>Mon, 08 Aug 2011 08:03:00 +0200</pubDate>
      <dc:creator>John Smith</dc:creator>
      <category>CDs</category>
      <guid>http://www.news2link.com</guid>
      <description>Description of news item 2</description>
      <content:encoded>The full content of News #2.</content:encoded>
    </item>
```

```
  <item>
    <title>News item 1</title>
    <link>http://www.news1link.com</link>
    <pubDate>Sun, 07 Aug 2011 08:48:00 +0200</pubDate>
    <dc:creator>John Smith</dc:creator>
    <category>Concerts</category>
    <guid>http://www.news1link.com</guid>
    <description>A bit more about news 1</description>
    <content:encoded><![CDATA[ The full content of News #1. In CDATA sections, ↵
     <a href="http://examp.com">markup code</a> can also be included. ]]></content:encoded>
  </item>
  </channel>
</rss>
```

The above example is for demonstration only, real-life applications usually contain many more item elements.

■ **Tip** Theoretically, an RSS channel can contain an arbitrary number of items. However, some RSS readers (such as the news feed reader gadget in Windows Vista and Windows 7) do not support RSS files larger than approximately 150KB or 2,800 lines, which corresponds to approximately 7 months of daily news. It is recommended that you keep the file size under this limit to maximize interoperability.

Some of the presented elements are required, while others are optional but highly recommended. First we'll examine the required elements.

Required Elements

As shown in the previous section, the rss element contains the channel element with all its contents. The required elements of the channel element in RSS 2.0 are title, link, and description.

The title Element

The title element represents the name of the channel. It often coincides with the title of the web site it is associated with. Listing 8-2 shows an example.

Listing 8-2. The Title of an RSS Channel

```
<title>John Smith Headlines</title>
```

The link Element

The link element is a URI representing the domain where the news feed is located. Listing 8-3 shows an example.

Listing 8-3. A Link in RSS

```
<link>http://example.com/</link>
```

The description Element

The description element contains a sentence or sentence fragment that describes the channel, as demonstrated in Listing 8-4.

Listing 8-4. A Channel Description in RSS

```
<description>The latest news about rock star John Smith.</description>
```

Optional Elements

In RSS 2.0 news feeds, the channel element has 16 optional subelements, including category, cloud, copyright, docs, generator, image, language, lastBuildDate, managingEditor, pubDate, rating, skipDays, skipHours, textInput, ttl, and webMaster. We'll look at all of these subelements in more detail here.

A common feature of all RSS 2.0 elements providing a URL is that they should begin with a URI scheme defined by IANA [10], for example, http://, https://, news://, mailto://, or ftp://. Note that the http:// and ftp:// schemes can be used from RSS 2.0 onward.

The category Element

One or more categories can be specified for RSS channels, which can be used for classification and filtering. For example, an RSS news feed of a web site dedicated to Semantic Web events might contain categories such as conferences, workshops, specifications, and so on. Another example might be a bookseller who uses categories to indicate the category of the latest book releases so that potential customers can easily track the latest books of a certain category (for example, fans of history books are not necessarily interested in technical books). The category element can be used for not only the entire channel but also for each item separately. Listing 8-5 shows an example.

Listing 8-5. A category Element in RSS

```
<category>Workshops</category>
```

The element has an optional domain attribute that is a URI identifying a taxonomy (Listing 8-6).

Listing 8-6. Category with Domain

```
<category domain="http://www.example.com/vocab">WS</category>
```

The value of the category element declared for the channel can be used by portals for classifying RSS news feed channels, while the values of category elements are often displayed as hyperlinks, or used as filters (considered as tags in feed readers). By clicking one of these links, the feed reader hides news entries from all other categories.

The cloud Element

To receive immediate notifications about channel updates, a publish-subscribe protocol can be written for RSS feeds with the cloud element. It specifies a web service that supports the rssCloud interface (which can be implemented in HTTP-POST, XML-RPC, or SOAP 1.1). Two request methods are supported: a client-to-cloud call to request notification and a cloud-to-client call to perform notification. A client request has five required parameters, including the name of the remote procedure to be called by the cloud when an update occurred, the TCP port of the client, the remote procedure call path of the client, the string xml-rpc (in case the client uses XML-RPC) or soap (in case SOAP is used), and the URLs of RSS files. The IP address used for the request for notification must coincide with the IP address that will receive the notifications. Listing 8-7 shows an example.

Listing 8-7. Using the cloud Element in RSS

```
<cloud domain="rpc.example.com" port="80" path="/RPC2" registerProcedure="pingMe" ↵
 protocol="soap"/>
```

The update notification sent by the cloud to the client contains one parameter: the URL of the RSS file that changed. As a response, the client must return the Boolean value TRUE.

The copyright Element

Copyright notice of RSS channels can be provided by the copyright element. Listing 8-8 shows an example.

Listing 8-8. Providing Copyright Information in RSS

```
<copyright>Copyright © 2015 Christina Sikos. All rights reserved.</copyright>
```

The docs Element

A hyperlink to the documentation of the applied RSS format can be provided by the docs element. The typical element value is http://www.rssboard.org/rss-specification.

The generator Element

RSS feeds generated by software tools can easily be recognized from the value of the generator element, where the generator software usually identifies itself (Listing 8-9).

Listing 8-9. An RSS News Feed Generated by Movable Type

```
<generator>Movable Type 4.34-en</generator>
```

If the element is omitted or contains a simple text editor, it usually shows that the feed is written by a hand-coder at the source level (as we do in this chapter). In such cases, the author provides a text editor such as Notepad++ and typically identifies himself or herself as the creator using the Dublin Core vocabulary. However, most people apply feed generators that can generate news feeds in both RSS and Atom, which is especially useful for companies that publish news feeds in both formats.

The image Element

An optional subelement of the channel element is image, which can be used to provide an image for the RSS feed. It has three required and three optional subelements:

- The URL of the image representing the channel is expressed by the url subelement.
  The image format can be GIF, JPEG, or PNG. Required.

- The alternate text of the image is defined by title. When the RSS is embedded into (X)HTML, this string is forwarded as the text for the alt attribute. The value of the title subelement should coincide with the value of the title element of the channel. Required.

- The image hyperlink to the site of the channel is determined by the link subelement. The value of the link subelement should coincide with the value of the link element of the channel. Required.

- The image width can be determined in pixels by the width subelement. The default value is 88, and the maximum is 144. Optional.

- The image height can be determined in pixels by the width subelement. The default value is 31, and the maximum is 400. Optional.

- The description of the image to be included in the title attribute of the hyperlink of the image in (X)HTML can be provided by the description subelement. Optional.

Listing 8-10 shows an example.

Listing 8-10. A Logo Image Specified for an RSS File

```
<image>
  <url>http://www.sikoswebconsulting.com.au/img/logo.png</url>
  <title>Sikos Web Consulting</title>
  <link>http://www.sikoswebconsulting.com.au</link>
</image>
```

■ **Note** The image declared for an RSS file is displayed in some RSS readers such as the ones implemented in browsers but not all (such as the feed reader in Outlook or the Windows feed reader gadget).

The language Element

The natural language of the news feed content can be declared by the language element. For example:

```
<language>en</language>
```

Table 8-1 summarizes the allowed values.

Table 8-1. *RSS-Specific Language Codes*

Language	Language Code
Afrikaans	af
Albanian	sq
Basque	eu
Belarusian	be
Bulgarian	bg
Catalan	ca
Chinese (Simplified)	zh-cn
Chinese (Traditional)	zh-tw
Croatian	hr
Czech	cs
Danish	da
Dutch	nl
Dutch (Belgium)	nl-be
Dutch (Netherlands)	nl-nl
English	en
English (Australia)	en-au
English (Belize)	en-bz
English (Canada)	en-ca
English (Ireland)	en-ie
English (Jamaica)	en-jm
English (New Zealand)	en-nz
English (Philippines)	en-ph
English (South Africa)	en-za
English (Trinidad)	en-tt
English (UK)	en-gb
English (USA)	en-us
English (Zimbabwe)	en-zw
Estonian	et
Faeroese	fo
Finnish	fi
French	fr
French (Belgium)	fr-be
French (Canada)	fr-ca
French (France)	fr-fr

(*continued*)

Table 8-1. *(continued)*

Language	Language Code
French (Luxembourg)	fr-lu
French (Monaco)	fr-mc
French (Switzerland)	fr-ch
Galician	gl
Gaelic	gd
German	de
German (Austria)	de-at
German (Germany)	de-de
German (Liechtenstein)	de-li
German (Luxembourg)	de-lu
German (Switzerland)	de-ch
Greek	el
Hawaiian	haw
Hungarian	hu
Icelandic	is
Indonesian	in
Irish	ga
Italian	it
Italian (Italy)	it-it
Italian (Switzerland)	it-ch
Japanese	ja
Korean	ko
Macedonian	mk
Norwegian	no
Polish	pl
Portuguese	pt
Portuguese (Brazil)	pt-br
Portuguese (Portugal)	pt-pt
Romanian	ro
Romanian (Moldova)	ro-mo
Romanian (Romania)	ro-ro
Russian	ru
Russian (Moldova)	ru-mo
Russian (Russia)	ru-ru

(continued)

Table 8-1. *(continued)*

Language	Language Code
Serbian	sr
Slovak	sk
Slovenian	sl
Spanish	es
Spanish (Argentina)	es-ar
Spanish (Bolivia)	es-bo
Spanish (Chile)	es-cl
Spanish (Colombia)	es-co
Spanish (Costa Rica)	es-cr
Spanish (Dominican Republic)	es-do
Spanish (Ecuador)	es-ec
Spanish (El Salvador)	es-sv
Spanish (Guatemala)	es-gt
Spanish (Honduras)	es-hn
Spanish (Mexico)	es-mx
Spanish (Nicaragua)	es-ni
Spanish (Panama)	es-pa
Spanish (Paraguay)	es-py
Spanish (Peru)	es-pe
Spanish (Puerto Rico)	es-pr
Spanish (Spain)	es-es
Spanish (Uruguay)	es-uy
Spanish (Venezuela)	es-ve
Swedish	sv
Swedish (Finland)	sv-fi
Swedish (Sweden)	sv-se
Turkish	tr
Ukrainian	uk

All RSS versions support these language codes except the original Netscape version (0.91), which does not contain the codes et (Estonian) and haw (Hawaiian). The language codes allowed in HTML language tags, defined in the HTML 4.01 specification [11], and originally in RFC 1766 [12], can also be used. Two-letter primary codes are reserved for ISO 639 [13] language abbreviations, including fr (French), de (German), it (Italian), nl (Dutch), el (Greek), es (Spanish), pt (Portuguese), ar (Arabic), he (Hebrew), ru (Russian), zh (Chinese), ja (Japanese), hi (Hindi), ur (Urdu), and sa (Sanskrit). Two-letter subcodes are ISO 3166 country codes [14].

The managingEditor Element

The managingEditor element can be used to provide the e-mail address of the news feed editor. Listing 8-11 shows an example.

Listing 8-11. Declaring the RSS Editor

```
<managingEditor>john@example.com (John Smith)</managingEditor>
```

The pubDate and lastBuildDate Elements

The publication date of the channel content can be provided by the pubDate element. The element value changes every time the news feed is updated. RSS applies the date and time specification defined in RFC 822 [15] except that the year can be expressed either in two or four characters (the latter one is preferred). Offsets should be provided according to the difference from Greenwich Mean Time (GMT)/Coordinated Universal Time (UTC). For example, an RSS channel updated on 24 November, 2010, at 08:04 a.m. in London, England (in other words, in the GMT time zone), can state the publication date shown in Listing 8-12, while another news feed published in Suva, Fiji (time zone 1200 GMT or UTC+12), at the same time can be written as shown in Listing 8-13.

Listing 8-12. A Publication Date in the GMT Time Zone

```
<pubDate>Wed, 24 Nov 2010 08:04:00 GMT</pubDate>
```

Listing 8-13. A Publication Date in the UTC+12 Time Zone

```
<pubDate>Wed, 24 Nov 2010 08:04:00 +1200</pubDate>
```

■ **Caution**   In countries where jurisdiction observes daylight saving time (summer time), the offset changes twice a year.

The date of the last modification of the news feed can be expressed by the lastBuildDate element in the same format as pubDate.

The skipHours and skipDays Elements

Periods without updates can be provided by the skipHours element and days by the skipDays element. Allowed values for skipHours are the integer numbers between 0 and 23 (the time in GMT) (Listing 8-14).

Listing 8-14. An RSS Channel That Should Be Checked for Updates During Business Hours Only

```
<skipHours>
  <hour>0</hour>
  <hour>1</hour>
  <hour>2</hour>
  <hour>3</hour>
  <hour>4</hour>
  <hour>5</hour>
  <hour>6</hour>
  <hour>7</hour>
  <hour>17</hour>
```

```
    <hour>18</hour>
    <hour>19</hour>
    <hour>20</hour>
    <hour>21</hour>
    <hour>22</hour>
    <hour>23</hour>
</skipHours>
```

The skipDays element has seven day subelements (the days of the week in full). They can be used to specify those days when the news feed channel is not updated and thus unnecessary to check for updates (Listing 8-15).

Listing 8-15. An RSS Feed That Is Not Updated on Weekends

```
<skipDays>
  <day>Saturday</day>
  <day>Sunday</day>
</skipDays>
```

■ **Note** The declared hours or days are hints only. RSS feed readers *may* read the channel during the listed periods.

The textInput Element

Another optional subelement of the channel element is textInput, which can be used to specify a search box. It has four required subelements:

- The label of the Submit button is determined by the title subelement.
- The text input area can be described by the description subelement.
- The name subelement identifies the text object.
- The link subelement provides the URL of the CGI script used for processing requests.

The textInput element is ignored by many RSS readers.

The ttl Element

The duration of caching before refreshing from the source can be expressed in minutes with the ttl element (which stands for "time to live"). In the case of three hours, for example, it can be written as shown in Listing 8-16.

Listing 8-16. 180-Minute Caching in RSS

```
<ttl>180</ttl>
```

The webmaster Element

The e-mail address of the webmaster responsible for the technical issues of the RSS channel can be expressed with the webMaster element.

Subelements of the item Element

The item element has ten subelements: author, category, comments, description, enclosure, guid, link, pubDate, source, and title. All subelements are optional; however, at least a title or a description should be provided for each **item** element.

The author Subelement

The e-mail address of the author of the news feed item can be provided by the author subelement. Listing 8-17 shows an example.

Listing 8-17. The RSS Author

```
<author>info@example.com (John Smith)</author>
```

The category and pubDate Subelements

The syntax of the category and pubDate subelements of the item element is the same as that of the corresponding subelements of the channel element (as discussed in earlier sections).

The comments Subelement

If there is a forum or blog that is related to a news entry (item element), a link to that page can be provided by the comments subelement of the item element. Listing 8-18 shows an example.

Listing 8-18. Comments of an RSS Item

```
<comments>http://example.com/blog/new-standard-released/</comments>
```

The description Subelement

The texts of items (news summaries) are delimited by the description subelement, as shown in Listing 8-19.

Listing 8-19. An RSS Item Description

```
<description>
 Reports from workshop sessions
</description>
```

The enclosure Subelement

The enclosure subelement of the item element can be used to describe files (usually audio or video) related to the news feed item. It has three required attributes: url (URL of the file), length (file size in bytes), and type (media type), as demonstrated in Listing 8-20.

Listing 8-20. An Enclosure

```
<enclosure url="http://example.com/download/words.mp3" length="4875577" type="audio/mpeg"/>
```

The guid Subelement

Each RSS item might have a string that uniquely identifies it, called the *globally unique identifier*. The guid subelement has no specific syntax rules, but its content is usually a URL (Listing 8-21).

Listing 8-21. A guid Specifying a Permalink Related to the News Entry

```
<item>
  <title>New HTML5 and CSS3 Tutorials</title>
  <link>http://www.lesliesikos.com/tutorials/</link>
  <pubDate>Mon, 06 Feb 2012 14:22:00 +0930</pubDate>
  <dc:creator>Dr. Leslie Sikos</dc:creator>
  <category>Website</category>
  <guid isPermaLink="true">http://www.lesliesikos.com/tutorials/</guid>
  <description>Tutorials on HTML5 video embedding and CSS3 transitions</description>
  <content:encoded>Several tutorials have recently been published on emerging ↵
  technologies such as HTML5 video embedding and CSS3 transitions.</content:encoded>
</item>
```

The guid subelement has an optional attribute, isPermaLink, that can be set to true or false. In the first case (which is the default), the attribute value must be a URL that points to the full article or story described by the item element). The false value is rarely used. In fact, the whole isPermaLink attribute is often omitted.

■ **Caution** The guid subelements, if provided, should be unique throughout the RSS file. This criterion might be difficult to meet if the frequent updates of the same web site are described multiple times in the file.

The value of a guid subelement is considered a string by RSS readers.

■ **Tip** Although the guid subelement is optional, it is recommended to provide it for all item elements in order to maximize interoperability.

The link Subelement

The URL of an item can be provided by the link subelement. Listing 8-22 shows an example.

Listing 8-22. A Link Declared for an RSS Item

```
<link>http://example.com/news</link>
```

The source Subelement

If the item content comes from an external RSS channel, it can be provided by the source subelement. The value is the title of the resource channel. The source element has one required attribute, url, which is the URL of the resource (Listing 8-23).

Listing 8-23. The Source of an RSS Item

```
<source url="http://www.example.com/news.xml">John Smith Headlines</source>
```

The title Subelement

The titles of RSS channel items can be declared by the `title` subelement of the `item` element. Listing 8-24 shows an example.

Listing 8-24. The Title of an RSS Item

```
<title>A new W3C standard</title>
```

Namespaces

The default namespace for RSS is `http://purl.org/rss/1.0/`, which is the *permanent URL* form of the RDF Site Summary (RSS) 1.0 namespace, `http://web.resource.org/rss/1.0/`. The namespace can be provided in the form presented in Listing 8-25.

Listing 8-25. Declaring the RSS Namespace

```
<rss version="2.0" xmlns:rss="http://purl.org/rss/1.0/">
```

Additional data on channel updates can be provided by the *web syndication namespace of RSS* (`http://purl.org/rss/1.0/modules/syndication/`). It extends the RSS channels with three elements:

- The period over which the news channel is updated can be described by the `sy:updatePeriod` element. Allowed values are `hourly`, `daily`, `weekly`, `monthly`, and `yearly`. If omitted, `daily` is assumed.

- The frequency of updates can be expressed in relation to the update period with the `sy:updateFrequency` element. Its value is a positive integer.

- To calculate the publishing schedule, a base date can be defined by the `sy:updateBase` element. It should be a #PCDATA date in one of the W3C date and time formats [16].

By default, news feed entries are plain-text contents. However, news aggregators often support (X)HTML markup that are not allowed in XML. Entity-encoded and CDATA-escaped contents can be provided with the `content:encoded` element defined by the `http://purl.org/rss/1.0/modules/content/` namespace. The `content:encoded` element is especially useful if the hyperlink delimited by the `link` element is not enough and additional hyperlinks are needed (in the news item content). Although text formatting and other markup codes can also be written this way, they are ignored by many RSS readers.

There is an element, `atom:link`, that can be used from another syndication format, Atom, to provide the self-link of the news feed channel. To apply this element, the Atom namespace `http://www.w3.org/2005/Atom` should be declared.

Advanced news feeds typically contain at least the namespace declarations presented in Listing 8-26.

Listing 8-26. Typical Namespace Declarations in RSS

```
<rss version="2.0" ↵
  xmlns:content="http://purl.org/rss/1.0/modules/content/" ↵
  xmlns:dc="http://purl.org/dc/elements/1.1/" ↵
  xmlns:sy="http://purl.org/rss/1.0/modules/syndication/" ↵
  xmlns:atom="http://www.w3.org/2005/Atom" ↵
>
```

Doing so, elements can be used from these namespaces in the `channel` as shown in Listing 8-27 or in `item` elements such as in the example in Listing 8-28.

Listing 8-27. Elements from External Namespaces in an RSS Channel

```
<dc:creator>Dr. Leslie Sikos</dc:creator>
<sy:updatePeriod>daily</sy:updatePeriod>
<sy:updateFrequency>1</sy:updateFrequency>
<sy:updateBase>2011-01-01T12:00+00:00</sy:updateBase>
<atom:link href="http://www.lesliesikos.com/sikos.xml" rel="self"
 type="application/rss+xml" />
```

Listing 8-28. An Element from an External Namespace in an RSS Item

```
<content:encoded><![CDATA[ An escaped RSS item can contain markup elements such as
 <a href="http://www.example.com/">hyperlinks</a> that work in all major news feed
 readers. ]]></content:encoded>
```

Styling RSS Feeds

The browsers that support news feeds usually provide a basic styling or no styling at all (rendering a tree structure instead). Developers who are not satisfied with that or want to ensure an advanced look (which is also similar in all browsers) can format RSS channels using CSS or XSLT.

In the first case, a CSS reference is required in the form presented in Listing 8-29.

Listing 8-29. Using a CSS File for Styling RSS

```
<?xml version="1.0" encoding="utf-8" ?>
<?xml-stylesheet type="text/css" href="css/feed.css" ?>
<rss version="2.0">
```

Writing the CSS rules is straightforward. For example, the font size of the main title can be increased by the CSS rule presented in Listing 8-30.

Listing 8-30. Setting the Font Size for the RSS Channel and Title

```
channel title {
  font-size: 1.4em;
}
```

The font of the document can be set as shown in Listing 8-31.

Listing 8-31. A CSS Rule for the Entire RSS Document

```
rss {
  font-family: Verdana, Helvetica, sans-serif;
}
```

Similarly, further styles can be set for other RSS elements. Much information is not always relevant and can be omitted, as for example in Listing 8-32.

Listing 8-32. Hiding RSS Elements with CSS

```
channel link, channel language, channel copyright, channel managingEditor, ↵
 channel webMaster, channel docs, channel lastBuildDate {
  display: none;
}
```

The second approach applies XSL Transformation, which provides more control. For example, hyperlinks can be activated, and node order can be changed. The XSL file can be linked as shown in Listing 8-33.

Listing 8-33. Using XSLT for Styling RSS

```
<?xml version="1.0" encoding="utf-8" ?>
<?xml-stylesheet type="text/xsl" href="css/feed.xsl" ?>
<rss version="2.0">
```

■ **Note**   Additional functionality such as searching or category listings provided by the built-in RSS reader of some browsers are not available when a custom style sheet is applied to a news feed.

Atom

The Atom news feed specification consists of two standards: the *Atom Syndication Format* and the *Atom Publishing Protocol* (AtomPub or APP). The first one is a web feed format in XML syntax defined by an IETF proposed standard (RFC 4287 [17]). The second one is an HTTP-based protocol that can be used for creating and updating web resources. It is also a proposed standard (RFC 5023 [18]). This section focuses on the Atom Syndication Format.

The file extensions of Atom feeds are `.atom` and `.xml`. The Internet media type of Atom is `application/atom+xml`. The Atom namespace is `http://www.w3.org/2005/Atom`.

Creating an Atom File

Atom files begin with an XML declaration. The root element of Atom files and the container of news feed entries (`entry` elements) is the `feed` element. Listing 8-34 shows the general structure of an Atom file.

Listing 8-34. General Structure of an Atom File

```
<?xml version="1.0" encoding="utf-8"?>
<feed xmlns="http://www.w3.org/2005/Atom">
  <title>An Atom news feed example</title>
  <link rel="alternate" type="text/html" href="http://www.example.com/" />
  <link rel="self" type="application/atom+xml" href="http://www.example.com/News/atom.xml" />
  <id>tag:www.example.com,2008-09-29://4</id>
  <updated>2011-08-08T08:03:00Z</updated>
  <entry>
    <title>News item 2</title>
    <link rel="alternate" type="text/html" href="http://www.expl.com/2011.html#entry-9167" />
    <id>tag:www.expl.com,2011://4.9167</id>
```

```
      <published>2011-08-08T08:03:00Z</published>
      <updated>2011-08-08T08:03:00Z</updated>
      <summary>Summary of news entry 2</summary>
      <author>
        <name>John Smith</name>
      </author>
      <category term="Home Page Stories" />
      <category term="Web of Services" />
      <content type="html" xml:lang="en" xml:base="http://www.example.com/">The full content ↵
        of News #2.</content>
    </entry>
    <entry>
      <title>News item 1</title>
      <link rel="alternate" type="text/html" href="http://www.example.com/news/#entry-9165" />
      <id>tag:www.example.com,2011://4.9165</id>
      <published>2011-08-07T08:48:00Z</published>
      <updated>2011-08-07T08:48:00Z</updated>
      <summary>Summary of news entry 1</summary>
      <author>
        <name>John Smith</name>
      </author>
      <category term="Publication" />
      <category term="Web design" />
      <category term="Press releases" />
      <content type="html" xml:lang="en" xml:base="http://www.example.com/">
        <![CDATA[ The full content of News #1. In CDATA sections, ↵
          <a href="http://example.com/markup/">markup code</a> can also be included. ]]>
      </content>
    </entry>
</feed>
```

These elements and attributes are described in the following sections in detail.

Text Constructs

Text constructs of Atom contain language-sensitive, human-readable texts. An optional attribute of text constructs is the type attribute. If provided, the attribute must have one of the following values: text, html, or xhtml. If omitted, Atom feed readers consider text constructs as if they were specified with the default value text. MIME types cannot be declared as attribute values for the type attribute.

Person Constructs

There are three person constructs in Atom that describe an entity such as a person or a corporation: name, uri, and email.

Atom news feeds must contain exactly one name element that provides the name of the author. The element content is language-sensitive.

The uri element is optional, and maximum one can be provided to link to the web site of the author. The content of the uri element is an Internationalized Resource Identifier (IRI) in the form defined by RFC 3987 [19].

The e-mail address of the author can be declared by the optional email element of which no more than one can be used in an Atom file. The content of the email element should conform to the standard Internet Message Format defined by RFC 2822 [20].

Date Constructs

The contents of date construct elements should be declared according to the date-time format defined in RFC 3339 [21]. Date and time should be separated by an uppercase T, while an uppercase Z should be used when the numeric time zone offset is omitted (Listing 8-35).

Listing 8-35. Some Valid Timestamps in Atom

```
<updated>2016-12-13T08:15:01Z</updated>
<updated>2016-12-13T08:15:01.25Z</updated>
<updated>2016-12-13T08:15:01+01:00</updated>
<updated>2016-12-13T08:15:01.25+01:00</updated>
```

All date values of Atom new feeds should comply with the ISO standard on date and time representation (ISO 8601:2004 [22]) and the W3C date and time format [23] specifications, as well as the ISO 8601 Conventions in the W3C Recommendation "XML Schema Part 2: Datatypes Second Edition" [24].

Containers

There are three container elements in Atom:

- The feed element, which contains the entire feed
- The entry element, which contains a simple news entry
- The content element, which contains a full story (the content of a news entry)

The next sections describe these containers in detail.

The feed Element

As mentioned earlier, the top-level element of Atom feeds is feed; it contains the news feed metadata and contents (all other Atom elements). One or more author elements are required for feed elements, except all child entry elements of the feed element contain at least one author element. Exactly one id element must be provided for all feed elements. The feed elements must contain exactly one updated element. Exactly one title element is required for all feed elements. The feed elements should contain one link element with a rel attribute value set to self.

An arbitrary number of category and contributor elements can be included in feed elements. Only one generator is allowed for each feed. The same holds for icon and logo elements as well.

The feed elements can contain a maximum of one link element with a rel attribute value set to alternate that has the same type and hreflang attribute values. Beyond such link elements, additional link elements might be included in the feed elements.

Only one rights and subtitle element is allowed for each feed element.

The entry Element

Atom news can be provided by the entry element. It can be a child of the feed element or a stand-alone, top-level element within the feed. The entry elements must have a minimum of one author element except when a source element is provided in the entry that has an author element or the feed element contains an author element. Optionally, entry elements have any number of category elements. The entry elements might have a maximum of one content element. Another optional subelement of the entry element is the contributor. An arbitrary number of contributors can be provided.

The entry elements must have an id element.

The entry elements without content must provide a minimum of one link element with the rel attribute and the alternate attribute value.

The entry elements cannot contain more than one link element with the rel attribute and the alternate attribute value with exactly the same type and hreflang attribute values. Optionally, additional link elements can also be provided for the entry elements.

The entry elements can contain a maximum of one published, rights, source, and summary element.

The summary subelement should be provided for entry elements if the entry contains a content element with the src attribute or the entry content is Base64 encoded.[1]

The entry elements must contain exactly one title and one updated element.

The content Element

The Atom news content can be provided by the content element. The content of this element is language-sensitive. The content element has two attributes: type and src.

The value of the type attribute on the content element might be text, html, or xhtml. If it is omitted, text is considered the default value by Atom readers. Another option is to provide a MIME media type (but not a composite type).

The content element has an optional src attribute. The value of this attribute should be an Internationalized Resource Identifier that conforms to RFC 3987. If the src attribute is provided, the content must be empty. The type attribute should also be provided with a MIME type along with the src attribute.

Metadata and Content Elements

Similar to RSS, there are several elements in Atom to express metadata and describe the contents of news entries, such as author, category, contributor, generator, icon, id, link, logo, published, rights, source, subtitle, summary, title, and updated. Those elements whose specification assigns meaning to the content and the ones with special restrictions are described in the following sections.

The author Element

The author in Atom feeds can be provided in three levels. If the author element is not provided as a subelement of an entry element, the author is derived from the author subelement of the source element. Otherwise, the author declared by the author of the feed element is used to display the author of the news (Listing 8-36).

Listing 8-36. Declaring the Author of an Atom Feed

```
<author>
  <name>John Smith</name>
</author>
```

The category Element

The category element has three attributes: the required term and the optional scheme and label (Listing 8-37).

---

[1]Although the type attribute of the atom:content element is an Internet media type, it neither is an XML media type nor begins with text/ or ends in /xml or +xml.

Listing 8-37. A Category Declaration in Atom

```
<category term="Publication" />
```

The value of the `label` attribute is language-sensitive. Character entities used in the attribute values are considered characters instead of markup.

The contributor Element

The person or company that contributed to an entry or the whole feed can be indicated by the `contributor` element (Listing 8-38).

Listing 8-38. A Feed Contributor

```
<contributor>
  <name>Alex Sikos</name>
</contributor>
```

The generator Element

If a software tool is used to generate the Atom news feed, it can be identified by the `generator` element. The `generator` element has two optional attributes. The value of the `uri` attribute should be an Internationalized Resource Identifier according to RFC 3987. The other optional attribute is `version` that represents the version of the Atom generator (Listing 8-39).

Listing 8-39. An Atom Generator Identified in the Feed

```
<generator uri="http://www.example.com/movabletype/" ver="4.34-en">Movable Type</generator>
```

The icon Element

Similar to the contents of the `uri` element and that of the `uri` attribute of the `generator` element, the content of the `icon` element should also be an IRI reference that conforms to RFC 3987. This element specifies an image file for the Atom news feed (Listing 8-40). The aspect ratio of the image should be 1:1.

Listing 8-40. An Icon for the Atom Feed

```
<icon>http://example.com/images/icon.gif</icon>
```

The id Element

The `id` element is a permanent identifier provided in lowercase (Listing 8-41). It is used as a subelement of both the `feed` element and the `entry` elements.

Listing 8-41. An Atom Identifier

```
<id>tag:example.org,2003:3</id>
```

Percent-encoding, the mechanism that encodes certain characters of a URI using a string that begins with a percent sign (%),[2] should be eliminated whenever possible.[3] Dots should be avoided in URIs. The Internationalized Resource Identifier should be NFC normalized, or NFKC normalized. Empty fragment identifiers should be preserved. The URIs in id elements are case-sensitive. Identifiers that apply percent-escaping are considered different from the ones that do not when comparing id instances.

The link Element

External hyperlinks related to an Atom entry or the whole feed can be provided by the link element. This element has six attributes: href, rel, type, hreflang, title, and length. The required href attribute contains the Internationalized Resource Identifier of the link. The optional rel attribute must have a nonempty string as a value according to either the *IRI* or the *isegment-nz-nc* syntax rules of RFC 3987. Allowed values are alternate, related, self, enclosure, and via. The type attribute, which is optional, must have a MIME media type as its value. The hreflang attribute is also optional. When provided, it must have an RFC 3066 language tag. The optional title attribute is language-sensitive. Character entities used in the title are considered characters instead of markup, and displayed rather than processed. A hint on the advisory length of the linked content can be provided by the optional length attribute in octets. Listing 8-42 shows a typical link element.

Listing 8-42. A link Element in Atom

```
<link rel="self" type="application/atom+xml" href="http://example.net/atom.xml" />
```

The logo Element

An image that visually identifies your Atom news feed can be provided by the logo element (Listing 8-43). Its content is an IRI reference (RFC 3987). The aspect ratio of the logo image should be 2:1 (horizontal to vertical).

Listing 8-43. A Logo Image of an Atom Feed

```
<logo>http://example.com/images/icon.gif</logo>
```

The published Element

The time when the first version of a news entry was written can be specified by a date construct of the published element (Listing 8-44).

Listing 8-44. A published Element

```
<published>2014-10-27T10:24:24Z</published>
```

Such timestamps might coincide with the content of the updated element in the entry.

The rights Element

Custom copyright information can be written as a text construct and added to your Atom news feed using the rights element (Listing 8-45).

---

[2]One of the most well-known examples for percent encoding is the %20 string that appears in place of space characters in poorly designed URIs.

[3]If percent encoding is essential and cannot be eliminated, letters should be uppercase characters A–F.

Listing 8-45. Copyright Information in Atom

```
<rights>Copyright © 2014 Leslie Sikos. All rights reserved.</rights>
```

The source Element

If an entry is derived from an external Atom news feed, the metadata of the original entry can optionally be used as the subelements of the source element. The author, contributor, rights, and category elements should always be preserved.

The subtitle Element

Atom feeds can be described by a string provided as the content of a subtitle element, which provides a longer description than the title element (Listing 8-46).

Listing 8-46. The Description of an Atom News Feed

```
<title type="text">Leslie Sikos News</title>
<subtitle>
 The news feed of Leslie Sikos. Web design news, publications, and more.
</subtitle>
```

The summary Element

A short description can be added to each Atom entry with the summary element (Listing 8-47).

Listing 8-47. A Summary of an Atom Entry

```
<summary>The W3C released the updated specification of HTML5.</summary>
```

RSS or Atom?

Both RSS and Atom are widely supported in all major consumer feed readers. From the standards points of view, the RSS 2.0 specification is copyrighted by Harvard University and is considered finalized. Significant changes are unlikely, although the specification was released under the Creative Commons license. In contrast, Atom 1.0 is a more feature-rich syndication format which can easily be extended.

The Internet media type application/rss+xml is unregistered while application/atom+xml is registered by IANA.

In contrast to RSS 2.0, which supports the RSS document format only, the Atom Entry documents of the Atom news feeds can apply any network protocol. As a result, the aggregation and extraction of Atom news feeds have more possibilities.

Although the namespace of RSS 2.0 is not an XML namespace, it can optionally contain elements from external XML namespaces (as discussed earlier). The namespace of Atom 1.0 is an XML namespace itself and might also have elements and attributes from other XML namespaces. The implementation of these external elements and attributes is clearly defined by specification guidelines. It can be concluded that Atom is more extensible than RSS.

RSS does not support relative URIs, while Atom reuses the xml:base attribute, which allows relative references.

There is no schema defined in RSS 2.0. Atom 1.0 applies the RelaxNG schema, which is the non-normative ISO-standard ISO/IEC 19757-2:2008 [25]. It can be used to validate the data provided in the Atom news feed. Optionally, further schemas can be generated from RelaxNG.

Correctly written RSS and Atom files are well-formed XML files that can be processed in many ways and can be extended using the namespace mechanism. Users usually do not notice the difference between the two formats when using a feed reader application.

Summary

This chapter took you through the RSS and Atom new feed formats with all the background information and practices required to not only create standard-compliant feed channels but also maintain them manually without interrupting the strict XML syntax, the RSS or Atom format requirements, or the highest level of interoperability.

In the next chapter, you will learn how to secure the layout of your web sites, use advanced typography features on the Web, and optimize image files to maximize user experience. You will also learn standard-compliant, cross-browser video and multimedia embedding techniques.

References

1. Ellerman C (1997) Channel Definition Format (CDF). Microsoft Corporation.
   http://www.w3.org/TR/NOTE-CDFsubmit.html. Accessed 13 October 2014

2. Guha RV, Bray T (eds) (1997) Meta Content Framework Using XML.
   http://www.w3.org/TR/NOTE-MCF-XML/. Accessed 13 October 2014

3. Winer D (1997) Scripting News in XML. Dave Winer.
   http://scripting.com/davenet/1997/12/15/scriptingnewsinxml.html. Accessed 23
   November 2010

4. RAB (2008) RSS 0.90 Specification. Transferred from original specification of Netscape
   published in 1999. RSS Advisory Board. http://www.rssboard.org/rss-0-9-0.
   Accessed 13 October 2014

5. Asman P, Cannon S, Sommo C (2010) Extending RSS to Meet Central Bank Needs.
   In: Proceedings of the International Conference on Dublin Core and Metadata
   Applications. Dublin Core Metadata Initiative, Pittsburgh

6. Cadenhead R, Smith G, Hanna J, Kearney B (2006) The application/rss+xml Media Type.
   The Internet Society. http://www.rssboard.org/rss-mime-type-application.txt.
   Accessed 13 October 2014

7. Beged-Dov G, Brickley D, Dornfest R, Davis I, Dodds L, Eisenzopf J, Galbraith D,
   Guha RV, MacLeod K, Miller E, Swartz A, van der Vlist E, et al (2008) RDF Site Summary
   (RSS) 1.0. RSS-DEV Working Group. http://web.resource.org/rss/1.0/spec.
   Accessed 13 October 2014

8. RAB (2008) The current version of the RSS Specification. RSS Advisory Board.
   http://www.rssboard.org/rss-specification. Accessed 13 October 2014

9. RAB (2010) Specification History. RSS Advisory Board.
   http://www.rssboard.org/rss-history. Accessed 13 October 2014

10. The Internet Corporation for Assigned Names and Numbers (2010) Permanent URI
    Schemes. Internet Assigned Numbers Authority.
    http://www.iana.org/assignments/uri-schemes.html. Accessed 13 October 2014

11. Raggett D, Le Hors A, Jacobs I (eds) (1999) Language codes. In: HTML 4.01 Specification.
    World Wide Web Consortium. http://www.w3.org/TR/REC-html40/struct/
    dirlang.html#langcodes. Accessed 13 October 2014

12. Alvestrand H (1995) Tags for the Identification of Languages. Internet Engineering Task
    Force. http://www.ietf.org/rfc/rfc1766.txt. Accessed 13 October 2014

13.   ISO (2002) ISO 639-1:2002. International Organization for Standardization. http://www.iso.org/iso/iso_catalogue/catalogue_ics/catalogue_detail_ ics.htm?csnumber=22109. Accessed 13 October 2014

14.   ISO (2006) ISO 3166-1:2006. International Organization for Standardization. http://www.iso.org/iso/iso_catalogue/catalogue_tc/catalogue_ detail.htm?csnumber=39719. Accessed 13 October 2014

15.   Crocker DH (ed) (1982) Standard for the format of ARPA internet text messages. University of Delaware. http://asg.web.cmu.edu/rfc/rfc822.html. Accessed 13 October 2014

16.   Wolf M, Wicksteed C (1997) Date and Time Formats. World Wide Web Consortium. http://www.w3.org/TR/NOTE-datetime. Accessed 13 October 2014

17.   Nottingham M, Sayre R (eds) (2005) The Atom Syndication Format. Proposed standard. The Internet Society. http://tools.ietf.org/html/rfc4287. Accessed 13 October 2014

18.   Gregorio J, de Hora B (eds) (2007) The Atom Publishing Protocol. Proposed standard. The Internet Society. http://tools.ietf.org/html/rfc5023. Accessed 13 October 2014

19.   Duerst M, Suignard M (2005) Internationalized Resource Identifiers (IRIs). The Internet Engineering Task Force. http://tools.ietf.org/html/rfc3987. Accessed 13 October 2014

20.   Resnick P (ed) (2001) Internet Message Format. The Internet Society. http://tools.ietf.org/html/rfc2822. Accessed 13 October 2014

21.   Klyne G, Newman C (2002) Date and Time on the Internet: Timestamps. The Internet Society. http://tools.ietf.org/html/rfc3339. Accessed 13 October 2014

22.   ISO (2004) Data elements and interchange formats – Information interchange – Representation of dates and times. ISO 8601:2004. International Organization for Standardization. http://www.iso.org/iso/iso_catalogue/catalogue_tc/catalogue_ detail.htm?csnumber=40874. Accessed 13 October 2014

23.   Wolf M, Wicksteed C (1998) Date and Time Formats. World Wide Web Consortium. http://www.w3.org/TR/NOTE-datetime. Accessed 13 October 2014

24.   Biron PV, Malhotra A (eds) (2004) ISO 8601 Conventions. In: XML Schema Part 2: Datatypes Second Edition. W3C Recommendation. World Wide Web Consortium. http://www.w3.org/TR/xmlschema-2/#isoformats. Accessed 13 October 2014

25.   ISO (2008) ISO/IEC 19757-2:2008. Information technology – Document Schema Definition Language (DSDL) – Part 2: Regular-grammar-based validation – RELAX NG. International Organization for Standardization. http://www.iso.org/iso/iso_catalogue/catalogue_ tc/catalogue_detail.htm?csnumber=52348. Accessed 13 October 2014

CHAPTER 9

■ ■ ■

Optimized Appearance

Design has always been an important factor in web site development, partly because appearance is responsible for the first impression. If the design of a web site catches the eye, it is more likely that visitors will become customers or clients. Web typography has recently started to attract attention, especially though proper whitespace handling and the introduction of web fonts. Images that are fundamental parts of web sites should be optimized for web publishing in order to achieve a reasonable quality to file size ratio and minimize download time. Since high-speed Internet connections have become widespread, the need for sharing multimedia content has increased enormously. Until the new elements introduced in HTML5, general objects have been used to embed audio and video content. Although design and multimedia are extremely popular, the basic usability principle should always be kept in mind: functionality over design.

In this chapter, you will learn how to create multiple-column layouts and fixed menus without the now-obsolete approaches, such as the ones that applied tables and frames. This chapter also describes a CSS property, called z-index, which provides full control over the appearance of layers above each other.

Until recently, most web sites used one or more fonts from a small list, resulting in a kind of monotony. There have been many methods for using a greater variety of fonts over the years, but not one was very satisfactory or dependable. You can now improve the appearance of text by declaring font files to be used for rendering textual content, which makes it possible to display web pages with carefully selected fonts in superior quality. However, web sites can contain not only text. You will learn how to optimize images for web publishing and embed multimedia files such as audio and video.

Layout

The layout of web content determines the overall appearance and has a large impact on functionality, usability, accessibility, mobile-friendliness, and design. Ideally, web layouts are reliable, as well as browser- and resolution-independent.

Positioning and Floating

Some web page components are placed on the page in relation to a corner of the browser window, such as the top-left corner (the 0, 0 position), while the position of others depends on the position of their parent elements (*containers*). There are various options including relative, absolute, and fixed positioning. Beyond the appropriate positioning, you must be careful to provide browser- and resolution-independent solutions.

On your web site, perhaps certain components should "float" on the web page, and the content should appear next to, rather than above or below, the main text. Typical examples are images, which frequently apply the float property to wrap text around images.

Absolute and Fixed Positions

Depending on the design and site structure, some page components (logo, menu, header, footer, and so on) are intended to be fixed and should not move when the page is being scrolled.

The CSS rule `position: fixed;` is very similar to `position: absolute;` but the first one prevents element scrolling when the user scrolls the page while the second does not. The `position: fixed;` rule is not supported by Internet Explorer 6 or earlier, which was a major layout problem in web site development for years. Instead of reverting it to `position: absolute;` to provide a similar effect, `position: fixed;` has been considered as `position: static;` which results in no positioning at all. Consequently, a layer at the bottom of a web page with `position: fixed;` which is intended to be a footer that remains intact when the user scrolls the page, appears on the page according to the DOM structure in older browsers (prior to IE7), resulting in an unaesthetic appearance or degraded functionality. Modern browsers support positioning correctly.

Tableless Web Layout

Until recently, especially before HTML5, a significant number of web sites applied presentational markup rather than semantic code. (X)HTML tables have been used for arranging web site elements and ensuring pixel-by-pixel layout. This easy and quick "development" was also encouraged by WYSIWYG development tools. However, using tables for layout has many drawbacks. Web sites whose layout relies on tables waste bandwidth and take longer to download and render. The document structure is illogical, making semantic data harder or impossible to retrieve. These web sites are not accessible and are difficult to maintain. Generally speaking, the table-based layout is not mobile-friendly either.

Tableless web layout eliminates the use of tables for page layout and web page element positioning [1]. This does not mean that tables are not allowed on web pages, but tables should be used exclusively for tabular data.

The positioning and layout of web page components can be fully controlled by layers that are represented as `div` elements in the markup. In HTML5, sidebars and widget areas can also be separated logically within the main layout of a web site using the aside element, which is suitable for contents aside the main page content.

The following sections describe the two most common types of web site layouts. Naturally, developers can create other layouts, too, i.e., arbitrary layouts can be described by `div` elements.

Fixed-Width Layouts

Traditional web sites typically have a main container, often aligned or floated to the center, with a predefined width in pixels (or other units). This approach worked satisfactorily until the early 2010s when mobile browsing gained so much popularity that mobile support became a fundamental need, introducing a new era of web layouts. However, many applications, especially industrial sites and web interfaces of older but widely adopted commercial software, are still based on a fixed-width container.

Multiple-Column Layouts

A typical web page arrangement is the *multiple-column layout with floating divisions* [2]. Multiple-column sites usually have a header at the top of each page. The menu is often provided on the left (or right). Additionally, a footer is a frequently used component on the bottom of each page. The usual number of columns is one, two, or three. Figure 9-1 shows a typical three-column layout.

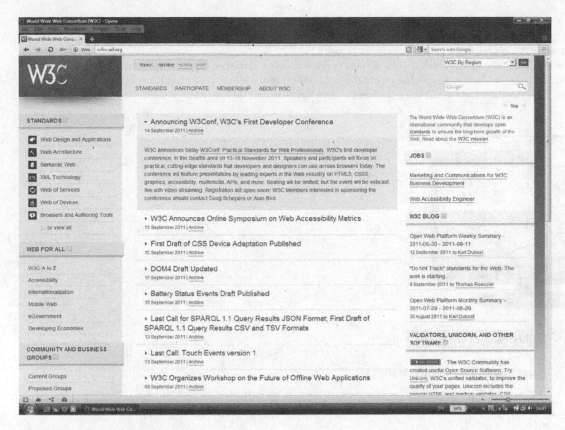

Figure 9-1. *A three-column layout*

You can see the main menu on the top of the page. Underneath the main menu there is the main content. On the left there are submenus, while on the right there are additional functions, such as a search box and blog entries.

Centralized-Column Layouts

Another typical arrangement applies *a centralized column with a width of approximately 700–1000 pixels (typically 760 or 960 pixels)*. Ideally, such centralized columns are not wider than about 1000 pixels to ensure that the main content remains visible on resolutions back to 1024×600 (WSVGA)[1] or smaller, without truncating the sides or adding too much empty space to the sides. As you will see in the next section, modern web sites use columns proportional to the screen rather than columns with a fixed width, which was the common practice for a decade and a half.

---

[1]The next standard and de facto standard resolutions such as 1366×768 (FWXGA) are larger than some screen resolutions of modern mobile devices with Internet browsing capabilities, however the typical resolution is constantly growing, and even medium-size tablets usually support 1920×1080 (full HD) or higher resolution. For smaller smartphone or tablet screen resolutions, web sites can also be optimized using alternate style sheets, as discussed earlier in Chapter 5.

Sites with centralized columns usually have the header and the main menu on the top. Optionally, there might be a secondary or submenu on the left (or right) within the main column. Quite often there is a footer at the bottom, usually within the main container (not affecting the layout).

There are various possibilities to horizontally center page content. A frequently used method applied the attribute value auto to the left and right margins of the container (Figure 9-2). This technique was introduced in the errata of the CSS2 specification [3]. Listing 9-1 shows an example.

Figure 9-2. *Centralizing with autowidth margins*

Listing 9-1. Centralizing with Autowidth Margins

```
#content {
  width: 720px;
  margin: 0 auto;
}
```

This method works on all browsers that support CSS2+.

Another method for centralizing the content, introduced by Simon Coggins, was to use offsets and negative margins. After declaring the width of the container element (similar to the previous method), its left edge is horizontally centered within the page by the combination of absolute positioning and a 50 percent left offset. Since the content begins on the second half of the page, the left margin of the layer should be set to the opposite of half the width of the layer. For example, if the width of the layer to be centralized is 780px, the left margin should be set to -390px (Figure 9-3).

Figure 9-3. *Centralizing with negative margins*

The corresponding CSS ruleset can be written as shown in Listing 9-2.

Listing 9-2. Centralizing with Negative Margins

```
#main {
  position:absolute;
  width: 780px;
  left:  50%;
  margin-left: -390px;
}
```

Flexible Layouts with Responsive Web Design

The first attempt to allow access to content and basic functionality of a web site and provide an advanced version of the same site to browsers with better or more complete web standards support is known as *Progressive Enhancement*, which was introduced in 2003. The corresponding approach is often referred to as *Graceful Degradation*. By applying best practices such as creating a correct document structure in the markup, web designers can contribute not only to Progressive Enhancement, but also accessibility and overall code quality.

To provide the highest level of interoperability and usability, web sites should be created by applying techniques that support an optimal user experience through device-, browser-, and/or feature-detection, so the website will be easy to navigate and read regardless of the device used for browsing (smartphone, tablet, desktop PC, etc.). As a result, the textual content of the website won't be tiny on a phone, and the large pictures will be automatically resized depending on the screen size and resolution.

Until recently, a large share of web sites have been designed with fixed-width layout (as described in the previous section) that might provide precise pixel-by-pixel representation, but cannot use the full surface of today's large-resolution monitors. It also has serious usability issues on the now widespread mobile devices such as smartphones and tablets that come with a relatively small screen size. Even on standard resolutions, the user might use a resized (not maximized) browser window. The endless variety of screen resolutions makes it practically infeasible to support all resolutions with a design that is optimized for a certain resolution.

More and more people will access digital services via a smartphone or tablet rather than a computer. In well-developed countries such as Australia, mobile browsing is over 50%, which represents extraordinary growth in mobile technology.

One of the approaches to address the issues of barely readable texts, inconsistent layout, and inconvenient scrollability is *Responsive Web Design* (RWD), which applies a *flexible grid layout* that is scalable (also known as *responsive layout*, *liquid layout*, or *fluid layout*). With the standardization and widespread implementation of CSS3 properties in browsers, and the growing need for mobile support, Responsive Web Design became popular in the early 2010s.

Responsive Web Design aims to achieve optimal user experience in terms of convenient reading and easy navigation, and "respond" to device features (hence the name). Depending on the characteristics of the device being used, different layouts are used, along with automatically scaling website elements, including text and images. Because some web site elements such as Flash headers containing raster graphics and video clips cannot be fully optimized for automatic scaling, the applicability of Responsive Web Design depends on the web site. In case a reliable fixed-width layout is used, support for mobile devices can still be provided by creating additional, device-dependent style sheets.

The use of flexible grid layout provides advanced mobile support while using only one style sheet per site with conditional styling for the various screen resolution ranges. Flexible layouts provide a way to create multiple column arrangements that are re-rendered vertically (while maintaining the logical flow) when browsing the site on a smaller resolution screen (or resizing the browser window). The columns that are adjacent on a high-resolution screen appear under each other and the text reflows when browsing the same site on a smartphone (Figure 9-4).

Figure 9-4. Flexible layouts adopt to screen size

This technique is advantageous not only for mobile support, but also contributes to (although won't guarantee) user experience, accessibility, and usability. While responsive web sites are not necessarily accessible, and not all accessible web sites are responsive, the proper use of standards results in web sites that are accessible and responsive at the same time.

Another approach, *elastic layout* applies fully scalable elements expressed in em rather than % in the style sheets. Because 1em is the currently specified font size, web page components of elastic layouts can adopt proportionally to the font size the reader uses.

Set the Viewport

Using the initial scale on mobile browsers can lead to unpredictable layout. To ensure that the device screen width is used as the viewport width, the meta tag can be used in the document head (Listing 9-3).

Listing 9-3. Set the Device Screen Width As the Viewport Width

```
<meta name="viewport" content="width=device-width, initial-scale=1.0" />
```

Create Markup For Responsive Layouts

The first liquid layout designs were based on fixed pixel widths and arbitrary percentage values. If you go one step further and calculate the appropriate proportions precisely, all elements of the resulting layout will resize their widths proportionally in relation to one another, regardless of the browsing device.

The proportions for each element can be calculated by dividing the target element by its context. A common technique is to draw an accurate web comp or mockup in Photoshop or Illustrator, calculate or measure the page element, and divide it by the full width of the page.

For example, if the layout is 960 pixels wide ("container"), and we have a 300 pixel wide sidebar, the width CSS property of the target element should have a value of 31.25% (300/960=0.3125) rather than 300px. The sidebar in this example will always be 31.25% of the width of the main container, regardless of the current width of the container (the items of the web site remain proportional to each other even if the entire page is rescaled).

Fluid grids are important in Responsive Web Design, but if the width of the browser becomes too narrow, the layout can start to collapse (a three-column layout, for example, wouldn't work very well on a small mobile phone). To address this issue, conditional CSS styling can be applied using CSS3 Media Queries.

Conditional Styling with CSS3 Media Queries

With CSS3 Media Queries, web sites can automatically detect features and feature support, and maximize user experience by applying different CSS rulesets based on the detected values. A frequently used CSS3 media query checks the minimum width (min-width), making it possible to apply specific CSS styles if the browser window reaches a particular width (Listing 9-4).

Listing 9-4. CSS Rules For Mobile Devices Using a Media Query

```css
@media screen and (min-width: 480px) {

  .content {
    float: left;
  }

  /* ... */
}
```

Such rulesets typically change the width of certain elements, change the floating to ensure that the desired elements will appear below each other, or disable elements (e.g., social media icons are not displayed when browsing the site on a mobile) or features (e.g., background image is disabled when browsing the site on a mobile). By creating similar rulesets for different de facto standard screen resolution ranges, web designers can cover pretty much any kind of device while providing an ideal user experience.

Older browsers such as Internet Explorer 8 and earlier do not support CSS3 Media Queries. To address this, it is popular to use a JavaScript fallback mechanism like `css3-mediaqueries.js` [4] or `Respond.js` [5].

Responsive Images

One of the approaches to use optimized images for mobile browsing is applying the `srcset` attribute of HTML5 [6], which can switch between different versions of the same image depending on the resolution and can be used on the `img` and `picture` elements (Listing 9-5).

Listing 9-5. Displaying Different Image File Versions Depending on Resolution

```
<img src="ferrari-400.jpg" alt="The Ferrari"
  sizes="(min-width: 600px) 60vw, 100vw"
  srcset="ferrari-200.jpg 200w,
          ferrari-400.jpg 400w,
          ferrari-800.jpg 800w,
          ferrari-1200.jpg 1200w">
```

The photo width will be 60% of the actual viewport width for browser windows that are at least 600 pixels wide. On smaller resolutions or browser windows, the photo width will correspond to the full viewport width. The browser applies the image with the resolution closest to the viewport width from the set of images optimized with a width of 200px, 400px, 800px, and 1200px, respectively, while considering not only the image width, but also the pixel density of the screen.

If the image is not huge and you want to use the same image file for mobile and desktop, the maximum width should be set to 100% (Listing 9-6).

Listing 9-6. A Responsive Image Implementation

```
img {
  max-width: 100%;
}
```

If the container around the image becomes narrower than the width of the image, then the image will scale down to match the width of its container. The 100% `max-width` also ensures that the image does not scale larger than its native size, which would significantly reduce the image quality (pixelated image).

There are many problems associated with responsive images, such as performance problems due to multiple image versions downloaded unnecessarily through browser preloading, bandwidth problems if only one huge image is used, and the Art Direction Problem, when the main object of the image is relatively small compared to the entire image, and becomes way too small when resizing the image for mobile browsing (e.g., a face becomes tiny while irrelevant background details are preserved).

Two popular JavaScript approaches are Picturefill and HiSRC. Picturefill is a responsive image polyfill for the HTML5 `picture` element that requires some special markup, namely `div` elements to represent the image variations, differentiated by `data-media` attributes that act like CSS3 Media Queries [7]. HiSRC is a jQuery plugin that enables you to create low-, medium-, and high-resolution versions of images, and the script will show the appropriate image version based on Retina-readiness and network speed [8].

A server-side approach is Adaptive Images, which uses a PHP script to intercept any image request and will resize it on the fly as needed to specified breakpoint sizes and serve the image on your pages automatically [9].

A solution to the Art Direction Problem is to use `min-width` for the full-size photo and provide a small, cropped image for resolutions smaller than the specified minimum width (Listing 9-7).

Listing 9-7. Cropped Image Version for Low-Resolution Displays, Full Version for High-Resolution Screens

```
<picture>
  <source media="(min-width: 960px)" srcset="bridge-full.jpg">
  <img src="bridge-closeup.jpg" alt="The Sydney Harbour Bridge">
</picture>
```

For browser windows with a width of 960 pixels and wider, the big-resolution photo is used while smaller browser windows will display the close-up version.

Text Around Objects

In many cases, web page text should "wrap around" an object or image. You can achieve this effect by using the `float` property; in other words, the image (or its container) should float (Listing 9-8).

Listing 9-8. Styles for Containers of Floating Images

```
#onleft {
  float: left;
}

#onright {
  float: right;
}
```

Figure 9-5 shows an image without styling and two floating images that use the previous rules. Without floating, the text does not wrap around the image: only the first line of the text appears next to the image (top photo). The second image applies the first rule of Listing 9-8 and is rendered on the left, surrounded by text on the right. The third image uses the second rule of Listing 9-8 and appears on the right, while the text surrounds the image on the left.

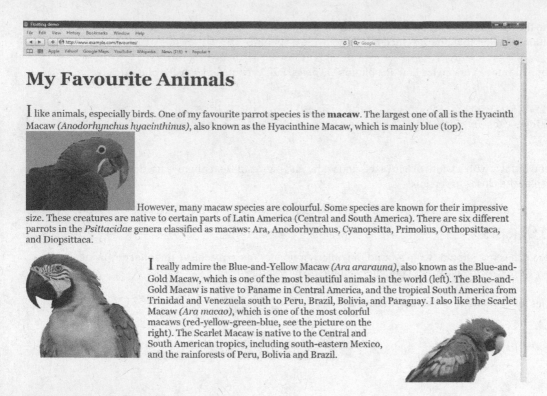

Figure 9-5. *Floating images*

Since the text would be rendered right next to the floating images, you should declare margins to get the final result shown in Listing 9-8. If you intend to display all images of a page on the right side, you can specify the float:right; rule on images without identifiers or classes as img { float:right; }.

If you want to ensure that the next paragraph is displayed below a floating image, you can use the clear property to stop the float on the left (clear: right;), on the right (clear: left;), or on both sides of the image (clear:both;).

Layers Above Each Other

Web site components can also be considered in a virtual space where the component order can be set by a CSS property that represents depth (the third dimension). This property is called z-index. It is frequently used for setting layer order. The larger the value, the higher the elements in the stack order. The element with the largest z-index appears above all other elements of the page. This property works on positioned elements only (elements that have a position rule). For example, the rulesets in Listings 9-9 and 9-10 put the layer with the logo above the main content.

Listing 9-9. The Lower Layer (Compared to Listing 9-10)

```
#main {
  position:absolute;
  width: 780px;
  left: 50%;
  margin-left: -390px;
  z-index: 1;
}
```

326

Listing 9-10. The Upper Layer (Compared to Listing 9-9)

```
#logo {
  position: absolute;
  width: 146px;
  height: 120px;
  margin-top: 20px;
  margin-left: 20px;
  z-index: 2;
}
```

■ **Caution**   Flash content requires an additional parameter that allows the developer to override the default setting that renders Flash content in front of other elements (see the section "Embedding Flash in XHTML").

Typography

Text has always been a fundamental web page feature. The first web documents contained mainly (if not exclusively) text with black fonts over a white background. In the next few years, the Web gradually transformed to a full multimedia platform. At the same time, more sophisticated whitespace handling and character encoding have appeared.

In contrast to books and other printed media where proper type arrangements and type design have always been ensured by typography, until recently the Web lacked these features.

After the introduction of TFT monitors and the ClearType fonts designed for them, characters have become really clear on the screen. With the increasing popularity of web fonts, an endless variety of fonts appeared on the Web.

You must be careful to provide not only eye-catching fonts and type but also legible text. The technique required to achieve that aim is known as *web typography*, which should also guarantee the proper appearance of characters and whitespace.

Misused Characters

According to the World Wide Web Consortium, you should be careful to apply the proper punctuation marks on the Web instead of their misused equivalents (Table 9-1) [10]. Which punctuation marks are typographically correct depends on the natural language of the web page. For example, in British English, single quotes are often preferred to double quotes, and commas generally park outside rather than inside the closing mark. In other languages, the quotation marks might be inverted. Similar differences exist in the use of en and em dashes.

Table 9-1. *Frequently Applied Punctuation Marks and Their Misused Equivalents*

Character	Name	Entity/Entities	Misused Equivalent(s)
"	Opening quote	&#8220;	"
"	Closing quote	&#8221;	"
'	Apostrophe	&#8217;	'
–	En dash (ranges)	– or –	-
—	Em dash (change of thought)	— or —	- or --
…	Horizontal ellipsis (an omission or a pause)	… or …	...

The opening and closing quotation marks appear identical in certain typefaces, known as the straight, vertical, or typewriter quotation marks, which should not be used in the text flow. On the other hand, these characters are used in the markup as the delimiters of attribute values.

■ **Tip**   Many text editors do not support typographic (curly) quotation marks and insert their misused equivalents. One of the options for getting the proper quotation marks is to insert them in a word processor (usually by pressing Shift+2) and then copy the characters to the source code through the clipboard.

Even if the proper quotation marks are used in the markup, browsers might render them incorrectly. Although it is a straightforward idea to apply the q tag for short quotations,[2] browsers render it differently. Firefox 3.6.6 renders both the opening and the closing quotes correctly. However, IE8 incorrectly applies the character „ for opening the quote (the closing is correct). In Safari 5 and Opera 10.6, the misused equivalent " is used for rendering. However, rendering quotes also depends on the language being used and relies on proper language settings in the markup.

Web Fonts

Originally, the Web was developed as a text-based medium. Initially, the selection of fonts available to web designers was limited to the intersection of fonts natively installed on all major platforms. In 1998, the CSS2 specification introduced a font matching and downloading mechanism (which has been dropped in CSS 2.1). In CSS3, external fonts can be applied, along with the declaration of multiple (similar) fonts as a fallback option if the specific fonts cannot be downloaded or are not installed on the user's computer. The technique has both legal and technical issues, however.

Fonts are generally copyrighted; thus, their font files cannot be stored and used on web sites. Even the ones that are advertised as free fonts cannot be used for web sites in many cases [11]. Since a standard font pack has been released under the "Core fonts for the Web" program by Microsoft, the fonts Arial, Georgia, and Verdana (among others) have become *de facto* fonts on the Web.

■ **Caution**   The character repertoire of typefaces varies greatly. While the English alphabet and the common punctuation marks are supported by most font files, the list of supported characters should be a major concern for sites written in a natural language other than English. Multilingual sites should not apply font files that do not support the full range of required characters, which would make it possible to apply the same fonts for the different language versions. One of the options to avoid nonsupported characters is to apply Unicode fonts. However, not all fonts presented on font collection sites as "Unicode fonts" support a really wide range of Unicode characters. In fact, the ones that do are typically 20MB to 25MB in size (compared to the typical font file size of 50KB to 300KB), which is inadequate for web publishing: the fonts won't appear while the font files are being downloaded, and this would take much more time than downloading the entire page with all of its components, including images.

From the technical point of view, the browser support for font embedding and downloading varies from browser to browser. However, the differences are decreasing because of standardization and the growing popularity of implementations. *Embedded OpenType* (*EOT*) font embedding is supported by Internet Explorer from version 4. Other browsers have introduced font linking for *TrueType* (TT) and *OpenType* (OT) fonts (Firefox 3.5+, Opera 10+, Safari 3.1+, Google Chrome 4.0+). Internet Explorer 9+ also supports TT/OT fonts but only those that have embedded

---

[2]If the quotation is longer than one line, the blockquote tag should be used instead.

permissions set to installable. TT has been extended to support additional metadata and gzip compression, known as the Web Open Font Format (WOFF). WOFF is a cross-browser, web-only format being standardized by the W3C [12] and supported by Internet Explorer 9+, Mozilla Firefox 3.6+, and Google Chrome 5+.

■ **Note** The semistructural details appearing on the ends of certain strokes of letters and symbols are known as *serifs* in typography. The typefaces that use serifs, such as Times New Roman, Cambria, Garamond, and Georgia, are known as *serif typefaces*. The typefaces that do not have these small projecting features are the *sans-serif typefaces*,[3] for example, Verdana, Tahoma, and Helvetica. Declaring one of the generic font families (serif, sans-serif, cursive, fantasy, monospace) is an excellent fallback mechanism [13].

Two different fonts (or the same font in two different formats[4]) can be declared with a fallback mechanism, as shown in Listing 9-11, and can be applied as demonstrated in Listing 9-12.

Listing 9-11. Using Fonts Stored in Different Formats

```
@font-face {
  font-family: "Csuff";
  src: url("http://example.com/fonts/csuff.ttf");
  src: url("http://example.com/fonts/csuff.eot");
}
```

Listing 9-12. Applying Web Fonts with a Fallback Mechanism

```
p {
  font-family: "Csuff", "Helvetica", sans-serif;
}
```

Note that a widely available font is also provided, along with the font family declaration that always works, in case neither of the external fonts can be used.

■ **Tip** Serif fonts are easy to read[5] and adequate for long text blocks published on web pages in medium or large font size, as well as for printer style sheets. Sans-serif typefaces are more suitable for short texts in small font size, such as copyright information in the page footer, which is often written in Verdana or a similar font. Monospace fonts like Courier and DejaVu Sans Mono are ideal for preformatted text, computer codes, and typewriter effects. Cursive fonts, such as Comic Sans MS and Brush Script, are used for cursive handwriting such as signatures. Fantasy fonts are best used for headings and artistic texts (for example, Impact and Copperplate).

---

[3]The word *sans* means "without" in French.
[4]Although there are tools for converting fonts from one format to another, it is often legally prohibited.
[5]This is the reason for their widespread application in books, newspapers, and magazines.

The normal, bold, and italic versions, as well as the bold and italic fonts, of a typeface are generally stored in separate files. Consequently, multiple declarations are needed to download and apply the appropriate font styles of the selected typeface (Listing 9-13). Without that, the content of headings and strong elements will be rendered using normal fonts rather than bold ones, em elements will be displayed with normal rather than italic fonts, and so on.

Listing 9-13. Multiple Declarations for the Same Typeface

```
@font-face {
  font-family: Calluna;
  src: url('fonts/Calluna-Regular.otf');
}

@font-face {
  font-family: Callunab;
  src: url('fonts/Calluna-Bold.otf');
}

@font-face {
  font-family: Callunai;
  src: url('fonts/Calluna-It.otf');
}

body {
  font-family: "Calluna", "Helvetica", serif;
}

h1, h2, h3, strong {
  font-family: "Callunab";
}

em {
  font-family: "Callunai";
}
```

There are also some alternatives for web fonts. A technique called *image replacement*, which is considered legal by many, is applied by some web designers to use rendered images of fonts. However, image replacement prevents text selection, has searchability and accessibility issues, and increases bandwidth use.

Another approach applies the Flash-based solution *Scalable Inman Flash Replacement* (*sIFR*). It is similar to image replacement, but the text is selectable and rendered as a vector graphic. A big disadvantage is that this method relies on a Flash plug-in on the client side.

The text can also be replaced by SVG or VML[6] (for Internet Explorer up to version 8) with JavaScript.

In SVG 1.1, fonts can be created within the SVG document. SVG fonts can improve the semantics of graphics that represent texts, such as logos. SVG fonts are partly supported by Safari 3+ and Opera 8+.

---

[6]SVG was not supported by earlier versions of Internet Explorer, which supported the Vector Markup Language (VML) instead (now obsolete).

Similar to (X)HTML documents, CSS can also be applied in SVG documents so the @font-face rule can be used for SVG texts too [14]. Listing 9-14 shows an example.

Listing 9-14. An Example for Using the @fontface CSS Rule in SVG

```
<?xml version="1.0" encoding="UTF-8" standalone="no"?>
<!DOCTYPE svg PUBLIC "-//W3C//DTD SVG 1.1//EN"
 "http://www.w3.org/Graphics/SVG/1.1/DTD/svg11.dtd">
<svg xmlns="http://www.w3.org/2000/svg" version="1.1">
  <defs>
    <style>
      <![CDATA[
        @font-face {
          font-family: Calluna;
          src: url('fonts/Calluna-Regular.otf');
        }
      ]]>
    </style>
  </defs>
  <text x="20" y="40" style="font-family: Calluna, serif; font-size: 1.2em; stroke: #0f0;
  fill: #0f0;">SVG text with Web Fonts</text>
</svg>
```

Embedding External Content

The majority of web sites contain not only formatted texts but also graphics and multimedia content, audio and video clips, and Flash animations. In contrast to formatted text content described by markup languages in text files, this type of content is retrieved from binary files. Although the format and features of such binary files are not standardized for web publishing, their optimization has a huge impact on overall appearance, look and feel, file size, and download time.

Raster Graphics

Bitmap graphics (also known as raster images), which are stored in a mapped array of bits and represent a grid of pixels, are common web site components. On the Web, bitmap file formats are used mainly for storing photographs and other images that are not line art. There are several image file features to be optimized for web publishing, such as pixel density, color depth, and resolution. You should choose the file format according to the content and the desired quality.

The Golden Rule of image processing and retouching for the Web is that whatever will be modified, the original master file should not be overwritten (even if it has a large file size). For example, a title in a compound image created on multiple layers in Photoshop cannot be modified later if you don't preserve the .psd file. Similarly, a heavily retouched or compressed photograph cannot be restored to its original state (which might be useful sometimes) if you haven't saved the original file.

■ **Note**   The following sections describe the major features and possibilities; however, a detailed description of image processing is beyond the scope of this book.

Pixel Density

Not just text content but also graphics can and should be optimized for web publishing. The measure of *spatial dot density* is dots per inch (dpi), which means the number of individual dots represented in a line within the span of 1 inch (2.54 cm). Although dot density correlates with image resolution, it is related indirectly. Instead of the dots that are used for printing, computer screens apply pixels to build up images. Their density can be expressed in pixels per inch (ppi). Although confusing, pixel densities standardized for computer screens are often expressed incorrectly in dpi rather than ppi (72, 96, and 120 dpi). The lowest value, 72 ppi, derives from typography where 1 point (pt) is defined to be 1/72 inch ($\approx$ 0.0139 inch or 352.8 µm). An image displayed on a 72 ppi screen has the same physical dimensions as the printed version in 72 dpi; in other words, 1 pt on paper is equal to 1 px on the screen. However, this is just a theoretical approach; it is not accurate and has lost its significance. Since the pixel density affects not only the quality of image rendering but also text readability, higher values provide better user experience. Modern operating systems and computer screens usually support 96–120 ppi. The pixel density of a screen can be calculated by the ratio of the diagonal resolution in pixels (using the Pythagorean Theorem) and the diagonal size in inches:

$$PPI = \frac{d_p}{d_i} = \frac{\sqrt{w_p^2 + h_p^2}}{d_i}$$

where

d_p is diagonal resolution in pixels,

w_p is width resolution in pixels,

h_p is height resolution in pixels, and

d_i is diagonal size in inches.

For example, the 10.1" display of the Lenovo ThinkPad 10 business tablet with WUXGA (1920×1200) resolution features 224 ppi, the 12" display of the Microsoft Surface Pro 3 with 2160×1440 resolution 216 ppi, while a 23" full HD (1920×1080) monitor 96 ppi.

Smartphones are very competitive from this aspect. In 2010, the Apple iPhone 4 featured the largest resolution screen, called the *Retina display* (640×960), which gave a high 326 ppi[7] pixel density for the 3.5" screen. From 2013 onward, high-end smartphones such as the HTC One and the Samsung Galaxy S5 introduced a full HD display with a resolution of 1920×1080 on a typical screen size of 4.7–5.1", achieving an even higher pixel density (432–468 ppi).

While the optimal pixel density for web publishing is not standardized, computer screens and operating systems generally support 120 ppi as a maximum and typically use 96 ppi. Larger pixel densities needlessly increase the file size.

Resolution

On the screen, resolution determines image size, not quality in general (printing is the opposite). As a general rule, the smallest image size that provides the desired details should be applied. The usual 8–16 MP photos taken by modern digital cameras are usually too large for web publishing and should be resized to a smaller resolution. Because huge-resolution photographs are large in size (a few megabytes depending on compression ratio and file format), it would take too long to download them. Moreover, they have too much detail that might cause legal issues considering faces, number plates, and so on, in the background. The high-resolution depiction of a human face can be used for fraudulent purposes because it can be easily retouched and printed (especially in passport size).

Providing `width` and `height` attributes on img elements for faster and robust rendering of web page images is highly recommended. However, these attributes should not be used for resizing photos. Online galleries and albums should apply small thumbnails linking to the full-size image files.

---

[7]At a distance of 12 inches from one's eye, this is the maximum amount of detail the human retina can process (hence the name).

Aliasing

Resizing digital images can result in distortions and quality loss. A high-resolution image displayed at a lower resolution, for example, might cause distortion artifacts called *aliasing*. *Anti-aliasing* allows the edges of objects to be rendered smoothly. On the Web, anti-aliasing is often applied to fonts and curved web graphics such as rounded corners.

Anti-aliasing requires additional colors with gradually decreasing intensity that merge with the background (Figure 9-6).

Figure 9-6. *Aliased vs. anti-aliased fonts and circles. The original images are shown above, the magnification below. Note the pixelated edges on the left images*

Using anti-aliased fonts on the Web has pros and cons. The most important advantages are smoother fonts, many of which are easier to read because of reduced blurring, the similarity with printed types (depending on the font being used), and often a more aesthetic appearance. However, small fonts become too fuzzy to read, and sharp edges are not always precise.

■ **Caution**   The readability of different web fonts is very different, and even the same typeface might look gorgeous in medium size but becomes unreadable when used with a small font size. There is often a transition between the two states: some parts of the font curves disappear, while others remain visible. Moreover, the rendering of the same web fonts is different in various browsers.

Color Depth

The number of bits required for representing the color of a single pixel in a bitmap image or video frame buffer typically varies from 1 to 2^{32} and is known as *color depth*. The higher the color depth, the larger the file size, which is an important factor in image optimization.

Monochrome (binary) images such as line art with black lines and no tonal contrast should be stored with 1 bit color depth, in other words, two possible values for each pixel.

Black-and-white photographs, which are composed exclusively of 256 shades of gray, should be represented as 8-bit grayscale images ($2^8 = 256$).

24-bit color depth (*true color*) applies red, green, and blue colors with various intensity values between 0 and 255 per channel (RGB color model) to reproduce $2^8 \cdot 2^8 \cdot 2^8 = 2^{24} = 16,777,216$ different colors with *additive color mixing*. Since the human eye cannot distinguish any two adjacent intensity values of these channels, this color depth is suitable for storing photographs.

Photorealistic images with partially transparent parts can be represented in 32 bits with an additional channel called the *alpha channel*[8] (that is, RGBA color space).

The color depth of logos, pictograms, and icons varies, depending on the complexity and image content.

Compression

To reduce file size, digital bitmap images are usually compressed. Compressed images are popular not only for storage but also for web publishing because of the smaller bandwidth requirement.

Image compression can be lossy or lossless. In the case of *lossy compression*s, part of the original information is lost and cannot be restored, which might affect image quality. *Lossless compression* algorithms allow the reconstruction of the original data from the compressed data, which is a nice feature but not always needed. The resulting files of lossy compression algorithms are generally smaller in size than the ones using lossless compression. As you will see, JPEG is the most popular lossy image format, and PNG is the most popular lossless image format on the Web.

Image-processing software tools usually provide the option to adjust the degree of compression, making it possible to select a trade-off between storage size and image quality. For example, Adobe Photoshop has a scale for a JPEG compression ratio with values 0–12. The supported quality ranges are Low (0–4), Medium (5–7), High (8–9), and Maximum (10–12). The settings are available after determining the name and destination of the file in the File ➤ Save As... dialog window (Figure 9-7).

Figure 9-7. *Excellent quality with small file size*

JPEG typically achieves about 10:1 compression with barely noticeable loss in image quality.

---

[8]There are also other approaches to provide transparency, but for partially transparent photographs, it is the common solution.

Interlacing

Certain bitmap formats such as GIF and PNG provide the option to display a degraded fast preview of an image before it is fully downloaded. The method is known as *interlacing*. Advanced image-processing software applications support interlacing and offer the choice to save such files either as *interlaced* or as *noninterlaced*. A similar effect can be achieved in photographs by applying a *frequency decomposition hierarchy* in *progressive JPEG* files. In the era of slow, dial-up connections, interlacing was a useful feature but lost most of its significance after the widespread distribution of broadband Internet access.

Transparency

Partially transparent images are very popular, and can be used for design effects and images that can be displayed on different background colors or textures (Figure 9-8).

Figure 9-8. *An image on three different backgrounds (first row). The second row is magnified to 600 percent. The transparent shadow perfectly fits to all backgrounds*

Not all raster image formats support transparency, though. GIF is generally a good (sometimes the best) option for partially transparent geometric shapes and cartoon-style images, while PNG is ideal for more complex (photorealistic) partially transparent images. With the exception of really simple shapes with relatively large areas of the same color, PNG is the better option.

Raster File Formats

The most common raster image file formats on the Web are JPEG, GIF, and PNG.

Joint Photographic Experts Group (JPEG) is a common lossy compression format for digital photographs. Part 1 has been standardized in ISO/IEC 10918-1:1994 [15] and ITU-T T.81 (09/92) [16], Part 2 in ISO/IEC 10918-2:1995 [17] and ITU-T T.83 (11/94) [18], Part 3 in ISO/IEC 10918-3:1997 [19] and ITU-T T.84 (07/96) [20], Part 4 in ISO/IEC 10918-4:1999 [21] and ITU-T T.86 (06/98) [22], and Part 5 in ISO/IEC FCD 10918-5 [23].

The original version of the Graphics Interchange Format, GIF87a, was introduced in 1987 [24], and the enhanced version with transparency and interlacing support, GIF89a, was introduced in 1989 [25].

The Portable Network Graphics (PNG) format was standardized by IETF RFC 2083 in 1997 [26] and ISO/IEC 15948 in 2004 [27]. However, the PNG format has not gained full support until recently. Although Internet Explorer supports PNG images from version 4.01b, the implementation was neither complete nor correct until IE9 (for example, IE6 had a buggy support for alpha-channel transparency). There were color inconsistencies between various browsers, partly because of the different handling of gamma correction (for example, colors of PNG images were displayed incorrectly on Safari for Windows). Fortunately, modern browsers overcame these issues.

To choose the right file format for a given image, the main features of file types and compression algorithms should be considered (Table 9-2).

Table 9-2. *Quick Comparison of JPEG, GIF, and PNG*

	JPEG	GIF	PNG
Maximum color depth	24-bit	8-bit	48-bit
Palette	Full	Restricted	Optional
Compression	Lossy (in most cases)	Lossless	Lossless
Transparency	–	+	+
Interlaced mode	+ (progressive JPEG)	+	+
Animation	–	+	–[9]
Optimal usage	Photographs	Icons, logos, diagrams (geometric shapes), clipart, cartoon-style images, and small animations	Photographs, partially transparent photographs, icons, and logos

For example, a simple image such as a solid circle can be stored with two colors in GIF with a very small file size compared to other formats such as JPEG. For images that have no complex content, the color depth can be reduced with color palettes (selected/indexed colors) in file formats such as GIF, TIF, and PNG. Anti-aliased images need a larger color depth resulting in a larger file size. Although GIF and PNG formats are usually better than JPEG for storing icons and logos, the SVG vector format should be preferred for such content (see the section "Vector Graphics").

Although it is very efficient on photographs, the JPEG compression algorithm adds additional pixels to the whole image, including solid areas. As a result, simple images become more complex than they were originally. This is the main reason why a solid circle stored in JPEG has several times larger file size than a GIF file with the same content even if the compression is high. Moreover, if the compression ratio is high, JPEG artifacts become noticeable, resulting in lower image quality. On the other hand, JPEG works perfectly on complex images. If the compression is set properly, the image quality to file size ratio is excellent.

File Size Optimization

Pixel density, resolution, dimensions, color depth, compression ratio, image complexity, and file format all have a large impact on file size.

The width and height should be optimized by cropping irrelevant parts of the image especially for scanned and high-resolution images where image parts can often be removed without losing information.

The required color depth must be used; 24-bit color depth is the default setting in many software tools, which can be reduced in many cases without affecting image quality. For example, black-and-white drawings should not be stored with 16 million colors.

The proper compression ratio must be used for all images.

The size-quality ratio can be effectively optimized with the File ➤ Save For Web & Devices... function of Photoshop (Figure 9-9).

---

[9]There is an extension called Animated Portable Network Graphics (APNG) that supports animation. APNG is natively supported by Firefox 3+ and Safari 8+.

Figure 9-9. *Comparison of file formats and settings for web publishing in Photoshop*

Photoshop also offers optimization to a desired file size, but it should be kept in mind that image content and complexity determine the optimal level of compression.

Beyond the compression settings of JPEG files available in Photoshop or GIMP, some software tools (such as JPEG Optimizer [28]) are capable of optimizing the file size to quality ratio by applying different compression ratios to various image areas.

The goal of file size optimization is to achieve the perfect balance between file size and picture quality. Large-resolution images can be frustratingly slow to download while a fast web page with low-quality images won't meet visual expectations.

Small, highly compressed versions (thumbnails) should be provided with links to a larger, high-quality version in online photo galleries and albums. This approach allows users to determine whether the image is relevant for them and reasonable to download the larger version, which will naturally take longer.

Vector Graphics

Vector and bitmap images have different application areas. Bitmaps are best suitable for photographs and photorealistic images, while vector images can be applied for artwork and illustrations that consist of lines and curves. Nonetheless, bitmaps are still used widely on the Web for all kinds of images, including the ones that should be provided in a vector format instead. The situation has started to change with the widespread support of SVG in browsers and the native SVG support in HTML5.

Scalable Vector Graphics should be preferred for all images that require basic shapes such as circles and polygons, Bézier paths and curves, text, opacity, transformations (rotation, skew, scale, and so on), gradients, and animations.[10] SVG content can also be combined with bitmap graphics.

Similar to PNG, the browser support of SVG should be taken into account in web design for the sake of backward compatibility. The SVG support of older browsers was different for inline SVG, external SVG files, and SVG used as a CSS background image. Prior to HTML5, external SVG files were usually embedded via the object element, while in HTML5 you can embed external SVG files also with img or the newly introduced svg or embed element, or write the SVG code directly in the markup (inline SVG). The browser support of the different SVG versions (1.0 and 1.1, Tiny and Full variants) was also different across older browsers. The Gecko layout engine supports SVG 1.1 Full since 2005, while WebKit since 2006, but early implementations were incomplete. Opera supports SVG 1.1 Tiny from version 8, SVG 1.1 Basic fully and SVG 1.1 Full partially from version 9, and SVG Tiny 1.2 (including compressed SVG) partially from version 9.5 onward. Modern browsers support SVG 1.1 Full correctly, which has a standardized second edition since 2011.

Flash

Before HTML5, Flash used to be one of the most popular technologies for publishing active content on the Web. For live video streaming, Flash is still the most popular. Unfortunately, the default embedding code provided by Flash development tools is often not standard-compliant and has some browser-dependent issues. For Flash contents, it is important to provide an alternate textual content that can be automatically activated if the Flash content cannot be displayed.

Embedding Flash in XHTML

The first Flash implementations applied the embed element, which was deprecated in HTML 4 and XHTML in favor of the object element but then was reintroduced in HTML 5.

To avoid browser- and vendor-specific code, various implementation methods have been introduced, including duplication (the *twice-cooked method*), the *nested objects method*, and *Flash Satay*. The latter one, Flash Satay, provides robust and standard-compliant Flash implementation by including an additional movie parameter, and suggested by the W3C [29]. Listing 9-15 shows an example.

Listing 9-15. Embedding Flash Using Flash Satay

```
<object type="application/x-shockwave-flash" data="australia.swf" width="735" height="677"↵
 id="flash">
  <param name="movie" value="australia.swf" />
</object>
```

Note that the same Flash file is specified both as a data attribute value on the object element and as a movie parameter value. Note that the classid and codebase parameters used by older methods are eliminated. If the codebase parameter is left in the code when modifying a traditional Flash embedding code, it prevents Firefox from rendering the Flash content, and the optionally provided alternate content appears instead (or nothing at all).

One of the known issues of the Flash Satay method is that the Flash movie is not streamed by some browsers such as Internet Explorer. Waiting for the whole file to download and start to play afterwards works fine for small files and fast Internet connections only.

If you develop a web page with layers above each other, it might be rather frustrating that Flash content appears above all other web site elements by default. If you want to set the layer order on web pages with Flash content, an additional parameter (wmode) is needed (Listings 9-16 and 9-17).

---

[10]Similar effects are also supported by CSS3.

Listing 9-16. Setting the wmode for Nontransparent Flash Content

```
<param name="wmode" value="opaque" />
```

The parameter value opaque indicates that the content is not transparent. If it is transparent, the attribute value should be changed to transparent (Listing 9-17).

Listing 9-17. Setting the wmode for Transparent Flash Content

```
<param name="wmode" value="transparent" />
```

Although it seems that there is no correlation between the transparency of Flash content and the stack position of the Flash content in the layer order, the wmode parameter should be used for setting both. Either the opaque or the transparent attribute value is used on the wmode parameter, Flash content can be sent behind any layer within the web page (or in any desired position in the layer order). The only problem associated with wmode is that the Flash content becomes inaccessible to users with screen readers and is therefore best avoided whenever possible.

Similar to (X)HTML markup, Flash content should be accessible and search engine friendly. The version of the installed Flash plug-in of the browser should be detected to determine whether it is up-to-date. Outdated plug-ins might encounter functionalities that are supported in higher plug-in versions only, and have vulnerabilities addressed in newer versions. This should be considered to eliminate broken and missing content.

As for the version dilemma, Adobe provides the Flash Player Detection Kit [30]; however, the code generated by the kit is not standard-compliant.

DOM scripting can address these issues. An open source example is the *SWFObject* by Geoff Stearns et al [31]. SWFObject provides a cross-browser method to embed SWF files into web pages using a very small JavaScript code. This JavaScript code detects Flash Player, declares alternate content, improves search engine indexing, assists Flash Player downloading if it is not installed, includes Adobe Express Install, and offers an API for JavaScript developers. However, version detection with JavaScript relies on scripting, results in longer code, and overcomplicates Flash embedding. As a conclusion, there is no better standard-compliant, cross-browser Flash embedding method than Flash Satay.

Embedding Flash in (X)HTML5

HTML5 has an embed element for embedded content that requires plug-ins. It supports all the standard attributes and event attributes of HTML5. Additionally, it has the specific attributes src, type (which specifies MIME type), height, and width. You can use it as shown in Listing 9-18.

Listing 9-18. Basic Flash Embedding in (X)HTML5

```
<embed src="australia.swf" />
```

The embed tag also supports the global and event attributes of HTML5, which have already been discussed in Chapter 3.

Audio

Prior to HTML5, there has never been native markup support for playing audio on web pages. Most audio content is played through a plug-in such as Flash. The major problem with this approach is that not all browsers have the same plug-ins.

HTML5 offers a standard way to include audio content in the markup: the audio element. It can be used to play sound files as well as audio streams, and adds semantic meaning to the markup. Three major audio formats are supported by the audio element: MP3, Ogg Vorbis, and WAV. However, the browser support of these formats varies (Table 9-3).

Table 9-3. *Audio Format Support for the audio Element in Different Browsers*

Format	IE	Firefox	Chrome	Opera	Safari
MP3	9+	3.5+[11]	3.0+	–	3.1+
WAV	–	3.5+	3.0+	10.5+	3.1+
Ogg Vorbis	–	3.5+	3.0+	10.5+	3.1+

The basic use of the audio element is straightforward (Listing 9-19).

Listing 9-19. Basic Audio Embedding in (X)HTML5

```
<audio src="valerie.mp3">
</audio>
```

Beyond the src attribute that specifies the source URL of the audio content to play, there are further attributes for automatic playing (autoplay="autoplay"), control buttons (controls="controls"), repeating (loop="loop"), and loading at page load (preload="preload"). The last one is ignored if autoplay is present.

To achieve a higher level of accessibility, alternate content should be provided (Listing 9-20).

Listing 9-20. Alternate Content for Audio

```
<audio src="valerie.mp3" controls="controls">
  <p><a href="valerie.mp3">Valerie by Joy</a></p>
</audio>
```

Since certain formats supported by a browser cannot be played in another, the audio element allows multiple source declarations that link to different audio files. Listing 9-21 shows an example.

Listing 9-21. Multiple Source Declaration for Different Formats

```
<audio controls="controls">
  <source src="valerie.mp3" type="audio/mpeg" />
  <source src="valerie.ogg" type="audio/ogg" />
  <p><a href="valerie.mp3">Valerie by Joy</a></p>
</audio>
```

Browsers can play the first supported format from the different audio formats.

Video

For many years, publishing videos was possible through general object embedding only. Because of the variety of video and audio codecs and the varying browser support, there is still no ultimate solution for publishing videos on the Web.

---

[11]To avoid patent issues, Firefox has no native MP3 support, and relies on a decoder from the OS.

Embedding Video in XHTML

Content from video-sharing services such as YouTube or Google Video, which serve movies through the Flash Player,[12] can be embedded using the Flash Satay method discussed earlier. Listing 9-22 shows an example.

Listing 9-22. Embedding a Flash Video Using Flash Satay

```
<object type="application/x-shockwave-flash"
 data="http://video.google.com/videoplay?docid=4226784084458819393#" width="400"
 height="326" id="VideoPlayback">
  <param name="movie" value="http://video.google.com/videoplay?docid=4226784084458819393#" />
  <param name="allowFullScreen" value="true" />
  <param name="allowScriptAccess" value="always" />
</object>
```

Window Media Video files (.wmv) can be embedded by using the MIME type video/x-ms-wmv (Listing 9-23).

Listing 9-23. Embedding a WMV Video File

```
<object type="video/x-ms-wmv"
 data="http://www.example.com/dreamcar.wmv"
 width="320" height="260">
  <param name="src" value="http://www.example.com/dreamcar.wmv" />
  <param name="autostart" value="true" />
  <param name="controller" value="true" />
</object>
```

For QuickTime videos, there are dedicated MIME types: the video/quicktime and the application/x-quicktime. IE tends to open such videos through an ActiveX control. To embed QuickTime videos in a browser-independent way that also validates, you can use the method presented in Listing 9-24.

Listing 9-24. Embedding a QuickTime Video File

```
<object classid="clsid:02BF25D5-8C17-4B23-BC80-D3488ABDDC6B"
 codebase="http://www.apple.com/qtactivex/qtplugin.cab" width="352" height="288">
  <param name="src" value="http://www.example.com/video/dreamcars.mov" />
  <param name="controller" value="true" />
  <param name="autoplay" value="false" />
  <!--[if !IE]>-->
    <object type="video/quicktime" data="http:// www.example.com/video/dreamcars.mov"
     width="352" height="288">
    <param name="autoplay" value="false" />
    <param name="controller" value="true" />
  </object>
  <!--<![endif]-->
</object>
```

The code provided as IE-style conditional comments[13] is used by all browsers except Internet Explorer, in which these comments are hidden and the outer object is displayed.

---

[12]Adobe Flash Player is widely used for streaming video playback on web sites.
[13]The method was suggested by Lachlan Hunt.

Embedding Video in (X)HTML5

In contrast to the complexity of video embedding with the object element in XHTML, (X)HTML5 provides the video element, which is easy to use, has full control over the video being embedded, and adds semantic meaning to the markup. The video element is supported in IE9+, Firefox 3.5+, Chrome 3.0+, Opera 10.5+, and Safari 3.0+. However, its usability depends also on the supported codecs. If you just think of DivX, Xvid, WMV, FFmpeg, 3ivx, Sorenson, or Flash Video from the enormous variety of video file formats, the video codec support of web browsers is undoubtedly in its infancy (Table 9-4).

Table 9-4. *Overview of Video Format Support for the* video *Element in Different Browsers*

Format	IE	Firefox	Chrome	Opera	Safari
H.264	9+	3.5+[14]	*Dropped*	–	3.1+
Ogg Theora	*Installable*	3.5+	3.0+	10.5+	*Installable*
WebM	*Installable*	4.0+	6.0+	10.6+	*Installable*

While there is no need to maximize the number of natively supported video formats on the Web, the reliable support for the most widely used, advanced formats would be desirable.

■ **Note**   Many video files are stored in container formats that are not restricted to one kind of video and audio codec. Consequently, the full support for a video container should include the support for all kinds of video and audio codecs allowed in that container format. For example, if browser vendors would like to introduce support for .flv Flash videos, it would require support for the H.264/MPEG-4 AVC, Sorenson, Screen Video, and VP6 video codecs, as well as the AAC, ADPCM, Linear PCM, Nellymoser, MP3, and Speex audio codecs. Moreover, many codecs have proprietary licenses or are encumbered by patents (this is the reason why Chrome dropped the H.264 support). The different associations of audio and video codecs along with the licensing issues make it rather complex to standardize video implementations on the Web. Different formats are suitable for different purposes and application areas, and there is no ultimate choice for video publishing as it depends on the scenario.

Listing 9-25 shows the basic code for the video element.

Listing 9-25. Basic Video Embedding in (X)HTML5

```
<video src="sample.ogv">
</video>
```

Features such as height or width can be added optionally. An image representing a frame from the video (alternate content) can be defined as the value of the poster attribute (displayed when the video cannot be rendered). Alternate markup can be defined as the element content between the opening and closing video tags (Listing 9-26).

---

[14]To avoid patent issues, Firefox has no native H.264 support, and relies on a decoder from the OS.

Listing 9-26. Additional Properties and Alternate Content for (X)HTML5 Video Embedding

```
<video src="sample.ogv" width="320" height="240" poster="sample.jpg">
  <p>Download the <a href="video.ogv">sample video</a> (OGV, 5.34 MB)</p>
</video>
```

Video controls can be shown or hidden in the browser by using the `controls` attribute on the `video` element (Listing 9-27).

Listing 9-27. Controls Set to Be Displayed for (X)HTML5 Video Embedding

```
<video src="xyz.mov" controls="controls">
</video>
```

Since the video codec support is different in each browser, the same video can be provided in various formats, avoiding the need to download videos that cannot be played on the system. Listing 9-28 shows an example.

Listing 9-28. The Same Video in Different Formats

```
<video>
  <source src="video.mp4" type="video/mp4" />
  <source src="video.ogv" type="video/ogg" />
  <p>Download the <a href="video.ogv">sample video</a> (OGV)</p>
</video>
```

However, the MIME type cannot reflect the codecs of videos stored in container formats (for example, H.264 in MPEG-4). They can be provided by the `codecs` parameter (Listing 9-29).

Listing 9-29. Declaring Video Codecs in (X)HTML5

```
<video controls="controls">
  <source src="video.mp4" type='video/mp4; codecs="avc1.42E01E, mp4a.40.2"' />
  <source src="video.ogv" type='video/ogg; codecs="theora, vorbis"' />
  <p>Download the <a href="video.ogv">sample video</a></p>
</video>
```

Care must be taken to apply single and double quotes alternately for the `type` attribute values.

The `video` element of (X)HTML5 provides playback support detection, including the `canPlayType()` method on the `media` element or the `onerror` event listener. Listing 9-30 is an example of the second method.

Listing 9-30. Video Plackback Support Detection in (X)HTML5

```
<video controls="controls">
  <source src="video.mp4" type='video/mp4; codecs="avc1.42E01E, mp4a.40.2"' />
  <source src="video.ogv" type='video/ogg; codecs="theora, vorbis"' ↵
  onerror="fallback(this.parentNode)" />
  <p>Download the <a href="video.ogv">sample video</a> (OGV)</p>
</video>
```

Since the video support in browsers varies, there is no ultimate cross-browser video-embedding code.

Although one of the major advantages of the `video` element is to eliminate the `object` element and plug-in declaration in video embedding, the `object` element can still be useful sometimes. If plug-ins are preferred to simple error messages, the `object` element can be embedded into the `video` element. Flash supports MPEG-4/H.264/AAC playback, so an `.mp4` file can usually be played by the code presented in Listing 9-31.

343

Listing 9-31. MPEG-4 Plackback

```
<video controls="controls">
  <source src="video.mp4" type='video/mp4; codecs="avc1.42E01E, mp4a.40.2"'↵
   onerror="fallback(this.parentNode)" />
  <object data="videoplayer.swf">
    <param name="flashvars" value="video.mp4" />
    <p>Download the <a href="video.ogv">sample video</a> (OGV)</p>
  </object>
</video>
```

Some browsers cannot stream the video or automatically download the whole video file even if playback has not been started yet. One of the exceptions is Firefox 3.6+, which downloads only a fragment necessary to determine duration and render a frame from the video. This behavior can be overridden by the preload attribute. The none attribute value forces the browser to avoid downloading. The metadata attribute value hints that enough data should be downloaded only to show a frame and determine duration. The auto value downloads the whole video. The effect of preload="none" can be simulated in browsers that do not support it by omitting the src attribute and source elements that are provided only if the user clicks a button (Listing 9-32).

Listing 9-32. Loading Video on User Click

```
<video controls="controls">
  Video not supported
</video>
<input type="button" value="Load video"↵
 onclick="document.getElementsByTagName('video')[0].src = 'video.mp4';" />
```

Additionally, customized controls can also be added to the video embedding since the DOM API for video in (X)HTML5 supports several events that can be handled through JavaScript. Listing 9-33 shows an example.

Listing 9-33. Customized Video Controls

```
<script>
  var video = document.getElementsByTagName('video')[0];
</script>
<input type="button" value="Play" onclick="video.play()" />
<input type="button" value="Pause" onclick="video.pause()" />
```

Playback can be started automatically by the autoplay attribute of the video element (Listing 9-34).

Listing 9-34. Video Playback to Be Started Automatically

```
<video src="abc.mp4" autoplay="autoplay"></video>
```

However, not all users want to download the video, and a start button is usually preferred. Additionally, if there are multiple videos on the same page, automatic playing is out of the question, especially if there are at least two that are not mute.

Currently, the src attribute value of the video tag should be a physical file, which makes it impossible to embed your favorite video from YouTube directly. For example, the code in Listing 9-35 cannot be used.

Listing 9-35. A YouTube Video Cannot Be Played Using the video Tag (Demonstration Only)

```
<video src="http://www.youtube.com/watch?v=WgL7DMiTCAY"></video>
```

(X)HTML5 videos can be dynamically drawn on a canvas with JavaScript using the drawImage method, such as in Listing 9-36.

Listing 9-36. Video Drawn on the Canvas Using JavaScript

```
<video src="video.mp4" controls="controls">
  Video not supported
</video>
<canvas id="canvas">
  Canvas not supported
</canvas>
<script>
  var ctx = document.getElementById('canvas').getContext('2d');
  var video = document.getElementsByTagName('video')[0];
  video.onloadeddata = function(e) {
  ctx.canvas.width = video.videoWidth;
  ctx.canvas.height = video.videoHeight;
  ctx.drawImage(video, 0, 0);
  }
</script>
```

Summary

In this chapter, you learned how to provide an advanced user experience through optimized appearance using standards. You became familiar with many web site components that contribute to user experience and affect web site usability and functionality. You know that it is a real challenge to ensure proper appearance across devices, which can be achieved by creating browser- and resolution-independent web sites with robust layout. You are well aware that many of the once popular techniques are obsolete, and tables should be used for tabular data only, not for layout. CSS provides full control over the appearance of web site components, and responsive layouts should be used in place of fixed-width documents. You also know how to optimize images for your web sites and embed Flash and video files in a browser-independent, standard-compliant manner.

In the next chapter, you will learn accessibility techniques that maximize user access to your web sites. By following the accessibility guidelines, you will be capable of supporting not only people with disabilities and mobile users but also all the others, because everyone benefits from an advanced level of web accessibility.

References

1. Hazaël-Massieux D (2005) Tableless layout HOWTO. World Wide Web Consortium. http://www.w3.org/2002/03/csslayout-howto. Accessed 15 October 2014

2. Cederholm D (2009) CSS layouts. In: Web standards solutions, Special edn. Friends of ED, Berkeley

3. W3C (2003) Errata in REC-CSS2-19980512. World Wide Web Consortium. http://www.w3.org/Style/css2-updates/REC-CSS2-19980512-errata.html. Accessed 15 October 2014

4.   Google (2014) css3-mediaqueries-js. https://code.google.com/p/css3-mediaqueries-js/. Accessed 16 October 2014

5.   Jehl S (2011) Respond.js. https://github.com/scottjehl/Respond. Accessed 16 October 2014

6.   Hickson et al (eds) (2014) The picture element. In: HTML 5.1 Nightly. A vocabulary and associated APIs for HTML and XHTML. World Wide Web Consortium. http://www.w3.org/html/wg/drafts/html/master/embedded-content.html#attr-picture-source-srcset. Accessed 16 October 2014

7.   Jehl S et al (2014) Picturefill. https://github.com/scottjehl/picturefill. Accessed 16 October 2014

8.   Grabanski M, Schmitt C (2014) HiSRC. https://github.com/teleject/hisrc. Accessed 16 October 2014

9.   Wilcox M (2014) Adaptive Images. http://adaptive-images.com/. Accessed 16 October 2014

10.   W3C (2010) English Typography. W3C Cheat Sheet. World Wide Web Consortium. http://www.w3.org/2009/cheatsheet/#typo. Accessed 15 October 2014

11.   Mason B (2009) When Free Fonts Aren't Free. Small Batch Inc. http://blog.typekit.com/2009/06/11/when-free-fonts-arent-free/. Accessed 15 October 2014

12.   Kew J, Leming T, van Blokland E (2012) WOFF File Format 1.0. W3C Recommendation. World Wide Web Consortium. http://www.w3.org/TR/WOFF/. Accessed 15 October 2014

13.   Bos B, Çelik T, Hickson I, Lie HW (2011) Generic font families. In: Cascading Style Sheets Level 2 Revision 1 (CSS 2.1) Specification. W3C Recommendation. World Wide Web Consortium. http://www.w3.org/TR/CSS2/fonts.html#generic-font-families. Accessed 15 October 2014

14.   Dahlström E, Dengler P, Grasso A, Lilley C, McCormack C, Schepers D, Watt J, Ferraiolo J, Jun F, Jackson D (eds) (2011) The 'font-face' element. In: Scalable Vector Graphics (SVG) 1.1 (Second Edition). W3C Recommendation. World Wide Web Consortium. http://www.w3.org/TR/SVG/fonts.html#FontFaceElement. Accessed 15 October 2014

15.   ISO (2011) Information technology – Digital compression and coding of continuous-tone still images: Requirements and guidelines. ISO/IEC 10918-1:1994. International Organization for Standardization. http://www.iso.org/iso/iso_catalogue/catalogue_tc/catalogue_detail.htm?csnumber=18902. Accessed 15 October 2014

16.   ITU-T (1992) T.81: Information technology – Digital compression and coding of continuous-tone still images - Requirements and guidelines. International Telecommunication Union. http://www.itu.int/rec/T-REC-T.81. Accessed 15 October 2014

17.   ISO (2008) ISO/IEC 10918-2:1995 Information technology – Digital compression and coding of continuous-tone still images: Compliance testing. International Organization for Standardization. http://www.iso.org/iso/iso_catalogue/catalogue_tc/catalogue_detail.htm?csnumber=20689. Accessed 15 October 2014

18.   ITU-T (1994) T.83: Information technology – Digital compression and coding of continuous-tone still images: Compliance testing. International Telecommunication Union. http://www.itu.int/rec/T-REC-T.83. Accessed 15 October 2014

19. ISO (2008) ISO/IEC 10918-3:1997 Information technology – Digital compression and coding of continuous-tone still images: Extensions. International Organization for Standardization. http://www.iso.org/iso/iso_catalogue/catalogue_tc/catalogue_detail.htm?csnumber=25037. Accessed 15 October 2014

20. ITU-T (2006) T.84: Information technology - Digital compression and coding of continuous-tone still images: Extensions. International Telecommunication Union. http://www.itu.int/rec/T-REC-T.84. Accessed 15 October 2014

21. ISO (1999) ISO/IEC 10918-4:1999 Information technology – Digital compression and coding of continuous-tone still images: Registration of JPEG profiles, SPIFF profiles, SPIFF tags, SPIFF colour spaces, APPn markers, SPIFF compression types and Registration Authorities (REGAUT). International Organization for Standardization. http://www.iso.org/iso/iso_catalogue/catalogue_tc/catalogue_detail.htm?csnumber=25431. Accessed 15 October 2014

22. ITU-T (1999) T.86: Information technology – Digital compression and coding of continuous-tone still images: Registration of JPEG Profiles, SPIFF Profiles, SPIFF Tags, SPIFF colour Spaces, APPn Markers, SPIFF Compression types and Registration authorities (REGAUT). International Telecommunication Union. http://www.itu.int/rec/T-REC-T.86. Accessed 15 October 2014

23. ISO (2013) ISO/IEC FDIS 10918-5 Information technology – Digital compression and coding of continuous-tone still images: JPEG File Interchange Format (JFIF). International Organization for Standardization. http://www.iso.org/iso/iso_catalogue/catalogue_tc/catalogue_detail.htm?csnumber=54989. Accessed 15 October 2014

24. CompuServe (1987) GIF – Graphics Interchange Format. A standard defining a mechanism for the storage and transmission of raster-based graphics information. CompuServe Incorporated. http://www.w3.org/Graphics/GIF/spec-gif87.txt. Accessed 15 October 2014

25. CompuServe (1990) Graphics Interchange Format Version 89a. CompuServe Incorporated. http://www.w3.org/Graphics/GIF/spec-gif89a.txt. Accessed 15 October 2014

26. Boutell T et al (1997) PNG (Portable Network Graphics) Specification Version 1.0. RFC 2083. Internet Engineering Task Force. http://tools.ietf.org/html/rfc2083. Accessed 15 October 2014

27. ISO (2004) ISO/IEC 15948:2004 Information technology – Computer graphics and image processing – Portable Network Graphics (PNG): Functional specification. International Organization for Standardization. http://www.iso.org/iso/catalogue_detail.htm?csnumber=29581. Accessed 15 October 2014

28. xat.com (2014) JPEG Optimizer: The JPEG Image Compressor for Windows. xat.com Internet Technology. http://xat.com/jpegopt/. Accessed 15 October 2014

29. W3C (2012) How can I include flash in valid (X)HTML Web pages? In: Help and FAQ for the Markup Validator. World Wide Web Consortium. http://validator.w3.org/docs/help.html#faq-flash. Accessed 15 October 2014

30. Adobe (2010) Flash Player Detection Kit. Adobe Systems Incorporated. http://www.adobe.com/products/flashplayer/download/detection_kit/. Accessed 07 December 2010

31. Google Inc (2010) Swfobject. Google Project Hosting. http://code.google.com/p/swfobject/. Accessed 15 October 2014

■ ■ ■

Accessibility

With the rapid evolution of web services and technologies, the number of Internet users is constantly increasing. Since many people suffer from various temporary or permanent disabilities and deficiencies, advanced web development practices should be applied to provide content that is accessible for all. The importance of web accessibility is being recognized by an increasing number of web designers and developers. W3C provides useful guidelines to ensure content accessibility. The accessibility support implemented in modern software tools and web sites should be clearly indicated so people living with disabilities can easily identify them. HTML5 markup also supports accessibility through advanced structuring elements, metadata, and Accessible Rich Internet Applications (ARIAs). Web accessibility techniques are not limited to the visually impaired or people with other disabilities. In fact, they also ease mobile access to web content and improve overall web page quality.

In this chapter, you will learn the criteria of accessible web sites, along with the techniques to fulfill them. You will understand the concept of web accessibility and become familiar with the most widely adopted official guidelines. The corresponding guidelines provide access to your web sites for the disabled and improve the user experience for people using devices with limited hardware capabilities, such as mobile users. The content of your web sites should remain legible even if the style sheets are turned off, can be read out loud effectively by screen readers, and rendered also in text-based browsers such as Lynx. Moreover, the techniques that support accessibility have a nice side effect: they improve web site usability and user experience as well.

Defining Web Accessibility

By default, web sites containing a variety of components, especially the ones with nontextual content such as videos, cannot be used by all people. Even common web site components like text might be difficult, and sometimes impossible, for some people to read. Not all users can see colors or move the mouse. Everybody knows how frustrating a web site can be when it does not work or has functionality that is very difficult to use for whatever reasons. Now imagine that feeling magnified by a factor of ten or a hundred, which is what people with disabilities suffer from when using inaccessible web sites. The degree of frustration varies from person to person, because some people live with visual impairment, while others with mobility, dexterity, auditory, or cognitive impairment.

More and more countries have introduced legislation addressing the need for web sites to be accessible to people with disabilities or the requirement to be nondiscriminative against people with disabilities. Some examples are the *Disability Discrimination Act 1992* in Australia [1], the *Disability Act 2005* in Ireland [2], the *Disability Discrimination Act* 1995 in the United Kingdom [3], or *Section 508 Amendment to the Rehabilitation Act of 1973* in the United States [4].

Web accessibility covers those web site development practices that provide web content usable ("accessible") for everybody, including people with disabilities. W3C director Tim Berners-Lee announced the launch of the International Program Office (IPO) for the Web Accessibility Initiative (WAI) [5] at W3C in 1997 by defining accessibility as follows: "The power of the Web is in its universality. Access by everyone regardless of disability is an essential aspect" [6].

While the brightly contrasting colored strips on the steps of buses provide improved visibility for the visually impaired, such strips can be useful to other people too (for example, in poor light conditions or when someone is in a hurry). Many ramps might be useful not only for people in a wheelchair but also for parents with children, skateboarders, in-line skaters, or people moving heavy goods. Similarly, the improved accessibility of web content is useful not only for people with disabilities but for any user in general. For example, web accessibility contributes to a higher level of user experience in mobile browsing, and mobile devices are used by everybody, not only people with disabilities.

There are several software tools and hardware devices used by people with disabilities for web browsing (and using the computer in general). Such tools and devices are referred to as *Assistive Technology* (AT).[1] This umbrella term covers screen readers, screen magnifiers, switch mechanisms, alternative and adaptive keyboards such as large key keyboards with simplified keyboard layout and approximately four times bigger (and often colored) keys than the keys on standard keyboards, high-contrast keyboards, keysets (chorded keyboards), keyboards with mousepads or keyguards, trackballs, mouthsticks, handsticks (keyboard aids, type aids), head pointers (head wands), and so on (Figure 10-1).

Figure 10-1. *Examples for assistive technology*

According to the 2010 World Standards Day Message, at least 650 million people around the world are affected by some kind of disability, and accessibility is not only an issue for the elderly or disabled. Anybody at any stage in life might experience temporarily reduced accessibility [7].

In contrast to the common misbelief, web accessibility authors address much more than just visual impairment. Many people have motor, mobility, auditory, or cognitive problems. The Web is just as, if not more, important to people with disabilities than it is to anyone. The reason is that the Web provides access to services and/or information that cannot be obtained easily without it (for example online ordering) [8]. However, badly designed web sites create barriers that exclude many people from using the web services [9].

The World Wide Web Consortium provides accessibility guidelines and techniques for web content (*WCAG*), authoring tools (*ATAG*) [10], and user agents (*UAAG*) [11]. Accessibility test results can be expressed in a special language called *Evaluation Language* (*EARL*) [12].

---

[1]Sometimes the term Adaptive Technology is also used.

The accessibility of dynamic contents and advanced user interfaces developed in a combination of HTML, JavaScript, Ajax, and other technologies is defined by the collection of specifications released by the Web Accessibility Initiative (WAI) at the W3C. This collection is known as the *Accessible Rich Internet Applications Suite*, which includes the following documents [13]:

- *WAI-ARIA technical specification*: Accessibility tips for the authors and editors of web standards, as well as developers of user agents and accessibility evaluation tools [14]

- *WAI-ARIA Primer*: The technical approach of WAI-ARIA with detailed descriptions of accessibility problems that can be solved by applying WAI-ARIA [15]

- *WAI-ARIA Authoring Practices*: A practical guideline for developers about accessible rich Internet applications developed using WAI-ARIA [16]

- *WAI-ARIA User Agent Implementation Guide*: Accessibility requirements for user agents [17]

Standards such as Synchronized Multimedia Integration Language (SMIL), which is an XML markup for describing multimedia presentations [18], or the Timed Text Markup Language (TTML), which provides text in synchrony with media such as video [19], can also be used to improve site accessibility.

WCAG 1.0

The first version of the Web Content Accessibility Guidelines (WCAG 1.0) became a W3C Recommendation in 1999 with the slogan "how to make web content accessible to people with disabilities." WCAG 1.0 consists of fourteen guidelines [20]:

1. Equivalent alternatives must be provided for auditory and visual content.

2. Information expressed in colors must also be available and perceivable without colors.

3. Markup and style sheets must be applied properly.

4. The natural language(s) of web documents must be declared.

5. Tables must be created in a way that they transform gracefully.

6. Pages that apply new technologies must transform gracefully.

7. User control must be provided for time-sensitive content changes.

8. Direct accessibility of embedded user interfaces must be ensured.

9. Web site design must be device-independent.

10. Interim solutions must be used.

11. W3C technologies and guidelines must be applied.

12. Information must be provided on context and orientation.

13. Navigation must be easy-to-understand.

14. Documents must be clear and simple.

Each guideline is subdivided into checkpoints that serve as the basis for checking WCAG conformance. There are 65 checkpoints, each of which has a priority from 1 to 3. As you will see in the next section, they are very similar to the conformance levels introduced in WCAG 2.0. The three priority levels are the following:

- *Priority 1 (cf. Level A conformance)*: Developers *must* satisfy these requirements, or else one or more groups cannot access the content.

- *Priority 2 (cf. Level AA (Double-A) conformance*: Developers *should* satisfy these requirements; otherwise, the content will be difficult to access for some groups. This level removes significant barriers.

- *Priority 3 (cf. Level AAA (Triple-A) conformance*: Developers *may* address these checkpoints in order to maximize accessibility.

WCAG 2.0

The second version of the Web Content Accessibility Guidelines (WCAG 2.0) became a W3C Recommendation in 2008 [21]. WCAG 2.0 can be summarized with twelve guidelines following four principles [22]:

Principle 1: User interface components and published information perceivable to anyone.

1. Alternate text must be provided for nontext contents, making it possible to change it into other forms.

2. Time-based media must have alternatives.

3. Web content must be available through different presentations without losing information or structure.

4. Both visual and aural contents must be easy to distinguish.

Principle 2: Operable user interface and usable navigation.

5. All functionality must be available from the keyboard.

6. Users cannot be forced to perform actions within time limits.

7. Designs that might cause seizures must be avoided.

8. Guidance and help must be provided for users to navigate through the site.

Principle 3: Understandable content and operation of the user interface.

9. Text content must be convenient to read and easy to understand.

10. Content appearance and operation must be predictable.

11. Assistance must be provided for users to avoid, find, and correct mistakes.

Principle 4: Robust content with high interoperability that can be used reliably on any kind of user agent, including assistive technology.

12. Compatibility must be maximized with current and future user agents and assistive technology, including the ones running on limited resources [23].

These guidelines contain 61 *success criteria*. WCAG 2.0 conformance can be achieved by applying a series of techniques [24]. Some of them are required to meet success criteria (*sufficient techniques*), while others are optional only (*advisory techniques*). W3C claims that none of the accessibility techniques can be marked as *required* or *mandatory* [25]. They are recommended only, and developers may choose to apply them.

In contrast to WCAG 1.0, which has three priority levels, WCAG 2.0 success criteria are organized into three *levels of conformance*. The *conformance requirements* of all levels of WCAG 2.0 are summarized in the following sections. Generally, the word *must* in the following sections—similar to the word use of the WCAG specifications published by the W3C—corresponds to Level A conformance, which is the minimum level of accessibility in WCAG 2.0 (for example, text alternative for nontext content). The word *should* correspond to Level AA conformance (for example, captions for live synchronized media). The words *may* and *can* correspond to Level AAA conformance (for example, optional sign-language interpreters).

The higher the accessibility conformance level, the more requirements or higher restrictions apply. For example, Guideline 1.4 describes distinguishable color use and the requirements for separating foreground from background. To meet level A, you should not rely on color alone for conveying information. Level AA has a stricter requirement and prescribes a minimum contrast ratio of 4.5:1 (3:1 for large text), while Level AAA demands an even higher contrast ratio of 7:1 (4.5:1 for large text).

Note that some requirements are general, while others are technology-specific and apply to a certain technology only, such as Flash. Some techniques can be used either individually or in combination with a similar technique, such as short and long descriptions, but the corresponding implementation requirements depend on the desired level of accessibility.

Level AAA conformance is not recommended as a general policy, because there are content types that cannot be published in a way that the document meets all AAA criteria due to the nature of the content or special technology features and limitations. In other words, using certain content types might limit the maximum achievable level of accessibility to WCAG 2.0 AA, while WCAG 2.0 AAA cannot be met if certain content types are present. For example, section headings can contribute to AAA conformance; however, they cannot be added to all kinds of documents (for example, a long letter [26]). Naturally, site structure or markup elements should be reorganized, added, or modified when creating an accessible web site or redesigning a nonaccessible site to become accessible, but there is no reason for a content author to modify the textual content of a web page just to make the site accessible or more accessible. Another example is Flash, which had known accessibility barriers at the time the WCAG specifications were introduced, and generally it was infeasible to provide Flash content and achieve level AAA conformance at the same time.

Additionally, WCAG conformance can be limited to a *conforming alternate version* instead of the whole web site. For example, if the complex design of a web site makes it infeasible to meet WCAG requirements, the site can still be accessible by providing an alternate style sheet or, in the case of more sophisticated design, an alternate, accessible version of each page within the site. Consequently, determining WCAG conformance requires deep site analysis and cannot be judged by simply opening the home page [27].

■ **Note**   In contrast to documents with tag soup and bad markup, well-structured, standard-compliant web sites with properly written content provide a basic level of accessibility by default, which can be further extended to achieve the desired (advanced) level of accessibility.

Site Structure Requirements

All web pages (not only the home page) must have descriptive titles provided by the `title` element. Ideally, page titles are short, identify the subject, logical, and understandable without context. Moreover, titles should be unique and identify the page within the site. Table 10-1 shows an example.

Table 10-1. *Unique and Short, but DescriptiveWeb Page Titles Within a Site*

URI	Page	Title Example
`http://www.example.com`	Index page	Professional consultants
`http://www.example.com/about/`	About page	About Professional consultants
`http://www.example.com/contact/`	Contact page	Contact Professional consultants

A hyperlink pointing to the index page must be provided at the top of each web page within a site.

■ **Tip** This requirement can be easily provided without interrupting the content or design by adding the link to the web site logo as `<a href="http://www.example.com"><img src="images/logo.png" alt="Pro Consultants" /></a>`.

Links to all other pages of the site must be available directly or indirectly from the home page. The relationship between the currently visited web page and other parts of the web site can be clearly indicated with properly selected web site components and well-written element content (descriptive URIs, descriptive titles, metadata provided with `link rel`, breadcrumb trails, chapters added using headings, and so on).

Breadcrumb trails may be applied to help the user visualize content structure, ease navigation, and identify the current location within the site structure as well as within the current web page. This can be obtained by displaying locations in the path or the location of the current web page within the site structure. Breadcrumb trails might provide links to previously visited web pages. They are placed in the same location within each web page. Typical separators used for breadcrumb trailing are ▼, ▲, >, |, ∷, and /. For example, it can be clearly indicated that the web store user is browsing LCD monitors with a screen size equal to or larger than 22 inches as Electronics ➤ Computers & Accessories ➤ Monitors ➤ LCD ➤ 22 Inches & Up (Figure 10-2).

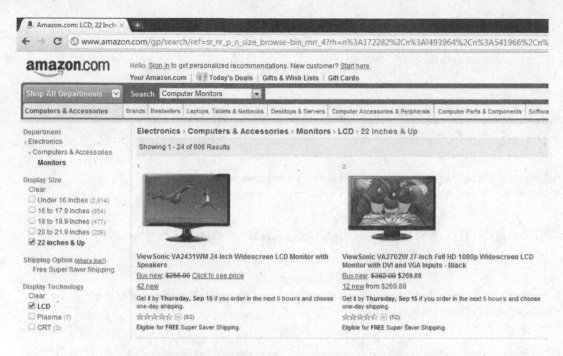

Figure 10-2. *Breadcrumb trails to ease navigation*

The current location may be presented within navigation bars too. The list of all other pages of the site as well as links to related web pages can also ease navigation. The link element may be applied for clearly indicating multiple relationships between the current web page and other web pages within the web site (with values of the rel attribute such as Start, Next, Prev, Contents, and Index). Listing 10-1 shows an example.

Listing 10-1. Declaring Web Page Relationships in the Document Head

```
<head>
  <title>Chapter 4</title>
  ...
  <base href="http://www.example.com/" />
  <link rel="prev" href="chapter3/">
  <link rel="next" href="chapter5/">
  ...
</head>
```

A logical tab order must be added to web sites that allows the user to easily navigate through links, objects, and form controls (Listing 10-2).

Listing 10-2. Tab Order Declared for the Menu, Search Box, and Flash Header of a Web Page

```
...
  <base href="http://www.example.com/" />
...
<ul>
  <li>
    <a href="http://www.example.com/" title="Home" accesskey="h" tabindex="1">↵
      <span class="ak">H</span>ome</a>
  </li>
  <li>
    <a href="about/" title="Introduction" accesskey="a" tabindex="2"> ↵
      <span class="ak">A</span>bout</a>
  </li>
  <li>
    <a href="services/" title="Wedding photography" accesskey="s" tabindex="3"> ↵
      <span class="ak">S</span>ervices</a>
  </li>
  <li>
    <a href="portfolio/" title="Samples and testimonials" accesskey="p" tabindex="4"> ↵
      <span class="ak">P</span>ortfolio</a>
  </li>
  <li>
    <a href="contact/" title="Address, mail, and phone" accesskey="c" tabindex="5"> ↵
      <span class="ak">C</span>ontact</a>
  </li>
</ul>
...
<form method="get" action="http://www.google.com/search">
  <fieldset>
    <label for="q">Search query</label>
    <input type="text" name="q" id="q" size="19" maxlength="255" value="Type to search" ↵
      tabindex="6" />
    <input type="submit" name="btnG" value="Search" tabindex="7" />
    <input type="hidden" name="domains" value="http://www.example.com/" />
    <input type="hidden" name="sitesearch" value="http://www.example.com/" />
  </fieldset>
</form>
...
<object type="application/x-shockwave-flash" data="flash/header.swf" width="720" ↵
 height="300" id="flash" tabindex="8">
  <param name="movie" value="flash/header.swf" />
  <param name="wmode" value="transparent" />
  <div>
    <a href="longdesc/"><img src="images/alter.jpg" alt="The image alternative for the ↵
      flash header." /></a>
  </div>
</object>
```

A search function is vital for all web sites because it might help users find content. A popular approach for providing a search function to web sites is to create a site-specific Google search field (also shown in the previous example). The Search button should be adjacent to the search field.

Content sections must begin with a heading element to provide structure (h1–h6). Descriptive headings and labels must be provided that allow users to select the information relevant to them. Pages can be organized efficiently with headings. In (X)HTML5, document introductions should apply the header element.

Content Requirements

The order of content in the source code must coincide with the default visual presentation of the content; in other words, the DOM order must match the visual order. Dynamic content inserted into the Document Object Model right after the element used to activate the dynamic content insertion ensures a correct tab order (and thus a correct reading order for screen readers) through the exploitation of the default tab order of user agents. Web page content must be ordered in a meaningful sequence. This also holds for interactive elements. Page section reordering must be performed by using the DOM. Repeated components should always be presented in the same order. Users must be allowed to skip repeated menu items through expandable and collapsible menus. Flash contents must apply the tabIndex property in order to specify a logical reading order and a logical tab order.

User Assistance

A site map and a table of contents also contribute to accessibility. A help link may be added to every web page. A dedicated help page can be used to collect information that can be helpful for less experienced users but omitted from the main content, because they are evident (and even disturbing) for most users. Moreover, a help page might provide information about special web site features that are not common on the Web. For example, a user of a highly accessible web site can be informed about the option to control the menu with keyboard buttons, which is not available on every site. Help may also be provided in the form of an assistant who gives a tour to new visitors on the functionality and content of the site. Such an assistant can be presented as an animation with a digital character (also known as a multimedia avatar) or a video clip with a real person, who gives instructions or a service overview or explains concepts related to the company portfolio (Figure 10-3).

Figure 10-3. *An assistant (video clip with a real person) [28]*

Ensured Readability

Ideally, text is easy to read. Complex text content may be summarized in a form that requires a reading ability less advanced than the upper secondary education level. For example, a technical article can be too complex to read for some people, and a text summary containing shorter sentences and more common words might be helpful for them. To achieve AAA conformance, text lines may not exceed an average of 80 characters even if the browser window is resized.

People with certain cognitive disabilities who have trouble tracking single-spaced lines might find 1.5× or double line spacing more convenient to read. Web pages may have buttons to improve readability by increasing line spaces and paragraph spaces (Listing 10-3).

Listing 10-3. Sample Buttons for Manipulating Line Space and Paragraph Space

```
...
<script type="text/javascript">
  function inclineh() {
    document.getElementById('main').style.lineHeight="200%";
  }

  function incpars() {
    var get_ps = document.getElementsByTagName("p");
    for (var i = 0; i < get_ps.length; i++) {
      get_ps[i].style.marginBottom="40px";
    }
  }
</script>
...
<div>
  <a href="javascript:inclineh();"><img src="images/lineh.png" alt="Line height" ↵
   title="Increased line height" /></a>
  <a href="javascript:incpars();"><img src="images/pspacing.png" alt="Paragraph spacing" ↵
   title="Increased paragraph spacing" /></a>
</div>
...
<div id="main">
  <p>
    This is the first paragraph of the main content.
  </p>
  <p>
    This is the second paragraph of the main content.
  </p>
</div>
```

Additionally, the `letter-spacing` CSS property must be used to control spacing within words (whitespace between characters) that can further increase readability. Font sizes are best provided in relative units (% or em). The em unit is preferred for text sizes of containers such as tables where percent-based fonts might result in a way too large font size when resizing the window. Information presented by text formatting such as font face, font size, or text decoration must also be accessible without formatting. Basic text formatting should apply not only for (X)HTML documents but also for plain text. Text files must have text formatting that represents paragraphs, lists, and headings.

The visual presentation of texts should be controlled with CSS properties such as `font-family`, `font-size`, `font-style`, `font-weight`, `color`, `letter-spacing`, `line-height`, `text-align`, `text-transform`, and `background-image` and the `:first-line`, `:first-letter`, `:before` and `:after` pseudoclasses. These properties and pseudoclasses can eliminate the need for image text.

Color Use

Web content must be accessible without the ability of sensory perception required for recognizing locations, shapes, sizes, or sounds.

Justified text aligned to both the left and right margins can be hard to read for people with certain cognitive disabilities. Consequently, text aligned to one side only contributes to the highest level of accessibility. If it is not feasible due to layout purposes, a mechanism may be added to remove full justification upon request.

If users are allowed to use the default colors of their browsers, that is, no background color, text color, or text background color is specified by CSS rules, users with vision disabilities can override certain colors that they have trouble seeing. This technique guarantees text readability presented over a background. It is allowed to specify container layout and border colors, though.

A cross-browser color selector solution may be applied that allows users to change the foreground and background colors of text sections.

The text-background contrast ratio should be 4.5:1 to achieve AA conformance (3:1 for large text) and may be a minimum of 7:1 (4.5 for large text) for AAA conformance (including images of text). A high-contrast control should always be provided that allows users to switch to a presentation with sufficient contrast. You can easily calculate the contrast ratio between arbitrarily selected colors by considering the differences in luminosity.

The relative luminance is defined by the WCAG 2.0 specification as "the relative brightness of any point in a colorspace, normalized to 0 for darkest black and 1 for lightest white." In case of the sRGB color space, the relative luminance of a color is defined as $L = 0.2126 \times R + 0.7152 \times G + 0.0722 \times B$, where the R, G, and B components are defined as follows [29]:

$$R_{sRGB} = \frac{R_{8bit}}{255} \text{ If } R_{sRGB} \leq 0.03928 \text{ then } R = \frac{R_{sRGB}}{12.92} \text{ else } R = \left(\frac{R_{sRGB} + 0.055}{1.055} \right)^{2.4}$$

$$G_{sRGB} = \frac{G_{8bit}}{255} \text{ If } G_{sRGB} \leq 0.03928 \text{ then } G = \frac{G_{sRGB}}{12.92} \text{ else } G = \left(\frac{G_{sRGB} + 0.055}{1.055} \right)^{2.4}$$

$$B_{sRGB} = \frac{B_{8bit}}{255} \text{ If } B_{sRGB} \leq 0.03928 \text{ then } B = \frac{B_{sRGB}}{12.92} \text{ else } B = \left(\frac{B_{sRGB} + 0.055}{1.055} \right)^{2.4}$$

If you don't want to calculate the color contrast, there are many useful tools that can check it for you, for example the WebAIM Color Contrast Checker [30], the Luminosity Colour Contrast Ratio Analyser of Juicy Studio [31], or the Luminosity Contrast Ratio Analyser 1.1 of WAT-C [32].

Information expressed in colors must also be available and perceivable without colors. Additional visual cues must be available when text color differences are used to convey information. Semantic markup must be added whenever color cues are used to convey information.

An optional multicolor selection tool added to pages to change the foreground and background colors arbitrarily allows users to specify colors according to their personal preference (Figure 10-4).

Color Picker

```
┌─Colors──────────────────────────
│
│  Foreground: pick    #000
│
│  Background: pick    #FFF
│
└─────────────────────────────────
```

[Change colors]

Random Text

Demonstrate persistence on a

Lorem ipsum dolor sit amet, c   t. Pr
ullamcorper, velit nulla porttit   elit p
et malesuada fames ac turpis   rutru
non lorem. Pellentesque sit amet augue. Phasellus leo turpis
hendrerit eget, tempus in, porta vel, turpis. Phasellus urna l

Figure 10-4. *A color picker example suggested by W3C [33]*

Information and structure must be separated from presentation to enable different presentations. Various color combinations can be provided for the text and background of the main content along with component groups within the web page.

Abbreviations, Definitions, and Foreign Words

The full form of words may precede their shortenings. Abbreviations might have an inline expansion or explanation they are associated with the first time they occur within a web page. Definitions may be provided by the abbr and acronym elements for all abbreviations. Defined words can be enclosed by the dfn element. Terms, abbreviations, initialism, and acronyms can be linked to their definitions in order to provide the highest level of accessibility. Terms and phrases written as definition list items are the most accessible. They may be collected on a glossary page available through a simple hyperlink provided by the link element. Alternatively, a search function can be embedded that provides the definitions through an external online dictionary. Beyond abbreviations, all words or phrases used in an unusual way or restricted manner can be made more accessible with a definition.

The pronunciation of a special or foreign word provided immediately after the word at least the first time it occurs within a web page contributes to AAA conformance. Other instances can alternatively provide a link to a list of pronunciations.

The default language of web documents must be identified in the HTTP header as well as by the lang and/or xml:lang attribute on the html element in the markup. This is also vital for web pages with Flash content because embedded Flash objects inherit the language settings provided by the lang and/or xml:lang attributes. Document sections written in a language other than the default language must be clearly identified on their containers.

To ensure text direction for bidirectional inline content, the right-to-left Unicode marks (‏, ‏, or U+200F) and left-to-right Unicode marks (‎, ‎ or U+200E) must be applied.

Text direction of inline content must apply the dir attribute to clearly indicate text direction.

In many languages, such as Arabic, Hebrew, or East Asian languages, text meaning largely depends on pronunciation. Web content written in such languages may apply Ruby annotation with ruby, rt, and rp elements in order to provide information about the pronunciation and meaning of text fragments.

■ **Note**   Ruby annotations were introduced a long time ago in Far Eastern textbooks to provide hints for students about complex characters. For example, Japanese texts written in the Kanji syllabary (writing system) often contain characters that are known only by those Japanese who have at least a high school diploma. Ruby texts written in Hiragana, which is a syllabary all Japanese are familiar with, can make the text clearer. Similarly, traditional Chinese texts can be displayed in simplified Chinese using Ruby annotations.

Using Ruby, a base text can be declared within the Ruby markup (the content of the ruby element), along with the associated Ruby text (the rt element), and optionally the Ruby parentheses (rp), that can be declared for browsers that cannot render Ruby text correctly. For example, pronunciation hints can be provided for words on an educational portal, while foreign words or unusual names can be transliterated into English (Listing 10-4) or represented using the International Phonetic Alphabet (IPA) (Listing 10-5).

Listing 10-4. Ruby Annotation for Tokyo

```
<ruby>
  東京
  <rp> (</rp>
  <rt>Tō kyō</rt>
   <rp>)</rp>
</ruby>
```

In the case of simple Ruby markup, user agents should render the Ruby text above the base text at approximately half the font size. In our case, the result should look like Figure 10-5.

Figure 10-5. *The Ruby annotation for the word Tokyo rendered in IE9*

■ **Note**   Ruby annotations are rendered most accurately by Internet Explorer.

Browsers that do not support Ruby annotations will render the previous code inline without interrupting the text flow (Figure 10-6).

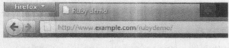

東京（Tō kyō）

Figure 10-6. *The fallback mechanism of the Ruby annotation in action*

Listing 10-5 is rendered in compliant browsers as presented in Figure 10-7.

Listing 10-5. The IPA Representation of an Eastern-European Name Using Ruby Annotation

```
<p>
  Count
  <ruby>
    István Széchenyi
    <rp>(pronounced: </rp>
    <rt>'iʃtvaːn 'seːtʃeːɲi</rt> <rp>)</rp>
  </ruby>
  was one of the greatest statesmen of Hungarian history.
</p>
```

Figure 10-7. *Pronunciation hint provided by Ruby annotation*

In browsers that do not recognize Ruby markup, the same example would be rendered inline (Figure 10-8).

Figure 10-8. *Pronunciation hint rendered inline in browsers that do not support Ruby annotations*

More complex Ruby annotations can specify not only the default display and fallback mechanism shown earlier but also positioning offsets, alignment, spacing, and overhang. The Ruby annotation was introduced as an XHTML 1.1 module and can also be used in HTML5. The Ruby annotations can also be styled using CSS3, which provides precise positioning and line breaking, defines the Ruby box model, and supports the vertical-ideographic layout mode [34].

The most accessible documents apply standard diacritical marks that can be turned on and off.

Properly selected positioning and units should be applied that support the zooming and text resizing features of browsers.

Accessible web sites have controls that allow users to incrementally change the size of all text (up to 200 percent). Loss of content or functionality is not acceptable when the text is resized, and the proportions of the text containers must remain the same.

User Interface

Content must be accessible through alternate user interfaces. Properly written markup must be provided that allows assistive technology to understand the content, expose information such as form control IDs, and control certain elements through an API (for example, the DOM).

Standard DOM functions must be applied to dynamically add content to web pages instead of scripting as script-generated contents are often inaccessible by screen readers.

■ **Note** Screen readers may not automatically read dynamically added content. Reading of dynamically added new content can be ensured by setting the focus to the new element or adding it below the current location where it will be encountered as the user continues browsing.

Liquid layout should be used on all web sites to present content without introducing unnecessary horizontal scroll bars. Page content should adapt to the available horizontal space. Layout regions should be resized with text and reflow as needed to display the page section. Highly accessible web sites eliminate horizontal scrolling even if the user resizes the browser window. One of the options to achieve such a foolproof layout is to specify proportional text containers through Responsive Web Design. If it is not feasible on the default screen, an alternate layout may be provided that does not require horizontal scrolling.

Content positioning should be based on structural markup. The appearance can be enhanced with CSS, but the content structure must also remain meaningful without style sheets.

If the content of the default version of a web page is not accessible but an alternate, WCAG-conforming version is, that web page must be linked at the beginning of the nonconforming page. If inaccessible objects cannot be eliminated from the content, a link must be added adjacent to or associated with these objects that link to an alternate, WCAG-compliant version. User preference must be saved in a cookie. The accessibility of the alternate version must always be ensured with `.htaccess` or the HTTP referrer header. A style switcher must be provided to ensure an alternate version with WCAG-compliant styles.[2] Three different types of style sheets are required to create a style switcher:

1. *Persistent CSS file:* The base styles that are used to share common styles throughout the site. The rel attribute is set to stylesheet, while the title attribute is omitted (Listing 10-6).

    Listing 10-6. A Persistent CSS File

    ```
    <link rel="stylesheet" type="text/css" href="styles/main.css" />
    ```

---

[2]Since not all functionalities can be provided through CSS, a conforming alternate version of a web site cannot always be provided by simply creating additional style sheets.

2. Preferred CSS file: Styles enabled by default when the page is loaded. The attribute value of the rel attribute is stylesheet, and the title attribute is provided (Listing 10-7).

Listing 10-7. A Preferred CSS File

```
<link rel="stylesheet" type="text/css" href="styles/main.css" title="Preferred" />
```

3. Alternate CSS files: CSS files designed for alternate versions of the site that reuse the styles declared in the main style sheet file but overwrite some of them (for example, set the font size to a larger value, or modify the font color to achieve higher contrast) or add new ones on top of the reused ones (for example, define a maximum width for mobile devices). They can be used not only for increasing accessibility but also for design or media-specific versions of the site (as hinted earlier in Chapter 3). Alternate CSS files have the rel attribute value alternate stylesheet instead of stylesheet, and a title attribute identifies them (Listing 10-8).

Listing 10-8. Alternate Style Sheets

```
<link rel="alternate stylesheet" type="text/css" href="styles/large.css" ↵
        title="Large" />
<link rel="alternate stylesheet" type="text/css" href="styles/contrast.css" ↵
        title="Contrast" />
```

First, create three CSS files, one for the main styles (Listing 10-9) and two for alternate styles that will provide large font size (Listing 10-10) or huge font size with high contrast (Listing 10-11), respectively.

Listing 10-9. The Main CSS File (main.css)

```
body {
  background-color:#004c25;
  color: #cff;
  font-family: Garamond, serif;
  font-size: 1.2em;
}

#wrapper {
  width: 800px;
  margin: auto;
}

#wrapper a:link {
  color: #ff0;
}

#wrapper a:hover {
  color: #ffa000;
}
```

```
#wrapper a:visited {
  color: #fff;
}

#colorswitch a:link {
  padding: 10px;
}
```

Listing 10-10. *The CSS File for the Large Font Version* (`large.css`)

```
@import ("main.css");

body {
  font-size: 1.8em;
}
```

Listing 10-11. *The CSS File for the High-Contrast Version* (`contrast.css`)

```
@import ("main.css");

body {
  background-color: #000;
  font-size: 2em;
}

#wrapper a:hover {
  color: #ff2121;
}
```

Next, we need a script that sets the styles from the selected CSS file and stores the choice in a cookie that can be read if the user returns to the page (Listing 10-12). Without cookies, the alternate styles would be applied for the current page of the current session only, which is not practical. If a visually impaired user selects the "high-contrast theme," he or she would probably like to read all the pages of the site with the same setting.

Listing 10-12. *The* `styleswitcher.js` [35]

```
function setActiveTheme(title) {
  var i, a, main;
  for (i = 0; (a = document.getElementsByTagName("link")[i]); i++) {
    if (a.getAttribute("rel").indexOf("style") != -1 && a.getAttribute("title")) {
      a.disabled = true;
      if (a.getAttribute("title") == title) a.disabled = false;
    }
  }
}
```

```javascript
function getActiveTheme() {
  var i, a;
  for(i = 0; (a = document.getElementsByTagName("link")[i]); i++) {
    if(a.getAttribute("rel").indexOf("style") != -1 && a.getAttribute("title") && ↩
    !a.disabled) return a.getAttribute("title");
  }
  return null;
}

function getPreferredTheme() {
  var i, a;
  for (i = 0; (a = document.getElementsByTagName("link")[i]); i++) {
    if (a.getAttribute("rel").indexOf("style") != -1
        && a.getAttribute("rel").indexOf("alt") == -1
        && a.getAttribute("title")
        ) return a.getAttribute("title");
  }
  return null;
}

function createCookie(name,value,days) {
  if (days) {
    var date = new Date();
    date.setTime(date.getTime() + (days*24*60*60*1000));
    var expires = "; expires=" + date.toGMTString();
  }
  else expires = "";
  document.cookie = name + "=" + value + expires + "; path=/";
}

function readCookie(name) {
  var nameEQ = name + "=";
  var ca = document.cookie.split(';');
  for (var i = 0; i < ca.length; i++) {
    var c = ca[i];
    while (c.charAt(0)==' ') c = c.substring(1, c.length);
    if (c.indexOf(nameEQ) == 0) return c.substring(nameEQ.length, c.length);
  }
  return null;
}

window.onload = function(e) {
  var cookie = readCookie("style");
  var title = cookie ? cookie : getPreferredTheme();
  setActiveTheme(title);
}
```

```
window.onunload = function(e) {
  var title = getActiveTheme();
  createCookie("style", title, 365);
}


var cookie = readCookie("style");
var title = cookie ? cookie : getPreferredTheme();
setActiveTheme(title);
```

Finally, we put all the components together and get the style switcher functionality on our site (Listing 10-13).

Listing 10-13. The Markup Code Featuring the Style Switcher

```
<!DOCTYPE html>
<html xmlns="http://www.w3.org/1999/xhtml" xml:lang="en-us" lang="en-us">
  <head>
    <title>Style switcher demo</title>
    <meta charset="UTF-8" />
    <link rel="stylesheet" type="text/css" href="styles/main.css" />
    <link rel="stylesheet" type="text/css" href="styles/main.css" title="Preferred" />
    <link rel="alternate stylesheet" type="text/css" href="styles/large.css" title="Large" />
    <link rel="alternate stylesheet" type="text/css" href="styles/contrast.css" ↵
     title="Contrast" />
    <script type="text/javascript" src="scripts/styleswitcher.js"></script>
  </head>
  <body>
    <div id="wrapper">
      <h1>Style switcher demo</h1>
      <p>This is the content.</p>
      <div id="colorswitch">
        <a href="javascript:void(0);" onclick="javascript:setActiveTheme('Preferred'); ↵
         return false;" id="default">Default CSS</a>
        <a href="javascript:void(0);" onclick="javascript:setActiveTheme('Large'); ↵
         return false;" id="larger">Large fonts</a>
        <a href="javascript:void(0);" onclick="javascript:setActiveTheme('Contrast'); ↵
         return false;" id="contrast">High contrast</a>
      </div>
    </div>
  </body>
</html>
```

Content scrolled with scripts, such as banners, must have a mechanism to pause or stop scrolling.

Web pages that apply image replacement for text fragments from CSS should have an interface that allows users to switch between the two versions.

Web content structure should contain proper semantic markup elements. The elements must be used according to their meaning rather than their (default) appearance. Semantically meaningful markup such as em or strong must be used for emphasized and special texts. The ol, ul, and dl elements must be applied for both lists and link groups. Links must be grouped using the map element.

Keyboard users must not be stopped by a web site section accessible exclusively with a mouse. The same holds for Flash objects that are not keyboard accessible by default.

■ **Note** Duplicated attributes on the same element might cause key errors for assistive technology and must be eliminated.

The appearance of elements receiving focus or being hovered over with a pointing device should be changed (for example, highlighted) to provide visual feedback to the user (such as changed background or border color). Flash content should also provide highly visible focus indication.

Alternate texts, labels, and names should be shared among components with the same functionality.

An optional sign language version provided for all information required to use the content can improve accessibility for people who are deaf or have cognitive disabilities. It can be either a multimedia avatar using a technology such as Flash or a video clip of an animated or real sign language interpreter (Figure 10-9).

Figure 10-9. *A signing avatar [36]*

Web site components such as markup, style sheets, and XML files must be validated to guarantee the proper use of formal specifications, grammar, syntax, and vocabulary. Opening and closing tags must be used according to the markup specification. All web pages must be well-formed.

Markup Requirements for Nontext Content

Images, photos, graphics, and symbols can be applied to improve user experience and help the user understand the content. However, all nontext contents, such as images, embedded objects (Flash content, applets, audio, video, and so on), *ASCII arts*, *emoticons*, and *leetspeaks* must have alternate texts.

All images must have an `alt` attribute. For those images that can be safely ignored by assistive technology, the `title` attribute must be omitted and the `alt` text set to null (`alt=""`). If an image and its associated text have the same link, they must be combined in order to avoid unnecessary duplication.

Spacer images such as 1×1 pixel GIF files should be totally eliminated in favor of CSS margins and padding.

For those images and objects where a short description is not sufficient, a long description must be added using the `longdesc` attribute or a regular a element with a link to the description.

Nontext content represented in colors must also be available with patterns that can be understood without colors.

Alternate text must be provided for nontext content that identifies its purpose (even for the content that requires sensory experience). Additionally, both a short and a long description must be provided for nontext content with an identical purpose that presents the same information.

If the original nontext content is too long or the same information cannot be achieved with text alone, short alternate text must be written that briefly summarizes the nontext content.

Images used exclusively for decoration, such as background images, image rollovers, or tab images, must be provided using CSS. Since there is no additional markup, assistive technology can ignore this nontext content.

Alternate text must be written for all `area` elements within image maps.

A text or nontext alternative must be provided for all objects. Alternate texts can be written directly in the content of the `object` element. Nontext alternatives can be provided by nested objects.

Adjacent nontext content sharing information or functionality must be described by alternate text in order to avoid unnecessary duplication.

Blinking and Flashing Content

Photoepileptic seizures caused by strobing or flashing effects should be eliminated. A link or button must always be added to web pages with blinking content that loads equivalent pages without blinking content. Blinking contents can be included on web pages only by using a technology that provides the option to turn off blinking with a browser feature. Blinking content must be minimized below 5 seconds using scripts and, if possible, totally eliminated. The same holds for animated GIF images.

Flashing content must also be minimized. A maximum of three flashes is allowed within 1 second. If it is not feasible because of the content features, the flashing area must be less than 25 percent of 10 degrees of the visual field. The content is not allowed to violate the general flash threshold or red flash threshold, which avoids photosensitive seizures. There are tools, such as the Photosensitive Epilepsy Analysis Tool (PEAT) [37], that can be used to evaluate flashing content to reduce the risk of seizure.

Flash Objects

The dimensions of embedded Flash objects may be specified in relative units (em or %).

Nontext objects marked with the `name` property must be applied in Flash to allow assistive technology to access them. A long text alternative must be provided by the `description` property for nontext objects in Flash. Text alternatives must be provided for clickable image hotspots that serve the same purpose. The accessible description of DataGrids has been used for years to provide information readable by screen readers.

Flash graphics must be marked in a way that they can be ignored by assistive technology if needed. This can be accomplished by directly exploiting the accessibility features of Flash objects or by applying textual alternatives using ActionScript.

If adjacent text and image buttons (icons) serve the same purpose, they must be combined into a single button symbol instance.

Forms written in markup are preferred to Flash forms. However, if you have to use Flash forms on your site, the following guidelines should be considered. Flash controls must be understood out of context. To achieve this, control labels can be changed via scripting to provide additional information. Similar to their markup equivalents, the required fields of Flash forms must be clearly indicated. Related Flash form controls must be grouped together to provide semantic meaning. Flash forms must be validated on the client side. If errors are found, a description must be added to the controls containing invalid data. Flash form controls must have an associate text label (for example, via auto labeling). Only `CheckBox` and `RadioButton` components get labels by default.

There must be an option to pause scrolling Flash contents controlled by a script.

Blinking of Flash contents must be controlled by scripts to stop within a maximum of five seconds.

Link Requirements

Hyperlink anchors must always have a text description that clearly identifies the purpose of the link. Links must apply the `title` attribute to provide additional link text. Hyperlinks must have a descriptive alternate text that clearly indicates the purpose of the link.

Additional link text added for advanced screen reader and Braille display support can be hidden using CSS selectors (without `visibility:hidden` or `display:none`). This link text can also be applied in combination with a style switcher. Repetitive content must be avoided.

A control must be added to the top of each web page providing an alternate page version with link texts that are sufficient to determine their purpose even without context.

The purpose of a link must be clear even without context (applying a descriptive link text), and the container context (paragraph, preceding heading, list item, table cell, and its associated table heading) must also be written in a way that further improves the clarity of the purpose of the link.

The minimum contrast ratio of 3:1 should be ensured between link colors and text colors. Moreover, additional visual cues must be provided on focus for links and controls where color alone is used to identify them.

Destination URIs are generally not descriptive enough. The link text `Read more...` is, for example, not sufficient to understand a link. If the description precedes the link in the same sentence, such link texts can be understandable, however, screen readers would still read "Read more". The link purpose must be identified using the combination of link text and the text of the enclosing sentence to ensure a logical text flow for screen readers. Link text changed dynamically upon context must be provided whenever necessary.

Links should be added to all web page elements and objects that do not support long descriptions as attribute values. The links must be next to the nontext content. The location of the long description must be indicated in the short description (if applicable). For example, the short description of an image provides the text "Comparison of smartphone operating systems—see details below," while the long description below the image states "In Figure 1, you can see the market share of smartphone operating systems, including Android, iOS, Windows Mobile, and BlackBerry OS."

If a web page contains blocks of repeated content such as navigation links or table of contents, a link must be added to the beginning of the blocks that allows users to bypass them. The top of the web page must contain links to the different sections of the content.

Dialog messages must be device-independent. Pop-up windows should be eliminated whenever possible. If a new window cannot be eliminated, an advanced warning may be provided. To avoid confusion, new windows opened on user request with the `target` attribute may have a proper link text clearly indicating that the content will be opened in a new window. As a general rule, however, links should be opened in the same window rather than a new window or tab. While this approach contributes to accessibility, it might lead to loss of visitors (if you point to an external site and the visitors forget to return to your site

User Input and Form Requirements

Form controls and links must be provided using (X)HTML elements rather than other technologies such as Flash.

Text inputs of forms must have a `title` attribute that can be used for providing context-sensitive help.

An accessible name must be applied for labeling Flash form controls. Flash buttons must always have an accessible label that describes the purpose of the link. Flash image buttons must have accessible names that provide information about the function of the buttons but do not describe the images in general.

The `label` property must be set for the `Button`, `CheckBox`, and `RadioButton` Flash form components explicitly. As a result, the label text appears next to the component and becomes available for assistive technology.

Groups of form controls must have a description provided by the `legend` element and must be grouped with `fieldset`.

A button must be applied along with `select` elements to perform an action. The `option` elements must be grouped with `optgroup` within `select` elements.

To keep proportions, textual form elements such as input boxes and buttons should be resized when the text size has significantly changed in the browser.

Beyond enumerated options, forms sometimes allow user-defined values (typically with the text `other, please specify`) for which text descriptions must be provided.

Text instructions must be added to the beginning of forms and fieldsets that clearly indicate the required input. Text input elements may have a spell checker. Required fields must be clearly indicated, for example with an asterisk (*) character. The user must be informed through a text description if the input is a prohibited value, falls outside the allowed limits, or is provided in a nonsupported format.

When using technologies that support Accessible Rich Internet Applications (WAI-ARIA), the allowed range of entry fields should be identified with the `aria-valuemin` and `aria-valuemax` properties. User agents typically do not permit users to enter values outside the specified range and generate a validation error if users do so.

Expected data formats presented with examples minimize the probability of incorrect or insufficient user input. The same holds for review and correction options offered before form submitting. A mechanism should be provided for web applications so that users can recover information deleted by mistake.

Multipart forms must provide a checkbox on the first page that gives users more time if they need it or completely avoids session time limits.

User input should be validated by means of client-side scripting. If errors are found, an alert dialog must be used to inform the user. Error messages can also be added via the DOM. Additionally, a mechanism should be provided that helps users find the location of input errors. If the information supplied by the user is not adequate and cannot be accepted, correct text should be suggested (if available).

If a Captcha is used on a form, alternate text must be added that describes the purpose of the test such as "the test determines whether or not the user is human". There should be an option to refresh the Captcha, i.e., generate another distorted image if the user cannot read the first one.

A checkbox provided in addition to Submit buttons encourages users to review their input before submitting. If confirmation is required to continue a selected action, form submission problems can be minimized or eliminated. After submission, a stated time period should be provided when the order/request can be updated or canceled by the user. A success feedback should always be provided when data is submitted successfully.

The `aria-describedby` WAI-ARIA property can be applied to attach descriptive information to one or more elements. Form controls must be associated with text labels by the `label` element. When the `label` element cannot be used, the `title` attribute must be applied. Labels must be positioned immediately before the field (with text direction taken into account) except the labels of radio buttons and checkboxes that are positioned after the field. Form fields and the buttons that clearly indicate their purpose must be adjacent.

A text cue must be added to colored form control labels to combine color and text or character cues to convey information. For example, required field labels represented in red can be quickly recognized by most people, but not all people can see colors. However, they can still read text cues or listen to them.

A description must be associated with form controls indicating context changes in advance. A submit button must be used in order to allow users to explicitly request changes of context. The aria-required WAI-ARIA property can be used to indicate that user input is required before submission. Text descriptions must be provided to identify required fields that were not completed.

Table Requirements

Tabular information must be presented with the table element. Table captions must be associated with tables by using the caption element. Data cells and header cells must be associated with the id, header, and scope attributes in tables. In Flash, the DataGrid component must be used to associate column headers with cells. These components must have a caption text. The summary attribute must be applied on the table element to provide a short description of the table (which is used by screen readers).

User Control Requirements

Every web site's functionality must be accessible not only with pointing devices such as a mouse but also with the keyboard. This also holds for Flash contents (using the click event on standard components).

A control must be provided on all web pages that allows users to stop moving or blinking contents, or prevent automatic content updates.

Both a pause and a restart option must be provided for all automatically refreshing or disappearing contents such as banners or flash headers. A link to the alternate content for the time-based media must be placed immediately next to the nontext content. Users should not be forced to complete any activities within time limits. Users must always be warned by a script if the time limit is about to expire. This also holds for Flash content.

Users must always have the option of setting time limits to ten times the default value. The option for extending the default time limit also applies for Flash contents. There must be a mechanism to turn off time limits.

The actions of markup elements such as anchors and form elements must be keyboard-accessible. Event handlers must be device-independent and allow not only the mouse but also keyboard access to full content functionality (for example, drag and drop). This can be achieved using redundant keyboard and mouse event handlers. The same holds for Flash contents as well as all scripting functions.

Web servers that require user authentication often terminate sessions for security reasons after a certain period of time spent without user activity. If the user cannot provide the input quickly enough, the session times out before data submission, and reauthentication is required. Servers should store such data in a temporary cache and retain them after a successful user reauthentication, so the user can continue filling in the form rather than starting it all over again, because all previously entered data is restored. Reauthorization pages may hide and encrypt user data.

Context changes must apply predictable actions. For example, if data entries of a form cannot be presented on a single page, the second page should not be loaded automatically after the user presses the Tab key on the last entry of the first page, because it can confuse screen reader users, which must be avoided.

Automatic redirections should be eliminated whenever possible. Both client-side (meta refresh) and server-side (HTTP response) redirections have accessibility issues that can confuse users.

Certain user interface components are highlighted by some browsers when they receive focus. For example, a form input is slightly highlighted in Google Chrome and strongly highlighted in Safari by default but not highlighted at all in IE, Firefox, and Opera (Figure 10-10).

Figure 10-10. *Default browser highlighting of the same input field in Firefox and Safari (the second text input is selected)*

Since highlighting varies from component to component and from browser to browser, the high visibility of focus indicators should be ensured by web developers.

Form components, links, and all elements with a `tabindex` attribute greater than 0 can receive focus. However, the default focus indicator of some platforms is not highly visible and may be difficult to see against certain backgrounds. The visibility of focus indicators should always be ensured.

Nonessential alerts are optional. Ideally, users are not disturbed with unnecessary modal pop-up windows (dialog windows that require the user to click the OK button to disappear).

Time-based media such as presentations must always have an alternate textual version or description. Automatically updated contents may be eliminated and a mechanism provided to postpone automatic content update. Moving and scrolling texts must also be available in a static page section or window

Live Media, Audio, and Video Requirements

Prerecorded synchronized media such as video clips must have captions. Sounds can be played on user request only. Sound effects must automatically be turned off within three seconds. Additionally, an easily discoverable control must be located near the beginning of the page for turning sound on/off. Flash contents must also have a control for the same purpose.

In Flash movies, screen reader detection with the `flash.accessibility.Accessibility.active` property can be used to turn off sounds that are played automatically if assistive technology is used (by default, the sound can still be played automatically).

Nonspeech sounds in audio files may be at least 20 dB lower than the speech audio content.

An additional, user-selectable audio track must be provided with audio descriptions.

A spoken version of the text can significantly improve site accessibility because it is more accurate and perceivable than the speech of screen readers.

Live audio-only contents may have text alternatives. This can be achieved by a *real-time caption service* with a trained human operator who can type the text with small delay. Note that such services are very rarely used in practice.

A link to a text transcript of a prepared statement or script may be provided for scripts followed by live audio contents. These scripts can be more accurate and complete than live transcriptions; however, care must be taken to ensure correct synchronization.

Accessible alternatives must be provided for time-based media presenting audio-only or video-only contents.

A descriptive label must be provided for live audio-only and live video-only content.

Videos must be provided with extended audio comments that fully describe the video content. Additionally, a second version of video content must always be provided with audio descriptions to maximize accessibility. This also holds for Flash audio-visual materials. Gaps of dialogue must be filled with extended audio descriptions using SMIL.

Video-only content, which is inaccessible to blind and some visually impaired people, must have an audio alternative in a common audio format such as MP3. Video stream accessibility can be maximized with sign language interpreters through a synchronized video whose display can be selected by the user.

Captions must be added for video contents that can be turned on and off upon request because they maximize availability. Captions must provide information for the hearing impaired not only about the dialogue but also the sound descriptions (unlike conventional subtitles).

Migrating from WCAG 1.0 to WCAG 2.0

Some projects require web site upgrade from WCAG 1.0 to WCAG 2.0. Several WCAG 1.0–compliant sites require little or no changes at all to meet WCAG 2.0. WCAG 2.0 is based on WCAG 1.0; however, there are some differences in the approach and requirements.

Sites that meet WCAG 1.0 partly fulfill WCAG 2.0 by default. The two versions of WCAG are compatible. Consequently, it is possible to meet both WCAG 1.0 and WCAG 2.0 requirements at the same time. Because of the advanced flexibility of the second version, however, a WCAG 2.0–compliant site does not automatically meet the requirements of WCAG 1.0. Some WCAG 2.0 success criteria are very similar to WCAG 1.0 checkpoints. On the other hand, there are WCAG 1.0 requirements that are not needed in WCAG 2.0. Some WCAG 2.0 requirements are more specific than the related requirements in WCAG 1.0 [38].

WCAG 1.0 is technology-specific [39], while WCAG 2.0 applies to W3C and non-W3C technologies as long as they provide accessibility [40].

WCAG 1.0 uses interim solutions ("until user agents. . ."), while WCAG 2.0 success criteria compliance assumes user agent support.

In WCAG 1.0, JavaScript is considered a technology with accessibility problems [41]. In fact, JavaScript can be accessible, depending on the application and functionality being used (which we'll discuss in more detail later). Scripting techniques successfully tested with screen readers are considered in WCAG 2.0.

The major steps of migrating from WCAG 1.0 to 2.0 can be summarized as follows [42]:

1. Conformance parameters should be determined.

2. Applied technologies should be determined.

3. The application potential of technical requirements should be analyzed.

4. WCAG 1.0 checkpoints should be checked related to WCAG 2.0 requirements.

5. WCAG 2.0 success criteria should be checked.

Finally, strange as it sounds, not everyone is enthused over the highest level of web accessibility. Although WCAG 2.0 is very impressive from the accessibility point of view, it is criticized for many reasons. For example, the specifications are very long and complex, the technology-neutral descriptions are rather difficult to implement for developers, very special requirements are included (especially for AAA conformance, like the real-time caption service), some definitions are difficult to understand, inaccessible page versions are tolerated when an accessible version is present, testing is far too complex, and not all content can be written in a way that conforms to the strictest requirements [43].

U.S. Section 508

Beyond W3C standards, there are country-specific standards and/or legislations on web accessibility around the world. In the United States, a basic requirement for government web sites is Section 508 compliance. Subpart B of the Amendment describes technical standards. The most important part for web developers is §1194.22 (Web-based Intranet and Internet Information and Applications) [44].

The web-based technology and information criteria defined by Section 508 are based on W3C WAI guidelines. Consequently, §1194.22 and WCAG 1.0 checkpoints are consistent [45].

There are no limitations on graphic or animation use, but they must be provided in an accessible form. Beyond the text labels and descriptions provided for graphics, this section also addresses usability of style sheets, forms, scripting, multimedia contents, image maps, languages, and plugins.

An alternate text should be written for all nontext elements. Multimedia presentations should be synchronized with their equivalent alternatives. Information cannot be expressed in color alone.

Information representation cannot rely exclusively on associated style sheets.

Row and column headers should be declared for data tables.

Data cells and header cells of data tables should be associated.

Client-side image maps should be preferred to server-side image maps except where the regions cannot be defined with an available geometric shape.

Redundant text links should be provided for all active regions of server-side image maps.

Frames should have unique titles.

Screen flickering with a frequency of 2–55 Hz should be eliminated.

A text-only page should be provided with equivalent information and functionality.

Assistive technology must be able to access content generated by scripting.

Web content that requires third-party software such as plug-ins must provide a link to the plug-in web site.

Forms should be accessible for assistive technology.

Users should be allowed to skip repetitive navigation links.

Users should be notified on timed response requirements and allowed to extend time limits.

Semantic (X)HTML5 Elements and WAI-ARIA

The new semantic markup elements introduced in the HTML5 specification such as header, footer, article, section, aside, and nav involve accessibility potential.

The support for ARIA roles is also increasing. ARIA roles can be applied as additional markup to improve accessibility potential; in other words, their presence does not cause any problems on systems without ARIA support. ARIA roles are added as attributes to elements such as banner, complementary, contentinfo, form, main, navigation, or search. Several ARIA roles describe document structure, namely, article, columnheader, definition, directory, document, group, heading, img, list, listitem, math, note, presentation, region, row, rowheader, separator, and toolbar.

The role of structuring elements can be provided by the role attribute. Listing 10-14 shows an example.

Listing 10-14. Using the role Attribute

```
<header role="banner" />
```

Certain roles must be unique within a page. The banner header code shown is a good example. While developers can use an unlimited number of headers, only one header can be a banner header.

JavaScript Accessibility

Hidden content, navigation, and strange user control behavior provided by scripting can cause confusion and accessibility problems. For example, the onblur event used for checking user input can override the default behavior of user agents and maintains focus until the correct answer is given, which makes it impossible for screen readers to access any other parts of the page (including the feedback text provided elsewhere) without entering the correct answer. Not all event handlers are device-independent, and some rely on the mouse (onmouseover, onmouseout, ondblclick) or keyboard (onkeydown, onkeyup), and cannot be triggered on all devices. If device-independent event handlers are used (such as onfocus, onblur, onselect, or onchange), content and functionality provided through scripting are accessible, full keyboard control is provided, and the scripts do not cause confusion by modifying or overriding normal browser functionality, then scripts can be accessible [46]. When JavaScript cannot be made natively accessible, an accessible alternative must be provided.

Drop-down and fly-out menus are commonly used throughout the Web. However, the onmouseover and onmouseout event handlers cannot be made directly accessible to keyboard users. Thus, an alternative must be provided.

The onfocus and onblur event handlers can be inconvenient or inaccessible for keyboard users to trigger.

The onclick event handler is a device-independent event handler; however, some applications rely on the mouse. In contrast to links or form controls, where the onclick event handlers can be triggered by pressing the Enter key, plain text and table cells cannot gain focus while navigating with the keyboard. Consequently, keyboard users cannot activate the onclick event for elements other than links or form controls. If this event is used with a form element (for example, for form validation), it is not a problem, and the Submit button using the onclick event can be activated by both pointing devices and keyboards.

The ondblclick event handler is generally mouse-dependent, because it is associated with the double-click of the mouse, and there is no equivalent event on some other input devices such as on keyboards.

Drop-down selection lists such as language selectors usually apply the onchange event handler. Going directly to the corresponding version by selecting an option from the list with a single click is very convenient for mouse users. However, these lists are not accessible for keyboard users who cannot select anything else but the first option (after pressing the cursor down key on the keyboard, the first option is selected immediately). One possible solution for the problem is to add a button to be the trigger of the onclick event handler. However, in this case all users should press the button after selecting the desired option to trigger the event handler.

The onselect event handlers can also be applied in a device-independent way.

Certain event handlers such as onkeydown and onkeyup can be triggered exclusively by the keyboard. The actions associated with them cannot be accessed by the mouse.

Dynamic content, such as the current time presented by document.write, cannot be read by screen readers.

■ **Note**   Some features of dynamic web pages can also be achieved by pure CSS (especially CSS3) and some JavaScript code block eliminated (for example, transitioning effects or transforming menu items). However, screen readers can handle certain CSS features poorly, for example, elements hidden by display: none; or visibility: hidden;.

PDF Accessibility

Adobe Acrobat and Adobe Reader provide accessibility (Figure 10-11) as well as screen reader options. They are available under Edit ➤ Preferences or directly with the shortcut Ctrl+K. You can find the screen reader option under View ➤ Read out loud.

Figure 10-11. *Accessibility preferences in Adobe Acrobat/Acrobat Reader*

Special features such as the Setup Assistant can be set under Edit ➤ Accessibility ➤ Setup Assistant (Figure 10-12).

Image-only PDF files, which are usually created by scanning paper documents, have accessibility issues. In such files, text cannot be searched and colors cannot be adjusted. Screen readers cannot read the image-only PDF files. Authors should use the OCR capabilities of Acrobat to provide text documents as text and preserve structure at the same time.

Figure 10-12. *Accessibility Setup Assistant*

The accessibility of *unstructured PDF files* varies. Their reading order can be changed. They provide automatic tagging and authors can optionally use manual tagging. Protected files cannot be saved to accessible formats.

Texts of *structured PDF files* are fully accessible. Hyperlinks are functional. The alternate text of images is accessible (if present). Page numbers are correct. Screen readers can read basic data tables correctly. If provided, the optional bookmarks can further improve accessibility. Protected files are also accessible. However, even structured PDF files have some known accessibility issues. Paragraphs, for example, cannot be located perfectly, and font attribute information is not available.

Flash Accessibility

Although accessibility was a weak point of the Flash technology for years, eventually both the developer environment and the free player had been improved. Adobe Flash Professional and Adobe Flash Player have several features to support assistive technology.

The layout and structure can be rather complex in Flash movies, making it very difficult for screen readers to read the content. A description added for the entire movie can give hints for screen readers about the movie structure.

Text equivalents must be added for graphic elements such as names for graphic icons or descriptions for gesturing animations. Element groups must have a single text equivalent.

Movies that never stop moving cause screen readers to refresh frequently. Even on web pages that contain a movie at the bottom, screen readers might interpret motion as a page update and return to the top to start reading again. This behavior can be eliminated by making the child objects of movie clips or entire movies inaccessible [47].

To allow users to control motion, Next buttons must be added to movies instead of displaying information for a limited time.

Several user interface components are accessible in Flash that automate common accessibility tasks such as labeling or providing keyboard access. The accessibility object can be enabled with the class `enableAccessibility()`.

The FLVPlayback component provides the option to include a video player in Flash applications to play downloaded Adobe Flash Video (FLV) files and streaming FLV files. The FLVPlaybackCaptioning component associates captions to your video. The captioning component supports the Timed Text Markup Language (TTML) W3C standard, along with multiple captioning and toggle control.

There are various approaches for providing control over reading order in Flash such as limiting stage size, providing an additional, linear version of the content or specifying reading order via ActionScript.

User controls must be accessible through the keyboard. Keyboard shortcuts must be added to buttons. In order to consider the limitations of screen readers, scripts must be kept within frames and empty movie clips used as buttons must be avoided.

In Flash Professional CS5, a new component was introduced to display audio captions contained either in Timed Text format (DFXP) or integrated with the FLV file as cue points. Flash Professional CS5 also added native support for accessible video player skins.

User controls such as the Play and Pause buttons are mandatory for audio playback.

For all controls, it is important to provide the user with feedback on the control as it changes.

The general rules for color selection described earlier in the WCAG requirements also apply for Flash contents.

Accessibility of Mathematical Notations

Mathematical equations provided in GIF images can be hard to read for the visually impaired and, if provided without a textual description, are inaccessible for screen readers.

In contrast, MathML equations are accessible. The accessibility potential of MathML is clearly demonstrated by the accessibility features of a free MathML plug-in for Internet Explorer,[3] Design Science MathPlayer [48]. The software provides audio or Braille descriptions for mathematical notations to screen readers. MathPlayer also has native speech capabilities (`speak expression` from the local menu). It allows keyboard navigation. MathPlayer 2 also contains MathZoom that allows users to magnify individual expressions. The matching algorithm ensures that the font size of mathematical notations is increased when the surrounding text is zoomed. Additionally, MathPlayer supports line breaks, which can improve readability if the font size is increased. It provides synchronized highlighting of subexpressions that are being read out loud, which helps people with certain learning disabilities such as dyslexia or dyscalculia

---

[3]Since Internet Explorer has native MathML support from version 9, a MathML plugin is required for earlier versions only. Design Science also provides tools for creating mathematical notations such as MathType (see section "MathType").

Summary

In this chapter, you learned the accessibility guidelines for the markup, style sheets, client- and server-side scripting, and multimedia content. You are now capable of creating web sites with the desired level of accessibility that can be used by anyone, regardless of user disability or browsing device limitations.

In the next chapter, you will learn about fundamental programs for your web design toolbox. You will become familiar with the core software features for choosing your advanced text editor, specific editors, and other web development tools that can ease your work significantly.

References

1. AustLII (1992) Disability Discrimination Act. Australasian Legal Information Institute. http://www.austlii.edu.au/au/legis/cth/consol_act/dda1992264/. Accessed 13 October 2014

2. Office of the Houses of the Oireachtas (2005) Disability Act. The National Parliament of Ireland. http://www.oireachtas.ie/documents/bills28/acts/2005/a1405.pdf. Accessed 13 October 2014

3. OPSI (1995) Disability Discrimination Act. The UK Statue Law Database. http://www.statutelaw.gov.uk/content.aspx?activeTextDocId=3330327. Accessed 13 October 2014

4. U.S. Access Board (2010) Section 508 Homepage: Electronic and Information Technology. United States Access Board. http://www.access-board.gov/508.htm. Accessed 13 October 2014

5. Henry SL (ed) (2011) Web Accessibility Initiative (WAI). World Wide Web Consortium. http://www.w3.org/WAI/. Accessed 13 October 2014

6. W3C (1997) World Wide Web Consortium Launches International Program Office for Web Accessibility Initiative. World Wide Web Consortium. http://www.w3.org/Press/IPO-announce. Accessed 13 October 2014

7. Régis J, Morrison A, Touré H (2010) World Standards Day Message. International Organization for Standardization. http://www.iso.org/iso/wsd2010/wsd2010_message.htm. Accessed 14 October 2010

8. Paciello MG (2000) Web Accessibility for People with Disabilities. CMP Books, Lawrence

9. Henry SL, McGee L (eds) (2010) Accessibility. In: Web Design and Applications. World Wide Web Consortium. http://www.w3.org/standards/webdesign/accessibility. Accessed 13 October 2014

10. Richards J, Spellman J, Treviranus J, May M (eds) (2010) Authoring Tool Accessibility Guidelines (ATAG) 2.0. World Wide Web Consortium. http://www.w3.org/TR/ATAG20/. Accessed 13 October 2014

11. Allan J, Ford K, Richards J, Spellman J (eds) (2010) User Agent Accessibility Guidelines (UAAG) 2.0. World Wide Web Consortium. http://www.w3.org/TR/UAAG20/. Accessed 13 October 2014

12. Abou-Zahra S, Squillace M (eds) (2009) Evaluation and Report Language (EARL) 1.0 Schema. World Wide Web Consortium. http://www.w3.org/TR/EARL10-Schema/. Accessed 13 October 2014

13. Henry SL (ed) (2011) The WAI-ARIA Documents. In: WAI-ARIA Overview. World Wide Web Consortium. http://www.w3.org/WAI/intro/aria.php#is. Accessed 13 October 2014

14. Craig J, Cooper M, Pappas L, Schwerdtfeger R, Seeman L (2011) Accessible Rich Internet Applications (WAI-ARIA) 1.0. World Wide Web Consortium. http://www.w3.org/TR/wai-aria/. Accessed 13 October 2014

15. Pappas L, Schwerdtfeger R, Cooper M (2010) WAI-ARIA 1.0 Primer – An introduction to rich Internet application accessibility challenges and solutions. http://www.w3.org/TR/wai-aria-primer/. Accessed 13 October 2014

16. Scheuhammer J, Cooper M (2010) WAI-ARIA 1.0 Authoring Practices – An author's guide to understanding and implementing Accessible Rich Internet Applications. World Wide Web Consortium. http://www.w3.org/TR/wai-aria-practices/. Accessed 13 October 2014

17. Snow-Weaver A, Cooper M (2010) WAI-ARIA 1.0 User Agent Implementation Guide – A user agent developer's guide to understanding and implementing Accessible Rich Internet Applications. World Wide Web Consortium. http://www.w3.org/TR/wai-aria-implementation/. Accessed 13 October 2014

18. Bulterman D, Jansen J, Cesar P, Mullender S, Hyche E, DeMeglio M, Quint J, Kawamura H, Weck D, Pañeda XG, Melendi D, Cruz-Lara S, Hanclik M, Zucker DF, Michel T (eds) (2008) Synchronized Multimedia Integration Language (SMIL 3.0). W3C Recommendation. World Wide Web Consortium. http://www.w3.org/TR/SMIL/. Accessed 13 October 2014

19. Adams G (ed) (2013) Timed Text Markup Language (TTML) 1.0 (Second Edition). W3C Recommendation. World Wide Web Consortium. http://www.w3.org/TR/ttaf1-dfxp/. Accessed 13 October 2014

20. Chisholm W, Vanderheiden G, Jacobs I (eds) (1999) Web Content Accessibility Guidelines 1.0. World Wide web Consortium. http://www.w3.org/TR/WAI-WEBCONTENT/. Accessed 13 October 2014

21. Caldwell B, Cooper M, Reid LG, Vanderheiden G, Chisholm W, Slatin J, White J (eds) (2008) Web Content Accessibility Guidelines (WCAG) 2.0. World Wide Web Consortium. http://www.w3.org/TR/WCAG20/. Accessed 13 October 2014

22. Vanderheiden G, Reid LG, Caldwell B, Henry SL, Lemon G (eds) (2010) How to Meet WCAG 2.0. A customizable quick reference to Web Content Accessibility Guidelines 2.0 requirements (success criteria) and techniques. World Wide Web Consortium. http://www.w3.org/WAI/WCAG20/quickref/. Accessed 13 October 2014

23. Vanderheiden G, Reid LG, Caldwell B, Henry SL (2008) How to meet WCAG 2.0. A customizable quick reference to Web Content Accessibility Guidelines 2.0 requirements (success criteria) and techniques. World Wide Web Consortium. http://www.w3.org/WAI/WCAG20/quickref/20081211/. Accessed 13 October 2014

24. Cooper M, Reid LG, Vanderheiden G, Caldwell B, Chisholm W, Slatin J (eds) (2010) Techniques for WCAG 2.0. Techniques and Failures for Web Content Accessibility Guidelines 2.0. World Wide Web Consortium. http://www.w3.org/TR/WCAG20-TECHS/. Accessed 13 October 2014

25. Cooper M, Reid LG, Vanderheiden G, Caldwell B, Chisholm W, Slatin J (eds) (2010) Appendix A. How to refer to WCAG 2.0 from other documents. In: Understanding WCAG 2.0. A guide to understanding and implementing Web Content Accessibility Guidelines 2.0. World Wide Web Consortium. http://www.w3.org/TR/UNDERSTANDING-WCAG20/appendixA.html. Accessed 13 October 2014

26. Cooper M, Reid LG, Vanderheiden G, Caldwell B (eds) (2010) Section Headings: Understanding SC 2.4.10. In: Understanding WCAG 2.0. World Wide Web Consortium. http://www.w3.org/TR/UNDERSTANDING-WCAG20/navigation-mechanisms-headings.html. Accessed 13 October 2014

27. Abou-Zahra S et al (eds) (2005) Conformance Evaluation of Web Sites for Accessibility. World Wide Web Consortium. http://www.w3.org/WAI/eval/conformance.html. Accessed 13 October 2014

28. WebsynergiDesign (2011) Accessibility – Our Experience & Accessible web site Design Portfolio. WebsynergiDesign Ltd. http://www.websynergi.com/accessibility/accessibility-bobby-w3c.aspx. Accessed 13 October 2014

29. Caldwell B, Cooper M, Reid LG, Vanderheiden G (eds) (2008) Relative luminance. In: Web Content Accessibility Guidelines (WCAG) 2.0. W3C Recommendation. World Wide Web Consortium. http://www.w3.org/TR/2008/REC-WCAG20-20081211/#relativeluminancedef. Accessed 13 October 2014

30. WebAIM (2011) Color Contrast Checker. Utah State University. http://webaim.org/resources/contrastchecker/. Accessed 13 October 2014

31. Juicy Studio (2011) Luminosity Colour Contrast Ratio Analyser. Juicy Studio. http://juicystudio.com/services/luminositycontrastratio.php. Accessed 13 October 2014

32. WAT-C (2005) Luminosity Contrast Ratio Analyser 1.1. Web Accessibility Tools Consortium. http://www.wat-c.org/tools/CCA/LCRA/index.html. Accessed 13 October 2014

33. Cooper M, Reid LG, Vanderheiden G, Caldwell B, Chisholm W, Slatin J (eds) (2010) Color Picker. Working example. In: Techniques for WCAG 2.0. Techniques and Failures for Web Content Accessibility Guidelines 2.0. World Wide Web Consortium. http://www.w3.org/WAI/WCAG20/Techniques/working-examples/G175/index.php. Accessed 13 October 2014

34. Ishida R (ed) (2011) CSS3 Ruby Module. World Wide Web Consortium. http://www.w3.org/TR/css3-ruby/. Accessed 13 October 2014

35. Sowden P (2001) Alternative Style: Working With Alternate Style Sheets. A List Apart Magazine. http://www.alistapart.com/d/alternate/styleswitcher.js. Accessed 13 October 2014

36. W3C (2004) Demonstration of Signing Avatar Technology as used in the Signing Science Project. TERC. http://www.w3.org/2004/Talks/0628-rdig-sims/vcom3d-signsci.mov. Accessed 13 October 2014

37. Trace Center (2011) Photosensitive Epilepsy Analysis Tool (PEAT). The University of Wisconsin. http://trace.wisc.edu.peat/. Accessed 11 September 2011

38. EOWG, WCAG WG (eds) (2009) Comparison of WCAG 1.0 Checkpoints to WCAG 2.0, in Numerical Order. World Wide Web Consortium. http://www.w3.org/WAI/WCAG20/from10/comparison/. Accessed 13 October 2014

39. Chisholm W, Vanderheiden G, Jacobs I (eds) (1999) Guideline 11. Use W3C technologies and guidelines. In: Web Content Accessibility Guidelines 1.0. World Wide Web Consortium. http://www.w3.org/TR/WAI-WEBCONTENT/#gl-use-w3c. Accessed 13 October 2014

40. Cooper M, Reid LG, Vanderheiden G, Caldwell B, Chisholm W, Slatin J (2008) Understanding Accessibility Support. In: Understanding WCAG 2.0. A guide to understanding and implementing Web Content Accessibility Guidelines 2.0. World Wide Web Consortium. http://www.w3.org/TR/2008/NOTE-UNDERSTANDING-WCAG20-20081211/conformance.html#uc-accessibility-support-head. Accessed 13 October 2014

41. Chisholm W, Vanderheiden G, Jacobs I (eds) (1999) Guideline 6. In: Web Content Accessibility Guidelines 1.0. World Wide Web Consortium. http://www.w3.org/TR/WCAG10/wai-pageauth.html#tech-scripts. Accessed 13 October 2014

42. Swan H, Henry S (2010) How to Update Your Web Site from WCAG 1.0 to WCAG 2.0. World Wide Web Consortium. http://www.w3.org/WAI/WCAG20/from10/websites.html. Accessed 13 October 2014

43. Clark J (2006) To hell with WCAG2. A List Apart. http://www.alistapart.com/articles/tohellwithwcag2. Accessed 13 October 2014

44. The United States Government (2010) § 1194.22 Web-based intranet and Internet information and applications. In: Section 508 Standards Guide. The United States Government. http://www.section508.gov/docs/Section%20508%20Standards%20Guide.pdf. Accessed 04 February 2011

45. The United States Government (2010) Note to §1194.22. In: Section 508 Standards Guide. The United States Government. http://www.section508.gov/index.cfm?fuseAction=stdsdoc. Accessed 04 February 2011

46. WebAIM (2014) Creating Accessible JavaScript. Overview of Creating Accessible JavaScript. Web Accessibility in Mind. http://webaim.org/techniques/javascript/. Accessed 13 October 2014

47. Adobe (2014) Adobe Flash accessibility design guidelines. Adobe Systems Incorporated. http://www.adobe.com/accessibility/products/flash/best_practices.html. Accessed 13 October 2014

48. Design Science (2014) MathPlayer Can Speak! MathPlayer: Speech instructions and examples. Design Science. http://www.dessci.com/en/products/mathplayer/tech/accessibility.htm. Accessed 13 October 2014

■ ■ ■

Developing with Standards

After learning the specifications required for creating standard-compliant web site components, you have to bring theory to practice. In this part of the book, you analyze the most common web site errors and master techniques and best practices through step-by-step guides to be able to plan and create standards-compliant web sites with confidence. You write well structured markup and core web sites components such as lists, tables, forms, and news feeds.

You get useful tips to set up a convenient and efficient web designer environment, and learn the distinctive features of advanced text editors that make them suitable for hand coding, such as correct whitespace handling, UTF-8 and UTF-16 support, and syntax highlighting. You see free and commercial web development tools, the most common semantic editors and reasoners for ontology development, and Responsive Web Design frameworks to design fluid grids for mobile-friendly web sites. You see how to analyze the DOM tree and modify the element containers with the built-in development tools of modern browsers, or update the CSS of a site on-the-fly in Firefox Inspector to get an instant preview without modifying any physical files. It will be demonstrated why and how to test site robustness in a text-based browser, under multiple browsers, and without style sheets.

You learn the best practices to create mobile-friendly layout, set font size proportional to the viewport size, properly combine CSS units, embed YouTube videos and Google Maps as valid HTML5, and ensure backward-compatibility and robustness through fallback mechanisms.

You learn about the fundamental validation services to check the markup, the style sheets, links, semantics, and news feeds individually or together using Unicorn, the unified validator. You become familiar with sophisticated accessibility validators such as Wave to identify accessibility barriers, and tools to evaluate the contrast ratio between foreground and background. You learn how to check semantic annotations by extracting machine-readable metadata using Indice. Once you achieve standard compliance, you can express validity and represent technologies with official icons and logos.

CHAPTER 11

■ ■ ■

Development Tools

Since modern markup elements and attributes are becoming more and more sophisticated, complex development software tools are used to generate web pages. Advanced text editors are fundamental programs in the toolbox of every web designer. Advanced text editors can be used for a variety of tasks, and provide very useful features such as syntax highlighting, line numbering, filters, uppercase-lowercase converters, spell checker, and so forth. They can also be integrated as the default editor of FTP clients, providing the option to directly edit files stored on the web server in an advanced environment. The implementation of Semantic Web technologies is efficient with semantic editors and reasoners. Markup correctors can be used to improve code quality. WYSIWYG editors and content management systems can be useful for rapid development; however, their code quality varies greatly.

In this chapter, you will learn about software tools that can help you develop standard-compliant web sites. You will become familiar with those vital features that should be considered when selecting your development tools, optimizers, and testing environments.

Feature Requirements

Although experienced web designers can write valid code in any text editor, the editor you select for your toolbox needs some advanced features that are vital for efficient hand-coding:

- Comprehensive character encoding support, including full Unicode support

- Whitespace character support

- Control character support, for example, CR+LF (Windows), LF only (UNIX), and Apple (CR only) break rows

- Multifile editing with tabs

- Customizable color schemas for *syntax highlighting* (XHTML, CSS, XML, scripts, and so on)

- Undo/redo

- Forced word wrap

- Line numbering

- Auto indent

- Guides for tag pairs and element nesting

- OS integration (adds application to right-click menu)

The selected editor should be integrated with at least one of your browsers as the default source code editor, which you can use to open the currently rendered web document for editing with a button or hotkey.

There are additional features of text editors that are not vital but can be useful:

- Customized color and font settings
- Customizable toolbars
- Spell checker
- Templates
- Bookmarks
- Full drag-and-drop support
- Built-in FTP client or integration with an (S)FTP client
- Conversions (uppercase, lowercase, invert case, and initial caps)
- International versions (can be convenient for some developers)
- Support for double-byte character systems (DBCS) used in Far East languages such as Chinese or Japanese (if required)
- Browser preview[1] (launching the default or selected web browser for debugging and testing)

Text Editors

In contrast to word processors such as Microsoft Word or OpenOffice.org Writer, *plain-text editors* cannot be used for document formatting, but they are suitable for creating web pages. However, basic text editors are not convenient for web design, because some vital features are missing from them. For example, many of them do not handle control characters and whitespaces correctly. The most well-known examples are Notepad under Windows and vi under Linux.

Advanced text editors such as WordPad provide text formatting and other additional features. *Source code editors* are advanced text editors with additional tools specifically designed for hand-coders and programmers. The most common feature of them is syntax highlighting for a variety of markup languages, style sheets, and programming languages. These full-featured editors are comprehensive tools suitable for hand-coding web pages. The following are some examples:

Linux

- BlueFish [1]
- Komodo Edit [2]

Mac OS

- BBEdit [3]
- TextWrangler [4]

---

[1]Some developers do not use this feature and open the desired browser(s) manually.

Windows

- EditPad Lite (free [5] and low-cost versions [6] are available)
- EditPlus [7]
- NotePad++ (free, open source [8])
- TextPad (low cost, free evaluation [9])

Cross-platform

- Arachnophilia (available for Windows, Linux, Unix, FreeBSD, and Mac OS [10])

As an example, let's look at the major features of Notepad++. It is a multifile editor with convenient file manager options. Notepad++ saves multiple files with a single click, opens recently edited files, and provides tabs for each opened file. It has a fully customizable interface with advanced features such as line markers, guides for opening and closing tag pairs, structuring guides to collapse or reveal the currently edited level of the DOM tree, and syntax highlighting (Figure 11-1).

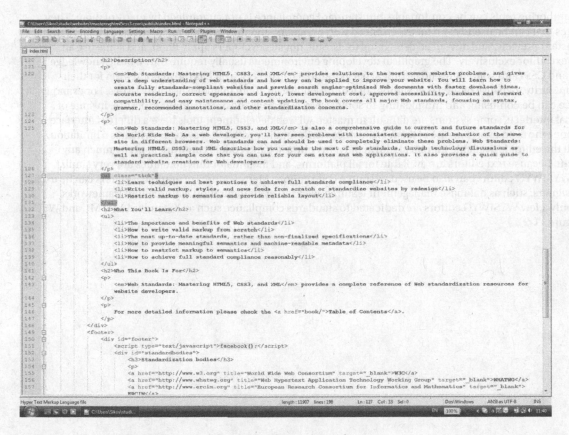

Figure 11-1. Syntax highlighting and tag pair guides in Notepad++

There are a variety of programming and web development languages supported in syntax highlighting from HTML to XML and from PHP to Ruby. There are several predefined color themes you can select from, or you can create new ones to your taste. The different document components (indent guidelines, marks, carets, whitespaces, tag pairs, active and inactive tabs, and so on) can be styled individually. Notepad++ can change text direction of documents. It also supports a variety of character encodings, can add and remove byte-order marks, supports big-endian and little-endian Unicode files, and converts files from one encoding to another.[2] The documents opened in the application can be previewed in any installed browsers.

Notepad++ also provides advanced text transformation functionalities, such as escaping certain characters, transforming lowercase characters to uppercase (or vice versa), searching for matching strings, converting decimal numbers to their hexadecimal equivalents, inserting the current date and time, sorting lists ascending or descending, automatically converting leading spaces to tabs, and so on. Notepad++ also supports macros, which you can run multiple times. The list of features can be extended through additional plug-ins, such as the MIME tools for Base64 encoding and decoding.

WYSIWYG Editors

Graphical authoring tools can be comfortable, but standard compliance is not guaranteed by many of them. They have features that can be useful even for experienced web designers, and they provide an interface with markup window, instant preview, and advanced debugging tools. Still, not all developers apply them, and some use an advanced text editor exclusively. The graphical developing environments usually require only a basic knowledge of markup and CSS (and sometimes no technical background whatsoever), which is the major reason for their extreme popularity. Because of the large number of features, however, there might be usability issues. For example, the interface can be confusing and intimidating to some users, especially the ones without expertise. In spite of the graphical interface, some systems are difficult to master. All web development tools have a different interface, and someone who is an expert in one of them is not necessarily familiar with other systems, which is a limitation, especially if the editor is available for one platform only. In contrast, hand coders can work in pretty much any environment, because text editors are available for all platforms, and their major functionalities are very similar.

Most WYSIWYG editors can also be used as source code editors. Many features of graphical editors can be useful for web designers, such as database management features, web server configuration features, and frameworks. However, only a few WYSIWYG editors are dedicated to standards compliance such as XStandard XHTML and W3C Amaya (Figure 11-2).

---

[2]This feature can be used for those encodings that can be reasonably converted to another, more advanced encoding without sacrificing special characters (for example, ANSI to UTF-8).

Figure 11-2. *An SVG file in Amaya*

Many commercial and free editing tools exist [11]. Compared to advanced text editors and source code editors, however, many commercial WYSIWYG editors are not affordable to everyone. On the other hand, there are several graphical developers that are not only free but also open source. Here are some examples:

Windows

- Microsoft Expression Web [12] (commercial, free trial available)

- Microsoft WebMatrix [13] (freeware)

Cross-platform

- Adobe Dreamweaver, available for Windows and Mac OS (commercial) [14]

- W3C Amaya, a free, open source (X)HTML, MathML, and SVG editor [15]

- XStandard XHTML, the standards-compliant XHTML editor, available for Windows and Mac OS (free lite version) [16]

The standard compliance of Dreamweaver, the industry-leading authoring application is constantly evolving. However, it took several years for the development team to reach a high level of web standards support. The latest versions of Dreamweaver support HTML, CSS, XSLT, JavaScript, ActionScript, XML, ASP, ColdFusion, JSP, and PHP. Some features and tools in Dreamweaver are useful not only for development in general but also for standard-compliant development. Some examples are invalid code highlighting, syntax error alerts displayed in the info bar, the list of CSS properties associated with the currently selected element, and syntax highlighting. The program interface is highly customizable and features different modes for displaying the code, the result, or both at the same time (Figure 11-3).

Figure 11-3. *Code and design can be displayed simultaneously in Adobe Dreamweaver*

Content Management Systems and Bloggers

Content management systems are WYSIWYG tools developed mainly for web content authoring and blog publishing. Many of them are driven by PHP. The most well-known content management systems are cross-platform, such as Drupal [17], Joomla! [18], and WordPress [19]. Beyond the common tasks of web publishing, they provide modern functionalities to support semantic annotations, SEO, and accessibility. However, the standard support of content management systems varies, and these systems are responsible for a large share of invalid markup on the Web. Figure 11-4 shows a typical example.

⊗ *Line 164, Column 120*: **Bad value Windows Phone for attribute name on element a: An ID must not contain whitespace.**

```
.hone" class="search_link" name="Windows Phone" rel="nofollow"> Windows Phone</a>
```

Syntax of id:
    An ID consists of at least one character but must not contain any whitespace.

⚠ *Line 164, Column 120*: **The name attribute is obsolete. Consider putting an id attribute on the nearest container instead.**

```
.hone" class="search_link" name="Windows Phone" rel="nofollow"> Windows Phone</a>
```

⚠ *Line 171, Column 108*: **The name attribute is obsolete. Consider putting an id attribute on the nearest container instead.**

```
.search?q=Symbian" class="search_link" name="Symbian" rel="nofollow"> Symbian</a>
```

⊗ *Line 180, Column 116*: **Bad value First Class for attribute name on element a: An ID must not contain whitespace.**

```
.st+Class" class="search_link" name="First Class" rel="nofollow"> First Class</a>
```

Syntax of id:
    An ID consists of at least one character but must not contain any whitespace.

Figure 11-4. *Errors and warnings in every tenth row of the markup generated by a CMS*

Although there are more and more content management systems that claim to generate standard-compliant code (LiveStoryboard [20], WebDandy [21], sNews [22], and so on), most of them do not provide a holistic approach to standards implementation.

Web Standards Support

The standards support of editors varies. Several tools implement certain markup versions or variants only, while others have limited CSS support (Table 11-1). No ultimate solution exists, but any comprehensive tool can be a good choice for hand-coders. For example, BlueFish supports not only all (X)HTML versions and variants but also RSS, Atom, MathML, CSS, JavaScript, Java, XSLT, XForms, and XPath.

Table 11-1. *Markup Language Support of Some Editors with Validation Feature*

	HTML 4.01			XHTML			1.1	2	HTML 5
					1.0				
	S	T	F	S	T	F			
Amaya	−	+	−	+	+	−	+	−	−
BlueFish	+	+	+	+	+	+	+	+	+
Dreamweaver	+	+	−	+	+	−	+	−	+
Freeway	+	+	−	+	+	−	−	−	+
KompoZer	+	+	−	+	+	−	−	−	−
Expression Web	+	+	+	+	+	+	+	−	+

Specific Editors

Beyond advanced text editors, there are other programs that cannot be missed from the toolbox of web designers. Such tools are semantic editors, semantic reasoners, MathML editors, and markup correctors.

Semantic Editors and Reasoners

Along with the increasing popularity of OWL, more and more tools are appearing on the market for OWL development. Web ontologies are machine-processable, and *semantic reasoners* (also known as reasoning engines or rules engines) can be used to infer logical consequences from facts or axioms described by the ontologies. Some of the most useful *semantic editors* and *reasoners* are described next.

Protégé is a free open source framework [23] and one of the most widely used OWL editors. It is an efficient tool for developing and testing ontologies. Protégé supports several file formats and syntaxes, including OWL, OWL in functional syntax, OWL in Manchester syntax, RDF/XML, OBO flat file, KRSS2, Latex, and Turtle. It can directly open not only saved files but also online ontologies.

HermiT is an OWL Reasoner that can be used to determine ontology consistency, identify relationships between classes, and perform further tasks. It can be used from the command line, in Java applications, or as a Protégé plug-in (Figure 11-5).

Figure 11-5. *The HermiT reasoner running in Protégé*

HermiT is released under the LGPL license [24]. *TopBraid Composer* is a graphical development tool for data modeling and semantic data processing that supports standards such as RDF, OWL, and SPARQL [25]. *Pellet* is an OWL 2 Reasoner for Java [26]. *Racer 2.0* supports standards such as RDF, RDFS, OWL Lite, OWL DL, and SPARQL. Connectivity with external software is also possible [27]. FaCT++ is a Description Logic reasoner compatible with OWL DL and OWL 2 [28].

MathType

MathType is an advanced editor for mathematical notations developed by Design Science. The equations and annotations can be edited through a powerful graphical user interface (Figure 11-6).

Figure 11-6. *Equation editing in MathType*

The software is available for Windows and Mac OS [29]. The editor is often embedded into Microsoft Word to replace the Equation Editor (either as a new menu or as a new ribbon, depending on the Word version), but it can also be used in other word processors such as OpenOffice, Google Docs, or Apple Pages. The mathematical annotations edited in MathType can also be exported to MathML and LaTeX. In fact, using MathType is one of the easiest ways to generate MathML. Beyond MathType, the W3C browser/editor Amaya can also be used to generate MathML.

Markup Correctors

Although sophisticated markup components such as metadata require human decision, conventional (X)HTML markup elements and attributes can be reliably corrected automatically. They can be useful in many cases; however, markup correctors do not replace hand-coder web standards experts. In contrast to developers, software tools do not always support the latest standards; some of them are discontinued or will be updated several years after the release of a standard.

395

HTML Tidy

HTML Tidy is a markup corrector that fixes invalid HTML and improves the layout and indent style of the markup. The tool was developed by *Dave Raggett*, the coauthor and editor of several markup specifications at W3C. Since it is written in ANSI C, precompiled binaries are available for a variety of platforms and can be compiled for further ones. HTML Tidy is available under the W3C license at Sourceforge.net (both as a downloadable binary and as the source code) [30] or as an online service at W3C [31].

The software can identify and correct missing or mismatched end tags, mixed-up tags, and quotes, as well as change markup layout according to predefined styles [32].

Tidy for PHP

The HTML markup generated by PHP scripts can be checked and corrected by the PHP extension *Tidy*. As an example, functions can be written to take HTML markup fragments as strings and run them through HTML Tidy. The output is a valid markup. This approach makes automatic page processing and standardization possible. If there are errors in the code, the location (line, column) and the error cause are clearly indicated or automatically corrected [33].

Log Validator

W3C Log Validator "combines a Server Log analysis engine with batch validation, link checking, and other quality-oriented processing, for step-by-step improvement and maintenance of Web Site Quality" [34]. It finds the most frequently downloaded invalid documents, broken links, other errors, and inconsistencies, and it sets a priority list for fixing them. This feature is designed for standardizing large-scale invalid web sites step by step by correcting only a certain amount of documents at a time. Eventually, the whole site will be fixed, but you can determine how to schedule development time and effort.

Log Validator applies processing modules that validate the latest server logs against markup and style sheet recommendations (according to W3C HTML and CSS Validation Services). The SurveyEngine module creates a summary of errors for the most popular documents that might affect the overall quality of the site. The basic processing module generates only a list of documents by popularity. Log Validator supports three types of output: raw, mail, and HTML.

Responsive Web Design Frameworks

Responsive frameworks are used by web designers to build a web site using a grid-based layout with predefined base code without spending a huge amount of time creating a grid structure from scratch. The following sections summarize some of the most popular Responsive Web Design frameworks.

Foundation

ZURB Foundation is one of the most popular free tool collections for responsive website and web application development [35]. It contains HTML and CSS-based design templates for typography, forms, buttons, navigation and other interface components, as well as optional JavaScript extensions.

Foundation is modular and based on Sass style sheets so that web designers can enjoy the benefits of variables, functions, operators, nested selectors, as mixins. From version 3.0 onward, Foundation can also be customized through a form to choose and modify the components needed for your project.

The default flexible grid layout of Foundation is 940 pixels wide, and supports the following device categories: mobile phones in portrait and landscape orientation, tablets, and PCs with low and high resolution screens. Selecting a device category adjusts the column width.

Bootstrap

Bootstrap is a free, open-source collection of tools for creating responsive web sites[3] and web applications [36]. The templates of Bootstrap are based on HTML5 and CSS3, and cover navigation, typography, forms, buttons, and other web site components (Figure 11-7), as well as optional JavaScript extensions. Bootstrap is compatible with all the modern browsers, and gracefully degrades when used on older browsers such as Internet Explorer 8.

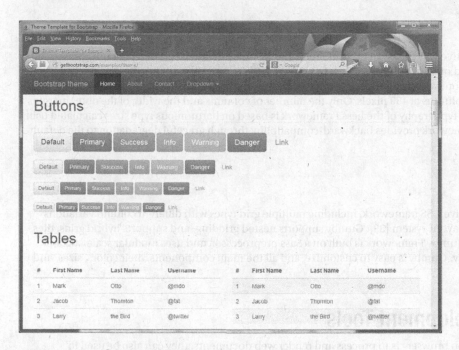

Figure 11-7. *A Bootsrap template*

The modular structure of Bootstrap relies on a set of LESS style sheets called bootstrap.less, making it possible to use variables, functions, operators, nested selectors, and mixins.

The default grid system for Responsive Web Design comes with a 1,170 pixels wide grid layout, however, web designers can choose a variable-width layout as well. The four target device classes in both cases are mobile phones with portrait and landscape orientation, tablets and desktop computers with low and high resolution screen. Selecting a device class modifies the width of the columns.

To use Bootstrap in the markup, you have to download the CSS file of Bootstrap and link it in the document head. Alternatively, the CSS file from the downloaded Less or Sass style sheets can be compiled with a special compiler. If you want to use the JavaScript components too, you have to load them on top of the jQuery library in your markup.

---

[3]Since version 2.

Skeleton

Skeleton is a boilerplate for responsive, mobile-friendly development [37]. The default grid of Skeleton is a variation of the 960 pixels wide grid system. Skeleton's typography feature supports strong hierarchy with basic styles. The default font is Helvetica Neue, which can be easily changed. Regular paragraphs have a font size of 14px and 21px line height by default. Skeleton also supports buttons, forms, and other responsive web site components through CSS3 Media Queries.

Less Framework

The Less Framework is an adaptive CSS grid system, containing four layouts and three sets of typography presets, all based on a single grid composed of 68 px columns with 24 px gutters [38]. The four layouts are the default, 992px wide 10 column layout, the Tablet layout with 8 columns at 768 pixels, the mobile layout with 3 columns at 320 pixels, and the wide mobile layout with 5 columns at 480 pixels. Only the number of columns and the width of the outer margins change in different layouts. The typography of the Less Framework is based on harmonious type sizes calculated using the Golden Ratio. The Less Framework provides backward-compatibility through graceful degradation to the default 992px layout.

Gumby

Gumby Framework is a responsive CSS framework, including multiple grid types with different column variations such as a 12-grid and a 16-grid layout system [39]. Gumby supports nested gridding, and supports hybrid grids, tiles, fancy tiles, and semantic tiles. Gumby Framework is built on a Sass preprocessor, and uses modular scale and a Golden Ratio tool for typography. Gumby is easy to customize, and all the main components, their colors, sizes, and fonts can be quickly changed.

Browsers as Development Tools

Although the primary aim of web browsers is to process and render web documents, they can also be used in development and standardization. Accessibility can be effectively evaluated by turning off style sheets and nontext content or by applying a text-based browser.

There are various built-in development tools in browsers such as the Developers Tools in Internet Explorer (F12) [40] which, among others, have a DOM Explorer, a Console, a Debugger, and Emulation. Emulation can be useful to test older web sites that targeted a particular version of Internet Explorer, or simply to test any web site for backward-compatibility. To do so, you can change the document mode, the browser profile, and the user agent string (Figure 11-8).

Figure 11-8. *Emulation in Internet Explorer*

In Firefox, you can launch the Inspector by pressing F12 or right-clicking any element of a web site and selecting Inspect Element (Q) from the local menu. The Inspector is a very useful tool, allowing web designers to analyze not only the DOM tree but also the style sheets applied to an element, including the rulesets declared explicitly and the ones inherited from parent elements (Figure 11-9). Those styles that are not applied are crossed out, making it easy to identify more specific styles. The CSS styles can be disabled and re-enabled by clicking on the checkbox in front of them. Any of the CSS styles can also be overwritten on the temporary files used to render the page, providing the option to check a different background color, font size, etc. without actually modifying any physical files.

Figure 11-9. *Firefox Inspector*

Safari's Developer Tools are available from Edit ➤ Preferences ➤ Advanced ➤ Show Develop Menu in menu bar [41], or by right-clicking an element of a web page and selecting Inspect element. Opera also offers a similar feature under Page ➤ Developer Tools [42] and by right-clicking an element and selecting Inspect Element. The Developer Tools of Google Chrome can show the DOM tree, the applied CSS rulesets, including the computed property values, and Event listeners (available under More tools ➤ Developer Tools or by pressing Ctrl + Shift + I).

Validator and Debugger Plug-ins

Browsers can also be extended with additional functionality by installing developer plug-ins, many of which are freely available.

There are numerous add-ons for Firefox that can be useful for developers [43]. For example, HTML Validator is an extension that adds HTML validation inside Firefox [44]. It clearly indicates the number of markup errors as an icon in the status bar when browsing. Live HTTP Headers displays HTTP headers of a page and while browsing [45]. FireFTP is a free, secure, cross-platform (S)FTP client for the browser [46]. The User Agent Switcher extension adds a menu and a toolbar button to switch the user agent of the browser [47]. The IE Tab extension supports Internet Explorer rendering from IE6 to IE9, which can be useful for testing purposes [48]. The Web Developer extension adds various web developer tools to a browser, such as the option to disable certain styles or display CSS by media type [49]. One of the most comprehensive developer add-ons for Firefox is Firebug [50]. It integrates several development tools to the browser to directly edit, debug, and monitor HTML, CSS, and JavaScript (Figure 11-10).

Figure 11-10. *Firebug in action*

Some of these Firefox tools are also available under Chrome (for example, Firebug [51], Web Developer [52]), and the ones that do not have a Chrome version have their equivalents for Chrome (such as IE Tab [53]). There are many other developer tools under Chrome [54], such as W3C HTML5 & CSS3 Validator [55], Validity that validates the markup from the address bar (or with hotkeys) [56], colorPicker [57], XML Tree [58], Resolution Test [59], just to mention a few.

Testing Web Pages in Text Browsers

Testing a web site in text browsers such as Lynx [60] is the best method to check information availability without styles and graphics[4] as well as accessibility. Properly designed web content remains usable in text browsers (Figure 11-11), while a large share of web sites do not.

---

[4]Lynx cannot display nontext contents by default, but external programs can be launched from Lynx such as image viewers or video players.

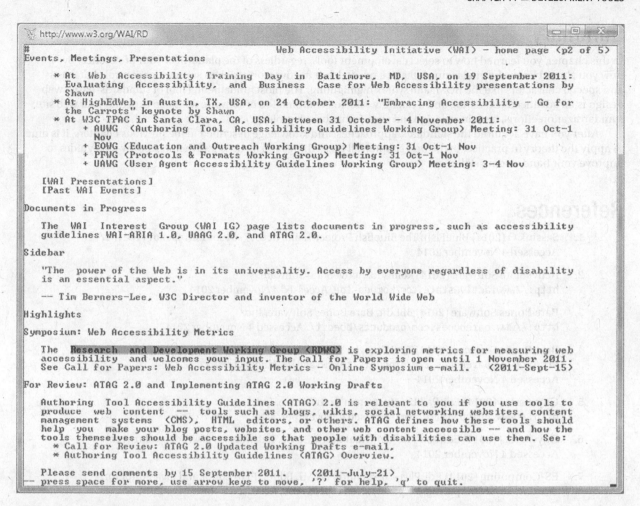

Figure 11-11. *Browsing an accessible site in Lynx*

View the Source Code

Web browsers provide the option to view the source code of the currently opened web page (usually by selecting View ➤ Source or Page Source, selecting a similar menu item from the local menu, or pressing Cmd/Ctrl+U or in Safari Cmd/Ctrl+Alt+U). This feature can be used to analyze the markup and other components of the site. Although it can be very useful to learn from other developers, it is crucial to keep in mind that a large amount of web sites are not standard-compliant and should not be considered as a reference or best practice.

There is a difference between the copyright of the web site content and that of the markup code that displays it. As a general rule, copying code of other web sites without permission is not allowed to be published unless there is a license that allows you to do so.

Summary

In this chapter, you learned how to select development tools, regardless of the platform of your preference. By now you should know the vital features that are needed for effective work, such as support for control characters and special characters like the BOM, and syntax highlighting. The most fundamental tool of standards-based web design is an advanced text editor, and a carefully selected combination of software tools can expedite your web site standardization efforts, both in redesign and start-from-scratch projects.

After you have acquired the standards, approaches, and knowledge described in the previous chapters, it is time to apply the theory in practice. In the next chapter, all these things will be used together in step-by-step guides to improve your hand-coding skills.

References

1. Sessink O (2014) BlueFish. The Bluefish Project Team. `http://bluefish.openoffice.nl/`. Accessed 4 November 2014

2. ActiveState Software (2014) Komodo. ActiveState Software. `http://www.activestate.com/komodo-ide`. Accessed 4 November 2014

3. Bare Bones Software (2014) BBEdit. Bare Bones Software, Inc. `http://www.barebones.com/products/bbedit/`. Accessed 4 November 2014

4. Bare Bones Software (2014) TextWrangler. Bare Bones Software, Inc. `http://www.barebones.com/products/textwrangler/index.html`. Accessed 4 November 2014

5. Goyvaerts J (2014) EditPad Lite. Just Great Software Co. Ltd. `http://www.editpadlite.com`. Accessed 4 November 2014

6. Goyvaerts J (2014) EditPad Pro. Just Great Software Co. Ltd. `http://www.editpadpro.com`. Accessed 4 November 2014

7. ES-Computing (2014) EditPlus – Text editor, HTML Editor, PHP Editor and Java Editor for Windows. ES-Computing. `http://www.editplus.com`. Accessed 4 November 2014

8. Ho D et al (2014) Notepad++. Don Ho. `http://notepad-plus-plus.org`. Accessed 4 November 2014

9. HELIOS (2014) TextPad. Helios Software Solutions. `http://www.textpad.com/products/textpad/`. Accessed 4 November 2014

10. Lutus P (2014) Arachnophilia. `http://www.arachnoid.com/arachnophilia/`. Accessed 4 November 2014

11. htmlArea (2014) WYSIWYG editor directory. htmlArea. `http://www.htmlarea.com`. Accessed 4 November 2014

12. Microsoft (2011) Microsoft Expression Web. Microsoft Corporation. `http://www.microsoft.com/en-us/download/details.aspx?id=36179`. Accessed 4 November 2014

13. Microsoft (2014) Microsoft Corporation. `http://www.microsoft.com/web/webmatrix/`. Accessed 4 November 2014

14. Adobe (2014) Adobe Dreamweaver. Adobe Systems Incorporated. `http://www.adobe.com/products/dreamweaver/`. Accessed 4 November 2014

15. Quint V, Carcone L (eds) (2012) Amaya. World Wide Web Consortium. http://www.w3.org/Amaya/. Accessed 4 November 2014

16. Belus Technology (2014) XStandard: free standards-compliant XHTML WYSIWYG editor. Belus Technology Inc. http://xstandard.com/. Accessed 4 November 2014

17. Buytaert D (2014) Drupal. Dries Buytaert. http://drupal.org. Accessed 4 November 2014

18. Moffatt S et al (2014) Joomla! The CMS Trusted By Millions for their Websites. http://www.joomla.org. Accessed 4 November 2014

19. Mullenweg M, Boren R, Jaquith M, Ozz A, Westwood P (2014) WordPress. http://wordpress.org/. Accessed 4 November 2014

20. liveSTORYBOARD (2012) liveSTORYBOARD web content management. Web standards save time, decrease costs, increase flexibility - don't ignore them. liveSTORYBOARD, Inc. http://www.livestoryboard.com/Benefits/CMS-standards-compliant.html. Accessed 4 November 2014

21. Web Dandy (2014) Web Dandy Content Management System - Accessibility Comes As Standard. http://www.webdandy-cms.co.uk/w3c-standards.htm. Accessed 4 November 2014

22. sNews (2014) sNews – Lightweight Content Management System. http://snewscms.com. Accessed 4 November 2014

23. Stanford University (2014) The Protégé Ontology Editor and Knowledge Acquisition System. Stanford Center for Biomedical Informatics Research. http://protege.stanford.edu/. Accessed 4 November 2014

24. Motik B, Shearer R, Glimm B, Stoilos G, Horrocks I (2014) Hermit OWL Reasoner. University of Oxford. http://hermit-reasoner.com/. Accessed 4 November 2014

25. TopQuadrant (2014) TopBraid Composer. TopQuadrant Inc. http://www.topquadrant.com/products/TB_Composer.html. Accessed 4 November 2014

26. Clark & Parsia (2013) Pellet: The Open Source OWL 2 Reasoner. Clark & Parsia LLC. http://clarkparsia.com/pellet. Accessed 4 November 2014

27. Haarslev V, Hidde K, Möller R, Wessel M et al (2014) Racer. http://www.ifis.uni-luebeck.de/~moeller/racer/index.html. Accessed 4 November 2014

28. Tsarkov D et al (2014) FaCT++. Dmitry Tsarkov et al. http://code.google.com/p/factplusplus/. Accessed 4 November 2014

29. Design Science (2014) MathType – equation editor. Design Science. http://www.dessci.com/en/products/mathtype/. Accessed 4 November 2014

30. Raggett D, Paehl D, Nelson C, Hennecke C, Teague T (2008) HTML Tidy Library Project. SourceForge.net: Find, Create, and Publish Open Source software for free. http://tidy.sourceforge.net. Accessed 4 November 2014

31. Connolly D, Hazaël-Massieux D (2014) Tidy your HTML. World Wide Web Consortium. http://services.w3.org/tidy/tidy. Accessed 4 November 2014

32. Raggett D (2012) Clean up your Web pages with HTML TIDY. Dave Raggett. http://www.w3.org/People/Raggett/tidy/. Accessed 4 November 2014

33. The PHP Group (2014) PHP: Tidy – manual. The PHP Group. http://php.net/manual/en/book.tidy.php. Accessed 4 November 2014

34. Thereaux O, Dubost K, Bless T, Skytta V, Cope AS, Rezic S et al (2007) LogValidator. World Wide Web Consortium. http://www.w3.org/QA/Tools/LogValidator/. Accessed 4 November 2014

35. ZURB (2014) Foundation | The Most Advanced Responsive Front-end Framework from ZURB. http://foundation.zurb.com. Accessed 4 November 2014

36. Otto M, Thornton J et al (2014) Bootstrap—The world's most popular mobile-first and responsive front-end framework. http://getbootstrap.com. Accessed 4 November 2014

37. getskeleton.com (2014) Skeleton: Beautiful Boilerplate for Responsive, Mobile-Friendly Development. http://www.getskeleton.com. Accessed 4 November 2014

38. Korpi J (2014) Less Framework. http://lessframework.com. Accessed 4 November 2014

39. Digital Surgeons (2014) Gumby - A Flexible, Responsive CSS Framework - Powered by Sass. http://gumbyframework.com. Accessed 4 November 2014

40. Microsoft (2014) Debugging HTML and CSS with the Developer Tools. Microsoft Corporation. http://msdn.microsoft.com/en-us/library/dd565627(v=VS.85).aspx. Accessed 4 November 2014

41. Apple (2014) Safari Developer Tools. Apple Inc. https://developer.apple.com/safari/tools/. Accessed 4 November 2014

42. Bovens A (2010) Opera extensions developer workflow. Opera Software ASA. http://dev.opera.com/articles/view/opera-extensions-developer-workflow/. Accessed 02 March 2011

43. Mozilla (2014) Web development :: Add-ons for Firefox. Mozilla Foundation. https://addons.mozilla.org/en-US/firefox/extensions/web-development/. Accessed 4 November 2014

44. Gueury M (2014) Html Validator. Mozilla Corp. https://addons.mozilla.org/en-us/firefox/addon/html-validator/. Accessed 4 November 2014

45. Savard D, Coukouma N (2014) Live HTTP Headers. Mozilla Corp. https://addons.mozilla.org/en-us/firefox/addon/live-http-headers/. Accessed 4 November 2014

46. Čuvalo M (2014) FireFTP. Mozilla Corp. https://addons.mozilla.org/en-US/firefox/addon/fireftp/. Accessed 4 November 2014

47. Pederick C (2014) User Agent Switcher. Mozilla Corp. https://addons.mozilla.org/en-US/firefox/addon/user-agent-switcher/. Accessed 4 November 2014

48. Mozilla (2014) IE Tab V2. Mozilla Corp. https://addons.mozilla.org/en-US/firefox/addon/ie-tab-2-ff-36/. Accessed 4 November 2014

49. Pederick C (2014) Web Developer. Mozilla Corp. https://addons.mozilla.org/en-US/firefox/addon/web-developer/. Accessed 4 November 2014

50. Hewitt J, Odvarko J, et al (2014) Firebug. Mozilla Corp. http://getfirebug.com/. Accessed 4 November 2014

51. Simonetti P (2014) Firebug Lite for Google Chrome. Mozilla Corp. http://getfirebug.com/releases/lite/chrome/. Accessed 4 November 2014

52. Pederic C (2014) Web Developer. Mozilla Corp. https://chrome.google.com/webstore/detail/bfbameneiokkgbdmiekhjnmfkcnldhhm. Accessed 4 November 2014

53. Blackfish (2014) IE Tab. Blackfish Software. https://chrome.google.com/webstore/detail/hehijbfgiekmjfkfjpbkbammjbdenadd. Accessed 4 November 2014

54. Google (2014) Google Chrome Developer Tools page. Google Inc. https://chrome.google.com/webstore?category=ext%2F11-web-development. Accessed 4 November 2014

55. Cebeci G (2014) HTML Validator. https://chrome.google.com/webstore/detail/html-validator/cgndfbhngibokieehnjhbjkkhbfmhojo?hl=en. Accessed 4 November 2014

56. Renyard I (2014) Validity. Ian Renyard. https://chrome.google.com/webstore/detail/bbicmjjbohdfglopkidebfccilipgeif. Accessed 4 November 2014

57. Dematte P (2014) colorPicker. Peter Dematte. https://chrome.google.com/webstore/detail/jegimleidpfmpepbfajjlielaheedkdo. Accessed 4 November 2014

58. Stroop A (2014) XML Tree. Alan Stroop. https://chrome.google.com/webstore/detail/gbammbheopgpmaagmckhpjbfgdfkpadb. Accessed 4 November 2014

59. Beckford B (2014) Resolution Test. Ben Beckford. https://chrome.google.com/webstore/detail/idhfcdbheobinplaamokffboaccidbal. Accessed 4 November 2014

60. Dickey T et al (2014) Lynx source distribution and potpourri. Internet Software Consortium. http://lynx.isc.org/. Accessed 4 November 2014

CHAPTER 12

■ ■ ■

Putting It All Together

Being familiar with web technologies and standards is not sufficient for standardizing invalid sites and developing valid sites from scratch. Web site standardization is always a complex project, and it takes into account a variety of requirements simultaneously. The list includes, but is not limited to, full standard compliance; optimal code length; interoperability; meaningful, structured, and accessible content; adequate metadata; and proper settings. Creating valid code can be learned most efficiently through the collection of step-by-step guidelines provided in this chapter.

After becoming familiar with web standards, it is time to learn how to create fundamental standard-compliant web site components from scratch in a text editor and extend them for your web pages. Most XHTML code fragments you will learn can be used as the basis for XHTML projects and HTML5 markup for new HTML projects. You will see how to use indentations to create clear, easy-to-maintain markup and provide the end tags immediately after the opening tags to avoid tags to be missed. The presented guidelines also demonstrate the proper, logical use of structural elements from paragraphs to lists and from tables to forms. Even if web development environments provide useful templates and functions, it is very useful to understand how to create core web site structures manually. After mastering the basic structure of lists, tables, objects, and forms, you will be able to extend, modify, and standardize the corresponding markup elements and never get lost in the details even if the markup is rather long and complex.[1]

Choosing the Relevant Standards

When it comes to the implementation of web standards, there is no ultimate choice. The browser support, the web design trends, and the user expectations are constantly changing. Most web designers consider W3C Recommendations as de facto standards; however, there are standards released by other standardization bodies as well, such as ERCIM, IETF, WaSP, or WSG (as discussed in Chapter 1). Even those web designers who know the mainstream web standards well do not necessarily implement them correctly.

The choice of standards has a serious impact on each phase of web site standardization and future extensibility. The decision-making has to precede the initial steps of design and coding by considering the features, strengths, and weaknesses of the various standards and technologies.

Switching Between Standards

It is a common misconception that implementing the latest technologies immediately at all costs is the key to developing modern web sites. In fact, the latest technologies without finalized specification are not recommended for use. The latest standards (with the W3C status "Recommendation") should be applied exclusively, and the Working

---

[1]Each step-by-step guide in this chapter focuses on a particular element or element group and the corresponding markup elements. The complexity of the markup will increase drastically when adding additional contents and attributes, but the basic structure always remains the same.

Drafts, which are subject to change, should not be used, unless you want to participate in the standards development as a *first implementer*. Since these technologies are at varying degrees of adoption and standardization, web site functionality cannot be guaranteed and the markup cannot be validated with full certainty (or validators provide this feature as an experimental tool only). User experience might degrade due to nonworking components, users might be prompted to download files of unknown types, and so on. Functionality and usability are more important than the incorrect use of the latest, often nonfinalized specifications (Figure 12-1).

Figure 12-1. Modern markup applied incorrectly. What is the point?

Naturally, web designers cannot fall behind if they want to remain competitive, but they should not rely on unofficial resources such as blog posts. Convincing clients and decision-makers to use the right standards can also be a challenge when it comes to the well-underestimated Web Quality Assurance and strict timeframes.

Step-by-Step Development

Creating a standard-compliant web site with valid markup, styles, semantic content, and accessible code should be the preferable way to develop a web site. You can verify whether individual technologies are standard-compliant by validating the markup, the style sheet, and further components such as the feed channel during development. However, the full standards compliance of a whole web site is more complex than that. As discussed throughout this book, full standards compliance covers valid character encoding declaration (preferably UTF-8), valid HTML or valid XHTML markup (the stricter, the better), valid CSS, valid RSS or valid Atom news feed, valid RDF, valid metadata, valid XML, valid object embedding, valid script embedding, WCAG 2.0 and Section 508 conformance, accessibility, mobile-friendliness, the application of Semantic Web technologies, browser- and resolution-independent code, and proper server settings, just to mention the most important ones.

Starting from Scratch

Typically, you should perform the following core tasks when creating a web site from scratch:

- Determine the document type.

- Create the `index.html` file. All required elements must be provided, along with the ones that are highly recommended for structuring.[2] As a general rule, the `html` element should be used as the `root` element for all HTML and XHTML documents. Markup documents should contain a document head (between `<head>` and `</head>`) and a document body (delimited by `<body>` and `</body>`). Beyond the general container `div` and paragraph `p` used in HTML 4.01 and XHTML, or the more specific HTML5 structuring elements `header`, `article`, and `section`, the cohesive parts of web page content should have headings. In (X)HTML, there are six levels of headings: `h1`, `h2`, `h3`, `h4`, `h5`, and `h6` (from the largest to the smallest). Levels should not be skipped (for example, applying `h4` in a document in which there is no `h3` but just `h1` and `h2`).

- Multiply files. Carefully applied copying and pasting reduces development time for hand-coders. It provides integrity throughout the site; however, modifications should be done on all files if the initial file has been modified. Such modifications are often easier on dynamic sites, which typically store the identical sections centrally.

- Create the primary style sheet file (for example, `main.css`) with an initial design for basic layout, colors, and font styles (they will be updated later). The main designing concepts should be determined in advance.

- Provide optional elements. Which optional elements are reasonable depends on the project. The various `meta` elements are recommended in most cases. Several `link` elements are also frequently applied including, but not limited to, links to external files such as the Atom or RSS news feed (`atom.xml`, `rss.xml`), the web site icon (`favicon.ico`), or optional metadata (`metadata.rdf`, `foaf.rdf`, `doac.rdf`).

- Add useful extensions. The number of useful—and free—web site extensions and APIs is constantly increasing. Some are Google Analytics tracking code (JavaScript), interactive Google Maps for contact details, or the Like and Tweet buttons for social networking. Although they are popular and used by millions, most of them are not standardized. Care must be taken to avoid invalid embedding codes provided by third-party software developers.

■ **Note** This doesn't mean you have to sacrifice third-party content, because many invalid embedding codes can be rewritten in a standard-compliant manner.

- Do additional tasks depending on client needs.

- Set up hosting on a web server.

- Beyond the simplest static sites, all web sites apply server-side scripting and applications with prerequisite technology support and configuration. These depend on the user needs.

---

[2]Development tools often provide templates and skeleton documents to begin your work with. Even text editors have options to insert markup elements, which can be faster than typing.

- Upload and install.

  - Static files can be directly uploaded to the web server.

  - Server-side applications usually have some installation files that should be uploaded to the server. These files can be executed on the server to install and configure the application.

- Share the web site through a domain.

Note that there is no fixed order for these tasks, although some always precede others. Furthermore, these steps apply for static web pages. If the site relies on server-side scripting, the steps depend on the type of the system. Content Management Systems such as WordPress or Joomla! generate the basic site structure during initialization. Such systems are usually based on PHP, so the index page of the site will be index.php rather than index.html, all web site data will be stored in a database such as MySQL instead of static HTML files, headings and footers are stored centrally, and new pages are typically created through the menu of the graphical user interface.

Following the basic principles discussed in the next sections can serve as the basis for developing standard-compliant code from scratch. The list of web site components is not complete by any means. However, most of these samples can be applied in a variety of markup languages and style sheets and are frequently applied in web design.

■ **Note**   The order of the step orders is a suggestion only.

XHTML

XHTML 1.0 Strict documents can be developed with the following steps. Other XHTML documents can be authored similarly by applying the desired document type.

1. Create XML declaration.

```
<?xml version="1.0" encoding="UTF-8"?>
```

2. Add document type declaration.

```
<?xml version="1.0" encoding="UTF-8"?>
<!DOCTYPE html
  PUBLIC "-//W3C//DTD XHTML 1.0 Strict//EN"
  "http://www.w3.org/TR/xhtml1/DTD/xhtml1-strict.dtd">
```

3. Add root element with default namespace and language setting.

```
<?xml version="1.0" encoding="UTF-8"?>
<!DOCTYPE html
  PUBLIC "-//W3C//DTD XHTML 1.0 Strict//EN"
  "http://www.w3.org/TR/xhtml1/DTD/xhtml1-strict.dtd">
<html xmlns="http://www.w3.org/1999/xhtml" xml:lang="en" lang="en">

</html>
```

4. Additional namespaces can also be added upon request.

5. Add document head and body.

```
<?xml version="1.0" encoding="UTF-8"?>
<!DOCTYPE html
 PUBLIC "-//W3C//DTD XHTML 1.0 Strict//EN"
 "http://www.w3.org/TR/xhtml1/DTD/xhtml1-strict.dtd">
<html xmlns="http://www.w3.org/1999/xhtml" xml:lang="en" lang="en">
<head>

</head>
<body>

</body>
</html>
```

6. Add document title.

```
<?xml version="1.0" encoding="UTF-8"?>
<!DOCTYPE html
 PUBLIC "-//W3C//DTD XHTML 1.0 Strict//EN"
 "http://www.w3.org/TR/xhtml1/DTD/xhtml1-strict.dtd">
<html xmlns="http://www.w3.org/1999/xhtml" xml:lang="en" lang="en">
<head>
<title>XHTML Document Sample</title>
</head>
<body>

</body>
</html>
```

7. Add head content, including metadata, base URI, links, and scripts. Although they are optional elements, many of them are used frequently. The most common one of all is the link to an external CSS file:

   a. Create a basic link with the file path or URI. If XHTML syntax is used, self-closing is required.

   ```
   <link href="styles/main.css" />
   ```

   b. Set the link type.

   ```
   <link type="text/css" href="styles/main.css" />
   ```

   c. Identify the link role.

   ```
   <link rel="stylesheet" type="text/css" href="styles/main.css" />
   ```

   d. Set the media type (optional).

   ```
   <link rel="stylesheet" type="text/css" media="all" href="styles/main.css" />
   ```

8. Head content can be arbitrarily extended upon request, for example with metadata from external vocabularies such as DC. A typical head section with highly customized content looks like this:

```
<?xml version="1.0" encoding="UTF-8"?>
<!DOCTYPE html ↵
 PUBLIC "-//W3C//DTD XHTML 1.0 Strict//EN"↵
 "http://www.w3.org/TR/xhtml1/DTD/xhtml1-strict.dtd">
<html xmlns="http://www.w3.org/1999/xhtml" xml:lang="en" lang="en">
  <head>
    <title>XHTML Document Sample</title>
    <meta http-equiv="Content-Type" content="application/xhtml+xml; charset=utf-8" />
    <meta http-equiv="Content-Style-Type" content="text/css" />
    <meta name="robots" content="noindex, nofollow" />
    <meta name="content-language" content="en" />
    <meta name="author" content="Dr. Leslie Sikos" />
    <meta name="keywords" content="Dr. Leslie F. Sikos, networking" />
    <meta name="description" content="Contact data of IT pro Dr. Leslie Sikos.↵
      Website  standardization, semantic websites, accessability, professional↵
      photography, videography, multimedia &amp; more." />
    <base href="http://www.lesliesikos.com/" />
    <link rel="alternate" type="application/rss+xml" title="Dr. Leslie Sikos IT↵
      professional" href="http://www.lesliesikos.com/sikos.xml" />
    <link rel="author" href="http://www.lesliesikos.com/" />
    <link rel="shortcut icon" href="favicon.ico" />
    <link rel="stylesheet" type="text/css" media="all" href="styles/sikos.css"↵
      title="Default style" />
    <link rel="stylesheet" type="text/css"  media="handheld" href="styles/mobile.css"↵
      title="Styles for mobile devices" />
    <link rel="stylesheet" type="text/css"  media="print" href="styles/print.css"↵
      title="Styles for printing" />
    <script type="text/javascript" src="js/help.js"></script>
    <script type="text/javascript" src="js/access.js"></script>
  </head>
  <body>

  </body>
</html>
```

9. Add body content.

```
<?xml version="1.0" encoding="UTF-8"?>
<!DOCTYPE html ↵
 PUBLIC "-//W3C//DTD XHTML 1.0 Strict//EN" ↵
 "http://www.w3.org/TR/xhtml1/DTD/xhtml1-strict.dtd">
<html xmlns="http://www.w3.org/1999/xhtml" xml:lang="en" lang="en">
  <head>
    <title>XHTML Document Sample</title>
    <meta http-equiv="Content-Type" content="application/xhtml+xml; charset=utf-8" />
    <meta http-equiv="Content-Style-Type" content="text/css" />
    <meta name="robots" content="noindex, nofollow" />
```

```
            <meta name="content-language" content="en" />
            <meta name="author" content="Dr. Leslie Sikos" />
            <meta name="keywords" content="Dr. Leslie F. Sikos, networking" />
            <meta name="description" content="Contact data of IT pro Dr. Leslie Sikos.↵
              Website standardization, semantic websites, accessability, professional↵
              photography, videography, multimedia &amp; more." />
            <base href="http://www.lesliesikos.com/" />
            <link rel="alternate" type="application/rss+xml" title="Dr. Leslie Sikos IT↵
              professional" href="http://www.lesliesikos.com/sikos.xml" />
            <link rel="author" href="http://www.lesliesikos.com/" />
            <link rel="shortcut icon" href="favicon.ico" />
            <link rel="stylesheet" type="text/css" media="all" href="styles/sikos.css"↵
              title="Default style" />
            <link rel="stylesheet" type="text/css"  media="handheld" href="styles/mobile.css"↵
              title="Styles for mobile devices" />
            <link rel="stylesheet" type="text/css"  media="print" href="styles/print.css"↵
              title="Styles for printing" />
            <script type="text/javascript" src="js/help.js"></script>
            <script type="text/javascript" src="js/access.js"></script>
          </head>
          <body>
            <p>
              An XHTML 1.0 Strict Document.
            </p>
          </body>
        </html>
```

(X)HTML5

(X)HTML5 documents can be developed with the following steps:

1. Create the Document Type Declaration. In XHTML5, the DTD can optionally be preceded
    by the XML prolog, which is not used in HTML5.

    ```
    <?xml version="1.0" encoding="UTF-8"?>
    <!DOCTYPE html>
    ```

2. Add the root element. In XHTML5, the xmlns attribute is used to define the XHTML
    namespace on the html element. In HTML5, this attribute is not used.

    ```
    <?xml version="1.0" encoding="UTF-8"?>
    <!DOCTYPE html>
    <html xmlns="http://www.w3.org/1999/xhtml">

    </html>
    ```

3. Add document head and body.

```
<?xml version="1.0" encoding="UTF-8"?>
<!DOCTYPE html>
<html xmlns="http://www.w3.org/1999/xhtml">
  <head>

  </head>
  <body>

  </body>
</html>
```

4. Add the document title. Similar to the example discussed in the previous section, metadata, base URI, links, and scripts can be added arbitrarily.

```
<?xml version="1.0" encoding="UTF-8"?>
<!DOCTYPE html>
<html xmlns="http://www.w3.org/1999/xhtml">
  <head>
    <title>Sample XHTML5 document structure</title>
  </head>
  <body>
  </body>
</html>
```

5. Add the character encoding declaration.

```
<?xml version="1.0" encoding="UTF-8"?>
<!DOCTYPE html>
<html xmlns="http://www.w3.org/1999/xhtml">
  <head>
    <title>Sample XHTML5 document structure</title>
    <meta charset="UTF-8" />
  </head>
  <body>
  </body>
</html>
```

In XHTML5, the character encoding declaration is terminated with the shorthand notation, which does not apply to HTML5 where **<meta charset="UTF-8">** is used.

6. Create the structure with a header, section, and footer.

```
<?xml version="1.0" encoding="UTF-8"?>
<!DOCTYPE html>
<html xmlns="http://www.w3.org/1999/xhtml">
  <head>
    <title>Sample XHTML5 document structure</title>
    <meta charset="UTF-8" />
  </head>
```

```
    <body>
      <header>
        <h1>Document sample</h1>
      </header>
      <section>

      </section>
      <footer>
        Copyright © 2015 John Smith. All rights reserved.
      </footer>
    </body>
  </html>
```

7. Provide content.

```
<?xml version="1.0" encoding="UTF-8"?>
<!DOCTYPE html>
<html xmlns="http://www.w3.org/1999/xhtml">
  <head>
    <title>Sample XHTML5 document</title>
    <meta charset="UTF-8" />
  </head>
  <body>
    <header>
      <h1>Document sample</h1>
    </header>
    <section>
      <article>
        <h2>Article1</h2>
          The first article of the document.
      </article>
      <article>
        <h2>Article2</h2>
          The second article of the document.
      </article>
    </section>
    <footer>
      Copyright © 2015 John Smith. All rights reserved.
    </footer>
  </body>
</html>
```

which can be written in HTML5 as follows:

```
<!DOCTYPE html>
<html>
  <head>
    <title>Sample HTML5 document</title>
    <meta charset="UTF-8">
  </head>
```

```html
  <body>
    <header>
      <h1>Document sample</h1>
    </header>
    <section>
      <article>
        <h2>Article1</h2>
          The first article of the document.
      </article>
      <article>
        <h2>Article2</h2>
          The second article of the document.
      </article>
    </section>
    <footer>
      Copyright © 2015 John Smith. All rights reserved.
    </footer>
  </body>
</html>
```

Links

Hyperlinks are fundamental elements of web pages that can be added to the markup as follows:

1. Provide the basic anchor. It can be a URI of an external site such as the following:

    ```html
    <a href="http://www.example.com">
    ```

    e. or a path within your site such as the following:

    ```html
    <a href="gallery/">
    ```

    f. Hyperlinks can also point to a document segment (identified by the id attribute) with a *fragment identifier*. Here's an example:

    ```html
    <a href="gallery/canada.html#calgary">
    ```

2. Set the target (if required). External links are often intended to be opened in a new window. Here's an example:

    ```html
    <a href="http://www.example.com" target="_blank">
    ```

3. Add a tabbing index to improve accessibility (optional).

    ```html
    <a href="http://www.example.com" tabindex="5" target="_blank">
    ```

4. Ensure that external links won't affect the PageRank of your site (optional).

    ```html
    <a href="http://www.example.com" rel="nofollow" tabindex="5" target="_blank">
    ```

    g. Steps 2 and 4 apply for external links only.

Images

Images are embedded with the img element. If XHTML syntax is used, self-closing is required. The location of the image file is determined by the src (source) attribute.

1. Embed a basic image.

   ```
   <img src="images/logo.png" />
   ```

2. Provide alternate content that can be rendered in case the image cannot be displayed (fundamental for accessibility).

   ```
   <img src="images/logo.png" alt="The logo of Big Profit Company" />
   ```

3. Provide a text to be displayed when the user moves the mouse over the image (optional). It can be the same as the alternate text or different.

   ```
   <img src="images/logo.png" alt="The logo of Big Profit Company" title="The logo of Big Profit Company" />
   ```

Lists

List items of both ordered (ol) and unordered lists (ul) are delimited by <li> and </li> (Listing 12-1).

Listing 12-1. List Item Structure in Ordered and Unordered Lists

```
<ol>            <ul>
<li></li>       <li></li>
<li></li>       <li></li>
...             ...
<li></li>       <li></li>
</ol>           </ul>
```

1. An unordered list can be created as follows:

   ```
   <ul>

   </ul>
   ```

2. The list items can be added arbitrarily.

   ```
   <ul>
       <li>Apricot</li>
       <li>Cherry</li>
       <li>Peach</li>
   </ul>
   ```

Definition lists define definition terms (dt) and their descriptions (dd) (Listing 12-2).

Listing 12-2. A Definition List Example

```
<dl>
  <dt>
    <label>Web site development</label>
  </dt>
  <dt>RDF</dt>
    <dd>A W3C acronym for Resource Description Framework, an XML specification for ↵
      metadata models.</dd>
  <dt>RSS</dt>
  <dd>Really Simple Syndication. An XML format for frequently updated content, e.g., ↵
    news headlines, blog entries.</dd>
</dl>
```

List Accessibility

You can improve the accessibility of lists by adding elements such as accesskey and tabindex. Here's an example:

```
<ul>
  <li>
    <a href="http://www.example.com/" title="Home" accesskey="h" tabindex="1">Home</a>
  </li>
  <li>
    <a href="about/" title="Introduction" accesskey="a" tabindex="2">About</a>
  </li>
  <li>
    <a href="gallery/" title="Gallery" accesskey="g" tabindex="4">Gallery</a>
  </li>
  <li>
    <a href="shop/" title="Webstore of oil paintings" accesskey="s" tabindex="6">Shop</a>
  </li>
  <li>
    <a href="exhibition/" title="Exhibitions" accesskey="e" tabindex="7">Exhibitions</a>
  </li>
  <li>
    <a href="contact/" title="Address and phone" accesskey="c" tabindex="7">Contact</a>
  </li>
</ul>
```

Styling Lists

You can use unordered lists for more general purposes than ordered lists. Unordered lists are often used to build menus.[3] Typical horizontal menus override the default display style, as shown in Listing 12-3, in order to render the list items next to instead of below each other.

---

[3]XHTML 2.0 also provides the more specific element nl for navigation lists, which is not supported by any other markup language.

Listing 12-3. Styling of List Items to Be Displayed Inline

```
li {
  display: inline;
}
```

A simple style frequently applied for the hyperlinks of such list items are bottom borders (Listing 12-4).

Listing 12-4. Bottom Border for Menu Hyperlinks

```
a:hover {
  color: #949295;
  border-bottom: 1px solid #949295;
}
```

Naturally, this style is seldom applied globally. Instead, it is extended with the identifier of the list or its container parent element such as #main a:hover or #navtabs li a:hover.

A usual technique for creating custom navigation effects is to add a background image to the list items. Listing 12-5 shows an example.

Listing 12-5. Custom Navigation Effect with a Background Image

```
li {
  background: url('images/navbg.png') 5px no-repeat;
  padding-left: 16px;
}
```

If certain links, such as the first, the last, or the currently selected one, have different styles than all the others, unique identifiers should be provided for them (Listing 12-6).

Listing 12-6. More Specific Rules for the First and Last Items

```
<ul>
  <li id="first">
    <a href="http://www.example.com/" title="Home" accesskey="h" tabindex="1">Home</a>
  </li>
  ...
  <li id="last">
    <a href="contact/" title="Address and phone" accesskey="c" tabindex="7">Contact</a>
  </li>
</ul>
```

The first ruleset can be styled as shown in Listing 12-7.

Listing 12-7. A Specific Ruleset for the First List Items

```
li.first {
  background: none;
  padding-left: 0;
}
```

If the project is more than just a small web page, these styles should not be applied globally, simply because these specific styles would be applied to all lists throughout the document, most of which should be overridden (there would be more styling rules to override than the inherited rules that suit our needs). Instead, an identifier should be added to the list such as shown in Listing 12-8.

Listing 12-8. An Unordered List Used for Navigation Is Identified to Be Styled Differently

```
<ul id="navtabs">
  <li id="first">
    <a href="http://www.example.com/" title="Home" accesskey="h" tabindex="1">Home</a>
  </li>
  ...
  <li id="last">
    <a href="contact/" title="Address and phone" accesskey="c" tabindex="7">Contact</a>
  </li>
</ul>
```

From now on, all styles should begin with #navtabs (Listing 12-9).

Listing 12-9. A Specific Ruleset for Styling the First List Items of the Unordered List navtabs

```
#navtabs li.first {
  background: none;
  padding-left: 0;
}
```

Alternatively, the styles can be declared at the container level and use inheritance to style the list.[4] This approach is useful when multiple lists are used within the document that have the same styles or are slightly different only. Such differences can be easily overridden by more specific styling rules.

Additional styles can be declared for access keys and further features. For example, the markup in Listing 12-10 can be styled with the CSS rules shown in Listing 12-11.

Listing 12-10. A Span Used to Style an Access Key

```
S<span class="ak">i</span>temap
```

Listing 12-11. CSS Rules for Access Keys

```
span.ak {
  color: red;
  background-color: #ffb;
  border-bottom: solid #000080 1px;
}
```

The default bullets can be changed to arbitrary characters or images by CSS. Listing 12-12 shows an example, which applies to unordered lists such as the one presented in Listing 12-13.

---

[4] Note that in this case the identifiers should be changed from id to class in the markup and from hash mark (#) to period (.) in the CSS.

Listing 12-12. Bullet Image

```
ul.tick {
  list-style-image: url('images/tick.png')
}
```

Listing 12-13. Application of the Custom Bullet Style Presented in Listing 12-12

```
<h1>The major benefits of standard compliance</h1>
<ul class="tick">
   <li>Resolution independence</li>
   <li>Browser independence</li>
   <li>Interoperability</li>
   <li>Robust functionality</li>
</ul>
```

The result is visually more appealing (and more specific) than a list with ordinary bullets (Figure 12-2).

The major benefits of standard compliance

   ✔ Resolution independence

   ✔ Browser independence

   ✔ Interoperability

   ✔ Robust functionality

Figure 12-2. Custom bullets with CSS

Tables

Let's assume that a 5×5 comparison table of the first 4 iPhone models needs to be presented on a web page (Table 12-1).

Table 12-1. A Sample Table to Be Coded

Model	iPhone	iPhone 3G	iPhone 3GS	iPhone 4
Preinstalled OS	iPhone OS 1.0	iPhone OS 2.0	iPhone OS 3.0	iOS 4.0
Display resolution	480×320	480×320	480×320	960×640
CPU clockrate	620 MHz	620 MHz	833 MHz	1 GHz
Camera	2 MP	2 MP	3 MP	5 MP (rear), 0.3 MP (front)

1. All tables should have an opening and a closing tag.

```
<table>
</table>
```

2. Table rows should be delimited by `<tr>` and `</tr>`. The first row starts like this:

```
<table>
  <tr>
  </tr>
</table>
```

3. Table header cells should be written between `<th>` and `</th>`. Since the desired table has five columns, five header cell elements are required:

```
<table>
  <tr>
    <th></th><th></th><th></th><th></th><th></th>
  </tr>
</table>
```

4. A new row should be started for the first row of data cells.

```
<table>
  <tr>
    <th></th><th></th><th></th><th></th><th></th>
  </tr>
  <tr>
  </tr>
</table>
```

5. Data cells should be provided by td tags. Since the desired table has five columns, five data cell elements are required for each row.

```
<table>
  <tr>
    <th></th><th></th><th></th><th></th><th></th>
  </tr>
  <tr>
    <td></td><td></td><td></td><td></td><td></td>
  </tr>
</table>
```

6.   Since the structure of rows is identical, the table row containing the five data cells can be
     copied three times with a simple copy and paste:

```
<table>
    <tr>
        <th></th><th></th><th></th><th></th><th></th>
    </tr>
    <tr>
        <td></td><td></td><td></td><td></td><td></td>
    </tr>
    <tr>
        <td></td><td></td><td></td><td></td><td></td>
    </tr>
    <tr>
        <td></td><td></td><td></td><td></td><td></td>
    </tr>
    <tr>
        <td></td><td></td><td></td><td></td><td></td>
    </tr>
</table>
```

7.   Finally, the cells should be filled with data:

```
<table>
    <tr>
        <th>Model</th><th>iPhone</th><th>iPhone 3G</th><th>iPhone 3GS</th><th>iPhone 4</th>
    </tr>
    <tr>
        <td>Preinstalled OS</td><td>iPhone OS 1.0</td><td>iPhone OS 2.0</td><td>iPhone ↵
        OS 3.0</td><td>iOS 4.0</td>
    </tr>
    <tr>
        <td>Display resolution</td><td>480x320</td><td>480x320</td><td>480x320</td> ↵
        <td>960x640</td>
    </tr>
    <tr>
        <td>CPU clockrate</td><td>620 MHz</td><td>620 MHz</td><td>833 MHz</td><td>1 GHz</td>
    </tr>
    <tr>
        <td>Camera</td><td>2 MP</td><td>2 MP</td><td>3 MP</td><td>5 MP (rear), ↵
        0.3 MP (front)</td>
    </tr>
</table>
```

Table Accessibility

You can further improve the markup to increase accessibility. Processing and understanding tables can be challenging for nonvisual browsers. You can use the table header (th) and the caption (caption) markup elements to increase table accessibility. The first element is useful for visual browsers too, while the second one is valuable for screen readers.

The table header element th not only adds meaning to the first row but is repeated by screen readers when each row of the table is read. It helps the visually impaired understand the correlations between table cells.

The textual description of the table can be provided by the caption element (Listing 12-14).

Listing 12-14. Table Caption

```
<table>
  <caption>
    A comparison table of iPhone models.
  </caption>
  <tr>
    <th>Model</th><th>iPhone</th><th>iPhone 3G</th><th>iPhone 3GS</th><th>iPhone 4</th>
  </tr>
  <tr>
    <td>Preinstalled OS</td><td>iPhone OS 1.0</td><td>iPhone OS 2.0</td><td>iPhone OS ↵
      3.0</td><td>iOS 4.0</td>
  </tr>
  <tr>
    <td>Display resolution</td><td>480x320</td><td>480x320</td><td>480x320</td> ↵
      <td>960x640</td>
  </tr>
  <tr>
    <td>CPU clockrate</td><td>620 MHz</td><td>620 MHz</td><td>833 MHz </td><td>1 GHz</td>
  </tr>
  <tr>
    <td>Camera</td><td>2 MP</td><td>2 MP</td><td>3 MP</td><td>5 MP (rear), 0.3 MP (front)</td>
  </tr>
</table>
```

You can also add access keys to the table cells if required.

Table Styling

Although table headers are usually rendered in bold by most browsers, the default styles of table cells, padding, and borders are different in each rendering engine, which is not always acceptable. All table features can be styled arbitrarily through CSS rulesets, however. For example, the default value of the border-collapse property, separate, can be overridden in order to make borders collapse into a single border whenever possible (Listing 12-15).

Listing 12-15. Set Borders to Collapse

```
table {
  border-collapse: collapse;
}
```

In this case, the `border-spacing` and `empty-cells` properties will be ignored. The padding and border of the header and data cells can be set as shown in Listing 12-16.

Listing 12-16. Padding and Border for Header and Data Cells

```
th, td {
  padding: 10px;
  border: 1px solid #13b141;
}
```

Drop-Down Selection Lists

Selection lists can provide options to choose from. Suppose a language selector is needed for a multilingual web site. It can be developed as follows:

1. Create a selection list with the `select` element.

   ```
   <select>

   </select>
   ```

2. Add the default option.

   ```
   <select>
     <option value="http://www.example.com" selected="selected">English</option>

   </select>
   ```

3. Add further options. Provide the URIs of each language version as the option values.

   ```
   <select>
     <option value="http://www.example.com" selected="selected">English</option>

     <option value="http://de.example.com">Deutsch</option>
     <option value="http://fr.example.com">Français</option>
     <option value="http://es.example.com">Español</option>
     <option value="http://ja.example.com">本語</option>
   </select>
   ```

4. To load the appropriate web page, the subdomains provided as the option values can be used as target URIs through an event handler. Although the use of the onchange event handler would be logical, it would be inaccessible for keyboard users. One of the solutions is to provide a button with an `onclick` event handler, which is device-independent. For example, the following function

   ```
   <script type="text/javascript">
     function goto_URL(object) {
       window.location.href=object.options[object.selectedIndex].value;
     }
   </script>
   ```

declared in the document head or a linked external file can be used by the onclick event handler on the input element as follows:

```
<form>
  <select id="langsel">
    <option value="http://www.example.com" selected="selected">English</option>
    <option value="http://de.example.com">Deutsch</option>
    <option value="http://fr.example.com">Français</option>
    <option value="http://es.example.com">Español</option>
    <option value="http://ja.example.com">本語</option>
  </select>
  <input type="button" value="Go!" onclick="goto_URL(this.form.langsel);" />
</form>
```

5. Note that other methods can also be applied such as server-side redirection, which eliminates the need for JavaScript.

Forms

Basic forms can be created with the following steps:

1. Create an empty form.

   <form>

   </form>

2. Specify the location of the server-side script used to process data from the form.

   ```
   <form action="register.php">

   </form>
   ```

3. Specify the method to be used for sending data. The form data can be sent as URL variables (method="get") or as an HTTP post (method="post").

   - The get method appends the form data to the URL as name-value pairs, which makes it possible to bookmark the result of the form submission. Because of the length limitations of URLs, however, it cannot be ensured that all form data will be transferred. Moreover, the get method is inadequate for transforming sensitive information such as passwords, because the data will be visible in the address bar of the browser.

   - The post method sends the form data as an HTTP post transaction. This method has no size limitations and is more secure than the get method.

   ```
   <form method="post" action="register.php">

   </form>
   ```

4. Create logical group(s) for form elements.

```
<form method="post" action="register.php">
  <fieldset>

  </fieldset>
  <fieldset>

  </fieldset>
</form>
```

5. Add the desired form controls such as text fields (text) and checkboxes (checkbox) and their attributes.

```
<form method="post" action="register.php">
  <fieldset>
    <input type="text" name="firstname" id="firstname" size="15" maxlength="255" />
    <br /><input type="text" name="lastname" id="lastname" size="20" maxlength="255" />
  </fieldset>
  <fieldset>
    <input type="checkbox" name="interests" value="1" id="photo" />
    <input type="checkbox" name="interests" value="2" id="video" />
    <input type="checkbox" name="interests" value="3" id="web" />
  </fieldset>
</form>
```

6. Improve accessibility. The label element adds a label to a form control. The legend element assigns a caption to a fieldset. The tabbing order can be set by tabindex attributes.

```
<form method="post" action="register.php">
  <fieldset>
    <legend>Personal data</legend>
    <label for="firstname">First name</label><br />
    <input type="text" name="firstname" id="firstname" size="15" maxlength="30" ↵
    tabindex="12" /><br />
    <label for="lastname">Last name</label><br />
    <input type="text" name="lastname" id="lastname" size="20" maxlength="50" ↵
    tabindex="13" />
  </fieldset>
  <fieldset>
    <legend>Main interests</legend>
    <input name="interests" type="checkbox" value="1" id="photo" tabindex="14" />
    <label for="photo">Photography</label><br />
    <input name="interests" type="checkbox" value="2" id="video" tabindex="15" />
    <label for="video">Videography</label><br />
    <input name="interests" type="checkbox" value="3" id="web" tabindex="16" />
    <label for="web">Web</label>
  </fieldset>
</form>
```

Flash Content

You can embed a Flash file with the general object tag in XHTML as follows:

1. Declare an application/x-shockwave-flash object.

```
<object type="application/x-shockwave-flash">

</object>
```

2. Add the source with cross-browser code.

```
<object type="application/x-shockwave-flash" data="flash/header.swf">
  <param name="movie" value="flash/header.swf" />

</object>
```

3. Provide attributes such as dimensions and an identifier (if required).

```
<object type="application/x-shockwave-flash" data="flash/header.swf" width="610" ↵
height="224" id="flash">
  <param name="movie" value="flash/header.swf" />

</object>
```

4. If the Flash content has a transparent background, it should be declared as an optional parameter. This is also required for providing the possibility to set layer order within the web page.

```
<object type="application/x-shockwave-flash" data="flash/header.swf" width="610" ↵
height="224" id="flash">
  <param name="movie" value="flash/header.swf" />
  <param name="wmode" value="transparent" />

</object>
```

5. Add alternate content such as a placeholder image and text descriptions to improve accessibility. If a short description is not sufficient, a good practice is to add a hyperlink to a resource that describes the object.

```
<object type="application/x-shockwave-flash" data="flash/header.swf" width="610" ↵
height="224" id="flash">
  <param name="movie" value="flash/header.swf" />
  <param name="wmode" value="transparent" />
  <a href="longdesc/"><img src="images/altheader.jpg" alt="The image alternative for ↵
  the Flash header." title="Our headquarters" /></a>
</object>
```

In (X)HTML5, the embed tag can be used instead of object.

1. Create an embed element. Since the parameters can be provided as attributes of embed, the self-closing tag can be applied in XHTML5 as follows:

```
<embed />
```

Evidently, the shorthand notation should be omitted in HTML5.

2. Add the path or URI of the file. It can be done by using the src attribute instead of data applied on object elements.

```
<embed src="flash/header.swf" />
```

3. Add dimension and optional parameters.

```
<embed src="flash/header.swf" width="550" height="400" wmode="transparent" />
```

RSS News Feeds

Creating RSS news feeds generally consists of the following steps:

1. Create the XML declaration. Since RSS 2.0 news feeds should be valid XML documents, the first line is the XML declaration:

```
<?xml version="1.0" encoding="utf-8"?>
```

The character encoding is optional but recommended.

2. Create the RSS channel. The contents of the RSS channel should be written within the rss and channel tags as follows:

```
<rss version="2.0">
<channel>

</channel>
</rss>
```

If additional namespaces are required, they should be added to the rss element. Interoperability can be maximized by providing escaped HTML markup, the creator with Dublin Core metadata, the update period and frequency defined by the syndication namespace, and the self-link from the Atom vocabulary. The following namespace declarations should be added:

```
<rss version="2.0"↵
 xmlns:content="http://purl.org/rss/1.0/modules/content/"↵
 xmlns:dc="http://purl.org/dc/elements/1.1/"↵
 xmlns:sy="http://purl.org/rss/1.0/modules/syndication/"↵
 xmlns:atom="http://www.w3.org/2005/Atom"
>
```

1. Provide feed information, including the required title, link, and description elements, as well as optional elements such as lastBuildDate and language.

```
<title>John Smith photography</title>
<link>http:// example.com/</link>
<description>The news feed of Alaskan photographer John Smith.</description>
<lastBuildDate>Fri, 10 Feb 2012 14:47:00 GMT-0900</lastBuildDate>
<language>en-US</language>
```

2. Provide news items. To create a valid RSS 2.0 feed channel with the highest level of interoperability, each item should have the following elements: title, link, description, pubDate, and guid.

```
<item>
    <title>Photo exhibition</title>
    <link>http://example.com/events/</link>
    <pubDate>Fri, 10 Feb 2012 14:47:00 GMT-0900</pubDate>
    <dc:creator>John Smith</dc:creator>
    <category>Events</category>
    <guid>http://example.com/events/</guid>
    <description>Best shots of 2011</description>
    <content:encoded><![CDATA[ My photo exhibition ↵
        <a href="http://example.com/events/">Best shots of 2011</a> takes place at the ↵
        Moose Hotel in Anchorage, AK, USA on 17-18 February 2012. ]]></content:encoded>
</item>
```

This is the section that can be copy-pasted and then modified each time the feed channel is updated with the latest news. The next news should be provided before the latest one, that is, earlier in the source code.

3. Validate.

4. Share. News feeds are usually used by linking to the XML file that contains them.[5] To use the built-in RSS reader of modern browsers, a link should be provided in the (X)HTML document head. Here's an example:

```
<link rel="alternate" type="application/rss+xml" title="John Smith photography" ↵
    href="http://www.example.com/rss.xml" />
```

This makes it possible for browsers to recognize that the current web page has an RSS news feed.

Making Web Sites Valid Through Redesign

The stricter the markup, the easier to upgrade it to a newer markup version. However, in certain cases, migrating to another standard is not feasible without completely rewriting the site. Regarding style sheets, valid CSS 2.1 can be easily extended with CSS3 features in most cases. Still, standardizing an existing site can be a difficult task.

---

[5]Another option is to retrieve the desired number of channel items with scripting. If you want to publish the latest news as part of a web page rather than a separate file, you need a script that opens the file, retrieves the contents of the news feed items, and generates the corresponding markup code.

Generally, there are two possibilities: rewrite the whole site from scratch or manually standardize each page (or page template) one by one. Both seem to need much more work than developers can afford. The first approach often results in broken links. The second approach requires lots of time and work (unless the site is very small) and can be performed in only a few cases.

The World Wide Web Consortium suggests a solution: carefully selected sections should be updated systematically [1]. The most frequently served (most popular) documents can be identified by the Log Validator, which also tries to find n invalid documents among the most popular ones (as discussed in the previous chapter). Certainly, the whole project is affected by the deadline and the affordable workload.

Summary

In this chapter, you saw a series of step-by-step guides for manually creating fundamental web site components character by character. By learning the semantic use of structural elements, you are now capable of creating meaningful markup with a logical flow and a perfect DOM. The carefully created markup provides a high level of interoperability and can be rendered in virtually any browser running on any kind of device without multiple site versions. Even if CSS is disabled, the headings, paragraphs, lists, and other site components remain legible, and the content is accessible to not only the latest browsers but also to very old versions and mobile browsers with limited capabilities and standard support.

In the next chapter, you will learn widely used standard-compliant best practices that can be applied in your daily work.

Reference

1. Thereaux O (2011) Making your web site valid: a step by step guide. World Wide Web Consortium. http://www.w3.org/QA/2002/09/Step-by-step. Accessed 2 November 2014

■ ■ ■

Best Practices

Beyond optimal markup and styles provided by the proper implementation of web standards, there are designing conventions that are browser-independent, reliable, and satisfactory, and considered as best practices. It is important to know the techniques that provide standard-compliant code and distinguish them from those tricks and hacks that cause incorrect markup or decrease interoperability.

By now you should know the major web standards for markup, styles, news feeds, and other web site components. It is time to learn how to apply these standards in practice, which can be used in the daily work of web designers. Even standard-compliant web pages do not necessarily provide content in a meaningful, logical manner; thus, you should learn the purpose of markup elements and CSS properties to maximize web page quality. The ultimate aim is to find the right combination of structure, presentation, and behavior and to separate them to maximize the benefits of web standards.

Appropriately Used Elements

A crucial decision in web design is which elements to implement for representing your content and achieving the desired web site behavior. The general rules can be summarized as follows:

- Tables for tabular data

- Floating elements instead of tables for positioned components (very bad practice)

- Headers instead of general paragraphs

- Paragraphs instead of separate lines with break rows (very bad practice)

- Paragraphs for text paragraphs instead of divisions

- Definition lists for terms and their descriptions instead of general paragraphs

- Headers, articles, and sections instead of general div containers (HTML5)

- The audio and video elements instead of general object embeddings (HTML5)

Violating any of these rules is usually a gross error even if the web site validates.

Content in Logical Order

Even though CSS styling makes it possible to arbitrarily position document sections and elements, content should be written in a logical order. This approach has the following advantages:

- Easier development and maintenance

- Higher efficiency in text-based browsers

- Legible and usable content even without CSS (in case the .css file cannot be loaded or the style sheets are turned off)

- Improved accessibility through advanced support for aural browsers and screen readers that will read the pages without breaking continuity

Mobile-Friendly Layout

In Responsive Web Design, you can create conditional styles with CSS3 to be applied depending on the screen resolution. On smartphones, even if the resolution is huge, it is more convenient to have a collapsed, easy-to-tap menu than a wide menu on a full-width page. Tablets usually have bigger screens, while desktop monitors are even bigger in size, but the resolution of smaller screens is not necessarily smaller than that of big monitors. The best practice is to create the core styles for the site, and create conditional style override for the different screen resolution ranges using min-width and/or max-width, and a font size proportionally bigger for smaller screens (Listing 13-1). *Mobile First Design* means that the core styles are designed for mobile devices and the style override adjusts the layout and font size to bigger screens while the standard approach is just the opposite.

Listing 13-1. Conditional CSS3 Styles for Different Screen Resolution Ranges

```
@media (min-width:320px) {

  body{
    background: none;
  }

  #content {
    width: 300px;
    font-size: 7.2vw;
  }
}

@media (min-width:480px) {

  #content {
    width: 460px;
    font-size: 5.9vw;
  }

}
```

```
@media (min-width:1025px) and (max-width: 2560px) {

  #content {
    width: 960px;
    font-size: 3vw;
  }

}
```

In this example, the first ruleset is applied on small-resolution screens of entry-level and older smartphones and phones in portrait orientation; the second ruleset is applied to smartphones in landscape orientation with a resolution anywhere between 480px and 1024px; while the third ruleset is used on high-resolution tablets in landscape orientation, as well as on ultrabooks, laptops, and desktop computers.

Browser-independent design with liquid layout is ideal in all cases where the design allows content positioning in a way that it spans the entire page width according to the available space (expands or contracts as required[1]). Note that high-resolution displays are often found on relatively small devices with very high pixel density such as modern tablets where the font size has to be changed proportionally, otherwise the text becomes illegible.

Sizes and Proportions

Style sheet validity does not guarantee proper sizes and proportions. The selection of CSS units has a large impact on the overall appearance of web page components, as well as the usability and readability of the content.

Lengths in Relative Units

The relative units of CSS (em and %), which are computed according to a feature of another element, should be used for lengths. In Responsive Web Design, the font size is set proportionally to the viewport size, as discussed earlier (vw, vh, vmin, vmax).

The absolute units such as inches, centimeters, points, and pica can be used only if the physical characteristics of the target media are known. A typical example is a printing option of a web page where the default output for an official document can be in 12pt Times New Roman with 2.5 cm margins on a standard-sized paper, such as the North American letter paper (8.5×11″) or standard A4 paper (210×297 mm, ISO 216 international standard [1]).

Combine Units Properly

The em unit can be used in CSS to provide scalable styles. It is a general unit for measuring lengths such as page margins or element paddings. It allows developers to specify several CSS properties relative to the current font size. Consequently, margins declared in this unit stay in proportion even if the user magnifies the font size.

To ease the calculation of font sizes expressed in em, user experience expert Richard Rutter introduced a technique that applies a font size of 62.5 percent on the body element (Listing 13-2) [2].

Listing 13-2. The Rutter Method

```
body {
  font-size: 62.5%;
}
```

---

[1]Liquid layout works not only for different resolutions, but also for resized windows on the same resolution.

Since 62.5 percent of the 16px default size used by many user agent style sheets is 10px, the previous rule makes the font size of the paragraphs styled by the rule in Listing 13-3 be 12 pixels because $1.2 \cdot 10 = 12px$.

Listing 13-3. Font Size Easily Calculated Using the Rutter Method

```
p {
  font-size: 1.2em;
}
```

■ **Caution**   Although widely implemented, this value is not completely reliable and might be different in some browsers.

Although em-based sizing could be used to ensure readable font sizes on any screen, this approach has a known issue. If the user changes the default font size or applies zooming in the browser, the text might become unreadable. On the other hand, font sizes set in pixels are robust in different environments but not proportional to other elements and the screen. The larger the resolution, the smaller the font size. Moreover, the built-in text zoom of browsers cannot be used in all cases for content with pixel-based font sizes.

■ **Note**   Because of the differences between browsers, font sizing on the Web is challenging. Absolute positioned content is not scaled uniformly in all cases by the magnifier feature in IE7+ (sometimes they are scaled smaller). IE supports both zooming and text size changes for fonts set with %, em, or named sizes. Firefox 3+ supports both zooming and text size changes. Opera 9+ also has a zooming feature. Zooming might give different results under different browsers, depending on the content and the styles associated with the page.

Embedding External Content Properly

Since the Web is a truly full multimedia platform, web pages often have embedded video clips, interactive objects, and other external components. Because of the incorrect embedding codes provided by the content resources, however, additional tasks are required in many cases to make them standard-compliant. Moreover, standardization cannot be performed sometimes because of the inadequate code provided along with the embedding code. Even if web developers standardize the invalid embedding code, they cannot correct the associated namespaces, scripts, and other components. A good example is the classic "Like" box of Facebook[2]. The namespace and vocabulary provided with the embedding code generated in the developers' section on Facebook.com are not consistent. One of the "solutions" developers use on the Web is to add the incorrect markup section to a JavaScript function such as the one in Listing 13-4, which writes the markup fragment delimited by apostrophes into the (X)HTML source.[3]

Listing 13-4. A Widely Used Trick to Embed Invalid Code

```
document.write('<script src="http://connect.facebook.net/en_US/all.js#xfbml=1"></script>↵
 <fb:like-box href="http://www.facebook.com/pages/Your-page/122946805997761" width="280"↵
 show_faces="true" stream="false" header="false"></fb:like-box>');
```

---

[2]Fortunately, Facebook provides a valid HTML5 embedding code for "Like" buttons and boxes since fall 2011. However, the classic embedding code is still used on many websites.
[3]Assuming that JavaScript is enabled.

The same fragment gives error messages in validators if it is written directly in the markup. The `iframe` version of the button has problems too because it cannot be used in XHTML. It can be rewritten as an `object` (with the same parameters), but then it stops working. Users of APIs and third-party software components often apply the previous trick if they want their web page to validate.

■ **Caution**   Providing markup code with `document.write` in JavaScript is a hack that you should not use. The same trick is applied for validating virtually any kind of otherwise incorrect markup that definitely cannot be accepted by real web standardistas. The document will validate only because the content written in the external `.js` file is ignored by the validator. This code is still not valid! How to provide such content without sacrificing either functionality or validity is an open question in many cases, though.

Embedding YouTube Videos as Valid XHTML or HTML5

YouTube, the popular video sharing portal offers two types of embedding codes for videos:

- The older-style embed code applies the `object` element with parameters and an `embed` element. It supports Flash playback only.

- The new embed code uses an `iframe` and supports both Flash and HTML5 video content.

Under each video on YouTube, there is a Share button that provides a link to the current video with options such as long link, HD link, and declaring a starting position for playback. After clicking on the Embed link, a text box appears with the selected new-type embedding code ready for copying to the clipboard. Below that text box there are further options for customizing the embedding code, such as declaring the size[4] or using the old-style embed code.

From the standardization point of view, both versions need some improvement.

In XHTML, the following issues should be addressed:

- The `embed` element contained by the older-style embedding code is invalid in XHTML.

- The `iframe` element used by the new-style embedding code cannot be used in XHTML 1.0 Strict or XHTML 1.1 (only in XHTML 1.0 Transitional, which should not be used). Moreover, the `data` and `type` attributes should be provided to maximize interoperability (without them, the embedding will not work under certain browsers). However, providing the `data` attribute while preserving the `movie` parameter from the suggested embedding code ensures browser-independence, because some rendering engines will use the outer declaration (the value of the `data` attribute on the `object` element), and others will use the inner declaration (the value of the `movie` parameter) to identify the resource URL (similarly to the Flash Satay method used for Flash embedding covered in Chapter 9).

In HTML5, the following issues should be addressed:

- If you prefer the new-style embedding code, the `frameborder` and `allowscreen` attributes should not be used on the `iframe` element.

- If you want to use the old-style code, the `data` and `type` attributes are missing from the `object` element. Moreover, the `param` elements as well as the `embed` element should be closed using the shorthand notation rather than the closing tags `</param>` and `</embed>`.

---

[4]The size can also be modified arbitrarily later in the markup when using the embedding code.

Suppose we want to embed the video with the embedding code presented in Listings 13-5 and 13-6.

Listing 13-5. New Embed Code for Example Video Suggested by YouTube

```
<iframe width="560" height="315" src="//www.youtube.com/embed/WgL7DMiTCAY" frameborder="0"
allowfullscreen></iframe>
```

Listing 13-6. Old-Style Embed Code for Example Video Suggested by YouTube

```
<object width="560" height="315"><param name="movie" value="//www.youtube.com/v/
WgL7DMiTCAY?hl=en_US&amp;version=3"></param><param name="allowFullScreen" value="true">
</param><param name="allowscriptaccess" value="always"></param><embed src="//www.youtube.com/v/
WgL7DMiTCAY?hl=en_US&amp;version=3" type="application/x-shockwave-flash" width="560" height="315"
allowscriptaccess="always" allowfullscreen="true"></embed></object>
```

In XHTML, the old-style embedding should be preferred and modified accordingly (Listing 13-7).

Listing 13-7. The Standardized Embedding Code in XHTML/HTML5

```
<p>
  <object type="application/x-shockwave-flash"
   data="//www.youtube.com/v/WgL7DMiTCAY?hl=en_US&amp;version=3"↵
   width="560" height="315">
    <param name="movie"↵
     value="//www.youtube.com/v/WgL7DMiTCAY?hl=en_US&amp;version=3" />
    <param name="allowFullScreen" value="true" />
    <param name="allowscriptaccess" value="always" />
  </object>
</p>
```

■ **Note** The nesting rules of the applied document type should not be forgotten. In XHTML 1.0 Strict, the `object` element should be wrapped in a container element such as `div` or `p`; otherwise, the code will not validate.

The same code can also be used in HTML5, where the embed element could also be preserved; however, it can be safely removed: the first two lines ensure browser-independence. In HTML5, the new-style embedding code can also be used. It can be standardized by removing the `frameborder` and `allowfullscreen` attributes (Listing 13-8).

Listing 13-8. A Standard-Compliant YouTube Embedding in (X)HTML5

```
<iframe width="560" height="315" src="//www.youtube.com/v/WgL7DMiTCAY?hl=en_US&amp;version=3">
</iframe>
```

Embedding Google Maps as Valid XHTML or HTML5

A popular way of defining the position of offices, restaurants, and so on, on web sites is embedding interactive Google Maps objects.

The source code provided by Google Maps looks like Listing 13-9.

Listing 13-9. A Google Maps Embedding Code Provided by Google

```
<iframe width="425" height="350" frameborder="0" scrolling="no" marginheight="0" marginwidth="0"
src="http://maps.google.com/maps?f=q&amp;source=s_q&amp;hl=en&amp;geocode=&amp;q=Honolulu,+HI,+United+
States&amp;sll=37.0625,-95.677068&amp;sspn=50.557552,89.208984&amp;ie=UTF8&amp;hq=&amp;hnear=Honolulu,
+Hawaii&amp;ll=21.306944,-157.858333&amp;spn=0.234454,0.479279&amp;t=h&amp;z=12&amp;output=embed">
</iframe><br /><small><a href="http://maps.google.com/maps?f=q&amp;source=embed&amp;hl=en&amp;
geocode=&amp;q=Honolulu,+HI,+United+States&amp;sll=37.0625,-95.677068&amp;sspn=50.557552,89.208984&amp;
ie=UTF8&amp;hq=&amp;hnear=Honolulu,+Hawaii&amp;ll=21.306944,-157.858333&amp;spn=0.234454,0.479279&amp;
t=h&amp;z=12" style="color:#0000FF;text-align:left">View Larger Map</a></small>
```

However, this code is not standard-compliant. In HTML5, the `frameborder`, `scrolling`, `marginheight`, and `marginwidth` attributes should be removed (styling should be achieved through CSS). In XHTML, the embedding code should be modified as follows:

- Since the inline frame element (`iframe`) cannot be used in XHTML 1.0 Strict and XHTML 1.1, it should be replaced by the `object` tag.

- The `type` attribute should be defined with the value `text/html`; otherwise, the map will not appear even if the code is valid.

- The `src` attribute should be replaced by the `data` attribute.

- The `frameborder`, `scrolling`, `marginheight`, and `marginwidth` attributes should be removed.

- The `object` element should be enclosed by a `p` or `div` container element.

- Styles should be defined by CSS to fit into page design (if the default appearance is not acceptable).

The result should be in the form presented in Listing 13-10.

Listing 13-10. A Standardized Version of the Embedding Code in Listing 13-9

```
<p>
  <object type="text/html" width="425" height="350" data="http://maps.google.com/maps?f=↵
  q&amp;source=s_q&amp;hl=en&amp;geocode=&amp;q=Honolulu,+HI,+United+States&amp;↵
  sll=37.0625,-95.677068&amp;sspn=50.557552,89.208984&amp;ie=UTF8&amp;hq=&amp;↵
  hnear=Honolulu,+Hawaii&amp;ll=21.306944,-157.858333&amp;spn=0.234454,0.479279&amp;↵
  t=h&amp;z=12&amp;output=embed">
  </object>

  <a href="http://maps.google.com/maps?f=q&amp;source=embed&amp;hl=en&amp;geocode=&amp;↵
  q=Honolulu,+HI,+United+States&amp;sll=37.0625,-95.677068&amp;sspn=50.557552,↵
  89.208984&amp;ie=UTF8&amp;hq=&amp;hnear=Honolulu,+Hawaii&amp;ll=21.306944,↵
  -157.858333&amp;spn=0.234454,0.479279&amp;t=h&amp;z=12">View Larger Map</a>
</p>
```

This embedding code works on all modern browsers and validates as XHTML 1.0 Strict, XHTML 1.1, and HTML5. There is just one issue with (X)HTML documents embedded with the object element: the layer order set by z-index in the CSS is ignored by older versions of Internet Explorer.

Semantic Web Best Practices

The World Wide Web Consortium provides Semantic Web best practices on implementing RDF Schema and OWL, and use them with object-oriented programming languages [3]. *Image Annotation on the Semantic Web* [4] describes the importance and advantages of image metadata, and provides guidelines for semantic image annotation and use cases. Further documents on Linked Data and controlled vocabularies are the *Best Practices for Publishing Linked Data* [5], the *Linked Data Platform Best Practices and Guidelines* [6], and the *Best Practice Recipes for Publishing RDF Vocabularies* [7].

WAI-ARIA Best Practices

The W3C WAI-ARIA Authoring Practices Guide describes best practices for developing rich Internet applications [8]. Approaches are recommended to create accessible widgets, keyboard navigation, form properties, drag-and-drop support, relationships, dialog boxes, and reusable component libraries.

Mobile Web Best Practices

More and more users browse the Internet on smartphones and tablets with smaller screen size, limited bandwidth, and a less convenient interface than desktop computers. Mobile-optimized web pages should be designed and served in the appropriate manner to provide a reasonable user experience. The specific features of mobile devices should be taken into account when designing for mobile media [9]. The most important considerations are as follows [10]:

- *Limited bandwidth*: Techniques such as compression, caching, and minimized data size can contribute to a better user experience for 3G and 4G mobile browsing[5]. Cookies and redirections should be eliminated whenever possible.

- *Limited processing capacity*: A large DOM, huge background images, a large number of scripts, and so on, can increase processing time. As a result, users will have to wait for relatively long periods of time, which should be avoided. Simple markup can be provided for mobile devices with XHTML Basic [11]. As for styles, CSS has a profile dedicated to mobile devices [12]. Note that smartphone processors became very powerful in the early 2010s, featuring multi-core architectures with a relatively high clock rate that do not have limited processing capacity anymore.

- *Limited technology support*: Do not rely on scripts, embedded objects, cookies, or style sheets. Tabular presentation should be minimized. Since mobile browsers usually support a small set of file types only, download sections should warn users of files provided in formats poorly supported by mobile devices.

---

[5]Smartphones are often connected to the Internet through WiFi unless the user is on the go.

- *Smaller interface*: The automatic sign-in feature and unchanged focus on dynamically updated pages can make the use of mobile applications more convenient. Preselected default values should be provided where possible. Default text entry mode, language, and/or input format should be specified [13]. The small screen size should be taken into account for sizing and positioning. Absolute units and pixel measures should be eliminated.

- *Harder navigation*: The simpler the top navigation, the easier to use on mobile devices. Link targets should be clearly identified. Access keys used for accessibility might also ease navigation.

- *Flexibility*: If devices are classified, the user experience can be boosted significantly. Providing alternate content for JavaScript is important.

- *Mobile-specific features*: Certain web page components can be exploited more on mobile devices than on computers. Telephone numbers, for example, should be provided with a direct calling feature. Physical addresses should be easy to forward to the GPS application.

Rendering web sites on mobile devices require optimization. Pop-up windows should be completely eliminated. Graphical components should not be used for spacing. The use of image maps should be reduced. Bad practices such as frames or table-based layouts should be avoided because they can make web pages unusable on mobile devices.

Providing Robustness

Web developers should ensure that the content can be used even if some technologies cannot be used or fail. Some common examples are discussed in the following sections.

Declaring Fallback Generic Fonts

Because of the endless variety of fonts available for computers, it cannot be guaranteed that a special font exists in each browser. One of the *generic font families* defined by the CSS specification, that is, serif, sans-serif, cursive, fantasy, and monospace [14], should always be specified. Let's look at an example of text provided in Gill Sans, which is not available for all users. The rule shown in Listing 13-11 can be applied; it ensures that the document text will be rendered with Gill Sans when available and any other sans-serif font when not. Depending on the browser and configuration applied, it might be Arial, Helvetica, or a similar font.

Listing 13-11. A Fallback Mechanism for Fonts

```
body {
  font-family: "Gill Sans", sans-serif;
}
```

Certainly, you can specify further (preferably similar) fonts of the same type as well (Listing 13-12), from which the first available will be applied, but the generic font family declaration will always work.

Listing 13-12. A List of Similar Fonts Preceding the Generic Font Family

```
body {
  font-family: "Gill Sans", "London", "Corinthian", sans-serif;
}
```

Declarations with Appropriate Specificity

Web developers often have to choose from a variety of settings and options. As a general rule, declarations should be defined in a way that obtains the desired effect or functionality on the widest range of devices and settings. For example, the color names reliably supported by CSS are limited to 16 colors (as discussed in Chapter 5). Although they are known by all browsers and seem developer-friendly, the hexadecimal notation should be preferred because there is no ultimate color list for the Web. Certain browsers support additional color names, but they are not standardized. There is no reason to mix the basic color names and other color notations in the CSS. After all, hexadecimal notation can produce virtually any color.

Testing

Since several web site features cannot be guaranteed by standardization, testing is vital in most cases.

Rendering in Multiple Browsers

Because of the differences of rendering engines, markup, and style, validity cannot ensure proper rendering under different user agents. Consequently, the legibility and functionality of web sites should be checked on all major browsers before publishing.[6] The more sophisticated the site design, the more complicated it is to provide similar rendering under different browsers. There are freely available, browser-independent style sheets that eliminate this time-consuming task. Good examples are the W3C Core Styles [15].

Readability Without Styles

An advanced method for testing web sites is to render them with the default style sheet of the browser. Properly structured, logically constructed web documents remain legible without the style sheet(s) developed for them. This test is also useful for checking content accessibility.

Summary

In this chapter, you learned standardized best practices that should be differentiated from the trends introduced by enthusiastic content authors and developers. You can safely apply these time-proven techniques in almost all scenarios and improve the overall web page quality, from code optimality to robust rendering.

The standard compliance of web sites created using the techniques and standards presented so far should be approved by validation, which will be described in the next chapter.

---

[6]As discussed in the previous chapter, some browsers provide the option to render web pages with different rendering engines, and there are more and more plug-ins available for testing browser-independence on tabs.

References

1. ISO (2011) Writing paper and certain classes of printed matter – Trimmed sizes – A and B series, and indication of machine direction. ISO 216:2007. International Organization for Standardization. http://www.iso.org/iso/iso_catalogue/catalogue_tc/catalogue_detail.htm?csnumber=36631. Accessed 2 November 2014

2. Rutter R (2004) How to size text using ems. Richard Rutter. http://clagnut.com/blog/348. Accessed 2 November 2014

3. Knublauch H, Oberle D, Tetlow P, Wallace E (eds) (2006) A Semantic Web Primer for Object-Oriented Software Developers. World Wide Web Consortium. http://www.w3.org/TR/sw-oosd-primer/. Accessed 2 November 2014

4. Troncy R, van Ossenbruggen J, Pan JZ, Stamou G (eds), Halaschek-Wiener C, Simou N, Tzouvaras V (2007) Image Annotation on the Semantic Web. World Wide Web Consortium. http://www.w3.org/2005/Incubator/mmsem/XGR-image-annotation/. Accessed 2 November 2014

5. Hyland B, Atemezing G, Villazón-Terrazas B (eds) (2014) Best Practices for Publishing Linked Data. World Wide Web Consortium. http://www.w3.org/TR/ld-bp/. Accessed 2 November 2014

6. Burleson C, Gutiérrez ME, Mihindukulasooriya N (eds) (2014) Linked Data Platform Best Practices and Guidelines. World Wide Web Consortium. http://www.w3.org/TR/ldp-bp/. Accessed 2 November 2014

7. Berrueta D, Phipps J (eds) (2008) Best Practice Recipes for Publishing RDF Vocabularies. World Wide Web Consortium. http://www.w3.org/TR/swbp-vocab-pub/. Accessed 2 November 2014

8. Scheuhammer J, Cooper M (eds) (2013) WAI-ARIA 1.0 Authoring Practices. An author's guide to understanding and implementing Accessible Rich Internet Applications. World Wide Web Consortium. http://www.w3.org/TR/wai-aria-practices/. Accessed 2 November 2014

9. Connors A, Sullivan B (eds) W3C (2010) Mobile Web Application Best Practices. W3C Recommendation. World Wide Web Consortium. http://www.w3.org/TR/mwabp/. Accessed 2 November 2014

10. W3C (2014) Mobile Web Application Best Practices Cards. World Wide Web Consortium. http://www.w3.org/2010/09/MWABP/. Accessed 2 November 2014

11. McCarron S, Ishikawa M (eds) (2010) XHTML Basic 1.1 Second Edition. W3C Recommendation. World Wide Web Consortium. http://www.w3.org/TR/xhtml-basic/. Accessed 2 November 2014

12. Bos B (ed) (2014) CSS Mobile Profile 2.0. World Wide Web Consortium. http://www.w3.org/TR/css-mobile/. Accessed 2 November 2014

13. W3C (2010) Mobile Web Best Practices. W3C Cheatsheet. World Wide Web Consortium. http://www.w3.org/2009/cheatsheet/#mwbp. Accessed 2 November 2014

14. Bos B, Çelik T, Hickson I, Lie HW (eds) (2010) Generic font families. In: Cascading Style Sheets Level 2 Revision 1 (CSS 2.1) Specification. World Wide Web Consortium. http://www.w3.org/TR/2010/WD-CSS2-20101207/fonts.html#generic-font-families. Accessed 2 November 2014

15. Bos B (2009) W3C Core Styles. World Wide Web Consortium. http://www.w3.org/StyleSheets/Core/Overview.html. Accessed 2 November 2014

Validation

The various computer languages used on the Web, including but not limited to (X)HTML, CSS, RDF, and RSS, provide structure, style, metadata, semantics, and other document features. Similar to natural languages, they have their own grammar, vocabulary, and syntax that need to be followed. However, just like the grammar, structural, or spelling errors that occur in documents written in natural languages, web documents might also have errors in them. Validation is the task of checking the source code of web documents against a DTD or schema. It contributes to error-free, clean code and increases overall web page quality.

Even a single character might affect your carefully created standard-compliant code, so it is important to regularly check your documents. After achieving the necessary routine, you are able to modify or extend web documents at the source level without violating standard compliance. In this chapter, you will learn about the tools that help you locate and correct errors if they occur and can assure you whether your code is error-free.

Concepts

Markup language grammar rules are defined by Document Type Definitions (DTDs). Prior to HTML5/XHTML5, developers should have provided a reference to the DTD associated with the document type being used (as discussed in Chapter 3).

Web documents can be verified against these rules, which is called *validation*. The tools used to perform validation are called *validators*. Documents successfully passing validation are claimed to be *valid*; in other words, they are free of errors and do not contain incorrectly used elements or attributes. However, validation guarantees neither well-structuredness nor proper element use [1]. A valid document follows the grammar rules outlined in the corresponding DTD, which makes it possible for user agents to construct the DOM correctly and render the document accurately.

Applying the grammar rules defined in DTDs is described in *technical specifications*, most of which are published by W3C.

Standard conformance is the feature of those web documents that fulfill all the requirements described by the appropriate DTD and specification. A web document is valid when it is correctly written in accordance to the *formal grammar* included in the technical specification of the corresponding markup language, whereas conformance relates to the entire specification. Since some conformance requirements, such as the proper use of attribute values, cannot be described by the formal grammar, validity is only part of conformance. Consequently, validity and conformance might be identical, but the latter one is a wider term.

Valid documents are written according to the formal grammar of the language being used. Standard-compliant documents apply the technology the recommended way.

Validation should not be considered as the final step right before web site launch. Instead, it should be performed as an essential part of web site development. For beginners who cannot write new markup elements and attributes correctly with 100 percent certainty, validation can help identify potential errors and prevent invalid markup from being duplicated or multiplied. Even experienced web designers might find validation useful and consider it an assistance rather than a mandatory task. After inserting new structural elements to the source, for example, it can be

445

more than inconvenient to identify the numerous—and often identical—closing tags (such as four to five or more consecutive `</div>` tags). While finding start tag–end tag pairs is very easy in a file containing 100–200 lines, the task can be overwhelming for larger files.[1]

No matter how experienced a developer is or how sophisticated development tools are used, errors are inevitable. This is where validators can help the work of web designers. As you will see, validators provide error locations, along with hints for possible causes and potential solutions.

Since validation contributes to overall web page quality, validators and advanced specific checkers are also known as *web quality assurance* tools [2].

Markup Validation

The primary validator for HTML/XHTML documents is the W3C Markup Validation Service at `http://validator.w3.org`. In fact, Markup Validation Service v1.3 can be used to validate several types of markup [3], including the following:

- *HTML*: ISO/IEC 15445:2000 ("ISO HTML"), HTML 2.0, HTML 3.2, HTML 4.01 Frameset, HTML 4.01 Transitional, and HTML5

- *MathML*: MathML 2.0

- *SMIL*: SMIL 1.0, SMIL 2.0

- *SVG*: SVG 1.0, SVG 1.1, SVG 1.1 Basic, SVG 1.1 Tiny

- *XHTML*: XHTML Basic 1.0, XHTML Basic 1.1, XHTML 1.0 Frameset, XHTML 1.0 Strict, XHTML 1.0 Transitional, and XHTML 1.1, XHTML Mobile Profile 1.2, XHTML Print 1.0, and XHTML5

- *Mixed-namespace documents*: XHTML + RDFa[2], XHTML 1.1 + MathML 2.0, and XHTML 1.1 + MathML 2.0 + SVG 1.1

The W3C Markup Validation Service offers three options to validate web documents:

- *Validation by direct input*: Validation of the markup provided in a textbox. The code can be either typed directly or copy-pasted from an advanced text editor. This is suitable for testing. Since there is no physical file to validate, neither character encoding nor server settings can be checked by direct input.

- *Validation by file uploading*: Validation of a file uploaded to a temporary folder. Character encoding can also be checked. Experienced web designers do not use this option frequently because the file can be uploaded to the host (final destination) with the same effort (in the case of static files).

- *Validation by URI*: Validation of an uploaded version on a web server. This is the ultimate validation that validates markup, character encoding, and server settings. It's ideal for final checking and the validation of web pages developed by others.

---

[1]Even if there are tools that represent the hierarchy with vertical dotted lines between the opening and closing tag pairs (e.g., Notepad++).

[2]The RDFa notation can be perfectly validated in XHTML documents. As of 2011, the Validator still does not recognize RDFa in HTML5, however, and gives errors.

The W3C validator supports the following character encodings: UTF-8, UTF-16, ISO-8859-1, ISO-8859-2, ISO-8859-3, ISO-8859-4, ISO-8859-5, ISO-8859-6-i, ISO-8859-7, ISO-8859-8, ISO-8859-8-i, ISO-8859-9, ISO-8859-10, ISO-8859-11, ISO-8859-13, ISO-8859-14, ISO-8859-15, ISO-8859-16, US-ASCII, EUC-JP, Shift_JIS, ISO-2022-jp, EUC-kr, gb2312, gb18030, big5, Big5-HKSCS, tis-620, koi8-r, koi8-u, ISO-ir-111, Macintosh, Windows-1250, Windows-1251, Windows-1252, Windows-1253, Windows-1254, Windows-1255, Windows-1256, and Windows-1257.

Both document type and character encoding are detected automatically and used for validation accordingly. If detection is not possible, the validator assumes the document type and/or character encoding; however, the results might be unreliable. Properly served standard-compliant web documents always provide both data; thus, the validator performs validation accurately. The validator can also be forced manually to use certain document type and/or character encoding; however, this feature should not be used in general cases. It should be considered a fallback mechanism rather than an overriding feature.

If there are errors in the markup, they are clearly indicated by the red stripe and the number of errors (Figure 14-1). Even the favicon of the page becomes a red square.

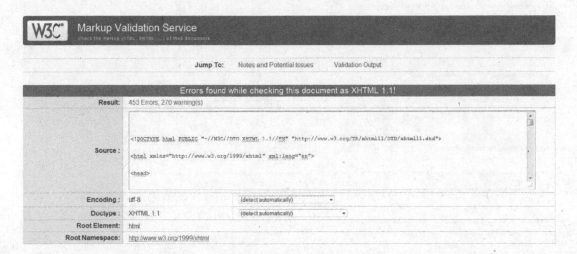

Figure 14-1. *The red stripe and the number of errors and warnings clearly show that the markup is invalid*

The consecutive errors and potential errors are listed under the summary sequentially by default, in other words, in the order of occurrence (location in the markup). This behavior can be overridden to group error messages by error type. Since many errors can cause further ones (such as a missing closing tag), sequential checking is appropriate in most cases.

■ **Tip** Because of the high potential of correlation between markup errors, it might be convenient to correct some errors only (especially if the document is full of errors) and then revalidate the document. The number of errors might decrease exponentially. Revalidation is also useful for testing implementations of special or new markup specifications as a direct input.

There are several advanced settings of the Markup Validation Service you can use for your standardization projects. The (X)HTML source code can be displayed with the error messages directly linking to the corresponding lines. This is a useful feature for developers. The tree structure of document headings can be visualized by the outline option, which makes it easier to realize which header is missed (if any). Custom 404 error pages sent by the server can be validated by ticking the checkbox "Validate error pages." Beyond the concise reports provided by default, more explanations and longer suggestions can be requested with the Verbose Output option. Another option of the W3C Markup Validation Service is to correct markup errors using the HTML Tidy tool discussed in Chapter 11.

Beyond the error location, the Markup Validation Service gives hints for corrections and links to the corresponding specifications and FAQs (Figure 14-2). Some of the characters might be highlighted, which is another aid, and sometimes makes the detection of invalid characters very easy.

Figure 14-2. *The W3C Markup Validation Service clearly indicates error locations and provides useful hints for correction*

The markup validation results and suggestions are useful not only for the less experienced developers but also for experts. Using the line numbers, it is fairly easy to find errors, which is a prerequisite for correcting them even for those who do not rely on the correction tips.

After the necessary corrections and the final revalidation, the result should look like Figure 14-3.

Figure 14-3. *The green stripe and the result "Passed" indicate that the markup is valid*

───

■ **Note**   Validating HTML5 is still an experimental feature at the W3C Markup Validation Service, and the validator will give a warning (not error) even if the web page being analyzed is valid. The validator does not recognize RDFa annotations in HTML5, nor XHTML5 documents.[3] Furthermore, in contrast to valid XHTML documents, the validator does not provide validation badges with hyperlinks for valid HTML5 documents. As will be discussed later, such badges can be downloaded from a separate site.

───

The W3C Markup Validator is not only free but also open source and available under the W3C Software License [4]. Anyone is welcome to set up mirrors of the service or contribute to its development.

Although there are other markup validators on the Web, such as the WDG HTML Validator [5], or offline tools such as Firefox's *HTML Validator* plug-in [6], using the W3C Markup Validation Service is recommended. It is part of W3C Unicorn, which can be used if styles sheets and feed channels are also validated (see later in section "W3C Unicorn").

───

[3]The XML declaration and all namespace declarations provided in XHTML5 result in an error message, even if they are valid. Moreover, the validation result of XHTML5 documents states HTML5 instead of XHTML5.

449

Validating markup is more complicated for developers of dynamic web sites since markup validators generally cannot deal with server-side scripts such as PHP. Checking the dynamically generated (X)HTML output, performing corrections, and revalidating documents are all real challenges. This is one of the major reasons why dynamically generated web pages are often invalid.

Validating XML

XML documents can be validated for conformance with a DTD, an XML schema, or the RELAX NG schema language. Syntactic well-formedness is a basic requirement, but it does not guarantee XML validity, which has several constraints, such as proper use of required and optional elements and attributes, correct document structure and syntax, and properly applied data types.

Although XML validation and parsing are logically independent tasks, both are often performed by XML parsers. Considering that even a single error can prevent the document from being parsed or its tree structure shown, XML parsers of web browsers can always be used as basic XML validators.

XML validity is not required by all XML parsers but by the XML parsers that check the document against its associated schema.

Batch validation of XML files can be performed by the xmlvalidate task of Apache Ant [7]. For example, the target in Listing 14-1 validates the .xml files in the directory specified by the dir attribute.[4]

Listing 14-1. Validating XML with xmlvalidate

```
<target name="validate-xml">
  <xmlvalidate lenient="no">
    <fileset dir="semweb/ont" includes="*.xml" />
    <attribute name="http://xml.org/sax/features/validation" value="true"/>
    <attribute name="http://apache.org/xml/features/validation/schema" value="true"/>
    <attribute name="http://xml.org/sax/features/namespaces" value="true"/>
  </xmlvalidate>
</target>
```

Validating RDF/XML

RDF documents written in the XML serialization format (RDF/XML) can be checked with the W3C RDF Validation Service at www.w3.org/RDF/Validator [8]. Validations can be performed by URI or direct input. The Validator not only checks the RDF code but also represents RDF triples (Figure 14-4).

---

[4]Relative to the Ant build file.

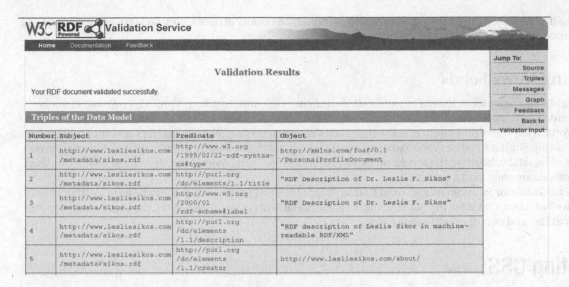

Figure 14-4. *Subject–predicate–object triples retrieved from a valid RDF file*

Optionally, the RDF graph can be generated in various formats, including embedded or linked PNG, SVG, GIF, PostScript, IsaViz/ZVTM, HPGL, and HPGL/2. Although the arcs look like hand-drawn curves and often overlap each other—which is not the most visually appealing representation—the image output can be useful for demonstrational or designing purposes (Figure 14-5). Note that there are only very few similar services available on the Web for generating graph images from RDF.

Figure 14-5. *Detail of an RDF graph generated by the W3C RDF Validation Service*

■ **Note** In contrast to the raster (PNG) output, the SVG output not only has incomparable quality but also contains the URIs as hyperlinks.

Optionally, the triples can be displayed in N-Triples format. The colors of nodes, arcs, and text, as well as font size and orientation, can be set as advanced options.

Validating News Feeds

Since RSS and Atom news feeds should be valid XML documents, care must be taken to provide error-free elements and well-formed XML structure.

The World Wide Web Consortium runs the *W3C Feed Validation Service, for Atom and RSS* at `http://validator.w3.org/feed/` [9]. Similar to other W3C validators, it provides not only validation by URI but also validation by direct input. After successful validation, the service provides a "valid RSS" or "valid Atom" logo (depending on the validated feed), an embedding code, and a text link.

The *FEED Validator for Atom and RSS and KML* at `http://feedvalidator.org` can also be used to validate RSS 2.0 as well as Atom 1.0 feeds [10]. Additionally, it validates elements of the `blogChannel`, `dc`, `itunes`, `mod_admin`, `mod_syndication`, and `mod_content`[5] namespaces.

Validating CSS

Style sheet validations should be performed according to the CSS level being used. Although valid CSS1 style sheets are also valid CSS 2.1 style sheets, some CSS1 rulesets should be written with slightly different semantics in CSS 2.1 [11]. Since certain CSS2 features are omitted in CSS 2.1, not all CSS2 styles are valid in CSS 2.1 [12]. Similarly, the new properties introduced in CSS3 are invalid in earlier CSS versions. Valid CSS style sheets must conform to the grammar rules of the corresponding version and must contain only at-rules, properties, and property values defined in that specification.

In spite of the relatively wide selection of markup language versions and variants, the document type to be used for markup validation can usually be selected automatically based on the Document Type Declaration. However, there is no similar mechanism in CSS, and determining the version of style sheets to be validated is not so straightforward. First, there is no version declaration in CSS, and second, there is a large overlap between the vocabularies of different versions, making automatic version detection impossible. Hence, the W3C CSS Validation Service at `http://jigsaw.w3.org/css-validator/` [13] validates style sheets against CSS3 by default. The CSS profile to be used for validation can be overridden or forced manually as an advanced option. For example, if you want to pass a CSS file to the validator as CSS3, you should construct a URI[6] similar to the one shown in Listing 14-2.

Listing 14-2. Explicitly Selected CSS Profile for Validation

```
http://jigsaw.w3.org/css-validator/validator?uri=www.example.com/styles/main.css↵
&profile=css3&usermedium=all&warning=0&lang=en
```

Similar to the Markup Validation Service, the CSS validator can perform the validation by URI, file upload, or direct input. The CSS validator can be used primarily to validate external CSS files, but internal styles can also be checked. However, in the latter case, the (X)HTML document should be validated first with the Markup Validation Service.

The CSS Validation Service supports CSS1, CSS2, CSS 2.1, and CSS3 style sheets, along with other document profiles. Media types can be selected manually, including `all`, `aural`, `Braille`, `embossed`, `handheld`, `print`, `projection`, `screen`, TTY, TV, or `presentation`. The default media type is `all`. Beyond errors, the validator might identify warnings as well. Since they might be false positives or the consequence of errors, warnings can be hidden.

---

[5]`content:encoded` only
[6]Naturally, you can select the profile "CSS level 3" from the drop-down list under "More Options." However, you need to construct a URI manually if you want to provide a validation link for your CSS3 button, because the default code assumes CSS 2.1.

The validation request applies parameters in conjunction with the base URI http://jigsaw.w3.org/css-validator/validator. The supported parameters are the following:

- uri: The URI of the document to be validated. It can be CSS or (X)HTML.

- text: The CSS document to validate.

- usermedium: The media type used for validation.

- output: html (HTML), xhtml (XHTML, default), soap12 (SOAP 1.2), text (plain text).

- profile: css1, css2, css21, css3, svg, svgbasic, svgtiny, mobile, atsc-tv, tv, or none.

- lang: The report language such as en (default), fr, it, ko, ja, es, zh-cn, nl, de, it, or pl.

- warning: Warning level with possible values no (hidden warnings), 0 (less warnings), 1 or 2 (more warnings). 2 is the default.

The output of the W3C CSS Validation Service is similar to the result page of the W3C markup validator. A green stripe indicates a valid file, while a red stripe means that the CSS file is invalid.

Validating I18N

The Internationalization Activity Group at the World Wide Web Consortium runs the W3C Internationalization Checker [14]. The I18N checker can be used to check web pages for *internationalization-friendliness* according to the following factors:

- *Character encoding*: HTTP Content-Type, byte-order mark, XML declaration, the Content-Type metadata, and HTML5 meta charset

- *Language settings*: the lang and xml:lang attributes on the html element, the HTTP Content-Language, and the content-language metadata

- *Text direction*: ltr (default) or rtl

- *The class and id names*: Non-ASCII as well as non-NFC classes and identifiers

- *Request headers*: Accept-Language, Accept-Charset

Validating Hyperlinks

One of the most disappointing experiences in web browsers is the broken hyperlink (dead link). W3C Link Checker at http://validator.w3.org/checklink is a useful tool for checking internal and external hyperlinks of web documents [15]. Linked documents can also be checked recursively throughout a maximum of 150 documents. URI fragments including a hash mark such as index.html#about are included in the test. Links forbidden by the *robots exclusion rules* declared in the robots.txt file are not checked (Figure 14-6).

		List of broken links and other issues

There are issues with the URLs listed below. The table summarizes the issues and suggested actions by HTTP response status code.

Code	Occurrences	What to do
(N/A)	19	The link was not checked due to robots exclusion rules. Check the link manually, and see also the link checker documentation on robots exclusion.
(N/A)	3	Accessing links with this URI scheme has been disabled in link checker.
404	2	The link is broken. Double-check that you have not made any typo, or mistake in copy-pasting. If the link points to a resource that no longer exists, you may want to remove or fix the link.
405	1	The server does not allow HTTP HEAD requests, which prevents the Link Checker to check the link automatically. Check the link manually.

⊘ Line: 196 http://www.assoc-amazon.com/s/link-enhancer?tag=w3geekweb-20&o=1

Status: 404 (no message)

The link is broken. Double-check that you have not made any typo, or mistake in copy-pasting. If the link points to a resource that no longer exists, you may want to remove or fix the link.

⬧ Line: 84 javascript:larger();

Status: (N/A) Access to 'javascript' URIs has been disabled

You must change this link: people using a browser without JavaScript support will *not* be able to follow this link. See the Web Content Accessibility Guidelines on the use of scripting on the Web and the techniques on how to solve this.

Figure 14-6. *Link Checker results*

Hyperlink validation is useful not only for checking entry points but also for important files such as style sheet files, scripts, or external URIs that might be modified by other site contributors or administrators any time without notification. For example, permanent redirections (HTTP response status code 301) are also identified by Link Checker, and although they work, such links should be updated. The results can be useful for improving user experience by eliminating broken links and accessibility barriers associated with links of the analyzed web page.

Validating Accessibility

Unlike other web site features, accessibility cannot be validated by validators with 100 percent certainty. While markup errors, such as incorrect element use, missing tags, or structural errors, can be identified automatically, accessibility is too complex and sophisticated to be validated automatically [16]. Many potential issues require human decision, checking, or confirmation. The equivalent functionality of scripts and noscript contents, adequacy of text descriptions, script functionality and effects, visual lists represented by paragraphs and break rows, and pause options in objects are some of the features that cannot be checked automatically with full certainty.

Even so, there are useful tools that can make the work of web designers easier [17]. Such tools should be used throughout the phases of web site development to prevent accessibility barriers, repair encountered barriers, and improve overall web page quality. The major task of accessibility tools is to identify accessible-friendly elements and attributes in the markup. Moreover, certain tools can assist developers in performing those checks that cannot be validated automatically [18]. Accessibility tools perform validation against the Web Accessibility Guidelines of W3C (WCAG 1.0 and/or WCAG 2.0) as well as Section 508.

A typical online accessibility checker is *AChecker* (http://achecker.ca [19]) that has been released by the Inclusive Design Research Centre at the University of Toronto, Canada. AChecker can test web sites for conformance to various accessibility guidelines, including WCAG 1.0/2.0 Level A/AA/AAA, Section 508, Stanca Act, and BITV. The interface provides accessibility checking by either URL or file upload. It identifies three types of errors: known, likely, and potential problems. Known problems are claimed to be errors that can be identified with certainty (for example, img element with missing alt attribute, missing label for the input element). Likely problems need human decisions (for example, misused elements, onchange event handler on the select element might cause extreme change in context). Potential problems are often not errors at all; however, they require human decision and confirmation (for example, dir attribute may be required to identify changes in text direction, data table may require th elements, script user interface may not be available from the keyboard). Unfortunately, not every suggestion would validate and some of them are incorrect (for example, the lang attribute on the html element is neither valid nor required in XHTML+RDFa if the natural language of the document is identified by the xml:lang attribute) (Figure 14-7).

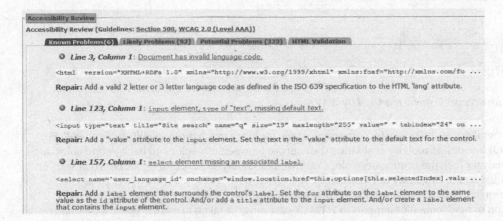

Figure 14-7. *AChecker provides good suggestions; however, not all of them would be valid*

AChecker also supports HTML validation. It provides error descriptions and suggestions for corrections.

The online accessibility validation tool Cynthia can perform validations by URI according to Section 508 and WCAG 1.0 with all priority levels [20]. Advanced options are also available such as browser emulation or line exclusions. Reports are clear and useful for developers dealing with accessibility (Figure 14-8).

13.1 Clearly identify the target of each link.	Yes		

o Rule: 13.1.1 - All Anchor elements are required not to use any of the defined link phrases in the link text.
   o No Anchor elements that use any of the defined link phrases in the link text were found in document body.
o Rule: 13.1.2 - All Anchor elements are required not to use the same link text to refer to different resources.
   o No Anchor elements that use the same link text to refer to different resources were found in document body.			

13.2 Provide metadata to add semantic information to pages and sites.		No	

o Rule: 13.2.1 - Documents are required to use the TITLE element.
   o Note: Document uses the TITLE element.
o Rule: 13.2.2 - Documents are required to use META elements, that are defined as required, in Head section.
   o **Failure** - Document does not contain a META element with the required name: language or language does not have a 'content' value.			

13.3 Provide information about the general layout of a site (e.g., a site map or table of contents).	Yes		

o Rule: 13.3.1 - Check for link to site map page within document.
    Site Map Link Text:
      o Note: This rule has not been selected to be verified for this checkpoint.			

13.4 Use navigation mechanisms in a consistent manner.			
Priority 2 - Tables	Yes	No	Other
5.3 Do not use tables for layout unless the table makes sense when linearized. Otherwise, if the table does not make sense, provide an alternative equivalent (which may be a linearized version).			
o Rule: 5.3.1 - Identify all Layout Tables. o Note: Layout TABLE Element found at Line: 337, Column: 1.			
5.4 If a table is used for layout, do not use any structural markup for the purpose of visual formatting.			
To assist with visual verification, we recommend that you refer to the detail of checkpoint 5.3 for locations of elements that apply to this checkpoint.			

Figure 14-8. *Detailed accessibility report with explanations and links to W3C guidelines*

One of the most comprehensive accessibility tools is WebAIM WAVE [21]. It is a free online tool at http://wave.webaim.org that renders web pages with accessibility errors, warnings, and information (Figure 14-9). It identifies accessible attribute values, inaccessible and potentially inaccessible content such as Flash or scripts, and device-dependent content such as keyboard traps.

Figure 14-9. *Section of an accessible menu rendered by WAVE*

While WAVE is a general accessibility tool focusing on markup, there are much more specific tools as well. For example, there are several free online tools for evaluating the contrast between text color and background color, such as the Color Contrast Analyzer [22], the Luminosity Color Contrast Ratio Analyzer [23], or the index of color texts on white background provided by the University of Wisconsin [24].

It is important to keep in mind that no accessibility tools can perform a complete evaluation by any means.

With the introduction of new semantic elements in HTML5, care must be taken to use the latest accessibility checkers available.

The final accessibility test is always a real-life test that involves evaluation performed by people with disabilities.

Validating Mobile-Friendliness

With the enormous popularity of mobile browsing, it is vital to test your web sites on mobile devices. However, it is practically infeasible to check web sites on all kinds of mobile devices. Fortunately, the W3C mobileOK Checker at `http://validator.w3.org/mobile/` can help you analyze the suitability of your web pages for mobile browsing [25]. The mobileOK Checker applies the tests defined in the W3C Recommendation "W3C mobileOK Basic Tests 1.0" [26], categorizes failures, and gives useful error descriptions (Figure 14-10).

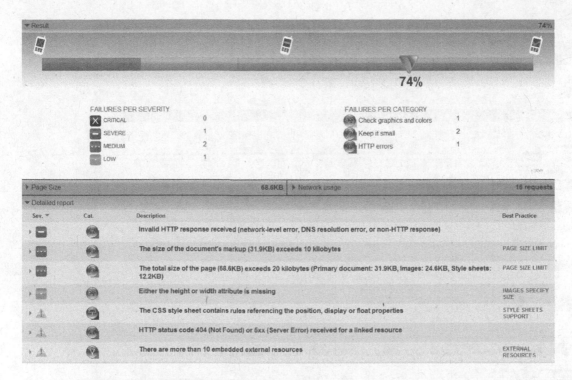

Figure 14-10. *The W3C mobileOK checker gives useful hints when evaluating web site suitability for mobile browsing*

After correcting the flagged issues, the web site will fulfill the fundamental requirements for providing a reasonable mobile browsing experience.

Unified Validators

Although individual validators could be used in combination for validating full web sites, in the case of large projects, it would be inconvenient and slow. Developers can apply unified validators to perform multiple validations easily and effectively.

W3C Unicorn

On 27 July 2010, W3C released Unicorn, a unified validator available at `http://validator.w3.org/unicorn/` [27] with the slogan "Improve the quality of the Web." Unicorn is the ultimate markup, CSS, and news feed validator and mobileOK checker. Validations can be performed by URI, by file upload, or by direct input individually or simultaneously. The advanced options are identical to the ones provided by the individual W3C validation services discussed earlier. Unicorn is available in many languages [28].

Depending on the tests chosen, the output provides information about the validity of the markup, style sheets, and news feeds, as well as the mobile-friendliness of the web page (Figure 14-11).

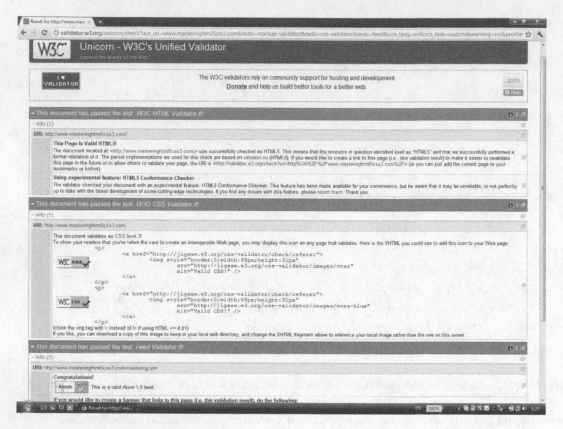

Figure 14-11. *The heaven of web standardistas: valid markup, valid style sheet, and valid news feed*

Similar to the individual W3C validators, valid documents are indicated by a green stripe, while invalid documents are indicated by a red stripe. By clicking the stripes, the validation test results can be collapsed/uncollapsed by category (they are uncollapsed by default). On the right side, on each stripe you can see the number of errors, warning, and information (if any). These numbers are hyperlinks and can be used to jump to the corresponding section on the page. In case of a valid web page, the validators provide not only reassuring information but also W3C badges with evaluation links that can be embedded to your valid web page. In other words, the output of Unicorn is identical to the output of the separate validators.

Total Validator

Another unified validator is Total Validator, which once was an online service. In contrast, the current version is available exclusively as a desktop software tool for different platforms [29]. The basic version can be downloaded free of charge. Total Validator is available for different platforms, including Windows, OS X, and Linux.[7] Total Validator is a small and powerful tool that combines a markup validator, an accessibility validator, a spell-checker, and a link validator (Figure 14-12).

---

[7]The basic tool is Java based and requires Java 1.5 or later.

Figure 14-12. *The configuration interface of Total Validator*

This interface is used for starting the process only. After declaring the URI of the web page to validate, along with the parameters, Total Validator opens a browser window and displays the validation results. Errors and warnings are shown in the markup code with hyperlinks to the corresponding entries of the long description after the markup code (Figure 14-13).

```
14      <script type="text/javascript" src="js/click.js">
14      </script>
15      </head>
16      <body>
17        <div id="wrapper">
18          <header>
19            <div id="header">
20 ⊡ ⊕ E801 [WCAG v1 6.3 (A)] Put some content between the start and end tag to provide a text equivalent for
   non-text items:
              <object type="application/x-shockwave-flash" data="flash/header.swf" width="940" height="300">
21              <param name="movie" value="flash/header.swf" />
22              <param name="wmode" value="opaque" />
23            </object>
24          </div>
```

More Information

WCAG v1 A Errors

E801 - 1 instance(s): When using <object> or <applet> you should put some content between the start and end tag to a provide a text alternative. With the <applet> tag this is in addition to any 'alt' text you may have defined. See http://www.w3.org/TR/WCAG10-HTML-TECHS/#applet-text-equivalent (displayed in new window).

Parsing Warnings

W001 - 1 instance(s): There should not be any white space at the start or end of an attribute's value. This is a minor issue and can probably be ignored. See here (displayed in new window) for more info.

WCAG v1 A Warnings

W800 - 1 instance(s): This warning appears if you have defined a <script> and there is no <noscript> alternative following it. You should ensure that pages are usable when scripts are turned off or not supported. Using <noscript> is a common way of doing this, but if you have used an alternative mechanism you can ignore this warning. See http://www.w3.org/TR/WCAG10-scripts (displayed in new window), and +http://www.section508.gov/index.cfm?fuseAction=stdsdoc#Web (displayed in new window).

Figure 14-13. *Validation results with a segment of the markup code (top) and the long description at the bottom of the page*

Beyond common markup languages such as XHTML 1.0 Strict, XHTML 1.1, and HTML5 (and many older versions), Total Validator also supports HTML + RDFa 1.1, XHTML + RDFa 1.1, HTML5 used as a polyglot language, and even XHTML5. Accessibility can be checked at all levels of WCAG, as well as according to Section 508. The spell checker supports American and British English, French, Italian, Spanish, and German.

Total Validator provides screenshots for analyzing web page appearance in different browsers, including various versions of Firefox from version 1.5, Internet Explorer from version 5.5, Konqueror 3.5, Lynx 2.8, Opera, and Safari.

An interesting option is that the validation result can be saved as HTML and opened with a single click on the button Last Results the next time the tool is executed.

SortSite

A comprehensive commercial validator is SortSite, developed by PowerMapper [30]. Its main features can be summarized as follows:

- *Accessibility*: Check conformance against WCAG 1.0, WCAG 2.0, and Section 508.

- *Broken links*: Check for broken links and incorrect server configuration.

- *Compatibility*: Check for browser-specific code, scripts, and image formats.

- *Compliance*: Check for compliance with EU and U.S. law.

- *Markup and styles*: HTML, XHTML and CSS validation.

- *Search engine optimization*: Check Google, Yahoo!, and Bing content guidelines

- *Usability*: Check against Usability.gov guidelines

Extracting Semantic Content

Semantic content of web sites can be checked with the W3C Semantic Data Extractor [31]. It can extract semantic data such as following:

- Generic metadata

  - Title, author, and description provided in the document head

  - RDFa metadata embedded in the document body (also generated in RDF/XML)

- Related resources

  - Linked files, for example, RSS or Atom news feeds

- Glossary, copyright, and bookmarkable points provided in the document head

- Outline of the document

- Quotes and citations

Menu points and URIs are provided with hyperlinks.

Another comprehensive semantic data extractor tool is the Sindice Web Data Inspector at http://inspector. sindice.com [32]. The tool can be used to extract RDF triples from markup, RDF/XML, Turtle, or N3 documents provided either by URI or by direct input. Sindice Web Data Inspector can be used for retrieving semantic data (Inspect button), combined semantic data extraction and validation (Inspect + Validate button), or ontology analysis and reasoning (Figure 14-14).

Figure 14-14. *Comprehensive options on the start screen of Sindice Web Data Inspector*

As a result, the tool provides the full list of subject–predicate–object triples retrieved from the file (Figure 14-15). The output format can also be changed to N-triples or RDF/XML.

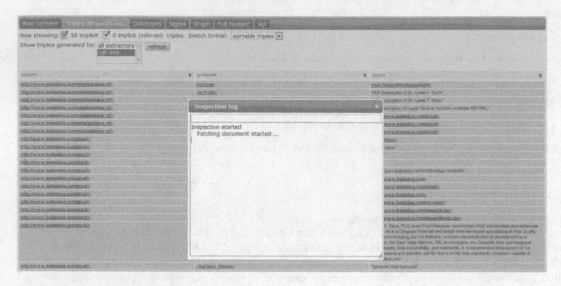

Figure 14-15. *Semantic data extraction in progress*

The "Sigma" option is a really good demonstration of machine-readable metadata. Software tools can extract structured data from properly written semantic documents and display them arbitrarily (Figure 14-16). This is the true essence of the Semantic Web!

Figure 14-16. *A personal description extracted from RDF and displayed in a visually appealing manner*

A very nice feature of Sindice Web Data Inspector is that a scalable graph can be generated from the semantic document (Figure 14-17). The graph not only presents the triples but also provides a quick summary of the ontologies and vocabularies used in the file.

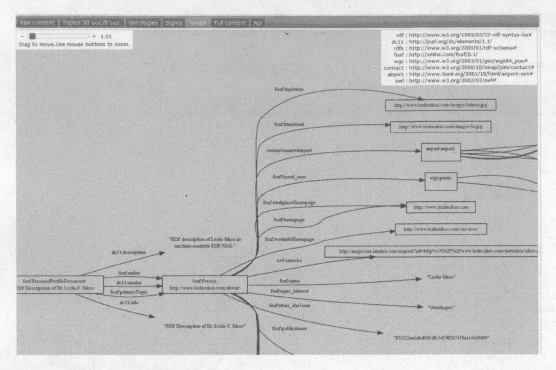

Figure 14-17. *A scalable graph generated from an RDF file*

The Sindice Web Data Inspector also has a validation feature with two different options. The first one, called "RDF syntax validation," performs an RDF syntax validation according to the W3C specification. The second option is the "Pedantic validator," which is a validation over the extracted triples. In case of a valid document, both validators give the result "Valid document."

Expressing Validity

Standard conformance of web sites can be expressed easily by the "valid" icons (also known as *validity badges* or *validity logos*). In addition to notifying readers, they can also be used as instant validation links if implemented correctly. The expected hyperlink is listed in the sample code provided by W3C validators themselves when validating web documents (Figure 14-18).

Figure 14-18. *W3C validation icons with embedding code*

Note that the codes are just suggestions. For example, the `style` attribute on the `img` element can be omitted in favor of external CSS rules. The recommended embedding code for XHTML [33] is presented in Listing 14-3.

Listing 14-3. Embedding Code for W3C Validation Icons

```
<p>
  <a href="http://validator.w3.org/check/referer">
  <img src="http://www.w3.org/Icons/valid-xhtml10" alt="Valid XHTML 1.0!" height="31"↵
    width="88" />
  </a>
</p>
```

W3C Icons

The W3C "valid" icons represent a W3C logo on the left and the Recommendation on the right (Figure 14-19). In many cases, the version or the Recommendation is also shown.

W3C logo   *Recommendation*

Version

Figure 14-19. *Structure of conventional W3C validity icons*

The default size of the icons is 88×31 pixels. The World Wide Web Consortium provides two versions for each icon: a gold one and a blue one. Web designers are free to choose which one to use. The W3C Trademark License as well as the logo and icon usage policies apply to all W3C validity icons. Modifying icons is not allowed.

The W3C valid logos can be used exclusively on web pages that pass validation. They are designed for verification. The icons must provide a hyperlink that validates the web page according to the corresponding W3C technology or standard. Consequently, clicking a correctly set "valid markup button" should pass the URI of the page to the W3C Markup Validation Service, which gives the same result page as if the URI was used directly for validation on the validator web page. The same holds for CSS validation buttons. Consequently, these buttons can also be used by web designers to revalidate pages every time they are modified. Experts can use this facility to reassure themselves about the latest modifications without the need for loading the corresponding validator and adding the URI manually, or copy-pasting the code.

The World Wide Web Consortium does not verify the validity of web pages; thus, it is the Web designers' responsibility to ensure consistency and conformance.

The full list of W3C validation icons is listed on the W3C Quality Assurance site [34] and includes the following:

- *Markup icons*: "HTML 2.0", "HTML 3.2", "HTML 4.0", "HTML 4.01", "ISO-HTML" for ISO/IEC 15445 (legacy missing), "XHTML 1.0", "XHTML 1.1", "XHTML Basic 1.0", "XHTML-Print 1.0", and "XHTML+RDFa"

- *CSS icons*: A general valid "CSS" icon and more specific icons for "CSS level 1" and "CSS level 2"

- *XML icons*: "XML 1.0", "XML 1.1"

- *SVG icons*: "SVG 1.0", "SVG 1.1", "SVG 1.2", "SVG Tiny 1.1", and "SVG Tiny 1.2"

- *MathML icon*: "MathML 2.0"

The validity icons are also available directly at the W3C Icon Repository (along with other images) [35].

Representing Technologies

Beyond validation, numerous icons are available to represent web technologies used on a web site. They can express not only underlying technologies but also dedication, initiatives the site developers agree with, or projects and organizations they sympathize with. Such icons can also be used to proudly present rarely implemented but advanced features that can hardly be seen on other sites. The most frequently used W3C technology icons are the following:

- "HTML5"

  - "HTML5 Powered with CSS3/Styling"

  - "HTML5 Powered with Semantics"

  - "HTML5 Powered with Offline & Storage"

  - "HTML5 Powered with Connectivity/Realtime"

  - "HTML5 Powered with Multimedia"

- "HTML5 Powered with Graphics, 3D, and effects"

- "HTML5 Powered with Device Access"

- "HTML5 Powered with Performance & Integration"

Technology names are optional and can be combined (by adding the word "and" prior to the last technology selected). The badges can be generated with Badge Builder 5000 in both horizontal and vertical orientations. The HTML5 mark with or without wordmark, supporting elements, technology classes, and sticker templates are available as separate SVG and PNG files. The HTML5 logo is also available as a one-color version. All badges are released with the Creative Commons Attribution 3.0 License [36].

- "Made with Cascading Style Sheets".

- Accessibility icons: "WAI-A WCAG 1.0", "WAI-AA WCAG 1.0", "WAI-AAA WCAG 1.0" [37], "WAI-A WCAG 2.0", "WAI-AA WCAG 2.0", and "WAI-AAA WCAG 2.0" [38].

- Semantic Web technology buttons: "GRDDL", "OWL", "POWDER", "RDF", "RDFa", "RIF", "SKOS", and "SPARQL" [39].

However, W3C is not the only institution that releases technology icons and logos. Here are some examples:

- "Unicode encoded"

- "Dublin Core used here"

- "Java—Get it now"

- "HCARD", "XFN FRIENDLY", and icons and logos for other microformats [40]

- "Cynthia tested" [41]

- "SEO friendly"

- "NO popups, NO spyware"

- "Powered by PERL"

- PageRank n/10—PRchecker.info (where n is a number between 1 and 10) [42]

Summary

In this chapter, you learned that there are powerful, efficient tools to check your web documents for errors. They can be used during development and are very useful for redesign. Many of these validators are free tools and are available online. The most commonly used ones are markup validators and CSS validators, because the markup and style sheets are core web site components and can be validated automatically. Validating web site accessibility is a real challenge, because several aspects of WCAG often require human decision.

The last chapter will enumerate the most common errors that result in invalid markup, style sheets, news feed channels, and accessibility barriers.

References

1. Murphy C, Persson N (2009) Valid code is not necessarily well-structured code. In: HTML and CSS Web Standards Solutions – A Web Standardistas' Approach. Friends of ED, Berkeley

2. Thereaux O et al (ed) (2012) Web Quality Assurance Tools. http://www.w3.org/QA/Tools/. Accessed 30 October 2014

3. W3C (2014) The W3C Markup Validation Service v1.3. World Wide Web Consortium. http://validator.w3.org. Accessed 30 October 2014

4. W3C (2014) Source code availability for the W3C Markup Validator. World Wide Web Consortium. http://validator.w3.org/source/. Accessed 30 October 2014

5. Quinn L (2007) WDG HTML Validator. Liam Quinn. http://www.htmlhelp.com/tools/validator/. Accessed 30 October 2014

6. Gueury M (2010) The HTML Validator add-on for Firefox. Marc Gueury. https://addons.mozilla.org/en-US/firefox/addon/249/. Accessed 30 October 2014

7. The Apache Ant Project (2014) XMLValidate. The Apache Software Foundation. http://ant.apache.org/manual/Tasks/xmlvalidate.html. Accessed 30 October 2014

8. Prud'hommeaux E (2006) W3C RDF Validation Service. http://www.w3.org/RDF/Validator. Accessed 30 October 2014

9. Thereaux O et al (2014) W3C Feed Validation Service, for Atom and RSS. World Wide Web Consortium. http://validator.w3.org/feed/. Accessed 30 October 2014

10. Ruby S, Pilgrim M, Walton J, Ringnalda P (2009) FEED Validator for Atom and RSS and KML. Sam Ruby, Mark Pilgrim, Joseph Walton, and Phil Ringnalda. http://feedvalidator.org. Accessed 30 October 2014

11. Bos B, Çelik T, Hickson I, Lie HW (eds) (2010) Grammar of CSS 2.1. In: Cascading Style Sheets Level 2 Revision 1 (CSS 2.1) Specification. W3C Working Draft. World Wide Web Consortium. http://www.w3.org/TR/CSS/grammar.html. Accessed 05 January 2011

12. Bos B, Çelik T, Hickson I, Lie HW (eds) (2010) Conformance: Requirements and Recommendations. In: Cascading Style Sheets Level 2 Revision 1 (CSS 2.1) Specification. W3C Working Draft. World Wide Web Consortium. http://www.w3.org/TR/CSS/conform.html. Accessed 05 January 2011

13. W3C QA (2009) CSS Validation Service. World Wide Web Consortium. http://jigsaw.w3.org/css-validator/. Accessed 30 October 2014

14. W3C I18N Activity Group (2013). World Wide Web Consortium. http://qa-dev.w3.org/i18n-checker/. Accessed 30 October 2014

15. W3C (2011) W3C Link Checker. World Wide Web Consortium. http://validator.w3.org/checklink. Accessed 30 October 2014

16. Abou-Zahra S (ed) (2013) Evaluating Web Sites for Accessibility: Overview. World Wide Web Consortium. http://www.w3.org/WAI/eval/Overview.html. Accessed 30 October 2014

17. Abou-Zahra S (ed) (2012) Complete List of Web Accessibility Evaluation Tools. World Wide Web Consortium. http://www.w3.org/WAI/ER/tools/complete.html. Accessed 30 October 2014

18. Abou-Zahra S (ed) (2012) Selecting Web Accessibility Evaluation Tools. World Wide Web Consortium. http://www.w3.org/WAI/eval/selectingtools.html. Accessed 30 October 2014

19. ATRC (2011) AChecker (Web Accessibility Checker). University of Toronto. http://achecker.ca. Accessed 30 October 2014

20. HiSoftware (2014) HiSoftware Cynthia Says Portal. HiSoftware Inc. http://www.cynthiasays.com. Accessed 30 October 2014

21. Kasday L, Andersen A, Smith J, Hernandez D, Bohman P, Anderson S, Maturi N, Varanasi B, Parija J (2014) WAVE. Web accessibility evaluation tool. Web Accessibility in Mind. http://wave.webaim.org. Accessed 30 October 2014

22. Johansson D (2010) Color Contrast Analyzer. Donald Johansson. http://www.colorsontheweb.com/colorcontrast.asp. Accessed 30 October 2014

23. Lemon G (2014) Luminosity Colour Contrast Ratio Analyser. Juicy Studio. http://juicystudio.com/services/luminositycontrastratio.php. Accessed 30 October 2014

24. UoW (2014) Index of Color Contrast Samples. The University of Wisconsin. http://trace.wisc.edu/contrast-ratio-examples/index.htm. Accessed 30 October 2014

25. W3C (2010) W3C mobileOK Checker. Is your Web site mobile-friendly? World Wide Web Consortium. http://validator.w3.org/mobile/. Accessed 30 October 2014

26. Owen S, Rabin J (eds) (2008) W3C mobileOK Basic Tests 1.0. W3C Recommendation. World Wide Web Consortium. http://www.w3.org/TR/mobileOK-basic10-tests/. Accessed 30 October 2014

27. W3C (2014) Unicorn - unified validator. World Wide Web Consortium. http://validator.w3.org/unicorn/. Accessed 30 October 2014

28. W3C (2014) Translations of Unicorn. World Wide Web Consortium. http://validator.w3.org/unicorn/translations. Accessed 30 October 2014

29. Total Validator (2014) Total Validator. http://www.totalvalidator.com. Accessed 30 October 2014

30. Powermapper (2014) PowerMapper – Website Testing and Site Mapping Tools. Powermapper Software. http://www.powermapper.com. Accessed 30 October 2014

31. Hazaël-Massieux D (ed) (2011) W3C Semantic Data Extractor. World Wide Web Consortium. http://www.w3.org/2003/12/semantic-extractor.html. Accessed 30 October 2014

32. Sindice (2012) Sindice Web Data Inspector. Sindice Ltd. http://inspector.sindice.com. Accessed 30 October 2014

33. W3C (2012) "Valid" icons. In: Help and FAQ for the Markup Validator. World Wide Web Consortium. http://validator.w3.org/docs/help.html#icon. Accessed 30 October 2014

34. Thereaux O (2009) List of all W3C Validation Icons. World Wide Web Consortium. http://www.w3.org/QA/Tools/Icons. Accessed 30 October 2014

35. W3C (2014) W3C Icon Repository. World Wide Web Consortium. http://www.w3.org/Icons/. Accessed 30 October 2014

36. W3C (2011) W3C HTML5 logo. World Wide Web Consortium. http://www.w3.org/html/logo/. Accessed 30 October 2014

37.   W3C (2008) W3C Web Content Accessibility Guidelines 1.0 Conformance Logos.
       World Wide Web Consortium. `http://www.w3.org/WAI/WCAG1-Conformance`.
       Accessed 30 October 2014

38.   W3C (2012) W3C Web Content Accessibility Guidelines 2.0 Conformance Logos.
       World Wide Web Consortium. `http://www.w3.org/WAI/WCAG2-Conformance`.
       Accessed 30 October 2014

39.   Jacobs I (2012) W3C Semantic Web Logos and Policies. World Wide Web Consortium.
       `http://www.w3.org/2007/10/sw-logos.html`. Accessed 30 October 2014

40.   Messina C, Baranovskiy D, Dibble G, Bartelme W (2013) Icons. Microformats Wiki.
       Microformats Community. `http://microformats.org/wiki/icons`.
       Accessed 30 October 2014

41.   HiSoftware (2010) Cynthia Tested Button Guidelines – When, Why, and How to use.
       HiSoftware Inc. `http://www.cynthiasays.com/org/cynthiatested.htm`.
       Accessed 04 February 2011

42.   Page Rank Checker (2014) Google Page Rank Checker. `http://prchecker.info/`.
       Accessed 30 October 2014

■ ■ ■

Most Common Errors

Several factors should be considered to achieve web site validity. The code is written either manually or generated automatically, and errors are inevitable. Errors occur in the markup, in the style sheet, in the XML files, in scripts, in server settings, and so forth. By analyzing and learning the most common errors, many of them can be eliminated or at least minimized. As a result, they can be recognized, identified, and corrected quickly and efficiently.

Even the most carefully created web pages can contain errors. In this chapter, you will learn about the most common errors and their solutions. It is really beneficial to know them, because they occur rather frequently, and learning how to correct them will decrease the time required for corrections and ease your standardization efforts.

Common Serving Errors

One of the most common serving errors is to serve XHTML as text/html. For many years, web browsers handled XHTML markup as if it were HTML. This is known as the "dirty secret of XHTML." Self-closing tags and other XHTML specific notations were ignored, and XHTML documents were rendered by SGML parsers instead of XML parsers [1]. As a result, none of the beneficial features of XML was used.

In contrast, modern browsers support the proper MIME type. XHTML documents should be served as application/xhtml+xml instead of text/html, as discussed in Chapter 4.

Common Markup Errors

Web designers should know all the common markup errors in order to easily identify, find, and correct them. Incorrectly used elements, wrong document structure, incorrectly closed tags, missing alt attributes, directly provided ampersand characters, ignored case sensitivity, nonunique identifiers, and misspelled keywords are among the most common markup errors. Many of them are clearly indicated by markup validators and can be corrected easily. Validators also provide useful hints on the correction. However, some errors can cause many others. For example, a missing end tag for a division makes not only the document collapse in the browser but also the nesting to become incorrect. Consequently, it might happen that an invalid document with 18 errors indicated by a validator has 2–3 errors only. So, do not be frightened by the initial number of errors!

Incorrectly Used Elements

As a golden rule, extended care must be taken to eliminate unnecessary containers in the markup. For example, images positioned to the right side of the page with the text "wrapping around" can be styled directly instead of putting them onto floating divisions. Another example is the p tag, which should be used for a paragraph container and not for carriage return. Look at the (really bad) example shown in Listing 15-1.

Listing 15-1. A Bad Practice That Should Never Be Used

```
<p>This is a very bad practice
<p>dating back to the early days
<p>of the Web
<p>unfortunately it is still in use
<p>even if it has many drawbacks, e.g.,
<p>illogical
<p>hard to identify related content
```

The technique of omitting end tags should be forgotten. Although it is allowed in HTML, it is not a clean code and is invalid in XHTML. Beginners with a basic (X)HTML knowledge might think that br elements should be added to the end of each line instead of incorrectly forcing line break with paragraphs. They are wrong.

Web content should be logical. The first five rows should belong to a paragraph, and the last two should belong to an unordered list. The previous example should be written as shown in Listing 15-2.

Listing 15-2. The Correct Markup for Listing 15-1

```
<p>This is a very bad practice dating back to the early days of the Web. Unfortunately it ↵
 is still in use even if it has many drawbacks, e.g.,</p>
<ul>
  <li>Illogical</li>
  <li>Hard to identify related content</li>
</ul>
```

Text width can be set by external style sheets in order to achieve similar (or exactly the same) effect expected from the original example. It all depends on the content and the publishing needs. In this case, the markup in Listing 15-3 with the appropriate style in the external CSS file shown in Listing 15-4 would be a standard solution.

Listing 15-3. A More Advanced Solution

```
<div id="thinbox">
  <p>This is a very bad practice dating back to the early days of the Web. Unfortunately it ↵
    is still in use even if it has many drawbacks, e.g.,</p>
  <ul>
    <li>Illogical</li>
    <li>Hard to identify related content</li>
  </ul>
</div>
```

Listing 15-4. CSS Ruleset for Listing 15-3

```
.thinbox {
  width: 400px;
  height: 600px;
  font-size: 14px;
}
```

Incorrect Structure

Incorrectly used elements often violate the DOM model. Required elements should be provided, and nesting rules should be followed. Moreover, the document structure should be maintained by using correct containers and elements in the proper manner. Take a look at the code in Listing 15-5.

Listing 15-5. List Items Without Structure or Semantic Meaning (Incorrect)

```
- first item <br />
- second item <br />
- third item <br />
```

Since the previous rows are items of a list, they evidently should be collected into an unordered list (Listing 15-6).

Listing 15-6. The Correct Markup for Listing 15-5

```
<ul>
  <li>first item</li>
  <li>second item</li>
  <li>third item</li>
</ul>
```

The default bullets provided by the li elements can be changed in CSS to an arbitrary character or image (see the section "Styling Lists"). CSS completely separates presentation from structure; thus, any elements can be arbitrary styled.

Incorrect HTML5 Structuring

Many of the new structuring elements of HTML5 are often used incorrectly, partly due to code distribution in blog posts that are not standard-compliant, and described elements and attributes before the finalization of the HTML5 specification.

Using section as Wrapper

With the introduction of section and article, there is a misbelief that the div elements should be completely eliminated (Listing 15-7).

Listing 15-7. The section Element Used Incorrectly as Document Wrapper

```
<body>
  <section id="wrapper">
    <!-- Page content -->
  </section>
</body>
```

In fact, div is still the right element to be used as the document wrapper as well as the generic wrapper of separate document parts (Listing 15-8).

473

Listing 15-8. Correct Document Wrapper

```
<body>
  <div id="wrapper">
    <!-- Page content -->
  </div>
</body>
```

Overuse of header

Some web designers incorrectly use header elements as containers of headings (Listing 15-9).

Listing 15-9. Too Many Headers

```
<article>
  <header>
    <h2>Blog post title</h2>
  </header>
  <!-- Article 1 content -->
</article>
<article>
  <header>
    <h2>Blog post 2 title</h2>
  </header>
  <!-- Article 2 content -->
</article>
```

Code optimality can be achieved by omitting the header container around headings (Listing 15-10).

Listing 15-10. Headings Without header

```
<article>
  <h2>Blog post title</h2>
  <!-- Article 1 content -->
</article>
<article>
  <h2>Blog post 2 title</h2>
  <!-- Article 2 content -->
</article>
```

Wrap All Lists in nav

The nav element is ideal for major navigation blocks only and should not be used as a container of all unordered lists.

Incorrectly Used figure Elements

Some web designers incorrectly use figure elements as containers of img elements. However, image such as logos are not figures, and a figure can be not only an image but also a piece of prose, a code block, a chart in SVG, and so on.

Misused Tables

Tableless layout: the Web standardistas' motto. Tables are for organizing data, not for controlling layout. For that purpose, div and other structuring elements should be used instead. Their positions, sizes, colors, layer orders, transparencies, and other features can be set via style sheets (Listing 15-12 instead of Listing 15-11).

Listing 15-11. Fragment of a Misused Table

```
<table border="1" bgcolor="#898989" width="400">
<td align="center" valign="top" spanning="2">  
<td>
```

Listing 15-12. Correct Structure of Tabular Data in the Markup

```
<table>
  <tr>
    <td>Meaningful content in data cell</td>
    <td>Content of other data cell</td>
  </tr>
</table>
```

The position of the table is determined by the content elements, text, and images as well as the container div element. The parameters should be given as CSS rulesets in the external style sheet associated with the document (see the section "Table Styling").

Nonoptimal Code Length

Analogously to the "tag soup" discussed in Chapter 1, the more specific "div soup" refers to the misuse and overuse of divisions (Zeldman calls it *divitis* [2]). Listing 15-13 shows an example.

Listing 15-13. A Divitis

```
<div class="maincontainer"><div class="nounderlineleftmargin"><div class="container"><div class="top
headlinesleftalign">The Latest News</div><div class="maintextthickborder"></div></div></div>
</div>
```

The major problem is that there is no structure at all (even if the code might be valid). Unnecessary divisions should be removed. Moreover, the names in the preceding example are far too long (although descriptive). They should be kept within reasonable limits.

Remember that in (X)HTML5 other elements dedicated to structuring should be used as the main containers except the general wrappers that should still be divs.

Element and Attribute Errors

A gross element error is when elements defined in another specification are used. Elements should be used according to the document type.

Incorrectly nested elements break the document structure and should be avoided. The location and order of elements within (X)HTML documents are not arbitrary and should meet the criteria of nesting rules discussed in Chapter 3.

Both errors can cause the message "document type does not allow element here" in the W3C Markup Validation Service.

Similar problems are associated with attributes as well. The W3C Markup Validation Service gives the error "there is no attribute 'attrib_name'" message. The selection of allowed attributes depends on the document type being used. For example, several attributes defined in the specification of the Transitional variant of XHTML are not allowed in Strict XHTML documents, as described in detail in Chapter 3. Similarly, several HTML attributes are prohibited in XHTML. Styling attributes should be provided in the CSS rather than the markup. Applying vendor-specific extensions such as `marginheight` can also cause similar problems. If an element is undefined, its attributes are considered invalid too.

End Tag Errors

The W3C Markup Validation Service clearly indicates the missing end tags by the message "end tag for element omitted, but its declaration does not permit this." Additional (unnecessary) end tags are identified as "end tag for element which is not open" by the W3C Markup Validation Service.

One of the easiest ways to ensure proper element closing is to write the closing tags immediately after opening them, such as shown in Listing 15-14.

Listing 15-14. Closing Tag Provided Before Any Child Elements

```
<div>

</div>
```

Element content should not be written until the closing tag is provided. It might seem evident, but consider that there could be hundreds of code lines between the opening and closing tags. Moreover, there might be several identical subsequent closing tags whose opening pairs can be difficult to identify even if indentation is used, or syntax highlighting is available in your markup editor.

Identifiers

Generally, there are two types of identifiers used in the (X)HTML markup. Naturally, `class` identifiers used mainly for styling multiple elements can be applied several times within the same document—not so with the `id` attribute, which should be unique throughout the document (such as a fragment identifier).

Common Style Sheet Errors

Although CSS parsers have a mechanism for handling style sheet errors [3], they should be eliminated by proper authoring and confirmed by validation. Writing declarations with incorrect properties and nonexisting property values are among the most common errors in CSS.

Nonexisting Properties

One of the most common CSS errors is the application of nonexisting style properties. The W3C CSS Validator clearly indicates these errors with the message "Property doesn't exist."

CSS name convention differs from the ones used in (X)HTML markup. The less experienced might type a CSS property name that is logical and "should be correct." For example, the left margin can be set with the `margin-left` property, although `left-margin` (which does not exist) would be more logical. Even if it seems to be straightforward, the result would be incorrect. If somebody is not familiar with the whole vocabulary of Cascading Style Sheets, all properties should be checked in the appropriate CSS specification before applying them. Another good example is a table data cell with vertically centralized content. In the early days of the Web when many styles were provided on HTML attributes directly, the `valign` attribute was used on the `td` element. In CSS, however, there is no property with the name `valign`. The corresponding property has a different name: `vertical-align`.

Nonexisting or Incorrectly Used Property Values

To avoid errors caused by incorrect CSS property values, the allowed values as well as the associated data types should be known. Additionally, it is very useful to know the initial (default) value. For example, one of the three attribute values, collapse, separate, or inherit, can be set for the border-collapse property used to set whether table borders are collapsed into a single border or rendered next to or above each other. The ruleset border-collapse: yes; cannot be used, because the attribute value yes would be illegal. Since this is an inheritable property, a corresponding ruleset is needed only if the inherited value is not appropriate for our purposes and needs to be overridden (or ensured).

Ignored Inheritance

Redundancy often occurs in badly written CSS. Although such style sheets might even be standard-compliant, they are longer than necessary, use more bandwidth, and are harder to maintain. *Code optimality* can be achieved only if inheritance is considered properly. Assume the style rulesets presented in Listing 15-15.

Listing 15-15. Redundant Rulesets (Should Be Optimized)

```
body {
  font-family: Verdana, Arial, sans-serif;
  font-size: 1.2em;
  color: #351801;
}

p {
  font-family: Verdana, Arial, sans-serif;
  font-size: 1.2em;
  color: #351801;
}

div {
  font-family: Verdana, Arial, sans-serif;
  font-size: 1.2em;
  color: #351801;
}
```

The previous rules are obviously redundant. Some developers would write them in the form shown in Listing 15-16.

Listing 15-16. A Better Yet Still Redundant Solution

```
body, p, div {
  font-family: Verdana, Arial, sans-serif;
  font-size: 1.2em;
  color: #351801;
}
```

Since browsers apply the same styles for the child elements (p and div in this example) as defined for the parent element (body), the code is still redundant and should be written as shown in Listing 15-17.

Listing 15-17. The Correct Element Selector

```css
body {
  font-family: Verdana, Arial, sans-serif;
  font-size: 1.2em;
  color: #351801;
}
```

In other words, the second and third rulesets of the original example are not needed and should be deleted. Note such identical, redundant rules are much more difficult to notice in long CSS files where there are hundreds of other rulesets between them. That's why it is important to think the major CSS rules over at the very beginning and later override those rules only where inherited values are not appropriate for the overall design and layout.

Because the previous ruleset has two properties that can be written with a shorthand property, the code can be optimized further (Listing 15-18).

Listing 15-18. The Correct Solution

```css
body {
  font: 1.2em Verdana, Arial, sans-serif;
  color: #351801;
}
```

Descendant selectors (also known as *contextual selectors* [4]) should be used for optimum code length. Examine the markup shown in Listing 15-19 and CSS rules in Listing 15-20.

Listing 15-19. Standard-Compliant but Nonoptimal Markup (Classitis)

```html
<div id="main">
  <p class="maintext">The is the main content of the site.</p>
  <p class="maintext">The second paragraph should look like the first one.</p>
  <p class="maintext">In fact, all paragraphs of the document have the same styles.</p>
</div>
```

Listing 15-20. Standard-Compliant but Nonoptimal Styling Rules

```css
.maintext {
  margin-left: 15px;
  margin-right: 15px;
  margin-top: 10px;
  margin-bottom: 5px;
  font-size: 1.4em;
  color: #1d4c90;
}
```

Although both the markup and the style rules are presented in a standard form, the code is far from optimal. This kind of class overuse is called *classitis* [5]. A much shorter, easier to understand, optimal solution could be the markup presented in Listing 15-21 with the CSS rules shown in Listing 15-22.

Listing 15-21. The Correct Markup for Listing 15-19

```
<div id="main">
  <p>The is the main content of the site.</p>
  <p>The second paragraph should look like the first one.</p>
  <p>In fact, all paragraphs of the document have the same styles.</p>
</div>
```

Listing 15-22. The Optimal CSS Rules

```
#main p {
  margin: 10px 15px 5px;
  font-size: 1.4em;
  color: #1d4c90;
}
```

If this is not a unique section of the page, the id attribute could be omitted, and the CSS ruleset could be modified in order to be applied to p elements in general.

Color Errors

CSS validation often results in color warnings that indicate potential problems with foreground and background colors. For example, if a very light font color is used on a white background, it might be hard or even impossible to read the content. In such cases, the W3C CSS Validator gives the message "Same colors for color and background-color in two contexts."

However, some of these messages can be considered as false positives since there are cases when visibility is not a problem at all (transparent or overlapping layers, text on background image, and so on). To be on the safe side, the text must remain readable even if other components of the page (for example, background image) cannot be downloaded.

Incorrect Locations

Incorrect location errors are typically caused by not properly closed rulesets. They should be checked one by one near the line indicated by the W3C CSS Validation Service error message "The element can't appear here in the context CSS 2.1."

Transparent Backgrounds

Transparent surfaces are popular throughout the Web. The transparency of a div is usually set as shown in Listing 15-23.

Listing 15-23. A Typical but Nonstandard, Browser-Dependent Ruleset for Transparency

```
#transdiv {
  opacity: 0.7;
  filter: alpha(opacity=70);
  -moz-opacity: 0.7;
  -khtml-opacity: 0.7;
}
```

In modern browsers it works fine. However, when validating as CSS 2.1, the validator would give errors. Even in CSS3, only the first one (opacity) is valid, which works in Firefox, Opera, and Safari but not in IE (which requires the filter property). Thus, validity can be obtained by removing the last three properties; however, the result won't work under Internet Explorer and older versions of other browsers.

A valid, cross-browser solution could be the transparent background image such as the one shown in Listing 15-24.

Listing 15-24. A Transparent PNG Background File Is a Robust Solution

```
#transdiv {
  background-image: url('images/transpbg.png');
  background-repeat: repeat;
}
```

Miscellaneous Errors

Not all documents can be checked by validators. Incorrect serving or temporary server errors are the most common reasons. Without providing data required for automatic document type detection or character encoding detection, validation cannot be performed or provides unreliable results.

Common News Feed Errors

Valid news feed channels should be well-formed and meet all general XML criteria. Even so, some errors might occur in manually updated news feeds because of human error. One of the most common errors is an incorrect date. If the publication date is earlier than the date of updating, validators give an error. This is referred to as an *implausible date*. Care must be taken to apply the proper offset whose misuse can lead to the same problem.

Common Script Errors

Scripts are out of the scope of markup validators. Consequently, extended care must be taken to ensure correctness and proper functionality. It should be ensured that a web page remains usable even if the scripts cannot be executed for whatever reason. It is important to keep in mind that alternate content written for scripts cannot be checked by software tools, and their evaluation depends on human decision.

Common Accessibility Errors

In contrast to markup or CSS errors where errors depend on the language version being used, accessibility errors are determined by the version and level of guidelines considered. A comprehensive overview of accessibility errors and their solutions ("Failures of Success Criteria") is collected in the W3C group note describing techniques and failures for WCAG 2.0 [6]. The most common accessibility errors can be summarized as follows:

- Lack of structured markup or table layout

- Images that convey important information are embedded through CSS

- User control is missing to stop or pause blinking, scrolling, and automatically played sound files or videos

- Missing captions or labels for sound effects and synchronized media
- Inadequate user guidance for forms
- Difficult navigation and traps
- Time limits
- Information representation relies exclusively on color, shape, location, or graphics
- Inaccessible custom controls
- Nonunique identifiers (not only inaccessible but also invalid)
- Missing alternate content and long description for nontext content and scripts
- Functionality that might disturb the user with nonrequested features such as a new window
- Text is not legible or clear enough, too small font size, or insufficient contrast difference between foreground and background colors or images
- Missing document title
- Missing or inadequate text alternatives such as filenames or placeholder
- Missing labels
- Whitespace or control spacing used to create multiple columns in plain text or within words
- Automatic form submission without warning
- Missing or incorrect tab order declaration
- Missing header cells, captions, and summaries in tables
- Pointing device-specific event handlers
- Nonspecific links such as "Click here" or "More"

Summary

This chapter enumerated the most common errors you might face in your daily work as a web developer. You are well aware by now how to eliminate them when you develop from scratch and correct them when you redesign a site.

After thoroughly reading this book, you have learned the importance and benefits of web standards and techniques for writing valid markup from scratch. You know how to recognize standards and differentiate them from nonfinalized specifications. You now have all the skills required to provide meaningful semantics and machine-readable metadata, restrict markup to semantics, and achieve full standard compliance in your projects.

References

1. Hickson I (2009) Sending XHTML as text/html Considered Harmful. Ian Hickson. `http://www.hixie.ch/advocacy/xhtml`. Accessed 14 October 2014

2. Zeldman J, Marcotte E (2010) The Heartbreak of Divitis. In: Designing with Web standards, 3rd Ed., New Riders, Berkeley

3. Bos B, Çelik T, Hickson I, Wium Lie HW (eds) (2011) Rules for handling parsing errors. In: Cascading Style Sheets Level 2 Revision 1 (CSS 2.1) Specification. W3C Recommendation. World Wide Web Consortium. `http://www.w3.org/TR/CSS21/syndata.html#parsing-errors`. Accessed 14 October 2014

4. Murphy C, Persson N (2009) HTML and CSS Web Standards Solutions – A Web Standardistas' Approach. Friends of ED, Berkeley

5. Zeldman J, Marcotte E (2010) Classitis: The Measles of Markup. In: Designing with Web standards, 3rd Ed. New Riders, Berkeley

6. Cooper M, Reid LG, Vanderheiden G, Caldwell B, Chisholm W, Slatin J (eds) (2014) Failures for WCAG 2.0. In: Techniques for WCAG 2.0. Techniques and Failures for Web Content Accessibility Guidelines 2.0. World Wide Web Consortium. `http://www.w3.org/TR/WCAG20-TECHS/failures.html`. Accessed 14 October 2014

Index

■ D

I

J

K

L

■ W

Y

 Z

Get the eBook for only $10!

Now you can take the weightless companion with you anywhere, anytime. Your purchase of this book entitles you to 3 electronic versions for only $10.

This Apress title will prove so indispensible that you'll want to carry it with you everywhere, which is why we are offering the eBook in 3 formats for only $10 if you have already purchased the print book.

Convenient and fully searchable, the PDF version enables you to easily find and copy code—or perform examples by quickly toggling between instructions and applications. The MOBI format is ideal for your Kindle, while the ePUB can be utilized on a variety of mobile devices.

Go to www.apress.com/promo/tendollars to purchase your companion eBook.